Information Sources in Engineering

A series under the General Editorship of
Ia C. McIlwaine,
M. W. Hill and
Nancy J. Williamson

Other titles:

Information Sources for the Press and Broadcast Media
    edited by Sarah Adair
Information Sources in Architecture and Construction (Second edition)
    edited by Valerie J. Nurcombe
Information Sources in Art, Art History and Design
    edited by Simon Ford
Information Sources in Development Studies
    edited by Sheila Allcock
Information Sources in Environmental Protection
    edited by Selwyn Eagle and Judith Deschamps
Information Sources in Finance and Banking
    by Ray Lester
Information Sources in Grey Literature (Fourth edition)
    by C. P. Auger
Information Sources in Law (Second edition)
    edited by Jules Winterton and Elizabeth M. Moys
Information Sources in Music
    edited by Lewis Foreman
Information Sources in Official Publications
    edited by Valerie J. Nurcombe
Information Sources in Patents (Second edition)
    edited by Stephen R. Adams
Information Sources in Polymers and Plastics
    edited by R.T. Adkins
Information Sources in the Earth Sciences (Second edition)
    edited by David N. Wood, Joan E. Hardy and Anthony P. Harvey
Information Sources in the Life Sciences (Fourth edition)
    edited by H.V. Wyatt
Information Sources in the Social Sciences
    edited by David Fisher, Sandra P. Price and Terry Hanstock
Information Sources in Women's Studies and Feminism
    edited by Hope A. Olson

Information Sources in
Engineering

4th edition

Editors
Roderick A. MacLeod
and
Jim Corlett

K · G · Saur München 2005

Bibliographic information published by Die Deutsche Bibliothek
Die Deutsche Bibliothek lists this publication in the Deutsche Nationalbibliografie;
detailed bibliographic data is available in the internet at http://dnb.ddb.de.

⊗

Printed on acid-free paper
© 2005 K. G. Saur Verlag GmbH, München

Typesetting by Florence Production Ltd., Stoodleigh, Devon, Great Britain.

Printed and bound by Strauss GmbH, Mörlenbach, Germany.
ISBN 3-598-24442-8

Contents

Series Editor's Foreword

In the first years of the 21st century, there is a popular belief that the Internet gives us easy world-wide access to all the information anyone can reasonably need. Experience, especially by those researching topics in depth, proves otherwise. It is ironic that, despite all the technical advances in information handling that have been made and the masses of information that assail us on every side, it remains as difficult as ever to ensure that one has what one wants when one needs it.

Of course the computer and the Internet have made a huge difference to our information gathering habits, especially in the hands of those who, through experience, have gained skill in their use, an ability to contain the amount of information within manageable limits and discrimination in assessing the reliability and adequacy of the resources accessed. No one nowadays would be without the Internet but it is only one among several sources each of which has its value according to the searcher's needs. In all cases, the speed and effectiveness of a search can be greatly enhanced by the advice of those who are experts in the techniques and in the subject field involved.

The aim of each volume of this K. G. Saur series of *Guides to Information Sources* is simple. It is to reduce the time which needs to be spent on patient searching; to recommend the best starting point and sources most likely to yield the desired information. To do this we bring you the knowledge and experience of specialist practitioners in the field. Each author regularly uses the information sources and services described and any tricks of the trade that the author has learnt are passed on.

Like all subject and sector guides, the sources discussed have had to be selected. The criteria for selection will be given by the individual editors and will differ from subject to subject. However, the overall objective is constant: that of providing a way into a subject to those new to the field and to identify major new or possibly unexplored sources to those who already have some acquaintance with it.

Nowadays two major problems face those who are embarking upon research or who are in charge of wide-ranging collections of information. One is the increasingly specialised knowledge of the user and concomitant ignorance of other potentially useful disciplines. The second is the trend towards cross-disciplinary studies. This has led to a great mixing of academic programmes – and a number of imprecisely defined fields of study. The editors are only too aware of the difficulties such hybrid subject fields raise for those requiring information and Guides for these sectors are being established as well as those for the traditional "hard disciplines". In addition to commissioning new titles, constant attention is given to the production of updated editions for subject fields which are fast moving and subject to rapid development.

The Internet now gives access to many new sources (and to some, but not all, of the old ones) and being discipline-free can be particularly attractive to those working in new fields. At the same time it gives access to an overwhelming mass of information, some of it well organized and easy to interrogate, much incoherent and ill-organized. On top of this there is the great output of new information from the media, advertising, meetings and conferences, regulatory bodies, letters, reports, office memoranda, magazines, junk mail, electronic mail, fax, bulletin boards and so on and so on. Inevitably it all tends to make one very reluctant to add to the load by seeking out books and journals. Yet they, and the other traditional types of printed material, remain for many purposes the most reliable sources of information. Quality encyclopaedias are excellent for an overview of a topic but there are also many other time saving reviews and digests of information. One still needs to look things up in databooks, to consult the full text of patent specifications, standards and reports, both official and commercial, and to study maps and atlases. Increasingly these are available on CD-ROM as well as in print and choice depends on one's circumstances. Some archives are becoming available electronically but the vast majority are still in paper form. Many institutions are making some at least of their expertise available on websites but contact with individuals there is often still necessary for in depth studies. It is also worth remembering that consulting a reference book frequently produces a more rapid result than consulting an online source.

Fortunately, in these times when the amount being published is increasing rapidly, it is rarely necessary to consult everything that has been published on the topic of one's interest. Usually much proves to be irrelevant or repetitive. Some publications (including in that term websites and e-journals) prove to be sadly lacking in important detail and present broad generalizations flimsily bridged with arches of waffle. Many publications contain errors. In such cases the need to check against other publications, first making sure that they are not simply derivative, adds greatly to the time of a search. In an academic field there is normally a "pecking order" of journals, the better ones generally having a "peer review" system which self-published articles on the web do not (though there are moves to intro-duce a peer review process to some web-published journals). Research workers soon learn – it is part of their training – which sources in their field of study to use and rely on, which journals, co-workers and director-ies are trustworthy and to what extent. However, when searching outside their own field of expertise and for other people, lay researchers and infor-mation workers alike, serious problems have to be overcome. This makes the need for evaluative guides, such as those in this series, even more essen-tial. The series attempts to achieve evaluation in two ways: first through a careful selection of sources, so that only those which are considered worthy are included, and second through the comments which are provided on those sources.

Guides to the literature and other sources of information have a long and distinguished history. Some of them retain their value for many years as all or part of their content is still relevant but not repeated in later works. Where appropriate these are included in the sources referred to in this series along with the wealth of new sources which make new Guides and new editions essential.

Michael W. Hill
Ia C. McIlwaine

Preface

A few changes have been made to the organisational structure of this fourth edition. A detailed Introduction sets the scene, and is followed by twelve chapters which examine different categories of primary and secondary information sources. A further fourteen chapters cover all of the main subject areas of engineering. Contributors range from specialist librarians to top academics, all with an expert knowledge of their particular field.

As with previous editions, contributions have not been subjected to restrictive editing, and the individual style of contributors has thereby been retained.

We would like to express our great thanks to all of the contributors, who have made this fourth edition a fascinating study of an important subject which often receives less attention than it deserves. Thanks also go to our publishing consultant, Geraldine Turpie, the editorial staff of K. G. Saur, and Michael Breaks, the University Librarian at Heriot Watt University.

Roddy MacLeod
Jim Corlett

About the Contributors

Kathy Abbott is Subject Librarian for Engineering and Mathematical Sciences at Queen Mary, University of London. A graduate of the Department of Engineering at Warwick University (1973), she trained at Hatfield Polytechnic Library, gaining experience in industrial libraries. She has enjoyed learning about the information needs of Aeronautical, Civil, Electrical, Electronic, Materials (including Biomaterials), Mechanical, Medical and Nuclear Engineering, and recently, Computer Science and Mathematics. Her membership of the UK JIBS User Group Committee (since 2000) utilises her knowledge of electronic information resources. In 2000, she received the Queen Mary Drapers' Award for Outstanding Service.

Michael F. Ashby was educated at Cambridge University, and subsequently held professorships at the University of Gottingen (1962–65) and at Harvard University (1965–73), before returning to the Engineering Department in Cambridge, UK. Since 1989 he has held the post of Royal Society Research Professor of Engineering at Cambridge. His interests are in material properties and in the selection of materials for engineering design.

Anne Bell holds the position of Collections Development Manager with the Information Services Division of Cardiff University. She has been with the university since 1984, holding first the position of Assistant Science Librarian, then from 1988 Science Librarian, and has published on the subject of electronic information sources and academic researchers.

David Cebon is a Reader in Mechanical Engineering in Cambridge University Engineering Department. He leads an active research group which is concerned with the design and dynamics of heavy commercial vehicles, traffic instrumentation, damage mechanisms of pavement materials and the effects of vehicles on the response and damage of roads and bridges. Dr Cebon is the Research Director of the Cambridge Vehicle Dynamics

Consortium. He also has interests in the use of computers in engineering design and education. He coordinates development of the Cambridge Engineering Selector and is the Managing Director of Granta Design Limited. Dr Cebon has written numerous papers on the dynamics of heavy vehicles, weigh–in–motion, road materials, road damage and materials selection.

Mike Chrimes is currently Head of Library and Information Services at the Institution of Civil Engineers, where he has worked since 1977. He has been heavily involved in the computerisation of library services, most recently managing the digitisation of all ICE journals from 1836 to date. He is currently seeking funding for further digitisation of journals. He has written extensively on the history of civil engineering and regularly lectures on the subject.

Dr Nigel Clarke has an honours degree in physical chemistry and carried out research in neutron scattering. After university he moved into metallurgy and materials science working in nuclear and defence R&D. He is a Chartered Chemist, Chartered Physicist, a Member of the Royal Society of Chemistry, and of the Institute of Physics and is registered as a European Physicist. He joined the EPO in The Hague as an examiner, transferred into IT project management, and later settled into patent information at the EPO in Vienna. He has organised many international patent information events, and managed projects supporting patent information (PATLIB) networks in Europe. Currently he is involved in market research, and the promotion of the EPO's internet services such as *esp@cenet*®. He has been heavily involved in the development and delivery of EPO training courses especially for Eastern European countries and non-member states. He maintains a strong personal interest in raising awareness of IPR among scientists and engineers in universities and SMEs.

Jim Corlett was born and bred in Southampton. After completing a degree in Modern and Medieval Languages at Cambridge University, and a graduate trainee year at Southampton University, he achieved a postgraduate diploma in librarianship and information science at the North London Polytechnic. Seven years at the Lyon Playfair Library at Imperial College was followed by twenty-three years as engineering librarian at the Nottingham Trent University. During this time, he was active within the SCITECH Group and worked with EEVL, the Internet Guide to Engineering, Mathematics and Computing. He has also produced and edited the Recent Advances in Manufacturing database for the past decade and more. He now works for his own company.

Steve J. Culley is Head of Design in the Department of Mechanical Engineering at the University of Bath in the UK. He has particular research interests in the supply of information to Engineering Designers and in particular is a champion of the Electronic Catalogue for technical data. He is a member of the Innovative Manufacturing Research Centre (IMRC) at Bath, dealing with Design Information and Knowledge and a non executive director of the information spin out company Adiuri Systems (www.adiuri.com). Other interests include performance modelling and automatic configuration of engineering assemblies and design for agility through changeover. He has organised the workshop 'Future Issues on Design Research (FIDR)' with the support of the Department of Trade and Industry (DTI) and the EPSRC. He is a Fellow of the Institution of Mechanical Engineers and member of the IMechE Manufacturing Industries Divisional Board.

Jonathan Dell is a Chartered Engineer, a member of the IEE and IEEE and is a lecturer in the Department of Electronics at York University. He specializes in digital electronics and microprocessors, their application in embedded systems and also industrial measurement techniques and systems. His current research centres on parallel computing architectures for application in real-time reconstruction of the images obtained through industrial tomography systems. He previously worked as a lecturer at Sheffield Hallam University and as an applications specialist at Tektronix International, Amsterdam, and Texas Instruments Ltd., Bedford.

Andy Garland is Head of Information at the Institute of Nanotechnology (IoN), and Contract Manager for the Technology Transfer Centre Ltd. He is author of the reports 'Nanotechnology in the UK', 'Nanotechnology in Europe', 'Nanotechnology in North America', 'Nanotechnology in Asia Pacific' and 'Nanotechnology and Government'. He has also led a number of industrial and government contracts including Nanotechnology and Nuclear Decommissioning, The UK Nanolandscape, Nanotechnology and Opportunities for Scotland, and produced the ground-breaking CD-ROM 'What is Nanotechnology?'

John Harrington is the Information Services Manager based at Cranfield University's Kings Norton Library, and is currently chair of the Aslib Engineering Group. He has considerable experience of research and other professional activities concerned with aerospace and engineering information. These include EURILIA – EC Framework III project (1992–1994), as well as two major studies of Aerospace Information Management in the UK and Europe (AIM-UK 1998–99, AIM-Eu 2001–2002). John has been involved in the Cranfield led Managing Access to Grey Literature Collections (MAGiC) project phases I and II (2000–2004). John is a member of the team that maintains the AERADE (Aerospace & Defence) internet information service, which is also part of EEVL, the Internet Guide to Engineering, Mathematics and Computing.

Ruth Harrison is the Senior Library Assistant at the Civil and Environmental Engineering Library, Imperial College London, where she has worked since 1998. She previously worked at the library of the Royal Society of Medicine. She wrote 'Internet Civil Engineer' in 2000/01, an online tutorial that forms part of the RDN's Virtual Training Suite. She has provided module content for the Imperial College London Library online information and learning skills programme, and has been involved in the teaching of this programme. She is a member of the Statutory Requirements & Legal Compliance task group, which contributes to the M25 Consortium of Academic Libraries staff training and development programme, CPD25.

Jill Lambert is the Team Leader for Science & Engineering and Head of Public Services in the Library & Information Services at Aston University. She has a science degree from Bristol University and a Masters in Librarianship from the University of North London. Jill has held professional posts in a range of organisations including University of Central England, Staffordshire University, OCLC Europe, and the Universities of Northumbria and Westminster. Her publications include 'Finding information in science, technology and medicine', 'Scientific and technical journals', 'Information resources selection' and a number of articles.

Roddy MacLeod is Senior Subject Librarian at Heriot Watt University, where he is also Manager of EEVL, the Internet guide to engineering, mathematics and computing. He edits the Internet Resources Newsletter, is Associate Editor of the *New Review of Information Networking*, and has written for numerous other publications including *Information World Review*, *Ariadne*, *Online Information Review*, *Program*, and *The Electronic Library*. In 2000, he was awarded the title of Information Professional of the Year by *Information World Review*.

Stephanie McKeating was an Academic Librarian at Loughborough University where her responsibilities include the provision of information services and support to departments in the Science Faculty. She has previously co-compiled an 'Aslib Guide to Online Engineering databases' and co-authored a chapter on online engineering resources for the 'Manual of Online Search Strategies.' She was a member of the JISC Advisory Group for the Resource Guide for Engineering, Maths and Computing.

Chris A. McMahon is a Chartered Mechanical Engineer who worked initially as a production engineer, then as a design engineer in an automotive consultancy, but for the last 20 years he has been an academic, being currently Reader in Engineering Design at the University of Bath. His teaching and research interests are in the application of computers to engineering design, in particular in assisting engineers in the organisation and management of design information and in improvement of the design process. This work has led to a number of articles on information and knowledge management in design, on the automation of the design process and on materials applications in design, in addition to a textbook on Computer-aided Design and Manufacture.

Christine Middleton is the Engineering Librarian at the University of Nottingham. Originally a Chartered Mechanical Engineer working in the manufacturing industries, Christine changed career in 1993, becoming a Chartered Librarian in 1997. She is greatly indebted to Dr. Sophie Hide, formerly of the Health and Safety Ergonomics Unit at Loughborough University, for her considerable help with the subject specialist content of the chapter, and also to Dr John Sutherland, Safety and Radiation Protection Officer at the University of Nottingham, for his comments and contributions.

Arnold Myers holds the position of Senior Information Scientist on the staff of Heriot Watt University Library. He organised the Offshore Information Conferences of 1978, 1980, 1982, 1986, 1990 and 1994. He compiled the 'INFOIL Thesaurus, English language version' for the UK Department of Energy. He was the principal contributor to the 'Petroleum and Marine Technology Information Guide' and now maintains the 'Offshore Engineering Information Service website'. He was presented with the Jason Farradane Award of the Institute of Information Scientists in recognition of services to information science in 1991.

Paul A. S. Needham is employed as an Electronic Information Specialist by the Information Services Division at Cranfield University. In 1978, Paul became a food technician at Spillers Research and Technology Centre in Cambridge, helping to develop novel proteins. In 1980, he gained computer-programming qualifications and, from 1981 to 1985, was employed as an analyst programmer at an insurance brokers in Swindon. Following a number of short-term posts, in 1987, Paul became a director of a waste recycling company and, from 1989 to 1993, was a director of a printing co-operative. In 1994, he started working for the University of Bath, first as a CAL development assistant and then as a network administrator, before finally joining Cranfield University in 1998. Since then, Paul has worked on a number of electronic information projects and initiatives, including the MAGiC project (Managing Access to Grey Literature Collections) and AERADE – the UK portal which provides integrated access to key aerospace and defence information sources on the internet, and contributes resources to EEVL.

Peter O'Reilly is the Manager of the Business and Intellectual Property Information team at the British Library, and has worked in the business information field for the past fourteen years. He is currently studying for his MA in Information Services Management at London Metropolitan University.

Martin Pitt is a Chartered Chemical Engineer and Chartered Chemist who has worked in both roles in industry, but has been an academic for the last eighteen years, being currently Coordinator of Design Teaching in Chemical and Process Engineering at the University of Sheffield. He was Chairman of the Institution of Chemical Engineers Education Subject Group and Secretary of the Working Party on Education of the European Federation of Chemical Engineering. He has published books on process instrumentation and waste disposal, and is the compiler for Bretherick's handbook of reactive chemical hazards.

Peter Rayson is divisional head for design and process innovation (DPI Division) at Birmingham's Technology Innovation Centre (**tic**) – the major City-centre technology campus of the University of Central England. With an M.Sc. in Manufacturing Technology from UMIST and a BEng in Systems Engineering from UWIST, prior to taking up his current post, Peter was Senior Fellow with Warwick University's Manufacturing Group (WMG). Peter Rayson began his career with Rolls-Royce, and rapidly gained his extensive engineering experience in the machine tool, automotive and aerospace sectors. This led him into higher education teaching and, subsequently, to consultancy with McDonnell Douglas Information Systems in the USA. A specialist in CAD/CAM/CAE (computer aided design, manufacturing and engineering) and product data management (PDM), Peter went on to become vice-president of worldwide aerospace operations for Computervision and senior vice-president for the Parametric Technology Corporation, in charge of industry marketing. He then returned to the academic sector firstly with WMG and subsequently through his current role at the **tic**.

Bob Rhodes is a Chartered Engineer, Chartered Librarian and a Member of the Institute of Materials, Minerals and Mining. He was until recently Sub-Librarian and Academic Services Manager for the Engineering Faculty at Loughborough University. His publications include a 'Student Guide to Engineering Information Resource Centres' in association with Aslib Engineering Group and the Engineering Institutions Librarians Committee; a number of guides on engineering design in association with other members of SEED (Sharing Experience in Engineering Design); and 'Aslib Guide to Online Engineering Databases' (co-compiler). Now supposedly retired, he continues to do occasional work, including being a book reviewer for *CILIP Update*.

Michael Richards is Information Management Officer at Cosworth Technology, the UK and North American engines and powertrain consultancy.

Before joining the company, he was a journalist in local newspapers and a teacher with a degree from Warwick University and postgraduate qualification from Manchester. He created Cosworth Technology's Library and Information Services in 1990, which has since absorbed its archives and developed knowledge-based data systems. He is also responsible for the company's website and automotive industry market intelligence reporting.

Recently retired, **Peter Richards** trained as a Zoologist in Aberdeen. After a spell in Industry in the area of Cell Culture (one of the foundation subjects for Tissue Engineeering) he studied Marine Biology in both Polar Regions before spending twenty-five years as the Biological part of a Biomedical Engineering Group. He has researched on Microscope Techniques, Heart-Lung Bypass, Heart Valves, Biocompatibility and Micro-electrodes. In the last few years, he has been heavily involved in the day-to-day running of an M.Sc. Course in Biomedical Engineering.

Penny Rowe, part-time information consultant, was formerly User Education Librarian at Imperial College, London, responsible for a co-ordinated programme of information retrieval in science, technology and medicine across the campuses. Previous posts included Science and Techno

logy Reference Librarian responsible to the Joint Imperial College and Science Museum Libraries and Engineering Subject Librarian. She was a founder collaborator and participated extensively in the European project EDUCATE (INTO INFO), a system of programs hosted on the Internet, providing multiple pathways for learning how to obtain and handle information in engineering, science and medicine efficiently. She was also a member of the development team of EEVL, the Internet guide to engineering, mathematics and computing, and continues to provide material for it as a Subject Consultant.

Keri Rowles has an honours degree in Physics from the University of Exeter. He joined the EPO in The Hague as an examiner working on patents in the field of electrotechnology. He has worked for the Patent Information branch of the European Patent Office (EPO) since 1994, during which time he has been extensively involved in the electronic publication of patent information produced by the EPO, and numerous national patent offices with which the EPO co-operates. He holds a Certificate in Intellectual Property Law, and a Masters degree in the Management of Intellectual Property from Queen Mary and Westfield College, University of London.

Ottilia Saxl is founder and CEO of the Institute of Nanotechnology (IoN). Ottilia has led nanotechnology missions to the US and Germany on behalf of the UK government and serves on the UK Basic Technologies panel, and the EU 6th Framework Advisory Committee for Thematic Priority 3, which focuses on nanotechnology. A renowned international speaker on micro and nanotechnology, as CEO of the IoN Ottilia has overseen the IoN's rise to its current position the as the world's leading nanotechnology information provider and network coordinator.

Tim Shaw (Prof. C. Tim. Shaw) is Emeritus Professor of Mining Engineering in the Department of Earth Science and Engineering, Royal School of Mines, Imperial College of Science, Technology and Medicine, and Honorary Professor, Institute of Archaeology, University College, London University. Between 1991 and 1995 he was Dean of the Royal School of Mines. He is a Fellow of the South African Institute of Mining and Metallurgy (SAIMM), an Associate Member of the Mine Managers Association of South Africa (AMMSA), Member of the American Institute Of Mining, Metallurgy and Petroleum Engineering, Fellow of the Institution of Materials, Mining and Metallurgy, Fellow of the Institute of Quarrying, and Foundation Member of the Society of Mining Professors-Societät der Bergbaukunde. He has written extensively on mining.

Ewan Smith is the Business & technical Librarian at the Central Library, Aberdeen. Prior to this role has was a Project Manager at British Standards Institute, London. He is responsible for general and specialist business information services, including intellectual property and standards. Ewan changed career, moving from engineering to information, and became a chartered librarian in 1997. He is also a chartered member of the Chartered Management Institute. He has written a conference paper for Patlib and is a member of the European Patent Office Organising Committee for Patlib 2004 (Portugal), where he will be chairing a number of events.

Sarah Vinsen is an Information Officer at the Institution of Mechancial Engineers, where she has worked since 2000. Previously she has worked at the Imperial Cancer Research Fund and Barnet College.

Martin Ward has spent most of his working life as an Information Specialist at Ricardo Consulting Engineers, the international consultancy for the motor industry, with a keen interest in i.c. engines and transmissions, and latterly the whole of the motor vehicle. He has initiated and now edits four industry-wide newsletters, *Components News*, *Transmissions News*, *Vehicle Engineering News* and *Alternative Powertrain News*, which summarize current literature, based on the input to Ricardo's large database of engineering references, 'POWERLINK'. Martin is the author of a book on adult user surveys of public libraries, based on his M.Lib. thesis for the (then) College of Librarianship Wales, which he attended as a student. He has also published articles on knowledge management, indexing techniques and the use of information by Ricardo's engineers, as well as a number of book reviews on knowledge-related subjects. He has a special interest in cataloguing technical articles in French, Italian, German and Japanese, and also in commissioning translations.

Martin Wolf is the Social Sciences Librarian at the University of Warwick. He has published on the subject of electronic journals and spoken at conferences on issues related to web-based library catalogues.

Information and the Engineer

Martin Ward

▶ INTRODUCTION

The purpose of this keynote chapter is to provide a unified context for the diverse and detailed surveys which follow in Parts 1 and 2 of this book. It attempts to describe the interrelationships between the specialist bibliographical information sources discussed in Part 1, and to outline the world of the engineers whose disciplines are the subject of Part 2. It presents some themes which apply to all engineers, their work and their roles within a Western society. It goes on to discuss the current state of the engineering knowledge base, and the role of specialist bibliographical information sources within it. These sources are shown working together in a model of engineering knowledge activities. This is followed by a first-hand account of the use of information sources by engineers within the writer's own company, Ricardo, which is intended to show their practical integration. The chapter concludes by stressing the need for a broad awareness of the problems engineers face, and circumstances within which they work, when dealing with the information sources which serve them.

▶ THE ROLE OF ENGINEERS IN SOCIETY TODAY

Engineers have an ambivalent role within our society. Some of them perform routine tasks which maintain the infrastructure of our lives, and which we are glad to leave to them, without any particular desire to understand their work or their needs. Others, as in the motor industry, are linked with iconic and glamorous products – the names of Porsche, Ferrari and Rolls-Royce come to mind. Similar examples are to be found in other consumer sectors such as pens and cameras. Throughout the civil population, there are individuals and groups who, while not engineers themselves, are fascinated by engineering techniques and products, whether these are cars, the latest PC software, or the London Eye. Failures (for example in rail or aerospace engineering) are as spectacular as they are unusual. There is a fair segment of the population who are engineers by profession. Not many of the engineering disciplines, however, are known well by single individuals.

Anonymity is sharpened by the fact that engineers, unlike artists, usually work in teams, and have to contend with regulatory and commercial constraints. Like all other professionals, there is an objectivity in the things they produce which looks away from the guesses and stresses of the latters' subjective origin. In terms of Erving Goffman's model of performance dynamics (Goffman, 1969), the engineering product is in the 'front of house', while the engineer himself toils away in the 'back region'. The fate of Rudolf Diesel's name indicates the price of engineering fame: reification.

Engineers add value to life. Mobility via private cars enlarges the scope of our activities, and, in the process, of ourselves. It is this that makes legislation on private transport such a hot political subject. Life is complex, and its aims are frequently contradictory. We somehow want fewer (of other peoples') private cars, because of the congestion, energy wastage and pollution which they entail, at the same time as we cherish our own. Such conflicting social goals are daily reflected in the work of engineers: more comfort, but with lower weight; lower weight, but with more space; more speed, yet more safety. A recent report on the Swiss car market showed the conflicting trends of increasing weight on the one hand, and decreasing fuel consumption on the other (Blessing and Schick, 2002). In this sense, engineering is not a wholly rational enterprise. Where design engineering has an aesthetic aspect, this follows, or even influences, current trends and tastes. More seriously, although technology is intrinsically neutral, its application both reflects and sharpens the unequal distribution of social resources and life chances in the world.

Technology as a whole has a high status in our society. Technological progress has for many people a hopeful connotation in itself. Social change is often prompted by technological change, even if changing values are required in order to enable the technology to take root. We owe to software engineers the tools for the vast changes that are bringing about two of the major revolutions of our time: the information society and the knowledge economy. To bioengineers, we owe the legal and ethical controversies which the realization of genetic manipulation has brought about. European history over the last fifty years might have been very different without the prospect of universal destruction via nuclear weapons.

There would be no technology without engineers. Technological change has advanced so far (with no prospect of it slackening) that the social infrastructure is now largely a synthetic one. There is no longer any clear interface between ourselves and our technology. Technology has entered our tacit lives, and has become a necessity rather than an optional aid. Our dependence on it emerges when things go wrong. Major power cuts have the status of natural disasters. The US is reluctant to enact legis-lation which would sacrifice high fuel consumption, even though it is certain that this contributes to the greenhouse effect. Engineering products feed the need of the socially mobile for conspicuous consumption, and a visitor from a developing country could well accuse us of living in an excess society. Technology, however, goes deeper than this for us; it is close to the core of our way of life, and our collective being.

Although we can temporarily turn our back on selected technologies, such as genetically-modified foods, nuclear weapons, and (after Chernobyl) nuclear power, knowledge is irreversible. Industrious historians and information specialists will ensure that Pandora's box is un-closable.

Technological advances tend to have a human cost. A recent article in *The Engineer* noted the ill effects of electromagnetic radiation to which modern electronic equipment has exposed us (Johnson, 2002). The great engineer Charles Kettering left us with two doubtful gifts: fluorocarbons for refrigerators, and TEL for gasoline. Some technology has caused as much conflict as it has been a boon. Mobile phones are used universally, yet strong opposition is offered to the siting of aerials near schools and hospitals. Airliners are essential to many business travellers, while the construction or extension of airports nearly always creates a furore.

Anthony Giddens has reminded us in his Reith lectures for 1999 that advancing technology has increased the ratio of man-made to natural risk in Western society (Giddens, 1999). After a series of environmental disas-ters including BSE, in May 2001 Lord Woolf, the Lord Chief Justice, conjured up the prospect of a legal body which would openly assess the scientific basis of controversial government policies (Verkaik, 2001). The suggestion reflected the intense popular mistrust which has arisen of the role of government advisers. In principle, his idea brings knowledge towards the centre of political life, a trend which may grow.

The consequence of the increasingly synthetic, or hybridized, nature of our world is to emphasize the responsibility of people (and the role of engineers) in sorting out its problems, at least insofar as those problems are solveable by the application of knowledge.

▶ A CLOSER LOOK AT THE ENGINEERS THEMSELVES

Despite the multi-faceted nature of engineering, some themes and aspects are common to engineers generally. A glance at the social context of tech-nology reminds us that engineers are very often not the initiators of ideas. Society is largely responsible for what they do. Engineers can produce monsters, like the hydrogen bomb, but not on their own. There is an uneasy, yet *pari passu*, link between broadening technical possibilities, social and commercial policy, economic resources, and the development of social needs and purposes.

To start with, engineers in our kind of society work within a commercial framework. What is made is closely linked with who is paid. Even for humanitarian purposes, the market may impede the progress of a good engineering idea, such as a special robot arm for people affected with muscular diseases. The more expensive the resources required (including knowledge), the higher the price of the end product. Luxury boats are laden with more and more must-have gadgets. Not that the link between engineering and costs is wholly disadvantageous to society, in that useless ideas are sometimes killed off. The availability of resources is a key factor in every engineering project.

The practical consequences for engineers of commercial and contractual constraints are considerable. They set a limit to the extent to which consulting engineers can take their helpfulness to clients, even though the engineering solution is clear. At worst, contractual difficulties can distort or block the application of engineering skills. Also, and this is a keenly-felt question of their role, engineers may resent spending time on unwrapping red tape.

Engineers also have a powerful matrix of regulations with which to contend. Contractual restraints are the most obvious. Patent and copyright laws put some barriers around knowledge transfer. Safety laws are intended to reduce the harmfulness of engineering products. There are professional regulations about ethics and the level of qualifications which engineers must have. Industrial standards, discussed in Part 1 of this book, represent the collective decisions of engineers, which usually have a mandatory force. On a day-to-day basis, the engineer has to conform to work procedures required by the quality assurance certification, which customers are increasingly demanding. All modern engineers have experienced that tingle of excitement which precedes the visit of quality assurance auditors. Confidentiality is also a constraint on what may or may not be written or said. During the closed share dealing season, this is legally enforced, but for the rest of the time embarrassment or financial loss must be avoided by taking care about what is communicated.

The effect of the regulatory framework extends to aspects of the engineering knowledge base. Rules on copyright affect photocopying, the use of the Internet, and the distribution of newspaper articles for current awareness services, among other information activities. The pressures on information specialists, characterized by the recent EU decision on commercial copying, are growing rather than diminishing, with the paradoxical result, that while IT is getting ever slicker, information transfer is in some bureaucratic ways more difficult than it was in the era of card catalogues.

The management context in which many engineers operate has consequences for responsibility in decision making, relationships and most other aspects of work. As with contractual affairs, there is sometimes a keen sense of the tension between managerial and engineering roles, which often leads to a separate career route for highly-qualified engineers ('Technical Specialists') who would otherwise be promoted into managerial posts they may not want.

Nor are engineers unaffected by the surrounding social, economic, political and cultural environment. Government policies affect the objectives and resources of engineers, as defence expenditure, for example, fluctuates from year to year. Many engineers participate in EU-funded research work. Legislation creating a European market has led many engineers to migrate to other EU countries. Global discrepancies in educational provision determine, often unfairly, who will become an engineer. Economic recession may curtail the output of engineering products. Engineers have to respond to the changing requirements of customers, partly in order to maintain brand differentiation. This has involved huge changes in the structure and practices of many industries (for example, the motor industry) in recent years. Although graphics and mathematics are universal, and English is used widely, language and other cultural differences significantly impede knowledge transfer.

▶ ENGINEERS VERSUS SCIENTISTS

There is a traditional place in the survey literature for comparisons between engineers and scientists. (Comparisons between engineers and other communities are rarer.) The differences described in the older literature are often nugatory, and dated. The claim, for example, that engineers are less well academically qualified than scientists has been superseded in an era of engineering PhDs (there are thirty-one in the author's company, out of a population of 900). In any case, as we shall see, this is an age of convergence, in which, for example, DaimlerChrysler employs physicists to work alongside engineers, often as co-authors of technical papers. In the German motor industry, senior academics and senior engineers form a single community. Engineering consultants in mechanical engineering often employ first-class chemists.

There is a lurking stereotype in the literature that engineers are nut-and-bolts people with a limited interest in ideas, who prefer a chat with someone to reading technical papers. The suggestion is that they are rather simple fellows compared with physicists, the toiling gnomes in Middle Earth's fiery depths, rather than the wizards. The writer's experience, based on a survey of engineers' information activities, as well as personal encounter, is that, despite outward sociological similarities, engineers are primarily individuals, with an equal range of cultural interests to members of other communities; there are artists, singers and other musicians, music-lovers, novel-readers and theatre buffs among them.

Paul G. Allen, co-founder of Microsoft, for example, is also the founder of Experience Music Project, an interactive music museum in Seattle.

Engineers are like other professionals. Each follows a unique path, towards a common métier, goes through similar processes of socialization and acculturation, and passes from stage to stage through a dynamic career. Engineers in a given discipline will share a common literature. They look back to leading engineers of the past, who can provide role-models, and to contemporaries, who act as reference groups. They possess a specialized vocabulary. Certain key professional activities are rituals of solidarity. They share in communal events like conferences. They work within a range of common problems and solutions. Some key problems are collectively seen as 'holy grails' yet to be attained.

Personal qualities underlie success and failure. Individual judgement, memory, decision-making skills, problem-solving skills, insight, experience, consistency and rationality are inseparable from practical achievement. A look at the careers of successful engineers shows the key importance of such qualities. Sir Harry Ricardo, for example, whose life has been the subject of a recent biography by John Reynolds (Reynolds, 1999), showed the vision of a pioneer and the gifts of a diplomat, as well as communication skills of a high order.

Engineers usually operate in teams. In work-groups, personal qualities can compensate for, reinforce, and complement each other. Groups can to some extent take on a life of their own, indeed such communities of practice are essential for achievement. One of the paradoxes of a capitalist economy is that its constituent companies pursue impersonal ends (even if these ends concern the personal satisfaction of the customer), but are forced to use personal means. There is consequently a permanent, dialectical relationship between the achievement of objective, corporate goals, and the life-quality and morale of the working community, without which these goals are (in practice) unattainable. The tacit knowledge of the community, for example, is vital to the company. Managers have the unenviable task of balancing these impersonal and personal demands. If the manager fails in this, engineers will apply their own market prerogative, and leave.

That engineers have ethical and social contributions to make was exemplified by the vogue for appropriate technology (Schumacher, 1973). The writings of Professor M.W. Thring, for example, also show a keen, informed awareness of the moral consequences of high technology (Thring, 1980.)

► THEORY AND PRACTICE

The following discussion offers a way of looking at engineering knowledge in the context of knowledge as a whole. It is also needed to explain a point of view which runs through the rest of this chapter. This consists of a broad distinction between formal knowledge, which is contained in many of the information sources discussed later in this book, and the practical contingencies of everyday life in which engineers apply this knowledge, with information specialists to help them. In some ways, each side of this distinction occupies its own territory, to the extent that there are certain tensions between the world of theory and abstract reason and knowledge, and the world of everyday encounter.

Each 'world' can be linked with characteristic values, knowledge, skills (especially reasoning), and life-styles. Abstract ideas appeal to some people, while practical problems attracts others. In the world of theory, things tend to be worked out in a systematic fashion; but attempts to apply theoretical models and structures to the world of practical affairs may lead to frustration, as the lack of match between theory and practice is revealed. Explicit knowledge is characteristic of the world of theory, while tacit knowledge is often of key importance in everyday life. Engineering know-how is the kind of knowledge which mediates between engineering principles and specific problems. Reasoning in the world of theory requires skills with abstract concepts, while reasoning in the world of encounter is also tied to particular contingencies. The world of encounter requires many skills of a tacit, personal and practical kind which are not needed in the world of theory.

The above distinction is reflected by Introna, who notes how inadequate formal management education is in certain circumstances of the world of work (Introna, 1997). Since management theory is rarely applicable in all its pristine fullness, the manager falls back on 'satisficing', which is a parody of the original, but a tactic which is essential for survival. A rather different aspect of this topic is reflected in the case of an inventor (known to the writer) who sees theory (and particularly formal engineering education) as a barrier to creative thinking and innovation. He goes straight from intuitions to engineering ideas, largely by-passing formal knowledge, which he values only in terms of working out the calculations needed for his inventions.

Engineering success partly depends on the interplay between theory and encounter – what one takes from theory and applies to encounter, how one takes it, how one applies it, and what one leaves behind. Information specialists are positioned at the confluence of the two worlds. Many aspects of their work are designed to mediate abstract, text-based knowledge to engineers in practical situations. Classification systems are an example: pre-coordinated systems assume a greater degree of pre-existing order in the world than post-coordinated ones. The schemes have to be updated, like this book, as the world-order changes. Reference interviews provide an interface between the language of information sources, and the natural language of users. Thesauri and taxonomies seek to erect proactive, semi-permanent verbal structures around fast-changing actualities. Information units actively manage the outputs of a host of information streams, which may be both self-contained and general in character, for the benefit of a particular group of users in their changing situations. Information specialists are required to be expert in both reasoning skills and encounter skills, as they seek to marry the two worlds.

There is no sharp division between the theoretical and the practical spheres. We inhabit both of them. Broadly speaking, they merge into each other, to form a spectrum from pure theory at one end to individual events and encounters at the other. This concept of a spectrum will reappear later in the discussion.

▶ THE ERA OF CONVERGENCE

The situation of engineers has changed in the last few years as the knowledge-economy has grown in importance. The value of physical objects as a proportion of the total value of the engineer's work, at least in western societies, has declined. It is now true to say that the engineer's knowledge, in terms of virtual engineering, computational fluid dynamics, e-collaboration, finite element analysis, computer-aided engineering and simulation, has become the most valuable asset he or she possesses, more valuable than many specific products.

Loaded with software and electronics, engineering products reflect our convergent times, by combining intangible and tangible content, material existence with formal knowledge. This is increasingly true for many branches of engineering. Looking at the huge range of routes, roles and life-chances reflected in the surveys in Part 2 of this book, it would be easy to detect more diversity than commonality in the careers and activities of engineers. Because of the pressures of competition, however, engineers today are working closer together than ever before. In this, they reflect the tendency of our times towards convergence and holism. At the abstract, 'top' end of the knowledge-encounter spectrum, scientists are working towards a unified theory for all particles and forces. Slightly downstream of this, and within range of direct interest for engineers, the fairly new discipline of multiphysics is now established. This envisages the common solution of physical problems involving different, traditionally separate, physics sub-disciplines, such as thermodynamics and acoustics, where a problem involves more than one of them. The new engineering discipline of mechatronics, further downstream, searches for a blend of mechanical and electronic solutions.

Still further downstream, engineers are combining their disciplines as never before. Mechanical engineers in the motor industry are finding solutions to hoary problems via the introduction of electronics and of software expertise. This has enabled such achievements as bringing the direct injection gasoline engine to production. Interdisciplinary studies are a feature of engineering education; for example, the US College of Engineering and Applied Science has set up an Integrated Teaching and Learning Laboratory, in which engineering students can gain hands-on experience of a range of specialisms. Engineers are making as good use as other groups of the potential for collaboration offered by e-mail and the Internet.

In yet more local terms, simultaneous engineering has taken over from the sequential execution of development steps, so great is the pressure to reduce development cycles. The old days of the 'over the wall' attitude to work, i.e. completely isolated, self-contained departmental activity, have been replaced by project groups, matrices, inter-disciplinary teams, outsourcing, and the use of consultants and contractors. Massive mono-liths based on a bureaucratic model have given way to spin-offs and joint ventures, giving greater flexibility (and greater anxiety). Engineers are now having to constantly widen the scope of their interests.

A look at Part 2 of this book will superficially indicate ever greater specialization. Engineers seem to be going ever further away from the general knowledge base and vocabulary of civil society. But the actual results are paradoxically taking us nearer to what we want, and to each other. Today's engineering products sell because, though ever more special-ized, they increasing mirror our intuitive needs and wishes. Mobile phones and the Internet have brought us close across space. Modern vehicles are increasingly offering the conveniences of home or office. The subjective is converging with the objective, as engineers find ways to quantify the emotional reactions of those who use engineering products. Competition ensures that the distance between the customer's wish and its attainment is continually shrinking.

▶ SOME WAY TO GO WITH INFORMATION LITERACY

Against these progressive tendencies, the role of the engineer is incomplete, insofar as it does not explicitly embody information literacy as a universal, mandatory and integrated component. While many engineers are informa-tion-literate, their literacy is sometimes acquired haphazardly. Others seem never to acquire it. The enormous deficiencies resulting from lack of infor-mation awareness among engineers surface from time to time. Schuchman's massive 1981 report on the information behaviour of US engineers was prompted by official uneasiness that their levels of knowledge were less than they might be (Schuchman, 1981). In 1998, Derwent reported on the parlous state of patent knowledge and its management in Europe, and particularly the UK. The report cited massive litigation costs and wastage of R&D resources as the result (Derwent, 1998). A 1996 survey in the writer's company revealed lack of basic knowledge of the (then) command language of the Information Services Department's bibliographic database. This extended even to those engineers who most enthused about the Library (Ward, 1996).

Dying for Information, the famous report by Paul Waddington for Reuters, seems to point to the opposite weakness: 'information overload' (Reuters, 1996). The failings cited by the report, however, reflect poor information management, as much as a superfluity of information. The failures noted extended to organizational structures which impeded information flow, the existence of multiple media of communication without proper control, and inefficient searching. Information overload may simply be poor information literacy or inept information and knowledge management in another form. If quality of information is considered, i.e. 'fitness for purpose', then the problem may result from a mutual failure, of the content of the information, and the skill of the searcher.

In an information society with a knowledge economy, shortcomings in information literacy are all the more painful. The present time emphasizes more than in the past the roles of information and knowledge management, transfer and use among engineers (and others). The knowledge that engineers possess is today even more the main characteristic of their social role. To some extent, modern engineers are (like information specialists, knowledge managers and lecturers) knowledge workers.

There is room for a pincer movement of legislation and public education, to ensure that information literacy becomes part of the engineer's role. Starting with the curriculum in schools and universities, literature searching skills should be demanded by employers, quality assurance assessors and senior managers. Evidence of literature searching, in appropriate cases, should be built into contract law.

► THE ENGINEERING KNOWLEDGE BASE

The 'engineering knowledge base' is simply a way of referring to the total sum of engineering knowledge and knowledge activities, i.e. the 'engineering information environment'. In this discussion, the concepts of data and information are taken to be subsumed within the concept of knowledge.

The engineering knowledge base is set within the general knowledge base of society. It is subject to time, it is close to action, and it is inseparable from being. It also reflects the convergence of three major concepts: knowledge, communication and learning. It is not a single entity, but has many divisions and sub-structures. Its state of health can be assessed, and the financial measurement of its value is a problem which management accountants are starting to tackle. The specific sources discussed in Part 1 of this book take their place alongside other elements of the knowledge base.

Broadly speaking, the engineering knowledge base consists of explicit knowledge, such as that contained in the sources discussed in Part 1 below, and tacit knowledge, inside people's heads, or embedded in organizational structures and practices, cultural and other objects (such as engineering products), techniques and instruments.

The engineering knowledge base is set within the general knowledge base of society, which engineers draw upon like anyone else, both (as in this discussion) as engineers, and also as citizens, people, readers, consumers etc. Engineering has grown out of practices and skills which lie close to tradition and common sense (the quality that the great innovator, James Watt, is credited with). Over time, it has become more and more differentiated from common sense, but the latter quality is still an essential ingredient in engineering success.

We have already noted the regulatory and commercial environments within which engineers work; these also affect the knowledge base. The knowledge in it consists of both public and confidential knowledge.

The engineering knowledge base is changing all the time, due to internal growth, or the impact of other disciplines. Because the knowledge base depends on an infrastructure which includes people, institutions, government ministries and firms, changes in these affect the growth, direction and transfer of knowledge. Daily innovation on all fronts, and in all ways and directions, has an enormous, if not precisely measurable, cumulative effect. The need to publish a fresh edition of this book is an explicit outcome of this ceaseless process.

Knowledge leads to action in the world of encounter, or it remains in the loftier realms of the world of theory. Information specialists and engineers can 'know' roughly the same things, but it is the engineer who is qualified to act on them. One can only act successfully on the knowledge one really knows. Action divides 'really knowing' from just 'knowing about'. Searching for knowledge in information sources is one of the actions that characterize the use of knowledge in the world of work.

The fact that people and their minds are so crucial to the generation, transfer, acquisition, development and use of knowledge indicates the inseparability of knowledge and being. Knowledge, and particularly innovation, are related to 'softer' concepts such as aspirations, insight, and perception. Being is both individual and collective: people leave, but their contribution to the knowledge base (hopefully) remains behind. The cultural basis of engineering activity is also of key importance.

Knowledge and communication are convergent concepts. Unless knowledge is communicated and promoted (by knowledge workers such as information specialists) it will never leave the theorist's head, and never end up as action. Therefore, communication systems, including organizational structures, are an intrinsic part of the knowledge base. People are necessarily involved as well, tying knowledge once again to being.

An even more rarely noted link is that between knowledge and learning. We now live in a learning society as well as an information society. Learning is one of the outcomes of engineering, which, in today's knowledge economy, is even more highly prized than some of the concrete products, however successful. Real life is prone to partial success, and even failure; but this is the way that new insights are often learned, and how the engineering knowledge base grows.

The knowledge base is not a single entity. Engineers have a commonalty in their shared, fundamental knowledge, while individual disciplines, like those surveyed in Part 2 of this book, have their own, more specialized knowledge bases. Knowledge bases can exist within individual companies, institutions, groups of companies, temporary corporate alliances, at conferences, and even in individual relationships. Within firms, they can exist in departments, teams, libraries, communities and invisible colleges. The engineering knowledge base is therefore a complex, living, fluctuating entity, and its life has cyclic and dynamic qualities.

Its state of health can be reflected in the amount and quality of research and development. The existence of professional information services within firms, their staff numbers and their budgets, the number of engineers with higher degrees either achieved or in prospect, and the generation of patents, are three of the ways that the condition of the company and industry knowledge base can be reckoned.

The knowledge database is knowledge capital. The assessment of the value, quality and role of knowledge assets is a point of debate in management accountancy. Intangible assets, intellectual property and the extent and value of tacit knowledge, are of increasing importance in a knowledge economy.

▶ WHERE DOES THE KNOWLEDGE COME FROM?

This book is largely concerned with text-based knowledge sources. The chapter on professional societies represents the role of organizations in the engineering knowledgebase. Clearly, the existence of the texts implies some kind of human organizational activity. Independent research institutions, university departments, professional organizations, government offices, quangos, pressure groups, dot.coms, management consultancies, industrial firms and their representative organizations and publishers are a handful of the organizations which make up the infrastructure, without which knowledge workers would have no knowledge to pass on and use.

Two of the aspects which control the working of the system are costs and change. Some of the sources, such as many reference works and journals, as well as abstracting and indexing services, journal subscription services, and a vast array of databases, such as those run by Dialog, stand or fall by the market forces which are the basis of their existence. They fulfil a variety of roles and purposes, but near the top of these is the need of engineers for information. If this need falters – and it must be perceived as a need by the engineers – or if the knowledge-providers cease to meet it effectively, the latter will decline or perish. Alternatively, the need may be clear, but resources may seem to be too scanty to acquire the information.

Content, format and inner structure are shaped by the need to meet information needs. Quality, accuracy, coverage, cost-effectiveness, accessibility and currency are some of the key features which determine whether the services for sale meet market requirements. The economics of the engineering knowledge industry are complex. Many providers, for example, have a niche existence, as they depend on specialist rather than general readerships.

Other sources are less dependent on the market. Many technical reports issue from government offices, pressure groups, think tanks and other research institutes, professional institutions and academic departments, whose on-going existence relies on other means than the texts they produce. Of particular value to knowledge workers are the statistical series which government departments are compelled by law to publish. Also of major interest are the technical papers and theses which emerge from academic institutions, often prompted by the need to contribute original research to the knowledge base. Many technical papers published by firms have only an indirect relationship with the need to make money. Professional institutions produce key reference books, such as membership lists.

Conferences and meetings and their written proceedings, often in the form of 'grey' literature which may be hard to obtain, are a frequent by-product of business life. Product literature is the outcome of the marketing needs of manufacturing and other companies. Workshop manuals are an essential element of the contractual relationship between sellers and customers of engineering products. Patents, which fulfil a legal requirement, are also outcomes of technological and commercial activities. Standards emerge from professional consultations between engineers which generally ride above the immediate need for profit, even though they affect nearly every aspect of what is made and sold. In this sense, they are similar to government legislation, which itself is the outcome of social, economic and political pressures and trends, of which the market is only one, if a key, feature.

There is, thus, almost as great a variety of reasons for publishing information as there are information sources. While some information is provided 'from above', most is supplied by a complex network of free enterprise, based on many separate perceptions of multiple needs. The result is an incredibly rich, and ever-growing range of knowledge resources, which, while serving specific needs, do not display an intrinsic organization. That is why the information sources themselves give rise to secondary resources such as reviews of work in progress, bibliographies, and abstracting and indexing services. The need which the latter meet is that of controlling the vast resources of primary information. One of the great debates of recent years has (broadly) been about the extent to which the filtered information can then safely pass directly to the end-user, and the extent to which the final arbiter of what he or she receives should be a person – the information specialist.

Any impression of a steadily on-going system is misleading, since social and technological change ensure that the engineering knowledge-base is in permanent, and sometimes radical, flux. The structures in which each knowledge source is embedded are constantly changing. The development of new media, such as CD-ROMs, on-line databases, intranets, e-mail and the World Wide Web have reshaped the knowledge landscape within the last 20 years. Competition itself is sufficient to bring new, and hopefully better, versions of existing services, or alternatives to them. Acquisitions and failures are major features of the knowledge industry. Its personnel change frequently. Business cycles affect the pattern of resources available to fund the production and purchase of information. The ever-increasing costs of publishing original research have led to a lively debate on e-versions of, and self-produced alternatives to, conventional learned journals. Such changes often not only involve a change in medium, but also challenge well-established values and norms. The content of the texts is, of course, always changing as well, as new ideas and discoveries supplant traditional views and approaches. The tendency to add more and more new knowledge is only matched by the constant re-evaluation of existing knowledge. Some of the reasons for changes such as the rise of the information society and of the knowledge-based economy seem obvious, but others are obscure to those, like ourselves, who are caught up in them.

▶ A CLOSER LOOK AT SOME OF THE CONTENTS OF THE ENGINEERING KNOWLEDGE BASE

The sources discussed in Part 1 of this book are an essential segment of the engineering knowledge base: they account for many of the explicit, bibliographical (mainly publicly available) information sources which are available for engineers. The preceding discussion suggests the context in which they are set. A survey carried out by the author in 1996 (Ward, 1996) identified the various information sources used by twenty-seven senior engineers in his own company. Some additional ones are also included in the following discussion.

Sources of tacit knowledge included:

- Memory – the first resort
- Other engineers – the survey identified groups of engineers ('knowledge clubs') whose knowledge and opinions were particularly valued by individuals. Specific individuals acted as gatekeepers, due to their long experience and good memories ('memory men'). Contacts with other engineers were made at work, in communication with clients, suppliers and colleagues in other companies (including those who had previously worked at Ricardo), and also at conferences and social events outside work. In the background, but of key importance, was the overall culture at Ricardo, which is notably open and communicative.

Sources of explicit knowledge included both confidential and publicly available materials.

Immediately surrounding the engineers were:

- Confidential personal files,
- Personal books,
- Confidential departmental files,
- Departmental books,
- Confidential departmental databases.

Other sources included:

- The Library.

The Library's stock of publicly-available items included:

- Textbooks and other books,
- Periodicals (which were circulated by the Library), plus an extensive, if selective, set of back issues,
- Trade literature (including a set of workshop manuals),
- Reference works,
- Standards,
- Legislation,
- A collection of papers written by Ricardo engineers,
- Other technical papers,
- Journal articles,
- Magazine articles,
- Videos,
- Tapes,
- Software,
- CD-ROMs.

The Library's stock of confidential material included:

- Internal reports,
- Presentations, reports and memoranda from other companies,

- Software,
- Films,
- Videos,
- Tapes,
- A very extensive collection of test sheets and other data from previous projects.

The Library's other services included:

- The extensive POWERLINK bibliographical database, (the largest database on powertrains [=engines and transmissions] in the world). This was available to all engineers within Ricardo, and also (for a fee) to clients,
- Databases indexing the confidential material,
- Services providing selective dissemination of information.

In addition, the Library provided reference, translating and circulation services, as well as acting as the company's major link with the whole range of external information sources.

Most of these services and sources are still available. Key additions since the survey include the Internet, which is available to all engineers, and is used heuristically for information retrieval, and also for e-commerce. The company now has its own website, from which POWERLINK is available. Other additions are e-mail, and the company Intranet, which is available to engineers in the now much enlarged Ricardo Group. The Intranet has since taken over the storage of internal reports, in electronic form, rather than the paper format used previously and stored in the Library, and acts (for example) as an internal newspaper, noticeboard, directory of personnel, telephone directory, and repository for the company's operations manual. POWERLINK is also internally accessed via the Intranet.

It is quite useful to identify and list, as above, some of the constituents of the engineering knowledge database. Clearly, the sources discussed in the first part of this book can be found a place among them, but it can be seen that the latter are only a segment of what is available. Before discussing the relative usefulness of the sources listed, and the relationships between them, it is helpful to note some general features.

Firstly, it is of interest that the list is a mixture of information sources and communication media, an entanglement which reflects the close relationship between knowledge and communication. E-mail, printed and hand-written texts, videotapes, CD-ROMs, software, audio tapes, drawings, graphs, tables, databases, photocopies, films and the spoken word, for example, are media; there is no indication of content. Legislation, reference books, technical papers and standards, however, are terms indicative of content. The reason why such a jumble is acceptable as a list of information sources lies in the third layer, the discourses, data, information, knowledge, opinions, formulae, programs, analysis and descriptions for which the others exist. Unconsciously, we use this layer to validate the other two.

The relationship between these three layers is subtle and complex (a fourth, mental layer probably lies behind them all). Ideas – intellectual content – are independent of any particular embodiment, whether text-based or electronic. The same intellectual content can be gathered from a textbook, the Internet, a post-it note, a library book or a diary. This is the case in principle, but total interchangeability is not what we experience as knowledge workers. In practice, distinctive formats, whether physical or literary, tend to imply some distinctions between the intellectual contents they embody. These depend on the kind of packaging which suits the content, on the physical nature of the media, on costs, on information life-times, and on conventions established by the knowledge industry. Formats are influential in their effect on information behaviour, as we will see later.

It is also important to remember the range and complexity of the knowledge within a given format. Two examples are:

- 'the Internet', which is in one sense a pigeon hole for survey-writers, but has a scope, variety and unpredictability which is global in breadth, and
- 'periodicals', which sound like a meaningful category, until one considers that periodicals include both learned, refereed journals (like the *British Medical Journal*), technical periodicals (like *Computing & Control Engineering Journal*) semi-technical journalism (like *Eureka*), serious news channels (like *New Scientist*) and popular magazines (like *Flight*). All of these will be useful at different points in the engineers' working lives.

The division of information sources into primary and secondary tells us something useful about the closeness of the source to the original work which it describes. However, it is also beneficial to range our sources along the slightly different spectrum of theory-to-encounter, which we have introduced earlier. This gives us a model of the sources in the engineering knowledge base, founded on some of their key functions.

Textbooks, and some reference books, for example engineering handbooks, largely belong to the basic-principle end. They are the least time-bound.

Engineering standards encapsulate specific requirements for engineering products and processes. They have a collective authority, and their revision is only undertaken with extreme care.

As this knowledge is worked on, it turns into individual technical papers and journal articles, with sometimes limited applicability.

Reviews (like this book), research-in-progress surveys and bibliographies summarize the knowledge-flow up to this point, but they, too, are time-bound.

Knowledge in an academic context remains, in principle, a public affair, but achieves specific, time-bound embodiments in theses and papers.

As knowledge is worked on by individual companies, it emerges in technical reports which are guarded from public view. Patents have a two-way function in both enshrining and revealing new knowledge, or new arrangements of previous knowledge, and also in protecting the knowledge gained: hence their classic ambiguities.

E-journals, e-books, self-published research studies and Internet and other digital resources (e-commerce, e-collaboration, virtual engineering) are somewhat closer in terms of recency to the competitive world of encounter than their slower, perhaps more expensive, paper equivalents.

Knowledge may later appear in the form of physical products, and generate a literature of product data and press releases. The physical object, far away from, but ultimately generated by, the world of basic principles, embodies a range of knowledge and know-how: it is a commitment which suffers from obsolescence almost immediately. It is less valuable than the knowledge which creates it, and which is already being used to make the next object. Key products and processes may have an irreversible effect on the way future work is conducted, through benchmarking and other means.

The professional press rounds up knowledge (and gossip) along the whole knowledge-spectrum: but emphasizes the world of encounter. Articles in engineering magazines are often reformulations of earlier conversations and of press releases.

Conferences, meetings and symposia are more fleeting events of communication. They tend to be closer to every-day experience and thinking than formal literature. The (often grey) literature which is their tangible product sometimes looks similar to the technical papers and journal articles already mentioned, but is often issued in forms, e.g. PowerPoint slides, which imply or require the oral context in which the papers were delivered. Literature is in any case only a small part of the reason why conferences are held; what counts for the engineer is the moment-by-moment interaction, the informal exchange of tacit knowledge, and the contractual and other possibilities which they create through personal encounter.

Individual notebooks, diaries, records of contract work, scraps of paper, and signed free-hand drawings may be essential to competitive success, even though they never see the public light of day. These are fragmented jottings from the life of encounter.

Conversations are sometimes crucial to the solution of an immediate problem. Knowledge sharing creates a community of understanding in which new ideas are born.

The thoughts of individuals, in their more finished, or rawer forms are fundamental. Here, we are in the world of everyday life, biography and existential commitment. This is prior to both primary and secondary sources, and reflects the dual roles of tacit and explicit knowledge. Ideas have a three-way existence, somewhere within, and also between, the consciousness of a group or an individual, and the texts which feed back into the explicit knowledge system.

With the exception of, for example, reverse engineering, knowledge seems to flow from the more static and abstract end of the spectrum (theory), towards the more dynamic and pragmatic end (encounter). The speed at which it does so is increasing all the time, under the pressure of competition.

▶ A SURVEY OF ENGINEERS' USE OF KNOWLEDGE SOURCES

Having looked at engineering knowledge sources in terms of the patterns of knowledge as a whole, let us now turn to their use by real engineers, as they carry out testing, design, research and development projects in the writer's company, Ricardo. No longer will we wrench them out of their working environment, useful as it has been to do so. This concluding section presents and interprets the survey mentioned earlier, which the present writer carried out at Ricardo in 1996 (Ward, 1996). Although the intervening years have been enriched by e-mail, the Internet and the company Intranet, the basic findings are still valid for the bibliographical sources mentioned in Part 1 of this book. It is also likely that the overall picture of engineers and of their relationship to information still holds good.

The world in which information is used seems to be a discontinuous one. A small sub-survey identified the large number of projects and concerns, both business and personal, which simultaneously preoccupied the minds of the engineers. While the themes themselves were ongoing and structured, they could only be attended to intermittently.

Another of the discontinuities reflected was in the overlap of the sources used. For example, company reports were held by individuals and departments, as well as by the Library. The world of work is untidy, however immaculate the engineering products.

A further discontinuity was shown in the complex relationship between formal (i.e. explicit) knowledge-sources (such as articles from journals), and tacit (i.e. informal ones) such as conversations between members of the 'knowledge clubs'. One engineer may recommend a bibliographical source, or offer an evaluation of it. Another may seek, through browsing in the Library, the kind of intellectual stimulus that someone else would look for in conversation.

There was tension between the two kinds of sources. Possibly according to temperament, some engineers went to textual sources more willingly than others, and the ranking of the popularity of the two kinds was complex. From a fellow engineer, one can get an instant, pre-digested slant on a problem, a facility which led one of the respondents to say that 'ten minutes with the right person is worth a week in the Library'. But the ability of individuals to remember streams of hard data is limited: that is a function for explicit information sources to fulfil, and for this, the Library is frequently essential.

The very varied purposes for which the knowledge is required may affect the use of sources most of all. In desk research, for example, the proportion of Library work may be nearly 100%, while a self-contained contract task may require no external knowledge. Engineers will use different sources seamlessly, and with complementary effect. The more experienced ones, who have been round the knowledge circuit many times, will be able to offer guidance to newcomers: knowing leads to learning.

In the above analysis there is a considerable loading of personal preference and personal knowledge, reflecting the convergence of knowledge and being. The individuality of the engineers' views and preferences, in spite of their sociological similarities, is reflected in the fact that not one question in the survey was answered in the same way by everybody.

There is also a linked convergence of knowledge and activity. Going to the Library, searching the database, choosing a source, reading a report, all reflect the fact that, within the narrative of the engineers' working lives, knowledge converges with action. In the same context, the knowledge gained, then tacitly absorbed, is enacted in the workflow.

The real-life situation under study revealed some barriers, as well as channels, to information and knowledge. Examples are the existence of projects confidential even to other Ricardo engineers, which represented knowledge-islands protected by security. Only in a generalized form did the work there contribute to the company's explicit knowledge base. The human equivalent was encountered in the (hopefully exceptional) engineer who hugged private knowledge as a means of political power. It was also clear that intra-company communication was less than perfect, resulting in work being duplicated. Their roles as administrators, and the pressures of the quality assurance system, were perceived by some engineers as a hindrance to their 'real work'.

We turn now to the engineers' use and appreciation of the knowledge sources at their disposal. As far as explicit knowledge is concerned, the presentation of data is often the key to its usefulness: material in an animation in a CD-ROM may contain the same data as a patent, but bring more immediate understanding. Purpose, level, type, presentation, depth, detail and immediacy are some of the key factors which lead to the use of one source rather than another.

The wide range of responses to the question as to how useful 'periodicals' are reflects the problem of dealing with such a heterogeneous collection of sources, as was noted above (and also by one of the respondents). Some questioned their technical value, while others praised their news and currency. One respondent said that, due to pressures of time, he relied on the recommendations of others when selecting articles to read.

Another said that he had given up reading them altogether, because of information overload. Thus contingencies impinge on knowledge transfer.

In the Ricardo environment, textbooks (seen at the static end of our formal-knowledge/encounter model) have less value than they would have in an academic context (academic libraries tend to have far more of them). They are like wise, trusty but retired engineers. Respondents valued them for their reliability (a prime quality of good information), comprehensiveness, theory, historical insights and the ability to stimulate ideas. Books, however, were unable to supply the timeliness which was found in periodicals, and which the engineers also required.

The thousands of technical papers published annually by the US Society of Automotive Engineers (SAE) represented a special category of value for the engineers. The SAE brand image confers a degree of status prior to actual content. In them, to some extent, the knowledge-principles enshrined in the books have moved down the theory/encounter line into specific projects and components, without (as with some of the periodicals) losing their technical value. The papers themselves vary widely in quality, and may occasionally hide the 'guesses and stresses' of encounter behind a mask of corporate perfection.

When aspects of the Library's retrieval system were tested objectively, results were disappointing, even from those engineers who were strongly supportive of the Library's role. The conventional subject arrangement of the books, involving the use of codes, represented a hindrance to many of their users. Also reported were problems with obtaining basic engineering information from the Library. A further barrier was offered by the simple absence from the shelves of documents which were on loan to other people. These factors must have sometimes reduced the usefulness of the Library as a knowledge source.

The survey produced some insights into what engineers do with the documents they obtain. One respondent emphasized that personal qualities of judgement and perception are involved in the crucial decision about relevance. 'Relevance' is a concept which belongs to the world of encounter, and links the latter with formal knowledge. The most popular recourse was reading the abstract, followed by looking at graphs and other figures, which are often so important in engineering texts (one respondent went to them first). Some respondents relied on the title, while the length, style and format of an article were also seen as important. Four respondents selected documents by trusted authors. The opinions of colleagues also enriched the evaluation process. *Current Contents* was used as well.

The survey also compared tacit with explicit knowledge sources. Although the two types can hardly be ranked in a clear hierarchy (as reflected in the respondents' inability to agree on this point), the discussion above has already shown that, while each fulfils specific needs, there are many ways in which they are linked or interwoven. Explicit knowledge often takes over where tacit knowledge leaves off. Articles can also provide a broader background to problems than can conversation; on the other hand, personal information is often more recent than the printed variety. Accumulated knowledge and experience are essential, underlining the fact that, before it can be of use, explicit knowledge has to be internalised, to become, in a sense, tacit. One respondent attributed success 70% to memory, 20% to people and 10% to paper knowledge, while another estimated that he solved 25% of problems using the Library alone, 25% using people alone, and 50% using both.

We earlier set a range of engineering knowledge sources according to their closeness to the world of abstract principles on the one hand, and to the world of problem-solving on the other. By contrast, the user survey showed what was apparently a highly discontinuous bundle of knowledge activities. Sometimes the relative distance of the knowledge from the immediate circumstances of its use came across (textbooks are 'out of date' but 'still essential'). But all sorts of personal and practical contingencies and concepts were mixed in with the knowledge; 'relevance' is one example. The two analyses show that theory and practice are interdependent, and that the marriage of the two in real time by the knowledge worker is a crucial activity.

► CONCLUSIONS

This chapter sets the scene for the detailed discussions which follow. While the engineers' roles and lives are very varied, there are common features. The pressure of competition is bringing diverse disciplines together. While the means used are increasingly specialized, and seem to be moving forever further from society's common knowledge base, engineering products are paradoxically breaking down the barriers between our intuitive desires and their fulfilment. This is the age of the information society, the Internet and the mobile phone. The ever-richer knowledge of engineers is becoming their chief resource, ahead of physical resources and financial capital. The transfer of this knowledge is, however, still wastefully constrained by limitations in information literacy which have yet to be properly tackled. This chapter has identified some of the aspects and implications of engineering knowledge and knowledge sources, by looking briefly at their relationship with knowledge as a whole, and in more detail as they relate to the practical needs of the engineer. The theoretical discussion was supported by a look at how some real engineers have used the sources at their disposal in the work context.

Thinking globally again, it seems that we are in the process of irretrievably committing human society to a future in which technology plays a predominant role. Through this, we have fundamentally altered our relationship with the natural world, time and space. We have ensured that the threats to human life are going to come increasingly from human sources, and that disputes about knowledge will form an increasingly important component of social debate.

To some extent this marks human progress towards a world of closer relationships, greater understanding, education, peace, comfort and the enhancement of the life chances and being of our children. There are many glowing accounts of the human achievement which knowledge and technology represent, with every prediction of their continuing to benefit us.

On the other hand, we have not yet come near to solving the problems which stem from the darker side of our individual and collective human nature. These remain, even today, in stark contrast to technological progress. Technology merely magnifies them. The problems we are currently living through are partly the result of huge imbalances and injustices in the distribution of the world's resources of all kinds. Influential writers like Martin Heidegger have stated that happiness and technology lie in opposite directions, but offer no assistance in coming to terms with the world as it is actually turning out to be (Heidegger, 1971). All we can say with certainty, on the basis of too much experience, is that technological progress is not enough.

Therefore we cannot expect engineers alone to provide the answers to the most difficult social and ethical questions. We have each to decide for ourselves our alignment to life's ultimate challenges, but a collective step forward will be taken if we can emulate the convergence that is setting in everywhere, and not shut ourselves in air-proof boxes of this or that social or occupational role. It is the privilege of knowledge workers to perceive, and work in terms of, a whole range of human concerns. The knowledge worker stands uniquely at the confluence of formal knowledge and the world of encounter. Let us exercise the power which this standpoint gives us to encourage in our colleagues a more holistic frame of mind.

▶ REFERENCES

Blessing, R. and Schick, H.P., 2002. Studie Entwicklung des Flottenverbrauchs in der Schweiz. *EMPA conference on I.C. Engine R&D in Switzerland, Dubendorf.*

Derwent Information Limited, 1998. *Managing patent information. The gulf between theory and practice.* London: Derwent Information.

Giddens, A., 1999. *Runaway world: how globalisation is reshaping our lives.* London: Profile Books.

Goffman, E., 1969. *The presentation of self in everyday life.* London: Allen Lane.

Heidegger, M., 1971. *Poetry, language, thought.* New York: Harper & Row.

Introna, L.D., 1997. *Management, information and power: a narrative of the involved manager.* Basingstoke: Macmillan.

Johnson, E., 2002. Killer hertz? *The Engineer,* 30 August–12 September, pp. 32–35.

Reuters Business Information, 1996. *Dying for information? An investigation into the effects of information overload in the UK and worldwide.*

Reynolds, J., 1999. *Engines & enterprise: the life and work of Sir Harry Ricardo.* Stroud: Sutton Publishing.

Schuchman, H.L., 1981. *Information transfer in engineering.* Glastonbury, Connecticut: The Futures Group.

Schumacher, E.F., 1973. *Small is beautiful. A study of economics as if people mattered.* London: Blond and Briggs.

Thring, M.W., 1980. *The engineer's conscience.* Bury-St.-Edmunds, UK: Northgate Publishing.

Verkaik, R., 2001. Judges want to scrutinize science advisers. *The Independent,* 29 May 2001, p.4.

Ward, M.L., 1996. A survey of engineers in their information world. *Journal of Librarianship and Information Science,* 33 (4), pp. 168–176.

2 Journals and Electronic Journals

Anne Bell and Martin Wolf

▶ INTRODUCTION

The range of engineers' information needs has already been discussed (Chapter 1). Journals have traditionally played a key part in satisfying those needs. They are a crucial source of current awareness information, used by engineers to keep up to date with new products, processes and research developments. Journals are suited to this role because they appear at regular intervals and their frequency (usually weekly, monthly or quarterly) will enable them to publish new information while it is still current. In addition, journals also constitute a permanent record of research and knowledge which can be consulted retrospectively to determine the provenance and authority for a process, material or concept.

Engineering journals can be subdivided by type – into trade, academic and professional journals – according to their frequency, the type of content that they carry and their readership. These different types of journal will be discussed in greater detail later, but it is worth noting that the majority of journals appearing weekly are trade journals, and they are mainly read by engineers in industry, while academic journals are mainly read by research engineers and they have a special role in the scholarly communication process.

Since the publication of the last edition of *Information Sources in Engineering* the most important change involving journals has been the development of electronic publishing. Many long-standing print journals now have electronic counterparts. There is also a growing number of electronic-only journals, meaning journals that have never been published in a print version and appear only in electronic form. E-journals have rapidly become so pervasive that many publishers now offer electronic-only subscriptions, and many library services are seriously considering taking these up in preference to maintaining their print journal collections. A significant part of this chapter will be concerned with developments in e-journals, so great has been their impact. The latest initiatives in scholarly electronic publishing will also be covered, particularly their impact on traditional engineering journals, and the likely future trends.

► TYPES OF JOURNAL

Engineers use two broad types of journal: trade journals and academic/ professional journals. It has already been noted that engineers have a vital need for up to date information on which to base new product designs and marketing. This kind of information is traditionally found in trade journals.

Trade journals

Trade journals contain material such as industry news and analysis, product and market information, technical information about materials and processes, reviews of software, products and trade literature and advertisements, including job opportunities. The term 'trade journal' also encompasses specialised newspapers and internal house journals and newsletters, all of which carry similar content. As they perform a current awareness role and contain material that will time-expire, trade journals need a rapid publication process, and generally they appear weekly or monthly.

Trade journals may be either general or specialised in coverage. Some of the more wide-ranging trade journals include: the weekly *The Engineer* (www.e4engineering.com/engineer), which contains news, features, and analysis of technologies and applications across industries; *Engineering* (www.engineeringnet.co.uk), a monthly containing editorials and news covering the full spectrum of the manufacturing industries; and the monthly *Eureka* (www.eurekamagazine.co.uk), which covers engineering mechanics and materials, mechanical engineering, electronics, and Computer Aided Design that those engaged in various facets of design might use. More specialised trade journals are mentioned in later chapters.

Trade journals are often supported financially by advertising, which means that they are inexpensive or may even be available free of charge. Some are 'controlled circulation' journals, meaning that they are free to those who apply and fulfil certain criteria determined by the publisher. This also means that many engineers receive personal copies, and the journals concerned are less likely than academic journals to be found in libraries.

House journals are those produced by organisations, businesses and public service providers. Their primary audiences are organisations' customers and/or employees (though this role is now often performed by company websites or intranets). They range from peer-reviewed titles such as *IBM Journal of Research and Development* (www.research. ibm.com/journal/) which is equivalent to academic/scholarly journals (see next section), to corporate newsletters such as *Adhesives and Sealants Newsletter*. The contents of newsletter-style house journals are rarely covered by abstracting and indexing services (see Chapter 9).

In addition to appearing in printed form, many trade journals now also exist in an electronic version or as part of manufacturers' and suppliers' websites. As engineers primarily use them for scanning to keep up to date, trade journals are not normally indexed for future use. Increasingly, though, trade journal content can be found in searchable sources such as websites and news databases. For example, LexisNexis Executive (www.lexis-nexis.co.uk/site/LN_Executive.asp) is a full-text online service providing access to business and trade information, and includes the facility to search by industry and product name. Information about which trade journals exist in electronic format can be found via EEVL, the Internet Guide to Engineering, Mathematics and Computing (www.eevl.ac.uk). EEVL includes a fairly comprehensive list of trade publications organised by industry, title, keyword or geographic eligibility, and there is a facility to register with selected publishers to receive free copies (eevl.tradepub.com).

Given their content, trade journals are primarily of interest to engineers in industry, though engineers in the academic arena may often consult them if their research or teaching so requires. Detailed research and development work, however, is not generally published in trade journals as it requires a quality control process before first publication. This role is undertaken by academic and professional society journals.

Academic and professional society journals

Academic publishers include engineering professional institutions and societies as well as commercial organisations. Academic and professional journals publish papers reporting and discussing research work that makes a new contribution to knowledge in the field of engineering. Such papers may be lengthy and normally include a list of bibliographic references to earlier published work. Before a paper is published it is reviewed by engineers who are authorities in the field and who assess its quality. A paper may only be published when it has been revised in the light of comments from the referees. For academic and research engineers this is a key element in peer recognition, which is derived from publication in quality peer-reviewed journals. A common criticism of the academic journal is that the peer review process takes time and can lead to significant delays in the publication of papers.

The relative importance of an academic journal in its field is determined by its impact factor. This is calculated annually by taking the total number of citations to a journal in any one year, and dividing it by the total number of papers published in the journal during the previous two years (Institute for Scientific Information, 1994). The leading academic journals are those with high impact factors. Journal rankings in science and engineering disciplines are published annually in *ISI Journal Citation Reports* (www.isinet.com/isi/products/citation/jcr/). In the field of mechanical engineering the highest ranked journal in 2002 was *Progress in Energy and Combustion Science* with an impact factor of 3.061, followed by *Journal of Microelectromechanical Systems* (impact factor 2.835), *International Journal of Plasticity* (impact factor 2.464) and *Advances in Applied Mechanics* (impact factor 2.400).

Two of these four are review journals, a special type of academic journal comprising papers that review previously published work rather than reporting new research. Review journals are commonly published annually and have titles such as *Advances in . . .* or *Progress in . . . .* Individual review papers may appear in almost any academic journal. A key characteristic of review papers is an extensive bibliography, the outcome of a comprehensive search of the relevant subject literature by the author. Review papers are widely read and generally are cited more frequently than typical research papers. Therefore review journals have some of the highest impact factors.

It is generally easy to discover which academic and professional journals exist and what their subject coverage is (see next section, *Finding information about journals*). The contents of these journals are well covered by abstracting and indexing sources (which are examined in more detail in Chapter 9). Some academic and professional journals cover a range of subjects of relevance to most engineers, such as *Journal of Engineering and Technology Management* and *Professional Engineering* (www.profeng. com). Specific journals of particular significance to individual fields are covered in the later chapters on engineering specialisms.

Commercially published academic journals can be very expensive, particularly those in specialised fields. Those published by professional societies may be less expensive, and available at reduced prices for members of the institutions or societies concerned.

▶ FINDING INFORMATION ABOUT JOURNALS

For those searching for information on particular subjects that are likely to be contained in professional and academic journals, the abstracting and indexing services examined in Chapter 9 are the major tools for information discovery. For those seeking information on journals themselves, there are a number of different services that can be used.

Ulrich's Periodicals Directory is one of the main sources for finding information about journals. Commonly known as Ulrich's, the directory is available as a multi-volume print reference work, a CD-ROM (updated quarterly) and a web-based service (www.ulrichsweb.com, updated weekly). The directory contains information on over 175,000 active journals in all fields. Information for each journal includes publisher, basic description of the journal's coverage, frequency of publication, subscription costs, whether the journal is refereed, which databases abstract and index their contents, and whether the journal is available electronically. It can be searched for information on specific journals, or browsed by subject to give an indication of the range of journals available in a particular subset. Along with the general heading *Engineering* there are ten subject based subdivisions, and separate information on abstract and review journals.

Ulrich's also provides some tools for the management of an organisation's journals subscriptions. For example, the Serials Analysis System allows organisations to compare their journal holdings with a set of core journals in a subject or all of the journals in the Ulrich's database. This can allow organisations to identify where they have gaps or overlaps in their collections.

Bowker, the company responsible for the *Ulrich's Periodicals Directory*, also publish *Magazine for libraries*. This is a reference book containing similar information about journals to that included in the Ulrich's Periodicals Directory. It is a single volume work and therefore does not hold as much information as Ulrich's, but it is also less expensive.

There is a free database of journal information available on the web called *JournalSeek* (genamics.com/journals), provided by Genamics. Users can search for information on specific titles, or browse through lists of journals in specific categories. There are seventeen subject sub-divisions for engineering, and eighteen subject sub-divisions for electrical and electronic engineering. The information for each journal is more basic than that of Ulrich's – a description of the journal's content is provided, along with a link to the journal publisher's website. The database can also be combined with e-journal management products from Openly Informatics (which will be discussed in more detail later).

As mentioned earlier, information on a journal's impact factor can be obtained from the *Journal Citation Reports*, produced by the Institute of Scientific Information. This database, available via the web or on CD-ROM, contains data comparing the relative impact made by different journals on the general body of scholarly literature. This can prove useful for managing an organisation's journal subscriptions.

▶ ELECTRONIC JOURNALS DEVELOPMENTS

The rapid expansion in the number and importance of electronic journals has been the most significant development in journals publishing since the previous edition of *Information sources in engineering*. Greater access to the World Wide Web now makes accessing journal content through a computer often more convenient and beneficial than consulting a print journal.

An electronic journal, or e-journal, is defined here as a periodical publication containing the full text of articles distributed through electronic means, usually the web but sometimes via other formats such as CD-ROM. As previously noted, many trade magazines have their own websites which often provide the full text of some or all of the print magazine's content for free. There is often little real difference between an electronic trade journal and an ordinary trade website. This section primarily considers the electronic equivalents of academic and professional society journals.

As with print magazines and journals, there are both free and subscription-based electronic journals. Many subscription-based print journals will have an electronic equivalent. Subscribers may have free access to the electronic version of a journal as part of their subscription to the print version, or a separate electronic-only subscription might be available. Different subscription options will be covered later in this section.

E-journals provide their content in a variety of different formats. Some might use basic html (Hypertext Mark-up Language), presenting their content in the same way as a standard web page, while others might use formats such as Adobe's PDF. These require the user to download (for free) a piece of software in order to display a journal's content on screen. The advantage of these formats is that they preserve exactly the style and layout of printed journals, and as such they are often used in the electronic version of a journal available in print.

Unlike print journals, you cannot pick up an e-journal and flick through its pages to see if something strikes your interest. However, e-journals will often provide a set of searching options that allow you to find articles about a specific topic of interest, written by a specific author, or published between specific dates. E-journals are therefore especially helpful if you want to find material on pre-determined topics quickly.

As electronic-only journals become more important to the overall body of information in engineering, they are increasingly editing and refereeing their contents to ensure that they are of the same quality as printed academic and professional journals.

Hosts and aggregators

One of the most important aspects of electronic journals to understand is the concept of *host* or *aggregator* services. These are web-based services that provide access to a range of different journals. Some of these services will provide access only to journals published by a certain institution, while others will provide access to the content of journals from a range of different organisations.

Some publishers licence their journal content to more than one aggregator service. This means that some print journals might have electronic versions available from different hosts and in different formats such as PDF, html or xml (eXtensible Mark-up Language). They may also cover different time periods – for example, content from 1995 to 1999 might be available on one aggregator service, while content from 1997 to the present might be available on another.

When using host or aggregator services, the contents of individual journals can be browsed, or you can search for articles containing your specific keywords, regardless of which journal(s) might have published those articles. The specific search features will vary from service to service, but will typically allow the user to:

- Search for articles by certain authors;
- Search for articles in specific journals;
- Search for articles containing certain keywords in their title, abstract or full text;
- Search for articles published between certain dates.

In addition, some e-journal services allow you to set up a personal profile. These offer options such as automatically sending you email alerts containing the contents list of new editions of your chosen journals, or saving search statements that can be re-run at a later date to find new material since added to the host's content. Personal profiles and alerting services are often available to non-subscribers as well, who may be able to purchase individual articles if they so wish.

Some examples of electronic journal host services are those provided by professional associations, such as *Xplore* (ieeexplore.ieee.org) from the IEEE (Institute of Electrical and Electronics Engineers), and the *ACM Portal* (portal.acm.org) of the Association for Computing Machinery. These subscription services provide access to the full text of articles from journals published by these associations. These particular services also provide access to the content of other material, such as conference proceedings and newsletters.

Aggregator services such as ingenta (www.ingenta.com) and ProQuest (www.proquest.com) provide access to the article content of journals from a wide range of different publishers, including small learned and professional societies that might not otherwise have the finances to make their journal content available electronically. As with host services, aggregator services allow users both to browse the contents lists of specific journals and to search for articles containing keywords related to their research topic.

Services such as these provide subscribers with access to a large number of titles and a number of added-value services. Subscriptions to these services are often very expensive, and as such might not be practical for smaller institutions. It is therefore worth noting that, as with personal profiles and alerting services, some host and aggregator services grant non-subscribers free searching of their material to abstract level before allowing the user to download an article of their choice in return for a credit card payment.

Version control

As noted above, some e-journals are electronic versions of print journals (this is currently the most common form of electronic journal) while others are *only* available electronically. In the case of the former, it is important to be aware of the issue of version control. This arises when the content of the print and electronic version of a journal differ in some way. For example, the electronic version of an article might include some multimedia elements, such as short video clips, that could not be provided in a print journal. Similarly, elements of a print journal such as advertisements and vacancies information may not be included in the electronic equivalent.

Features and characteristics of electronic journals

Greater accessibility – as e-journals are accessed over computer networks, rather than in physical locations like libraries, they can be used at any time of day or night. Additionally, the use of passwords to authorise access to content means that journals can be searched and articles read from anywhere in the world as long as the user has a connection to the Internet. This has the added benefit of ensuring that no-one is disadvantaged by geographical location, which can sometimes lead to engineers in one part of the world having access to a print journal a month or more before those in other areas. Such access may also ensure that more than one person from the same institution can access content from the same journal at the same time – an impractical option with print journals.

Possible cost-savings – unlike print journals, e-journals do not incur physical maintenance costs. They do not take up office or library space, and do not require any special maintenance beyond ensuring that the institution's computer hardware is functioning properly. In those situations where budget restrictions make it unfeasible to subscribe to a journal just in case some of its content might prove useful, the facility offered by some providers to buy individual articles (mentioned above) might also be attractive.

Value-added services – as indicated earlier, electronic journals can provide more than just full text article content on the desktop. Value-added services such as table of contents alerting services can help engineers maintain awareness of current developments in their field, while the collection of usage statistics can help those providing an information service to engineers to pinpoint which journals are popular with their user community and which are not.

Technical problems – as with much other information available on the web, technical problems can cause frustration. For example, some journal services might require the latest versions of the main Internet browsers in order to be displayed properly on screen. Image quality might also not be to high enough standards for some purposes.

Continuity of long term access – as the content of e-journals most often resides on the computer servers of the publisher, rather than in an institution's library or information centre, access to the information in e-journals is more unstable than access to print journals. Professional mailing lists often feature debate and concern over issues such as publishers stopping access to a title if a subscription renewal invoice has not been received, despite payment having been sent. To combat this problem, most publishers provide some form of 'grace period' to allow for continued access while subscription renewals are arranged, but access may still be blocked at times.

If it is decided not to renew a subscription to an e-journal, subscribers may find that they lose access to material for which they have already paid. Policies on continued access to previously paid-for material vary between journal providers. This can prove particularly troublesome in the case of subscriptions to multi-title deals from aggregator services, which may drop or add titles to a particular subscription without warning.

If a publisher were for some reason to cease trading, it is possible that all access to its electronically-published material might be lost. At the time of writing there are no firm industry standards as to the long-term archiving of electronic journal content. There are moves in the library sector to address this issue – for example, the Dutch National Library (Koninklijke Bibliotheek) has agreed to archive the entire output of the publisher Elsevier Science in perpetuity, and the International Publishers Association is working with the International Federation of Library Associations to explore ways of preserving digital information (IFLA and IPA, 2002)

Expense and complexity of subscription offers – smaller organisations may not have the budgets necessary to subscribe to all the host and aggregator services relevant to their interests. It is worth noting that electronic journal providers offer a bewildering array of different subscription options, where costs can be based on percentages of spend on print titles, or dependant on number of electronic titles taken, or relative to time of the year, etc. The management of these different options can be a time consuming and potentially frustrating experience.

Managing electronic journal subscriptions

As the paragraph above indicates, organisations need to consider a wide range of factors when taking out subscriptions to e-journal services. Consortia may be able to negotiate cheaper access to electronic journals depending on the number of organisations willing to subscribe to a service.

For instance, the JISC (Joint Information Systems Committee) and CHEST (Combined Higher Education Software Team) have negotiated deals on behalf of the higher and further education communities in Britain. Some consortium deals go further than this – a project of Iceland's Ministry of Education, Science and Culture, using a mixture of consortium buying and government funds, has resulted in all Icelanders using one of the country's eight Internet Service Providers having full access to the content of e-journals from large aggregators such as ABI Inform/Proquest and ScienceDirect.

There are products available that aim to simplify the management of e-journal subscriptions. For example, some maintain a watch on an organisation's subscriptions to ensure that all e-journals that should be available to its users through hosts and aggregators are accessible (this helps combat situations like those outlined above where titles may be added or dropped from aggregator services with no warning). Others might also provide a single point of access for the tables of contents of all an organisation's e-journal subscriptions, regardless of their aggregator.

Another feature of e-journals that can be exploited by subscription management products is OpenURL linking. OpenURL is a standard for bibliographic information about journal articles contained within URLs from indexing databases and other citations taken from the web. Pieces of software called OpenURL resolution software can examine the bibliographic data contained in a URL (Uniform Resource Locator) and immediately create a link to the relevant journal if the organisation subscribes to it. This can be a difficult concept to grasp, and is best illustrated by example:

A reader finds information on an interesting e-journal article while searching an aggregator database, but the full text of the article is not available through that service. OpenURL resolution software will examine the bibliographic information in the URL of the web page containing information about the article and compare it with the e-journal subscriptions of the reader's organisation. If the reader's organisation subscribes to the e-journal through a different aggregator, the OpenURL resolution software will automatically create a link to the full text of the e-journal.

Some examples of e-journal management products are TDNet (www.tdnet.com), SerialsSolutions (www.serialssolutions.com) and 1cate (www.openly.com/1cate).

▶ RECENT DEVELOPMENTS IN E-JOURNAL PUBLISHING

Perceptions of the present journal publishing system

E-journal developments such as those discussed above have mainly been led by traditional journal publishers, and largely informed by traditional commercial practice. Some recent developments in e-journal publishing are responding to perceived failings in the present scholarly journal system. The driving force of these initiatives is to make content freely available in electronic form, such that neither the reader, nor his/her organisation, need subscribe to journals in the conventional way in order to read reports of original research. In this context, a distinction is made between original research and other journal content such as review papers, editorials, etc.

The 'open access' movement has two strands: firstly, *open access journals* – achieved either by creating new journals whose content is freely available, or by encouraging publishers of existing journals to make their research content freely available; secondly, *author self-archiving* – meaning that authors deposit copies of their papers in an electronic archive. The archive could be institution- or discipline-based.

Advocates of open access argue that under the present system, high costs and restrictive policies result in limited access to research information. There is also a perception that publishers give a poor service – they supply little added value, and the whole publication process is unacceptably slow. In a report (Office of Fair Trading, 2002) produced in September 2002, the Office of Fair Trading noted the following concerns with respect to scholarly journals:

- price increases above inflation;
- a large price disparity between commercial and non-commercial journals;
- high levels of profitability for commercial STM (scientific, technical and medical) publishing (around 10–15 per cent above other forms of commercial journal publishing);
- the possibility that the bundling of a large selection of their journals by commercial publishers might result in others being inhibited from entering the market.

Some of these issues (particularly spiralling costs and slow publication) were present in the pre-electronic environment. What is possibly different now is that in the electronic world there are greater expectations – and a belief that electronic publishing should solve some of these problems. Instead, the perception is that the electronic medium is not producing the expected benefits for scholarly communication – it is driving costs up further, but not making information available more widely or more quickly.

A further issue of concern to the advocates of open access is copyright transfer. Publishers do not pay academic authors, but they often require authors to assign copyright when work is submitted. Publishers therefore obtain a 'free' benefit in which they claim copyright, and in the form of journal subscriptions they charge the research community to read it. While this has consistently been a characteristic of scholarly journal publishing, it has particular significance for the development of alternative electronic publishing. It is the basis of the distinction between original research content, which is created by researchers and given freely to publishers, and the journal content (reviews, editorials) to which publishers do add value.

The Office of Fair Trading report concluded that change could come about through new technology and that 'the Internet . . . is increasingly allowing the academic community to bypass expensive commercial publishers'. These are the initiatives already noted: open access journals and author self-archiving. In December 2003 the House of Commons Science and Technology Committee launched an inquiry (House of Commons Science and Technology Committee, 2003) into these issues, looking particularly at access to journals within the scientific community, and the impact of e-publishing on the integrity of journals and the scientific process. The Committee's report was published in July 2004.

Open access journals: SPARC –The Scholarly Publishing & Academic Resources Coalition

SPARC (www.arl.org/sparc) describes itself as 'an alliance of universities, research libraries, and organisations built as a constructive response to market dysfunctions in the scholarly communication system.' Originally US-based, SPARC is also active in Europe and has campaigned in favour of the open access ideal (SPARC, 2002) in addition to promoting journals known as SPARC Alternatives. These are competitively-priced e-journals that represent an alternative to existing high-priced titles and embody the open access ideals advocated by SPARC. Some examples from the engineering field are:

- *IEEE Sensors Journal*
  (www.ewh.ieee.org/tc/sensors/SJSensors_journal.htm) – an alternative to *Sensors and Actuators, A and B.*
- *Journal of Machine Learning Research (JMLR)*
  (www.ai.mit.edu/projects/jmlr) –
  an alternative to *Machine Learning.*
- *Theory and Practice of Logic Programming* (www.cs.kuleuven.ac.be/-dtai/projects/ALP/TPLP/index.html) – an alternative to *Journal of Logic and Algebraic Programming.* (In November 1999 the entire 50-strong editorial board of the *Journal of Logic Programming* resigned in order to launch *Theory and Practice of Logic Programming. Journal of Logic Programming* ceased at the end of 2000, and was succeeded by *Journal of Logic and Algebraic Programming.*)

Open access journals: the Budapest Open Access Initiative

The Budapest Open Access Initiative (www.soros.org/openaccess/) gets its name from a meeting convened in Budapest by the Open Society Institute (OSI) in December 2001. The purpose of the meeting was to 'accelerate progress in the international effort to make research articles in all academic fields freely available on the internet.' The outcome, which has become known as the Budapest Declaration, was dated February 14, 2002 and has been signed by dozens of institutions and hundreds of researchers. The declaration does not oppose commercial publishing, but seeks an alternative system of free access journals and self archiving set up in parallel.

Open access journals: the Public Library of Science

The Public Library of Science (www.publiclibraryofscience.org) has produced an open letter urging publishers to allow their journal content to be distributed freely by 'independent, online public libraries of science'. More than 30,000 scientists and engineers in over 180 countries have signed the letter, which in effect is a petition urging researchers and libraries to support the journals that have adopted the policies being advocated.

Arising from these initiatives, commercial journals are increasingly making some of their content available to non-subscribers, but few engineering journals are currently among them. One notable example is *BioMedical Engineering OnLine* published by BioMed Central (www.biomedcentral.com). Life science journals are to some extent leading the way with open access policies, and BioMed Central is currently unique as a commercial publishing house committed to providing immediate free access to all its research information. Another novel development is that this policy is financially supported by author charges.

Author self-archiving via e-print archives

The author self-archiving initiative means that authors deposit copies of their papers in electronic archives (distribution servers on the Internet) and readers can retrieve papers from the archive either through a web interface, or by sending commands to the system via e-mail. E-print archives are discussed in greater detail in Chapter 8.

With respect to their relationship with journals, the archives may include both pre-publication versions of papers and final versions as actually published in journals. In the first and best known e-print archive – the Los Alamos Preprint server for physics and related disciplines (now known as arXiv and located at Cornell University) – the concept was that pre-publication versions of papers would be deposited in the archive to speed up the communication process. The final peer-reviewed version would be published in a traditional print journal which would constitute the scholarly record and the source of peer recognition.

Therefore e-print archives were not established with the aim of challenging commercial publishers (unlike SPARC), but to provide rapid and free access to new information for fellow researchers. Advocates of the initiative maintain that it is not an alternative to publishing in traditional high-impact journals, but a parallel development arising from the need for free and quick communication of research results.

Potential copyright conflicts do arise from this process, but increasingly publishers are adopting open access policies that allow authors to deposit either pre-publication or published versions of their papers in e-print archives. Some examples of such publishers in the engineering field are the Association for Computing Machinery, the Institute of Electrical, Information and Communication Engineers, the Institution of Chemical Engineers and the Society of Photo-optical Instrumentation Engineers.

Although arXiv has been highly successful, there is no other discipline-based electronic archive of comparable stature. More recently, institutional archives have been established to promote the self-archiving ideal and one of their challenges is to convince authors of the benefits in terms of the visibility and impact of their work. The perception of many academic authors that self-archiving is self-publishing, and that content is not peer-reviewed quality material, means that at present a majority of researchers prefer to publish in traditional high-impact journals rather than engage in self-archiving.

A decade ago it was not uncommon to read of the predicted demise of traditional journals in favour of Internet-based alternatives. Most current observers believe that journals will co-exist with the new initiatives because they fulfil complementary roles and together can meet the needs of future engineers and scientists.

> Publishers should not object to web archives, and authors should not abandon journals. Researchers should use multiple distribution channels, including self-archiving and publishing in traditional journals. Journals provide a stable archive of the literature, quality filters and other valuable aspects; web e-print servers allow quick access to more sources of information. (Tenopir and King, 2001)

Developments such as these, along with the greater access to traditional journals also facilitated by web technology, should ensure that engineers are able to locate information relevant to their needs in the wide body of journal literature.

▶ REFERENCES

House of Commons Science and Technology Committee, 2003. *Inquiry into Scientific Publications.* (www. parliament.uk/parliamentary_committees/science_and_ technology_committee/scitech111203a.cfm)

IFLA and IPA, 2002. *Preserving the Memory of the World in Perpetuity: a joint statement on the archiving and preserving of digital information* (www.ifla.org/V/press/ifla-ipa02.htm)

Institute for Scientific Information, 1994. *The impact factor.* (www.isinet.com/isi/hot/essays/journalcitationreports/7.html)

Office of Fair Trading, 2002. *Can the scientific journals market work better?* PN 55/02 9th September 2002. (www.oft.gov.uk/News/Press+releases/2002/ PN+55–02+Can+the+scientific+journals+market+work+better.htm)

SPARC, 2002. *Gaining Independence: a manual for planning the launch of a nonprofit electronic publishing venture* (www.arl.org/sparc/GI)

Tenopir, C. and King, D.W., 2001. *Lessons for the future of journals* (www.nature.com/nature/debates/e-access/Articles/tenopir.html)

3 Reports, Theses and Research in Progress

Paul A. S. Needham

▶ **INTRODUCTION**

Reports, theses and details about research in progress have much in common: they are all relatively inexpensive to produce, available in timely fashion, and are able to provide cutting-edge information about research on a particular topic. They are frequently the sources of choice for fast, early access to research. These attributes make them important media of communication for engineers.

There have been numerous studies of the information seeking behaviour of engineers, including one recent review (Needham, 2002) which explained the popularity and importance of these types of resources. These studies suggest that engineers use information primarily to solve problems and they need reliable, preferably validated, answers to normally very specific questions.

While the types of resources used will vary according to the particular phase of the work or research being conducted, there is often a strong inter-relationship between the degree of technical complexity or economic uncertainty and the information required to support that activity. Engineers therefore tend to favour sources that in terms of content and format present information in a way that can be easily assimilated, applied or transferred. Reports and theses meet these criteria because they are often produced with a specific readership in mind. They typically contain a high level of detail, such as problem definition, error analysis and a discussion of favoured solutions (as well as any tried and discarded options). This is essential for a thorough understanding of the work and speedy appraisal of the outcomes and recommendations. Moreover, reports can be produced with a minimum of delay, either at the conclusion of a research project or at various agreed milestones while work is still in progress. Reports are frequently produced in response to a particular requirement, and their distribution may be restricted to those who have a vested interest or involvement in that requirement for commercial or security considerations.

Given that engineers value access to timely information, keeping up to date is important to avoid potentially wasteful duplication of effort, for effective competitor intelligence, and to ensure that work isn't compromised by ignorance of recent advances in techniques and thinking. It should be noted, however, that the importance placed on the usage of validated information and data means that engineers will often seek to better the state-of-the-art rather than find the 'best' solution, and may therefore choose to ignore new information unless its relevance to their work can be clearly demonstrated.

▶ DEFINING GREY LITERATURE

Reports, theses and research in progress are all, to a certain extent, 'grey areas' and they involve that body of materials known as grey literature.

Although it is impossible to give a perfect definition, there are a couple of working definitions of grey literature that have gained prominence and are widely quoted:

- Auger (1998) includes reports, technical notes and specifications, datasheets, trade literature, pre-prints, conference proceedings and supplementary publications in his definition, all of which are characterised by poor bibliographic control and information, low print runs and a non-professional layout and format. This means they are difficult to identify and locate, and, as they are not available through normal book-selling channels, they are difficult to obtain.
- A second definition, known as the 'Luxembourg Convention on GL' (named after the location of the 3rd International Conference on Grey Literature) states that 'grey literature is produced at all levels of government, academia, business and industry, in print and electronic formats, and is not controlled by commercial publishers'. (Farace, 1997).

In referring to 'print and electronic formats', this second definition highlights an important point: traditionally, information was distributed via a physical exchange of documents. In the last few years, in common with all sectors, the engineering community has gained enhanced access to electronic information resources. The rise of the Internet, particularly the World Wide Web, and the increasing creation, acceptance and use of electronic full text documents have opened up new possibilities for the virtual dissemination of information far more quickly and widely than most of us could have dreamt.

Within the last decade, in the US, there have been strenuous efforts to disseminate the results of federal research. In the UK, compared to other resource types such as electronic journals from mainstream publishers, the body of grey literature has received until recently a lower level of attention.

Happily, in the last five years, the lack of attention given to reports and theses in the UK has been rectified somewhat through the work undertaken by a number of projects and initiatives, including the Managing Access to Grey Literature Collections (MAGiC) project (www.magic.ac.uk) and the University Theses Online Group (UTOG) (www.cranfield.ac.uk/cils/library/utog/).

A word of caution: while reports, theses and research in progress, like other information sources, have all been affected (and benefited to varying extents) from these changes, we must not forget that a vast store of knowledge is still locked up in documents produced on paper, microfilm and microfiche. And, while we now live in the 'age of the electronic document', attention still needs to be paid to unlocking this huge bank of legacy research.

The following sections of this chapter will examine, in turn, reports, theses and research in progress, before concluding with a brief discussion of the outlook for the future.

▶ REPORTS

Introduction

An exact definition of the term 'report' is difficult, if not impossible. In the context of engineering, the word is used as an umbrella term for a variety of documents including technical reports, progress reports and translations, as well as company annual reports, market research reports, and too many other document types to list.

Technical reports may contain experimental procedure, production data, specifications, standards, operating plans, drawings and/or raw results (Mildren and Hicks, 1996). They will set out the conclusions and recommendations arising from the research, and include coverage of all aspects of the research. This means that the information they contain is very specific, addressing a particular problem, and very rich in experimental detail.

King and Griffiths (1991) characterise technical reports as containing very specific, very new information, as they are often the first place information is recorded, before (if ever) being presented to conferences or published as journal articles. They tend to be used over a longer period of time after publication than journal articles; although one-half of readings involve reports under six months old, the average age of technical reports read is two years.

Most engineering research, technology acquisition and development address a particular need or problem. Generally, technical reports are generated as a by-product of the process, rather than the end-product of research.

Within many organisations, the report is the primary means of technical communication, as it is cheap and quick to produce. Reports must be detailed enough to satisfy the requirements of the funder or contractor of the research, and their detailed nature is their greatest strength as an information source. Once the report has been circulated within the organisation, if appropriate, it is then distributed to a wider audience, without peer-review or editing. Of course, some reports will be held in confidence if there are commercial or military restraints.

A large amount of valuable information contained in reports is never formally published as a journal article or within a book. Even if refined versions appear later, twelve to eighteen months' delay is common due to the publishing cycle, so reports are frequently at the cutting edge of engineering research, design and development.

While engineers undoubtedly need to access and use information they are not generally renowned as large generators of published literature, in comparison for example to the scientific community. This is a reflection of the different cultures and environments in which engineers and scientists tend to operate. Scientists are encouraged to publish in order to establish their reputation and to set precedence for original work. Funding agencies such as research councils and charitable trusts positively encourage scientific researchers to look outward and to disseminate findings in order to advance knowledge. Within this environment rewards and status are often directly influenced by the number and quality of papers published.

In contrast, engineering research is more often than not carried out by commercial organisations, often on behalf of sponsors, who are primarily concerned with the end product. Typically in the UK, any data or information produced as a result of the research is deemed to be the intellectual property of the company carrying out the work. There is little motivation to widely disseminate results, as commercial or contractual restrictions often prevent external publishing. Rewards systems for engineers are normally internal to their organisations, so that individuals have less incentive to publish as their reputations are based on contributing to the company's profits and profile. Technology-based companies involved in applied research are often reluctant to risk the loss of perceived commercial advantages, and prefer to rely on the end-product to demonstrate their skills and competencies rather than formally disseminate the knowledge and supporting information and data on which those products are based. In an environment in which commercial and sometimes defence restrictions are so prevalent, the technical report is seen as an ideal medium for ensuring targeted and controlled dissemination of information.

Moreover, those journal articles and conference papers which do emanate from engineering research may give a compressed summary of the work undertaken, stripped of most of the really important and useful technical detail. They are intended largely to provide a shop window for the technical expertise or competence of the author's organisation or company, and hence put a positive gloss on the final results. They tend not to give experimental detail of exactly how the results were arrived at, the raw data or the mistakes that were made along the way. This can make understanding or validation difficult.

The MAGiC project (Needham, 2002) observed that most engineers use technical reports at some time. On occasions that reports are used, these often prove extremely useful to the engineer and the MAGiC findings suggest that reports are just as important to an engineer's work as more traditional information sources such as journal articles and conference papers. Reports can be invaluable to an engineer who has specific queries about an experimental method, who wants to know about the latest developments in a field, or who needs to disseminate results promptly.

Consequently, the technical report is one of the most common and important types of grey literature within the engineering sector.

Translations are frequently treated like reports, which, in many cases, they are not.

Wood (1976) found that roughly half of the world's scientific and technical literature is published in languages other than English and this literature is vital to English speaking scientists.

History

Despite its importance now, the report as a medium of communication scarcely existed a century ago. Some of the earliest documents that would now be considered as reports literature were produced by the Admiralty Experimental Works (one of the many predecessors of the Royal Aerospace Establishment) in the late 1870s. Within the aeronautics sector, reports became an important and accepted form of communication and technology transfer in the early decades of the twentieth century. Extensive series were produced by the ARC (Aeronautical Research Council) in the UK and NACA (National Advisory Committee for Aeronautics) in the US. However, it wasn't until the 1940s that the importance of the report, as a major tool of communication, was more generally recognised and widely established.

The *Dictionary of Report Series Codes* (Godfrey and Redman, 1973) picks up the story, from a US perspective, tracing the development of the report literature from the Second World War which was the catalyst for a huge increase in the production of reports. The Office of Scientific Research and Development (OSRD) fashioned the shape of government-sponsored research, widely spreading scientific effort through contracts issued to research teams. The unpublished report was deemed the most appropriate means of recording and disseminating the results of these research efforts.

At the same time, large numbers of reports were also produced by Allied teams investigating enemy scientific and technological research.

In the decade following the war, expenditure on research and development doubled. By 1950, the results of US government-sponsored research were being published in reports at the rate of more than 75,000 per year. The onset of the Cold War and especially the development of the nuclear industry fuelled further scientific and engineering research. At this time more than ten independent departments and agencies of the US Government were conducting significant research and development programs of actual or potential military value, including the National Advisory Committee for Aeronautics (NACA), the Wright Air Development Center (WADC), and the Atomic Energy Commission (AEC). The disbanding of the OSRD left no central agency to control or monitor research reports, though new agencies were created in specific areas, such as atomic energy and naval research.

Thompson (2001) describes US grey literature and reports at length. During the 1980s and 1990s, some report series that were freely available as part of a Federal Depository Library Program were given to the National Technical Information Service (NTIS) to maintain and distribute. Reports from the Department of Transportation (DOT) and the Environmental Protection Agency (EPA) were amongst those transferred. NTIS supplied reports from US government agencies and departments on a commercial basis, and many libraries ceased collecting reports when a charge was introduced.

In the UK, the Technology Reports Centre provided access to unpublished reports by government research establishments until it closed in 1981. Its function was split between the Defence Research Information Centre (DRIC) and the British Library. DRIC (succeeded by Dstl Knowledge Services) disseminated scientific and technical information to the UK defence community for more than seventy-five years, and is the focus for exchange of scientific and technical defence reports with other countries, publishing the *Defence Reports Abstracts* and *Defence Technology Abstracts*. The British Library used to publish 'R&D Abstracts' twice a month, but this has now ceased.

The continuing use of, and growth in, reports emphasises their importance as a means of communication for engineers. In 1963, estimates of the number of reports issued annually in the US varied from 50,000 to 150,000. In the next ten years to 1973, estimates ranged as high as 500,000, but no reliable figures were obtained. The British Library estimates that 50,000 UK local authority documents are produced each year, and about 70,000 US scientific and technical reports are added to NTIS each year. The British Library itself acquires approximately 19,000 UK reports each year, compared with 7,500 UK doctoral theses and 17,000 conference proceedings.

As their numbers have grown, reports have become accepted as a respected means of communication, as evidenced by the increasing inclusion of high profile report series in standard abstract and indexing services.

Obstacles to using technical reports

The organisations producing reports effectively control their distribution, so despite the proliferation of report sources, and the numbers of reports produced, the lack of a controlling and standardising body means that a large proportion of reports can be very difficult to find and obtain. Concerns over intellectual property and competition dictate that organisations operating in the corporate sector are generally far less willing to collaborate and share information externally than their counterparts in government or academia. This urge to restrict commercial and defence information in the UK means that many reports are never made publicly available. Reports can be subject to embargo until the company decides the information cannot be used for commercial gain by its competitors. Often company reports can only be accessed by direct contact with the company, and can only be discovered from citations or recommendation.

The situation is made worse by the manner in which many libraries and institutions have gathered reports, by gift or exchange. Gaps in series are often not chased or claimed, and so holdings are often incomplete.

Reports Series

Literally thousands of organisations issue reports in the course of their activities. Each organisation creates its own scheme(s) for identifying the reports that it produces.The Report Series Codes Dictionary, for example, lists tens of thousands of reports series held by the participating organisations.

The British Library has, in the past, produced several editions of the *Alphanumeric Reports Publications Index (ARPI)*. The third edition (British Library, 1995) lists over 12,000 report series, and of these more than 2,000 are series produced by organisations in the UK. Entries in ARPI link corporate sources to report series prefixes and their BL shelfmark. While the corporate sources are not classified into subject areas, by cross-referencing with other directories and indexes, it is possible to identify organisations that produce reports relevant to engineers. Also, report series often include reports that act as indexes to the series.

Although it is unlikely to be applied retrospectively, a further possibility for improving access to technical reports, now and in the future, would be the promotion and adoption of the International Standard Report Number (ISRN) as recommended in the ANSI/NISO standard Z39.23–1997 (National Information Standards Organization, 1997).

Reports collections

Dstl (Defence Science and Technical Laboratory)/Qinetiq hold reports produced by their predecessors (DERA, DRA, RAE, and many more) as well as relevant reports from other organisations.

The British Library (BL) holds more than 240,000 reports from 1980 onwards, from more than 4,000 sources, most of which are housed at the British Library Document Supply Centre (BLDSC) in Boston Spa in Yorkshire.

Even within the British Library the full extent of the reports collection is unknown, as items prior to 1980 are not on the computer catalogue. The holdings of US reports are not catalogued at all. According to one estimate, (Auger, 1998), the BL's collections number more than four million items from some 12,000 reports series, mainly from NTIS (from 1940s), NASA/NACA (from 1900s), AIAA, US DoE/AEC (from 1940s), ERIC and INIS (from 1970). These are much larger than their holdings of UK reports.

Apart from these substantial holdings at the BL, major collections of technical reports tend to be scattered across academia, government and industry. These resources are difficult to identify, locate and access, as there has been little co-ordination across or within sectors and there is no national database of holdings.

The UK National Archives (formerly the Public Record Office – PRO) preserves the records of central government. Technical reports that are produced by government departments and so form a part of those records are collected and recorded, but are only available to access if they are more than thirty years old.

Reports in libraries

In its investigations, the MAGiC project noted that the cataloguing of engineering technical reports tends to be of poor quality and inconsistent, both within and between libraries.

In general, academic libraries treat reports series as periodicals and have only a single catalogue entry at series level. The practice of treating report series as serials adds to the difficulty in identifying, locating and accessing reports. Where there is item level cataloguing, report numbers are entered inconsistently and information about the authors, publishers and corporate sources varies greatly. In general, records (metadata) are 'thin' in terms of detail as they rarely include abstracts, and few library catalogues allow collections to be searched by reports as a separate resource type.

Libraries in industry and government generally catalogue reports individually. However, access to their catalogue records is problematic for reasons of commercial sensitivity and security.

Academic libraries are short of space and some libraries in industry are being rationalised or closed down, so their collections are being discarded in the hope that someone else will have them. This is leading to a reduction in potentially searchable resources. The pressure of meeting ever-decreasing budgets has forced the search for short-term savings; at what cost, in the long term, remains to be seen.

Reports availability and supply

The format in which reports are published and distributed has changed over the years, from paper to microfiche to CD-ROM, and soon to DVD. The sources for finding reports have also largely evolved from print to predominantly electronic. Before the advent of databases, key printed sources included the US produced *Government Reports Announcements and Index (GRA&I)*, *Scientific and Technical Aerospace Reports (STAR)*, *Energy Research Abstracts* and the international *INIS Atomindex*, and in Germany, *Forschungsberichte*. These are all described in some detail by Auger (1976).

Increasingly, organisations are making lists and indexes of their reports, and in many cases the reports themselves, available on the Internet through their websites. The US Defense Technical Information Center's Technical Reports Automated Information List (TRAIL) (www.dtic.mil/trail/) for example, is a free electronic mailing list that automatically disseminates citations to unclassified/unlimited technical reports recently added to the DTIC technical reports database. Other organisations that now publish their reports on the Internet include, for example, NIREX (2001), AEA Technology Environment (2002), Council for the Central Laboratory of the Research Councils (2002) and UKAEA Fusion (2002).

The proliferation of these new web-based report collections have added both to the availability of information and arguably to the complexity of resource discovery by requiring would-be users to search multiple sources. It has also brought into question the role and future viability of the large reports handling agencies, who have dominated the document supply scene, in some cases for the past several decades.

International initiatives

The International Nuclear Information System (INIS) promotes peaceful uses of nuclear energy and has a membership of 107 states. It processes the world's scientific and technical information within its area and produces a bibliographic database with a full text service on 'non-conventional' sources like technical reports.

The Energy Technology Data Exchange began in 1987 and has eighteen member countries which exchange energy research and technical information through the creation of a common database. In addition to ETDE's traditional Energy Database, web access is provided through ETDEWEB (www.etde.org/etdeweb/). This includes information on the environmental impact of energy production and use, including climate change; energy R&D; energy policy; nuclear, coal, hydrocarbon and renewable energy technologies. It contains over 3,057,400 bibliographic records and over 99,400 full text documents.

Another notable online collection of reports is provided by the RTO (Research and Technology Organization), which is the focus for defence research and technology activities within NATO. The RTO website provides access to a collection of full text documents produced by the NATO Research and Technology Organization and its predecessor, AGARD (Advisory Group for Aerospace Research & Development). In fact the RTO has stopped distributing hardcopy reports, so the only access to its material is through the Internet.

The major European project for raising the visibility of reports is SIGLE (System for Information on Grey Literature in Europe), which is co-ordinated by EAGLE (European Association for Grey Literature Exploitation). SIGLE's aim is to provide access to European grey literature, which it does by means of a network of national centres, one of which is the BLDSC (The British Library Document Supply Centre). SIGLE has centres in sixteen countries. Each centre is responsible for collecting grey literature in its own country and providing bibliographic details for entry into the SIGLE database, which now comprises about 630,000 citations (Wood and Smith, 1993). Over 100,000 of these citations refer to reports from the UK. Reports, dissertations, and other grey literature found in SIGLE can be ordered from the source indicated in each record. The dial-up online version of the SIGLE database is hosted by STN International and can be accessed directly via STN or EINS (European Information Network Services) GEM. A CD-ROM version of SIGLE is available from Ovid (a Silverplatter platform).

The UK

There are cultural differences between the US and UK. The US can drive disclosure and dissemination through the federal agencies within a polit-ical culture of freedom of information. Within the UK, the need to publish is not necessarily recognised by the agencies carrying out the research and there can be debate over who owns the intellectual property rights of the research. Even if the government has funded the research, the agency or company can be reluctant to divulge information which it sees as being its property and of commercial advantage. Additionally, in contrast to the scientific community, engineering publication is not linked to a reward system, and so there is no personal professional gain in publishing results.

The *British National Bibliography for Report Literature* (BNBRL), which was formerly known as *British Reports, Translations and Theses* until its title changed in 1997, lists reports and other material published in the United Kingdom by non-trade publishers such as research organisa-tions, universities, charities and pressure groups which have been acquired by the British Library.

MAGiC, sponsored by the British Library Co-operation and Partnership Programme, has been addressing the challenge of demystifying engineering grey literature to 'enhance awareness, access and utilisation of key collections of technical reports for the benefit of the UK engineering community' (Needham, 2002).

US initiatives

In comparison with the situation in the UK and Europe, organisations in the US have been more effective in making report literature accessible. The government has a responsibility to disseminate the results of federally sponsored research as broadly as possible, for the public good. Recognising the Internet as a powerful means to increase dissemination, the US government funded digitisation projects such as NTRS and the GrayLit Network.

The OSTI GrayLIT Network was launched as a response to recommendations from a DOE (Department of Energy) workshop in May 2000. Providing access to the grey literature of US federal agencies, OSTI GrayLIT allows cross-searching of more than 100,000 full-text technical reports located at DOE, the DOD (Department of Defense), the EPA (Environmental Protection Agency), and NASA.

The US is leading the way, taking advantage of the opportunities of new technologies and partnership arrangements to increase the availability of technical reports, with major US sources offering free full text access via the web. Many US Federal Agencies now provide web access to their documents via technical report servers. Amongst the best known and most heavily used are the NASA Technical Report Server (NTRS), the US department of Transportation's TRIS Online, and the Department of Energy's Information Bridge.

▶ THESES

Introduction

Theses or dissertations (the terms are increasingly interchangeable) are the documents produced as the result of student research carried out in order to gain a degree at masters or doctoral level. The latter are generally held in higher regard than the former. The fact that theses are reviewed by competent, qualified supervisors, and the existence of close relationships between industry and academia in the engineering arena, means that the contents of theses are often relevant to practising engineers.

Theses are frequently placed in the category of grey literature, though not everyone will agree with this. Their bibliographic control is generally well-managed – doctoral theses more so than masters – and is often superior to that of reports. Nevertheless, theses do have much in common with reports. As noted by Auger (1998), theses are often announced in journals devoted to grey literature, they share many characteristics of reports in terms of format, are issued with identifying numbers, and, at times, can be difficult to identify and obtain.

Abstracting and indexing

Two of the longest established resources used for searching for theses are:

UMI/Proquest's *Dissertation Abstracts* database, which covers doctoral dissertations and masters' theses, holds over 1.6 million entries divided into three sections. Section B encompasses Science and Technology, but only covers United States and Canadian doctoral dissertations. Since Vol.41(1), July 1980, it has been published on microfiche. Section C (formerly known as *European Abstracts*) includes a growing number of theses from around the world and covers all disciplines.

The *Index to Theses* describes theses accepted for doctoral and masters' degrees which have been submitted to Universities in the UK and Ireland. It is available in both print and web versions. The printed edition covers theses from 1950 onwards, while the website covers theses dated from 1970 (Volume 21) onwards. Since 1986, entries have included abstracts, as prior to that only bibliographic citations were given. The online index is only available to members of organisations that subscribe to the printed version. In the past, the *Index* has also been produced in CD-ROM format, however this is no longer supported or updated.

E-theses

There are many initiatives around the world looking at the development of electronic theses. The best known of these is the Networked Digital Library of Theses and Dissertations (NDLTD) which is an open federation of about 130 universities constructing a global digital library of electronic theses and dissertations. The main objectives of the NDLTD are to increase the availability of student research and to preserve it electronically; to encourage universities to unlock their information resources; to improve graduate education by helping students to produce electronic documents, use digital libraries and understand issues in publishing. The NDLTD database is open and can be searched at: hercules.vtls.com/cgi-bin/ndltd/chameleon

Other e-theses initiatives include the following:

UNESCO has funded the creation of a Guide for Electronic Theses and Dissertations available at: etdguide.org.

The Australian Digital Theses project is based at University of New South Wales, see: adt.caul.edu.au.

Funding from the Joint Information Systems Committee (JISC), as part of the Focus on Access to Institutional Resources Programme (FAIR), is enabling three project teams in the UK to study the issues and challenges associated with the deposit and management of theses in electronic format.

The growth in interest in e-theses can be traced back to the University Theses Online Group (UTOG) which was formed following a proposal to the Follett Implementation Group on Information Technology in 1994. UTOG, which was a working group of librarians, representing eleven UK university libraries and the British Library Document Supply Centre British Thesis Service, investigated 'the technical, cultural and administrative issues involved in the storage and delivery of theses in digital form'.

The findings of the group confirmed that making the digital full text of theses available could improve the situation considerably. These led directly to a number of further projects sponsored by the Joint Information Systems Committee (JISC) which aim to develop recommendations for UK universities in order to make theses available electronically. These are all part of the FAIR (Focus on Access to Institutional Resources) programme.

A consortium led by The Robert Gordon University is evaluating a wide range of existing practices and methods of e-theses production, management and use against a set of criteria in order to produce recommended models for use within the UK information environment. Building particularly on recent work undertaken by the aforementioned NDLTD, it is also considering the potential developments and opportunities offered by the production of 'born digital' theses, and ways of creating an electronic theses resource base at national level.

Edinburgh University is carrying out an e-theses pilot project which will employ e-theses submission software to create a body of e-theses content in several universities, and advise universities across the UK of the steps involved in introducing an e-theses service. Theses Alive! as the project is called is taking a practical route, by developing Electronic Thesis and Dissertation (ETD) submission software customised for use by UK HE institutions, and piloting that software within a number of institutions. The project will concentrate on developing an interface to the chosen software which achieves a number of objectives including: that it is simple to use by both theses authors and their supervisors; it permits secure storage of work in progress, and version control; it allows interaction between supervisors and authors; it allows for the generation of metadata records.

In addition to the development of a submission system, the Project will run an ETD help service with an 'ETDs FAQ' as its central component. This knowledge base will assist institutions to move towards creating their own ETD services, by addressing issues such as IPR, advocacy with academic staff, publisher policies, digital preservation and other key issues in addition to technical questions regarding software and hardware requirements.

Glasgow University is implementing an e-theses service as part of a research project called DAEDALUS, which will develop a range of OAI

(Open Archives Initiative) compliant services. The project will establish a network of freely accessible Digital Collections at the University, including: published and peer reviewed academic papers; Pre-prints and grey literature; Theses; and Research resource finding aids.

While much information can be derived from reports and theses, they are, of course, the outcomes of research that has already taken place either recently or in an increasingly distant past. Discovering what research is currently taking place – right here and now – is another matter.

▶ RESEARCH IN PROGRESS

There is, at any given time, a vast amount of research being undertaken by thousands upon thousands of researchers. Before beginning any new research or development project, whether a student, a scientist, or a skilled engineer, it is important to discover what other research is taking place that relates to the work. The student working towards a Masters or PhD needs to know that his/her research is new and original. The problem-solving engineer needs to avoid 're-inventing the wheel', to come up with workable solutions quickly and to keep costs down.

Unfortunately, much information on research in progress is simply not available: commercial organisations will not share information that they perceive will give them a competitive edge over their rivals, and details of current military and defence research will, in most cases, not see the light of day for many years to come.

Having said that, there is much that can be discovered about current research, and a variety of methods that can be employed to find out what research projects are currently being undertaken at institutions and organisations in the UK and around the world.

Directories

There are various directories which can aid the identification of international research centres and organisations. These include *Current research in Britain* (CRIB), a register of current research arranged by subject (physical sciences, biological sciences, social sciences and the humanities), with author and keyword indexes. *European Research Centres*, previously published by Longman, is now out of print. *Research Centers Directory*, published by Gale, lists nonprofit research organisations in the US and Canada. HERO (Higher Education & Research Opportunities in the United Kingdom) (www.hero.ac.uk) is the official gateway site to the UK's universities, colleges and research organisations and is a useful source of information.

Internet subject portals

In the UK, subject portals such as EEVL (www.eevl.ac.uk) and Aerade (aerade.cranfield.ac.uk) are run from specialist academic centres and scan the latest subject websites for details of new research groups and projects.

Email lists

Email discussion lists sometimes include postings detailing research projects. *The Directory of Scholarly and Professional E-Conferences* (www. kovacs.com/directory/index.html) is one source of information about lists, and another is the *Locating electronic mail discussion lists* (www.lboro. ac.uk/library/subj/disclist.html) webpage, produced by Loughborough University Library. In the UK, JISCmail (www.jiscmail.ac.uk) provide many thousands of lists for the UK Higher and Further Education communities.

Pre-prints

Auger's definition of grey literature included pre-prints. Whereas formerly pre-prints were produced as limited distribution hardcopy documents, in the course of the 'information revolution', this particular unconventional document type has risen to prominence under the burgeoning 'e-print movement'. These 'born digital' documents have an impact on the availability of all information sources, but particularly on the discovery of recent and current research in progress. Researchers submitting articles to peer-reviewed journals can now self-archive in an ever-increasing number of digital repositories. Engineers seeking current research articles need no longer wait for up to a year and a half for this body of work to appear to the world at large.

Other sources

The UK Research Councils plan, fund and execute research in a variety of areas. Their websites will normally provide information on current research programmes. In the UK, the Engineering and Physical Sciences Research Council (EPSRC) (www.epsrc.ac.uk) is the government's leading funding agency for research and training in engineering and the physical sciences. It publishes the *EPSRC Newsline* and also *Spotlight*, both of which focus on current research issues and projects. Other research councils can be located through Research Councils UK (RCUK) (www.rcuk.ac.uk), a strategic partnership set up to champion science, engineering and technology which is supported by the seven UK Research Councils.

CORDIS, the Community Research and Development Information Service (www.cordis.lu), is a European Commission information service providing access to complete information on EU research and exploitation possibilities. CORDIS provides a central source of information for any organisation wishing to participate in the exploitation of research results, participate in EU funded research programmes and/or seek partnerships. Information on all research and technological development activities in the EU is provided through a range of databases.

The Community of Science (www.cos.com) is designed to help identify and locate researchers with similar interests and expertise. The COS Expertise database covers researchers, inventions, and facilities around the world.

Web of Science contains the three citation indexes – Arts and Humanities, Science and Social Science. Most references obtained by searching these indexes will list the institutional addresses of the authors. These can be used to trace other research conducted by either the authors or institutions. Many university websites, for instance, will list the research undertaken by various academic departments.

▶ OUTLOOK FOR THE FUTURE

E-prints

The established and traditional method of scholarly information transfer is the journal article. What began as an effective method of communicating scientific discoveries and experimental results in the 17th century has been challenged in recent years by the widespread use of the Internet and the rapid communication and exchange of documents it allows. Coupled with large price increases, delays in publishing articles due to peer review and the number of articles awaiting publication, and the growing awareness that transferring all intellectual rights to publishers diminishes rather than encourages dissemination of results, an alternative has evolved in the form of e-print (or pre-print) archives.

The idea originated at Los Alamos National Laboratory in the US, where what is now known as arXiv.org was created in 1991 to allow authors to deposit ('self-archive') research papers in physics, mathematics and computer science. It is now the largest collection of non-peer reviewed research in the world, containing 203,751 documents on 26th July 2002, with an average of three million connections per month.

In the UK the JISC funded Focus on Access to Institutional Resources (FAIR) programme is supporting a number of e-print related projects. ePrints UK plans to develop a national service through which the UK higher and further education community can access the collective output of e-print papers available from OAI compliant Open Archive repositories provided by UK universities and colleges. The project team are working closely with other projects in this area including: HaIRST (Harvesting Institutional Resources in Scotland Testbed)(hairst.cdlr.strath.ac.uk), which will provide e-prints UK with a single point of access to metadata repositories of thirteen Scottish institutions, the SHERPA (Securing a Hybrid Environment for Research, Preservation and Access)(www.sherpa.ac.uk) project, which aims to support the development of a number of institutional e-print archives in the UK, and RoMEO (Rights Metadata for Open Archiving) (www.lboro. ac.uk/departments/ls/disresearch/romeo/), which is exploring intellectual property issues surrounding institutional e-prints archives.

► REFERENCES

Aea Technology Environment, 2002. *Research Information.*
    laburnum.aeat.co.uk/archive/reports/list.php
Auger, C.P., 1998. *Information sources in grey literature.* 4th ed., London: Bowker-Saur.
British Library, 1995. *Alphanumeric reports publications index (ARPI).* 3rd ed., Boston Spa:
    BLDSC.
Council for The Central Laboratory of The Research Councils, 2002. *Technical Reports.*
    www.clrc.ac.uk/Activity/ACTIVITY=Publications;SECTION=225;
Farace, D.J., ed., 1997. *Perspectives on the design and transfer of scientific and technical
    information.* GL 97 3rd International Conference on Grey Literature, Jean Monnet
    building, Luxembourg, November 13–14, 1997, Amsterdam: TransAtlantic, 1997.
Godfrey, L.E., and Redman, H.F., eds., 1973. *Dictionary of Report Series Codes.* 2nd ed.,
    New York: Special Libraries Association.
King, D.W., and Griffiths, J.-M., 1991. *Indicators of the use, usefulness and value of scientific
    and technical information.* Online information 92: 15th international online
    information meeting proceedings, Oxford: Learned Information.
Mildren, K., and Hicks, P., eds., 1996. *Information sources in engineering.* 3rd London:
    Bowker-Saur.
National Information Standards Organisation (NISO), 1997. *Standard Technical Report
    Number Format and Creation.* Bethesda, MA: NISO Press
    www.niso.org/standards/resources/Z39-23.pdf
Needham, P., 2002. *Management of access to grey literature collections (MAGiC) Final
    Report.* www.bl.uk/concord/docs/magic-final.doc
Nirex, 2001. *Nirex Publications: The Bibliography*
    www.nirex.co.uk/publicn/pdffiles/01biblio.htm
Thompson, L.A., 2001. Grey literature in engineering. *Science & Technology Libraries,*
    19(3/4), pp. 57–73.
UKAEA Fusion, 2002. *UKAEA FUS Reports.* www.fusion.org.uk/cgi-bin/listfus.pl
Wood, D.N., 1976. The foreign language problem facing scientists and technologists in
    the United Kingdom. *Journal of Documentation,* 23(2), pp. 117–130.
Wood, D.N., and Smith, A.W., 1993. SIGLE: a model for international cooperation.
    Interlending and document supply 21(1), pp. 18–22.

4 Conferences

Kathy Abbott

Conferences are an important information source and this chapter reviews the following topics:

- Why do engineers attend conferences and similar events? Networking, exposure, keeping up-to-date
- What happens at conferences? Sharing information versus confidentiality
- Where are conferences held?
- Who organises conferences and why?
- Examples of engineering conferences
- Conferences in a particular subject area: electrical and electronic engineering
- Trade exhibitions
- How do engineers find out about forthcoming conferences?
- Conference publications, and their different formats
- Discovery tools for conference publications and papers
- How do engineers obtain conference type papers and whole publications?

► WHY DO ENGINEERS ATTEND CONFERENCES AND SIMILAR EVENTS?

Attendance at a conference provides an opportunity to make contact and network with other people from similar and varying backgrounds. Meetings bring together experts and specialists, often from different subject fields, and so are major sources of the latest available information, up-to-date thinking and practice. The first time that a new idea or research result is made public is often at a conference. Conference papers may be presented a long time before comparable material is published in periodicals.

With the rapid rate of change in engineering, practitioners find it increasingly difficult to keep up with developments. Conferences may provide product reviews and updates, and papers may include promotion of industrial products. The world is changing for engineers, with the most recent information being of growing importance. Engineers often used to say that you could look back twenty years and find relevant information that had not been developed or applied in the intervening time. This is not so much the case now. Conference proceedings seem to be of more importance to engineers than to pure scientists.

Conferences often address new, developing, interdisciplinary or multi-disciplinary areas, such as parallel computational fluid dynamics, or control applications in marine systems. The topics often border scientific as well as technological areas, where innovative fields spring up:

- Applications of algebraic geometry to coding theory, physics and computation
- Artificial neural networks in image processing
- Fabrication and metrology in nanotechnology
- Fluid flow and transport in porous media, mathematical and numerical treatment
- Fuel cell science, engineering and technology
- Mathematics in signal processing
- Microgravity transport processes in fluid, thermal, biological and materials sciences
- Mobile video, delivering rich media to mobile devices
- Molecular, cellular and tissue engineering
- Problems arising from accidents in the chemical industry
- Statistics and analytical methods in automotive engineering
- Waste management and the environment
- Web delivering of music

Subject coverage may be extremely specific. The American Society of Mechanical Engineers plans a workshop on the use of elevators in fires and other emergencies, for 2004. On the other hand, a conference may be an overview in a wider field such as mobile communications. Long-standing regular conferences in broad areas have general titles, e.g. *World Telecommunications Congress*, or American Institute of Aeronautics and Astronautics/American Society of Mechanical Engineers *Joint Thermophysics and Heat Transfer Conference*, but will include sessions on emerging topics.

Giving a paper presenting the results of investigation to one's peers provides status and personal recognition in your field. In the commercial sector, becoming known may help an engineer obtain a different job. Modern day life requires presentation skills and the ability to expose and explain your ideas publicly. In academia, it is important for young researchers to progress their careers by giving papers, often written jointly with supervisors. It may be a requirement of a research grant to present a conference paper.

The particular value of a conference is the chance to ask questions, make comments and to discuss current issues. Ambiguous points can be more easily dealt with face to face than by electronic mail. You can normally ask questions during the conference session. Alternatively, if you think your question might be better asked privately, or if you are a nervous newcomer, you can take the opportunities provided by coffee breaks, poster sessions, evening meals, tourist excursions and the bar. You can talk and communicate with an expert or another person with an interest in your topic, which is agreed to be an excellent way to learn and find information.

Engineers can benefit from all the social environments provided by conferences to find congenial friends, often from different countries. Business contacts and possible research collaborators can be sought out. Newcomer or first-timer teas and meetings provide a gentle introduction to other participants.

▶ WHAT HAPPENS AT CONFERENCES?

Opinions on the value of attending conferences and reading conference proceedings vary. Without question, the best information source of all is other people. The published journal literature gives evaluated, refereed state-of-the-art research findings. Conference information may be riskier, consisting of work in progress, which is not complete enough or even intended for refereed publication. But the very latest innovative ideas, theories and solutions may be communicated.

The information conveyed may be considered superficial and not technical enough compared to periodical articles, but attending meetings and writing papers to present are popular with engineers. One factor may be that it is less onerous to write a conference contribution than a periodical paper.

- Conferences
- Symposia
- Congresses
- Conventions
- Seminars
- Colloquia
- Workshops
- Meetings

All of the above can provide a fast track into what an engineer might be missing, and a method of current awareness. National or local seminars may be one-day events for a small group of specialists in a narrow field.

For example, the Institution of Electrical Engineers published Seminar Digests on *Advances in carbon electronics* and *Programmable electronics and safety systems: issues, standards and practical aspects.* In contrast, international conferences may last a whole week with thousands attending. The *International SAMPE Technical Conference* (Society for the Advancement of Material and Process Engineering, US based) lasts for five days. The Society of Automotive Engineers (US based) conference is four days and attracts over 40,000 attendees.

An informal atmosphere promotes the free exchange of ideas, often in the company of fellow enthusiasts. These enthusiasts may also be competitors, so the commercial pressures against sharing information and knowledge must be remembered. This consideration is particularly important in the engineering field, because of its close industrial connections. In the current climate, other university academics as well as industry based engineers may unfortunately be seen as rivals. The degree of confidentiality varies, with defence being at one end of the spectrum. Some of the North Atlantic Treaty Organization's Research and Technology Organisation (RTO) conferences are closed, with only invited participants. The proceedings remain restricted for varying periods of time. RTO was previously AGARD, the Advisory Group for Aerospace Research and Development.

In Computer Science, and Electrical and Electronic Engineering, the Association for Computing Machinery (ACM) and the Institute of Electrical and Electronics Engineers (IEEE) referee conferences fairly rigorously, using a panel. Some conferences announce the number of papers submitted and the number accepted, which may emphasise that papers are often rejected. However, the level of refereeing of conference papers varies considerably, and the intellectual level therefore also varies. An individual's management may require a paper to be presented before funding attendance. Organisers increase the number of active participants by running simultaneous, parallel sessions and having poster sessions.

Conferences often have plenary sessions with keynote presentations, which may be attended by all delegates. Prestigious invited speakers may present more carefully prepared papers, to give an overview or insights into present and future developments.

Sessions are often held on particular aspects, with a knowledgeable chairperson, a series of presented papers, and questions either after each paper or after groups of papers. For large conferences, there will be separate threads, with several papers being given at any one time in parallel sessions. Delegates must work hard to listen to all the papers they have marked on their programmes. Chairpersons must keep to time, so that attendees can sprint between simultaneous sessions. Coffee breaks may be intensive, busy periods to make contacts and obtain a quick injection of caffeine for the listening challenges ahead. Participants may be fighting jet lag.

Conferences may convene in plenary sessions to present conclusions, which will not necessarily be reported in the proceedings. Much of the value of conferences is gained only by attending. Delegates may benefit from educational opportunities such as formal courses, seminars, tutorials or master classes, either free or at supplementary cost, before, during or after the main conference. As a result of all this activity, conferences do not usually last more than four or five days. With life's increasing pace, conferences tend to be shorter, so that delegates are not away from matters requiring attention for too long. They may need to remain in contact with work, by reading e-mail, connecting laptops to the Internet, and checking mobile phone voice mail.

As an example of a large conference, *SAMPE Symposium/Exhibition 2003* took place in Long Beach, California, USA, and invited a mixed audience of industry, government, academia and entrepreneurs. The wide range of facilities offered included a job fair, book store, tutorials, a full-scale banquet, site/factory visits and a hospitality night, with commercially sponsored entertainment. Some papers are closed, and only open to US citizens.

▶ WHERE ARE CONFERENCES HELD?

Conferences may be local, national or international events. Attendance at international conferences is prevalent, since air travel is relatively cheap. Conferences are often held in pleasant surroundings set in attractive places. A suitable time of year is chosen to take advantage of good weather, during 'the conference season'. So work and a holiday break can be efficiently combined, sometimes with a special post-conference tour. Cultural, tourist or leisure centre activities may be offered, and a 'partners' programme provided. Conferences may offer ice-breaking activities such as karaoke, discos, country dancing, country or town walks. Recreational activities are appropriate if the conference spans a weekend.

Some events are housed in hotels, often with a range of standards to suit financial means and delegate status. Others are accommodated in university rooms built with the conference trade in mind. Some hotel-based conferences in cities are very expensive, but may have reduced rates for students and delegates from developing countries. Overall value for money to one's employer is an important factor in conference attendance.

Popular venues in recent years have been major European cities such as Copenhagen, Florence, Lisbon, Vienna, St Petersburg, which are popular with all, including USA delegates. Wessex Institute of Technology organises many useful conferences in well-chosen locations, such as Crete and Halkidiki, Greece. India in the 1980's, South Africa and China in the 1990's have been major destinations, opening up new collaborations between developed and developing countries. Japan and South America are venues for more adventurous planners, usually if local representatives can be found. Some other conferences are always held in the same location, usually because so many attend. The *Offshore Technology Conference* of the Society of Petroleum Engineers has been held in Houston, Texas, USA since 1970, attracting up to 25,000 visitors every May.

As the number of engineers and scientists grows, conferences have a tendency to become bigger, requiring larger venues appropriate to their stature. Conferences previously run by volunteers may need professional support. Local organisers are usually essential. Some larger university-based conferences in the United Kingdom, attracting over a thousand delegates, can only be accommodated in the few universities providing suitable meeting and dining capacity. UK universities prominent in the conference trade include Exeter, Heriot Watt, Manchester, and Warwick.

International conferences held in countries such as Russia may have English as the conference language, with simultaneous or delayed translation into the host language. English has taken over as the language of engineering and science.

► WHO ORGANISES CONFERENCES AND WHY?

Many conference type events are promoted by national bodies, including government agencies and the European Union, and independent organisations such as universities, learned societies, research establishments and trade associations. Dissemination of knowledge and information is usually part of the mission statement. Major professional engineering institutions run hundreds of events as part of their professional development programmes, to fulfil their responsibility to members, and to contribute to knowledge. These include:

- Institute of Electrical and Electronics Engineers (IEEE, US based), www.ieee.org
- Institution of Electrical Engineers (IEE, UK based), www.iee.org
- American Society of Civil Engineers (ASCE), www.asce.org
- Institution of Civil Engineers (ICE, UK based), www.ice.org.uk
- American Society of Mechanical Engineers (ASME), with divisions such as the Design Engineering Division which organises the *Design Technical Conference* every year, www.asme.org
- Institution of Mechanical Engineers (IMechE, UK based), www.imeche.org.uk
- Society of Manufacturing Engineers (SME, US based), www.sme.org
- Institution of Chemical Engineers (IChemE, UK based), www.icheme.org
- Institute of Petroleum (IP, UK based), www.petroleum.co.uk
- American Institute of Aeronautics and Astronautics (AIAA), www.aiaa.org

- Royal Aeronautical Society (RAeS, UK based), www.raes.org.uk
- Verein Deutscher Ingenieure (VDI, Germany), www.vdi.de

Some examples of different types of conference bodies are:

National associations:
American Society for Testing and Materials (ASTM – many *Special Technical Publications* are proceedings of conferences, up to STP 1200 in 2003), www.astm.org
American Wind Energy Association (AWEA), www.awea.org
British Wind Energy Association (BWEA), www.bwea.com
Royal Society (UK), www.royalsoc.ac.uk

National trade associations:
RAPRA Technology Ltd (UK based), www.rapra.net
Society of Motor Manufacturers and Traders (SMMT, UK), www.smmt.co.uk
TWI (World Centre for Materials Joining Technology, UK based), www.twi.co.uk

National government organisations:
United States' National Aeronautics and Space Administration: NASA has a wide variety of conferences as part of its mission to disseminate knowledge, and makes information about its NASA CP conference publications available on the web, www.nasa.gov
National Science Foundation (USA), www.nsf.gov
Engineering and Physical Sciences Research Council (EPSRC, UK), www.epsrc.ac.uk

European organisations:
EuroMech, www.euromech.cz
European Association of Geoscientists and Engineers, www.eage.org

International research associations:
International Federation for the Theory of Machines and Mechanisms (IFToMM), www.caip.rutgers.edu/IFTOMM/indexa.html
International Federation of Automatic Control (IFAC), www.ifac-control.org
International Society for Optical Engineering (SPIE – previously the Society of Photo-Optical Instrumentation Engineers), www.spie.org
International Society for Soil Mechanics and Geotechnical Engineering (ISSMGE), www.issmge.org

The UK's *Engineering Recruitment Show* (www.engrecruitshow.co.uk), sponsored by the Institution of Electrical Engineers and the Institution of Mechanical Engineers, offers a wide range of vacancies in the engineering arena.

Commercial congress bureaux often support organising bodies. Conferences may be arranged by self-perpetuating committees. Helpful permanent websites may be provided, e.g.

Intelec: International Telecommunications Energy Conference, www.intelec.org

Annual Symposium on Engineering Geology and Geotechnical Engineering, coe.isu.edu/geosym

Many conferences are regular events, annual or every two, three or four years. Frequency may be determined by the energy of those willing to plan and participate, or resources in organising institutions. Individuals may contribute much time, for career development, and to contribute to the profession and knowledge. Some conferences take place back-to-back with other related conferences, sometimes leaving one venue for another city. The American Institute for Aeronautics and Astronautics advertises several conferences taking place at the same time in the same location. As well as the established *AIAA/ASME/ASCE/American Helicopter Society's Structures, Structural Dynamics, and Materials Conference,* four other more specialised conferences were held at the same time in 2003. Such factors contribute to librarians' confusion.

▶ EXAMPLES OF ESTABLISHED CONFERENCE SERIES

One example of a long running series of prestigious conferences, held in interesting locations, is *International Mineral Processing Congress (IMPC).* Held every two or three years since 1952, the 22nd was held in 2003. Venues have included: 1960 London, 1963 Cannes, 1964 New York, 1968 Leningrad, 1970 Prague, 1973 London, 1975 Cagliari, 1977 Sao Paulo, 1979 Warsaw, 1982 Toronto, 1985 Cannes, 1988 Stockholm, 1991 Dresden, 1993 Sydney, 1995 San Francisco, 1997 Aachen, 2000 Rome, 2003 Cape Town.

Demonstrating the community's interest in the subject and in international travel, *International Conference on Soil Mechanics and Geotechnical Engineering,* previously the *International Conference on Soil Mechanics and Foundation Engineering,* has taken place all over the world. The locations rival the Olympic Games. 1 Harvard 1936, 2 Rotterdam 1948, 3 Zurich and Lausanne 1953, 4 London 1957, 5 Paris 1961, 6 Montreal 1965, 7 Mexico 1969, 8 Moscow 1974 (2355 specialists from 51 countries took part, including 1877 foreign specialists), 9 Tokyo 1977, 10 Stockholm 1981, 11 San Francisco 1985, 12 Rio de Janeiro 1989, 13 New Delhi 1994, 14 Hamburg 1997, 15 Turkey 2001. The responsible body is the International Society for Soil Mechanics and Geotechnical Engineering (ISSMGE).

The Fédération Internationale des Sociétés d'Ingénieurs des Techniques de l'Automobile organises the *FISITA World Automotive Congress* every two years. FISITA is an independent world body representing over 167,000 automotive engineers through its membership of national automotive societies in thirty-three countries. Its 29th congress was held during June 2002 in Helsinki, Finland.

The International Federation of Automatic Control (IFAC) is responsible for the *IFAC Symposium on Robot Control (SYROCO)* every three years, with the proceedings published by Pergamon.

In transportation, the *PTRC European Transport Forum* (previously the *PTRC Summer Annual Meeting)* is held in Europe. The United States *Transportation Research Board Conference* is a world conference, and the *World Conference on Transport Research* every three years is for academics.

Other examples are:

Parallel CFD (Parallel computational fluid dynamics): 14th conference in 2002.

International Conference on Turbochargers and Turbocharging, Institution of Mechanical Engineers in the United Kingdom: 7th conference in 2002.

Computational methods in water resources, proceedings of the XIVth International Conference on Computational Methods in Water Resources (CMWR XIV): June 2002 in Delft, the Netherlands.

Advances in manufacturing technology XVI, proceedings of the eighteenth National Conference on Manufacturing Research: September 2002 at Leeds Metropolitan University, UK.

▶ CONFERENCES IN A PARTICULAR SUBJECT AREA: ELECTRICAL AND ELECTRONIC ENGINEERING

The majority of conference type events is organised by the IEEE and the IEE. The events include:

- about 150 one day IEE seminars held on specific topics in London every year.
- the IEE's twenty annual conferences.
- the IEEE's 300 annual conferences, e.g. *IEEE Conference on Decision and Control*, with many conferences held outside the USA. Activities include technical conferences, workshops, professional / careers / technical / policy meetings, and standards working group meetings. Events are hosted by a range of IEEE groups, including Technical Societies (e.g. IEEE Instrumentation and Measurement Society), Sections and Chapters, Regions, the Standards Association, the Educational Activities Board, and IEEE-USA.

- prestigious international conferences run jointly by the IEE and the IEEE, held in the UK, elsewhere in Europe, North America or all over the world.
- international conferences held jointly with other organisations, e.g. *International Broadcasting Convention* held annually in Europe, by the IEE, IEEE and the European Broadcasting Union.

Electric Power Research Institute (EPRI, USA): *International Conference on Electrical Machines (ICEM)*, held in even years in Europe or North America.

International Telecommunication Union (ITU): *ITU Telecom World, ITU Plenipotentiary Conference, World Summit on the Information Society.*

Union Radio-Scientifique Internationale (URSI): *General Assembly*, and sponsored conferences such as the *International Symposium on Microwave and Optical Technology*, which are announced in its publication *Radio science bulletin.*

Power Systems Computation Conference, up to the 14th by 2002, is run by a Technical Programme Committee and a Local Organising Committee. Earlier proceedings were published non-commercially, then by Butterworths, and more recently all the papers are freely downloadable from the web in pdf format.

▶ TRADE EXHIBITIONS

Chapter 7 on Product information provides useful relevant information. Commercial concerns, such as DMG World Media (www.dmgworldmedia. com), promote trade exhibitions, consumer shows and fairs worldwide. Trade events often include product promotion receptions sponsored by commercial companies, with presentations, refreshments and social interaction. Detailed exhibition catalogues promoting new and improved products are a good information resource. Free seminars are an attractive added feature.

Trade conferences, attached to lavish, major exhibitions, may be so large that they can only be held in national exhibition centres such as the National Exhibition Centre, Birmingham in the UK. The huge *ACHEMA Exhibition and Congress on Chemical Engineering, Environmental Protection, and Biotechnology* is held every three years in Frankfurt, Germany. The world's biggest industrial fair is the *Hannover Messe*, with 233,000 professionals from more than eighty countries attending in 2002. It included eight trade fairs in 2003: Factory Automation, MicroTechnology, Motion, Drive & Automation, Energy, Compressed Air & Vacuum Technology, Factory Equipment & Tools, Subcontracting, Research & Technology. In the United Kingdom, the *Commercial Vehicle Show* is a three-day show organised by the Society of

Motor Manufacturers & Traders Ltd., with 22,500 visitors at the National Exhibition Centre, Birmingham. *Nepcon* (www.nepcon.co.uk) is the UK's largest annual electronics exhibition.

Useful websites providing search tools to track down and investigate trade events worldwide include TSNN (www.tsnn.co.uk), with more than 5,000 trade shows and conferences and over 30,000 seminars, Expo 24–7 (www.expo24-7.com) and Exhibitions.com (www.exhibitions.com). Trade fairs & exhibitions UK (www.exhibitions.co.uk) is the official website for the UK exhibition industry, sponsored by Trade Partners UK, the United Kingdom government organisation responsible for trade promotion and development work.

▶ HOW DO ENGINEERS FIND OUT ABOUT FORTHCOMING CONFERENCES?

The World Wide Web has transformed information about forthcoming conferences. Paper submission is often managed electronically. Websites are often in English as well as the native language. The conference website may be hosted by local organisers (facilitating immediate updating), or the sponsor.

Academic journals and trade publications in a field usually list relevant upcoming events, and may include prominent advertisements. Many Elsevier periodicals such as *Composites Part A* include a calendar. Professional engineering institutions provide meeting calendars in their member printed publications and on their websites. The Institution of Electrical Engineers has an Events calendar (www.iee.org/Events/Calendar) and the Institution of Mechanical Engineers an Event Directory (www.imeche.org.uk/conferencesandevents). Engineers will receive relevant announcements on e-mail lists to which they choose to subscribe, by direct mailshots, and possibly via the UK's Learning and Teaching Support Network (LTSN) subject centres (www.ltsn.ac.uk).

Informal personal recommendations by management and colleagues probably influence engineers on which events to attend.

Several specialist printed publications provide listings of forthcoming conferences. Emerald in association with Aslib, the Association for Information Management in the UK, produce the printed *Forthcoming international scientific and technical conferences*, covering international conferences and British national conferences. The main issue is published in February, superseding and updating previous issues. The February issue is followed by a May supplement, with cumulative supplements in August and November. Conferences are listed in date order with date, title, locations and address. Subject, location and sponsor indexes are provided. The ISSN is 0046–4686, and 2003 subscription €349.

The *International congress calendar* has been published quarterly by the Union of International Associations in Brussels since 1982. 7,000 meetings a year are covered, across all fields.

The ISSN is 0538–6349, 2003 subscription €260, and a web version is being tested.

In North America, the World Meetings Information Center has produced a series of quarterly journals, now published by Thomson Gale, New York. *World meetings* covers medical, scientific and technical meetings two years ahead, including *World meetings: United States and Canada* (1963-, ISSN 0043–8693, 2002 subscription $195) and *World meetings outside the United States and Canada* (1968-, ISSN 0043–8677, 2002 subscription $195). One aim is to aid conference scheduling and to avoid conflicts. Each entry gives the conference title, date, location, sponsoring body, contents, deadlines for papers, expected availability of the proceedings, and details of any accompanying exhibition. Conference titles, keywords (up to four), date, location, publication and deadline indexes are provided.

The British Library has a database of forthcoming conferences. Services provided to search the database are described on the website.

Information about forthcoming meetings in specific subject areas includes *Meetings on atomic energy*. Vienna: International Atomic Energy Agency, 1969-, with the printed version published quarterly. The same information is available on the web with more frequent updating (www.iaea.org), and this reflects what must be the future trend. The Offshore Engineering Information Service (OEIS), a free service based at Heriot-Watt University Library, and made available through EEVL: the Internet guide to engineering, mathematics and computing, includes information about forthcoming and earlier meetings (www.eevl.ac.uk/offshore/welcome.htm/meetings). *Radio science bulletin* is produced by URSI, and since September 2002 is available on the URSI website in pdf format (www.intec.rug.ac.be/ursi/).

▶ CONFERENCE PUBLICATIONS, AND THEIR DIFFERENT FORMATS

Published conference proceedings can form a significant part of the literature and information, perhaps in fast moving fields such as nanotechnology. As part of the conference fee package, delegates often receive a printed copy of the proceedings, or a book of abstracts, sometimes in advance. CD-ROM proceedings are often a welcome substitute for printed volumes, which can be heavy to transport home. Alternatively, proceedings may be published after the conference, and possibly supplied later to delegates. Conference proceedings can be usefully passed around colleagues to fuel reporting back, or placed in the Library.

Proceedings may only be provided to delegates attending the conference, and not be available for sale subsequently. Some non-refereed papers may not be submitted by their authors for inclusion, or may be withdrawn. Selected papers only may be published, possibly leaving out poorer quality papers or those submitted late. The requested paper which is not included is a familiar problem for librarians. Some published papers bear little relation to the papers presented. Sometimes, a summary or transcript of the discussions is included, which can prove very useful. Conference papers tend to be in a different style to papers published in periodicals. However, many conference papers are published either within ordinary periodicals or as special issues. The *International Conference on Ferroelectric Liquid Crystals* has been published in *Ferroelectrics*. The IEEE Summer and Winter Power Meetings form part of the *IEEE Transactions on Power, Apparatus and Systems*. The British Library Document Supply Centre routinely checks all incoming periodicals for conference papers, to add to its database.

The World Wide Web is transforming the availability of conference papers. Authors may put their conference papers up on their home pages, either legally or illegally. Whole conferences, or archives of series of conferences, may be on the World Wide Web, usually in pdf format. The Society of Automotive Engineers (SAE, USA), the American Institute of Aeronautics and Astronautics (AIAA) and the American Society of Mechanical Engineers (ASME) now publish most of their conference papers as separate papers via the web, individually priced. A searchable index is provided, and subscriptions are often also available. Nearly all IEEE conference papers since 1988 are in the comprehensive product *IEL (IEE/IEEE Electronic Library)* and sold individually to non-subscribers. Purchase from 'digital stores' via the web with electronic payment and delivery is fast and convenient.

The American Institute for Aeronautics and Astronautics provides a range of formats for its conferences and those of some associated bodies, e.g. *ASME Wind Energy Symposium Technical Papers*. Individual conference papers can be purchased immediately via the web. Complete sets of printed papers may be purchased by standing order. Annual collections of conference papers, arranged by groups of conferences, may be purchased as CD-ROMs. For some of the most important conferences, in certain years, the AIAA publishes a printed volume of proceedings, e.g. *AIAA Applied Aerodynamics Conference Technical Papers 2000*. The *35th Intersociety Energy Conversion Engineering Conference (IECEC)* for 2000 was published in two volumes by the American Institute of Aeronautics and Astronautics, with every paper having an individual AIAA paper number. This conference has six sponsors: AIAA, Institute of Electrical and Electronics Engineers, American Institute of Chemical Engineers, American Nuclear Society, Society of Automotive Engineers and American Society of Mechanical Engineers. The printed proceedings can be purchased for engineers to browse conveniently on the train.

Conference proceedings may occupy a large number of printed volumes. The *Peaceful uses of atomic energy* series was sixteen volumes in 1955, growing to thirty-three volumes in 1958, providing an invaluable source of up-to-date information in a new interdisciplinary field. The *International Conference on Soil Mechanics and Geotechnical Engineering* is usually four or more thick volumes.

The American Society of Mechanical Engineers' publication mode mirrors its structure, with thirty-seven separate Technical Divisions and Subdivisions publishing conferences in numbered sub-series. The divisions and their acronyms include Advanced Energy Systems (AES), Applied Mechanics (AMD), Fluids Engineering (FED), Heat Transfer Division (HTD), and Internal Combustion Engine (ICE).

The American Institute of Chemical Engineers (AIChE) has published its conferences since 1951 in the *Chemical engineering progress symposium series*, a colourful publication of varying thicknesses.

Some conferences previously published by conference organisers on a relatively informal basis, perhaps by the host university, have been taken over by major commercial publishers and marketed widely. Camera ready copy makes this a commercial proposition, although commercial publications are often expensive. University publication usually means an inexpensively produced soft-cover. In either case, publication can be admirably quick.

Pergamon publishes the prestigious *BOSS – Behaviour of Offshore Structures*. *BOSS* is planned every three years, on a rotating basis by four universities: the Norwegian University of Science and Technology, the University of London, Massachusetts Institute of Technology, and Delft University of Technology.

MATADOR – Machine Tool Design and Research was previously published by the University of Manchester Institute of Science and Technology, but Springer published the 33rd conference (2000). The International Federation for Information Processing (IFIP)'s publications are a Kluwer imprint.

The American Chemical Society (ACS) only produces volumes containing abstracts, in the expectation that material will be published subsequently in periodicals, the favoured publication method in chemistry. *American Chemical Society abstracts of meetings papers*. Washington, D.C.: American Chemical Society, 1947–, annual.

Since the author may retain copyright, it is common to publish subsequently in journals. Papers may be longer or shorter, with more experimental evidence, and the same or similar titles. Searching an abstracting and indexing publication may deliver both an American Society of Mechanical Engineers conference paper and an ASME periodical article, sometimes with a slightly changed title.

► DISCOVERY TOOLS FOR CONFERENCE PUBLICATIONS AND PAPERS

The published proceedings of conferences have often been difficult to track down, and may form part of 'grey literature'. The British Library Document Supply Centre (BLDSC) at Boston Spa, Yorkshire, UK has been very successful in building a comprehensive conference proceedings collection. Discovering published proceedings may require detailed information including: full name, acronym name (e.g. *AAAI90, SISPAD, ICA 2001, QRM 2002, CMWR XIV, IDEAL 2002, IEA/AIE 2002)*, editors, sponsoring bodies, number in a series, exact beginning and end days, month and year, exact location, place of publication, publisher, date of publication (often different from the event date), ISBN/ISSN.

Invaluable sources of information about available conference proceedings are produced by the BLDSC, utilising its data in different formats. BLDSC has published *Index of conference proceedings received* since 1973, listing conference proceedings newly acquired by the British Library. Published monthly, it has a February annual cumulation for separate purchase. ISSN 0959–4906, monthly subscription 2003 £120 in the UK, annual volume £99 in the UK.

The British Library produces the *Inside* database, updated daily, for the global market. Paper level bibliographic information, without abstracts, for all subjects from more than 20,000 research journals and over 100,000 conference proceedings from 1993, is searchable online. It is possible to order directly over the web and to receive articles within two hours. The same data provides UK higher education's *Zetoc* service, and OCLC's *ProceedingsFirst Database* and *PapersFirst Database*.

The *British Library Public Catalogue*, containing Document Supply Material holdings, is freely accessible on the web. Copies of papers and loans of proceedings can be provided worldwide by the BLDSC, providing an excellent service to industry and academia.

The online host STN provides FIZ Karlsruhe's *CONF* database which contains information on past, present and future conferences and meetings in science and technology. Records contain the conference title, sponsoring organization, conference location and dates, contact for further information, notes on related publications and, to some extent, keywords describing the conference topics. Coverage is from 1976, updated weekly with 200 new conferences and 200 updates. *Dialog ondisc engineering conferences and reports* is a CD-ROM collection (also available via the Internet) combining conference papers and proceedings from *Ei Compendex* (Elsevier Engineering Index), FIZ Karlsruhe's *CONF* database and the European Association for Grey Literature Exploitation's *SIGLE Tech Database*. Pricing for online products is often complex, depending on the number of sites and the number of simultaneous or potential users. As an indication, *Dialog ondisc engineering conferences and reports* 2003 price is $2,300 for one user on one site.

The *Directory of published proceedings* has been published by the InterDok Corporation, New York since 1965. It is produced ten times a year, from September to June, with a cumulated annual volume, and a cumulated index supplement three times a year. One of the three sections is *SEMT: science/engineering/medicine/technology*, covering any publication published worldwide that is the result of a conference, with a combined subject and sponsor index, plus editor and location indexes. ISSN 0012–3293, monthly edition $595, cumulated index supplement $180, annual cumulated volume $375. From 2004, InterDok (www.interdok. com) will introduce the *Directory of published proceedings* as an online database. One month, three months, six months and annual subscriptions will be available.

▶ ABSTRACTING AND INDEXING OF CONFERENCE PUBLICATIONS AND PAPERS

Most subject abstracting and indexing publications' scope information claim inclusion of conference proceedings. Whether they index each conference proceedings as a whole or each paper individually is often unclear. The BLDSC collects 16,000 conference proceedings a year, a high proportion of which must be in science and engineering. Numerical coverage of conference literature in abstracting and indexing sources is difficult to estimate, but is far below the whole output. *Aerospace Database* (Cambridge Science Abstracts) includes all the AIAA conference papers. *Ei Compendex* (Elsevier Engineering Index) indexes many conference proceedings (more than 1,000 entries for 2002 publication year, 1,100 for 2001). *Inspec* (Institution of Electrical Engineers) has complete coverage of all Institution of Electrical Engineers and Institute of Electrical and Electronics Engineers conference papers. From all publishers, 41% of *Inspec* engineering subfile source documents are conference papers, 9% of documents being conference papers in journals.

An example of an abstracting and indexing product which does not index conference proceedings or papers is the United States National Library of Medicine's *Medline*, which only includes periodical papers. This demonstrates the greater importance of conference publications to the engineering community, compared to the medical community.

The Institute for Scientific Information (ISI, USA) publishes *ISI proceedings* (previously *ISTP: Index to scientific and technical proceedings*), which provides web access to bibliographic information and author abstracts from papers delivered at prestigious international conferences, updated weekly, with a quarterly CD-ROM. The *Science and technology edition* is relevant. With the *Social sciences & humanities edition*, over two million papers from over 80,000 conferences since 1990 are included. About 17,000 conferences in science and technology were added in 2001–2002.

Inside (British Library) and *ISI proceedings* do not provide intellectual subject indexing, using controlled vocabulary and other assigned subject keywords, and therefore are quicker to include papers from conference proceedings than subject indexed abstracting and indexing sources.

▶ HOW DO ENGINEERS OBTAIN CONFERENCE PAPERS AND PUBLICATIONS?

Having heard about a conference paper or proceedings, an engineer may use informal personal contacts or formal channels through libraries to obtain the full text. Some conferences require authors to sign away their copyright, but the majority does not. Many authors put their own individual conference papers up on their own websites or in web repositories. A highly developed web archive in a related area is arXiv.org e-Print archive (arxiv.org).

Efficient web search engines with the technology to index pdf papers, e.g. *Google*, provide effective retrieval for papers on authors' sites. With the time-saving possibility of contacting authors personally by e-mail and convenient electronic transmission, obtaining obscure conference papers can sometimes be easy and fast.

Since the British Library conference index contains the records of 400,000 conference proceedings held in stock, with 16,000 new records added each year, the British Library's Document Supply service is an excellent resource for gaining access to conference type publications. The British Library website (www.bl.uk) provides expert guidance on the bibliographic information which helps to obtain required material. Its services area (www.bl.uk/services/document/conference.html) states: 'The British Library endeavours through its own scanning to obtain all 'worthwhile' conference publications, whatever the subject or language, and covers all types of publication formats with the exception of audio-visual. However, we still rely on speculative orders sent in by our customers to alert us to many publications we would not otherwise know of. Because of this, we always encourage customers to place an order, even if they cannot find the item entered in our catalogues.'

5 Patent Information

Nigel Clarke and Keri Rowles

▶ **INTRODUCTION**

Any analysis of the evolution of our modern industrial world must acknowledge that changes in the means of information transmission, storage, processing, and ownership have been amongst the most far-reaching in their consequences for mankind.

This chapter focuses upon one aspect of these changes by providing an introduction to the information contained in patent documents. It explains how patent documents can provide a valuable source for engineers faced with the barrage of information that is available today. As David Shenk so succinctly put it in 'Data Smog': *'By and large, over our long history, people have been able to examine and consider information about as quickly as it could be created and circulated. ... In the mid twentieth century this synchrony was abruptly knocked off track ...'* (Shenk, 1997).

This chapter provides pointers for accessing patent information that can be used as part of a general strategy to keep on the right information track. It does not attempt to teach the law of patents. Patent law is extremely complex, and the financial consequences of mistakes can be enormous. We strongly recommend seeking the advice of a qualified professional when dealing with patent law matters.

One of the first reactions of many engineers, when presented with the suggestion to consult patent information, is to draw a comparison with other more familiar information sources, and especially with technical journals. Their willingness to abandon basic scientific principles when making such comparisons is surprising, and a remarkable number of normally rational engineers dismiss patent information without further thought.

Several explanations have been put forward for this phenomenon, including:

- unfamiliarity with the patent system,
- general lack of empirical studies comparing patent information with other sources,
- unwillingness to depart from known information sources.

Some basic studies (Allen and Oppenheim, 1979) do suggest, however, that patent information is worth consulting.

▶ PERSPECTIVES ON PATENTS

A patent is not a piece of real property like a book, which can be controlled by possession. Patents are 'intellectual property', and the exploitation of the ideas contained in a patent is controlled through more subtle exclusionary rights granted by the state. A patentee has the right to exclude others from infringing upon the subject matter claimed in the patent. However, there are always two sides to an allegation of patent infringement, and arguments about where the boundaries of protection for a particular patent lie can be extremely technical, long, and expensive. Specialist advice from a qualified professional is essential.

The technical nature of patented subject matter can be contrasted with copyright, trademarks, and the many other forms of intellectual property (exclusionary right) that are granted by the state. Other forms of intellectual property are generally intended to protect the fruits of quite different categories of mental labour. One example of the confusion that can exist is the often-heard assertion that someone has 'copyrighted an invention'. This is nonsense. Copyright is a right to prevent the copying of a specific category of works such as literary, artistic, musical, and the like. A patented invention relates to a technical idea, whilst copyright protects the form of expression of an idea.

Not only do the various forms of intellectual property relate to different types of material, though occasionally there may be some overlap between categories, but the nature of the rights that they confer are quite diverse.

For a more detailed introduction to the legal concepts involved, the relevant sections of the Patent Office website (www.patent.gov.uk) are helpful.

Patents as a legal construct

Many observers seem happy to talk of patents as one type of a general class of 'intellectual property', or 'intangible asset', with little more than a passing thought given to the deeper implications. However, studies of the origins of our intellectual property system reveal that it was only in the nineteenth century that our modern concepts of what should be the object of patent protection crystallised (Sherman and Bradly, 1999). Previously, a dominant consideration had been the mental labour involved in the creative act, with patent protection reserved for creations that were derived from more substantial mental labour. The role of a written description of an alleged invention was rather unclear, and often neglected.

Today, when speaking of patents, we are referring to specific subject matter that lies within legal boundaries set out by Acts of Parliament, and other legal sources. What is important today is not so much the quantity of mental labour, but the characteristics of the end product of that mental labour as described in a patent document. Is the alleged invention, *as described*, sufficiently different to what has gone before? Is it industrially applicable, etc? What is protected is that which is clearly claimed in the patent document, and if the patent document is poorly drafted, then protection may be lost for some of all of what was intended. Under this modern view, the importance of consulting a qualified professional when drafting a patent application cannot be overestimated.

Patents and public policy

An excellent study of the patent system that was prepared for the United States Senate Judiciary Committee (Machlup, 1958), examined four of the main positions that often recur in public policy debates:

- Natural justice dictates that an inventor should receive rights in the fruits of mental labour because it is unfair that others can 'steal' ideas.
- An elaboration on the justice theme links new innovations to the general public benefit that results. The inventor is rewarded for providing a benefit to society, and the reward takes the form of an exclusionary right to work the invention. As John Stuart Mill put it ' . . . *an exclusive privilege, of temporary duration, is preferable; because it leaves nothing to anyone's discretion; because the reward conferred by it depends upon the invention's being found useful, and the greater the usefulness, the greater the reward; and because it is paid by the very persons to whom the service is rendered, the consumers of the commodity*' (Mill, 1848).
- As technological development is generally accepted to be beneficial, a reward in the form of exclusionary rights for those who develop new and useful inventions would seem to be a sensible approach to public policy. It will motivate people to invest effort, and other resources in the innovation process.
- An inventor may keep an invention secret. Patents, by granting exclusionary rights, may render the keeping of secrets unnecessary. The patent law specifically requires that patent applications be published with a certain delay after the application is filed at the Patent Office. As a result, the pool of publicly available knowledge is increased.

The techno-economic aspect of patents

The World Intellectual Property Organization (WIPO) considers that patents *'not only provide incentives to individuals by ensuring recognition, and material reward, they also help enrich the total body of technical knowledge in the world. Patent owners are obliged to publicly disclose information on their invention, this provides valuable information for other inventors as well as inspiration for future generations of researchers and inventors.* **This leads to further invention and innovation** . . .' [Authors' emphasis].

▶ INTERNATIONAL ARRANGEMENTS

In a global economy, the international dimensions of Intellectual Property rights cannot be ignored. Some key elements are discussed below.

The Paris Convention

The Paris Convention for the Protection of Industrial Property was first concluded in 1883. It provides the basis for numerous common rules between signatory states for patents designs, and other forms of intellectual property. Most countries have now signed the Paris Convention, and in many ways it is the foundation of modern international intellectual property harmonisation. One very important principal introduced by the Paris convention is 'convention priority' that gives a grace period for filing subsequent patent applications in other countries. In the words of the convention: *'Any person who has duly filed an application for a patent, . . . in one of the countries of the Union, . . . , shall enjoy, for the purpose of filing in the other countries, a right of priority during the periods hereinafter fixed'.* The grace period for patents is fixed at twelve months.

Because of the priority principle, a whole family of patent applications that relate to the same invention can be filed in several countries. Such 'patent families' are discussed below.

The European Patent Convention (EPC)

European patents are granted by the European Patent Office (EPO) under the EPC. A single application in one of the official languages of the EPO (English, French, or German) can lead to protection in as many member states as the applicant designates. By March 2003 there were twenty-seven EPC contracting states. These were Austria, Belgium, Bulgaria, Cyprus,

Czech Republic, Denmark, Estonia, Finland, France, Germany, Greece, Hungary, Ireland, Italy, Liechtenstein, Luxembourg, Monaco, the Netherlands, Portugal, Romania, Slovakia, Slovenia, Spain, Sweden, Switzerland, Turkey, and the United Kingdom. An excellent starting point for further information is the website of the European Patent Office (www.epo.org). The EPC system is one of the world's major patenting systems, and European Patent application documents are a key source of patent information.

Patent Co-operation Treaty (PCT)

Concluded in 1970, the PCT is open to States party to the Paris Convention. The PCT enables patent applicants to request patent protection in many countries simultaneously using an 'international patent application'. At the beginning of 2003 there were 118 PCT contracting states. The administrative, and other strengths of this system mean that it is used by a very large number of patent applicants, and in 2002 there were almost 100,000 PCT patent applications published. PCT publications are therefore an extremely important source of patent information. For further information, consult the WIPO website (www.wipo.int). The PCT, as the EPC, is one of the world's major patenting systems. PCT patent documents figure highly on the list of patent documents that patent information users consult.

Major patent offices

In addition to the European (EPC), and International (PCT) systems mentioned above, almost every country has a national patent office that will publish national patent applications. The two very large patent offices of the United States, and Japan, will probably be relevant in almost any case.

Trade Related aspects of Intellectual Property Rights (TRIPS)

During the Uruguay round of the General Agreement of Trade, and Tariffs (GATT) negotiations (1984 -1994), a consensus was reached that ideas and knowledge now form an important part of world trade. From recorded music, and films, to branded clothes, software, and medicines, the protection of the related intellectual property was considered to be an essential part of the modern international trading system. The World Trade Organisation agreement that emerged from the Uruguay round therefore contains a large part (TRIPS) relating to the protection of intellectual property, and the enforcement of minimum standards in all signatory states. This agreement, with its associated enforcement procedures, is a powerful force behind the global movement to promote the recognition of intellectual property.

▶ PATENT TERM, AND PUBLICATION OF PATENT DOCUMENTS

The extent of the exclusionary rights granted by patents is limited in both technical scope, and time. Under the TRIPS standards, the minimum term of patent protection is twenty years, which is in line with the long established practice of many western countries. In return for the possibility of enjoying exclusionary rights over such an extended period, a patent application will be published by the Patent Office concerned – normally within eighteen months of the priority date defined by the Paris Convention. The TRIPS agreement further contains provisions relating to the sufficiency of patent documents:

> *'Members shall require that an applicant for a patent shall disclose the invention in a manner sufficiently clear and complete for the invention to be carried out by a person skilled in the art and may require the applicant to indicate the best mode for carrying out the invention known to the inventor at the filing date or, where priority is claimed, at the priority date of the application.'*

The 'sufficient disclosure' principle is fundamental to patent information.

▶ PATENT DOCUMENTS

We now discuss some of the common conventions relating to the way that patent documents present information.

WIPO Recommendations – harmonising patent documentation

WIPO is, in its own words *'an international organisation dedicated to promoting the use and protection of works of the human spirit ... intellectual property'*. It has its headquarters in Geneva, and is one of the specialised agencies of the United Nations. At the end of 2002, WIPO was responsible for the administration of twenty-two treaties in the field of intellectual property. The WIPO website (www.wipo.int) is a rich source of information on many aspects of intellectual property.

The activities undertaken by WIPO include the establishment of various Guidelines, Standards, and Recommendations relating to patents. Some of these recommendations are intended to harmonise technical aspects of the presentation, and electronic distribution of patent information, and a few are mentioned below.

A full set of WIPO Recommendations is included in the *WIPO Handbook on Industrial Property Information, and Documentation*, which is available on CD-ROM, and can be ordered via the WIPO website.

The front page

Most patent offices, the UKPO included, consolidate key bibliographic information on the front page of patent applications, and granted patents. Bibliographic data include the publication number, inventor's name, date of filing, etc. Each individual patent document has a set of bibliographic data which identifies that patent document.

WIPO Standard 9 states: *'Users of patent documents and Patent Gazettes often encounter difficulties in identifying the bibliographic data on or concerning patent documents. The aim of this Recommendation is to overcome these difficulties. The Recommendation covers a list of approximately 60 distinct bibliographic data widely used on the first page of patent documents or in Patent Gazettes. They are identified through code numbers, the so-called 'INID Codes' or 'INID Numbers.'* ('INID' is an acronym for Internationally agreed Numbers for the Identification of bibliographic Data.)

Three commonly used INID codes are:

(11)Number of the patent, SPC or patent document
(22)Date(s) of filing the application(s)
(32)Date(s) of filing of priority application(s)

INID codes are especially useful when the front page of the document is printed in a language with which you are not familiar.

The front page is followed by a description, drawings, claims, and possibly a search report. In order to become familiar with the structure, and layout of patent application documents, we recommend taking a look at the *esp@cenet*® database on the EPO website (www.epo.org).

Description

The description of the invention is intended to be an enabling disclosure (see TRIPS agreement). In a manner analogous to the way that a scientific

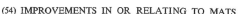

PATENT SPECIFICATION   (11)   1 413 714

1 413 714

(21) Application No. 18508/73   (22) Filed 17 April 1973   (19)
(31) Convention Application No. 722 669   (32) Filed 19 April 1972 in
(33) South Africa (ZA)
(44) Complete Specification published 12 Nov. 1975
(51) INT. CL.² A47L 23/22
(52) Index at acceptance
    A4S 1F 1G 1H

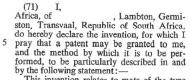

(54) IMPROVEMENTS IN OR RELATING TO MATS

(71)   I,
Africa, of   , Lambton, Germi-
ston, Transvaal, Republic of South Africa,
do hereby declare the invention, for which I
5 pray that a patent may be granted to me,
and the method by which it is to be performed, to be particularly described in and
by the following statement:—
    This invention relates to mats of the type
10 which comprise a plurality of generally parallel slats separated by strips of rubber or other
flexible resilient material each of which is

cables or the like may be employed to enable the mat to be rolled up. The spacers
may be of resiliently flexible material.
    The use of tubular spacers provides a
means for holding the strips in position 55
against the slats and eliminates the labour
and expense of extensively riveting each strip
to a slat. Manufacture is effected simply by
correctly locating the spacers between the
slats and the strips, and threading connecting 60
wires through suitably punched holes in the
strips and slats and the spacers.

Fig. 5.1: An example of the front page of a patent document

paper should allow another experimenter to reproduce the results of the author, the technical description in a patent document is intended to allow a person familiar with the technology (a person skilled in the art) to reproduce the invention.

Drawings

Where appropriate, the patent document should include 'drawings' which indicate how the invention is constructed, operates or is used. The term 'drawings' is used in the general sense to mean a non-textual representation. With this definition 'drawings' can mean engineering drawings, but also electron micrographs, circuit diagrams, chemical formulae, crystal structures, flow charts, graphs, DNA sequences, and so on. In a patent document, a picture truly is worth a thousand words.

Claims

The claims of a patent document are the most legalistic part. The claims indicate exclusive 'territory'.

Search report

If available, a search report is usually included with a published patent application. If the search report is not ready before the end of the eighteen-month publication delay, then it will normally be published later as a separate document. The search report summarises the examiner's initial findings on comparing the patent application, as filed, with previously published material 'prior art'.

In addition to indicating similar technical material, a search report can also yield other information such as the identities of others working in the field. It is also a very important element in the subsequent examination of a patent application by the examiner.

▶ TYPES OF INFORMATION FROM PATENT DOCUMENTS

Patent documents yield varied information to different users, and its significance is greatly influenced by the context, and information from other sources. For example, a patent application naming Peter Ingenious as inventor, and Wamo Widgets as applicant could yield more than just technical information. If Peter Ingenious works for another company, and has not told them about his moonlighting for Wamo, then the consequences could be more than merely technical for Peter. Four general categories of information often extracted from patent documents are technical, legal, administrative (procedural), and commercial.

Patents as technical literature

The initial technical disclosure in the patenting process is the patent application document. A printed patent specification is published later if the patent is granted. The application is therefore normally of greater interest for technical searches. Furthermore, empirical studies have suggested that the overlap between patent documents and journals is surprisingly small (Allen and Oppenheim, 1979).

Legal information

As discussed above, patents are an essentially legal construct. The patent examiner undertakes a quasi-judicial role in deciding whether a patent application is to be granted or not. As with any judicial process in England, there are numerous checks and balances in place to ensure that justice is served. One of the most important is the possibility to appeal against an unfavourable decision that may be delivered against a patent application. It is also possible to appeal against the decision to grant a patent to someone else if it is felt that this decision was not justifiable. One example of a patent that attracted a large number of 'oppositions' was filed at the EPO by The President, and Fellows of Harvard College in relation to a 'Method for Producing Transgenic Animals' (EP0169672, 1986).

Procedural

The patent examination procedure is complex, and a single application can be processed for several years before grant, and completion of appeals. A very important aspect to this procedure is the payment of fees. There are many different steps to be taken when prosecuting a patent application, and even more if it is decided to take the international route. Failure to pay the appropriate fees on time can have catastrophic consequences, and information about fees is therefore very important. Once paid for, the various procedural steps may also result in the production of various documents, and other statements. The public part of a patent application file at a patent office can be consulted in a process known as 'file inspection', if available. There is also a patent register that can be consulted.

Patents as commercial literature

As patents serve to grant a form of control over the exploitation of inventions, it is not surprising that many patentees opt to exercise that control. Potential economic gains are a major motivating factor for technical research, and patenting. Statistical techniques such as plotting intellectual property landscapes can yield both general information about commercial trends, and specific information about the behaviour of individual patent applicants.

For example, statistical analysis of patent applications can be an aid to analysing investment trends. It is also not uncommon for companies negotiating joint ventures, and other forms of co-operation, to undertake a patent counting exercise to aid in the establishment of their respective bargaining powers.

▶ SOME BASIC AIDS TO ANALYSING PATENT INFORMATION

Before reviewing some practical examples of patent information exploitation in the next section, a few basic tools of the trade are introduced to offer some 'handles' for the manipulation of otherwise unwieldy data.

Patent classification codes

During the 19th century it became increasingly clear that a system would be required to classify the ever more numerous patent documents into technical fields of manageable size. The development of the first such system in England is generally attributed to the former Superintendent of the Great Seal Patent Office, Bennett Woodcroft (1803–1879).

Classification systems have become necessary in the same way that labels on filing cabinet drawers identify the contents, and hanging files subdivide the contents of the drawers.

International Patent Classification (IPC)

In Woodcroft's day, steam engines formed the basis of numerous important categories, however as technology moved ahead, so the range of classifications required expanded. Since Woodcroft, many classification systems have appeared around the world, and the most widely used today is the International Patent Classification (IPC) administered by WIPO. Detailed information about the IPC is available on the WIPO website (www.wipo.int/classifications).

The IPC is revised every five years, and by 2003 the 7th revision had been adopted by fifty-three countries.

The IPC is a hierarchical classification system used to classify, and search patent documents (patent applications, specifications of granted patents, utility models, etc). The 7th revision contains 70,000 entries for distinct technical areas, which are organised as follows:

- Eight sections have been created to identify the 'top-level' general fields of technical activity. For example, 'A' includes 'Human Necessities', 'D' includes 'Textiles, and Paper', and 'G' covers 'Physics'.
- The 7th edition divides the eight sections into 120 classes. For example, 'D03' covers 'Weaving'.
- The 120 classes are further subdivided into over 600 sub-classes. For example, 'D03D' covers 'Woven Fabrics, Methods of Weaving, and Looms'.
- Subclasses are divided into main groups, and subgroups.
- Main groups always end with '/00' e.g. main group 'D03D01/00' covers 'Woven fabrics designed to make specific articles'.
- The subgroups are listed below the main group headings, and their descriptive titles are preceded by dots with more dots indicating a lower level in the hierarchy. For example, '1/06. Curtain heading tapes' is listed directly below 'D03D01/00'.

The IPC has a catchword index that can be very helpful for finding classification codes when it is not obvious where to start. Alternatively, try drilling down through the classification hierarchy using the IPC version available on the WIPO website.

Normally one patent document will contain material corresponding to more than one IPC code. In this case the document will be assigned several IPC codes. Many patent offices include the IPC code allocated by their patent examiners on the printed front page of the patent documents. It is also very common to include these codes in the electronic indexes of patent information products.

A word of warning; different patent examiners in different patent offices may assign different IPC codes for the same, or similar material. This effect may influence the results of a search based upon too narrow a range of IPC values.

European Patent Classification (ECLA)

The ECLA system is used by the EPO for carrying out patent application searches (European Patent Office, 2000). Whilst *based* on the IPC, it is *not the same*. The essential point about ECLA is that it is designed for searchers. Documents are given ECLA classifications by examiners. An examiner may at any time create new classifications, or assign different classifications to existing patent documents. This ensures that documentation is classified, and reclassified, and remains easily searchable.

UK Patent Classification

In addition to the IPC, the UK also assigns classification codes according to a distinct, nationally designed system, to UK patent documents. For further details see the UKPO website.

US Patent Classification

In addition to the IPC, the USPTO also assigns classification codes according to a distinct nationally designed system to US patent documents. For further details see the USPTO website. In general, the USPTO classification is based on function rather than form.

Patent families

Roughly, a patent family is a group of patent documents that relate to the same invention. One of the most obvious methods of achieving this is to group documents filed in different patent offices with the same Paris convention priority into one family. However, this is not the whole story, and the practice of the information supplier being used should be ascertained.

Search report citations

Search report publication is one of the first public results of the patent examiner's work. The search report indicates the examiner's first opinion on the patentability of the claimed invention. The documents cited by the examiner are important for the searcher, in that the citations indicate whether the claimed invention is thought to be novel, and/or inventive. Most patent offices examine patent applications, but it is by no means a foregone conclusion that if one patent office considers that a given invention is patentable, that another will reach the same conclusion. Different examining practices are studied in the work of Michel and Bettels (2001).

▶ COST-BENEFIT

Extensive studies indicate that engineers seldom consider patent information, preferring to consult traditional professional and learned journals or even word-of-mouth. However, there is a financial cost associated with traditional literature sources, and the reliability of word-of-mouth sources can be difficult to assess. Engineers would be well advised to weigh up the costs, and benefits of all sources available.

Value-added patent information distributors generally charge for their services, but a great deal of patent information is available for little or no cost. In this respect, when analysing various information options with a view to cost-benefit, patents may score very highly. A number of free patent information databases are publicly available via the Internet. The first obvious choice would be that of the Patent Office (www.gb.espacenet.com). This is a part of a much wider Internet based patent information resource, established under the European Patent Organisation, (www.espacenet. com). These free databases allow access to the technical ideas of many thousands of patent applicants, and inventors worldwide.

Advantages of the *esp@cenet*® services include their extensive coverage (geographically, and chronologically), and the vital 'key' to the EPO databases; the European patent classification scheme ECLA (N3. espacenet.com/eclasrch).

When consulting any of the resources listed in Annex 1, it is good idea to check the help facilities to ensure that the nature of the data being accessed is fully understood. Critical database characteristics include; languages of the indexes, time period covered, publishing offices covered, searchable data fields, and more. A useful review of patent information resources has been produced by Goodchild (2003).

▶ PRACTICAL EXPLOITATION OF PATENT INFORMATION

The grant of a patent is a bargain struck between the inventor, and the state (patent granting authority). In return for the right to prevent others, for a finite time in a finite territory, from working the invention, the patentee agrees to make details of his invention public. The cumulative volume of published patent documents over hundreds of years, and from hundreds of thousands of inventors is included in the enormous body of 'patent information'. Indeed it has been argued that patent information is the largest resource of technical information.

Different national and regional systems entail different kinds of publications. The EPC, and the British system, call for the publication of patent applications, and patent specifications. The German system has three different kinds of patent document; *Offenlegungschrift, Auslegeschrift*, and *Patentschrift*. Until recently, the US system allowed for the publication of only the granted patents, but after much debate the USPTO now also publishes patent applications.

The enormous volume of patent documentation published annually (for example, the EPO received over 150,000 patent applications in 2001), and the sheer number of copies to be made available, have driven patent information publications away from paper documents, towards electronic media.

In addition to the traditional paper pamphlets, patent information is now available on CD-ROM, DVD-ROM, on-line databases, and the Internet.

▶ PATENT-INFORMATION – EXAMPLES OF PATENT SEARCHES

If you are an inventor, or patentee, there are many very good reasons for consulting patent information. These include; registration, protection, defence, technology watch, competitive intelligence, exploitation, trade, and disposal.

If you were a potential patentee, then you would want to make sure that no one has previously come up with your idea, and patented or published it. You would want to ensure that what you claim to have invented is novel, and inventive. After having obtained your patent you would want to ensure that nobody infringed it. The responsibility for policing your patent portfolio is yours, and yours alone. There is no such thing as 'the patent police'. It is up to you to detect, and identify infringers, and then take the appropriate action after consultation with your qualified legal advisor. It is to be hoped that you would also take precautions to avoid infringing others' patents. You may want to know in which countries you may exploit your invention/technology so you would try to identify countries/territories in which patent protection does not exist, or no longer exists (due to lapses, revocations, etc.).

Knowledge of the instantaneous patent landscape in your field is an invaluable support for all decisions needed at each stage of the Innovation Process.

Do not underestimate the complexity and level of skill required in making patent searches. It is possible to make some progress using, for example, free Internet databases, where available. However, the best advice (where critical decisions have to be made, or perhaps more importantly, where money is concerned) is that you should have your searches carried out professionally.

Prior art, or state-of-the-art searches

This kind of search provides an overview of the latest developments within a technical field. It reveals results achieved, and protection obtained by competitors. Documentation can be built up containing the most relevant patent documents for a field of activities.

Technology watch/competitive intelligence searches

To update technical documentation, to regularly receive the latest published patent documents in a technical domain (technology watch), or to follow a specific company (competitive intelligence), a specially adapted search profile can be defined. It can be carried out at regular intervals. For example, the EPO publishes patent applications every Wednesday – unless the office is closed that day. A European patent watch could therefore be activated every Wednesday.

Novelty search

This kind of search, which is based on the description of an invention, can help when deciding whether it will be economically worthwhile to continue with R&D efforts. The search result can help in finalising a patent application by taking into account the appropriate, current, state-of-the-art, and distinguishing an invention from it.

Legal status, and family member search

The search result can reveal the geographical protection initially sought for an invention. At the same time it can identify where a given patent is still valid. There is the opportunity to analyse portfolios of other patent applicants. The EPO produces patent family, and legal status databases under the INPADOC® brand.

Freedom of exploitation (freedom to act):

When commercialising a technology at home or abroad, such a search would reveal the extent of existing patent activity in the intended market area.

The freedom to act search:

- can prevent unpleasant surprises.
- can support opposition to the grant of a patent, or revocation of a granted patent.
- can provide results with which to defend against an accusation of infringement.
- can affect the decision on patentability by providing supplementary state of the art documents entering an evaluation procedure.

▶ CONCLUSIONS

Research has repeatedly shown that engineers do not consult patent information sufficiently to fully support innovation. Surveys indicate that patents are often in last place as a source of technical information. Paradoxically, the same surveys report that the two most frequently consulted sources of information are 'within the enterprise' or 'competitors'.

Many engineers have not yet realised that patent information offers a unique entry into intra-enterprise technical information, and competitor activities, on a much wider scale than is possible with simple word of mouth. Engineers who rely on the 'grapevine' for such information, when patent information would be more reliable, comprehensive, and up-to-date, are missing out, to their detriment.

▶ BIBLIOGRAPHY

Derwent Information, 1998. *Managing Patent Information: The Gulf Between Theory and Practice.*

European Patent Office, 2002. *Directory of patent information centres in the member states.* European Patent Office.

European Patent Office and ITM/Motivaction, 2003. *Survey on the usage profile of patent information 2002–2003* (Unpublished results).

Hewish, J., 1980. *The Indefatigable Mr Woodcroft: The Legacy of Invention.* British Library Publishing.

European Commission, 1993–1996. *Community Innovation Surveys I and II.*

Lev, B., 2001. *Intangibles, Management, Measurement and Reporting.* Brooking Institution Press.

▶ REFERENCES

Allen, A., and Oppenheim, C., 1979. The overlap of US and Canadian Patents with Journal Literature. *World Patent Information* 1(2), pp. 77–80.

European Patent Office, 2000. *Epidos News,* Issue 1.

Goodchild, D., 2003. Patent truths in the hunt for information on the Web. *Materials World.* 11(2), pp. 29–31

President and Fellows of Harvard College, 1986. *Method for Producing Transgenic Animals,* EP0169672, 29 January 1986.

Machlup, F., 1958. *An Economic Review of the Patent System.* US Government Printing Office.

Michel, J., and Bettels, B., 2001. Patent Citation Analysis. A closer look at the basic input data from patent search reports. *Scientometrics,* 51(1), pp. 185–201.

Mill, J. S., 1848. *Principles of Political Economy with some of their applications to social philosophy.* London: J.W. Parker, 1848.

Shenk, D., 1997. *Data Smog.* Abacus.

Sherman, B., and Bently, L., 1999. *The Making of Modern Intellectual Property Law.* Cambridge University Press.

▶ ANNEX I – SOURCES OF PATENT INFORMATION

Internet Resources

Selected general information relating to patent information:

Name of organisation	Website	Description
The Patent Information Users Group (PIUG)	www.piug.org	Not for profit international society dedicated to promoting the use of patent information
UK Government Intellectual Property Web-site	www.intellectualproperty.uk.gov	Policy, Practice, and Procedure
The Intellectual Property Institute	www.ip-institute.org.uk	Think tank for generators of, users of, and those who study IP

Selected Patent Information, and Documentation resources:

Name of organisation	Website	Description
The Patent Office's internet server	gb.espacenet.com	Full patent documents
The European Patent Office server	www.espacenet.com	Full patent documents from EPO, and other offices
The European Patent Office epoline® service	www.epoline.org	A range of electronic products, and services produced by the EPO
The US Patent Office patent information site	www.uspto.gov/main/patents.htm	Full US patent documents
WIPO Intellectual Property Digital Library	www.ipdl.wipo.int	Various intellectual property collections
Japanese Patent Office Industrial Property Digital Library	www.ipdl.jpo.go.jp/homepg_e.ipdl	Various industrial property information
Intellectual Property Office of Singapore	www.surfIP.gov.sg intro-e.html	Intellectual Property Portal
NERAC	www.nerac.com	Information service that aims to deliver targeted results
DEPATISNet	www.depatisnet.de	Full patent documents from various patent offices
Canadian Patent Office	patents1.ic.gc.ca/intro-e.html	Full Canadian Patent Documentsintro-e.html

Many of the web resources mentioned above are free at the time of writing, however there are numerous alternative fee paying, and free, information providers that you may wish to consider.

Optical media

CD-ROM, and DVD-ROM are amongst the most widely used patent document archiving technologies. One of the most significant efforts to harmonise the formats, and retrieval software used by various patent offices is the MIMOSA software. Further details can be found on the EPO website.

Paper documents

Only a few of the larger patent information libraries still receive paper copies of new patent documents. However, older documents are often only available in paper form.

Patents Information Network

There is a network of specialised patent information centres throughout the UK. This is known as the 'patents information network' or PIN. Details are available at: www.bl.uk

It is true that these centres can provide access to patent information, and that they are supplied with patent data from The Patent Office, and the European Patent Office. However, their resources allow much more than that. They can provide information on trademarks, and other related IP information. They are staffed by qualified experienced personnel who can instruct on how to search the relevant databases. Moreover, they can help interpret the significance of information retrieved. For modest fees they can carry out searches using Internet, CD-ROM, and on-line database sources. They can also provide document delivery services (hard copy, fax, fax-modem, e-mail).

In addition, the Patent Office has its own helpdesk, and commercial search services:

> The Patent Office
> Concept House
> Cardiff Road
> Newport
> South Wales NP9 1RH
> Tel: (+44 1633)814 000 (Switchboard)
> E-mail: enquiries@patent.gov.uk
> URL: www.patent.gov.uk
>
> Search & Advisory Service
> Concept House
> Tel: (+44 1633) 811010
> Fax: (+44 1633) 811020
> E-mail: commercialsearches@patent.gov.uk

Patent information networks, actually a network of national networks, exist throughout Europe, and could also assist with finding that elusive publication. Details of the European network are published by the European Patent Office.

6 Standards

Ewan Smith

Ewan Smith

▶ INTRODUCTION

Standards are off-the-shelf technical documents agreed by consensus, and contain precise criteria that ensure those materials, products, processes and services are made to a certain quality to be fit for their purpose. As Sir David John (BSI's Group Chairman) stated ' . . . standards aid the competitiveness of British Industry' (Longworth, 2002). Standards contribute to making life simpler, and to increasing the reliability and effectiveness of the goods and services we use. For example, smart cards (smart card is a term used to describe a credit card sized identification card with an embedded microchip) made to ISO standards BS EN ISO 7816: 1999 – *Identification cards, integrated circuit cards*. Standards are produced at local, regional and international level and the main organisations involved are the national, European and international standards bodies.

▶ INTERNATIONAL

The three most important international agencies for standardisation are the International Organisation for Standardization (ISO), the International Electrotechnical Commission (IEC), and the International Telecommunication Union (ITU), all of which are described in detail below.

International Organisation for Standardisation (ISO)

The ISO is an international organisation of national standards bodies from more than 140 countries, represented by one from each country. ISO is a non-governmental organisation which was set-up in 1947. Its mission is to promote the development of standardisation and related activities in the world by facilitating the international exchange of goods and services, and encouraging co-operation in the areas of technological and economic activity. ISO's work results in international agreements that are published as International Standards. There is a seeming lack of correspondence between the official title when used in full, International Organisation for Standardisation, and the short form, ISO. This is because ISO is used around the world to denote the organisation, whatever the country.

The origin of the establishment of ISOs was to rationalise trade between well-established technologically advanced states in such diverse fields as information, communications and technology, textiles, packaging, distribution of goods, energy production and utilisation, shipbuilding, banking and financial services. There are numerous reasons for this growth in standardisation activity. Firstly, global progress in trade liberalisation in current laissez-faire economies is increasingly encouraging a wide range of sources of supply, and provides opportunities for expanding sectors. Fair competition needs to be based on common terms and criteria that are identified by all countries. An industry-wide standard, internationally recognised, developed by consensus among trading partners, along with World Trade Organisation (WTO) agreements, serves as the facilitator of trade.

Secondly, cross-fertilisation in a sector is another reason to encourage standardisation, as no industry can be completely independent of components, regulations, and such like. For example, bolts are used in aviation, civil and general engineering. Environmentally friendly products and processes, and recyclable or biodegradable packaging are significant concerns, as governments strive for economies that promote sustainable development.

Thirdly, communications systems and the computer industry provide a good example of developments that require speedy standardised solutions at an international level. Compatibility among open systems promotes healthy competition among producers, and results in good offers to users. Such activity, support and co-operation facilitate international standards for emerging technologies. Standardisation programmes in completely new fields are now being developed. Such fields include advanced materials, the environment, life sciences, urbanisation and construction. This in turn assists developing countries and agencies, as standardisation of an infrastructure is a basic condition for the success of economic policies aimed at achieving sustainable development. Industry-wide standardisation is a condition existing within a particular industrial sector when the large majority of products or services conform to the same standards. It results from consensus agreements reached between all parties in that industrial sector – suppliers, users, and often governments. They agree on specifications and criteria to be applied consistently in the choice of products, the manufacture of goods and the provision of services.

The aim is to facilitate trade, exchange and technology transfer through enhanced product quality and reliability at a reasonable cost. In turn, this should improve health, safety and environmental protection, and reduction of waste. The result of such co-operation is greater compatibility and interoperability of goods and services, to name but a few reasons and benefits. Furthermore, users have more confidence in products and services that conform to International Standards. Quality Assurance of conformity can be provided by manufacturers' declarations, for example CE mark, etc., or by audits carried out by independent bodies.

ISO has produced more than 13,700 documents in partnership with 146 organisations such as the national standards bodies: International Commission on Radiological Protection (ICRP); the International Telegraph and Telephone Consultative Committee (CCITT); the International Maritime Organisation (IMO); and the International Labour Organisation (ILO). International regulations and standards are produced to assist all parties including industry, consumers and engineers. They can, however, also act as technical barriers to trade, preventing the free flow of goods and services. Harmonisation between international, regional and national levels of standardisation is proceeding apace, but much still needs to be done to prevent unnecessary duplication, contradiction or wasteful rewriting. De facto international standards are being adopted unilaterally and already exist. For example, standards issued by bodies such as the American Society of Mechanical Engineers (ASME) are now quoted worldwide.

An ISO standard is the result of an agreement between member bodies of ISO. The standard may be used as such, or, perhaps, implemented by adoption as a national standard of the different countries. For example, in the United Kingdom, the British Standards Institution catalogue indicates the following symbols to show correspondence:

π An identical standard: a national standard identical in every detail with the corresponding international standard: published with dual numbering.

= A technically equivalent standard: a national standard in all technical respects the same as corresponding international standard: the wording and presentation may differ quite extensively.

$\neq$ A related standard: a national standard, the content of which, to any extent at all short of complete identity or technical equivalence, covers subject matter similar to that covered by the corresponding international standard: it is emphasised that while the subject matter is similar, the standard may deal with it in a different manner.

An ISO standard begins as a Draft Proposal (DP), becomes a Draft International Standard (DIS), and then, with 75 per cent voting in its favour, the DIS is sent to the ISO Council for acceptance as an ISO International

Standard. Every agreed ISO standard is reviewed at not more than five-yearly intervals except where it is necessary to have more frequent revision, e.g. because of new methods or technological development. Electronic balloting is now in operation in ISO as a response to internal customer requirements.

ISO Technical Committee TC 1 covers Screw Threads and TC 2 Other Fasteners are examples showing that international standards development has mirrored the United Kingdom engineering experience. Other standards bodies frequently refer to ISO standards, and they may also be adopted as their national standards. Similarly, national standards may form the basis for an international standard. Good examples of these are the BS EN ISO 9000 and BS EN ISO 17799 series of standards that were British Standards BS 5750 and BS 7799 respectively.

ISO standards are issued in A4 size, printed format, and micro-form versions are also available. Two main languages that are used are English and French, but a few selected standards are in multilingual versions, e.g. ISO 1891–1979: Bolts, screws, nuts and accessories; terminology and nomenclature, which appear in English, French, Spanish, Italian and Russian.

ISO series references use the prefix ISO followed by a number, e.g. ISO 1–2002 *Geometric product specification (GPS) – Standard reference temperature for geometrical product specification and verification*. ISO standards can be purchased from the International Organisation for Standardisation in Geneva or from the national standards bodies who act as agents. They are listed in the *ISO Catalogue* (annual) as well as in ISO subject bibliographies, and current information on them is given in the *ISO Bulletin* (monthly) as well as their website. The *ISO CataloguePlus 2003* is now available as a CD-ROM and includes drafts and the work programme of the committees.

The *ISO Handbooks* are subject collections of standards and *ISO Guides* cover subjects related to international standardisation. Other useful publications include *ISO Memento* (annual). In the United Kingdom, complete sets of ISO standards can be consulted at the British Standards Institution, London; the Science Reference & Information Service (SRIS) at the British Library, London and certain provincial public libraries. Selected ISO standards are held by many technical libraries but the facility for borrowing them depends upon the policy of the libraries concerned.

International Electrotechnical Committee (IEC)

On 15 September 1904, delegates to the International Electrical Congress in St. Louis, USA, adopted a report that included the following words 'steps should be taken to secure the co-operation of the technical societies of the world, by the appointment of a representative Commission to consider the question of the standardisation of the nomenclature and ratings of electrical apparatus and machinery.' As a result, the IEC was officially founded in June 1906, in London, England, where its Central Office was set up.

By 1914 the IEC had formed four technical committees to deal with Nomenclature, Symbols, Rating of Electrical Machinery, and Prime Movers. The Commission issued a first list of terms and definitions covering electrical machinery and apparatus, a list of international letter symbols for quantities and signs for names of units, an international standard for resistance for copper, a list of definitions in connection with hydraulic turbines, and a number of definitions and recommendations relating to rotating machines and transformers. In between the First and the Second World Wars, a number of new international organisations came into being, and the IEC recognised the need for co-operation to avoid overlapping efforts. In some cases, joint technical committees were formed, such as the International Special Committee on Radio Interference (CISPR).

IEC is the next most significant international standards authority after the ISO, with whom it works in close liaison. From sixty-two national committees, representatives are sent to the IEC Council, and through the IEC Committee of Action, technical standards are prepared. All the members of the more than seventy technical committees are volunteer engineers and scientists. More than 5,000 IEC standards are currently available.

IEC liases with many other major international electrotechnical and related standards bodies, including the International Commission on Illumination (CIE); the International Commission for Conformity Certification for Electrical Equipment (CEE); the International Telecommunications Union (ITU) and others.

IEC publications are available for sale from the IEC office in Geneva, or from IEC National Committee offices in the various countries. The series reference for IEC standards is simply IEC followed by a running number and date, e.g. IEC 60110–1998 *Power capacitors for induction heating installations – general.*

International Telecommunication Union (ITU)

ITU has its headquarters in Geneva, Switzerland and is an international organisation within the United Nations System where governments and the private sector co-ordinate global telecom networks and services. The ITU is the leading publisher of telecommunication technology, regulatory and standards information.

At the 1932 Madrid Conference, the Union decided to combine the International Telegraph Convention of 1865 and the International Radiotelegraph Convention of 1906 to form the International Telecommunication Convention (CCITT). It was also decided to change the name of the Union to International Telecommunication Union. The new name, which came into effect on 1 January 1934, was chosen to properly reflect the full scope of the Union's responsibilities, which by this time covered all forms of wireline and wireless communication. It consists of three sectors, as follows; radiocommunication, telecommunication standards and telecommunication development. ITU works closely with ISO and IEC. ITU currently produces over 200 Recommendations each year and continues to be progressive in its approach to standards activity.

World Trade Organisation (WTO)

The WTO is the only global international organisation dealing with the rules of trade between nations, and provides a platform for the use of international standards. At its heart are the WTO agreements, negotiated and signed by the bulk of the world's trading nations and ratified in their parliaments. The goal is to assist producers of goods and services, exporters, and importers with conducting their business.

GATT (the General Agreement on Tariffs and Trade) has adopted an agreement to overcome such barriers. The GATT secretariat monitors developments and advises countries, encouraging them to use international standards whenever possible. GATT also tries to discourage unnecessary duplication of standards and to prevent the growth of malpractice. However, the agreement on Technical Barriers to Trade (TBT) aims to reduce barriers to trade, resulting from differences between regulations and standards. The ISO/IEC information centre records acceptance of this code by the national standards institutes on behalf of WTO.

► REGIONAL

Americas

In the Americas, Pan American Standards Commission (COPANT) has representatives from sixteen states, and ICAITI (Central American Standards) has five constituent nations. COPANT is based in Buenos Aires and its standards are issued in Spanish. The *Catalogue of COPANT Pan American Standards and Recommendations* lists the current publications. Like those of COPANT, Normas Centroamericana, issued by ICAITI, are in Spanish and the organisation is based in Guatemala.

Asia (Pacific)

The Pacific Area Standards Congress (PASC) comprises countries bordering on the Pacific Ocean. It does not issue standards, nor is it a regional standards body as such, but it does endeavour to represent the views of the region in relation to possible standardisation needs. International standardisation is the wider stage on which political as well as economic decisions has influence in the various organisations. It is unlikely that 100 per cent agreement can be reached but a 75 per cent consensus is often achieved without too great a loss of practical technical usefulness. However, national standards are still the level of standardisation for most countries, commercial firms and for the engineer.

Austrialasia/Africa

In the Far East, Japan has a dominant position in standards. Australasia was formerly influenced by its historical links with the United Kingdom but, increasingly, Australia and New Zealand are refocusing their view of standards, whilst keeping some BS-like series. They are adopting more American practices and developing their involvement with international standards.

In Africa, although having a standards organisation is essential, European, American and international standards are freely quoted. In South Africa the main producer is the South African Bureau of Standards (SABS).

More than 100 countries have national systems of standardisation, and these are usually national bodies. Most country systems consist of official and unofficial, mandatory and voluntary standards, plus a regulatory framework. No country's system is identical, and engineers will need to supplement them with some international (or foreign) standards plus a positive awareness of technical and local regulations. What is more, many organisations prepare and use their own specifications, and these often form the basis for national standards.

Europe

The major West European national standards series are produced by the British Standards Institution in Britain; Deutsches Institut fur Normung (DIN) in Germany, and Association Francaise de Normalisation (AFNOR) in France.

The three larger national standards bodies, BSI, DIN and AFNOR contribute to *Perinorm*, a CD-ROM of bibliographical details of all standards published by national standards bodies. Other European countries continue to use their own standards within their own confines.

The major influence in Eastern Europe is the USSR State Committee for Standards (GOST) in Russia. Most Central and Eastern countries now have a national standards office.

European Committee for Standardization (CEN)

CEN's mission is to promote voluntary technical harmonisation in Europe in conjunction with worldwide bodies and its partners in Europe. Harmonisation diminishes trade barriers, promotes safety, allows interoperability of products, systems and services, and promotes common technical understanding. In Europe, CEN works in partnership with CENELEC – the European Committee for Electrotechnical Standardisation and ETSI – the European Telecommunications Standards Institute. CEN was established in 1961 and has published over 8,000 standards and has 276 active committees.

European Committee for Electrotechnical Standardisation (CENELEC)

CENELEC was set up in 1973 as a non-profit-making organisation under Belgian Law. It has been officially recognised as the European Standards Organisation in its field by the European Commission in Directive 83/189/EEC. Its members have been working together in the interests of European harmonisation since the late fifties, developing alongside the European Economic Community. CENELEC works with 35,000 technical experts from twenty-two European countries to publish standards for the European market. The electrotechnical standards currently developed in Europe result in no real technical barriers to trade due to electrotechnical standards in the European Economic Area (EEA).

European Telecommunications Standards Institute (ETSI)

ETSI is a not for profit organisation whose mission is to produce the telecommunications standards that will be used throughout Europe. Based in Sophia Antipolis, in the south of France, ETSI unites 912 members from fifty-four countries inside and outside Europe, and represents administrators, network operators, manufacturers, service providers, research bodies and users. Its members, who are also responsible for approving its deliverables, determine the Institute's work programme. As a result, ETSI's activities are maintained in close alignment with the market needs expressed by its members.

ETSI plays a major role in developing a wide range of standards and other technical documentation as Europe's contribution to worldwide standardisation in telecommunications, broadcasting and information technology. ETSI's prime objective is to support global harmonisation by providing a forum in which all the key players can contribute actively. ETSI is officially recognised by the European Commission and the European Free Trade Association (EFTA) secretariat.

▶ NATIONAL

United States (USA)

In America, the standards issued by the American National Standards Institute (ANSI) are important but are not the exclusive nor the most influential sources of information, since there are powerful US Government and sectional standards in demand. Provision in Central and South America is fragmented, and it is not unusual for American/European standards to be freely used, depending on political, economic or industrial influence.

The standardisation scene mirrors very closely the economic, geographic, political and technical conditions of that nation. Standards are an important discipline, and US standards have great influence both domestically and abroad. There is a strong federal input into standardisation, both civil and military, but the voluntary principal is also well marked. Many engineering standards are voluntary, but through the circumstances of their use and citation they often turn out to be mandatory in practice. Whilst most cover the whole of the United States, some are limited to specific local areas.

The American National Standards Institute in New York is the national standards body, equivalent to, but not identical with, other standards organisations such as BSI, DIN and AFNOR. ANSI was known formerly as the American Standards Association (ASA), an abbreviation still used to indicate film speeds. ANSI co-ordinates the American federal standards system and, through its good offices, voluntary standards, prepared by relevant and respected professional and trade associations, are recognised and approved as official US standards.

The usual form of reference for ANSI standards is, for example, ANSI X9.16: *Formats for messages types, standard*. The symbol X9.16 above is a class reference from the ANSI classification scheme, but these are now given only to standards sponsored by ANSI directly. Nowadays ANSI uses the originating bodies' own reference numbers as sole identifier, which can lead to confusion when filing standards, especially when they are new editions of earlier ANSI titles. ANSI publications include the *ANSI Catalogue of American National Standards* (annual) and the *ANSI Reporter* (bi-weekly) which includes news of national and international standardisation activities.

United States Government Standards

Federal standards and specifications cover all the non-military procurement sectors, and are issued by the General Services Administration of the Federal Supply Service in Washington. They are printed in A4 format in white covers, and new editions are shown by the addition of a lower-case letter after the series number. There are different series number sequences for Federal Standards and for Federal specifications, a fact that can be a source of confusion for the non-American user. One of the most important government organisations producing standards is the National Institute of Standards and Technology (NIST). NIST is a non-regulatory federal agency within the U.S. Commerce Department's Technology Administration.

NIST's mission is to develop and promote measurement, standards, and technology to enhance productivity, facilitate trade, and improve the quality of life. NIST carries out its mission in four cooperative programs:

- NIST laboratories
- Baldrige National Quality Programme
- Manufacturing Extension Partnership
- Advanced Technology Programme

The other major producer of government standards is the Department of Defence (DOD), which issues military standards covering the Army, Navy and Air Force together with NATO standards and qualified products lists. DOD standards and specifications are published by the US Government Printing Office in Washington and are listed in *DOD Index of Specifications and Standards,* published annually by the Government Printing Office.

The form of reference is, for example, MIL-A-7021 C-1996. *Asbestos sheet compressed for fuel lubricant, coolant water, and high temperature resistant gaskets.* New editions are indicated by the addition of an upper-case letter after the series number. In the above example the letter 'C' indicates the 4th edition. DOD also publishes a series of handbooks on various subjects.

United States Voluntary Standards

The major publishers of voluntary standards are the American Society for Testing and Materials (ASTM); the American Society of Mechanical Engineers (ASME); and the Society of Automotive Engineers (SAE). ASTM is well known for the quality of its standards (it has produced over 16,000) and the efficiency and speed of updating. ASTM standards are recognised worldwide and many are treated as international standards. The *Annual Book of ASTM Standards* is arranged in sixteen sections, e.g. iron and steel products, rubber, electronics, test methods, magnetic properties, etc. Other publications include *ASTM Standardisation News* (monthly) and the *ASTM Journal of Testing and Evaluation* (bi-monthly).

ASME's major publication in the standards field is the *ASME Boiler and Pressure Vessel Code*, which includes standards, codes, case reports and inspection and test methods, affecting the safety of boilers, pressure vessels and nuclear plant components. The ASME Code is recognised worldwide as a *de facto* international standard.

SAE publishes the *SAE Handbook* (annual) in four volumes, containing more than 9,400 standards, recommended practices and information reports covering ferrous and non-ferrous materials, threads, fasteners, etc. It also publishes *Metals and Alloys in the Unified Numbering System* (1999).

United Kingdom

British Standards Institution (BSI)

British Standards Institution (BSI) is the United Kingdom (UK) national standards body, established by Royal Charter in 1929. BSI has expanded its operations, and now is a group of several complementary businesses, supporting business and trade worldwide. It is the organisation that represents standardisation to the British government and to represent the United Kingdom on the international forum. BSI believes in the 'universal adoption of best management practices, reduction of risk throughout the trading process and harmonisation and acceptance of international standards by consent as a means of achieving economic prosperity.' BSI Group facilitates standards development, training, assessment, testing products, certification and inspection services. These are the two main divisions of British Standards Institution that are concerned with standards development and facilitation.

British Standards are developed by BSI British Standards which is the UK national standards body and a participating member of the European and international standards organisations. BSI British Standards publish 1,800 standards each year. Standards are revised and re-issued to encompass new developments in technology and keep them current. There are eight business sectors that facilitate the development of standards, with a remit for providing a service to national, European and international bodies and committees.

BSI's first standard was for BS 1 *Rolled steel sections* (1903), followed closely by BS2 *Tramway and dock rails* (1904). Engineering interests were the motivation in the early years. There are currently more than 9,000 standards in print, each being subject to a programme of revision and review on a rolling basis. Like the national standards of most industrial nations, BSI standards are intended mainly for general use, with extra series developed for the more specialised user, e.g. BS CECC 00009: 1982 *Harmonised system of quality assessment for electric components. – Basic specification.*

BSI's standards fulfil the needs of industry and commerce, and protect the rights of consumers. They are essential for public service requirements as well as for individual professional technical responsibilities. British Standards are voluntary, but in certain circumstances, for example when quoted in regulations and legal documents, they become mandatory, e.g. BS 6658:1985 (1995) *Specification for protective helmets for vehicle users*. There are many categories of standards, the most basic being those of measurement, physical and mechanical data. In each engineering discipline, as they reflect the current state of the art, new editions, new standards and new codes of practice are constantly needed to keep them significant and helpful to users. British standards are issued in a number of series, of which the General Series is of particular importance to the engineer.

These standards are generally referred to in the form BS 0 Parts 1–3: 1997, *A standard for standards*, which describes the principles of standardisation, BSI and its committee procedures and the drafting and presentation of standards. The most quoted standards were as follows; BS 308 Part 1: 1972, which now falls into the BS EN ISO series. A guide (PD 308) provides guidance to the European standards for engineering drawing in the BS EN ISO series, BS EN ISO 9000:2000. *Quality management and quality assurance standards* and also BS EN ISO 14001: 1996 *Environmental management systems: specification with guidance for user*.

Draft standards are available for comment via BSI, London, by letter, telex, and also telephone can be purchased from the BSI sales agents. British Standards can be consulted for reference in more than seventy-six public libraries, universities and polytechnics throughout the United Kingdom, and may be borrowed from the British Library at Boston Spa, Yorkshire. BSI also produce an annual catalogue, a monthly journal called *Business Standards*, and *Update Standards*. There are several suppliers of standards information products such as Technical Indexes Ltd and Barbour Index.

BSI issues a number of other standards series in addition to the General Series. Codes of Practice (CP) have been issued for technical drawings. The history of the codes of practice for building, electrical and mechanical engineering reveals the co-operation between the professional institutions and BSI over more than 100 years. The codes were originally produced by the institutions, then continued by BSI as separate CPs. Now it is policy when revising a CP to include the new edition in the General Series, allocating a series number to it, but maintaining the name code of practice. Special series of standards have been issued in the areas of automobile engineering, marine engineering, to name a few.

BSI took over responsibility for automobile standards (BS AU) from the Society of Motor Manufacturers and Traders. The usual form of reference is, for example, BS AU 50–1.0.1 1999 – *Tyres and wheels: method of test for measuring type uniformity*. The BS Marine Series (BS MA) has eighty-eight standards currently in force, the form of reference being BS MA 12 Part 2: 1983 (1999). *Specification for welded steel bollards, cruciform type*. New editions are indicated by the date of the standard with a note of previous editions in the foreword. The BSI Aerospace Series uses capital letters plus numbers as a series reference. Only twenty-one letters or combinations of letters have been chosen; they are A; B; C; E; F; G; HC; HR; J; K; L; M;N; PL; S; SP; T; TA; V; W; and X. The series of BS Aerospace specifications are usually referred to in the form BS A 22: 1947 (1998). *Units of measurement in civil aviation.*

New editions are referred to by the prefix of a number before the series letter, e.g. BS 2G 180:1974. *Permanent splicing for aircraft electrical cables*, which can lead to confusion with other non-BSI standards series. The Aerospace Series is only one of the major series relevant to aviation. Engineers may also need to consult the specifications issued by the Ministry of Defence and specifications of the Society of British Aerospace Companies.

The large majority of Published Document (PD) have been withdrawn but there are a few new ones e.g. PD 5500:2000. There are also standards packs for educational purpose and these are prefixed with either a PP or KIT. Drafts for Development Series (DD) are issued in A4 format with orange covers. The numbering sequence begins at DD2: 1971 *Dynamic force calibration of axial load fatigue testing machines by means of a strain gauge technique*. BSI also makes available DD ENVs (ENVs are draft European standards) and Eurocodes. Many DDs are subsequently withdrawn and replaced by BSs, for example DD 67; 1982, is now BS 8206–2:1992 – *Code of practice for daylighting*

Government and the public sector use Public Authority Standards (PAS). The series is numbered 3–85: 2001. They are now being phased out, an example of the policy to encourage the use of existing British and international standards.

Delivering Information Solutions to Customers (DISC)

A separate division of BSI is called Delivering Information Solutions to Customers (DISC). It is the specialist information technology (IT) section of BSI British Standards. It offers guidance, codes of practice, seminars, etc. on subjects such as; Information security, Data protection, Scanning and storage, IT services, TickIT – software process and ETSI publications.

Government Standardisation

Government concern for standardisation and its importance for the economic success of the country, together with the need for an increased awareness and use of standards, have all been stressed in recent years. The Standards and Technical Regulations Directorate (STRD) is part of the Department for Trade and Industry (DTI), and its main aims are 'to secure a standards, testing and certification infrastructure which meets the needs of UK industry; to contribute to the removal of technical barriers to trade through EU legislation and other international agreements; and to act as budget holder for the BSI standards budget.'

These aims relate to DTI objectives on improvement of the efficiency and effectiveness of markets, the adoption of best practice, and removing unnecessary burdens from business in the regulatory framework for commercial activity. However, there is no co-ordinated approach to the work of the numerous standards-issuing bodies outside the scope of BSI. This includes professional, trade and research associations, nationalised industries, government departments and industry.

Military standards are the concern of the Ministry of Defence, whose 'Standards for Defence' embrace all standards, whether national, civil or international, which are relevant to the Ministry's needs. The Ministry has a policy of choosing existing standards wherever possible before initiating an MOD standard, and would not normally do so if a suitable standard or industrial specification already exists. Defence Standards (DEF STAN) are usually referred to in the form DEFSTAN 00–00 (Pt1)/3(1999) – *Standard for defence – MODUK standardisation policy, organisations and implementation*. This particular standard in all its parts and sub-sections explains the structure, policy and organisation of the standards system. Defence Standards can be purchased from the Directorate of Standardisation in Glasgow, and complete sets are held for reference by some of the depository libraries that hold British Standards.

Defence Specifications (Def Spec) are now being phased out and most will be absorbed or replaced by DEF STANs. These standards are now the responsibility of the MOD, Procurement Division, but were formerly produced by the Directorate of Technical Development in the Ministries of Aviation, Supply and Aircraft Production, and the Air Ministry.

France

Association Francaise de Normalisation (AFNOR)

The official body in France is the Association Francaise de Normalisation (AFNOR), based in Paris. AFNOR issues Normes Francaise (NF). More than 31,500 standards are currently in force, issued by AFNOR and it's associated bodies in A4 format with microfiche versions also available. The reference format is NF C 01–1O1: 1999 *Electrotechnical vocabulary*, where C = the major class, mathematics; 01 = sub-class; 101 = a unique number for the specification; and 1999 = edition date.

The AFNOR Standards Information Service is based in the head-quarters library in Paris, France. AFNOR holds copies of ISO and IEC standards and is the main agent in France for many other national standards bodies.

Publications include the *AFNOR Catalogue des Normes Francoises* (annual); *Catalogue of English Translations* (annual); *Enjou:* i.e. *Nouvel Mensuel de la Normalisation Francaise* (monthly); *Recueils de Normes Francaises* (one of a number of handbooks) and subject collections of standards, to name a few.

Germany

Deutsches Institut fur Normung (DIN)

The official standards organisation in Germany is the Deutsches Institut für Normung (DIN), based in Berlin. More than 40,000 DIN standards (DIN normen), plus hundreds of DIN EN, DIN IEC and DIN ISO standards are currently in force. The series reference for the general series is in the form DIN 820: part 1: 1994. *Normungsarbeit: Grundsatze* (standardisation procedure – principles). A prefix 'E' indicates a draft standard and 'V' a preliminary standard.

Publications issued by the Institut include the *DIN Katalog für Technische Regeln* (DIN Catalogue of Technical Rules), which appears annually and is arranged by UDC; *DIN Mitteilungen + Elektronorm* (monthly), which includes an update to the *DIN Katalog-*, and *DIN Taschenbücher*, which are subject collections of standards, of which some are also issued in English translation, e.g. DIN Handbook 1: 2001. *Mechanical standards*. Over 3,500 DIN standards are available in English translation, and selected standards are available in other foreign languages.

All DIN publications are printed and published by Beuth Verlag GmbH in Berlin. Deutsches Informationszentrum fur Technische Regeln (DITR) is the German information centre for standards, rules and regulations in Berlin, housed in the same building as the Institut. It has a major standards library, offers a comprehensive enquiry service and operates the DITR Datenbank online service. DIN standards are available in over thirty deposit collections in Germany, and are also held by the national standards bodies of more than seventy countries. They are often quoted by other countries. Their metals standards, for example, like those of BSI, are used worldwide and DIN standards are among the most influential in the world. However, because of the pervasive German insurance requirements and other legal regulatory services, they are often mandatory in practice. Germany has many other standards-issuing bodies in addition to DIN: for example, Verein Deutscher Ingenieure (VDI), Verband Deutscher Elektrotechniker (VDE) and the Bundesverband der Unfallkassen (BUK).

All European countries have standards organisations, other main ones being the Institut Beige do Normalisation in Brussels; Dansk

Standardiseringsraed in Hellerup; the Hellenic Organisation for Standardisation in Athens; the Institute for Industrial Research and Standards in Dublin; Ente Nazionale Italiano di Unificazione in Milan; and Nederlands Normalisatie-institut in Delft. There are also many non-official standards-issuing bodies in every country.

No complete description of all aspects of standardisation activities at all levels has yet appeared, but standardisation is here to stay.

▶ BIBLIOGRAPHY

Rankl, W., and Effing, W., 2000. *Smart card handbook*. Wiley.

Struglia, E. J., 1965. *Standards and specifications: a guide to information sources*. Gale.

Woodward, C. D., 1972. *BSI – the story of standards*. BSI.

▶ WEBSITES

Afnor, www.afnor.org

ANSI, www.ansi.org

ASME, www.asme.org

ASTM, www.astm.org

Barbour Index, www.barbour-index.co.uk

BL, www.bl.uk

CEN, www.cen.org

CENELEC, www.cenelec.org.ch

CIE, www.cie.co.at

Copant, www.copant.org

DIN, www.din.de

EFTA, www.efta.org

ETSI, www.etsi.org

ICRP, www.icrp.org

IEC, www.iec.org

ILO, www.ilo.org

IMO, www.imo.org

ISO, www.iso.org.ch

ITU, www.itu.org

NATO, www.nato.int

NIST, www.nist.gov

Pasc, www.pascnet.org

SAE, www.sae.org

Technical Indexes, www.tionestop.com

VDE, www.vde.de

VDI, www.vdi.de
WTO, www.wto.org

▶ **REFERENCES**

Longworth, D., 2002. Positive thinking, *Business Standards*, Oct/Nov 2002, 13–15.

7 Product information

Peter O'Reilly

► INTRODUCTION

In the global marketplace, it is vital to be aware of the tools for sourcing products, developing awareness of competitors and finding detailed product information.

In recent years the information market has changed dramatically, due to the emergence of the Internet, and it continues to evolve. Traditional printed and other electronic sources are being challenged by the proliferation of websites offering information to potential buyers.

► TRADE LITERATURE

Literature from a company providing a product or service is the obvious starting point in the hunt for information. Companies willingly send literature to interested parties and maintain mailing lists for future contact. Literature, from company to company, will vary in quality, frequency of publication and quantity. Websites are an ideal platform for providing vast amounts of information, which is often an exact copy of printed literature, to a potential audience of millions. The pitfall of websites, in comparison with printed or CD-ROM material is that the information is often here today but gone tomorrow. Many companies now use email alerts to advertise sale items, introduce new products, etc. Companies often list their foreign or local distributors and agents on their websites.

The Internet looks set to revolutionise the provision of product information and the relationship between manufacturers and customers. ISO 10303 is a standard promoting the production of product information, throughout a product's life cycle, in a form that can be interpreted by all computer systems. This lends itself to the sharing, and archiving, of data.

In industry the spirit of ISO 10303 manifests itself in the use of collaborative product commerce (CPC). A particularly exciting piece of research is the Shapesearch.net project (www.shapesearch.net), based at Heriot-Watt University. This project is developing a 3D search engine for the sourcing of engineering components.

Companies produce literature in many forms, including:

Full range product catalogues
Individual product brochures
Price lists
Research & test documentation
Technical specifications
Compatibility specifications
Health and safety data sheets
Advertisements
Press releases
Installation manuals
User manuals
Product samples
Corporate overviews
Annual reports
House journals

Companies often issue press releases to announce the arrival of a new product, product applications, etc. Releases may include detailed specifications and photographs of the product. Increasingly, companies are including press releases on their websites and some will provide keyword searchable archives, for example Lucent Technologies (www.lucent.com) includes a searchable archive dating from 1995 to the present.

House journals are produced to serve various audiences. Some will target the interests of a particular audience, for example employees, customers, shareholders or readers in industry. Consequently, the content and the quality can vary dramatically. Titles aimed at customers or members of the industry form vital sources of product information. House journals often contain detailed articles on products which would not appear in independent media sources, and can include new product launches, customer case studies and brand history. Some websites include house journals scanned as PDF documents. The ChevronTexaco website (www.chevrontexaco.com), for example, includes recent issues of the house journal *CVX*.

The websites of distributors are excellent tools for finding free information. For example the website of RS components (www.rscomponents. co.uk), a distributor of industrial components, has a database of 135,000 products from various manufacturers. The website provides photos, technical specifications and line drawings for most products. An online library of 40,000 data sheets, user manuals and other literature is freely available. A parametric search facility enables the sourcing of semiconductors.

▶ TRADE LITERATURE LIBRARIES

Many leading companies and industry associations keep libraries of trade literature. For example The Building Centre (www.buildingcentre.co.uk) keeps literature from several thousand companies.

The British Library Business Information Service holds a collection of trade literature, which contains catalogues from over 12,000 companies. The collection dates from the 19th century to the present. It covers a wide range of products including agrochemicals, paper, packaging, photographic equipment, computer graphics, banking and financial services, security equipment, street furniture and sports equipment. Most of the material is from British companies and has been acquired through donation.

The Science Museum Library has a large trade literature collection containing material from about 40,000 companies, large and small. The majority is British and from the late nineteenth and twentieth century but there is some foreign and older material.

▶ TRADE LITERATURE AGGREGATORS

Product literature aggregators, or package libraries, were first published in the 1970's on microfilm and provided access to the catalogues of companies. This still involved the reading of pages to identify the appropriate literature. Today a number of Internet and CD-ROM services allow the location of a single word within millions of catalogue pages.

Google Catalogs (catalogs.google.com) provides a free search facility to the content of over 5,800 print mail order catalogues from US companies. It includes both consumer and industrial catalogues from manufacturers, distributors and retailers. This service was launched in 2001. The selection policy restricts content to US catalogues that include prices and are designed to help customers make an immediate purchase. The catalogues can be searched as one group, by subject heading or individually. Individual catalogues, once identified, can be read page by page. Although the content is biased towards the consumer sector, it is apparent that the website is growing at a steady rate, and includes a number of industrial catalogues.

Technical Indexes (www.tionestop.com) offers 400 services providing technical data, standards, product and supplier information to industry worldwide. Many of the products on offer are aimed at specific sectors, but the following have broad appeal. Specify It (www.specify-it.com) is a subscription service providing 260,000 full text pages from the literature of over 5,500 UK manufacturers and suppliers to the construction and civil engineering sectors. The literature from these databases includes full catalogues, data sheets, manuals, handbooks, product specifications and CAD drawings. Companies are arranged in a classified directory of 67,000 activity headings. It is possible to search for keywords relating to the company name, trade name or product. The results can be refined by town name, postcode or to companies awarded ISO9000 accreditation.

The *Engineering Product Library CD-ROM*, also published by Technical Indexes, provides access to the pages of over 100,000 trade catalogues from over 11,000 companies in the fields of electronics, design, manufacturing and process engineering.

CatalogXpress (www.ihserc.com/catalogxpress/) contains three million pages from the catalogues of 16,000 suppliers based in the United States. This subscription database also lists 700,000 distributors and sales offices worldwide. The database is searchable by keyword, part or model number, brand name and manufacturer. One enhanced feature allows the addition of requested catalogues, not already on the database, to be maintained on the subscriber's behalf.

Solusource (www.solusource.com) is a subscription database of 23,000 catalogues from over 10,000 US manufacturers of mechanical and electro-mechanical products.

The Universal Parts Center (www.ihsparts.com) is a subscription database for sourcing over 100 million parts for defence, aviation, marine and other industries from commercial and government suppliers. The database is searchable by product keyword, part number or company name and the results can be filtered in a number of ways. In addition to product information and contact details the price and stock quantity is provided. Requests for quotes and custom-made parts can be placed. Many other sites exist for sourcing components, such as USBid.com (www.usbid.com), Partminer (www.freetradezone.com) and Dionics plc (www.dionics.com).

▶ PRESS RELEASE AGGREGATORS

Product News Network (www.productnews.com), a subscription service from Thomas Publishing, started in 1995. It is currently adding over 1,000 new product press releases each month from North American manufacturers to the 200,000 announcements already on the database. The database, of products new to the industrial marketplace, is searched using product or company name keywords. The product keywords are searched for in the full text of the press releases, and can be further refined by product heading. The results can also be limited to include releases that are current or up to six months old. A smaller number of releases, 10,000 in February 2003, are available free of charge at the Thomas Regional directory homepage (www.thomasregional.com), under the heading 'product news'. Searching is by keyword only.

Manufacturingtalk (www.manufacturingtalk.com) provides free access to the press releases of engineering manufacturers and distributors from around the world. The database currently lists 6,000 releases from over 1,400 companies dating back to January 2000. The partner database Electronicstalk (www.electronicstalk.com) provides free access to the press releases of electronics manufacturers and distributors from around the world. Close to 10,000 releases from over 1,100 companies dating back to January 2000 are listed. The releases are searchable by date, company name and subject. The sites are updated daily. There are another eight websites in the Pro-Talk stable covering various industries, including building, printing, subcontracting, computing, etc.

Businesswire.com (www.businesswire.com) provides free access to several thousand international news releases, covering a number of industries, published in the previous week. The industry headings of relevance are automotive, energy and high-tech. It has a keyword search facility which can be filtered by international region, country or date. Subscription services are also available.

Gale Group New Product Announcements Plus, available via Dialog (www.dialog.com), contains the full text of close to one million press releases relating to product information with a focus on new products. The database, dating from 1985, has an international coverage and is updated daily.

Gale Group Newswire ASAP, also available via Dialog, is a database that aggregates the press releases of various sources, including Business Wire and PR Newswire. In addition to other issues, the database covers company, product and industry news. Started in 1983, the database now boasts over 1.5 million press releases.

▶ TRADE DIRECTORIES

The current edition of *Directories in Print* lists over 15,000 publications. Many of these will be international, regional, national or industry specific titles vital to sourcing products and services.

Trade directories started life in printed form 200 years ago. Recent years have seen the transition to diskette, CD-ROM and DVD-ROM. However it is the advent of the Internet, which has provided new opportunities for traditional directory publishers and many other organisations to reach a wider audience and provide information on more companies, larger amounts of information on these companies and many other enhanced features.

The Internet has seen numerous printed directories transfer their content to free websites. Publishers will allow companies to add basic activity and contact details, free of charge, to their web directories but will derive revenue by selling the companies enhanced features, such as search sensitive advertising, links to the company website, direct email connection, fax back and the inclusion of pages from product catalogues. Publishers are increasingly relying on listed companies to use online accounts, on the directory websites, to keep their information accurate and current. Some Internet directories offer a basic service free of charge to users, with additional priced options. The priced option may offer details of more companies or further information about a particular company. Enhanced features for searchers can include facilities to save search strategies and companies found. Blank email forms for ordering products online or requesting quotes or further literature are common features.

▶ INTERNATIONAL DIRECTORIES

Printed Kompass directories are available for over seventy countries. CD-ROM versions are available for over forty countries and nine regions. Kompass United Kingdom 2002 (Reed Business Information) was established over forty years ago. The first volume, *Products & services*, identifies the activities of 45,000 manufacturers, importers, exporters, wholesalers, merchants, distributors and agents. It is classified by seventy-one industrial groups, comprising 1,800 product and service groups, further broken down into 50,000 activities. The company name and address is always supplied but rarely are phone or fax numbers given. This can be remedied by accessing the Kompass website (www.kompass.com), which is free to search and provides address, phone and fax numbers free of charge. The website is searchable by any one of the following: keyword, product, service, classified heading, company name, trade name or executive name. Results can be viewed by country, continent or worldwide. A searchable classified directory of product and service headings, as found in the printed directories, is provided. A classified directory is a vital tool when browsing a family of products in order to identify the most appropriate one. The website, of 1.7 million companies, also offers a subscription service to access detailed profiles of companies. The profiles can include a detailed list of products/services, overseas representatives, export markets, key executives, turnover band and employee number band.

Wand Global Trade Directory (www.wand.com) lists 1,000,000 firms from 177 countries. The database maintains a classified directory of 65,000 product and service headings. Keyword searching allows use of terms that form the stem of any word in the company name, product heading or service heading. The results are viewable by continent or worldwide, although the United States can also be viewed separately. The classified directory can be browsed to enable the selection of the most appropriate heading. The database also supports searching by harmonised system codes and allows searching in sixteen languages.

The Thomas Global Register (www.tgrnet.com) contains 500,000 manufacturers and distributors from twenty-six countries organised by 10,500 product and service categories. The database is searchable in nine languages, by activity or company name keyword. The directory is also available on CD-ROM free of charge. Address, phone and fax numbers, along with a list of activities, are always included. An email address, contact names and other data are sometimes given.

The *International Directory of Importers* 2003, published by Interdata, comprises nine volumes listing 150,000 importing companies from 160 countries. A classified directory of imported products is included. Interdata also publish the *International Directory of Agents, Distributors & Wholesalers* 2003, which lists 30,000 companies from 160 countries. The commodity index features 1,200 product headings. Both publications are available on CD-ROM.

In addition to traditional printed directories, and their electronic equivalents, trade lead websites have appeared serving global, regional, country and industry-specific markets. These sites enable suppliers to offer their products or services for sale, and potential customers the chance to specify their needs. An example is Europages (www.europages.net) which includes a trade leads section. Buyers and sellers can view leads on the website and in addition can request email alerts of relevant future postings. The adverts are usually arranged by broad activity heading and sometimes with the option of narrower headings. At this point, keyword searching of the text of the postings is used to find relevant offers to buy or sell. Some of these sites boast memberships of 250,000 or more companies. For some countries and regions these websites represent a first port of call, and examples include Asian Products (www.asianproducts.com), a directory of 150,000 Asian suppliers; Made in China (www.made-in-china.com); and Mercantil.com (www.mercantil.com), a directory of 1,500,000 companies from nine Latin American countries.

▶ EUROPEAN DIRECTORIES

The Thomas Register of European Manufacturers (www.tipcoeurope.com) contains 210,000 European industrial manufacturers and service providers organised by 10,500 activity headings. Searching is by activity or company name keyword. Companies of the fifteen European Union nations plus Norway and Switzerland are represented. It is searchable in six European languages and is available on CD-ROM free of charge. Standardised email forms with which to contact firms for a quote or product literature are provided.

Europages (www.europages.com) is a directory of 500,000 companies from thirty-three European countries searchable in sixteen languages. It can be searched using company name or activity keywords. Over 94,000 product and service keywords are indexed. A classified directory is available to browse. After performing an activity search, the results can be refined by turnover, number of employees or activity type (manufacturer, distributor, retailers, etc). These are welcome and unusual features.

WLW (web.wlwonline.de) is a directory of over 370,000 companies from fifteen European countries searchable in eleven languages. The database can be searched using company name or activity keywords, and has 43,000 product and service headings. It is also possible to refine by postcode or city name.

► UNITED KINGDOM DIRECTORIES

KellySearch (www.kellysearch.com) is a directory of over 150,000 UK firms classified under 110,000 activity headings. The website has a keyword search facility by product, service, company name, trade name, street, town or postcode. After performing a search for a product or service, it is possible to select firms located within a specified radius of a full postcode, e.g. five, ten, fifteen, twenty-five or fifty miles, etc. Company profiles include the address, phone number, fax number and products or services offered. When available, the website, email and trade names are also listed. *Kelly Industrial Directory* is available as a printed or CD-ROM directory.

Sell's Products & Services Directory 2001/2002, published by CMP Information, is a printed and CD-ROM directory of 60,000 UK firms classified under 8,900 consumer and industrial products and services.

► UNITED STATES DIRECTORIES

Thomas Register of American Manufacturers 2003, published by Thomas Publishing Co., is a thirty-one volume directory of 189,000 US and Canadian manufacturers arranged under 62,500 product and service headings. It is available free of charge at Thomas Register (www.thomasregister.com), although registration is a prerequisite. This is searchable by keyword relating to activity, company name or brand name. CD-ROM and DVD-ROM versions also exist. There is also Thomas Regional (www.thomasregional.com), a free-to-search database of 550,000 US manufacturers, distributors and service companies arranged under 6,000 activity headings.

► ENGINEERING DIRECTORIES

A number of freely accessible engineering directories exist as websites.

Look4industry (www.look4industry.com) is a website offering free access to the content of four printed directories from CMP Information, a division of United Business Media. Searching is by keyword relating to activity, company name or brand name. The chemical and offshore directories have additional search headings. Filtering of results by town, county or country is possible.

The *Engineering Industry Buyers' Guide* 2003 lists over 16,900 United Kingdom companies under 5,100 products and services. It includes an alphabetical list of 10,000 trade names and over 2,500 overseas manufacturers and their UK agents.

The *Electronics & Electrical Buyers' Guide* 2002/2003 lists 11,200 United Kingdom companies arranged under 1,900 activity headings. It also includes an alphabetical list of 7,000 trade names.

Chemical Industry Europe 2002 lists 10,500 European companies arranged under 4,100 activity headings. The directory contains manufacturers of chemicals, equipment manufacturers and service providers. An alphabetical list of 10,000 trade names is provided. This title incorporates the Laboratory Equipment Buyers' Guide.

Offshore Oil and Gas Directory 2002/2003 is a classified directory of 7,000 worldwide companies arranged under 3,600 product and service headings. It covers exploration, production, drilling, offshore engineering and other suppliers of equipment and services.

Look4industry also links to the Printing Trades Directory (dir. dotprint.com), and the Packaging Magazine Directory (dir.dotpackaging. com).

Applegate (www.applegate.co.uk) is a directory of 40,000 UK and Irish companies, arranged under 15,000 activity headings from the chemical, electronics, engineering, chemical engineering, recruitment, plastics & rubber industries. The directory has alphabetical indexes by company, activity, town, county, postcode and telephone area code. Lists of overseas manufacturers and their UK agents are available.

Dial Engineering (www.dialengineering.co.uk) lists over 20,000 UK companies, arranged under 5,000 product and service headings. *Dial Engineering* is available free to qualifying individuals, in print and CD-ROM. The 2001 print version lists close to 14,000 trade names and their owners.

Dial / Electronics Weekly Buyer's Guide (www.dialindustry.com) lists 23,000 UK suppliers arranged under 21,000 product and service headings. The 2002 print version lists 7,000 trade names. Both Dial websites have a keyword search facility by product, service, company name, trade name, street, town or postcode. It is also possible to browse using alphabetical indexes of activity headings, company names and town names. Contact information consists of address, phone and fax numbers, and direct email and website links.

EngNet (www.engnetglobal.com) is a database of engineering companies from around the world. Separate sites exist for the United Kingdom, South Africa and the United States. These countries contribute the majority of the companies listed. Simple searching is by activity, company name or trade name keyword. The advanced search facility allows filtering by international regions or individual country. It includes a classified directory of products and services.

Electronic Engineers' Master (www.eem.com) is a free directory of over 5,300 US companies providing electronic components, equipment and services. It is searchable by activity or company name keyword. A classified directory allows browsing of products and services.

FirstIndex (www.firstindex.co.uk), established in 1992, 'aims to be the most trusted global marketplace for custom-manufactured parts and the supply of industrial equipment.' Registering with the site is required but the service is free for prospective buyers and suppliers. Buyers are able to post detailed requests for quotes (RFQ) on the website. This can include CAD drawings and other documentation, which can be faxed or emailed to FirstIndex. The RFQ is forwarded to suppliers able to supply the product or service. The Buyer is able to choose between the companies who reply to the quote, or decline them all if they so wish. A printed directory, *First Index: the compendium for manufacturing suppliers 2002/2003* details the capabilities of 700 part and equipment manufacturers and processors in the United Kingdom and Ireland. FirstIndex have established databases to serve the engineering markets in Germany (www.firstindex.de), and the United States (www.firstindex.com).

MfgQuote (www.mfgquote.com) provides a US alternative to Firstindex. It is a free service for buyers, but manufacturers are charged a flat fee to appear on the database.

GlobalSpec (www.globalspec.com) is a database of 1,300 engineering product and service suppliers organised by 900 product and service headings. Headings can be selected by keyword search or browsing category lists. Once a heading has been selected, an additional search form appears enabling the selection of products or services satisfying a particular specification. The additional search form contains only specification options pertinent to that product. For example if 'waste pumps' is selected it is possible to specify the pump speed, power source, maximum fluid temperature, or maximum pressure, amongst others. However, not all suppliers provide information to enable searching by specification. Direct links to PDF documents and specific product web pages are often provided.

Industry specific directories are numerous, with many publishers only publishing one title. Many printed and electronic versions are only available at a price. Notable British directory publishers with an international output are Jane's Information Group (www.janes.com), which specialises in defence, aerospace, aviation, shipping and other transport issues; Metal Bulletin Books Ltd (www.metalbulletin.com), which specialises in minerals, metals, mining, scrap, other materials, etc; and BioCommerce Data (www.pjbpubs.com), which specialises in the biotechnology sector.

Sourcerer (www.sourcerer.co.uk) is a directory of the UK chemical industry provided by the Chemical Industries Association. Over 3,500 companies arranged under 100,000 activity headings are listed. Company names are searchable by keyword, but it is the activity searching facility that stands out. Aside from keyword searching for products or trade names, it is possible to use chemical formulas and chemical registration numbers (CAS and EINECS) to locate suppliers.

Product Selector Plus (www.productselector.co.uk), produced by the Royal Institute of British Architects (RIBA), is a directory of 8,000 British building product manufacturers and service providers. It is searchable by classified heading, company name, trade name, certification, etc. Filtering by company type is possible, e.g. manufacturer, installer, distributor or importer. Some company profiles include links to PDF files of trade literature. Building Product Expert (www.barbour-index.co.uk/bpe) allows keyword searching by product, company name and trade name.

Many associations have added buyers' guides of their members, to their websites, for example the Society of British Aerospace Companies (www.sbac.co.uk) provides a searchable directory free of charge. Products and services can be searched by keyword, or by consulting a detailed alphabetical list of activities. The Design Directory (www.britishdesign.co.uk), supported by the Design Council, is a directory of 4,000 design agencies from various disciplines, such as web design, graphics, engineering, etc.

Some government departments provide or sponsor directory websites, often for export promotion purposes. Examples of broad export promotion websites include TradeUK (www.tradeuk.com), a directory of 60,000 British companies provided by Trade Partners UK, and the Japan Trade Directory (www.jetro.go.jp) of 2,000 Japanese companies, available via the website of the Japan External Trade Organization. The British Defence Equipment Catalogue (www.bdec-online.com) is provided by BDEC Ltd in collaboration with the MOD's Defence Export Services Organisation.

Trade journals often include directories as part of the subscription, for example the journal *British Plastics & Rubber* is accompanied by an annual directory of 1,400 companies. The 2003 edition has a classified directory of 900 products and services which features manufacturers, service providers, distributors and agents providing materials, equipment, services and software. This directory is also available free of charge at (www.polymer-age.co.uk). Some publishers, with journals and directories in their portfolio, provide access to directories through the subscription sites of their journals, for example *New Civil Engineer*, (www.nceplus.co.uk) provides access to the *Concrete Yearbook* and *Roads, Rail and Transport Directory*.

▶ OTHER DIRECTORIES

In the event of a country being poorly covered by general or industry specific trade directories, yellow pages style directories provide an alternative option for sourcing products and services. Such directories exist for virtually all countries and are generally available via the Internet. These directories are not designed for sourcing detailed product specifications, but for finding the largest number of firms offering a broad product or service in a particular locality. For example Yell (www.yell.com) lists 1,700,000 UK businesses under 2,350 product and service headings. In developed economies it is common to see competing databases. Scoot (www.scoot.co.uk), ThomsonLocal (www.thomsonlocal.com) and BT directory enquiries (www.bt.com/directory-enquiries), amongst others, cover the UK. An interesting addition to this market is AskAlix (www.askalix.com/uk). Companies appearing on AskAlix complete a form that includes a description of their activities. This activity description is scanned when activity keywords are searched. This database design lacks the defined structure of a classified directory and will often produce irrelevant results, but will also find exact matches.

▶ SOURCING DIRECTORIES

Directories in Print 2003, from Gale Group, lists over 15,000 directories published in the United States and worldwide. *Current British Directories* 1999, from CBD Research, lists 2,450 directories, arranged under 1,750 subject headings, published in the United Kingdom and the Republic of Ireland. The *World Directory of Trade and Business Associations* 2002, from Euromonitor, lists 5,000 associations from 125 countries. All include directories of individuals or organisations from the fields of business, government, science and culture.

It is also worth consulting the websites of the Directory and Database Publishers Association (www.directory-publisher.co.uk), and the European Association of Directory and Database Publishers (www.eadp.be), which have lists of directories published by their members arranged by subject.

For website directories, consult the directory functions of Google (www.google.com), and Yahoo (uk.yahoo.com). Choose 'business' followed by 'directories'. The Open Directory project (dmoz.org) is another useful resource. Freedirectories.com (www.freedirectories.com) links to freely available web directories of people and companies. It is searchable by country, industry or interest. The Federation of International Trade Associations (www.fita.org/webindex/index.html) provides links to web resources for international trade, which include country, industry specific and trade lead directories. The Purchasing Research Service, (www.purchasingresearchservice.com) lists online directories by industry. To find Internet yellow & white pages directories worldwide consult Teldir (www.infobel.com/teldir/), or World Telephone Book (intrax.ch/telephone.htm). The

BRAD directory, published by EMAP Communications, includes a new media section that lists a number of directory websites.

▶ EXHIBITION CATALOGUES

Exhibition Catalogues offer an alternative to print and electronic directories for the sourcing of providers of products or services. The Association of Exhibition Organisers (www.aeo.org.uk) calculated that close to 2,000 business and consumer exhibitions, serving over seventeen million visitors, were held in the United Kingdom in 2001. Thousands more are held around the world each year. Exhibitions are usually staged to represent businesses from a particular industry or from a particular region within a country. Exhibitions are also staged overseas to represent foreign companies wishing to enter the markets of the host country.

Most exhibition organisers produce an accompanying printed catalogue or guide to the exhibition. Exhibition catalogues, like print or web directories, often provide detailed profiles of firms and their products and services. Many catalogues will also include an index of firms arranged by product or service. Some of the indexes include headings for specific products not found in the classification schemes of traditional directories. However even the largest of exhibitions will only showcase several hundred leading firms at a time. Increasingly, websites are being created for individual exhibitions offering searchable directories of exhibitors. Unfortunately some websites will be removed after the exhibition has been staged and some will be stripped of information in preparation for the next staging of the exhibition.

In the absence of a dedicated website, the obvious way to obtain a catalogue is to attend the exhibition. Catalogues are often provided free of charge to attendees, and if there is a charge it is usually negligible. Those unable to attend can contact the organiser just before or after the exhibition is due, to request a copy of the catalogue. There are several websites and printed sources devoted to providing a calendar of exhibitions around the world.

Trade Fairs & Exhibitions UK (www.exhibitions.co.uk) lists major Exhibitions held in the United Kingdom. TSNN (www.tsnn.co.uk) lists over 15,000 trade shows and conferences, and over 30,000 seminars held around the world. Expo 24–7 (www.expo24–7.com) lists 30,000 exhibitions held around the world. Exhibitions.com (www.exhibitions.com) lists exhibitions, conferences and meetings held around the world. Trade Partners UK (www.tradepartners.gov.uk) maintains an 'events' database which lists exhibitions, trade missions and other events supported by the UK government in the UK and overseas.

▶ TRADE MARKS, TRADE NAMES AND BRANDS

Trade marks, often referred to as trade names or brands, can be words, logos or symbols, or a mix of these forms. They are used to distinguish a product or service, or the corporate identity, of a firm from others.

It is a common occurrence to know a trade name for a product without knowing the name of the manufacturer. Taking a trade name for a firm's name is an easy mistake to make. The websites of the national and multinational trademark registration offices provide ideal starting points for broad searches.

The Patent Office (www.patent.gov.uk) oversees the UK trademark register. This is searchable via their website by trademark number, trade mark name or proprietor name. When searching by name, the term searched for has to be an exact match or the first word, or stem of the first word, in the trade mark or proprietor name. The Office for Harmonization in the Internal Market – Trademarks and Designs (oami.eu.int) manages the registration of European Community trademarks. By the end of 2002, 165,000 trademarks were registered. The website provides free access to CTM Online which is searchable by the trade mark number, trade mark name keyword or owner name. The trade mark keyword search offers greater flexibility of searching compared to the UK trademark register. When searching for the owner it is only possible to use terms that find an exact match or match the stem of the first word in the full name. The World Intellectual Property Organization (www.wipo.org) runs an international trade mark registration scheme signed up to by seventy-one states. The Madrid Express Database, available free of charge via the WIPO website, provides free access to information about all trade marks currently registered and those that have expired in the past six months. Searching is by keyword of the trade mark name or owner name. The United States Patent and Trademark Office (www.uspto.gov) provides free access to the Trademark Electronic Search System (TESS) of 3,000,000 registered, pending or dead federal trademarks. TESS offers numerous search options including trademark name and owner name. Name searching allows truncation before or after the search term. The trade marks link page (www.bl.uk/services/information/patents/tmlinks.html), on the British Library website, lists over twenty-five other national trademark databases available over the web. Some, but not all, are free to search. Other commercial databases exist, for example Trademarkscan.

The Kompass database (www.kompass.co.uk) allows keyword searching of 744,000 trade names. *Industrial Trade Names* 2002/2003, published by Reed Business Information is volume 4 of the Kompass Register Series for the United Kingdom, and lists over 46,000 trade names and their user companies. A separate section lists the 11,000 companies with their contact details and trade names used. It also lists 25,000 lapsed trade names. The final section lists over 3,500 overseas companies and the names of their UK agents or distributors. Both web and print versions provide brief descriptions of the nature of the product with each trade name.

Companies and their Brands 2002, from Gale Group, lists the trade names of 400,000 consumer products, available in the United States, and their 114,000 manufacturers.

A number of engineering directories list trade names, including Look4industry (www.look4industry.com); Dial Engineering (www.dialengineering.co.uk); and Dial/Electronics Weekly Buyer's Guide (www.dialindustry.com).

► TRADE JOURNALS

Trade journals represent the first port of call for numerous product information issues, including current legislation, best practice, new products, environmental issues, safety, testing, prices, project news, industry awards, manufacturing technology, contracts and tenders.

Many trade journals are distributed free of charge to qualifying individuals in the industry concerned. Websites arising from the print journals can be free or priced, with some offering a mixture of the two. Websites often include searchable archives of previous issues and offer news alerts by email. Discussion forums exist on many websites, allowing exploration of business opportunities and the exchange of ideas about products and other industry issues. One example is RFGlobalnet (www.rfglobalnet.com), from VertMarkets Inc., which serves the radio frequency and wireless design industry. A number of publishers publish several journals from related industries and offer single websites to search the archives of all their titles. The New Civil Engineer Plus (www.nceplus.co.uk), from EMAP Construct, has some free content and provides many additional features to subscribers. Issues of printed journals frequently include a mini buyer's guide, e.g. *Swimming Pool News* published by Market Link Publishing lists manufacturers of wavemakers, synthetic pool surrounds, custom made slides, roman end steps and other products which may not appear in general directories.

Trade journals often include a reply card service enabling readers to obtain free literature from selected companies. Many journals also offer this facility via dedicated websites, e.g. Industrial Engineering News Europe (www.ien-online.com) has a searchable archive of the printed journal and a reader reply service. Occasionally, literature can be requested for a broad product heading, resulting in literature being received from a variety of companies. Manufacturing.Net (www.manufacturing.net), from Reed

Business Information, is an online community serving manufacturing, e.g. design, plant management, logistics, procurement, etc. Company news, new products and buyers' guides are some of the available features. Access to twenty-three relevant magazines is provided.

Industry specific trade journals commonly feature adverts for offers to buy and sell new or used machinery, surplus stock and buildings. Specialist journals also exist to serve this market. For example the weekly journal *Machinery Market* (www.machinery-market.co.uk), from MM Publishing Ltd, which has been in existence for 123 years, is circulated to over 8,000 companies worldwide. The website has a keyword searchable database of auctions, products for sale and products wanted. There is also *Industrial Exchange and Mart* (www.iem-net.co.uk).

Machinery Magazine (www.machinery.co.uk), published by Findlay Publications, is the 'UK's leading production engineering journal', providing a supplier database of companies involved in new and used machine tools, tooling, workholding, contract manufacturing and engineering products and services. The database covers over 100,000 product entries from over 12,000 suppliers.

Engineering Capacity, published since 1959, is a monthly journal that features the activities of specialist engineering subcontractors in the United Kingdom. The journal has a controlled circulation of over 10,000 individuals within UK companies. The current edition of *Capacity Handbook* is a classified directory listing close to 500 sub-contractors. Some entries from the directory have been added to the website (www. engineering-capacity.co.uk) as a trial feature with a full web launch of the 2003/2004 edition scheduled for May 2003.

To identify trade journals relevant to your industry consult the directories *BRAD* and *Benn's Media*. Both titles list UK consumer and business magazines arranged under broad subject headings. *Benn's Media* includes two additional volumes for Europe and the rest of the world. Entries in both directories indicate the content and target readership of the journal concerned. The Purchasing Research Service (www.purchasingresearchservice.com) lists online journals and other sources of information arranged by industry. The Google directory function (directory.google.com) links to several hundred industry specific online journals. Choose 'business' followed by 'resources' and 'news and publications'.

Some online databases provide information about products. One example is Gale Group F&S Index, a bibliographic database of over four million records devoted to international company, product and industry news. Over 2,500 newspapers, journals and other sources are scanned.

Dialog Product Code Finder exploits the information held in other Dialog databases by searching within the product code and product name fields of those databases. The database contains over 500,000 references to product information articles and other records.

► STANDARDS

Standards provide an agreed way of producing materials or products or of providing services or systems. Sources of information about standards are covered in Chapter 6.

It is essential for companies to be aware of the standards commonly observed or in force in the geographical markets or industries in which they wish to operate.

Adoption of a given standard is normally a voluntary action. Occasionally legislation incorporates the provisions of a standard making it compulsory, e.g. the dimensions of credit cards. Companies often specify that a certain standard be observed within a contract.

Adoption of a standard by a company can confer numerous benefits, including the acceptance of a product in one or more markets, consumer confidence and adoption of efficient production methods.

► PATENTS

Sources of information about patents are covered in detail in Chapter 5. A patent can be granted, after successful application, to the inventor, to protect their novel products and processes. If granted, the patent gives the inventor a sole right to exploit the invention for a set number of years. There are over four million patents in force around the world, and many millions more no longer in force. For a patent to be granted, the product or process must be a new invention which can be used in industry. The information in a patent must be sufficiently detailed to allow for the product or process to be repeated. Such detailed information forms a vital source of product information.

► FORUMS AND ADVISORY SERVICES

Industryweb (www.industryweb.co.uk) is a free to access site providing the latest product information, industry news and discussion forums to industrial engineers in the United Kingdom.

Eng-Tips forum (www.eng-tips.com) is a US based discussion forum for engineering professionals. It is free to join but registration is required.

The Government-Industry Data Exchange Program (GIDEP) (www.gidep.org) is a joint government and industry initiative operating in the USA and Canada. The program fosters the exchange of information to help reduce or eliminate unnecessary expenditure of resources. Data relates to all stages of the product or service life-cycle, from research and development to full operation. To participate, organisations must be supplying products or services, directly or indirectly, to the US government or the Canadian National Department of Defence.

ESDU International (www.esdu.com) is a subscription service which provides validated engineering design data, methods and software for the engineer. These are presented in over 1,250 design guides with supporting software. Endorsed by professional institutions, ESDU data and software form an important part of the design operation of companies large and small throughout the world.

The Component Obsolescence Group (www.cog.org.uk) was established in 1997 to address the issues of electronic and mechanical obsolescence. One benefit of membership is the ability to draw on a pool of knowledge when sourcing obscure and obsolete products. The National Obsolescence Centre (NOC) (www.nocweb.org) includes a database of solution providers, e.g. product change notices, inventories of obsolete products, component lifecycle predictions, etc.

MatWeb (www.matweb.com) provides a mixture of free and priced information on material properties of over 30,000 metals, plastics, ceramics and composites. There are various search options including trade name or manufacturer.

AZOM (www.azom.com) is a free database of information on advanced materials. It includes properties' data, news releases and supplier profiles.

MSDS-Search (www.msdssearch.com) provides free access to 2,500,000 material safety data sheets from 5,000 manufacturers and others in the public domain.

8 Electronic Full Text Services

Jill Lambert

▶ INTRODUCTION

We have reached the situation in engineering and science where electronic full text services are the most popular source of information available for users. The reasons are clear – these services offer immediate, convenient access via the Internet. Defining exactly what electronic full text services are, though, raises a few questions – the terminology can mean different things to different people, now that so much information exists in digital format.

In its widest sense, these services can be taken to include all of the following resources:

- E-journals – periodicals published in electronic format. These can range from new Web based journals with no print equivalent, to well established, prestige titles, published both in paper and electronic form.
- E-print archives – electronic collections of research papers, accessible free on the Internet.
- Product information – technical specifications, component and equipment data sheets, and more generally the electronic equivalents of manufacturers' and suppliers' catalogues.
- Databases – a very wide category, which includes full text electronic versions of patents, standards, conference proceedings, reports and theses.
- Reference sources – the online versions of handbooks, encyclopedias, dictionaries and other referral sources, often re-packaged as subject collections.
- E-books – books that can be searched and read electronically. The e-book market is evolving rapidly, with several different formats and mechanisms available for displaying and reading the information on screen.

The potential scope of these resources is huge, and is still increasing as more and more information is created in, or converted to, digital format.

Many of these electronic full text services fall within the scope of other chapters in this book, and are covered elsewhere in the text. E-journals are covered in Chapter 2, reports and theses in Chapter 3, conference proceedings in Chapter 4, patents and standards in Chapter 5, and product information in Chapter 6. The aim of this chapter is to concentrate on the other full text electronic sources – e-books, electronic reference services and e-print archives, with the aim of explaining the background and structure of these resources, and giving an outline of what is available.

▶ E-BOOKS

Although there is a lot of interest in e-books, there is also a lot of confusion over what these actually are – a casual reading of newspapers throws up names such as Rocket ebook, Softbook, Palm, and so forth but without much more than the idea that these are devices for reading the digital versions of novels. The term 'e-book' means different things to different people – to some it is a text that can be displayed on a PC, to others it is an actual item of hardware, a 'reader' containing the text.

A short definition of an e-book is a book which can be downloaded and read electronically. A longer one is any piece of electronic text regardless of size or composition, but excluding journal publications, made available electronically (or optically) for any device (handheld or deskbound) that includes a screen (Armstrong, 2002). These electronic texts may have been converted from print – as is the case with the classic novels now being sold as e-books for reading on the train, etc. Alternatively, electronic texts can contain information 'born-digitally', i.e. that never existed as paper copies.

Defining an e-book as electronic text, regardless of its origin or the device used for reading the information, is helpful. It is still useful though, as part of the larger picture, to have an understanding of the range of formats and delivery mechanisms available.

Formats

Although formats and delivery mechanisms tend to become blurred together in any discussion of e-books, they are different entities. The format depends on the software used to display the information on screen. As you might expect with an evolving medium such as e-books, there is no established, standard format. The main formats being used by larger publishers and suppliers are:

- PDF (Portable document files) from Adobe Acrobat
- HTML (Hypertext Markup Language)
- XML (Xtensible Markup Language)

Other formats include Microsoft Reader, MobiPocket Reader and Palm PDB. Reader software – software compatible with the specific format – is also needed for text to be displayed on screen.

Efforts are being made to establish standards, to try to avoid the problems of the proprietary systems that have caused damage in other areas. These efforts have centred on developing the Open eBook Publication Structure. This is a non-proprietary specification, based on XML, and supported by the Open eBook Forum (www.openebook.org), an international trade and standards organisation for e-books. It covers the content, structure and presentation of e-books, to enable publishers to produce digital documents, which can be used without needing to be reformatted for each different reading system (Snowhill, 2001).

Delivery mechanisms

The delivery mechanism is the means by which an e-book can be viewed – essentially the hardware for displaying the information on screen. The choices include:

- A dedicated portable e-book reader. Some of the early, well known brand names in this area were 'Softbook', and 'RocketBook', later rebadged by their manufacturers.
- Hand held computers, palmtops and personal digital assistants (PDAs). These are all small pocket type devices, which can be used as e-books if reader software is installed.
- A desktop personal computer (PC) or laptop.

Much of the publicity and hype has been concentrated on e-books for the leisure/personal market, and the type of devices needed for this. On the whole, professional interest has centred on e-books that can be used from the desktop. These do not need proprietary devices, and have the advantage that they sit within a delivery mechanism, already used to access e-journals, free Internet sites and other electronic information resources.

Why use e-books?

Do e-books have any advantages? Are they a technology looking for an application? These are questions that naturally arise, given the convenience, relative cheapness and – more subjectively perhaps – the affection that people have for the printed book. For publishers, the cost factor is an incentive. E-books offer the chance to launch new titles much more cheaply, without paying for large print runs which might never be sold. The alternative problem faced by publishers of under supply – 'out of print' books – is also solved.

There are also benefits from a user's perspective in a work environment:

- Instant access (though this is dependent on the terms and conditions of the licensing).
- Integration with other electronic resources. E-books become available on the same basis as e-journals, and other full text resources through one window – the user's workstation.
- In universities and other educational environments, the ability to access texts off campus has great potential for distance learners.
- Searching facilities. Finding the relevant section in a text should be easy in an e-book. With a collection of e-books on the same topic, there is the added benefit of being able to retrieve information simultaneously from several different works.
- The technology can be an aid to partially sighted, physically disabled and other users with additional needs. Font sizes can be increased, pages can be turned with the click of a bar, and there is also the option of using screen reading or screen magnification software.
- Annotation. Users can make notes and drawings, and mark passages in a way that is not possible with printed books.
- Enhanced features. Some e-books have extra features such as interactive dictionaries, and it is likely that other additional features will develop over time.

The claims often made by vendors that e-books are portable and convenient are more arguable. It is hard to think of a more convenient, portable device than a printed book. The inconvenience of needing a reading device – whether this is a PDA, e-book reader or PC – is one of the major disadvantages of e-books. Another is eyestrain. Most people still find it uncomfortable to read on screen for any length of time.

Usability will be a key aspect in determining how successful e-books will be in the marketplace. Some very useful guidelines for designing electronic textbooks were developed by the EBONI (Electronic Books ON-screen Interface) Project, funded by JISC, the UK universities' Joint Information Systems Committee. EBONI focussed on the two principal factors affecting design – the appearance of information on-screen and the 'look and feel' of e-book hardware (Wilson, 2002).

Some of the guidelines which emerged from the project include:

- Having a table of contents and index as well as a search engine.
- Using hypertext links to improve navigation and cross-referencing.

- Ensuring clear headings, a lot of white space with a clean appearance, and avoiding 'busy' screens.
- Providing book-marking, highlighting and annotating facilities.
- Breaking text into small chunks.

An interesting comment by users was that it was easy to get 'lost' either within an e-book, or by straying from it into other areas of the Internet. EBONI guidelines suggest that e-books should be treated as closed environments, with no links to other sites (for example in a bibliography), unless clearly signposted. Within an e-book it is important to include orientation markers so that a user has an idea of a 'sense of place' in the same way that one has in a printed book.

For hardware, not surprisingly the guidelines propose using display technology with high resolution, high contrast and minimal glare, and designing reading devices ergonomically so that the user is comfortable when reading.

Pricing

Although it may be stating the obvious, vendors need to sell e-books at an economic price if they are to gain a stronghold in the marketplace. Getting the right economic model has presented a problem to publishers. Some fear a situation where academic libraries in particular could buy just one copy of an electronic book, making it accessible to many students, therefore replacing individual purchasing by students and multiple copy buying by organisations (Midgeley, 2002).

There is a wide range of pricing systems in use. For institutional buyers, one of the most common is an annual subscription for access to a specific collection of titles. Where an institution is willing to commit to a longer time period, the access fees are likely to be reduced accordingly. Other mechanisms include free browsing of a publisher or vendor's collection, with charges for printing and downloading and a one off purchase of an e-book, with a premium charge for on-going access.

One obvious question when considering the purchase of an e-version of a book, also available in print, is whether or not it is value for money. Exact comparisons are hard to make, but there are points to consider. E-books can provide immediate access for remote users, an inducement for engineers and computer scientists, who may not have the time to make regular visits to a library or information centre to borrow printed works. There are labour saving and storage benefits – no library staff time is spent on issuing, discharging or shelving the books. If the premium on the electronic version of a title is high though, the cost may be disproportionate to the benefits.

There are of course many free e-book Websites. The best known is Project Gutenberg (promo.net/pg/), with its large collection of novels, plays, poetry etc, all out of copyright. There are others, though, that are specifically relevant to engineering, and are listed below in the section 'What's Available?'

Digital Rights Management

Interlinked with pricing is the question of how access to the content of e-books is to be controlled. Pay by use is one method of controlling access but there are others – limiting to one user at a time, by length of content, or by time, are other options. Control over the intellectual property content – increasingly referred to as Digital Rights Management – is a critical aspect in the development of e-books (Neylon, 2001). The question of how this control should be enforced also applies to e-journals, but is more urgent for e-books because of their larger content and length.

Several Digital Rights Management Systems (DMRS) have been, or are under, development. These hardware and software systems include:

- Adobe Acrobat Web Buy for PDF documents
- XrML, a joint venture between Xerox and Microsoft
- ONIX, a book industry standard
- Open Digital Rights Language (ODRL) by the World Wide Web Consortium (W3C)

With a new untried and untested medium, it is understandable that publishers want to protect their investments by limiting the amount of downloading, copying and printing from e-books. If e-books are to be useful though, the information has to be easily accessible, particularly in a library setting. A balance will need to be achieved between the protection of digital rights and fair access and usage.

When selecting titles from publishers or vendors, there are numerous questions which can be asked:

- Is downloading permitted?
- Is it possible to print a section without paying extra?
- If so, how large a section can be printed?
- Is access limited to one person at a time?

Users are accustomed to the access situation with electronic journals, where there is usually no restriction on the number of individuals that can log in concurrently. Asking questions such as these is important, because the e-book industry is still evolving rapidly. Feedback to publishers and vendors on how users want to access e-books, their requirements for hardcopy, and what level of pricing is acceptable, is an important step in shaping development.

Discovering what is available

Given the fact that e-books are a new medium needing to be promoted to attract customers, you might expect that it would be simple to find out what titles are available from vendors. In fact bibliographical access is not that easy. A JISC Working Group on e-books identified the problem of tracing relevant material as a deterrent to purchase (Armstrong, 2002). With some vendors, it is not actually possible to see a list of books until you have joined the service.

The type of bibliographical data readily available for printed books is scarce, but the situation is gradually changing. BookFind-Online, one of the major sources used by UK libraries, now includes some e-books. In the longer term, the passing of the Legal Deposit Libraries Act in 2003 is likely to improve bibliographical access. This Act extended the rights of the British Library and the five other copyright libraries in the UK and Ireland to include electronic publications.

Traditional ways of identifying new titles still apply – promotional information from publishers and vendors, attending exhibitions, reading professional journals, contacts in other institutions and email discussion lists. There is also a growing number of websites – some specifically set up to sell e-books, others from traditional booksellers – listing e-book titles. Most are general in scope, but do include IT, science and engineering e-books, where these are available. Useful ones to try are:

- eBooks.com (us.ebooks.com), a commercial e-book seller, covering all subject fields, including technology and computers.
- EbookMall (www.ebookmall.com), also a commercial e-book seller and Internet publisher
- eBook Locator (www.ebooklocator.com), a site specifically covering e-books, with wide coverage and detailed information on content.
- Amazon (www.amazon.co.uk)
- Blackwell's Online ebookshop (blackwell.etailer.dpsl.net)
- WHSmith.co.uk eBooks (ebooks.whsmith.co.uk)

Bibliographical access is likely to improve in due course. In the meantime these less structured channels should be reasonably effective in keeping up to date with what is available.

E-book publishers

Computer science, engineering and technology are represented in the market, partly because of the benefits of quick, easy access to current information that e-books offer in these subject fields. Publishers with significant e-book coverage for engineering and IT include:

- Kluwer Online (ebooks.kluweronline.com)
- McGraw-Hill eBookstore (www.mhhe.com/)
- Taylor & Francis (www.eBookstore.tandf.co.uk), which includes the Routledge and Spon Press imprints.
- Wiley Interscience OnlineBooks (www3.interscience. wiley.com/)

Although not e-books as such, some publishers also provide additional information online, as an accompaniment to their textbooks. Pearson Education has 'Companion Websites' for many of its engineering books, (booksites.net/solutions/aboutcws.htm).

E-Book aggregators

Aggregators – organisations giving a single point of access to large number of e-books – are also prominent within engineering disciplines. Leading aggregators include:

- Ebrary (www.ebrary.com), one of the leading providers, with a database of over 10,000 titles from over 130 academic, professional and trade publishers, including a range of University Presses such as Cambridge, Yale, Harvard and MIT. It has content in the computing and technical fields, with a special collection of SME (Society of Manufacturing Engineering) working papers, books, and journals. Ebrary's pricing model is based on free access, with users paying fees to copy or print text.
- NetLibrary (www.netlibrary.com), owned and backed by OCLC. One of the first e-book aggregators, netLibrary covers a wide range of disciplines, which includes networking and telecommunications, computers, and some titles in engineering and manufacturing. The service is based on an annual subscription-pricing model, but also has a collection of free books.
- Safari: Tech Books Online (proquest.safaribooksonline.com), a joint venture between the publishers' O'Reilly and The Pearson Technology Group, which includes well known imprints such as Addison Wesley, Prentice Hall, Cisco Press, Sams and Que. Safari is aimed at the information technology sector – students, academics, programmers and other IT professionals – and includes programming, software engineering, Web administration and networking. It is hosted by Proquest (www.proquest.co.uk), an aggregator with long experience of providing a fast, reliable platform for accessing information on the Web. Pricing is based on a monthly subscription service.
- XanEdu (www.xanedu.com), also part of Proquest, is provider of e-books as course materials for higher education. Working with

publishers such as McGraw Hill, Pearson, Wiley and Prentice Hall, it supplies Web based versions of books in conjunction with virtual learning environments (VLEs), such as WebCT and Blackboard.

One of the problems for aggregators has been selecting titles that users need. Academics recommending titles to students, for example, want to see e-versions of the books they currently recommend. They are not usually willing to reverse the process, by choosing their reading lists according to what is available electronically. This situation is gradually changing as publishers become more willing to work closely with aggregators to provide electronic versions of their newest texts.

Free e-book sites

Although mainly general in content, there are also some relevant free e-book sites. One of the best is the Internet Public Library Texts Collection (www.ipl.org/div/books). Established as a development project for students in the School of Librarianship at the University of Michigan School, the site has a fairly wide spread of books, ranging from basic works such as an electronics text for beginners to technical reports.

Other sites with some engineering content include the On-Line Books Page (onlinebooks.library.upenn.edu), and Searchebooks.com (www. searchebooks.com). More specifically, the National Academies Press (NAP) Website (www.nap.edu), has nearly 3,000 full textbooks and reports from the US National Academy of Engineering, and other American national bodies in the fields of engineering, science and health.

► ELECTRONIC REFERENCE SOURCES

Engineering is a discipline that has been well supported by printed reference works, because of its need for reliable, accurate, validated data. There are numerous examples of high quality titles – *Machinery's Handbook*, the *ASM Handbook* and *Kempe's Engineers YearBook* are a few of the leading ones. All the advantages of e-books – instant access, easy precise searching – apply even more so to electronic reference works. It is not surprising therefore that engineering is one of the leading areas for online reference data sources.

Launching reference books on the Web, though, requires significant investment to support and promote a service. One estimate put the cost of operating a Web subscription service at over $500,000 per year (Hodgkin, 2001). The cost factor has been a strong influence on the development of aggregated reference services, pooling the content of a range of sources. These aggregated services share a website, with 'power searching', across all the titles simultaneously. Some aggregated services include the reference works of many publishers; others are based on the output of a single publisher. The main contenders include:

- Xrefer (www.xrefer.com), covering over 150 reference titles from a range of publishers such as Penguin, Macmillan and Butterworth-Heinemann. Xrefer is general in scope, but does include some engineering dictionaries, such as *Newnes Dictionary of electronics*.
- Knovel Scientific and Engineering databases (www.knovel.com), providing access to hundreds of reference books from publishers ranging from McGraw-Hill, CRC Press, American Society of Mechanical Engineers, Reed Elsevier, Society of Plastics Engineers, ASM (American Society for Metals) to Butterworth-Heinemann. It includes classics such as the *Machinery's Handbook, Marks' Standard Handbook for Mechanical Engineers* and *Perry's Chemical Engineers' Handbook*. The coverage extends from aerospace and radar technology, electronics, semiconductors, materials science and plastics through to chemical, ceramic, environmental, and mechanical engineering. Some titles are 'interactive deep searchable' (IDS), a facility allowing numeric searches to be performed by field, and data to be manipulated in tables.
- CRC Press (www.crcnetbase.com), licensing access to subject groupings of their online reference works. ENGnetBASE is one of the key collections, with more than 200 titles from all subject areas. Other relevant ones include CHEMnetBASE, ITKnowledgeBASE, POLYMERSnetBASE, ENVIROnetBASE, FOODnetBASE, InfoSECURITYnetBASE, MATHnetBASE and STATSnetBASE.
- Oxford Reference Online (www.oxfordreference.com) covers reference works from Oxford University Press, including dictionaries of mathematics and physics.
- Wiley InterScience Reference Works (www3.interscience.wiley.com/), with strong coverage of chemical technology. Subscribing institutions select their content from the range of Wiley reference works, including the Kirk-Othmer *Encyclopedia of Chemical Technology*.

Customisation – the ability to select content according to the needs of specific users – is becoming an increasingly important feature of aggregated services as they increase in size. Another aspect is the extent to which the collection is integrated. While aggregation can bring together reference material into one place for searching, cross-referencing is also needed if users are to navigate within and between sources. Xrefer, for example, has cross-references to other related sections, within a single reference work, plus links 'xreferences' to relevant sections in other dictionaries and encyclopedias in the collection.

Not all electronic reference books are aggregated services of course. One of the leading general resources in its field – the *McGraw Hill Encyclopedia of Science & Technology*, now in its 9th edition (2002), is available online as AccessScience (accessscience.com). A subscription is required to use AccessScience, which is updated daily. Validated engineering data is available from ESDU (Engineering Sciences Data Unit) International (www.esdu.com). A subscription is required to access the ESDU database, originally established by the Royal Aeronautical Society, and consisting of more than 1,100 design guides, and accompanying software.

E-print archives

E-print archives – sometimes referred to as pre-print servers – are stores of electronic collections of research papers, made freely available on the Internet. Some of the papers in an e-print archive may have already appeared in a journal, some may be awaiting publication but others will never have been formally published at all.

One of the main benefits for a researcher in contributing a paper to an e-print archive is the speed with which the work can be made public – papers are peer reviewed, so there are no delays for refereeing, or time lag before publication. Users also benefit from this very rapid dissemination of information, but also need to be aware that the data has not been 'quality assessed' in the way that papers published formally in journals will have been.

The largest and most well known e-print archive is 'arXiv', based at Cornell University (www.arxiv.org). arXiv, which was established in 1991, contains over a quarter of a million papers in computer science, non-linear systems, physics, and mathematics

Other e-print servers include:

- CERN Document Server (cdsweb.cern.ch), covering particle physics and related technologies.
- CogPrints (cogprints.ecs.soton.ac.uk), a collection of self archived papers by authors, which includes computer science.
- NASA Astrophysics Data System (ADS) (adswww.harvard.edu). This is a very large collection of both bibliographic references and pre-prints, which includes the physics and instrumentation subject fields.
- The E-print Network (www.osti.go/eprints/). This site has been developed by the US Department of Energy as a 'one-stop shop' for e-prints in technology and science, linking to a range of servers in these subject fields.
- Physics Documents Worldwide (de.physnet.net/PhysNet/physdoc.html), links to pre-prints, reports and other information, such as lists of publications, stored locally on servers in universities and other institutions.

The development of e-print archives is likely to be stimulated by the launching in 2002 of the Budapest Open Access Initiative (BOAI), (soros. org/openaccess). This initiative has $3 million available in grants to sponsor the development of new models for scholarly communication, including self-archiving.

▶ REFERENCES

Armstrong, C., Edwards, L., and Lonsdale, R., 2002. Virtually there? E-books in UK academic libraries. *Program; electronic library and information systems,* 36(4), pp. 216–227.

Dillon, D., 2001. E-books: the University of Texas experience, part 1. *Library Hi Tech,* 19(2), pp. 113–124.

Hodgkin, A., 2001. Reference books on the web. *Ariadne,* Issue 30. www.ariadne.ac.uk/issue30/ref-books/intro.html.

Midgeley, S., 2002. The end of books? *Guardian* Tuesday April 9th. guardian.co.uk/Archive/Article/0,4273,438951 0,00.html

Neylon, E., 2001. First steps in an information commerce economy: digital rights management in the emerging Ebook environment. *D-Lib Magazine* 7(1), dlib.org/dlib/january01/neylon/01neylon.html

Snowhill, L., 2001. E-books and their future in academic libraries: an overview. *D-Lib Magazine* 7(7/8). dlib.org/dlib/july01/snowhill/07snowhill.html

Wilson, R., and Landoni, M., 2002. *EBONI: Electronic Textbook Design Guidelines.* eboni.cdlr.strath.ac.uk/guidelines/index.html

9 Abstracting and Indexing Services

Bob Rhodes

Abstracting and indexing services first appeared in the late nineteenth Century as a means for researchers and others to find descriptions of documents relevant to their interests. By indexing a number of journals within a subject area, these services have enabled searchers then and now to cover the large and increasing quantity of publications in order to identify pertinent documents. Some services include an abstract or summary giving details of the content of papers. Many of the early services are still being published, including several in science and technology. The initiative to produce abstracting and indexing services often came from professional institutions and societies.

While the majority still cover journals, some have been extended to include other publications such as conference proceedings, reports, theses and patents. A number of services cover a different form exclusively. Other variables include geographical and language coverage.

From about the 1970's, these printed sources have been complemented by computerised databases and associated electronic sources. The result is that some are available in one form or the other while some are available in both, particularly those from the major services. These databases may be supplied by different routes including CD-ROM, or accessed via the Internet. Access via the Internet can be to nominated terminals, by passwords or unrestricted access. There are variations in the structure of databases but sometimes a common platform is used.

Databases are now the dominant form of abstracting and indexing services, but they have not entirely eclipsed the printed form. Change continues, and now some databases and services are being grouped together as 'aggregated' services. Although a few have existed for some time, the term is relatively new and descriptive.

While commonsense would suggest choice should be based on the most appropriate service rather than purely a preference for one form or the other, this might not always be the case. Two other factors come into play. One is the users, many of whom seem to prefer the convenience and advantages of databases, and the other is accessibility (availability, and ease of use). Databases now seem to dominate in some locations such as universities. Searches can be made in offices without the need to visit the library, and the results can be printed or stored at the press of a few buttons. Access is often limited, however, to staff and students of the subscribing organisation, in order that database producers can recover their costs plus margins. Consideration needs to be given to the users, real and potential, who do not have ready access to a sufficient range of subscription databases. Some freely available databases also exist, many of which cover their costs by charging for document delivery.

There is a trend for aggregation, which brings together a number of database services as one package, an early example being OCLC FirstSearch. Aggregation brings some advantages and possible simplification. One practical outcome is that the order of searching the abstracting and indexing services may, in part, be based on using the relevant parts of an aggregated service sequentially. In other words, once connected to an aggregated service, a searcher will often use all the appropriate features (Wiggins, 1998).

▶ USE OF ABSTRACTING AND INFORMATION SERVICES

Abstracting and indexing services have an important role to play in enabling engineers and others to keep up with published literature and information. Their effectiveness in achieving this has been studied, notably in recall (finding all appropriate documents), and relevance (inappropriate documents are screened out). These are quality factors, and there is currently reason for concern that despite thorough searching of on-line collections, some documents remain hidden. An example has been reported by Jensen in a case study in the geosciences (Jensen, 2001).

Purpose

Usage is likely to be part of the information gathering process, which in itself is normally a constituent of some other activity or project such as research, development, engineering design, manufacture or construction. This is often restricted to a particular field such as mechanical engineering or electrical engineering, but it might be in a more specific area such as avionics or hydraulics. It might be a small detail like checking a reference. The purpose of a search is important, as it helps set the parameters such as the period of dates covered, language, or selectivity (relevance and recall).

It is also the first step in a methodical approach to searching, particularly for more extensive searches. It is followed by:

- selecting appropriate services
- using them effectively, especially in the choice and use of search terms (keywords)
- recording details of potentially relevant papers/documents
- acquiring content for reading
- utilising with possible analysis and synthesis

Selection

Services should be selected to match the requirement, and help can be sought by using guides such as this one. More details can often be obtained from suppliers who normally have useful websites and support services. Familiarity with particular services is useful, otherwise some time should be spent reading the guidance notes provided by most services. It may be worthwhile getting advice from a librarian or information professional, ranging from advice on sources, to full involvement of the intermediary.

With a number of possible services relevant to many topics, the order of choice is a matter of preference, combined with ease of use and perceived relevance. There is likely to be duplication of material, but conversely, each service normally adds to the pool of references. Because of duplication and the need to obtain as full a record as possible, choosing to start a search in a database which includes abstracts is often advisable.

Keywords and headings

In printed sources, various arrangements are available, with some sort of alphabetical list of topics being the norm. There may be a constraint on the words used as headings to reduce problems of synonyms, with cross-references ('see' and 'see also') to direct the searcher.

An example of an unusual index is the Geodex Retrieval System used with *Geotechnical Abstracts and Structural Information Service*. Co-ordinate index cards are used to combine terms. Although the sources are in specialised areas they are worthy of mention here because of their now unusual nature and a reminder that there can be, and often are, significant variations between services and forms of service. Another, perhaps more important factor, is the ability to search by classification codes which is possible in Compendex, Inspec and some other databases.

Regardless of the possible use of classification codes, the searching of databases will often involve terminology, and care is needed. Different spellings and use of synonyms are one area of concern, e.g. aluminium/aluminum, and niobium/columbium. Using parts of words can help, as can 'help' pages or tips. One advantage of most databases is the combining of terms by the alternatives of 'and' 'or' and 'not' as in Boolean algebra. 'Not' needs particularly judicious use.

Terminology is a common cause of difficulties, and time should be spent ensuring appropriate keywords are used. Examples can be found in information management (or is it librarianship?). Engineering can be precise in terminology, but problems do arise. One wonders, for example, if two people interested in 'green' issues in engineering would put together identical searches. Perhaps more salutary is to search just one database and its printed alternative and repeat the search, say a week or so later, without reference to the previous search.

Recording

It may be appropriate to keep two sets of records, one of the findings, and the other a log of the search including sources and search strategy.

Most databases have a facility to save bibliographic details electronically or as prints. In some cases, they can be saved in a personal file using special software called personal bibliographic software, or sometimes, personal bibliographic managers. This can be obtained for the purpose or sometimes as an option from the provider. Some software packages may be readily available within an institution as part of a collective or site license.

The common elements of personal bibliographic software are:

- storage of references transferred from databases plus manual input of references, from for example, printed sources
- searching
- inserting and formatting references, to common styles such as MLA, into papers in conjunction with word processing software

There are differences between the various packages as exemplified by three of the major ones, Procite, EndNote and Reference Manager, now being owned by one provider – ISI Research Soft. Seeking advice from colleagues and in-house specialists is advisable particularly on current suitable products. There are useful websites which give guidance, such as users.ox.ac.uk/~ctitext2/service/workshop/bib-overview.html and www.biblio-tech.com/html/pbs_end_rm.html

Keeping a log as a record of the search is advisable, noting sources, search terms/keywords, dates and outcomes (e.g. number of references found). This does not need to be elaborate or take much time but can save effort if or when the need for checking, changes and clarification arises.

Acquisition

Traditionally, the searcher decides which papers need to be read. Some may be to hand, possibly in a local collection. Others can be obtained, often at a charge, by interlibrary loan or through some other document delivery service. A recent trend is for some databases to indicate availability in the subscribing institutions own library. Other databases incorporate a document delivery service which may be provided inclusive of the service subscription or for an extra charge.

Utilising

This can be a complicated activity as details are sorted, sifted, analysed, synthesised and reported together with any research results.

▶ GUIDES TO ABSTRACTING AND INDEXING SERVICES

Electronic

Publist (www.publist.com). Free to search source, which describes itself as a premier online global resource for information about print and electronic publications. It features 'Article Finder' (a free search service and some links).

Ulrichsweb (www.ulrichsweb.com). Electronic version of the established *Ulrich's International Periodicals Directory*. Part registered access, and part free access. Free access includes a listing of abstracting and indexing services. The details are 'refreshed' (updated) every month with a useful box for new abstracting and indexing services.

Jointly administered knowledge environment (jake) (jake.openly. com). This is a co-operative website created by a group of librarians. It has a number of features, and amongst other things it lists the databases which index particular journals.

In addition there are various listings of free databases, some of which are grouped by subject. One excellent list has been produced by Lewis which hopefully will be kept up to date to accommodate changes (Lewis, 2001). It should be noted that the distinction of free is less clear as some 'free' ones may have additional services such as document delivery for which charges apply; also charged services may provide limited free access. The websites of subscription agents may be useful as can the catalogues of large libraries and notable engineering libraries.

Printed

Ulrich's International Periodicals Directory. Bowker, annual with quarterly updates.

Index and Abstract Directory: an International guide to services and serial coverage. 1993. 3rd edition. EBSCO.

Gorman, G. E., and Mills, J. J., 1992. *Guide to current indexing and abstracting services in the third world.* Zell.

Accessing the services

It used to be a simple matter of finding a library with the various printed abstracting and indexing journals required, perusing them, recording relevant details and then going through the process of locating and obtaining the papers to read. Then access to computers at remote locations became possible. Sometimes the computer was situated in a nearby room and made use of a tape, and later a CD-ROM supplied by subscription. Sometimes the computer was part of a host service many miles away and access was shared with others. An intermediary assisted with the search. Then services were offered direct to users with the result that increased use reduced the cost per search. However, the cost to producers remains relatively high, and is reflected by subscription levels. The services can, and in many cases are, being enhanced by various means such as providing the selected documents and bringing groups of services together as a package. Ideally, this guide would indicate prices but this is not possible, and one reason is that it depends on the components of the package in question.

The situation is both flexible and convenient, but has also become complex. Take Inspec, for example, one of the core engineering information services. Inspec is currently available from nine hosts (suppliers) as pay-as-you-go or for an annual subscription from several other service suppliers, including EDINA (www.edina.ac.uk) and Ingenta (BIDS) (www.bids.ac.uk). A recent agreement now makes it available from another core information provider. A typical online host such as STN or Dialog may list over a hundred different databases and offer various added benefits.

In some cases none of this matters, as specialists in the organisation sort out the provision and provide both access and support. The newcomer, however, may be overwhelmed, or the situation can be confusing for an engineer who is used to databases being available in one organisation, discovering that they are not available in a new organisation.

These are situations of concern to all, from the producer to consumer (end user). Attention is being paid to this matter, and hence the availability of free databases and trials for subscription databases. There is another, possibly more important, factor – investment. This is the investment of both time and money. The case for investment is clear in engineering development and design. Critical decisions are made at an early stage in a project, these decisions usually have high cost implications, e.g. features, cost of manufacture route or experiment. Decisions are ideally made on a sound assessment of the available information. When the cost of obtaining and analysing that information is small relative to overall costs, then the investment is productive. This is often the case.

Regarding free databases, Lewis has produced one of several lists accessible via the Internet at: www.library.ucsb.edu/istl/01-winter/internet.html Some are excellent as exemplified by one of the specialised services: *ASCE Civil Engineering Database* (www.pubs.asce.org/cedbsrch.html).

The desirable investment in information exists, and the market is there for the range of appropriate services. The cost of searches using a whole range of sources is small compared to the potential savings from avoiding needless duplication of research and cost implications of decisions in development, design and manufacture. In nearly all cases it makes sense to use a number of services and the sources should be seen as complementary, and not as competing services.

▶ SELECTED ABSTRACTING AND INDEXING SERVICES

General abstracting and indexing services in engineering are covered in this section. More specialised sources are covered in other chapters, though some overlap is both likely and desirable. The services are given in three lists: core, main and a section with the emphasis on printed sources. The classes are not mutually exclusive so again there is some overlap.

Core abstracting and indexing services in engineering

These are some of the core sources for all engineering topics and together with specialised sources for particular engineering disciplines are good starting points. If access is not available, printed versions can be found in many libraries.

Because of the extensive range of services available, it is desirable to have this simple starting point. Researchers new to information seeking in engineering should welcome a selection. Companies looking to subscribe to services should similarly welcome guidance. The criteria are:

- to be an established service (though possibly with a different name and form)
- to have primarily general engineering coverage (at least two major areas and not dominated by the sciences)
- to cross national boundaries (cover publications from at least two countries)
- to be widely used and serve research and operational interests

Four services appear to meet the criteria but there are caveats:

- the four are no more and no less selected than meeting these criteria; a service (general or specific) listed separately can be, and often is, an ideal source

- services complement each other in building up details of a topic of interest
- seekers of engineering information should build up their own selections and keep flexible and aware of changes.

The four services are:

Abstracts in New Technologies and Engineering (ANTE) – (Cambridge Scientific Abstracts). Available with abstracts from 1993, though its origins go back much further as a UK source. It now covers UK and US based journals including some popular widely read ones. This makes it suitable for use with engineering freshers and those of the wider public with technical interests. Practical matters are covered with product reviews on industrial plant. The base is 350 journals, including the following selection which will give a flavour of the range of coverage. A complete list of journals can be found under 'Serials Source List' on the useful factsheet at: www.csa.com/csa/factsheets/ante.shtml

Aerospace International
Aviation Week and Space Technology
Building
Chemistry in Britain
Economist
Engineer
Engineering
Farmers Weekly
Hi-Fi News
Nature

Trial use is available via Cambridge Scientific Abstracts. There is a print version with the same name.

Applied Science and Technology Index/Abstracts/Full Text (ASTI/A). (Wilson). These are three services based on the same list of journals. Their origins are in a printed source called *Industrial Arts Index* 1946–1957, which became the printed *Applied Science and Technology Index* in 1958, with the database version available from 1983, and with the abstracts service introduced in 1993 and subsequently the full text service. The three services (four, if the print version of the *Index* is included) are US based, with subject and geographical coverage generally broader than ANTE. A list of the 574 journals (including non-current) covered as at April 2003 with dates is available at: vnweb.hwwilsonweb.com/hww/Journals/ The following is a selection to indicate some of the coverage of engineering:

ASHRAE Journal
Electronics World
Experimental Mechanics
Information and Management
Journal of Aeronautical Sciences

Compendex (Elsevier Engineering Information). 1970–. A large database with six million abstracts across engineering. It includes engineering management and is a useful starting point for many researchers and others. It developed from the printed version *Engineering Index* and is now one of a range of products from this producer and supplier. Other products include *Engineering Village 2* through which *Inspec* is now also available.

Inspec (Institution of Electrical Engineers). 1969– . A major database covering physics, electrotechnology (electronics and electrical engineering) and both computer science and control, produced by Inspec; the service and principal product having the same name. Obviously a good choice in the fields of coverage and for researchers in these and associated areas. Related services include the three abstracting journals (*Physics Abstracts*; *Electrical and Electronics Abstracts*; *Computer and Control Abstracts*) which make up the printed version of Inspec. The printed versions started much earlier than the database. Inspec is currently considering digitizing the earlier records. There is also a document delivery service; a full text service to the Institution's own journals and those of the Institute of Electrical and Electronic Engineers called *IEL* (IEEE/IEE Electronic Library). These journals are typical of Inspec coverage and it is worth pointing out the ability to search for software in this service. More details can be found at: www.iee.org/Publish/Inspec/ProdCat/index.cfm A Vendors Table is available and a useful means of perusing the twenty-four suppliers of Inspec services.

Abstracting and indexing services for engineering (databases and printed)

The following list is wide ranging and includes:

- some aggregated services
- comprehensive and multidisciplinary services
- science and combined science and technology services
- other areas of interest to engineers
- free services including some specialist ones
- national services
- some services for formats such as books

This section excludes publishers' databases which are listed separately. It is a developing area with changes and additional services, notably document delivery.

NOTES: Where two names are given together (*Abc Service/Ab Index*), the first is the name of the database version followed by the name of the printed version where this is different. In most cases, the emphasis is on the database versions which are often the preferred choice. The subsequent list addresses printed sources in more detail to redress any imbalance.

Details are very brief for services directed at fringe areas, but fuller details can be found at the indicated websites.

ABI Inform Global (American Business Institute). This is one of a number of databases covering management interests, any of which can usefully supplement searches for topics in engineering management. Some services may be available within the organisation e.g. a university. If not, pay-as-you access may be useful. *ABI Inform* is available in various forms, one of which is *Global* ... More details can be found at: www. umi.com

ACM Digital Library (Association for Computing Machinery). Includes bibliographic information, abstracts, reviews and full texts. ACM produced *ACM [Electronic] Guide to Computing Literature* in both digital and non-digital format which may now be encompassed in the Digital Library. Details at: www.acm.org

Agricultural Engineering Abstracts (Commonwealth Agricultural Bureau). Included here, because from a user's perspective the concern is periphery areas. It is one that serves the engineering interest, others for agriculture can be traced using *Publist*, *UlrichsWeb* and other guides.

AMR Journal Article Abstracts Database (American Society of Mechanical Engineers). 1989–. This is a companion service to established *Applied Mechanics Reviews* (see Chapter 10). The database covers 500 plus international journals in the engineering sciences with over 250,000 items. More details at: www.asme.org/pubs/amr/database.html

ArticleFinder. A large database from Infotrieve of twenty million references with ten million abstracts of scientific, technical, medical and other scholarly content. Details at: www.infotrieve.com/search/databases/newsearch.asp

BIOSIS Previews/Biological Abstracts (BIOSIS). An established major international service for the life sciences with some secondary products. It uses a unique indexing system and it is worth familiarising oneself with it. Details at: www.biosis.org

Chemical Abstracts (American Chemical Society). 1907–. Available as a database from 1967 with an additional database called *CAOLD* for the period 1907 to 1966 thereby completing the coverage. The coverage is extensive and more a case of anything of interest to chemists rather than just chemistry. The publishers claim 35% of its content is relevant to engineering with good coverage on materials, particularly plastics. Some coverage may not initially be obvious, such as water supply and building materials. The abstracts are informative. The printed version is relatively easy to use and benefits from five year indexes and the earlier ten year indexes.

ENGINE – Australian Engineering Database (RMIT Publishing). 1980–. Produced by the Institution of Engineers Australia, this is one of a number of databases from RMIT. Details at: www.rmitpublishing.com.au This website includes a list of journals, one of which is *Engineering*

Neighbours which might amuse those familiar with a certain Australian television 'soap' and is useful to anyone interested in the activities of the Indonesia/Australia Engineer Enhancement Program for which this is their newsletter.

Embase/Excerpta Medica. A large database covering medicine, including pharmacology, and linked to Medline. An established printed form. Details at: www.embase.com

Energy Citations Database (U.S. Department of Energy (DOE): Office of Scientific and Technical Information (OSTI)). 1948–. A freely available database for energy and energy-related scientific and technical information.

Fluidex (Elsevier Science). 1974–. Covers fluid engineering and contains about 410,000 records. More details at: www.info.sciencedirect. com/content_coverage/databases/fluidex.shtml

General Science Abstracts/General Science Index (Wilson). 1984–. These two cover science, as indicated in their titles. Engineering is covered more specifically in a companion pair of services *Applied Science and Technology Abstracts/ . . . Index*. Included here partly because of their coverage of computers.

History of Science and Technology (Research Libraries Group-Eureka). 1975–. An alternative title appears to be *History of Science, Technology and Medicine*. It is actually a database of three bibliographies updated annually. More details at: www.rlg.org/cit-hst.html and in Chapter 10 on Bibliographies and Reviews.

Japan Engineering Abstracts (Engineering Society of Japan).

Japanese Journal of Engineering: Abstracts. 1922–.

Medline/Index Medicus (US National Library of Medicine). Covers 4,500 biomedical journals. There are associated sources detailed at: www.nlm.nih.gov/hinfo.html

Pascal/Bibliographie Internationale (Inist-CNRS: Institut de l'Information Scientifique et Technique – Centre National de la Recherche Scientifique). 1973–. The Pascal database has 14.7 million references from 6,000 international titles. Although international, significant attention is given to French and European scientific and technical literature. More than 50% is biological and medical sciences. Analysis by field shows 17% of references are in engineering (metallurgy may be separate) and linguistic analysis shows 76% of references are in English, 9% French, 6% Russian and 5% German. Searching by keywords can be in French, English, Spanish or all three languages. There is access via the CNRS portal (gateway). Details are available at: www.inist.fr/PRODUITS/ pascal.php

Polymer Library formerly *RAPRA Abstracts* (Rapra Technology). 1972–. Produced from, and available in, computerised form from 1972. Coverage includes rubber, plastics and some associated materials such as adhesives. More details at: www.csa.cm/csa/factsheets/rapra.shtml

[Bibliographie Internationale] formerly *Bulletin Signalétique,* is the printed version from which *Pascal* (see above) was developed.

Referativnyi Zhurnal (All-Russian Institute of Scientific and Technical Information of Russian Academy of Sciences – VINITI). Published in printed form since 1952 in Russian, in over thirty subject-based sections with variations between levels of coverage. Database version introduced in 1981. More details can be found in English at: www.viniti.ru/welcome.html An added 'r' to make welcomer will give the Russian language version.

SCI Expanded (Science Citation Index) – (Thomson/ISI). c1980–. In spite of its origins as a citation index this can be searched by keyword. It has an advantage in being a large database which covers engineering as well as science. It covers 5,900 scholarly journals and emphasises its value in research. In practice, it has proved useful in a wide variety of searches including difficult and generally unproductive ones. It is part of the whole range of products called *ISI Web of Knowledge* which includes access to some other services such as methods of managing references. Further details and a list of journals can be found at: www.isinet.com/isi/

Scirus (Elsevier Science). This is a free science-specific search engine which targets sites such as university websites and author homepages and filters out non-scientific sites. Available at: www.scirus.com

TEMA (Technology and Management) – (FIZ Technik) 1990–. This is a bibliographic database with abstracts covering German and international literature (technical journals, conference papers, research reports, books and theses) in German and English. Information can be found at: www.stn-international.de/stndatabases/databases/tema.html

Printed

The areas in which *printed* abstracting and indexing services are particularly suitable include:

- *comprehensive* searches with a mix of printed and electronic sources
- for *early* work which is mainly prior to the 1970's
- when there is *uncertainty,* and *browsing* is an advantage
- as a *preferred* or the *only* option

Abstracts of New Technologies and Engineering (ANTE). Produced 1962–1980 as *British Technology Index,* then changed its name to *Current Technology Index* and in 1997 as its current title with a database version called ANTE Plus. Strong UK coverage including product reviews, particularly of industrial plant and vehicles. Good choice for starter service for students.

Applied Science and Technology Index. Produced 1946–1957 as *Industrial Arts Index* and as the current title from 1958. Strong US coverage and a broad subject area. Database options available from 1983. There is also a print version which started under a different name in 1946. The layout and indexing is typical of H W Wilson, the producer, and is easy to use within the constraints of terminology common to all abstracting and indexing services.

ASCE Publications Abstracts. Produced 1966–. Renamed *ASCE Publications Information* in 1983. Included here because it precedes the freely available CEDB database version which covers from 1970 onwards. It has broader coverage than is suggested by the title.

ASM Review of Metal Literature. Produced from about 1940 and merged with *Metallurgical Abstracts* to become part of *Metals Abstracts* in 1972 (listed separately). Although not much used now and held by few libraries, it was at one time a key source.

Bibliographie Internationale. Earliest sections produced from 1940 originally as *Bulletin Signalétique* until 1983 when it changed to its current name, and is the comprehensive French language service published monthly by the Centre National de la Recherché Scientifique in Nancy. It has sixty-five sections. The database version is called *Pascal* and has been available since 1973 with a reported 17% of content relevant to engineering.

Chemical Abstracts. 1907–. The publishers claim 35% of its content is relevant to engineering with good coverage on materials, particularly plastics. Some coverage may not initially be obvious, such as water supply and building materials. The printed indexes usually make searching quick, even over a number of years, and has useful items such as five year printed indexes and the earlier ten year indexes. There is a two-part database version.

Computer and Control Abstracts. 1966–. Originally called *Control Abstracts* and introduced as *Science Abstracts part C,* it changed to its current name in 1968. It is relevant to many engineers because of the wide interest in computers and control. Inspec are the producers and it is available as part of the Inspec database since 1966.

Electrical and Electronics Abstracts. Produced since 1898 originally under a slightly different title and for most of the period as *Science Abstracts part B.* It subsequently led to the Inspec services, and has been available as part of that database since 1966.

Engineer and *Engineering.* These are not abstracting or indexing services, but rather are two journals. They have annual indexes and cover major engineering developments from about the mid-nineteenth Century, thus extending further back than the early abstracting and indexing services. They are very useful for the history of engineering, with well-crafted articles and good illustrations.

Engineering Index. Produced since 1884 and claims to be the world's first choice for engineering. Since 1970 it has been available as a database called *Ei Compendex.* More recently the producers have broadened their services with *Ei Village.*

Fifty Year Index to ASTM Technical Paper and Reports. Covers from 1898 to 1950 and then supplemented by *Five Year Index*/es. This is a specialist index which can identify useful papers in areas such as testing and materials.

International Aerospace Abstracts. Established printed service now available as *Aerospace Database,* which also includes an electronic version of *Scientific and Technical Aerospace Reports* from 1962. Coverage extends beyond aerospace to include fields such fuels and metals.

Japanese Journal of Engineering Abstracts: Abstracts. 1922–.

Metals Abstracts. Formed in 1968 by merging *ASM Review of Metal Literature* from the USA, and *Metallurgical Abstracts* in the UK. The computerised version is called Metadex.

Rapra Abstracts. Established service for rubber and plastics, now available as the database *Polymer Library.*

Referativnyi Zhurnal. Published by the All-Union Institute of Scientific and Technical Information (VINITI) in Moscow, and is a large extensive service. There are over thirty sections relating to engineering, and some sections are more comprehensive than others.

Science Citation Index. This was the forerunner of the computerised version, and initially produced with an emphasis on science and linking citations. There are five-year printed indexes which are useful for early searches.

▶ AGGREGATED SERVICES AND MAJOR PROVIDERS

Academic Press/IDEAL (Academic Press). 1996–. This covered the publisher's science journals. From 2003 it is integrated into Elsevier ScienceDirect.

ACM Digital Library (Association for Computing Machinery). This is a service to members of the Association. Details at: www.acm.org/dl/

Cambridge Scientific Abstracts (CSA). More than fifty databases are available via their Internet Database Service (IDS) and those listed under engineering are: ANTE, Aerospace and High Technology Abstracts, Civil Engineering Abstracts, Environmental Engineering Abstracts, Engineering Materials Abstracts (including the three constituent parts), Mechanical Engineering Abstracts, NTIS, Polymer Library. Additional databases of possible interest are included under other headings such materials science. More details at: www.csa.com

Cambridge University Press Journals Online (CUP). A publisher's service with details at: www.journals.cup.org

Canadian Institute for Scientific and Technical Information (NRC-CISTI). Part of the National Research Council Canada, and provides three databases (articles, journals and a catalogue). Services include Table of

Contents, current awareness and document delivery. Sources include fifteen million articles, from 17,000 journals in all subject areas, almost two thirds of which are in science, technology and medicine. Sourced world-wide and from nearly every country from Argentina to Zimbabwe, and in most languages from Afrikaans to Swedish. Details at: cisti-icist.nrc-cnrc.gc.ca/cisti_e.shtml

Dialog. This is one of a number of online service providers to organisations. Available databases include Ei Compendex and Inspec. Details at: www.dialog.com

Elsevier ScienceDirect (sometimes referred to as Reed Elsevier Science Direct or just ScienceDirect). This service, from a publisher, lists four databases under engineering, namely: Ei Compendex, Fluidex, Inspec and Oceanbase (for marine science and technology). Other services are available, more details can be found at: www.sciencedirect.com/databases/index.shtml

Engineering and Applied Science (RMIT Publishing). 1936–. A compilation of ten Australian databases in collaboration with data providers. Released via SilverPlatter. Details at: www.rmitpublishing.com.au

Engineering Village 2 (Elsevier Engineering Information). Includes access to Compendex, Inspec and the two combined plus some specialised sources. The combined search is convenient, and includes elimination of duplicated references. Check UK and US spelling. Details at: www.engineeringvillage2.org

FIZ Karlsruhe (Fachinformationszentrum – FIZ). This is the STN Service Centre for Europe and offers access to more than 200 databases in science and technology. Details at: www.fiz-karlsruhe.de/about_fiz/aboutfiz.html See also STN in this list.

Infotrieve. This has search and document delivery services including *ArticleFinder*, which indexes over 30,000 journals, a table of contents service, and Ariel (a document delivery service). More details at: www.infotrieve.com

Institute for Scientific Information (ISI). Produces a range of products including databases and printed equivalents. Notable service is *Web of Science* which gives access to *Science Citation Index* amongst others. Also provides some software for managing references. Further details at: www.isinet.com/isi

Kluwer Online. This publisher provides access to over 650 of its journals including those in science, technology, humanities and law. Also, there are databases for reference works and books. One of these provides delivery of self-selected chapters of e-books. Details at: www.kluweronline.com

Networked Computer Science Technical Reference Library. 1976–. This is a collaboration of several organisations in the USA. More details at: www.ncstrl.org

OCLC FirstSearch. Founded in 1967 as a co-operative venture and now serves over 43,000 libraries in eighty-six countries. It provides access to seventy-six databases, both general and specific. These include ABI Inform, ASTA, ASTI, OCLC ArticleFirst, Basic BIOSIS, GSA, GSI, Inspec, Medline, WorldCat. Some are exclusive to OCLC FirstSearch. More details at: www.oclc.org/firstsearch/

Ovid. A range of services mostly for science and medicine. Includes a database of journals, some of which are technical. Details at: www.ovid.com

PubSCIENCE. This fairly well known database has been discontinued from November 2002.

Research Index – also known as *CiteSeer.* (NEC Research Institute). Mostly covers computer science. Details at: citeseer.nj.nec.com

RMIT Publishing. Based in Australia, providing a search and retrieval interface called *Infomit.* Details at: www.remitpublishing.com.au

SilverPlatter. Joined with Ovid in 2001 to become a single company.

STN International (Operated jointly by FIZ, Chemical Abstracts Service and Japan Science and Technology Corporation). Details at: www.stn-international.de The site lists 200 databases, including many relevant to particular areas of engineering.

▶ TRENDS AND CHANGE

The current situation is complex and subject to change, however, the result is a wide range of choice and flexibility. It is perhaps advisable for engineers to consult information specialists and librarians for advice on services. Many libraries, particularly in universities, maintain websites which can be consulted. For librarians, links with colleagues, service providers, conferences and discussion groups can all help.

The major engineering gateways are a useful source of information about online databases and one, EEVL, the Internet guide to Engineering, Mathematics and Computing (www.eevl.ac.uk) includes details of numerous databases and also provides free access to one specialised service *RAM (Recent Advances in Manufacturing).* These gateways are dealt with elsewhere in this book.

▶ REFERENCES

Jensen, K. L., 2001. Providing access to online government documents in an academic research library collection: a case study in the geosciences. *Science and Technology Libraries,* 20(2/3), pp. 15–25; and in: Schlembach, M. C., and Misco, W. H., eds., 2001. *Electronic resources and services in sci-tech libraries.* New York: Haworth, pp. 15–25.

Lewis, S., 2001. Science and technology sources on the internet. There is such a thing as a free lunch: freely accessible databases for the public. *Issues in Science and Technology Librarianship*, Winter (www.library.ucsb.edu/istl/01-winter/internet.html).

Wiggins, G., 1998. Chemistry on the internet. *Journal of Chemical Information and Computer Sciences*, 38(60), p.960.

10 Bibliographies and Reviews

Bob Rhodes

Bibliographies and reviews can help to save a lot of time and effort when searching for information, and can also prove useful when evaluating material. In addition, reviews also save effort in reading, analysing and synthesising information.

A bibliography is a listing of publications with a common feature, an example being the publications of a particular area, such as a country or subject. A bibliography may be annotated with an indication of content added to the basic (bibliographical) details of the publications. It may be a cumulative bibliography with the original being supplemented to extend it to include recent items. The result can be similar in content to an abstracting or indexing service. A bibliography may be published as a book, part of a book or in other forms such as a report. Catalogues, notably those of national libraries, have some elements in common with bibliographies and therefore also need brief consideration.

A review is a published paper or document which collects together the essence of papers on a subject, and provides a convenient digest of that subject. The author of a review is typically a specialist in that subject area and will have obtained and read all, or most, of the publications. This bringing together of the detail of the subject in an ordered and analytical fashion is valuable. Of importance are the credentials of the author, for a review is more than a mere listing. Ideally, a review will be carried out in conjunction with, or evaluation by, peers. References to documents (e.g. papers, books and reports) are provided and there might also be a bibliography or guide to further reading. Some of the variants include book reviews, product reviews and reviews of practices and techniques. Although not generally viewed as reviews, it is also worth considering engineering handbooks and yearbooks, as their contents can provide a useful digest of key areas.

Traditionally, the bulk of bibliographies and reviews cover particular themes. In many fields their role is fairly well established, but this is not necessarily the case in engineering.

Taking a pessimistic view, it might be said that 'engineers don't look for bibliographies and reviews because they don't exist; when they do they don't find them, and when they do find them, the publications are out of date or of little value'. There is an alternative and more optimistic view that they can be readily found using some key sources such as *Compendex* and *Inspec*. Whatever view is taken, the overall picture is complex and unpredictable.

▶ A BASIC APPROACH

The complexity is in the detail and the variables. A starting point in a literature search is to take a simplified approach that may apply in the majority of cases. A simple approach is to ignore bibliographies and reviews when searching, but with exceptions:

1. To note and make early use of them during searching. A number of abstracting and indexing services indicate items that are bibliographies or contain bibliographies. Similarly, some also indicate reviews.
2. If a search is producing an overwhelming amount of material, to make a deliberate search for bibliographies and reviews. Some sources use slight variations of the two terms. One indexes them as literature reviews, which is a more precise phrase and distinguishes them from product reviews. In some cases, there is a special field that allows the searcher to specifically select bibliographies and/or reviews.

Rather than exceptions, there are options when searches might use 'bibliography' and/or 'review' as a search term.

3. For problem searches, particularly where it is difficult to use well defined specific terms. An added option is to use a broader term with the field.
4. For browsing. Later in this chapter, review journals are considered separately to reviews.

▶ ADDITIONAL FACTORS

It is difficult to provide clear guidance beyond the basic practice. Complexity comes from the variables, which makes each case different. Given the limitations of generalisation, a look at some additional factors can help, in particular cases, to improve search results. These might include:

*   preparation of a bibliography or review
*   building special collections

- high potential value searches
- problem searches, notably terminology difficulties at the specific level
- subject areas with ample easy-to-find bibliographies and/or reviews
- as a wide ranging current awareness source

Researchers

Not all researchers are the same. Those seeking bibliographies and reviews at an early stage in the information retrieval process are the exception rather than the rule, and then only in selected cases. Such researchers tend to be information professionals, engineering writers and certain research engineers. Apart from engineers involved in research activities, others are concerned with development, design, construction and manufacture and have varied needs. There is recent evidence from Needham in a report on grey literature (i.e. technical reports) that, for engineers, accessibility is a factor and also that formal sources are used reluctantly (Needham, 2002). Though prior to accessibility, the matter of availability is a concern.

Not all researchers looking for engineering information will be engineers. Potential users might also include scientists, economists, managers, historians and writers. Some will have greater expectations of bibliographies and reviews.

Availability

There appear to be few bibliographies of wide general engineering interest. Lord lists twenty-nine in his guide to engineering information sources, which is less than 2% of the 1639 sources mentioned in the book (Lord, 2000). Of these, some are guides to literature, including an earlier edition of this book, and a number of others deal with computer science and topics of a cross-disciplinary nature.

The situation is similar for reviews. An authoritative source, *Ulrichweb/Ulrich's International Periodicals Directory*, includes just two review journals listed as general engineering.

Most bibliographies and reviews cover specific topics, and here the need is to match the topic to the interest of the searcher. The degree of match is important and so is the likelihood of a match. This tends to be patchy even on the unlikely assumption that sources for finding them are consistent. Some areas of interest, such as computer science, are relatively well served with bibliographies and reviews. However, there seems to be an overall impression that for many areas of interest there is not a matching bibliography or review. In contrast, scanning through a number of reviews will reveal interesting and potentially useful items.

Accessibility

Given the apparent scarcity of engineering bibliographies and reviews contrasted with the saving of time and effort, there is a need for easy, convenient and reliable strategies for finding those that do exist. Sources include:

- dedicated sources such as *Applied Mechanics Reviews* and *Index of Scientific Reviews*
- review journals
- catalogues, national bibliographies and booklists
- abstracting and indexing services
- search engines such as *Google*
- publishers' sources and services
- engineering gateways or electronic libraries such as *EEVL*, the Internet guide to engineering, mathematics and computing.

In total, this is a significant number of sources, and each might reveal further sources, rather than just bibliographies or reviews. Continuing the search would seem sensible but the net effect might be a case of diminishing returns. On the other hand, as is so often the case in information seeking, a bit more is often found with each step, and critical pieces of information can be located at any point. Judgement, care and potential value need balancing against each other.

Selection of sources is easier in some disciplines other than engineering. In science, for example, a chemist might use *Chemical Abstracts*, *Index to Scientific Reviews* and possibly one or two review journals or a search engine. For a civil engineer, however, the potential list is likely to be longer and dependant on specific interests, and be irrespective of the quality services at his or her disposal.

A suitable starting point is to ensure that basic document types are covered, including books, papers and reports. The core abstracting and indexing services are candidates for inclusion, as are specialised services, providing that bibliographies, reviews or both are indexed or indicated. Searching an unproductive source usually takes little time, though care has to be taken that the search is carried out diligently.

A key feature of a number of abstracting and indexing services is the ability to readily identify bibliographies, reviews or both, by treatment or keywords during a search. The searcher can then modify a search if appropriate and assign additional value to these items.

► SELECTED SOURCES FOR FINDING BIBLIOGRAPHIES AND REVIEWS

Here the concern is mostly with locating bibliographies and reviews on particular subjects. Product reviews and review journals are listed separately.

There is also very little in the way of evaluation because what is useful for one person researching a particular subject in a particular set of circumstances may well be irrelevant to another in a different situation. It may be said that *Compendex* and *Inspec,* amongst others, are consistently useful sources for subject reviews provided the material exists. On occasions some other sources will match and possibly surpass them.

It is worth a reminder that both bibliographies and reviews may be published in different forms, including books, and papers in journals and reports. Some of the sources are selective in their coverage.

In some of the details on sources, numbers of items found using basic keywords are given. These are to be taken only as an indication of their content because some bibliographies and reviews will not have 'engineering' as a keyword as they will be on specific topics such as aeronautics and corrosion. In addition, numbers may change over even a short period of a few days.

Abstracts in New Technology and Engineering – (ANTE) (Cambridge Scientific Abstracts). 1981– with abstracts from 1993. Available as a database and also in print. Previously *Current Technology Database/Index.* Good coverage of product reviews including industrial equipment, construction plant and specific models of cars/automobiles. A useful fact sheet is available from Cambridge Scientific Abstracts at: www.csa.com/csa/factsheets/ante.shtml

ACM Digital Library (Association for Computing Machinery). This comprises:

> *ACM Guide* (a database)
> *ACM Digital Library* (full text of ACM publications)
> *Online Computing Reviews Service*

There is an emphasis on computer science. This is available through the portal: portal.acm.org/portal.cfm. The portal also gives access to the *Online Computing Review Service.*

Aerospace and High Technology Database (Cambridge Scientific Abstracts). 1962–. Database version of *International Aerospace Abstracts* (IAA) and *Scientific and Technical Aerospace Reports* (STAR) for 1986 to 1993. Apart from the obvious coverage it extends to mechanical engineering and mathematical and computer sciences, amongst other areas. 'Bibliographies' is used as an index term. Useful fact sheet available from Cambridge Scientific Abstracts at: www.csa.com/csa/factsheets/aerospace.shtml

Amazon. One of a number of internet based booksellers. Amazon has a large range of stock and there are various country-specific versions. The UK site at: www.amazon.co.uk lists about 150 books as engineering bibliography. As they are available for sale, most ought to be reasonably up to date.

Applied Mechanics Reviews (American Society of Mechanical Engineers – ASME). (www.asme.org/pubs/amr/). Established printed source of reviews, and now available via the website. This website also includes

AMR Abstracts Database. Some indication of coverage is shown in the classification scheme used, which includes the following headings: dynamic and vibration, automatic control, mechanics of solids and fluids, heat transfer, earth sciences, energy and environment, and bioengineering.

Applied Science and Technology Full Text/Abstracts/Index (Wilson). This is a group of related databases with their origins in *Applied Science and Technology Index,* the original printed version, which is still available in print form as well as on Wilson Web (www.hwwilson.com) and WilsonDisc. There is good coverage across engineering. It can be useful and easy to use for searches where there is a geographical factor, such as, for example, water resources in Mexico. More details at: www.hwwilson.com/databases/applieds.htm

ArticleFirst (OCLC FirstSearch). 1990–. Details available at: www.oclc.org/home/ and then select 'Librarian's Toolbox'. This source covers papers and is a good partner for *WorldCat,* which covers books and is from the same supplier. It is also a large database which is often an advantage when searching for bibliographies and reviews. It has over 14.3 million references from 12,118 journal titles (March 2003), but it should be noted that it is multi-disciplinary, and so engineering interests are a fraction of the whole. The website includes a list of journals from which the following review journals have been taken:

- *Advances in Cement Research*
- *Advances in Electrochemical Science and Engineering*
- *Advances in Engineering Software*
- *Advances in Heat Transfer*
- *Advances in Nuclear Science and Technology*
- *Advances in Solar Energy*
- *Advances in Water Resources*

ASCE Annual Combined Index (American Society of Civil Engineers). For civil engineering and related subjects, closely related to *ASCE Database* which is freely available via the Web (see below). The latter is probably the preferred option, but it does list bibliographies and reviews, and indicates under subject terms any reviews.

ASCE Database (American Society of Civil Engineers). 1970–. Access at: www.pubs.asce.org/cedbsrch.html. This is a valued source for civil engineering and related topics, and all the more appreciated for being freely available. As of February 2003, it listed sixty-eight bibliographies such as 'Teaching hydraulic design', and book reviews is a designated document type with 265 listed, e.g. Bridge scour.

BiblioAlerts. (www.biblioalerts.com) This is a service provided by Cambridge Scientific Abstracts in association with a number of partners. It describes itself as a source for customised technical information. For elaboration, details are on the website. There is a searchable section on engineering.

Bibliographic Index (Wilson). Monthly print source with some items under engineering topics. A database version, the Bibliographic Index Plus, is available, which contains details of over 350,000 bibliographies and the full text of nearly 100,000 bibliographies. The coverage includes a significant number of languages. A dedicated database which is frequently updated will be welcome and should encourage more frequent searching for bibliographies. Details at: www.hwwilson.com/databases/biblio.cfmn

Bibliographies on the Web. This is the title of a paper in the journal *Civil Engineering*, May 1998, pp. 23–24. Web sources like this do appear occasionally in journals and might not be readily traceable. This one was found using *ASCE Combined Index*.

BIOSIS Previews/Biological Abstracts (Biosis). A life sciences source available in both database and print versions. Bibliographies and literature reviews can be sought. More details at: www.biosis.org

Biotechnology and Bioengineering Abstracts (Cambridge Scientific Abstracts). 1982–. Detailed fact sheet available from Cambridge Scientific Abstracts, at: www.csa.com/csa/factsheets/ante.shtml

British Library Public Catalogue. (blpc.bl.uk). This is a free access catalogue of a national (deposit) library. Bibliographies and reviews linked to engineering can be found. When these are limited to recent years, the number of items is very small. The Current Serials File (www.bl.uk/catalogues/serials.html) catalogue can be used to find 'review' within journal title search, which requires keywords in the language of the title. Using *Copac* (see below) instead makes sense as it includes the British Library Catalogue as well as other catalogues.

Chemical Abstracts (Chemical Abstracts Service, a division of the American Chemical Society). Available as a database and also in print. In the printed General Subject Index, there is a Heading 'Literature – bibliographies'. Under subject terms an indicator 'R' prefix to the abstract number indicates a review; prefix 'B' is for books, not bibliography. Given the title it might be thought to include limited engineering coverage, which to some extent is so, although coverage of industrial chemistry is good. It can be very useful for a wide range of topics – one example is 'Aircraft engines'. Not a source to be readily by-passed. More details at: www.cas.org

Clover Information Index. A smaller service in printed form which covers journals of interest to the technically minded. Included here because it can provide details of product reviews of domestic interest, such as cars, computers, and so-called 'white goods'. Engineering interest is mainly limited to engineering design of domestic products.

Collection of Computer Science Bibliographies (University of Karlsruhe). (liinwww.ira.uka.de/bibliography/index.html) For details of, and access to, approximately 1,400 bibliographies and 1.2 million references in computer science, with mirror sites around the world. This makes it a useful site in this field.

Compendex (Engineering Information Inc.). Database version of *Engineering Index* with details on the Engineering Village website at: www.engineeringvillage2.org Being both a major service, and extending across engineering, including engineering management, makes this a key site. One of the treatment codes (TC) is 'General review'.

Computing Reviews (Association for Computing Machinery – ACM). Details at: www.reviews.com/home.cfm This source gives reviews of books, articles and other forms of publication, on computing and related topics.

Copac (copac.ac.uk/copac/). This is a union catalogue of large university libraries in the UK, plus the British Library. Bibliography and review can be used as keywords. 'Bibliography' and 'engineering' gave 601 items and 'review' and 'engineering' gave 836 items in March 2003.

Cumulative Book Index (Wilson). This is a printed source, published monthly by H.W. Wilson that ceased publication in October 2000 after 101 years of existence. It may still be useful for those interested in the history of engineering.

Current Technology Index. Superseded in 1996 by *Abstracts of New Technologies and Engineering*. The keyword 'bibliographies' is used in the subject index but 'reviews' is not. In the main listing, useful product reviews can be found.

Electrical and Electronics Abstracts (Institution of Electrical Engineers). Now part of the *Inspec* database. In the print version, some bibliographies are listed under that heading. Reviews are indicated under subject headings.

Engineering Index. Ei is the print version of *Compendex*. There is a heading for 'bibliographies' in the subject index but not one for 'reviews'.

Findarticles (LookSmart and Gale Group). 1998–. Details and access at: www.findarticles.com A free service which includes details of some bibliographies.

General Science Index (GenSciIndex) (H.W. Wilson, and available via OCLC Firstsearch). As the name suggests, this focuses mostly on science. Coverage includes US and UK sources. More details at: www.oclc.org/firstsearch/databases/

Global Books in Print (Bowker). (www.globalbooksinprint.com). This is a subscription service listing of English language books available through booksellers.

IEEE Publications Online – IEEE Xplore (Institute of Electrical and Electronics Engineers). 1988–. Full-text access to IEEE Transactions and journals. Details at: ieeexplore.ieee.org/Xplore/DynWel.jsp

Index to Scientific Reviews (Institute for Scientific Information – ISI). Details at: www.isinet.com/isi/products/indexproducts/scientificreviews/ Subject coverage is similar to the more familiar *Science Citation Index* and extends into engineering. The material included is from more than 200 review journals and over 2,600 primary journals.

Ingenta. This is both a service and a supplier. The *Ingenta* database indexes over 27,000 academic and professional publications. Test searches produce an interesting mix of results. Details of the service are at: www.ingenta.com

Inspec (Institution of Electrical Engineers). This is a core abstracting and indexing service from which bibliographies and reviews can be found. Strengths in physics, electrical engineering, electronics, computers, control and associated areas. Details at: www.iee.org/Publish/INSPEC

International Aerospace Abstracts/ STAR. Two closely related print sources. Bibliographies are listed. Worth looking under the heading 'reviewing' for reviews. The database version is called *Aerospace and High Technology Database.*

International Catalogue of Scientific Literature. 1901–1914. Rather a specialised printed source in the context of this chapter. May be useful for the history of science and technology.

International Scientific and Technical Proceedings – ISTP (Institute for Scientific Information – ISI). Indexes conference papers in journal and book literature with abstracts. It is available in several delivery options including on-line via DIMDI from 1978. Details at: www.isinet.com/isi/products/indexproducts/istp Note that this has the same publisher as the *Index to Scientific Reviews.*

Library of Congress: On-line Catalog. A database of 110 million items, mostly books. Details and access at: catalog.loc.gov

Mathematical Reviews/Mathematical Reviews Database (American Mathematical Society). 1940–. Available as both a printed abstracting service and a database (www. ams.org/mr-database) with good coverage of reviews. Includes some engineering science topics, such as fluid mechanics.

Metadex/Metals Abstracts and *Alloys Index.* 1966–. Bibliographies do not appear to be listed but reviews are, and are also indicated under subjects. As the names suggests, this source covers various aspects of materials including both their production and use. There is a useful guide from a supplier at: www.csa.com/csa/factsheets/metadex.shtml

NTIS. 1990–. This is essentially a US Government reports database. Details and access at: www.ntis.gov

Physics Abstracts. See *Inspec*, of which this a part.

Polymer Library/RAPRA Abstracts Database (Rubber and Plastics Research Association – RAPRA). This is traditionally called *RAPRA Abstracts* and started as a printed source, but is now also known as *Polymer Library.* This is a useful established source for information on the rubber, plastics and polymer industries. Details at: abstracts.rapra.net/abs/absmaine.htm

Royal Society of London. Catalogue of Scientific Papers 1800–1900 (Royal Society). A printed source which is useful for historical research. There is a subject index, volume II of which is Mechanics and covers engineering science.

Science and Technology Aerospace Reports – *STAR*. Similar to *International Aerospace Abstracts* with which it is now combined in the *Aerospace and High Technology Database* – see under this title above.

Science Citation Index – *SCI* (Institute for Scientific Information – ISI). This is a large database for science and technology from the same publisher as *Index to Scientific Reviews*. It is available via a number of delivery options. Some backfiles start in 1945. In addition to conventional keyword searching it allows cited reference searching. This can be a useful facility in cases where an early bibliography or review is known and the searcher wishes to find references which cite it. Details at: www.isinet.com/isi/products/citation/sci

Swetscan (Swets and Zeitlinger). This is a 'table of contents' service from a library supplier and information provider, covering 14,000 journals in all disciplines world-wide. Details at: www.swetsblackwell.com/custss-about.htm

Web of Science (Institute for Scientific Information – ISI). This is part of *Web of Knowledge* and part of a range of products and services available from this supplier, some of which are included in this list. Details at: www.isinet.com/isi/

World Bibliography of Bibliographies (Societas Bibliographica). A traditional library reference source but only a small percentage of the bibliographies listed cover engineering, and there is nothing recent in this print source.

WorldCat (available via the subscription service OCLC FirstSearch). This lists some 48 million items. Essentially a very large collective (union) catalogue. Complements other FirstSearch sources such as *ArticleFirst*. Details at: www.oclc.org.worldcat

NOTES. Additional sources can be readily found by using search engines such as *Google* (www.google.com) to locate catalogues of national libraries and a variety of libraries of professional engineering institutions and research bodies, though in many cases their services are primarily for members. Many academic libraries provide guides for various subjects including engineering and its constituent disciplines. Just one example of many is the University of Delft in the Netherlands at: www.library.tudelft.nl/eng/resources/ As the situation is subject to change it is worth checking the date of the last amendment.

Virtual libraries, gateways and any other Web based access points are useful. Powell has described features and services of some of them (Powell, 2001).

Book reviews have been excluded as being an aspect more appropriately covered in texts on collection building.

▶ SELECTED REVIEW JOURNALS AND SERIES

Finding review journals in a subject field tends to involve browsing, with a choice of one or more sources devoted to journals. These include:

PubList. Available at: www.publist.com this usefully indicates publication type such as monographic series.

Ulrichweb/Ulrich's International Periodicals Directory. The former is at: www.ulrichsweb.com and the latter, i.e. printed version, is published annually (with quarterly updates) by Bowker. It can be scanned under appropriate subject headings.

Other sources include the catalogues of subscription agents. It is worth noting that Swets Blackwells has an agreement with the publisher Annual Reviews, though most if not all such catalogues are useful sources of information. Catalogues of major libraries can also assist. An example is the *British Library Public Catalogue,* available at: blpc.bl.uk Searching at advanced level can produce a list of manageable proportions.

Often the emphasis when considering publications dedicated to reviews is on journals, hence the term 'review journals'. However, some review publications are books, possibly in a series, and others might be included in conference proceedings, hence the inclusion of comprehensive catalogues as a source, and the value of *PubList* including publication type.

The following list is a sample of English language review journals and series.

Advances in Applied Mechanics (Academic Press)
Advances in Bioengineering (ASME)
Advances in Biotechnical Processes (Wiley)
Advances in Cement Research (Thomas Telford)
Advances in Chemical Engineering (Academic Press)
Advances in Computing Research (JAI/Elsevier)
Advances in Computers (Academic Press)
Advances in Cryogenic Engineering (Plenum) Based on a conference series
Advances in Electrochemical Science and Engineering (Wiley-VCH)
Advances in Engineering (SAE)
Advances in Engineering Software (Elsevier)
Advances in Environmental Research (Nelson & Commons Communication)
Advances in Environmental Science and Technology (Wiley)
Advances in Heat Transfer (Academic Press)
Advances in Materials Research (Springer)
Advances in Nuclear Science and Technology (Kluwer)
Advances in Polymer Technology (Wiley)
Advances in Powder Metallurgy and Particulate Materials (Metal Powder Industries Federation)

Advances in Solar Energy (American Solar Energy Society)
Advances in Technology of Materials and Materials Processing Journal (Ad Tech)
Advances in Thermal Engineering (Wiley)
Advances in Water Resources (Elsevier)
Annual Review of Biomedical Engineering (Annual Reviews)
Annual Review of Fluid Mechanics (Annual Reviews)
Annual Review of Materials Research (Annual Reviews)
Annual Reviews of Industrial and Engineering Chemistry (American Chemical Society)
Catalysis Reviews: Science and Engineering (Dekker)
Chemical Engineering, Concepts and Reviews (Gordon and Breach)
Computer Aided Engineering Review (Elsevier)
Control and Dynamic Systems – Advances in Theory and Applications (Academic Press)
Critical Reviews in Biomedical Engineering (CRC Press)
Journal of Recent Advances in Applied Science (Evoke)
Knowledge Engineering Review (CUP)
Progress in Aerospace Sciences (Elsevier)
Progress in Astronautics and Aeronautics (AIAA)
Progress in Biomedical Engineering (Elsevier)
Progress in Combustion Science and Technology (Medical and Technical Publishing)
Progress in Electromagnetics Research: PIER (EMW Publishing)
Progress in Energy and Combustion Research (Elsevier)
Progress in Environmental Science (Arnold)
Progress in Extractive Metallurgy (Gordon and Breach)
Progress in Materials Science (Elsevier)
Progress in Passive Solar Energy Systems (AS/ISES)
Progress in Technology Series (SAE)
Recent Advances in Engineering Science (Gordon and Breach)
Reviews in Chemical Engineering (Freund)
Reviews in Process Chemistry and Engineering (Taylor and Francis)
Structural Engineering Review (Elsevier)

The purpose of the above list is to give an indication of subjects covered by dedicated review publications. It is not intended to be a comprehensive list, and some reviews relevant to engineering may be included in publications covering areas such as biotechnical engineering, environmental issues and materials science. In comparison, there are relatively few titles matching traditional disciplines such as civil engineering and manufacturing.

Contact Websites

Academic Press, www.academicpress.com (now part of Elsevier)

American Institute of Aeronautics and Astronautics – AIAA, www.aiaa.org
American Society of Mechanical Engineers – ASME, www.asme.org
Annual Reviews, www.annualreviews.org
Applied Science, see Elsevier.
Arnold, www.arnoldpublishers.com
AS/ISES, www.ises.org
Blackwell, www.blackwellpublishing.com
Books on Demand, www.books-on-demand.com (websites in various languages)
Cambridge University Press – CUP, www.cup.org
CARL (Uncover) now available through Ingenta, www.ingenta.com
Dekker, www.dekker.com/index.jsp
Ebsco Information Services, www.ebsco.com (provider of services including serials subscription services and databases)
Edina, edina.ac.uk (database service provider)
EELS (Engineering E-Library Sweden), eels.lub.lu.se (formerly a Swedish based engineering gateway, which is no longer maintained)
EEVL, the Internet guide to engineering, mathematics and computing, www.eevl.ac.uk (a UK based gateway which includes *Recent Advances in Manufacturing (RAM)*).
Elsevier, www.elsevier.com (a publisher and service provider with a number of subsidiaries)
EMW Publishing, www.emwave.com
Freund, www.angelfire.com/il/freund (a publisher)
Gordon and Breach – see Taylor and Francis.
Kluwer, www.wkap.nl
Metal Powder Industries Federation, www.mpif.org (this organisation is based in Princeton, NJ, USA)
Pergamon, see Elsevier.
Plenum, see Kluwer.
Society of Automotive Engineers, www.sae.org
Springer, www.springer.de
Taylor and Francis, www.tandf.co.uk
Thomas Telford, www.t-telford.co.uk (a trading subsidiary of the Institution of Civil Engineers in the UK)
UMI, www.umi.com
Wiley, www.wiley.com

▶ PRODUCT REVIEWS

There are few journals devoted exclusively to product reviews, with UK examples being *Which* magazine published by the Consumers Association and *What to Buy for Business*. Others appear in a variety of journals including computer magazines and popular magazines such as *Good Housekeeping*. Product reviews often deal with highly competitive industries such as motor vehicles. In the UK there is a survey of consumers views produced as the *JD Power Survey*. Similar publications can be found in other countries. Other reviews can be found on the internet, particularly for domestic and sports products.

Guides to the scattered product reviews are useful, and the familiar databases can be used. One such is:

Abstracts in New Technologies and Engineering (ANTE) available as a database and printed version with the database usually being easier to search. Useful for a range of products, including industrial equipment.

▶ REVIEWS OF METHODOLOGIES AND TECHNIQUES

There are not too many publications which review methods and techniques in engineering. They are desirable because a survey can indicate good practice. Often there is not a strong motive for writing such material, with a possible exception being in the area of management techniques. In engineering, the manufacturing, building, construction and process industries can make particularly good use of them.

The producers are often organisations providing a collective service either to members, or if government backed, to the industry as a whole. Some examples with some typical reviews are:

Building Research Establishment – BRE. (www.bre.co.uk). The following examples can be found using the keyword 'review' in the search box at the BRE website.

> *A review of routine foundation design practice.*
> *Background ventilation of dwellings: a review.*

European Construction Institute – ECI (www.eci-online.org). Parts of this site are restricted to members. The use of the site map reveals a number of task forces with publications which could be considered reviews.

> *Long term partnering.*
> *Life cycle costing.*

There are other examples in other fields, and other countries, as well as the international level.

▶ REFERENCES

Gomersall, A., and Stewart, I., 2002. *Market research: a guide to the British Library collections.* 9th edition. London: British Library.

Lord, C. R., 2000. *Guide to information sources in engineering*. Englewood: Libraries Unlimited, 2000.

Needham, P. A. S., 2002. *The MAGiC project, managing access to grey literature. Final report; executive summary*. [British Library]. (www.bl.uk/concord/pdf_files/magicfinalexecsum.pdf).

Powell, J. H., 2001. Virtual engineering libraries. *In* Conkling, T. W. and Musser, L. R., eds, 2001. *Engineering libraries: building collections and delivering services*. New York: Haworth Press. Co-published simultaneously as *Science and Technology Libraries*, 19(3/4), pp. 105–128.

Internet Resources in Engineering

Penny Rowe

▶ INTRODUCTION

The Internet is both a receptacle for information and a medium for its delivery, providing a framework for exchange of all types of information media. Engineers will be familiar with the Internet's more obvious tools and resources and will have their favourite sites, but to maximize procurement in terms of information delivery, they need to be aware of the full range of facilities and end products available on the Internet.

Sections of this book focus on particular categories of literature or subject resources, all of which exist on the Internet. In view of overlap with such specialist sections, this chapter will take a general approach, providing a background to the others by focusing on the Internet as an entity, mapping their context within an overall information framework and their relationship with each other within the Internet. It will emphasize the Internet's comprehensiveness and diversity and the circular and interconnecting nature of the Web. It will highlight its unique strengths and characteristics, the extent and range of its capabilities and its potential in all aspects to be a 'goldmine' for engineers.

More specifically, it will discuss the value of the Internet in terms of its several major components, not least the World Wide Web. It will clarify the Internet jungle by displaying resources and tools in a generic context exemplifying them in the main rather than listing them, and will assume that readers will refer to specialist chapters for in-depth comprehensive coverage. It will also give brief guidance on appropriate search paths for efficient information retrieval and will indicate current trends and future developments.

This chapter will provide a snapshot of the Internet at the time of writing. Wherever possible it focuses on potentially persistent features, and areas deemed to expand. Resources without versions in English will not be covered.

Internet development

The Internet evolved from the US military's linking with area networks to form the NSF network, which greatly facilitated research communication between universities through file transference and email. Early connections required knowledge of a remote computer's existence, but tools grouping open-access resources into hierarchies later enabled searching by list browsing. Early Web software gained ascendancy when browsers exploited the full potential of hypertext linking. Its client/server software made information simple to disseminate and access and encompassed other facilities (FTP sites, Usenet groups etc). The advent of search engines enabled searching by novices, and business opportunities were exploited by commercial and financial sectors, initiating new facilities and resources.

Features of the Internet

The Internet's combination of shared and unparalleled characteristics make it unique. It shares with all electronic materials the advantages over print of speed of publication, ease of duplication through networking, capacity for data manipulation and user participation etc., but is unmatched in its facility for instant data dissemination and access worldwide, rapid updating and greater potential for interactivity. Its ability to support all kinds of media (text, graphics, video and sound, etc.), incorporate different platforms, host a variety of sites with a variety of disparate resources, is unrivalled. An engineer can receive data at his desk at his chosen location, manipulate it as required and forward it to a colleague across the world at the touch of a button.

Accessibility of material

An important distinction to bear in mind is that the term 'freely accessible' on the Internet means that something is generally accessible but not necessarily FREE. The vast majority of data is free, at the cost of being relatively unorganized and/or scattered. The more difficult to collect, specialized in nature or structured data is, the less likely it is to be free or freely accessible; the most significant intellectual information is generally accessible only to specialists and at a price, the Internet merely acting as a delivery service. Much is packaged specifically for, and only available to, academic institutions. Practising engineers in large corporations able to afford unsubsidized subscriptions to permitted material are in a better position than those in small concerns which cannot. Some 'freely accessible' material is available on a pay-by-item basis to individuals.

The Internet has spawned many free services which aim to bridge the gap between expensive scholarly tools and disparate free material, by pointing to and aggregating both free, freely accessible and non-free resources of use to both engineers in academia and outside. Even where full text may not ultimately be free, it is unlikely that an index to it will not be available to it somewhere on the Internet.

Constituent components of the Internet

The Internet currently provides these major tools:

- World Wide Web (WWW/Web)
- electronic mail (email)
- newsgroups/network news
- Internet Relay Chat (IRC)

The major part of this chapter will concentrate on the **Web**, it being the major purveyor of information in terms of quantity and variety.

It will follow with coverage of **email** and **newsgroups**, which exist for the exchange of communication and news announcements, and are employed extensively in informal contact between peers in academia (the 'invisible college'), thus playing an important part in scientific research. Email-based mailing lists and network news, (a development of the bulletin board system), enable rapid communication between groups with shared interests and will be described later in some detail.

IRC which exists solely for quasi real-time, quick-fire dialogue between participants will not be covered in this chapter as it is ephemeral and used primarily in the public domain, though it has potential for informal academic conferencing.

Although separate components, email, newsgroups and the Web can inter-relate; web pages can be accessed via email, email via the web, newsgroups announce web pages etc.

The following are recommended for those not familiar with the Internet:

- **Netskills** (materials.netskills.ac.uk) from the University of Newcastle, provides a comprehensive range of Internet training materials under academic licence.
- **What is the Internet, the World Wide Web, and Netscape?** (www.lib.berkeley.edu/TeachingLib/Guides/Internet/WhatIs.html). University of California at Berkeley's library guides are typical of University free guides about the Internet.

▶ WORLD WIDE WEB

Analogies of the Web as a warehouse of randomly organized goods or a telephone network, convey its size, chaotic nature or information exchange process but not its complexity. Millions of suppliers (both corporate and individual) load data in all sorts of guises and on all sorts of platforms onto the Web. Being a single channel for this diversity, the Web obscures the real differences between media, types of output, sites and pages, categories of material, sources, hosts, platforms, free and subscription material. Understanding the functions of different categories of research material and the relationships between them is crucial when conducting research, and knowing how and where they turn up on the Web makes it easier to organize a search strategy efficiently.

Complexity of resources

Information on the Web is complex on various fronts: the diversity of its location at server level, its ephemeral and ever-changing nature, the variety of its software base, content, packaging, function and relationship with other material.

A resource can be defined as something that supplies a want or as stock that can be drawn on. In terms of information and in the context of the Internet, which is structurally complex, a vehicle for different tools and media and supplies many different needs, the term resource can be interpreted variously. A narrow interpretation might restrict it to end products, i.e. specific documents, video clips, music etc., and their data content. But the tool that discovers the end product, the site hosting it and for that matter the software underlying all these elements, are an integral part of the information supply process and can be seen as resources with their own culture and identity. This inclusive interpretation results in almost anything with an identity being considered a resource.

Not only can anything from a piece of information to a document to a site be a resource but a resource can reside anywhere within the server folder hierarchy. It may be the site homepage comprising the root directory or a file branching directly from it buried deep down the tree structure. To add to the intricacy, the same type of file can exist at different hierarchical levels and be infinitely recursive (i.e. contain a resource containing a resource, which contains a resource) to the smallest unit of data, thus precluding mutually exclusive classes of resources.

In addition, with increasing exploitation of the Web and growth in competition, sites not only aggregate resources but create compound ones, blurring boundaries between resources. Pointing services are increasingly teamed with what they point to. For instance, bibliographic databases not only link to full text held elsewhere, but in some cases provide it as part of the site package. A journals' Table of Contents, which is essentially an index, may include abstracts and could be considered an end product for providing a degree of informative material. Thus resources become hybrids.

To add to the confusion, pages may move location and be difficult to trace. The URL works as a locator at a particular period, but does not definitively identify a document as some URLs only function for a few minutes. A further complication is the fact that many pages completely vanish with time (the average Web page lasting only seventy days) or the site itself may disappear.

However, some sort of classification is helpful, and resources will be divided as far as possible into the following not necessarily mutually exclusive categories:

- Websites
- End products
- Finding services

Websites

Websites vary enormously in size, complexity, content, function and background context, reflecting the variety of objectives of the very different bodies or individuals producing them.

Whatever meaningful criteria are applied to categorize sites, there are no clear cut or mutually exclusive distinctions. By definition, end products and finding services categorize themselves by content and function which could be applied to sites as well. Some sites are indeed synonymous with their function; a site equating with a search engine is essentially a finding tool. Typically, though, sites comprise a mixture of resources to cater for different user needs; a publisher of any size will include a site search engine, a catalogue of publications, full text of archived journal back issues etc., cutting across distinctions of content and function. A different denominator, exclusive of content and function, would be more appropriate: using context to categorize sites provides additional perspectives to the information scene by revealing background and responsibility for content.

Most websites emanate from academic, professional, governmental, commercial and other (unaffiliated or deriving from individuals') backgrounds, all of which can be the source of engineering-related information. Such sites incorporate scientific and technological R&D, engineering, chemical, manufacturing, production, exploration, refining and processing, transport, construction, geotechnical and public health engineering industry material, professional engineering, consultancy and related service industry matters dealing with feedstocks, components, procurement and supply, health and safety, and legislation etc. Finding tools for engineering information exist on government and education sites, institutional and commercial publishers, or in their own right as commercial or externally backed concerns.

The contexts of sites are categorized and described below but even here distinctions are not precise; for instance, professional institutions often act as commercial publishers supplying publications to the public as well as members and subscribers:

- **Academic** – encompass universities and equivalent, their departments and research centres providing organization, staff, research and course details. They may provide access to research reports, teaching material, technical databases, full text papers or other information. Most pages are available to anyone apart from sectional Intranets and subscription services available through libraries,
- **Institutional** – a wide ranging category including professional institutions, trade associations, societies etc. Sites typically provide basic information about the organization, its function, membership, activities and events such as conferences, and publications. Engineering institutions usually offer a wealth of other facilities including reference or technical information about processes and products relating to their area of interest, in some cases for free, and full text publications for subscribing members.
- **Commercial** – a very diverse category which includes commercial publishers, financial organizations, manufacturing and service companies, suppliers and consultancies etc. Sites may be mere advertisements of a company's existence with basic financial, organizational and service information, listings of products and publications. Many include detailed product data, with additional reference, statistical, applicatory and technical data, extensive directories and databases, and full text technical reports. Since many publishers are now offering full text on the Web, their sites are expanding from mere advertisements and catalogues into portals providing a mixture of catalogues of print works, TOCs of journals, conference proceedings and reference books together and more or less inextricably linked with the full text. Free technical material is available here and there but manufacturing companies may restrict it to customers, and publishers providing structured full text online services usually limit access to subscribers.
- **Governmental** – a range of international agencies, non-governmental organizations, national, regional and local branches of government, government funded research centres etc. Information about function and activities reflect the advisory, statutory and research roles of the individual organizations. They provide statistical, scientific and technical data quite often in the form of the full text of legislative and research reports.

- **Other** – some sites produced by individuals provide some indication of provenance and others give few clues as to origin. They may well be useful and of high quality but need to be used with more caution than a recognized source.

An organization, however small, needs a web presence these days to advertise its existence, services or products, either overtly or more covertly. This may consist solely of a single page with company contact details and a summary of products and/or services. More usually it will extend to several or hundreds of pages with each page representing perhaps a different aspect of the organization.

Increasingly, organizations use the Web as a vehicle for conducting business. They may limit themselves to a single server, or make use of several sites whose different servers are used for different purposes. Sites range in complexity from single entity specialist resources such as a full text document within a particular resource, a full-text multi-volume work, a search engine or a catalogue of different types of publication, or they may specialize in a collection of homogeneous resources, such as a journal TOCs service.

End products

Formats

At the most specific level, end products are available in a wide variety of formats:

- textual material
- numerical data including software – e.g. freeware, evaluation copies, upgrades of commercial products
- images – graphics, video clips, photographs etc
- sound – music, speech, & real-time radio

The format and function of a file is signalled by extension codes. The most common on the Web, htm or html, indicates text with embedded links. Increasing complexity in the form of dynamic pages, interactivity, use of images, is reflected in a variety of extensions such as asp, jpeg, cgi, png.

For explanations of file extensions see:

- **Every file format in the world**
  (whatis.techtarget.com/fileFormatA/0,289933,sid9,00.html)

End products – what they are

An end product can be a scientific document such as a technical report, courseware, video, software program, job advertisement etc.

Formal scientific documents – full text

Scientific documents are classified as primary or secondary literature. **Primary literature** comprises the first published reports of original research. **Secondary literature** essentially re-packages or re-organizes information reported in primary literature.

These traditional forms of scientific communication all undergo some form of validation conferring a guarantee of quality, and should be the first avenue for engineers seeking scholarly information.

Traditional types of formal scientific communication

Primary Literature
- **Scientific journal (periodical/serial) articles**
  Scientific journals published by commercial, professional and academic organizations present the significant facts on recent research in articles relating to the journal field. Journals were the first category of material whose full text was made available on the Web in a systematic way by commercial publishers. A developing trend is to publish 'accelerated' electronic issues substantially prior to print, enabling early pick-up by abstracting services.
- **Conference papers**
  Conference papers present preliminary research results and work-in-progress for the scrutiny of peers, at conferences (symposia, congresses, workshops etc.). Conferences are organized by learned societies and associations, professional and academic institutions and published as Proceedings.
- **Technical reports**
  Reports contain detailed results of work carried out or in progress, in relation to research, development, testing and evaluation. Applied research organizations often regard them as the prime means of technical communication enabling rapid dissemination of findings with little or no editing.
- **Theses and dissertations**
  Theses are reports examined for the awarding of higher degrees, PhD and equivalent-grade theses requiring original research, masters theses or dissertations, independent, but not necessarily original study.
- **Patents**
  A patent, often taken out at an early stage of R&D, provides statutory protection for a technical concept, process, equipment or product, preventing others from exploiting it for a number of years. It has been estimated that 85% of the information in patents is never published anywhere else (Turner, 1999). The Web makes available much patent data difficult or expensive to obtain elsewhere.

- **Preprints**

  Preprints are research manuscripts prior to publication which may have been reviewed and accepted or submitted in final form or intended for publication and are being circulated for comment. They may also be referred to as 'e-prints' as electronic versions of papers disseminated for peer review, journal publication, or prior to conference presentation. The term preprint can often be used loosely to describe any electronic work circulated by the author on the Internet or outside of the traditional publishing environment.

Secondary Literature

- **Books – reference works, textbooks, other monographs**

  Many reference works are now published in electronic format in addition to or instead of print. Textbooks and monographs, however, have been slow to go electronic particularly in engineering disciplines.

- **Review articles**

  A review article is an expert's evaluative overview of recent developments in a field of study which establishes their context, highlights particularly significant work and provides a wealth of references to the research reviewed.

- **Popular journals & magazines, newspaper articles**

  Popular science journals summarize recent developments and are useful overviews of particular subjects. Newspaper articles can provide useful overviews of particularly topical subjects.

- **Standards**

  Standards and specifications are documents declaring how materials and products should be manufactured, defined, measured or tested, laying down sets of conditions to be fulfilled. A standard is an evolution of a specification accepted by recognised authority and may be published by national and international issuing bodies and companies.

Many university library sites and the subscription-based **Into Info** (educate. lib.chalmers.se) provide information on scientific communication.

Hitherto, scientific literature has reflected, in structure and content, its communication function and the constraints of a paper document. However, apart from some innovations including increasing use of embedded linking, formal scientific documents, however hosted or creatively packaged on the Web, still largely reflect traditional categories of literature in all their distinct forms.

Other material of use in engineering

The categories below are a mixed bag and may be format, content or function oriented and not necessarily mutually exclusive. Non-scholarly material such as product information has become easier for researchers to locate with the arrival of commerce on the Web, initiating an explosion of financial, product, statistical and other material. Less formal types of scientific communication have expanded through the ease of dissemination offered by the Web and in some cases taken on more standardized identities.

- **Trade literature and product information**
  This is an indistinct but much-used category, defined by provenance and subject matter rather than format, which encompasses a range of material. It includes non-refereed trade journals and magazines providing industry news and product information, product and component catalogues, product and process FAQs, and news postings containing product, equipment, process, management and business information, and safety issues relating to engineering.
- **Courseware, learning materials, case studies etc.**
  Material pertaining to courses including lectures, assignments, case studies, assessment tests, examinations etc., which may be packaged into modules for availability on a fee-paying basis.
  The Web's ease of dissemination of different media and interactive capabilities are being increasingly exploited in courseware provision.
- **Numerical data, statistical material and software packages**
  Includes factual information especially that organized for analysis or for reasoning or decision making, values derived from scientific experiments, processed data and software packages.
- **FAQs**
  FAQs evolved from the permanent posting of answers to Frequently Asked Questions on newsgroups and comprise basic files on a topic or definitive pointers to resources. Newsgroup and mailing list FAQs by virtue of their collective evolution, are likely to be reliable. The concept permeated to the Web where a FAQ may comprise little more than introductory generalities relating to a site or subject and may not be particularly technical.
- **Newsgroup and Mailing list archives**
  Posted discussion aggregated or archived on dedicated individual list/group websites. Organized by topic thread within group or list and may include useful scientific data.
- **Blog (Weblog)**
  These short topical comments, in reverse chronological order, are becoming used by the academic community as an additional means

of informal communication, being arguably easier to follow than email or newsgroup forums, keeping colleagues in the communication loop, promoting group culture, and providing an informal voice to outsiders. Commentaries cover news and developments relating to companies, ideas, processes and events and Web links and may include a facility for receiving comment on postings.

- **News services**
  Include scientific and technical breakthroughs and developments, new processes, products and services considered especially topical etc. (Overlaps with trade literature category).
- **Legislation and recommendations**
  A subject based category which involves any material covering such engineering-related matters as health and safety regulations, building regulations, contract law, employment law etc.
- **Recruitment and job opportunities**
  Include jobs offered and sought, sector opportunities, information for clients and candidates on contract, job applications and CV writing, training opportunities, travel help etc.
- **Contracts and procurement**
  Include the drawing up and issuing of contracts and agreements, funding and requisitioning procedures, advice for gaining funding, consultant and contractor sources, commodity procurement etc.

Finding services

Indexes to end product

- **Library Catalogues**
  Catalogues of scientific and technical literature held in many university, national and institution libraries are available online. They index titles of whole works (rather than segments of works such as individual chapters or articles) including reference and textbooks, journals, conference proceedings, reports, local theses, and material such as standards etc. Increasingly, catalogues provide electronic links from journal and reference titles to full text on publishers websites, and are fast becoming an almost seamless channel to full text.
- **Abstracting and indexing services (bibliographic databases)**
  Abstracting and indexing services are specialized collections of bibliographic references with abstracts (summaries) of the full text of individual journal, conference and review articles, technical

reports and in some cases patents, theses and monographs, structured such that specific information can easily be found and retrieved. They are the main academic tools for identifying primary research material and to a lesser extent, secondary literature. Increasingly available on the Web, they are hosted directly by their publishers or by academic or commercial data services and accessed either via host URL or via subscribing libraries' web pages whose journal full text they may be set up to link to.

- **Bibliographies** similarly comprise references to literature but normally restrict themselves to a more specialist topic, do not usually summarize works and, like a set of references, often constitute part of a document whose context they relate to.

- **Tables of Contents Services (TOCS)**
  Single publishers or aggregator services providing online texts normally interface them with contents' indexing services known as Tables of Contents Services. Journal TOCS list chronologically by volume and issue the bibliographic details for each article, often accompanied by abstracts of the full text and occasionally article references. As more reference works appear online their TOCS provide summaries of the whole work accompanied by chapter or article titles and often chapter sub-headings and subject listings. Larger services include search facilities which may scan the full text as well as bibliographic details and abstracts (thus approaching a deeper level of indexing than abstracting services while (currently) limited as to material type).

  TOCS can be used as a way of keeping up to date and many users will regularly browse the latest issues of their chosen journals. At the same time, as more full text is archived TOCS are increasingly acting as a retrospective tool with the search engine function gaining more prominence.

Web search tools

Different search tools are available for different situations and purposes.

- **Keyword oriented searching**
  Search engines
  A Web search engine is a co-ordinated set of programs that includes a robot for harvesting websites, reading pages and embedded links, a program for copying the read data into a database (index), and a program to receive search requests, compare them with index entries, and return results, all without human intervention. **General search engines** index the content of a large portion of the Web down to deep page level

and produce a large number of hits. **Specialist search engines** are selective in their crawling and indexing of the Web.

Individual websites increasingly offer a search engine licensed from the large search engine providers for searching their own site.

- **Subject-oriented searching**
  Web directories

  Classified directories, or Web catalogues as they are also known, enable an alternative way of finding network-based resources – by browsing. While search engines require keyword input and are automatically produced, directories provide hierarchical browseable subject trees and usually have some form of human input in their classification. Specialist directories concentrate on particular areas of the Web or types of resource, or on a particular continent or country.

  Subject gateways

  Directories with a defined subject area are usually referred to as subject gateways (or subject catalogues/directories/index gateways/trees or subject-based information gateways (SBIGs), virtual libraries, clearing houses, pathfinders). Some aspiring to the name are merely lists of links constituting part of a site; some index their lists of links and provide a brief description of the resources and a simple search facility.

  Advanced gateways, typically products of the academic community, enhance their basic database with browseable indexes to a variety of fields created by human cataloguers describing the resource, and a search facility. Increasingly, gateways are adding additional services progressing towards being portals in their particular sphere. Non English-language sites are often neglected by leading gateways whose lingua franca is predominantly English.

  Most directories and gateways now also include a search facility to their resource database.

- **Portals**

  The term portal is variously interpreted in the Web commmunity and applied by sites varying functions. It can justifiably be categorized as both finding tool and/or a type of website. It is categorized in this chapter as a finding tool in that in the academic arena it is perceived as the extension of a subject gateway, leading the user to both internal and external sources.

  It is more than a subject gateway in that it leads the user not only to external websites, but aggregates links to a comprehensive range of services, and in some cases even provides full text on site.

In other words it aims to be the interface or hub through which users are channelled directly to external services, but in some cases also to act as a one-stop-shop in providing some end-products on the same site. Portals exemplify the Web's circular nature since they can evolve from either end of the spectrum, from gateways, online journals services, professional institution sites or government agencies. Publisher or government-based portals often provide both indexes to and full text of their own publications and place less emphasis on external resources than gateway-emergent portals.

▶ SEARCHING THE WEB

Different goals and approaches to study require different types of literature.

When searching for information the following should be taken into consideration:

- type of data required
- end products it may be contained in
- finding tools to track down the end product
- drafting an efficient search statement
- appropriate search techniques
- evaluation of material discovered

Resources in terms of need

The sheer volume of data on the Internet makes it easy to obtain some degree of information on practically any subject through the mere insertion of a keyword into a browser's search engine. However, other tools should be investigated as they may produce more relevant and higher quality results.

Price writes 'where you search is determined by what you need' (Price, 2001) but unhappily it is also determined by which tools you are permitted to access. A great variety of tools exist but not all are available to everyone, even should they be willing to pay. The widest range of material is available to members of well-resourced universities who normally have access to all of the following:

- Web search engines
- Web subject gateways
- library catalogues (OPACs)
- bibliographic abstracting or indexing services/bibliographic databases

When deciding on the type of end product and finding tool required, consider the implications for your needs, of weighing up and opting for alternative types of material such as those in the following non-mutually exclusive list:

- primary and/or secondary literature
- verified sources versus unknown quantity material
- indexes of material versus full text
- academic, commercial or government material
- aggregators versus single resources
- subscription, purchasable versus free material
- forthcoming, current or non-current (past publications) material

Appropriate search tools

Developments on the Web are multiplying the variety of approaches to finding scholarly and related information.

Finding scholarly research material

Full text research material is being made freely available to a greater extent on the Web and there are many freely available finding tools. Freely available government-sponsored research reports can be found through a subject or resource-type query in free-to-use subject gateways. A relatively small number of journals and conference proceedings provide free access online, others allow authors to post articles on the Web, and others allow authors to purchase the right to post their articles on the Web. Most journals are still restricted to subscribing institution or pay-per-view, but the expansion of aggregators brings with it the inclusion of in-house journal search engines which allow much searching to be conducted 'under-one-roof', in many cases by the general public who are only restricted as far as the full text is concerned.

However, for licensed users, web-based traditional abstracting and indexing services are still the prime means of identifying primary literature and still have the edge since they aggregate many different categories of material and are developing competitively with additional facilities including related Web links and virtually seamless links to the full text.

By subject

Via subscription services
New postgraduates needing an overview of their field and seminal papers would be wise to seek out a review in the first instance, and only later, original research material. A technical report may provide a wealth of technical detail, while a journal article will provide validation at the expense

of some loss of detail. Breaking research will be found in pre-print confer-ence papers. All of these can be identified using scholarly **abstracting and indexing services** and the **full text** of the original works can be retrieved via the subscribing **library's catalogue,** which links directly to online electronic full text services or points to library print copies.

Undergraduates needing textbooks and reference works for estab-lished facts and theories are advised to look directly for them (whether electronic or print) in the university **library catalogue.**

N.B. Contents of abstracting and indexing services and online library catalogues cannot currently be accessed by Web search engines although the latter can be manually searched online.

Via freely accessible and/or free services

A number of sites suggest key freely accessible or free search tools set against pre-determined user requirements. One such is: **Choose the Best Search for your Information Need** (www.noodletools.com/debbie/literacies/information/5locate/adviceengine.html). Such guides are useful pointers to a range of tools with specialist focus and functions, such as late-breaking news and biographical material, but should be used with caution as they can be too narrowly prescriptive, omitting alternative avenues to subject-related searching.

A **classified directory** or **subject gateway** for quality records is appro-priate for those with enough subject knowledge to choose relevant contexts in which to browse. A directory-based tool is appropriate to find sites specializing in a topic or a particular home page rather than documents which are buried deep in the site structural hierarchy. Be aware that you are searching a catalogue, and not the web pages directly; if your terms are found in a record the resource itself should prove highly relevant.

Free bibliographic databases / abstracting and indexing services are useful identifiers of primary material but are far less inclusive than subscrip-tion services and often restrict themselves to one category of material. Currently free databases are somewhat randomly listed by library sites and not necessarily categorized together by all gateways. A subject approach will help reveal them, however.

If you have a very specialist term and are unfamiliar with the subject, a preliminary search on a **Web search engine** may help you deduce its context from amongst the hits. Thus, equipped with an idea where to look in the subject hierarchy, you can then turn to subject gateways to unearth more 'seminal' sites.

By resource (report, patent etc) or treatment type (theoretical, experimental etc)

Via subscription services

You can specify categories of resource within many **abstracting services** enabling you, for example, to find a review. Some also allow you to specify treatment codes to limit records to experimental or theoretical work etc. Some services focus solely on particular resources, for example, *Index to Theses*.

Via freely accessible services

Some **Subject gateways** allow you to browse by category of resource to isolate, for example, bibliographic databases, government publications, associations, engineering companies, patents, standards, FAQs, full text documents etc.

By proper name

Both **Web search engines** and **engineering-related subject gateways** will pinpoint individually named resources such as company names, names of institutions, database etc. Individual people can be found by means of specialist people-finder tools.

Finding other material – e.g. products, statistical material

Material which is non-academic in origin such as product information, commercial and financial statistics, etc., may be found via subject gateways. Those with resource category indexes may specifically index products, statistical data etc. An increasing number of **search engines** specialize in particular types of material.

Keeping up-to-date with resources

To research efficiently, you need to be aware of current developments occurring in not only your subject, but in the packages through which research is communicated and in search tools. You may miss the latest research if, for example, you are unaware of search engine advances enabling more focused searching. Some developments are advertised by producers, others by monitoring services, and certain services only exist as current awareness and monitoring tools.

Keeping up-to-date comprehensively can necessitate regular scanning of a multiplicity of different types of resources involving anything from news postings, latest weekly updates on an abstracting service, reading a peer's blog, looking at a stop press notice on your local library's website, checking the TOCs of the current issues of relevant journals or publishers' catalogues for newly published titles, to investigating a search engine monitoring site on a regular basis, etc. Increasingly, pro-active services across the board communicate developments and URLs of updates, new products etc. direct to the user via email, many tailor-made to individual requirements.

Search statements

Creating a search statement is advisable whether you use a search engine or abstracting service. Many general engines have emulated search functions available on abstracting services and provide a choice of simple or advanced searching using Boolean and/or other operators allowing results' refining using set statements. Advice on devising search statements, use of focusing operators, consideration of grammatical and semantic factors, use of weighting factors, is available on many higher education library sites for use with abstracting services, and holds good for search engines for the major part. Typical sites include:

- University of Glasgow's /TLTP tutorial at University of Southampton: (www.ulst.ac.uk/library/training/uuonly/searchskills/frblurb3.html)
- Loughborough University Library's 'How to plan a search strategy' (www.lboro.ac.uk/library/subj/searchst.html)

You can adapt your search statement to dovetail with search facilities on offer by taking advantage of the variety of advanced features which only some 3–5% of search engine users activate. Help pages are useful here. Remember – no search engine covers the entire Web or makes 'everything' searchable. Nor are all the search engine databases up to date. That is why you should use more than one of the best search engines (Price, 2001).

Criteria for evaluating results

A certain intellectual standard may be assumed in relation to abstracting and indexing services' results. However, relevance criteria will still need to be applied.

A 'hit' from a Web search engine needs to be assessed for importance, accuracy, quality, currency etc., by conducting basic checks as suggested by this amended checklist (Tyburski, 2003):

- determine its origin
- discover the author and publisher
- ascertain the author's and publisher's credentials
- discover the date of writing for historical context
- verify it by comparison with similar information from another reputable source
- distinguish between fact, fiction, opinions etc.

A document's URL can convey a great deal. It 'can expose what kind of server and content management system or scripting language is used. It may contain original publication dates for articles, author names, ad companies, or search options.' (Notess, 2003). The host name portion can indicate provenance and authority of content. The homepage or introductory pages of responsible, particularly corporate, sites should provide actual information about their producer. An individual may include document references to the author's own and others' work, links to other organizations etc.

Accolades or being pointed to by other reputable and subject related sources, may suggest quality and importance or at the very least, popularity. Dated pages give an idea of currency though even good sites do not necessarily date pages.

▶ SPECIFIC RESOURCES – ACCESS AND EXAMPLES

Overviews of Web resources

Comprehensive guides which provide an overview of the range of resources on the Internet and list important sites, end-products, indexes and Web search tools, tend to be either divided on subject lines or in print format.

A gateway, which while not a guide, contains a wealth of academic-related information, is:

- **HERO (Higher Education and Research Opportunities in the UK)** (www.hero.ac.uk)
  which includes a Resources overview:
  (www.hero.ac.uk/reference_resources/resources413.
  cfm?menu=true) covering categories: Journals & publications, online dictionaries, Internet search facilities, local resources, resource databases, discussion lists.

For a more explanatory overview with selected examples, follow an engineering tutorial at:

- **RDN Virtual Training Suite** (www.vts.rdn.ac.uk) a set of free online tutorials to improve Internet information literacy providing an overview of the range of resources available.

Current awareness overviews

Some long established services provide an overview of current developments and new resources in relation to end-products and finding tools and their publishers, hosts, and sites.

- **Internet Resources Newsletter**
  (www.hw.ac.uk/libwww/irn/irn.html) provides free monthly current awareness of resources for students and engineers. It is also available as a free email newsletter to subscribers.

- **NSDL Scout Report for Math, Engineering and Technology** (scout.wisc.edu/nsdl-reports/met/current/) is a publication from the NSF's Internet Scout Project and part of the National Science Digital Library focusing on mathematical, engineering and technology online resources, published bi-weekly and also available by email.
- **BUBL Link Update** (www.bubl.ac.uk/link/updates/current.html) is bi-weekly, listing additions and changes to BUBL's catalogue of Internet resources.

Websites

Keeping up to date with websites

(See also Current awareness overviews at beginning of Specific resources section)

- Internet magazines and sections of broadsheet newspapers list new websites
- Directories and subject gateways often list new resources separately or alert users of updates through email newsletters.
- Intelligent agents

Types of websites

Academic

Identifying sites
UK sites – general information

- **HERO (Higher Education & Research Opportunities in the United Kingdom)** (www.hero.ac.uk) is the official gateway to the UK universities, colleges and research organizations. It provides information on universities, courses, research information etc. It links to the **Network for the Exploitation of Science and Technology (NEST)** (www.nest.ac.uk) which indexes Research Council funded research projects in universities providing project descriptions, dates etc.

Examples of sites
Lists of engineering departments world wide can be found through a search engine. Examples include:

- **Chemical Engineering Faculty Directory** (www.che.utexas.edu/che-faculty/World/inst-index.html) browseable alphabetically by name of universities worldwide

- **ICivilEngineer** (www.icivilengineer.com/
  Academic_Department_Index/) links to civil engineering
  department websites in universities around the world listed
  by country.
- **Departments of Electrical Engineering around the
  World** (www.elec.uq.edu.au/doc/universities.html)
- **European Geoscience University Departments**
  (www.sci.muni.cz/~sulovsky/euracad.html)
- **Mechanical Engineering Graduate Schools Directories**
  (www.gradschools.com/listings/menus/mech_eng_menu.html)

The variety of facilities and material displayed on many academic sites is
exemplified by the following:

- **Centre for Composite Materials, Aeronautics, Imperial
  College** (www.ae.ic.ac.uk/composites/)
- **The semi-conductor subway**
  (www.mtl.mit.edu/semisubway.html)
- **Superplasticity Homepage on the Web**
  (callisto.my.mtu.edu:591/FMPro?-db=sp&-format=sp.html&-view)

Institutional

Identifying sites
UK and main US sites:

- **EEVL** (www.eevl.ac.uk) choose Institutions/Societies within
  Engineering's 'Browse by Resource'.

An example of a directory which focuses on associations:

- **Gateway to Associations** (info.asaenet.org/gateway
  /OnlineAssocSlist.html) provides links to over 6,500 US
  associations.

Examples of sites
Some examples of the variety of associations available:

- **Fluid Power Society** (www.ifps.org) is an international
  organization for fluid power and related motion control
  professionals.
- **Foundation for Water Research** (www.fwr.org) an
  independent, not-for-profit organization that disseminates
  knowledge on all aspects of water, wastewater and related
  environmental issues.
- **Institution of Civil Engineers** (www.ice.org.uk) an
  independent UK-based international organization, representing
  over 80,000 professionally qualified engineers world-wide and the
  civil engineering industry.

Commercial

Identifying sites

Engineering-related companies:

- **EEVL** (www.eevl.ac.uk) browsing within Engineering section Resource category 'Commercial' reveals over 100 pages of commercial engineering-related sites.

Commercial publishers:

Most lists of publishers' sites fail to keep up with the constant shifts in the publishing scene caused by mergers and take-overs. The comprehensive:

- **ACQWEB's Directory of Publishers and Vendors** (acqweb.library.vanderbilt.edu/acqweb/pubr.html) although no longer updated can still prove useful in that it can lead to the new owners of taken-over sites.

Examples of sites

The following are examples of sites which can be used to find companies in specific technical areas:

- **Global Defense Directory** (www.afji.com/Services/ GDDirectory/index.htm) is an international directory of companies involved in defence, compiled by Armed Forces Journal International.
- **ProcessEngineeringOnline.com** (www.processengineeringonline.com) is a directory of process engineering companies, products, services and news for biotechnology, semiconductor, chemical, pharmaceutical, petroleum, food and drink and other process industries.

A random selection indicating the variety of engineering-related companies:

- **Boeing** (www.boeing.com) the largest aerospace company, provides company, market and product information for air, rotor and spacecraft plus much else including full text of press releases.
- **Key to Steel Database** (www.key-to-steel.com) a global database of steel materials.

Examples of a major and smaller specialist publisher:

- **Blackwell Science** (www.blacksci.co.uk) is the science division of a major general academic publisher
- **Imperial College Press** (www.icpress.co.uk) a joint venture with World Scientific Publishing to produce high-quality print and electronic books and journals.

Governmental

Identifying sites
- **Governments on the WWW** (www.gksoft.com/govt/) is a comprehensive database of multi-governmental institutions, parliaments, ministries, law courts, embassies, councils, etc. from over 220 countries.

Examples of sites
- **FirstGov** (firstgov.gov) is the official portal for U.S. Government, with state and local links. Search by keyword, or use subject tree directory which includes Science and Technology section.
- **UKOP** (www.ukop.co.uk/default.aspx) is the catalogue of UK official publications from over 2,000 bodies including Parliament, devolved administrations, government departments, quangos, agencies, and international bodies.
- **Engineering and Physical Sciences Research Council (EPSRC)** (www.epsrc.ac.uk).
- **British National Space Centre (BNSC)** (www.bnsc.gov.uk) works on behalf of the government to provide a focus for civil space policies and oversee the UK's position within space science.

Finding tools

Web search tools

The vast majority of Web search engines and directories are freely available and free to the user.

Keeping up to date with Web search tools
General search engines and directories undergo more continuous development than perhaps any other tool and any descriptions of them here will date correspondingly quickly. The following long established sites monitor both search engines and directories, providing up-to-date analyses, comparisons, advice and news of new functions etc:

- **Search Engine Showdown** (www.searchengineshowdown.com) features advice on searching and features of different engines and directories.
- **Search Engine Watch** (searchenginewatch.com) gives up-to-date information on and comparisons of different search engines and directories.

- **Search Engines Worldwide** (home.inter.net/takakuwa/
  search/search.html) includes over 3,000 listed by country.

Keyword searching

Search engines
Currently the following are important examples of the genre or exemplify
a type:

Single search engines
There are less than a dozen major search engines (not including commercial pay-per-click engines) which function in their own name and/or are the
power behind ISP, browser or directory search tools. The current most
acclaimed and outstanding general search engine is:

- **Google** (www.google.com) popular with professional and
  non-professional searchers alike. It is also the power behind many
  other engines. It provides various additional search services
  including **newsgroup, images** and **pdf** material identifying
  authoritative content from respected sources.

Search engine aggregation sites e.g.
- **Search Engine Colossus** (www.searchenginecolossus.com)
  links to search engines from 195 countries and 38 territories
  around the world.

Metasearch engines
Special tools and some major websites let you use a number of search
engines simultaneously and compile results in a single list with the number
of hits restricted to the most relevant e.g.:

- **Search.com** (www.search.com)

Subject specific search engine
- **Scirus** (www.scirus.com) restricts itself to scientific content deep
  indexing free web pages and seventeen million records from
  subscription sources including ScienceDirect, Medline, BioMed,
  Beilstein, SIAM, US Patent Office, NASA and others.

Resource specific engines
Images:

- **picsearch** (www.picsearch.com) is an example of a format based
  engine providing fast-loading images which on request display
  origin, image data and textual context. A search for suspension
  bridges brought up 604 images, and wavelet 533 images (though
  some were merely book cover images).

Software:

- **Shareware.com** (shareware.cnet.com) is in fact a metasearch engine covering over a dozen shareware directories searching for free downloadable software programs.

People:

There are hundreds of search engines for people and their attributes such as telephone number, email address etc., many of them such as **Yahoo People Search** offered by the larger engines and area restricted.

- **ISIHighlyCited.com** (isihighlycited.com) is a free tool from ISI Web of Science using citation analysis to identify individuals, departments and institutions that have made fundamental scientific advances in recent decades.

Subject-oriented searching

Directories/catalogues

General classified directories

- **Yahoo** (www.yahoo.com) is a popular directory with summary descriptions. The category 'Engineering' contains forty subcategories and a sub-section Companies usefully subdivides into subject-related areas as well as an alphabetical listing.

Academic-based general directories

Although general, they include substantial and/or high quality resources in their engineering sections. Some important examples:

- **WWW Virtual Library** (www.vlib.org/Home.html) is the oldest catalogue of websites. Individual general and specialist indexes are maintained by volunteer experts on hundreds of different servers around the world. Recognized as being amongst the highest quality guides to particular sections of the Web.
- **Infomine** (infomine.ucr.edu) from the University of California is a directory of scholarly resources of databases, electronic publications, mailing lists, library catalogues etc., described by librarians. Relevant subject sections include: Physical Sciences, Engineering, Computing etc.
- **Academic Info** (www.academicinfo.net) is a nonprofit US educational organization.
- **The Scout Report Archives** (scout.cs.wisc.edu/archives/) is a searchable and browseable database of over five years' worth of the Scout Report and subject-specific Scout Reports giving access to over 10,000 Internet sites and mailing lists.

Subject specific gateways

Identifying subject gateways

- **Pinakes: A Subject Launchpad**
  (www.hw.ac.uk/libWWW/irn/pinakes/pinakes.html) links to
  numerous gateways in all subjects.
- **Resource Discovery Network (RDN)** (www.rdn.ac.uk)
  funded by UK Higher Education Funding Councils comprises a
  series of single and collective gateways (hubs) covering most areas
  of academic study. Several focus on engineering-related subjects
  with a degree of overlap.

UK engineering and related gateways

- **Chemdex** (www.chemdex.org) from Sheffield University is a
  comprehensive gateway for chemical information.
- **PhysicsWeb** (physicsweb.org/resources/) is the Institute
  of Physics gateway providing physics resources, news and
  jobs.
- **PSIgate** (www.psigate.ac.uk), part of the RDN, offers high quality
  resources in the physical sciences which include earth and
  materials sciences.

More minor specialist directories like Geo-information Gateway (www.
geog.le.ac.uk/cti/info.html) may prove useful but their contents may be
already covered by larger inter-disciplinary gateways.

Non-UK general engineering gateways

- **Science.gov** (www.science.gov) hosted by US DOE's
  OSTI, is a gateway to authoritative selected science
  information provided by U.S. Government agencies, including
  R&D results. Links to over 11,000 Agency databases and
  websites.
- **ViFaTec Engineering Subject Gateway** (vifatec.tib.uni-
  hannover.de) includes a list of free bibliographic databases for
  which a meta-search interface is under construction, and a
  server of purchasable full text. It is a useful pointer to German
  sites.

Area specific gateways

Some gateways specialize in sites from a particular area scantily covered
by other gateways e.g.:

- **AVEL Sustainability Knowledge Network**
  (www.avel.edu.au) portal to quality resources in sustainable
  systems and engineering with emphasis on Australian resources.

Specialized subject gateways

Range from large discipline areas to very specific topics. More general gateways may identify the more specialist ones. Examples include:

- **MaterSci** (www.matersci.net) covers materials and metallurgy.
- **RadWaste.org** (www.radwaste.org) a source for radioactive waste management material.
- **Global Change Data and Information System (GCDIS)** (www.globalchange.gov) a gateway to global change data and information locating multi-agency news, data, publications, and research from the U.S. Global Change Research Program (USGCRP).
- **MEMSnet** (www.memsnet.org) an information service for the Micro-electrical-mechanical systems' development community. Includes a materials properties database.

Product Directories

Company directory:

- **EngNet®** (www.engnetglobal.com) incorporates a buyers guide for sourcing engineering products, services, and companies.

Portals

Portals may be freely available, publicly funded services, and/or offer material which is pay-per-view or subscription-based.

General engineering portals

Examples of major portals
Free services

- **EEVL** (www.eevl.ac.uk) provides a rich combination of information for engineers. The Engineering section alone has all the requirements of a portal acting as both a gateway and supplier of information. It offers a variety of indexes to catalogues of described Web resources enabling subject and resource type browsing and individual and combined searching. Facilities include several free bibliographic databases: Recent Advances in Manufacturing (RAM), Jet Impingement and Liquid Crystal, an Offshore Engineering Service, Web tutorials in specific disciplines, and an ejournal search engine etc. Other sections include: Literature search resource descriptions and links, current awareness, events, jobs and recruitment, Web tutorials, Learning and Teaching Subject Centres (LTSN), and contactable engineering librarians.
- **NASA Scientific and Technical Information** (www.sti.nasa.gov) is the homepage of the NASA STI program. The site centres around the STI database maintained by NASA Center for Aerospace Information (CASI), which provides publicly

available comprehensive worldwide scientific and technical bibliographic records covering basic and applied sciences from many sources. Over 3.5 million records, most with abstracts, index NASA reports, patents, conference proceedings, journal articles, and non-print materials including websites, as well as other aerospace-related NASA, US and international information. Full text of NASA material acquired since 1995 is linked to. The site also provides access to seven other NASA databases including NASA Image eXchange and the site catalogue, which gives details about NASA purchasable publications.

- **The Office of Scientific and Technical Information (OSTI)** (www.osti.gov) of the U.S. Department of Energy (DOE) provides access to a wealth of energy, science, and technology research and development (R&D) information from DOE-supported research and other technical information of interest. Access is provided to major DOE databases such as the Information Bridge, Energy Citations, Pre-print Network, GrayLit Network, covering journal articles, reports, pre-prints and other literature.

Subscription or part subscription

- **Elsevier Engineering Information Inc** (www.ei.org/eicorp/eicorp) is Engineering Information's own portal as distinct from other Elsevier owned sites. It provides access for subscribers to its own and other major bibliographic databases including Compendex and Inspec, both directly and indirectly on separate servers, and links to full text through ScienceDirect, full text databanks and websites. Some databases and databanks are searchable via single interfaces in three individual 'village' contexts – Engineering Village 2, Paperchem 2, Chemvillage – covering engineering of all kinds, specialist paper and pulp technology, chemicals and chemical technology and related business aspects, petroleum, petrochemical, natural gas and energy industries, patents, standards, industry news and relevant websites.

Specialist portals

Examples of free sites:

- **Aerade** (aerade.cranfield.ac.uk) is a portal specializing in aerospace and defence resources providing a browseable and searchable database of carefully described aerospace and defence Internet resources, a special collection of military and defence resources (DEVISE), abstracts of the ESDU databank for engineering design data and methods, an interactive aviation tutorial part of the RDN Virtual training suite series and aerospace and defence news.

- **eFluids** (www.efluids.com) is a one-stop resource for fluid dynamics and flow engineering. The site contains galleries of fluid flow images and experiments, software and various calculators. The directory element contains many different sections: around sixteen flow and turbulence archival databases and datasets world wide are described in detail and linked to; an education section lists tutorials, educational tools and materials, and students' competitions, as well as departments, laboratories and institutes and centres. Other directories cover products, companies, research and technology transfer organizations, professional societies, consultants, government agencies and specialist subject sites.

Indexes to end product

Library Catalogues
Library catalogues are free to use and referred to as Online Public Access Catalogues (OPACs).

Identifying OPACs

- **OPACs in Britain and Ireland (OBI)** (www.hero.ac.uk/reference_resources/opacs_in_britain_and_ireland_3795.cfm) – a directory of library catalogues and services in Britain and Ireland produced by HERO.
- **Worldwide library resources** (www.hero.ac.uk/reference_ resources/worldwide_library_resources3796.cfm?menu=true) A list of links provided by HERO to a selection of over sixty library-related resources (including some library catalogues) worldwide.

Identifying material held in research libraries
Mostly catalogues can only be searched one at a time but collaborations are being initiated for multiple-OPAC online searches. For example:

- **COPAC** (copac.ac.uk/copac) is the merged online catalogue of many of the largest university research libraries in the UK and Ireland, plus the British Library (CURL).
- The **British Library's** catalogue (blpc.bl.uk) covers both London Reference collections where science and technology material dates from 1974 and remote access material available through inter-library loan from the Document Supply Centre (DSC) where journals go back to 1700, conference proceedings to 1800 and books and reports up to 1950.

Abstracting and Indexing services
(See also Chapter 9) Most of the major abstracting and indexing services (bibliographic databases) are subscription based but there are some available free of charge.

Subscription services
(*N.B. Since some of these are available from several hosts, no URLs are given.*)
Major abstracting services/bibliographic databases for Engineering

- **Compendex** covers engineering. Available from several hosts.
- **Engineered Materials Abstracts** covers polymers, ceramics & composites. Sources include patents. Host: Cambridge Scientific Abstracts.
- **INSPEC** covers electrical and electronic engineering, physics, computing and information science. Hosts: Dialog, EBSCO, Elsevier Engineering Information Inc. (Ei), Edina.
- **METADEX** covers metals and alloys. Host: Cambridge Scientific Abstracts.
- **Science Citation Index** covers science and technology. Host: MIMAS Web of Science (WOS).

Specialist subjects – examples

- **ANTE (Abstracts in New Technologies and Engineering)** is topical and includes newspaper and popular journals in its coverage. Host: Cambridge Scientific Abstracts.
- **Computer & Information Systems Abstracts** covers computing and information systems. Host: Cambridge Scientific Abstracts.
- **Petroleum Abstracts** covers petroleum and offshore engineering. Self hosting.
- **International Civil Engineering Abstracts** covers civil engineering. Host: Emerald.

Specialist types of material – examples

- **NTIS** covers US Government **research reports** and government sponsored material (not necessarily in US). Host: Cambridge Scientific Abstracts.
- **Index to Theses** covers master's and doctoral **theses** in UK in all subjects. Self hosting.
- **ISI Proceedings** indexes papers presented at **conferences** (symposia, etc) worldwide including those in science and technology. It is searchable in relation to conference title and papers within it. Host: MIMAS Web of Knowledge (WOK).

- **CONF** covers forthcoming and past **conference title** information worldwide. Host FIZ Karlsruhe.

Freely accessible databases – Credit card open access

- **DialogWeb** (www.dialog.com/products/dialogweb/) is a search tool from Dialog Corporation for intermediate and advanced online searchers and novice users who can use a guided search facility. It offers Web access to all 600 Dialog databases covering patents, trademarks and technical and reference material in science and technology.
- **DialogSelect** (www.dialog.com/products/dialogselect/) is a search tool for end-users without search expertise needing routine answers in specific subject areas. Provides Web access to 300 Dialog databases covering energy and environment research, patents, and technology research

Free databases
A few examples:

- **ChemFinder** (www.chemfinder.com) includes 3 free databases – ChemFinder covering chemical structures, physical properties and Web links, ChemACX Net a collection of chemical catalogues from major suppliers searchable by name, formula or desired structure, and Organic Synthesis.
- **NTIS (National Technical Information Service)** (www.ntis.gov/search/advanced.asp?loc=3–0–0&q=) covers US government sponsored reports in science and technology. Free searching of all the content in the NTIS database published since 1990.
- **NTRS: NASA Technical Reports Server** (ntrs.nasa.gov) covers scientific and technical research reports, journal and conference papers, technical videos, mission-related operational documents, and preliminary data from NASA and external sources. NASA material can be isolated and individual archives searched.
- **MatWeb** (www.matweb.com) covers all kinds of properties of over 28,500 metallic and non-metallic materials. Searchable by material type, manufacturer, trade name, or metal composition.
- **SPE Online** (speonline.spe.org/cgi-bin/searchform.pl) from the Society of Petroleum Engineers covers oil exploration and production technology in 35,000 technical papers. Full text is purchasable.
- **TRIS Online** (199.79.179.82/sundev/search.cfm) from US Bureau of Transportation Statistics and Transportation Research Board, holds around 470,000 records from over 470 journals. Over 9,000 links to full text are backed up by document delivery.

- **RAM (Recent Advances in Manufacturing)**
  (www.eevl.ac.uk/ram/index.php) hosted by EEVL, covers
  manufacturing, mechanical engineering and related management
  areas such as CAD, product development etc, from over 500
  journals, books, videos and conference proceedings.
- **Earthquake Engineering Abstracts**
  (nisee.berkeley.edu/eea.html) from National Information Service
  for Earthquake Engineering (NISEE), University of California, offers
  100,000 abstracts of earthquake engineering articles from 1971.

Bibliographies
(See also Chapter 10)

- **The Collection of Computer Science Bibliographies**
  (liinwww.ira.uka.de/bibliography/)
  contains around 1,400 bibliographies with more than 1.2 million
  references to journal and conference articles, reports, many with
  BibTeX entries. Over 19,000 references contain cross references
  to citing or cited publications and over 150,000 link online. There
  are over 2,000 links to other sites.
- **Computer Hardware Testing On The Space Shuttle**
  (www.noodletools.com/noodlelinks/links/
  tu2ic81s_c3e0b855990334d89f93e4bbad3832f4.html) is a
  specialist bibliography from NoodleLinks Database of Academic
  Bibliographies.

Tables of Contents Services (TOCS)
(*N.B. Since TOCS are packaged together with full text they will be exemplified at the appropriate sections of **End-products** below i.e. **Journal** articles and **Books-Reference** . . .).*

End products

Journal and review articles

(See also Chapter 2)

Identifying journals in existence
The vast majority of online scholarly journals are not free, not least because
of their costly editing and refereeing processes, though there are a number
of collaborative initiatives to make scientific research more freely available
and consequently a few refereed titles are available free. Comprehensive
listings of journals can be found in:

- **Ulrich's Periodicals Directory** (www.ulrichsweb.com/
  ulrichsweb) lists a quarter of a million journal titles worldwide.

- **DOAJ (Directory of Open Access Journals)**
  (www.doaj.org) lists free, full text, scholarly journals whose
  bibliographic details are browseable and searchable with free full
  text available but not currently searchable. It includes a Technology
  and Engineering section.

Journal articles

Keeping up to date with recently published articles

Subscription service
A resource specializing in current awareness is:

- **ISI Current Contents Connect** (www.isinet.com/isi/
  products/cc/ccconnect/cccsitewide/), providing weekly coverage of
  bibliographic data (from articles, editorials, meeting abstracts,
  reviews etc) appearing in recent editions of over 8,000 scholarly
  journals and 2,000 books, and evaluated scholarly websites. One
  edition specializes in engineering, computing & technology.

Free service

- Articles in the **latest issue** of any journal can be browsed through
  in **Tables of Contents Services (TOCS) on e-journal
  online services** to keep up-to-date with specific journals.
  Keywords can be sought in TOCS which include search engines.

Identifying journal articles

Subscription services

- **Abstracting and indexing services** all cover journal articles
  (in addition to all kinds of literature) which can be searched in
  relation to a large number of fields (*See **Abstracting & Indexing
  Services** in **World Wide Web** and **Specific Resources** sections
  for more information and examples*).
- **Table of Contents Services (TOCS)** on journal online
  services provide browseable, and increasingly, searchable TOCs of
  journal articles on their sites (*N.B. Since TOCS are inextricably
  linked with full text they are exemplified within **Full text** section
  below – For more explanation about TOCS in general see TOCS in
  World Wide Web section*).

Free services
The following indexes articles in free e-journals:

- **Engineering E-journal Search Engine (EESE)** (www.eevl.
  ac.uk/eese/) searches the full text of over 150 free e-journals.
  A browseable A-Z list provides links to the journal homepages.

Full Text

(*N.B. Publishers overlay their Online (full text) Journal Services with a Tables of Contents Service (TOCS) to which they are inextricably linked. Thus TOCS and full text are exemplified together below. Many publishers provide alerting services in the form of regular emails to users advising them of all new titles. TOCs or a selection relevant to the users profile and such services are exemplified below*).

Subscription – Journal Online and Table of Contents Services (TOCS)

Conditions of access vary. Full text is restricted to subscribing institutions (who access it via their Web pages), by IP address recognition, or less usually, username and password. Institutions can opt to subscribe to the entire collection or to a specified selection. Individual items may be available for purchase to registering members of the public.

Most services provide free access to TOCs and alerting services, and increasingly to abstracts, site search engines and in some cases, additional data such as article references.

Single/simple publisher sites – examples

General

- **Springer LINK List of Journals** (link.springer.de/ol/index.htm) covers all scientific subjects.
- **Wiley InterScience** (www3.interscience.wiley.com/ journalfinder.html) covers scientific, technical, medical, and professional subjects in 300 leading journals. Engineering journals can be isolated. Individuals or professional association members may be licensed to access select publications.

Specialist publishers
Some important examples for engineers:

- **IEEE/IEE Electronic Library** (ieeexplore.ieee.org/ Xplore/DynWel.jsp) is a major, highly structured databank providing full text of journals, amongst all other categories of IEE/IEEE publications in electrical and electronic engineering, computing, physics and information technology. Full text is available to corporate, government and university subscribers, abstracts of publications and full text of IEEE Spectrum to members and TOCs are free to anyone.
- **Association of Computing Machinery (ACM) Digital Library** (portal.acm.org/dl.cfm) covers journals, reports, and conference proceedings on computing science and related subjects. TOCs are free and full text plus other services is available to subscribers and student members.

- **American Institute of Physics Online Journal Publishing Service** (ojps.aip.org) covers physics, engineering, science journals. Free TOCs service.
- **Institute of Physics** (www.iop.org/EJ/) covers physics journals. Both TOCs and full text are independently searchable. Full text access to *New Journal of Physics*, articles in This Month's Papers and IOP Select is free, as are TOCs and abstracts. Individual subscriptions are allowed. Access to full text 1874–1992, requires an additional fee.
- **SIAM (Society for Industrial and Applied Mathematics)** (epubs.siam.org) covers mathematics journals of which nine research titles are accelerated (issued early in advance of print version). A database of TOCs, abstracts and citations from 1994 is free with licensed access to full text from 1997.
- **Thomas Telford Journals online service** (www. t-telford.co.uk/jol/) covers journals in civil engineering and construction from Telford and Institution of Civil Engineers, including Proceedings and *Geotechnique*. Free TOCs and abstracts. Full text from 1997 is available to subscribers.

Aggregators of single publishers' various imprints

- **ScienceDirect** (www.sciencedirect.com) provides a fulltext online journal service of over 1,800 Elsevier and Elsevier owned imprint journals covered by a search engine (in addition to hosting major databases). Journal TOCs and abstracts are free to anyone.

Aggregators of many publishers
A major aggregation service whose facilities encompass a range of those provided by other services, is:

- **EBSCOhost Electronic Journals Service** (EJS) (ejournals.ebsco.com/Login.asp) provides TOCs, abstracts and full text of nearly 10,000 e-journals from 685 different publishers. Over 900 engineering journals can be browsed alphabetically, within subject or publisher groupings. Search facilities enable journal title, specific article, author and keyword searching.

Other major services:

- **IngentaSelect** (antonio.ingentaselect.com) is the electronic journal-only site of the Ingenta service (the same titles can also be found on the main **ingenta** site (www.ingenta.com)). It supplies access to 5,400+ full text online publications of which around 120 are engineering.
- **Emerald** (antonio.emeraldinsight.com/ vl=17631788/cl=73/nw=1/rpsv/journals/index.htm)

(MCB University Press) journal service provides full text of around seventeen Emerald-published Engineering and Materials science journals mostly in mechanical engineering, electronic and electrical engineering, back to 1989, and abstracts of articles from other publishers.

- **SwetsWise** (www.swetswise.com/public/login.do) from Swets Blackwell, another major journal subscription management tool provider, offers 7,428 full text publications from 258 publishers with the usual search and browse facilities.

Free e-journals

One example of the few initiatives for making scholarly journal articles openly available:

- **BioMed Central** (www.biomedcentral.com) is a commercial publisher committed to providing immediate free access to peer-reviewed biomedical research. Areas such as biotechnology, medical imaging and nuclear medicine may be of relevance to engineers.

Review articles

(See also Chapter 10) An example of a site which specializes in them is:

- **Annual Reviews** (www.annualreviews.org) which focuses on science. Areas relevant to engineers are biomedical engineering, energy and the environmental, fluid mechanics and materials research.

Conference Papers

(See also Chapter 4) The websites for individual conferences often provide abstracts and sometimes full-text of papers.

Keeping up-to-date – forthcoming conferences

A Bibliography of indexes to forthcoming conferences:

- **Keeping your research up to date – conferences and conference papers**
  (www.lboro.ac.uk/library/aware/conf.html) from Loughborough University Library.

Subscription

- **CIS** (www.fiz-informationsdienste.de/en/DB/conf/indexcis.html) (Conference Information Service) lists forthcoming meetings for the next two years emailed to you in the area of your choice.

Free services

- **ZETOC** (zetoc.mimas.ac.uk) Conference Search contains details of 16,000 conference proceedings published per year, received by the British Library.
- **AllConferences.com** (www.allconferences.net) is a directory focusing on forthcoming specialized scientific, medical and technological and academic conferences. Searchable and browseable amongst over thirty science and technical categories.
- **Association, institution and company sites** advertise their upcoming conferences for bookings and calls for papers, e.g. **ACM conferences** (www.acm.org/events/).

Identifying conference papers – past and recent

- **Abstracting and indexing services** routinely cover conference papers (See *Abstracting and indexing services*).
- Recently published conference papers in abstracting services may be able to be isolated by date or weekly input file.
- Specialist abstracting services are **ISI Proceedings** and **CONF** (See *Abstracting and indexing services*).
- Publishers' sites include **TOCs** of recently published proceedings.

Full text services

Subscription

- **IEEE/IEE Electronic Library** (ieeexplore.ieee.org/ Xplore/DynWel.jsp) (See also *Journal section- Single/simple Publisher sites*) provides full text of IEEE/IEE conferences of which IEEE alone publishes 400 a year.

Technical Reports

(See also Chapter 3)

Identifying reports – past and recent
Many of the services below provide news sections or allow update searching for recent reports.

(N.B. Identifying services which also hold full text are included below.)

Subscription service

- Many scientific and technological **abstracting and indexing services** list and summarize research reports along with other categories of material.

- A specialist abstracting service for reports is **NTIS (National Technical Information Service)** www.ntis.gov (a free version also available) which covers reports resulting from US government sponsored research in US and worldwide.

Free services

- **GrayLIT Network** (graylit.osti.gov) hosted by OSTI, cross searches five servers (the US Defense Technical Information Centre (DTIC), DOE Information Bridge, NASA Jet Propulsion Lab Reports, NASA Langley Technical Reports, and Environmental Protection Agency (EPA) Reports) which hold over 130,00 records, using a distributed search tool.
- **NTIS (National Technical Information Service)** (www.ntis.gov/search/advanced.asp) US government sponsored reports in all science and technical subjects. Free searching of all the content in the NTIS database published since 1990.
- **NASA Technical Reports Server (NTRS)** (ntrs.nasa.gov) provides free access to over 500,000 records from scientific and technical literature from around twenty NASA and external government programs.
- **Energy Citation Database (ECD)** (www.osti.gov/ecd/) is a bibliographic database covering energy and energy-related literature from 1948, from the Department of Energy (DOE) and its predecessor agencies.

Full text services

Free services

- **DOE Information Bridge** (www.osti.gov/bridge/) from the US Department of Energy and OSTI, allows anyone to access, locate and search the bibliographic records, abstracts and full-text of 65,000 DOE R&D reports from 1995.
- **Subject Portals** (www.osti.gov/subjectportals/) from US DOE's OSTI provide full-text DOE scientific and technical reports, links to journal literature, and other information sources. A selection of the portals includes: **Photovoltaic Energy (PHV)** (www.ost.gov/pv/); **Geothermal Energy Technology (GET)** (www.osti.gov/get/); **Superconductivity (SUP)** (www.osti.gov/sup/); **Wind Energy (WET)** (www.osti.gov/wet/); **Biopower Energy Systems (BEP)** (www.osti.gov/bmp/); **Biofuels Energy Systems (BMF)** (www.osti.gov/bmf/)

Theses

(See also Chapter 3)

Identifying theses

Some **abstracting and indexing services** include theses amongst their other coverage. Specialist abstracting services which focus entirely on theses are:

- **Index to Theses** (www.theses.com) theses for higher degrees in Great Britain and Northern Ireland accepted from 1970 to 2003
- **Dissertation Abstracts** (library.dialog.com/bluesheets/html/bl0035.html) covers North American masters and doctoral theses and a small number of European theses

Gateways can be particularly useful at picking up thesis material, particularly where it merely constitutes part of material on a website. An example to refer to is:

- **EEVL** (www.eevl.ac.uk) Engineering section. Click on Browse by Resource Type and choose Full text – Theses/Dissertations section.

Full text

Theses published from the outset in electronic form are in their infancy and full text *en masse* from educational institutions is usually restricted to university Intranets, though initiatives for digital libraries are on the increase. Individuals may post their own theses on their own web pages.

- **Digital Library of MIT Theses** (theses.mit.edu) a collection of **selected** MIT masters and doctoral theses available online.

Patents

(See also Chapter 5) There is extensive free general information, guidance on patent application, writing and searching, services by patent agents and commercial services, sites of patent granting bodies, and patent news on the Web, and also many free bibliographic databases covering patents applied for. Full text patent databanks tend to be subscription only, but a few are free. Many sites include some or many of these features, so it is difficult to categorize them precisely.

To find websites with all kinds of patent information refer to:

- **EEVL** (www.eevl.ac.uk) Engineering section. Click on Browse by Resource Type and choose the several sections referring to Patents.

Patent information

- **UK Patent Office** (www.patent.gov.uk) is the official body for the granting of patents in the UK. The site offers a wide variety of information about intellectual property, publications and services.
- **Patent Information Services** (www.bl.uk/patents) at the British Library are part of the most comprehensive patent print collection in the world with forty-seven million specifications from forty countries. It provides extensive introductory and advanced information on patents, patent application procedure and searching, the collections, UK libraries who help with patent research and links to key databases on free sites and other relevant links.
- **European Patent Office** (www.epo.co.at/epo/) created to establish a uniform patent system in Europe, allows patents to be applied for and granted simultaneously in different European countries. Searchable databases including European Patent Convention available.

Alerting Services
Examples:

- **Patent Alert** (www.patentalert.com) is a free (upon registration) email service based on the US Patent and Trademark Office database which provides descriptions of newly awarded US patents in areas pre-selected by the client.
- **Patent Alert! / Trade-mark Alert!** (strategis.ic.gc.ca/SSG/ed01599e.html) from Strategis, a Federal government service, is a free monthly email service containing links to all newly registered Canadian patents and trademarks matching previously submitted profiles.

Identifying patents – past and recent
Various kinds of services can be used for finding both recently awarded, ongoing and past patents, including:

Subscription

- **Derwent** (www.derwent.co.uk) provides international patent information and offers several patent search databases including World Patents Index with over eleven million patent records and Patents Citation Index. The databases are made accessible from database online hosts such as Dialog and Delphion.

Free services
Many **websites** provide free access to databases describing patent applications.

- **Patent Search Links** (www.paznet.com/neifeld/patsea.html) provide a comprehensive set of links to various patent search databases around the world and national patent websites, both organized by country. Maintained by patent attorney Richard Neifeld.
- **The Intellectual Property Digital Library (IPDL)** (pctgazette.wipo.int) hosted by the World Intellectual Property Organization provides access to various intellectual property data collections.

Full text
Some important examples:

Subscription

- **Delphion Research** (www.delphion.com) (Thomson subsidiary) is a comprehensive service offering full-text patent documentation, comprising over thirty-five million records from leading patent authorities and seventy patent offices worldwide.

Free service

- **US Patent & Trademark Office (USPTO)** (www.uspto.gov) USPTO's site gives extensive general information on patents and trademarks and on the Office's services in addition to full text.
- **Espacenet** (gb.espacenet.com) (via the UK Patent Office) or (ep.espacenet.com) is a free service from the European Patent Organisation through the EPO and member states offices providing access to many databases. It provides full text of EPO, France, Germany, Switzerland, United Kingdom, United States and WIPO patents, abstracts and bibliographic data for China and Japan and bibliographic data from another fifty countries.
- **PCT Full Text Database** (ipdl.wipo.int) hosted by WIPO, is a prototype of the PCT Gazette, and freely available for test purposes with the aim eventually of superceding the Gazette.

Preprints

Preprints are posted randomly on the Web in various locations – in formal repositories, on university department pages, on academics' own pages, etc. – and until recently there have been few attempts at indexing them.

Identifying preprints

- **PrePRINT Network** (www.osti.gov/preprint/) is a searchable gateway to preprint servers dealing with scientific and technical disciplines of concern to US Department of Energy (DOE). A document search facility allows users to search the category, title, top of document, and full text of over 120,000 PDF documents from 10,000 servers in thirty-five countries linked to the PrePRINT Network. Access is free.

The **Alerts service** will automatically notify you by email when new preprint information is available in your registered areas of interest.

Popular journal and magazine articles

- **New Scientist.com** (www.newscientist.com) is the free online weekly version of the subscription version print journal. It provides a large number of articles with news of new research and technical developments, collections of the latest articles on some twenty or more topical areas of science and makes available to personal print edition subscribers a ten year archive of issues.
- **Science News Online: Search** (www.sciencenews.org/search.asp) is the online version of Science News, a weekly newsmagazine covering the most important research in all fields of science. It provides free access to 18 percent of all articles in the print version, bibliographic references and sources for *all* articles published in *Science News*, and online-only features, since April 25, 1996.

Standards

(See also Chapter 6) International, national and corporate **standards issuing bodies** all provide a greater or lesser degree of information on their published and forthcoming standards. Some of them also provide **Alerting services.**

To find websites of standards' issuing bodies and those with standards' information refer to:

- **EEVL** (www.eevl.ac.uk) Engineering section. Click on Browse by Resource Type and choose sections referring to Standards.

Information on standards

- **BSI Group** (www.bsi-global.com/index.xalter) the issuer of British Standards, provides comprehensive information on standards and standards-based services to organizations worldwide.

Identifying standards

A leading subscription **abstracting and indexing service** identifying standards worldwide is:

- **Standards Infobase** (www.ili.co.uk/en) produced by ILI. It covers 400,000 standards from over 250 issuing bodies.

Examples of important standards' sites:

- **ILI** (www.ili.co.uk) features a searchable catalogue of hardcopy standards from a large number of issuing bodies including: ANSI, API, ASHRAE, ASTM, BS, CECC, EIA, DIN, IEEE, ISO, SAE, linked to an online ordering facility.
- **International Organization for Standardization (ISO) Online** (www.iso.ch) includes the catalogue of all ISO International Standards including drafts, complete lists of ISO members and technical committees and general background on ISO.
- **International Electrochemical Commission (IEC)** (www.iec.ch) is the leading global organization issuing international standards for all electrical, electronic and related technologies which serve as a basis for national standardization and international contracts.
- **NSSN** (www.nssn.org) a network collaboration between the American National Standards Institute (ANSI), US standards' organizations, government agencies, and international standards' organizations providing standards' information from more than 600 national, foreign, regional and international bodies.

Full text

- **British Standards (BS) Online** (bsonline.techindex.co.uk) Subscription full text databank of current, historic, and draft British Standards and more than 16,000 BSI adopted European and international standards.

Books – reference, textbooks, monographs

(See also Chapter 12) Publishers' catalogues and full text/content online services are typically on separate, though linked, servers. Full text is in the main a subscription service, pay-per-item but some academic organizations and enthusiastic authors provide some free.

Alerting services

Many publishers provide notification services of new titles, some personalized, mostly in the form of emails to users. An updated list of such services is available:

- Keeping your research up to date – new book titles (www.lboro.ac.uk/library/aware/books.html) is a bibliography of publishers with alerting services

Identifying books

- **Major Library OPACS** are a good way of identifying existing books (both print and electronic) (See **Library catalogues** within **Finding tools** in this section)
- **Abstracting services** and **TOCS** can help identify books. (See examples in **Abstracting & Indexing Services** and **TOCS** in this **Specific Resources** sections).

Full text

Full text is offered in a variety of ways – individual major opuses with their own sites, a collection of works by a publisher on the home site or as part of a collection by different publishers amassed by aggregators, such as Emerald or Knovel. TOCS and bibliographies are typically available at no cost. Full text is available to licensed institutional customers and often individuals or members of professional associations may also license content access for select publications.

Subscription services

Single opus site – example

- **AccessScience** (www.accessscience.com) is home to the *McGraw-Hill Encyclopedia of Science and Technology Online.* Updated daily. Full search capabilities.

Single publisher sites

- **CRCnetBASE** (www.crcnetbase.com) from CRC, a major publisher of engineering reference works, is the hub for many CRC sites focusing on different disciplines. Examples include: ENGnetBASE (www.engnetbase.com) where you can browse among different engineering disciplines for some 170 handbooks, etc. (N.B. Relevant handbooks may appear under categories not indicated as pertinent by CRC). Other sites include ENVIROnetBASE (www.environetbase.com) with 108 titles and CHEMnetBASE (www.chemnetbase.com) which includes Polymers: a property database (www.polymersdatabase.com). A forthcoming title is BIOTECHnetBASE.
- **Wiley InterScience** (www.interscience.wiley.com) is Wiley's full text content service. Major reference works include eight engineering works such as *Characterization of Materials, Encyclopedia of Space Science and Technology, Reference Manual for Telecommunications Engineering* (www3.interscience.wiley.com/reference.html).

Aggregator – a major example

- **Knovel** (www.knovel.com) is a major aggregator providing over 150 engineering reference handbooks and databases from twenty-three different publishers including for example, the Royal Society of Chemistry and McGraw-Hill (fifty titles). Of particular strength are chemical engineering with seventy-four titles, mechanical engineering, semiconductors, and electronics. It allows searching and retrieval of text and data, and some manipulation of data in Knovel's own publications including its *Knovel's Critical Tables* and the well known *International Critical Tables of Numerical Data, Physics, Chemistry and Technology*. Though freely searchable, full-text access is only available to the General Engineering and the Mechanical and Mechanical Engineering sections.

Free full text
Example

- **Scientific and technical acronyms, symbols and abbreviations** (www3.interscience.wiley.com/stasa/) is the online edition *of Scientific and Technical Acronyms, Symbols and Abbreviations* published as a free adjunct to content presented in Wiley Interscience.

Trade literature and product information

Identifying product literature and sites

- **Yahoo** (www.yahoo.com) Product Search enables searching by type of product amongst millions of items from thousands of merchants, to find products.
- **Froogle** (froogle.google.com) a product search engine from Google, currently in its infancy and restricted as to technology coverage.
- **EEVL** (www.eevl.ac.uk) Engineering section enables browsing by resource type to find Product Information and Product News sites.

Examples indicating a variety of sites containing product information:

- **E4Engineering** (www.e4engineering.com) is part of Centaur Publications' E4 Network of sites providing information and services to engineers based around several trade journals including *The Engineer*.
- **Engineeringtalk** (www.engineeringtalk.com) the homepage of the email newsletter, provides product information and news published by Pro-Talk Ltd., UK.

- **RS Online** (rswww.com) is the website of RS, a distributor of industrial components with a database of over 135,000 products supported by freely available enquiry services and technical information including over 40,000 data sheets and user manuals.
- **Chemical Equipment Online** (www.chemequipmag.com) is the electronic equivalent of the process industries' trade magazine published by Reed Business Information.

Courseware, training, learning materials and case studies

Courseware is available in different guises and accessible in different ways: restricted to Intranets or by password for local students or those taking distance learning courses, available freely in part or wholly and freely available. Free courseware is in a relatively embryonic stage, its development being led by US universities.

Identifying courseware etc

- **EEVL** (www.eevl.ac.uk) Engineering section enables browsing by Resource type to find Learning/ courseware

Sites supporting courseware development and learning activities:

- **The World Wide Web Courseware Developers Listserv Web Site** (www.unb.ca/wwwdev/) contains information for those developing courseware for Web delivery, including a list of members' courseware.
- **UK Centre for Materials Education** (www.materials.ac.uk) which supports and promotes innovative learning and teaching, lists online resources in materials providing starting points for learning activities

Free material

Examples showing the variation in extent and type of courseware and/or learning materials on offer:

- **MIT OpenCourseWare** (ocw.mit.edu) a pioneering scheme by MIT to make publicly available university engineering course materials with lecture notes, assignments, and solutions in pdf format.
- **World Lecture Hall** (wnt.cc.utexas.edu/~wlh/browse/index.cfm) is the University of Texas's gateway to courseware from faculty worldwide, in any language. Besides engineering, relevant sections include biomedical, chemical, civil, industrial, electrical, computer, mechanical, petroleum and geosystems engineering and environmental science.

- **RDN Virtual Training Suite** (www.vts.rdn.ac.uk) teaches key information skills for the Internet environment through tutorials covering major higher education disciplines including eight modules in major engineering subjects and related modules in physical sciences.
- **RDN Case Studies** (www.rdn.ac.uk/casestudies/eevl/) were created to illustrate ways in which RDN hub resources can integrate with further education. These engineering case studies include *Making Engineered Products, Role of New Technology in Engineering, Health and Safety in the Engineering Environment, Transmission Systems, Product Design,* and *Tyres and Tyre Technology.*
- **eFunda** (www.efunda.com/home.cfm) is a publisher offering engineering content and software in the form of over 30,000 pages of engineering fundamentals and calculators created by in-house staff. All kinds of materials and processes are covered.
- **Engineering Case Studies** (www.civeng.carleton.ca/ECL/) a catalogue from Carleton University in Canada and others of over 250 cases both in print and electronic form.
- **Engineer on a Disk** (claymore.engineer.gvsu.edu/~jackh/eod/index.html) provides a series of notes on a wide range of engineering topics including production planning, quality control and materials.
- **HowStuffWorks** (www.howstuffworks.com) is a guide to how things work aimed at young engineers and students with articles divided amongst automotive, computers, electronics, engines, internet, science and tech and transportation sections.
- **Knovel Quick Reference Guide** (www.knovel.com/knovel2/support.jsp) is typical of help pages on services provided by publishers.

Specialist subject sites

- **Downloads and Free Computer Training Materials** (www.customguide.com/downloads.htm) Computer training courseware.
- **Composite Materials Design** (callisto.my.mtu.edu/my4150/).
- **Electronics for Beginners and Intermediate Electronics** (ourworld.cs.com/gknott5413) includes descriptions and diagrams on general theory, components and projects.
- **aluMATTER: Strengthening Mechanisms** (aluminium.matter.org.uk) provides interactive web-based learning tools for aluminium science and technology.
- **Get a Grip on Robotics** (www.thetech.org/exhibits_events/online/robots/teaser/) provides graphics and text covering basic robotics including an introduction, robot basics, main parts of the robot, degrees of freedom, applications of robots, and other information.

Numerical and technical raw data – data databanks, images & video, statistics and software

Periodic tables

- **WebElements Periodic Table** (www.shef.ac.uk/~chem/web-elements/)
- **Periodic Table of Elements, EnvironmentalChemistry.com** (environmentalchemistry.com/yogi/periodic/)
- **The Periodic Table of the Isotopes** (ie.lbl.gov/education/isotopes.htm)
- **X-ray Properties of the Elements** (www.csrri.iit.edu/periodic-table.html)

Calculations and calculators

There are thousands of sites aiding calculations in all scientific and technical areas. Many American universities have helpfully aggregated them, and useful sites might include the all-subject:

- **Calculators On-Line Center** (www-sci.lib.uci.edu/HSG/RefCalculators.html) contains over 7,000 calculators from over 3,000 sources. 'Engineering' contains calculators for all topics e.g. bearings.

and the more specialist:

- **Nano, Quantum & Statistical Mechanics & Thermodynamics: Data & Property Calculation Websites** (www.uic.edu/~mansoori/Thermodynamic.Data.and.Property_html)

Databanks

Databanks, as a category, overlaps with other areas; for example, full text online journals' services are databanks:

Subscription

- **ESDU International** (www.esdu.com) provides extensive validated engineering data, methods and software in 1260 data items and 250 manipulative programs within twenty-three specific aerospace, process, structural, and mechanical engineering topics. The data is particularly useful in design.

Free databanks

- **Smithsonian Astrophysical Observatory, Central Engineering** makes available half a dozen databanks from its web pages entitled Online Engineering Resources: (ce-www.harvard.edu/online_resources/online.html) including:

- **Ceramic Material Database**
  (ce-www.harvard.edu/online_resources/materials/ceramic_frm.html)
- **Plastics Material Database**
  (ce-www.harvard.edu/online_resources/materials/plastic_frm.html)
- **UIUC Airfoil Data Site** (www.aae.uiuc.edu/m-selig/ads.html) provides the Airfoil Coordinates Database, which contains over 1,150 airfoils and covers a wide range of applications.

Images and video

Some random examples of sites concentrating on static or moving images.

- **Exploring the Nanoworld**
  (www.mrsec.wisc.edu/edetc/index.html) from the Materials Research Science and Engineering Center, University of Wisconsin – Madison.
- **Fluid Mechanics, Hydraulic and Environmental Engineering: Dr. Hubert Chanson's Gallery of Photographs** (www.uq.edu.au/~e2hchans/photo.html) comprises this extensive gallery of fully documented photographs of structures and phenomena in the fields of fluid mechanics, hydraulic and environmental engineering in addition to detailed overview articles and other information.
- **Get a Grip on Robotics** (www.thetech.org/exhibits_events/online/robots/teaser/) part of The Tech's interactive Museum of Innovation, provides a graphics-intensive exhibition covering the basics of the world of robotics.

Statistics

Statistics are one of the many elements provided on diverse sites. A relatively small number of sites focus entirely on statistics. Examples include:

- **Transport Statistics** (www.transtat.dft.gov.uk) from the UK Department of Transport provides extensive statistical and textual data on all aspects of transport and transport trends in Great Britain and personal travel.
- **Aerospace Industries Association (AIA)** (www.aia-aerospace.org), a trade organization representing the US aerospace industry, includes a section on statistics.
- **Airports Council International (ACI)** (www.airports.org). Amongst other data the site includes airport traffic statistics by passenger, cargo and aircraft movements, busiest airports, latest monthly ranking.

Software

- **Free Mechanical Engineering Software**
  (www.freebyte.com/cad/) provides details on and links to Windows based software including CAD/CAM finite element, dynamic simulation, thermal analysis, etc.
- **engAPPLETS** (www.engapplets.vt.edu) is a project from Virginia Polytechnic Institute and State University, comprising a collection of small software programs, written as Java 'applets', designed to teach various engineering concepts.
- **Odeon Room Acoustics software**
  (www.dat.dtu.dk/~odeon/index.html) is a program developed by the Department of Acoustic Technology, Ørsted Technical University of Denmark and six consulting companies. A demonstration version is available by ftp and includes a large database for coefficients of absorption.

Technical FAQs

Newsgroup/Usenet FAQs
The main archive site for all Usenet FAQs in full text is the ftp site (ftp://rtfm.mit.edu/pub/usenet/).

- **Internet FAQ Archives** (www.faqs.org/faqs/) archives 2,490 popular Usenet FAQs which are browseable by subject category (e.g. sci will produce around 100, technology only two). An advanced Usenet FAQ Archive search (www.faqs.org/faqs/faqsearch.html) covers the entire *. answers FAQ database (over 3,900 FAQs). Many FAQs are not updated.

Examples of newsgroup FAQs archives on the Web are:

- **Acoustics FAQ** (www.campanellaacoustics.com/faq.htm) a collaboration between participants of the alt.sci.physics.acoustics newsgroup dealing with all aspects of acoustics with links to related sites.
- **Active Noise Control FAQ** (users.erols.com/ruckman/ancfaq.htm) written for newsgroups news:alt.sci.physics.acoustics and news:comp.dsp, focusing on acoustics and digital signal processing, provides answers to common questions about active noise control referring to web links, magazine articles, technical references, and other sources of information.
- **Robotics Frequently Asked Questions List**
  (www.frc.ri.cmu.edu/robotics-faq/) is the FAQ list for the Internet robotics' newsgroups comp.robotics.misc and comp.robotics.research. Information is provided on robotics

resources on the Net, robotics organizations, periodicals and publications, conferences and competitions, as well as products and technical information.

- **Sam's Laser FAQ** (www.repairfaq.org/sam/lasersam.htm) is part of the Sci.Electronics.Repair FAQ provided by Samuel M. Goldwasser in the USA. The site covers topics such as safety, operating requirements, testing and maintenance, definitions of laser terminology as well as information on laser suppliers and how to build lasers at home. Different types of laser are described and also some schematics are provided.
- **Sci-Polymers Frequently Asked Questions** (www.theotherpages.org/poly-faq.html) contains sections on polymer basics including abbreviations, tradenames, properties, classification, processing methods, and recycling of polymers, a selection of polymer sites, some general information on organizations, producers, events, publications and a bibliography.

A random example of other FAQs:

- **Hybrid Electric Vehicle Program** (www.ott.doe.gov/hev) is a US Department of Energy program concerned with the development of HEVs.
- **OPEC (Organization of the Petroleum Exporting Countries) FAQs** (www.opec.org/FAQs/ AnswersAboutPrtroleumInd.htm) contains statistical and other information about the petroleum industry and non-OPEC oil producing countries.

Newsgroup and mailing list archives

(See also *Newgroups and Mailing Lists sections*)

Newsgroups

- **JISCmail** (www.jiscmail.ac.uk) is the UK's major electronic mailing list service.

Mailing Lists

- **Google Groups** (groups.google.com) contains the searchable archives of over 700 million newsgroup messages from 1981.

Blogs (Weblogs)

Identifying blogs

Directories of academic bloggers are maintained at (www.henryfarrell.net/ blog/) and (rhetorica.net/professors_who_blog.htm), though few actually focus on academic matters. While many blogs list other blogs, their names often do little to reveal their subjects.

Examples:

- **ENGLIB** (englib.info) from a 'scitech' librarian, provides news, technology, services, resources, education, databases, conferences, events, employment with searchable archives.
- **The SciTech Library Question?** (www.podbaydoor.com/engine/) maintained by 'scitech' Librarians at University of Alberta, provides occasional postings about 'scitech' issues of interest.
- **Confessions of a Science Librarian** (jdupuis.blogspot.com) by John Dupuis, 'scitech' librarian at York University, Toronto, features links and pointers of interest to science librarians.
- **Quark Soup** (www.davidappell.com) by freelance science writer David Appell, is a mixture of comment on scientific and political news and developments and encourages discussion.

News services, newsletters

They may comprise specialist magazines or newsletters or be included as an item on any site.

Identifying sites with news sections
A comprehensive gateway for news links on engineering sites is

- **Latest news in Engineering** (www.eevl.ac.uk/engineering/ newsfeed.htm) provided by EEVL. For each engineering discipline section it provides daily news headlines plus a list of Recommended News Sources (sites dedicated to news plus news sections on important engineering sites).

Services for news stories – examples

- **SciTechDaily Review** (www.scitechdaily.com) is a gateway for news stories providing informed science and technology coverage and analysis on a daily basis. Displayed in magazine format, summaries of topics link through to sources from many publications.
- **Environment News Service (ENS)** (ens-news.com) is the original daily international wire service presenting late-breaking environmental news, indexed by Reuters/Dow Jones Factiva, and the London Financial Times.

Legislation and recommendations

Government and institution sites may provide full text or summaries of regulations, provide updates or guidance on compliance, or merely advertise the existence of publications.

- **COSHH Essentials** (www.coshh-essentials.org.uk) developed by UK Health and Safety Executive, helps firms comply with the Control of Substances Hazardous to Health Regulations by advising on the use of chemicals.
- **The IEE Wiring Regulations** (www.iee.org/Publish/WireRegs/index.cfm) The IEE prepares regulations for the safety of electrical installations for buildings, the IEE Wiring Regulations (BS 7671), now the UK and many other countries' standard.

Contracts and procurement

Sites include government, university departments and other bodies responsible for C & P.

- **Constructionline** (www.constructionline.co.uk) from the UK Department of the Environment, Transport and the Regions, is a register of over 8,000 construction contractors and consultants qualified to criteria set and audited by DETR, ranging from architecture to demolition and in size from small specialists to the largest contractors.
- **Defence Advanced Research Projects Agency (DARPA) Tactical Technology Office** (www.darpa.mil/tto/) undertakes advanced military research for the US Department of Defense.

Recruitment and employment

Sites focusing on recruitment, etc., include agencies and organizations offering job opportunities, and are based around jobs and manpower databases which can be searched by a range of parameters which may include category, type, salary range, keywords and location and may be interactive. Job vacancies are routinely posted on organization sites.

Academic

- **jobs.ac.uk** (www.jobs.ac.uk) covers academic jobs in the UK, including engineering and technology posts.

Professional

- **Bulldog Engineering Recruitment and Management Services** (www.bulldog.co.uk) serves UK engineering maintaining a database of over 17,000 applicants and 3,000 companies.
- **Contracts Consultancy Ltd.** (www.ccl.uk.com) recruits for the oil and gas, power, process, food and brewing, telecommunications, railways, and pharmaceuticals industries in UK and overseas.
- **Engineers Online** (www.engineers-online.co.uk) contains a database of over 100,000 engineering businesses in the UK.
- **Executive Recruitment Services** (www.ers.co.uk) includes a searchable database of vacancies for contract or permanent employment within high technology industries.
- **Justengineers.net** (www.justengineers.net) provides access to job searches, career advice, e-mail alerts. Their newsletter includes engineering recruitment news, vacancies, employer profiles, and upcoming training.
- **The Engineer Jobs** (www.theengineerjobs.co.uk) is the recruitment section of the E4 Network.
- **Jobsite** (www.jobsite.co.uk) is a recruitment service providing details of UK job vacancies with sections for engineering, construction, electronics and IT.

Specific area recruitment

- **cad.uk.com** (www.cad.uk.com) advertises CAD & CAE vacancies for the United Kingdom.
- **Careers in Construction** (www.careersinconstruction.com) provides job advertisements, career advice, a CV service, company profiles, a courses' list and a free email alerting service.
- **CivilJobs.co.uk** (www.civiljobs.co.uk) specializes in the UK civil engineering industry recruitment.
- **Earthworks** (www.earthworks-jobs.com) provides job opportunities for geoscientists, petroleum engineers, hydro and engineering geologists, remote sensing professionals, oceanographers, and environmentalists in academia, upstream oil & gas and mining industry.
- **IEE Jobs Online** (www.iee.org/EduCareers/JobsOn/jobs_db.cfm) is a database of jobs listed in the IEE Recruitment newspaper sent out to IEE members.
- **Materials Edge** (www.materials-edge.net/html/index.php) is a recruitment company based in UK focusing primarily on the materials science, engineering, manufacturing and technology markets.

► MAILING LISTS

Email has greatly expedited and expanded informal scientific communication with obvious benefits for R&D. Also, by providing an additional communication forum, it has expanded the group discussion arena previously held by Usenet special interest groups prior to the development of the Internet.

Mailing or **discussion lists** have a similar function to Network News; users can post and reply to the list, conduct research through previous discussion, ask for assistance, etc; the difference being that once you have subscribed to a list, postings come directly as an email to you.

There are tens of thousands of mailing lists and no definitive list of lists. Lists on similar subjects and with the same title may not get picked up together by a list directory and a researcher must assume that there may well be others in their subject. Many mailing lists have evolved into conference or publication announcement services.

The Web facilitates mailing list organization by providing a base for mailing lists in the form of homepages for individual mailing lists or collective sites, where potential members can find out about the list, register and look up previous discussion organized into topic threads which may be indefinitely archived.

- **JISCmail** (www.jiscmail.ac.uk) aggregates UK academic lists. They are categorized as public, restricted or private; anyone can join a list but postings are restricted to members and may not be accessible by non-members. You can search by list names, keywords and for lists within a given discipline such as Engineering and Technology. An example of a UK list is:
- **Engineering-Geotech** (www.jiscmail.ac.uk/lists/ENGINEERING-GEOTECH.htm) for geotechnical engineers in research and industry.
- **Tile.Net/Lists** (tile.net/lists) covers worldwide discussion and information lists.
- **CataList** (www.lsoft.com/lists/listref.html) is the official catalogue of LISTSERV (software used particularly by US lists), providing information on 71,487 public lists out of 278,874 LISTSERV lists. A UK listserv example is:
- **Materials Science and Engineering list** (listserv.liv.ac.uk/archives/materials.html)

► NETWORK NEWS / DISCUSSION LISTS

The phrase Network News is used for Internet group discussion between people with similar interests and a quasi-interactive activity. The original

Usenet Groups, linking students with common interests, pre-dated the Internet and became one of its earliest clients. Network News may be referred to as **Usenet Discussion** even though it comprises an aggregation of Usenet discussion groups and other news including local sources, and may also be simply termed **Newsgroups**. In essence the 30,000 plus groups make up a huge continuously updated database for users to consult, share resources and ideas, forward questions and answers and pass on information and news. Messages are archived, arranged in threads (themes) following each particular line of discussion (which may coincide simultaneously with other topics within a group) and are available for browsing or searching.

Access to newsgroups

A news server collects and makes news available to your local server or ISP which then organizes the display of groups and related threads using a news reader program on your browser or email facility. Availability of newsgroups depends on the computer your newsreader uses as its news server. You can consult any newsgroup but will normally subscribe to those you want to see regularly. University servers are likely to restrict what they offer to academic interest groups. An ISP's offering may not include 'academic' groups and you may have to set up the software to download additional groups.

Newsgroups on offer will display under News on your browser's Tools pull down menu. To find suitable groups, you can simply browse down the hierarchies accessible to you.

Types of newsgroups

Newsgroup names reflect their hierarchical organization with the broadest grouping first, followed by any number of subgroupings separated by periods (.) The original seven categories have been added to by others as groups have spread worldwide.

Relevant groups for engineers fall within the **sci** category (research in the sciences), **comp** (computer software and hardware, computer science) and possibly **biz** (business) etc. Others like **alt** (alternative) may contain some topics of interest. More specialist groups with their own hierarchies are **hepnet** (high energy and nuclear physics with ten groups), **ieee** (IEEE related with fourteen subgroups). Within the umbrella groupings are subgroups relating to different disciplines or particular subjects. Some lists are moderated; submissions are automatically directed to a moderator who edits or filters and then posts the results ensuring irrelevant postings are excluded.

The science category embraces nearly 200 newsgroups. The following are just a selection:

sci.aeronautics* (2 groups),
sci.answers (useful for technical FAQs)
sci.chem* (6 groups)
sci.comp-aided
sci.electronics* (8 groups)
sci.energy* (1 group)
sci.engr* (24 groups)
sci.environment* (1 group)
sci.geo* (12 groups)
sci.materials* (1 group)
sci.mech* (1 group)
sci.nanotech

An alternative option to receiving selected newsgroups is to scan public Usenet services on the Web:

- **TileNet** (tile.net/news/) is a long-serving newsgroup provider. You can search by keyword or browse all groups by index, name hierarchy and description. The description usefully provides some idea of what you might be getting, which is important since once you click on a newsgroup within the description page, it displays all threads within your email, which can work out at several hundred.
- **Google Groups** (groups.google.com) provides access to newsgroup postings. Groups are aggregated beneath their main names with numbers of linkable subgroups and rate of activity indicated. Over 700 million messages back to 1981 are available.

▶ TRENDS AND DEVELOPMENTS

Large and small scale technological, economic and organizational developments are converging on the Internet with far-reaching implications for communication of scientific and technical information.

Currently, commercial and academic interests on the Web are pulling in different directions. The Internet's economic collapse resulted in much free information vanishing altogether, disappearing behind the commercial threshold or being restricted through user registration criteria. Services such as portals, gateways and search engines are remaining free through collaborations and support from advertising income. In commercial publishing, mergers and annexations have resulted in a relatively small number of major aggregation services.

Improved organization of information by portals and aggregators etc, is making resource identification easier but full text acquisition not necessarily cheaper. Many sites do offer a percentage of free information but it may be limited to cataloguing and indexing-type services rather than full text.

Simultaneously there are moves towards greater access to freely available/free full text research material.

By 2001 there were 'over a million research articles ... freely available on the web' (availability varying according to discipline) (Lawrence, 2001). Factors accelerating the rising tide of free research material, and calls for growth of and initiatives for research material on the Web, include the high cost of journals, the speed and ease with which authors can post work directly on the Web, and greater collaboration between greater numbers of widely distributed researchers using new methods of rapid communication and disseminating findings. Effecting changes in the economic model linking commercial publishers, university libraries, the peer-review system, etc. is problematic but events are to some extent already overtaking matters. Increasing dependence on pre-prints is illustrated by Andrew Odlyzko, citing work on a high temperature superconductor generating fifty e-prints from other laboratories before the original paper was even published, demonstrating informal peer review (Odlyzko, 2003). Faster communication is creating a continuum of publication requiring a continuum of peer review and the notion of a final definitive version of an article, so basic to scholarly publishing, is likely to fade away. Lawrence argues that free availability speeds scientific progress and 'articles freely available online are more highly cited' a finding mainly relating to computing science, a front-runner in posting e-prints and conference papers directly on the Web (Lawrence, 2001).

US Government sponsored research has been in the vanguard in making scientific research material freely available and encouraging exchange of information. In the academic sector, open access initiatives have been set up in the last few years including the Open ARCHIVE Initiative, Scholarly Publishing and Academic Resources Coalition (SPARC), FIGARO, DARE, Public Library of Science (PLoS) and others, culminating in the Budapest Open Access Initiative (BOAI) (Anon[2], 2003) which supported commitment to accelerate the making of research articles freely available on the Internet with reduced or no cost to the user.

Commercial publishers of both end-products and indexing tools are responding by making inroads into the middle ground occupied by librarians. Besides improving their product range and associated services including sophisticated search facilities, more archival material, accelerated electronic journal titles, seamless links to full text, etc, they are increasing emphasis on services based on individual user profiles. Chris Forbes, of Knovel, emphasizes this importance of moving towards end-user oriented services, indicating that aggregators should solve a problem or an information need, or provide answers (Hane, 2003).

This emphasis on problem-solving and specific data on request appears an expectation for the future in all spheres and requires use of interacting technologies. One such area that would benefit is higher education, where the complexity of resources and access methods for users constitutes a barrier to knowledge and is at odds with the speeds of data processing they are used to. The recognized need for internal services that are more integrated and connect to a wide variety of external services through transparent interfaces is generating interest in Web Services Technologies (WST) which allow services to interact with each other over the network (McDonald, 2003).

Evolving technology of all kinds is incrementally expanding ways the Internet is used, providing opportunities for enlarging the resource base for teaching and learning and aiding information recall. For example, video content can now be embedded in text, live broadcasting with replay ability is provided by over 700 TV broadcasting stations worldwide, and an increasing number of individuals are posting live streaming video on the Web (Frishberg, 2003). High-speed networking technology is making it possible to conduct interactive classes over the Internet with lecturers and students far removed from one another (Anon[1], 2003).

Other advances are helping to identify and trace information. Powerful and sophisticated search tools track communities of knowledge, metadata application is helping to standardize searching procedure and increase productivity, and perpetual tags such as the Digital Object Identifier (DOI) to bibliographic records, are helping to manage and track documents wherever and whoever is hosting them (International DOI Foundation, 2003). Developments impacting on user profiling and statistics' compilation and manipulation are improving targeting and tracking of users and general data usage analysis.

On the grand scale the GRID is set to transform scientific research. It will have a major impact on knowledge communication, and result in a sea change to the Internet. Grid computing applies the resources of many computers in a network (local or global) virtually simultaneously to a single scientific or technological problem (Anon[3], 2003), as exemplified in the human genome project. An example of a US joint effort between government, academia, and industry, is NASA's Information Power Grid (IPG), a network of high performance computers, data storage devices, scientific instruments, and advanced user interfaces (NASA, 2002). In the UK the National e-Science Grid Programme has established national and regional centres to promote and link grids. The expanded concept of the Grid is that it will link computers in academia and industry on a global scale, ultimately incorporating national and local grids 'producing a seamless pool of managed and brokered resources with an unprecedented level of flexibility and availability' (Anon[4], 2003).

The Web provides seamless access to information. Grid technology allows seamless access and use of computing resources as well as information. A Grid search engine will not only find data but also the data processing techniques and the computing power to carry them out before sending you the results. Grid computing and Web services may eventually converge until there is no distinction between them (Shread, 2003).

It remains to be seen whether specific developments on the Internet as it is now will be superceded or accelerated by those brought about by widespread expansion of grid computing but one thing is certain – there will be even more information to deal with at our fingertips.

▶ REFERENCES

Anon[1], 2003. *Making movies and music at the speed of light.* GlobalTechnoscan. www.globaltechnoscan.com/16thApr-22ndApr03/light.htm

Anon[2], 2003. Budapest Open Access Initiative (BOAI). www.soros.org/openaccess/

Anon[3], 2003. *Grid computing: the Whats.com word of the day: April 30 2003.* Global Grid Forum. www.gridforum.org/L_News/Details/whatis.htm

Anon[4], 2003. *Gridstart: background* DTI- e-SCIENCE National e-Science Grid Programme. www.gridstart.org/background.shtml

Frishberg, M., 2003. Roll-your-own Net TV takes off. *Wired News* July 15 www.wired.com/news/technology/0,1282,59623,00.html

Hane, P., 2003. InfoToday 2003 (Conference circuit). *InformationToday* 27(7) www.infotoday.com/it/jul03/hane2.shtml

International DOI Foundation, 2003. *The Digital Object Identifier System.* www.doi.org

Lawrence, S., 2001. *Online or invisible.* NEC Research Institute. Edited version appears in: *Nature,* 411(6837), p. 521. www.neci.nec.com/~lawrence/papers/online-nature01/

Mcdonald, D., 2003. *Web Services Technologies.* Joint Information Services Committee. www.jisc.ac.uk/index.cfm?name=techwatch_report_0304

NASA Advanced SuperComputing (NAS), 2002. *Information power grid.* www.nas.nasa.gov/About/IPG/ipg.html

Notess, G., 2003. Unlocking URLs: extensions, shortening options, and other oddities. *Online* 27(3). www.infotoday.com/online/may03/OnTheNet.shtml

Odlyzko, A., 2003. The Public Library of Science and the ongoing revolution in scholarly communication. *Nature webdebates* (www.nature.com/nature/debates/e-access/Articles/odlyzko.html)

Price, G., 2001. web search Engines FAQS: questions, answers, and issues. *Searcher* 9(9). www.infotoday.com/searcher/oct01/price.htm

Shread, P., 2002. A future when Grid computing, Web services are one. *Grid.earthweb.com: News.* www.gridcomputingplanet.com/news/article.php/3281_979701

Turner, E., 1999. Patent information on the Internet – can you afford to ignore it?
    Free Pint www.freepint.co.uk/issues/130599.htm#tips
Tyburski, G., 2003. Evaluating the quality of information on the Internet: checklist.
    The Virtual Chase 3 June 1997. www.virtualchase.com/quality/checklist.html

12 Reference Sources

Stephanie McKeating

The majority of resources included in this chapter have been chosen either because they cover more than one branch of engineering or because they are very broad subject-oriented works within the engineering field. In a few cases more subject specific works have been mentioned, but for specialized reference sources refer to the appropriate subject chapter elsewhere in this volume.

▶ GUIDES TO REFERENCE MATERIAL

For an overview of reference material in engineering a good starting point is a general guide to reference sources.

Mullay and Schlicke (1999) is probably the key guide to reference works with the first of its three volumes dealing with Science and Technology. It is international in scope although there is some bias towards British material. The entries are arranged in UDC (Universal Decimal Classification) order and of the 7,500 of them contained in Volume 1 around 1,300 are in the section on engineering. Some electronic resources such as websites and databases are included.

Balay (1996) does not have such a comprehensive engineering content since the bulk of the volume concentrates on reference books in social sciences and the humanities. There are some 300 entries in the guide, to books on engineering. Hurt (1998) covers all types of reference materials including electronic resources and websites. The guide concentrates on resources published after 1991, with nine of the twenty-one chapters being devoted to engineering disciplines. This title is also available as an e-book from netLibrary (www.netlibrary.com).

American Reference Books Annual (ARBA) is a serial publication which aims to review all reference books published in the United States during the course of the preceding year. Awe (1997) is compiled from ten years of the American Reference Books Annual (1986–1996). One of three main subject sections is devoted to science and technology, with the chapters containing reviews of relevant subject dictionaries and encyclopaedias.

American Reference Books Annual. 1970-, Englewood, Co.: Libraries Unlimited.

Awe, S. C., 1997. *ARBA Guide to subject encyclopedias and dictionaries.* 2nd ed. Englewood: Libraries Unlimited.

Balay, R., ed., 1996. *Guide to reference books.* 11th ed. Chicago: American Library Association.

Hurt, C. D., 1998. *Information sources in science and technology.* 3rd ed. Englewood: Libraries Unlimited.

Mullay, M. and Schlicke, P., eds., 1999. *Walford's guide to reference material, Vol. 1: Science and technology.* 8th ed. London: Library Association.

► ENCYCLOPAEDIAS

For background information on a subject of interest encyclopaedias can be helpful. A number of general encyclopaedias are available which contain technical information in various engineering disciplines. The principle encyclopaedia devoted to science and engineering is the *McGraw-Hill encyclopedia of science and technology* (2002). This twenty volume work is updated annually with yearbooks. A web-based version of the encyclopaedia is available on subscription. Known as AccessScience (access-science.com) the service is updated on a daily basis. Collections of articles taken from this work are published as separate volumes. Available on CD-ROM the *McGraw-Hill multimedia encyclopedia of science and technology* (1999) combines material from earlier editions of the *McGraw-Hill encyclopedia of science and technology* and Parker (2002) (see following section).

Meyers (2001) is published in eighteen volumes and is written at a more advanced level than the McGraw-Hill publication. A more concise, two volume scientific encyclopedia is Considine (2002) which is also available condensed into a single volume, Axelrod (2003).

Singh (1987) covers the theoretical concepts, technology and applications of systems and control in a wide range of scientific and engineering disciplines. Similarly, widely applicable Finkelstein and Grattan (1993) includes a catalogue of transducer devices and related systems as well as material on measurement and instrumentation.

The study of materials is of interest in many branches of engineering and thus Buschow *et al.* (2001) is a useful interdisciplinary work. Published in eleven volumes it is also available as a web version (www.elsevier.com/emsat) which is accessible via a site license. Regular updates are made to the web version. Schwartz (2002) brings together in one volume the most up-to-date information on materials, forms and parts, finishes, and processes utilized in industry.

There is a wide variety of encyclopaedias available which are subject specific in content and these will be dealt with in the relevant subject chapters elsewhere in this volume, however there is an online collection containing a wide variety of subject specific encyclopaedias which is worthy of description. Wiley Interscience makes a range of reference material available on the Internet (www.interscience.wiley.com/cgi-bin/browse byproduct?type=3) including a number of encyclopaedias. Institutional customers may take out an annual subscription to the online versions of these reference works with pricing dependent on the type of institution, user population and which titles are subscribed to. Titles include the following:

Encyclopedia of Bioprocess Technology
Encyclopedia of Polymer Science and Technology
Kirk-Othmer Encyclopedia of Chemical Technology
Ullman's Encyclopedia of Industrial Chemistry
Encyclopedia of Imaging Science and Technology
Encyclopedia of Smart Materials
Encyclopedia of Software Engineering
Reference Manual for Telecommunications Engineering
Wiley Encyclopedia of Electrical and Electronics Engineering

Forthcoming titles include:

Encyclopedia of Space Science and Technology
Encyclopedia of Telecommunications
Digital Encyclopedia of Applied Physics
Encyclopedia of Agrochemicals

Axelrod, A., 2003. *Van Nostrand's concise encyclopedia of science.* New York: Wiley.

Buschow, K. H. J. et al., eds., 2001. *Encyclopedia of materials: science and technology.* London: Elsevier.

Considine, G. D., ed., 2002. *Van Nostrand's scientific encyclopedia.* 9th ed. New York: Wiley.

Finkelstein, L. and Grattan, K. T. V., eds., 1993. *Concise encyclopedia of measurement and instrumentation.* Oxford: Pergamon.

McGraw-Hill encyclopedia of science and technology. 2002. 9th ed. New York: McGraw-Hill.

McGraw-Hill multimedia encyclopedia of science and technology. 1999. New York: McGraw-Hill.

Meyers, R. A., ed., 2001. *Encyclopedia of physical science and technology.* 3rd ed. San Diego CA: Academic Press

Parker, S. P., ed., 2002. *McGraw-Hill dictionary of scientific and technical terms.* 6th ed. New York: McGraw-Hill.

Schwartz, M. M., 2002. *Encyclopedia of materials, parts, and finishes.* 2nd ed. Boca Raton, Fla: CRC Press.

Singh, M. G., ed., 1987. *Systems & control encyclopedia.* Oxford: Pergamon.

▶ DICTIONARIES

There are three types of dictionaries covered in this section; defining dictionaries which provide definitions of engineering terms, translating dictionaries which cover terminology in more than one language and dictionaries of symbols and abbreviations.

Defining dictionaries

Dictionaries covering science and technology tend to be selective in their coverage of engineering terminology, however they can still be useful tools. One of the main works of this sort is Parker (2002), which is now in its 6th edition. Parker (2003) contains 17,500 entries derived from this title. Other examples of science dictionaries include Morris (1992) and Walker (1999).

For more specialist engineering terminology, Timings and Twigg (2001) covers engineering science, electrical and electronic engineering, workshop practices and mechanical engineering. This and a small collection of other scientific and technological dictionaries are included in the Xrefer online reference collection service (www.xrefer.com) which provides access to a collection of aggregated and integrated reference books from twenty-four publishers. Some thirty showcase titles from a total of 130 can be accessed free of charge but most of the service is available on institutional subscription and the bulk of the titles on offer are from the social sciences and humanities.

There are several dictionaries of terminology resulting from standards. *Industrial engineering terminology* (2001) is a revised edition of ANSI standard Z94.0–1989. The *ASTM dictionary of engineering, science and technology* (2000) contains all 22,000 standard definitions referenced in all ASTM terminology standards, and the *Authoritative dictionary of IEEE standards terms* (2000) is a similar work emanating from the field of electrical and electronics engineering. British Standards (2002) provides a glossary of building and civil engineering terms used in BS 6100. Further information on standards can be found in Chapter 6.

For dictionaries covering electronics, Gibilisco (2001a) includes illustrations and a companion CD-ROM containing a searchable, cross-linked version of the book in Adobe PDF format. Amos and Amos (2002) has illustrations and circuit diagrams as well as including TV, radio and computing terms, and is available as part of the Xrefer service. The Society of Automotive Engineers (SAE) publishes a number of dictionaries in engineering disciplines, Nayler (1996) covers mechanical engineering, Goodsell (1995) covers automotive engineering, Tomsic (1998) aerospace engineering including terms from SAE standards and the NASA thesaurus, and Tomsic (2000) is a dictionary of materials and testing.

An alternative dictionary for aerospace engineering is Williamson (2001). For materials engineering both Walker (1993) and Davis (1992) are useful volumes with the latter including sixty-four Technical Briefs that provide encyclopedia-type coverage of key material groups.

Many areas of research are today concerned with environmental issues, and Porteous (2000) covers the scientific and technical terminology associated with environmental science at a level accessible to a general reader as well as a student. Wyman and Stevenson (2001) covers similar subject areas, whereas Webster (1999) combines environmental science with civil engineering terminology. A good compact dictionary of civil engineering is Scott (1991). FOLDOC the free online dictionary of computing (wombat.doc.ic.ac.uk/foldoc/) is a valuable web-based dictionary of computing and information technology jargon. Entries are cross-referenced to each other and to related resources elsewhere on the Internet and can be searched either by direct entry or by browsing an alphabetical list.

Although not strictly a dictionary, the *EI Thesaurus* (Milstead, 2002) is an alphabetical list of the controlled vocabulary terms used by Engineering Information (Ei) in *Engineering Index* and Compendex. It includes cross-references and scope notes and is available as a print publication or an online tool as part of the Compendex database. See Chapter 9 for more information on abstracting and indexing services.

Amos, S. W. and Amos, R. S., 2002. *Newnes dictionary of electronics.* 4th ed. Oxford: Newnes.

ASTM dictionary of engineering, science and technology. 2000. 9th ed. W. Conshohocken, PA: ASTM.

Authoritative dictionary of IEEE standards terms. 2000. 7th ed. New York: Standards Information Network, IEEE Press.

British Standards Institution, 2002. *Glossary of building and civil engineering terms, BS 6100.* Oxford: Blackwell Scientific.

Davis, J. R., ed., 1992. *ASM materials engineering dictionary.* Materials Park, OH: ASM International.

Gibilisco, S., 2001. *The illustrated dictionary of electronics.* 8th ed. New York: McGraw-Hill.

Goodsell, D., 1995. *Dictionary of automotive engineering.* 2nd ed. London: Butterworths.

Industrial engineering terminology: a revision of ANSI Z94.0–1989. 2001. rev. ed. Norcross, GA: Industrial engineering and Management Press.

Parker, S. P., ed., 2002. *McGraw-Hill dictionary of scientific and technical terms.* 6th ed. New York: McGraw-Hill.

Parker, S. P., ed., 2003. *McGraw-Hill dictionary of engineering*. 2nd ed. New York: McGraw-Hill.

Milstead, J. L., 2002. *El thesaurus*. 4th rev. ed. Hoboken, NJ: Engineering Information.

Morris, C., ed., 1992. *Academic Press dictionary of science and technology*. San Diego, CA: Academic Press.

Nayler, G. H. F., 1996. *Dictionary of mechanical engineering*. 4th ed. London: Butterworths.

Porteous, A., 2000. *Dictionary of environmental science and technology*. 3rd ed. Chichester: Wiley.

Scott, J. S., 1991. *Penguin dictionary of civil engineering*. 4th ed. London: Penguin.

Timings, R. L. and Twigg, P., 2001. *The pocket illustrated dictionary of engineering terms*. Oxford: Butterworth-Heinemann.

Tomsic, J. L., ed., 1998. *SAE dictionary of aerospace engineering*. 2nd ed. Warrendale, PA: Society of Automotive Engineers.

Tomsic, J. L., ed., 2000. *Dictionary of materials and testing*. 2nd ed. Warrendale, PA: Society of Automotive Engineers.

Walker, P. M. B., ed., 1999. *Chambers dictionary of science and technology*. Edinburgh: Chambers.

Walker, P. M. B., ed., 1993. *Chambers materials science and technology dictionary*. Edinburgh: Chambers.

Webster, L. F., 1999. *Dictionary of environmental and civil engineering*. Carnforth: Parthenon.

Williamson, M., 2001. *Cambridge dictionary of space technology*. 2nd ed. Cambridge: Cambridge University Press.

Wyman, B. and Stevenson L. H., 2001. *Facts on file dictionary of environmental science*. New York: Checkmark Books.

Translating dictionaries

There are many translating dictionaries available, some of which are bilingual and others multilingual. As with other sources they also vary from those covering general engineering to those concentrating on a particular engineering discipline.

Two publishers which specialise in translating dictionaries are Elsevier and Routledge. Elsevier publishes mainly multilingual dictionaries and a comprehensive list of these titles can be viewed on Elsevier's dictionary website (www.elsevier.com/homepage/sae/dictionaries/start.htm). Each entry includes a description, sample pages and bibliographic and ordering information. The list can be accessed via author or keyword indexes and there is news about forthcoming titles.

Routledge publishes a wide selection of bilingual dictionaries. Worthy of mention are three general titles. The *Routledge French technical dictionary* (1994) is available as a two volume set, a diskette or CD-ROM containing some 100,000 terms in both French and English as well as 3,000 abbreviations. The *Routledge German technical dictionary* (1995) is the equivalent German publication and is available in similar formats. There is also a *Routledge Spanish technical dictionary* (1997).

Richard Ernst's *Dictionary of engineering and technology* has been published in a number of bilingual combinations including English-German/German-English and English-French/French-English. Möllerke (2000) is a bilingual German dictionary covering both electronic and mechanical engineering. An alternative dictionary for French is Forbes (1997). For Russian, Barinov (1997) is a recent general work. A multilingual technical dictionary covering the main European languages is *Five language technology dictionary* (1994).

Barinov, C. M., 1997. *Comprehensive English-Russian scientific and technical dictionary.* Moscow: Russo.

Ernst, R., 1984. *Dictionnaire general de la technique industrielle.* [*Dictionary of engineering and technology*]. English-French. Wiesbaden: Oscar Brandstetter.

Ernst, R., 1997. *Wörterbuch der industriellen Technik.* [*Dictionary of engineering and technology*]. 5th ed. English-German. Wiesbaden: Oscar Brandstetter.

Ernst, R., 2000a. *Dictionnaire general de la technique industrielle.* [*Dictionary of engineering and technology*]. 2nd ed. French-English. Wiesbaden: Oscar Brandstetter.

Ernst, R., 2000b. *Wörterbuch der industriellen Technik.* [*Dictionary of engineering and technology*]. 6th ed. German-English. Wiesbaden: Oscar Brandstetter.

Five language technology dictionary. 1994. London: Gale Research International.

Forbes, J., 1997a. *Dictionnaire des Techniques et Technologies Modernes.* [*Modern Dictionary of Engineering and Technology*]. 2nd ed. French-English. Andover: Intercept.

Forbes, J., 1997b. *Dictionnaire des Techniques et Technologies Modernes* [*Modern Dictionary of Engineering and Technology*]. 3rd ed. English-French. Andover: Intercept.

Mollerke, G., 2000. *Engineering dictionary: Elektrotechnik & Maschinenbau. Technik-Wörterbuch.* Berlin: VDE.

Routledge French technical dictionary. 1994. London: Routledge.

Routledge German technical dictionary. 1995. London: Routledge.

Routledge Spanish technical dictionary. 1997. London: Routledge.

Dictionaries of symbols and abbreviations

Of the many general abbreviations dictionaries, Bonk (2001) and Stahl and Kerchelich (2001) are useful sources.

Peschke (1999), Clark (2002) and Keller and Erb (1994) all provide good coverage of scientific and technological acronyms and abbreviations. There are many more subject-specific dictionaries particularly in the area of information technology and computing. Vlietstra (2002) covers technical terms in information and communication technologies. This book also lists abbreviated names of relevant organizations, conferences, symposia and workshops. Wennrich (1992) is a two volume dictionary of acronyms and abbreviations from electronics, electrical engineering, computer technology and information processing which contains some multilingual definitions.

Bonk, M. R., ed., 2001. *International acronyms, initialisms and abbreviations dictionary*. 5th ed. Detroit, MI: Gale Research.

Clark, J., ed., 2002. *Dictionary of technology acronyms*. Canterbury: Financial World Publishing.

Keller, H. and Erb, U., 1994. *Dictionary of engineering acronyms and abbreviations*. 2nd ed. New York: Neal-Schuman.

Peschke, M., 1999. *International encyclopedia of abbreviations and acronyms in science and technology*. Munich: K. G. Saur.

Stahl, D. A. and Kerchelich, K., eds., 2001. *Abbreviations dictionary*. 10th ed. Boca Raton, FL: CRC Press.

Vlietstra, J., 2002. *Dictionary of acronyms and technical abbreviations: for information and communication technologies and related areas*. 2nd ed. London: Springer.

Wennrich, P., 1992. *International dictionary of abbreviations and acronyms of electronics, electrical engineering, computer technology and information processing*. Munich: K. G. Saur.

► HANDBOOKS INCLUDING DATA SOURCES

One of the key sources of numerical data for engineering is the range of handbooks published by CRC Press in a wide variety of technical subject areas. Dorf (2003) is a collection of the most widely consulted tables from the more specialised CRC Handbooks already published. Subjects covered include electrical, mechanical, computer, biomedical, power, signal processing, electronics, mechatronics, communications, aerospace, and ocean engineering. This is a likely successor to Bolz (1973). Other CRC Handbooks of interest to more than one engineering discipline include Dorf (1995), Ross (1995) on software for engineers and scientists, Tucker (1996) on computer science and engineering, and Shackelford (2000) for materials science and engineering. Another useful CRC publication is Nasar (1991) which deals with engineering equations including practical examples of solved problems.

Many of the CRC Press publications are now being made available online as part of ENGnetBASE (www.engnetbase.com). This collection of e-books, one of several subject groupings from CRC including ITKnowledgeBase, POLYMERSnetBASE, ENVIROnetBASE and MATHnetBase, is available on annual subscription. All the titles, (some 166 as of February 2003, with more being added) can be cross-searched and the results displayed in a number of ways, including by relevance or chronologically. Results from keyword searches provide links to the PDF files of relevant chapters and the contents pages of individual books can also be browsed. Further information on e-books can be found in Chapter 8.

Although strictly a yearbook, as it is published annually, one of the standard data sources for engineering is Stephens (2002). Now in its 107th ed., it contains information on the principles of engineering, including more than 1,500 technical illustrations, diagrams, tables and graphs. Two further collections of data from a range of subject areas are James and Lord (1992) and Eshbach (1990). Ganic (2002) provides tables, formulas, charts, diagrams, figures, key methods and solutions for hundreds of engineering problems. All major engineering disciplines are covered. ESDU International provides validated engineering data, methods and software in the form of over 1,250 design guides available on subscription in hardcopy, on CD-ROM or via the web (www.esdu.com).

A concise book of formulas, functions, symbols, constants, and conversions is Gibilisco (2001b). Another handy pocket guide to engineering formulas is provided by Gieck and Gieck (1997), while Matthews (2000) includes various engineering-related websites offering technical data. Korn and Korn (2000) provides definitions, theorems and formulas from every area of mathematics. Introductions, notes and cross-references show how the various topics are related, and their significance to science and engineering. Another handbook dealing with engineering mathematics is Tuma and Walsh (1997).

A major collection of online engineering data and reference material is provided by Knovel (www.knovel.com) which offers the ability to cross search text, tables, equations, graphics and figures from electronic versions of handbooks, conference proceedings, databases and e-references by a number of different publishers using a web-based search engine. Results can be manipulated and saved in tabular or graphic formats. Subscriptions are available for subject collections or individual titles. Butterworth-Heinemann, ChemTec Publishing, Kluwer, McGraw-Hill and Noyes are among the publishers included in the service with the subject emphasis being weighted towards materials engineering, particularly plastics and rubber technology and chemical engineering.

Another major source of materials data is the series of handbooks published by ASM International. Currently available in twenty-one volumes plus an index, the series covers properties of metals and their alloys. The ASM Handbooks are also available in electronic format, on CD-ROM, DVD and online (www.asminternational.org/materialsinfo/). Another online service from ASM International accessible via the same address is the ASM Alloy Center Online. This provides access to property and corrosion data, charts, processing information and equivalent alloy designations for a variety of countries. Both services are available on annual subscription. A concise summary of the key data from the ASM handbooks can be found in Davis (1998). Further printed handbooks published by ASM include Bauccio (1993) for metals and alloys and Bauccio (1994) for composites, ceramics, plastics and electronic materials. Both volumes contain data helpful in the materials selection process.

For another concise work covering metallic data, Gale and Totemeier (2003) deals with the physical, electrical, mechanical and magnetic properties of metals. Brady *et al.* (2002) covers a much broader range of materials, (more than 13,000 in all) including ferrous and nonferrous metals, plastics, elastomers, ceramics, woods, composites, chemicals, minerals, textiles, fuels, foodstuffs and natural plant and animal substances. Data provided includes performance properties, principal characteristics and applications in product design.

A standard reference work in design and manufacturing is Oberg *et al.* (2000) which is also available on CD-ROM. Lingaiah (2002) provides charts on material properties and equations, formulas, calculations, and graphs designed to help solve machine design problems. Kutz (1998) not only covers most aspects of mechanical engineering but also a broad range of topics and specialized areas including aerospace, chemical, materials, nuclear, electrical, and general engineering.

There is a host of handbooks and data sources devoted to individual engineering disciplines. These are covered in more detail in the relevant subject chapters. However some key titles in the main subject areas are briefly referred to here. For mechanical engineering, Avallone (1996) has detailed coverage, while Marghitu (2001) is a concise volume. Laughton and Warne (2002) is an important source for electrical engineers, and Fink and Beaty (2000) offers practical information on electrical engineering including research and development, equipment and system design, operations, maintenance, properties of materials, and applications of electric power tool industry. For chemical engineering the key title is Perry (1998) while McMillan (1999) deals with process control and instrumentation. The latest edition of Merritt *et al.* (2003) is a standard guide to civil engineering and construction practices and Blake (1994) covers fundamentals, theory and practice in international construction industries.

ASM Handbook. 1991– Materials Park, OH: ASM International.

Avallone, E. A. and Baumeister, T., 1996. *Mark's standard handbook for mechanical engineers.* 10th ed. New York: McGraw-Hill.

Bauccio, M. L., ed., 1993. *ASM metals reference book.* 3rd ed. Materials Park, OH: ASM International.

Bauccio, M. L., ed.,1994. *ASM engineered materials reference book.* 2nd ed. Materials Park, OH: ASM International.

Blake, L. S., ed., 1994. *Civil engineers reference book.* 4th ed. London: Butterworths.

Bolz, R. E., 1973. *CRC handbook of tables for applied engineering science.* 2nd ed. Boca Raton, FL: CRC Press.

Brady, G. S., Clauser, H. R. and Vaccari, J., 2002. *Materials handbook.* 15th ed. New York: McGraw-Hill.

Davis, J. R., ed., 1998. *Metals handbook desk edition.* 2nd ed. Materials Park, OH: ASM International.

Dorf, R. C., 2003. *CRC handbook of engineering tables.* Boca Raton, FL: CRC Press.

Dorf, R. C., 1995. *The engineering handbook.* Boca Raton, Fl: CRC Press.

Eshbach, O., Tapley, B. D. and Poston, T. R., eds., 1990. *Eshbach's handbook of engineering fundamentals.* 4th ed. New York: Wiley.

Fink, D. G. and Beaty, H. W., eds., 2000. *Standard handbook for electrical engineers.* 14th ed. New York: McGraw-Hill.

Gale, W. F. and Totemeier, T. C., eds., 2003. *Smithells metals reference book.* 8th ed. Oxford: Butterworth-Heinemann.

Ganic, E. N. and Hicks, T. G., 2002. *McGraw-Hill's engineering companion.* New York: McGraw-Hill.

Gibilisco, S., 2001. *Mathematical and physical data, equations, and rules of thumb.* New York: McGraw-Hill.

Gieck, K. and Gieck, R., 1997. *Engineering formulas.* 7th ed. New York: McGraw-Hill.

James, A. M. and Lord, M. P., 1992. *Macmillan's chemical and physical data.* London: Macmillan.

Korn, G. A. and Korn, T. M., 2000. *Mathematical handbook for scientists and engineers.* Mineola, NY: Dover.Publications.

Kutz, M., ed., 1998. *Mechanical engineer's handbook.* 2nd ed. New York: Wiley.

Laughton, M. A. and Warne, D. F., eds., 2002. *Electrical engineer's reference book.* 16th ed. Oxford: Newnes.

Lingaiah, K., 1994. *Machine design data handbook,* 2nd ed. New York: McGraw-Hill.

Marghitu, D. B., 2001. *Mechanical engineers handbook.* San Diego, CA: Academic Press.

Matthews, C., 2000. *Engineers' data book.* 2nd ed. London: Professional Engineering.

Mcmillan, G. K. ed., 1999 *Process/industrial instruments and controls handbook.* 5th ed. New York: McGraw-Hill.

Merritt, F. S., *et al.* eds., 2003. *Standard handbook for civil engineers.* 5th ed. New York: McGraw-Hill.

Nasar, S. A. and Paul C. R., 1991. *Essential engineering equations.* Boca Raton, Fl: CRC Press.

Oberg, E., *et al.* eds., 2000. *Machinery's handbook.* 26th ed. New York: Industrial Press.

Perry, R. H. and Green, D. W., 1998. *Perry's chemical engineers' handbook.* 7th ed. New York: McGraw-Hill.

Ross, P. W., ed., 1995. *The handbook of software for engineers and scientists.* Boca Raton, Fl: CRC Press.

Shackelford, J. F. and Alexander, W., 2000. *CRC materials science and engineering handbook.* 3rd ed. Boca Raton, Fl: CRC Press.

Stephens, J. H., ed., 2002. *Kempe's engineers year-book for 2002.* 107th ed. Tonbridge: CMP.

Tucker, A. B., 1996. *The computer science and engineering handbook.* Boca Raton, Fl: CRC Press.

Tuma, J. J. and Walsh, R. A., 1997. *Engineering mathematics handbook.* 4th ed. New York: McGraw-Hill.

▶ DIRECTORIES AND YEARBOOKS

A number of general guides listing published directories are available. *Current British directories* (2000) (also available on CD-ROM), *Current European directories* (1994) and *Directories in print*, which is published annually, are examples.

The kind of information offered by directories and yearbooks tends to date quickly, such as contact details for individuals, associations or companies, product information, and current research being undertaken. Some of these subjects are covered in more detail in other chapters but some key resources in these areas are indicated in this section.

Details of associations, institutes, societies and professional bodies in the United Kingdom and Ireland can be found in the *Directory of British associations and associations in Ireland* and Atterberry (2001). There are two complementary publications covering Europe, the *Directory of European industrial and trade associations* (1997) and Greenslade (1995). Associations in the European Union can be found in *Trade associations and professional bodies of the continental European Union* (2002) and *The directory of 12500 trade and professional associations: in the European Union* (2002) which lists the details of some 750 EU associations as well as the national member organisations of each European association (some 11,750).

For worldwide coverage *World guide to trade associations* (2002) covers over 23,500 trade associations and trade unions based in 185 countries while the *World guide to scientific associations and learned societies* (2001) contains descriptions of 17,500 national and international associations active in science and technology in more than 170 countries around the world. Many associations and institutes from the various engineering disciplines publish their own directories and yearbooks, often covering membership or product information. For further information on professional societies see Chapter 13 or refer to one of the individual subject chapters.

For information about consultancies, Fullalove (2002) lists 500 engineering and technology consultancies in the UK and Europe recommended by the Engineering Council. Published by FIDIC (Fédération Internationale des Ingénieurs-Conseils), the worldwide federation of consulting engineering member associations, the *International directory of consulting engineers* (2003) gives information about consulting firms working both internationally and domestically which are FIDIC members. The latest edition of the directory has been published on the Internet and is available free of charge (www.fidicdirect.com).

For company and product information the *Engineering Industry Buyers Guide* (2003) (formerly the Engineer Buyers Guide) lists details on over 16,900 companies and more than 5,100 products and services. The guide also includes information on brands and trade names, overseas manufacturers and their agents and associations and organisations. A free web-based directory providing information on British engineering firms and their products is *Dial engineering* (www.dialengineering.co.uk). Searches can be made by company name, product or location or alternatively it is possible to browse a list of over 7,000 engineering product headings. Updates are made weekly. Product information is covered in more detail in Chapter 7.

It is sometimes difficult to trace information about current research but there are several directories which can help. Volume 1 of the publication *Current research in Britain* (1999) lists research being undertaken at UK universities and colleges. Edwards (2000) covers British bodies which are concentrations of effort and expertise, or which provide information to the general public and have 'centre', 'bureau' or 'institute' in their names. *The Research centers directory* (2002) covers North American research institutes, while information on Europe is given in *European research centres* (1995) and the *European research and development database – Directory of European research and development* (2002). Worldwide coverage is provided by *International research centers directory* (2002). The most widely used guide to worldwide academic institutions and research organizations is *World of learning 2003*. This is also available online (www.worldoflearning.com) on a subscription basis. For higher education establishments within Commonwealth countries there is the *Commonwealth universities yearbook 2002*. For more information on tracing research in progress see Chapter 3.

Commonwealth universities yearbook 2002. 2002. 77th ed. London: Association of
      Commonwealth Universities.
Current British directories. 2000. 13th ed. Beckenham: CBD Research.
Current European directories. 1994. 3rd ed. Beckenham: CBD Research.
Current research in Britain. 1999. Vol. 1. Boston Spa: British Library.
Directories in print. 2003. 23rd ed. Detroit, MI: Gale Research.
Directory of 12500 trade and professional associations: in the European Union. 2002. 5th ed.
      Genval: Euroconfidentiel.
Directory of British associations and associations in Ireland. 2002. 16th ed. Beckenham:
      CBD Research.
Directory of European industrial and trade associations. 1997. 6th ed. Beckenham: CBD
      Research.
Edwards. C., ed., 2000. *Centres, bureaux and research institutes: UK concentrations of effort,
      information and expertise.* 4th ed. Beckenham: CBD Research.
Engineering industry buyers guide. 2003. Tonbridge: CMP Data and Information Services.
*European research and development database, part 1: Directory of European research and
      development.* 2002. 3rd ed. Munich: K. G. Saur.
*European research centres: a directory of organisations in sciences, technology, agriculture and
      medicine.* 1995. 10th ed. London: Cartermill International.

Fullalove, S., ed., 2002. *Consultant engineers and technologists 500.* Twickenham: Anchorage Press.

Greenslade, S., ed., 1995. *Directory of European professional and learned societies.* 5th ed. Beckenham: CBD Research.

International directory of consulting engineers. 2003–2004. London: Rhys Jones Marketing Consultants [in press].

International research centers directory. 2002. 16th ed. Detroit, MI: Gale Research.

Research centers directory. 2002. 30th ed. Detroit, MI: Gale Research.

Sheets, T. E., ed., 2001. *Trade associations and professional bodies of the United Kingdom and Eire.* 16th ed. London: Gale Research International.

Trade associations and professional bodies of the continental European Union. 2002. 2nd ed. London: Gale Research International.

World guide to scientific associations and learned societies. 2001. 8th ed. Munich: K. G. Saur.

World guide to trade associations. 2002. 6th ed. Munich: K. G. Saur.

World of learning 2003. 2002. 53rd ed. London: Europa Publications.

► BIOGRAPHICAL INFORMATION

Naturally, biographical information about scientists and engineers can be found in standard reference sources such as *Who's Who*. However there are some works specifically devoted to individuals working in engineering and technology. The *Dictionary of scientific biography* (1981) is a multi-volume series containing more than 5,000 biographies of scientists and mathematicians from countries worldwide and covering all historical periods. Supplements are available. *A concise dictionary of scientific biography* (2000) is based on this work.

Porter and Ogilvie (2000) also covers the lives of men and women of science together with a series of chronologies which place the individuals' achievements in a broader context, while Millar (2002) is an alphabetically organized, illustrated biographical dictionary covering the work of over 1,500 key scientists from forty countries. *Who's who in science and engineering* (2002) includes details on some 26,000 individuals. *European research and development database – Who's who in European research and development* (2002) is the companion work to the *Directory of European research and development* mentioned in the previous section. It lists professionals all over Europe involved in research and technological development in science and engineering. Davis (1995) has good coverage of American engineers while *American men and women of science* (2002) contains details of workers in physical, biological and related sciences.

American men and women of science. 2002. 21st ed. Munich: K. G. Saur.

Concise dictionary of scientific biography. 2000. 2nd ed. New York: Scribner's.

Davis, G. 1995. *Who's who in engineering.* Washington: American Association of Engineering Societies.

INFORMATION SOURCES IN ENGINEERING 247▶

Dictionary of scientific biography. 1981. New York: Scribner's.

European research and development database, part 2: Who's who in European research and development. 2002. 3rd ed. Munich: K. G. Saur.

Millar, D. 2002. *The Cambridge dictionary of scientists.* 2nd ed. Cambridge: Cambridge University Press.

Porter, R. and Ogilvie, M. B., eds., 2000. *The biographical dictionary of scientists.* 3rd ed. Oxford: Oxford University Press.

Who's who in science and engineering 2002–2003. 2001. 6th ed. New Providence: Marquis Who's Who.

13 Professional Societies

Sarah Vinsen

▶ **INTRODUCTION**

This chapter will provide an overview of the role of engineering professional societies. It will describe the different types of information resources they produce. Subsequent chapters will give detailed information about specific societies and publications by subject area. Professional societies vary considerably in their age, structure, size and the role they play. Central to all is the 'Learned Society' function. They act as forums for discussion and dissemination of technical ideas and practices. They work to promote awareness of engineering issues and protect the rights of engineering practitioners. The majority are concerned with maintaining educational standards and providing training to ensure the competence and quality of engineers. On the whole they are independent, 'not for profit', democratic bodies, which adhere to a set of governing principles. They offer various grades of membership. These vary from those who simply have an interest in engineering, to professional grades, which are restricted to those who have reached a required level of education and experience. Membership of these organisations demonstrates a level of competence and status and provides a means of keeping abreast of new ideas. Some societies are very large, serving a major field of engineering such as 'chemical', 'civil', 'electrical' or 'mechanical', whereas others cater for very specialised fields such as 'building services' or 'lighting'. Other societies are cross-disciplinary, representing engineering roles such as 'design'. Finally there are societies which represent affiliated interests such as professional engineering publishers and libraries.

▶ ENGINEERING SOCIETIES IN THE UNITED KINGDOM

Engineering is one of the largest professions in the United Kingdom. It was estimated that there were 880,000 professional engineers in the UK. (Engineering Council, 2002). There are over forty different engineering societies. The Institution of Civil Engineers (ICE) was founded in 1818 and is the oldest specialised engineering institution in the world. It was followed by the establishment of the Institution of Mechanical Engineers (IMechE est. 1847), Institution of Gas Engineers (IGEM est. 1863), Royal Aeronautical Society (RAeS est.1866), Institute of Materials, Minerals and Mining (IOM^3 est.1869), Institution of Electrical Engineers (IEE est.1871) and Institute of Marine Engineering, Science and Technology (IMarEST est.1889), to name but a few.

The IEE is the biggest with over 130,000 members, closely followed by the Institution of Mechanical Engineers and the Institution of Civil Engineers, which have in the region of 80,000 members respectively. There are several smaller bodies representing specialised interests such as the Institute of Acoustics, which has 2,400 members and Institute of Measurement and Control, which has 5,200 members. The Institution of Incorporated Engineers (IIE) and the Society of Engineers are cross-disciplinary organisations with members from all the different sectors of engineering.

There are three organisations overseeing the whole of the UK engineering profession. Engineering Council (UK) is the lead body for the engineering profession in the UK. It is responsible for the regulation of the profession by co-ordinating and standardising the activities of the different engineering societies. It publishes various surveys of the UK engineering sector. The ETB membership is made up of representatives from business, industry, academia and the engineering professional institutions. It is a new body formed in 2001 aimed at proving one voice for the engineering profession. Its remit is to restructure the current UK engineering sector regulation and education processes. The Royal Academy of Engineering is the national academy of engineering. It has 1,200 elected members who are the elite of the engineering profession coming from all the different engineering disciplines. It acts as a learned society and works to promote engineering to the public.

▶ ENGINEERING SOCIETIES IN THE UNITED STATES OF AMERICA

In the USA there are approximately one hundred engineering societies representing all the types of engineering activity. The Institute of Electrical and Electronics Engineers (IEEE) is one of the largest engineering societies in the world representing over 377,000 members. One of the smallest is The Minerals, Metals and Materials Society (TMS) with only 10,000 members. The oldest US engineering societies are: American Society of Civil Engineers (ASCE est. 1852), American Institute of Mining and Metallurgical Engineers (AIME est.1871), American Society of Mechanical Engineers (ASME est. 1880), the IEEE (est.1884) and the American Institute of Chemical Engineers (AIChE est. 1908). They are known as the Founder Societies and together they make up the United Engineering Foundation Inc (UEF). The UEF was established to provide a united central home for the key engineering bodies. The National Society of Professional Engineers (NSPE) represents licensed engineering professionals across all the engineering disciplines. It services over 60,000 members. US engineers require a license to practise certain activities. The licensure requirements vary from state to state.

There are four bodies that oversee the US engineering profession. The American Association of Engineering Societies (AAES) co-ordinates the activities of engineering societies. It works to promote public awareness of engineering issues and publishes surveys reviewing the state of the US engineering profession. The Accreditation Board for Engineering Technology (ABET) is responsible for setting educational standards and accrediting engineering courses. The National Council of Examiners for Engineering and Surveying (NCEES) co-ordinates and standardises the activities of the individual state licensing boards. The National Academy of Engineering (NAE) provides leadership to the engineering sector as advisor to the federal government. Membership is by election and is restricted to leading engineers. It publishes many surveys of the engineering sector.

▶ ENGINEERING SOCIETIES IN EUROPE

France has a number of learned societies connected with engineering and two main umbrella bodies which represent and co-ordinate engineering activities. Commission des Titres d'Ingenieur (CTI) is a government sponsored body which accredits engineering programmes in France. The Conseil National des Ingénieurs et Scientifiques de France (CNISF) is a non governmental body which represents the French engineering and scientific community. It has approximately 150,000 members.

There are over 100 different engineering institutions in Germany. One of the best known is the VDI (Verein Deutscher Ingenienure) (VDI). This is a cross-disciplinary organisation, with over 126,000 members and eighteen different technical divisions. As the leading engineering society in Germany it represents engineers on the governmental and public stage.

The two main Dutch engineering organisations are Koninklijk Instituut van Ingenieurs (KIVI), and Nederlandse Ingenieursvereniging

(NIRIA). KIVI is the Royal Institution of Engineers in the Netherlands representing 15,000 graduates from the universities of technology. NIRIA, the Netherlands Association of Engineers represents 20,000 engineers from polytechnics. These bodies are learned societies which take an active role in governmental consultations.

There are two principal Pan-European professional bodies, EurEta (European Higher Engineering and Technical Professional Association), and FEANI (European Federation of National Engineering Associations). They work to promote international co-operation, the mobility of engineers and the recognition of engineering professional standards. FEANI represents over 1.5 million engineers from twenty-five countries. Its members are the national engineering governing bodies. It awards the title of 'Eur Ing' which is a qualification recognised by all its member countries. It produces the *FEANI Index* CD ROM. This lists accredited engineering courses in the European member states. EurEta membership is made up of individuals and eleven national engineering bodies. It maintains a register of professional engineers and awards the title 'Ing EurEta'

There are also Pan-European engineering bodies that work to unite the engineering societies for individual engineering disciplines. European Committee of Civil Engineers (ECCE), Convention of National Societies of Electrical Engineers of Europe (EUREL), and European Federation of Chemical Engineers (EFChE) are examples of these types of bodies. They aim to promote the dissemination of technical information and to provide a forum for multilateral co-operation by organising multi-national events and publications.

▶ REGULATION OF THE UK ENGINEERING PROFESSION

The role played by professional societies in the regulation of the engineering profession varies between countries. The requirements are influenced by the different educational systems and cultures. In some countries, the control over the licensing, regulation and education of engineers belongs to professional societies. In others this power belongs to central umbrella organisations, which are often government sponsored.

In the United Kingdom the regulatory role is shared between a central body Engineering Council (UK) and the individual professional associations. Engineering Council (UK) sets the standard of qualification required of UK professional engineers. These are set out in its *UK-SPEC* (Standard for Professional Engineering Competence). It then licenses professional societies to accredit education courses and provide initial and continuing professional development schemes. Details of accredited courses are available on most society websites. A few societies require members to pass a membership exam, for example the Institution of Structural Engineers (IStructE).

The Engineering Council (UK) maintains a national register of qualified engineers and technicians. The individual societies propose and submit candidates from their own areas of expertise to the Register. There are three main grades of membership, 'Chartered Engineer' (CEng), 'Incorporated Engineer' (IEng) and 'Engineering Technician' (Eng Tech). To obtain 'Chartered Engineer' status an engineer would require membership of one of the professional societies, to have achieved the required academic qualifications, demonstrated initial professional development, to agreed to abide by the society's professional code of conduct and shown a commitment to continued professional development.

Most engineering societies offer courses and training to enable engineers to develop their skills and obtain professional status. Both the IEE and the ICE have training arms running short courses. These are available to both members and non-members. All professional societies have a moral code of practice, by which their professional members agree to abide. Details of these are usually listed on society's websites, often as part of their bye-laws. In the UK the 'Chartered Engineer', 'Incorporated Engineer' and 'Engineering Technician' titles are protected by law but the generic term 'engineer' is not. There is no system of licensing within the UK and no legal limitation to practicing as an engineer.

► LEARNED SOCIETY ROLE

Engineering societies were established at the time of the industrial revolution. Connected with this growth in industry, engineers began to see the need to distinguish themselves and gain public recognition for their distinct knowledge and specialised role. Groups of like minded individuals came together to discuss new ideas and seek solutions to technical problems. Although they have now become much more formalised and carry out many different activities, professional societies' central role remains the same, to promote the profession, to provide a meeting place and disseminate and advance technical ideas.

► TRANSACTIONS, MAGAZINES AND NEWSLETTERS

All professional societies produce some form of professional journal to disseminate new information. These range from multi-volume transactions to less formal magazines and newsletters. Benefits of society membership include a regular publication to fulfil members' current awareness needs.

They also benefit from discounts on society 'subscription only journals' and other publications. The larger societies have considerable publishing arms, often these are set up as affiliated commercial companies. For instance, Thomas Telford Ltd, is the publishing arm of the ICE. The large societies produce transactions or proceedings. These are peer reviewed scholarly journals, which cover the latest research in their sector. These publications can be multi-volume series such as the *Proceedings of the Institution of Mechanical Engineers*, which is published in fourteen parts covering sectors from process engineering to railway engineering and the *IEEE Transactions* series which has over seventy different parts.

The larger societies also produce news and current affairs magazines which members receive. These publications include details of news about society events, courses, people, industry affairs, legislation, products and job advertisements. They are useful for researching the engineering market sector as they cover the key concerns affecting the engineering industry. For example, members of the IEE receive the *IEE Review* magazine. Members of ICE receive the *New Civil Engineer* magazine. Members of the Institution of Chemical Engineers (IChemE) receive the *tce magazine*. Members of the IMechE receive the *Professional Engineering* magazine.

Newsletters cover more limited intent society news, branch news and diaries of events. Many of these are freely available on society websites. Increasingly, free electronic only newsletters are being produced. Examples of these are *IMarEST News*, (IMarEST) (www.imarest.org/inews), *Agenda* produced by the IMechE (www.imeche.org.uk/media/agenda.asp) and the ICE's electronic only *Infoshare Newsletter* (www.infoshare.org.uk).

Whereas the larger societies publish professional transactions, magazines, and newsletters, the smaller societies tend to produce single volume publications, containing all the above content. They cover technical papers, society events, news and jobs. Examples are *Engineering Technology*, *Energy World*, *Structural Engineer* published respectively by the IIE, IStructE and the Energy Institute.

The majority of engineering society journals are now available electronically. Various access mechanisms exist. Many are available via aggregators such as Ingenta and Infotrieve. The larger societies have created their own electronic journal portals such as the IEE and AIChE.

▶ BOOKS AND STANDARDS

The publishing arms of professional societies produce textbooks, handbooks, standards, yearbooks, conference proceedings and design guides. Whole ranges of textbooks are produced to support the educational role of professional societies. These introduce students to engineering fundamentals such as thermodynamics, kinematics, and dynamics. Design guides and handbooks, which act as the main reference guides for engineering practitioners are produced. For example the *ASHRAE Handbook* published by the American Society of Heating Refrigerating and Air Conditioning Engineers, the *CIBSE Guide Series* produced by the Chartered Institute of Building Service Engineers(UK) and the IStructE *Design Recommendation Series*.

Key papers given at conferences and events are collected together and published as Conference Proceedings. These normally cover the latest technology areas although they are often published some time after the event.

Surveys and Yearbooks are published by some societies. These provide useful engineering market sector information. For example the *NDT Yearbook* published by the British Institute of Non-Destructive Testing (UK) and the *Instrument Engineers Yearbook* produced by the Institute of Measurement and Control (UK). These are annual publications which give details of products, markets, standards and services in these sectors. A number of societies and umbrella bodies, notably CIBSE, Engineering Council (UK) and IChemE publish salary surveys of their members. Sometimes these types of publications are available in limited formats via society websites.

In their role of promoting 'best practice', professional societies undertake standardization activities. They are involved in the formulation of both national and international standards. The IEE produces the UK electrical wiring standard the *IEE Wiring Regulations BS 7671*. In the UK the main engineering standards of contract such as the *Model Forms of Contract (IEE/IMechE/ACE, 2001)*, *IChemE Conditions of Contract* series and the *ICE Conditions of Contract* are developed and published by professional societies.

The American engineering societies play a much larger role in standardization activities than their European counterparts. They develop and publish standards, which are then accredited by ANSI (American National Standards Institute). Many of these standards are accepted internationally such as the *ASME Boiler and Pressure Code* and the American Society for Testing and Materials standards collection published as the *Annual Book of ASTM standards*. The IEEE produces over nine hundred current standards.

Most societies produce publication catalogues. The majority of large societies now have online bookshops allowing you to search across their publications to locate titles in a particular subject area.

▶ EVENTS

In keeping with their origins, professional societies not only disseminate information, but also act as a meeting place for practicing engineers. Professional societies normally have subject-based groups or committees and/or regional branches covering different technical and geographical areas. Such networks arrange conferences, seminars, courses, lectures, visits, social events and meetings at various locations. Many societies are establishing subject based virtual communities offering specialised chatrooms, news, factsheets and event listings via their webpages. These events bring engineers with similar interests together allowing them to discuss problems, obtain guidance and find out about the latest technology and the future developments. Some conferences are prestigious international events which are held regularly, such as the *ASME Offshore Mechanics and Artic Engineering Conference Series* and the *SAE/IMechE VTMS Vehicle Thermal Management Systems Conferences*. Others are informal one-off affairs, reviewing new legislation or technical developments. Although members receive preferential rates to attend events they are not normally restricted to members. Many of the technical papers given at these events will be published in the society's journals or conference proceedings. Many of the informal meetings and seminars produce no proceedings at all or if they do they remain unpublished.

▶ LIBRARIES

Most professional societies have a library service. Primarily they exist to serve the membership of the respective body by offering loan, document supply and technical enquiry services. They provide information to members to support their professional development needs. However, many provide document supply and enquiry services to non-members, normally for a fee or via interlibrary loan. Their collections cover society publications, trade literature, standards, engineering books, databooks, periodicals and historical manuscripts. The three main UK engineering societies – ICE, IEE and IMechE – have vast specialised libraries. Due to the history of these institutions their collections include important historical material describing the achievements of past generations of engineers in UK and abroad. These three main bodies, along with many of the other societies, have online catalogues freely accessible so that anyone can check their holdings. The IMechE Library Catalogue includes abstracts of the Institution's technical papers back to 1984 (www.imeche.org.uk/library). Detailed descriptions of UK professional society libraries are given in *ASLIB Directory of Information Sources in the United Kingdom* (Reynard, 2002)

In the USA the library collection of the United Engineering Foundation, which represents the ASCE, AIME, ASME, IEEE and AIChE, is held by the Linda Hall Library. This is possibly the world's largest engineering library collection. The Linda Hall Library provides an international document supply and reference search service. Its catalogue is available on the web at: leonardo.lindahall.org

► VIRTUAL LIBRARIES

Many societies are digitising their technical paper archives and allowing access to their conference and journal publications on a 'pay per view' basis. These are extremely valuable sources of information. They allow searches across specialised databases via subject headings, authors, titles or keywords. For instance you can search the *Institution of Civil Engineers Virtual Library* archive of papers published between 1836–2003 via its website (www.iceknowledge.com). The majority of the American engineering society websites contain technical paper archives. However, some societies are restricting their archive facilities to their members. For instance IEEE members have access to the *IEEE Xplore digital library*. Other societies publish subscription-only archive services such as the Society of Automotive Engineers (SAE) database of papers, and ASME paper's database. Commercial bibliographic databases are also produced by a number of professional societies. For instance *INSPEC*, which is produced by the Institution of Electrical Engineers and *WeldaSEARCH*, which is produced by The Welding Institute (TWI, UK).

► TECHNICAL ADVICE

Several societies have technical advice departments, which are staffed by engineering specialists. The IOM[3] runs a Materials Information Service. It has regional materials advisors who can answer queries concerning any aspect of materials technology. Typically, societies produce a 'Consultants Directory' or 'Membership Directory'. These are often available on society websites. IMarEST *International Directory of Marine Consultants* (www.imarest.org/idmc), the *CIBSE Consultants Database* (www.cibse. org) and the British Institute of Non-Destructive Testing *Directory of Quality Practioners* (www.bindt.org) are all available in this way.

The ICE, IEE, IMechE and IChemE all provide a dispute resolution service. They will put forward members to act as arbitrators, adjudicators and expert witnesses for court cases or to settle breaches of contract.

► CAREERS INFORMATION

Engineering societies actively promote the profession. They produce careers brochures and websites to explain engineering opportunities to school children to encourage them to join the profession. The IEE runs the *Micromouse competition* and provides various school resources via its website. *Engineering Opportunities for Students and Graduates* (IMechE) (www.pepublishing.com/magazines/eng-opps/index.htm) is an annual publication sponsored by the main UK professional engineering societies. It contains profiles of young engineers, details of undergraduate sponsorship schemes and explains the chartership process. The Royal Academy of Engineering runs schemes such as the 'Year in Industry Scheme' and the 'Headstart Scheme' which help young people gain engineering experience. Most engineering societies run undergraduate sponsorship and award schemes such as the ICE's 'QUEST Awards Scheme.'

As has been described, society magazines often contain job advertisements. Both the IEE and the ICE run Recruitment Agencies. A large number of societies also advertise these vacancies on their websites or via recruitment portals. Professional Careers.net (www.professionalcareers.net) contains the advertisements from the *Professional Engineering* magazine. The Engineering Recruitment Show (www.engrecruitshow.co.uk) is sponsored jointly by the IEE and IMechE. This event is held regularly at various UK locations showcasing the main engineering recruiters.

▶ REPRESENTATION AND MARKETING

Professional societies lobby governments on engineering issues and are involved in government consultations. They usually publish position statements, which draw together and summarise the key issues confronting decision makers and detail their own stance on socially important or topical issues. These papers are often freely available on society websites. Professional societies actively promote engineering technical issues to the public. Several societies publish free fact sheets on key subjects within their discipline. Again these are often freely accessible via their websites. For example the websites of the following bodies, Chartered Institution of Water and Environmental Engineers, ICE and the IStructE and the Institute of Energy currently have fact sheets available describing areas such as solar power, combined heat and power and structural failures.

▶ AFFILIATED BODIES

This chapter has focussed on the role of the societies responsible for the training and representation of professional engineers. There are a number of bodies which have affiliated engineering society roles such as publishing, libraries and education.

On the publishing side there is the Association of Learned and Professional Society Publishers. This is a UK body which represents the interests of 'not for profit' publishers. It provides guidance, codes of practice, representation and training for the publishing arms of professional societies. The International Council for Scientific and Technical Information (ICSTI) works to improve the transfer of technical information. It carries out research into the ways that engineers and scientists use information and the impact of new information technologies. It is also concerned with developing standards and promoting co-operation between the main engineering/ scientific information providers.

The International Association of Technological University Libraries (IATUL) represents worldwide technical librarians and suppliers to technical libraries. It provides a forum for the exchange of ideas and co-operation by holding regular conferences, publications and a discussion list.

SEFI is the European Society for Engineering Education. Its membership is made up of European universities and associations who provide engineering training. Its aims are to promote co-operation and the exchange of information between its members.

► SOURCES OF INFORMATION ABOUT PROFESSIONAL SOCIETIES

There are a number of directories available which provide details of professional societies. Most allow you to search by name or subject area. The following all give details of UK societies: *Directory of British associations and associations in Ireland* (2002), Ask Hollis, *The Directory of UK Associations* (2003), *Key organizations* (2003) and *A Guide to the Engineering Profession* (Engineering Council, 2003). For European bodies there is the *Directory of European professional and learned Societies* (2004). The following two annual directories cover worldwide bodies *Encyclopedia of associations: international organisations* (2003) and *Yearbook of International organisations* (2003). Information on US societies is available in *Encyclopedia of associations: national organizations of United States* (2003). The main umbrella type organisations such as the Engineering Council (UK), FEANI and ABET all publish details of their members on their websites.

► MAIN UK ENGINEERING SOCIETIES

British Computer Society (BCS)
1 Sanford Street
Swindon
Wilts SN1 1HJ
Phone Number: 01793 417417
Website: www.bcs.org.uk

British Institute of Non-Destructive Testing (BINDT)
1 Spencer Parade
Northampton NN1 5AA
Phone Number: 01604 630124/5
Website: www.bindt.org

Chartered Institution of
Building Services Engineers
(CIBSE)
Delta House
222 Balham High Rd
London SW12 9BS
Phone Number: (020) 8675 5211
Website: www.cibse.org

Chartered Institution of Water and
Environmental Management
(CIWEM)
15 John Street
London WC1N 2EB
Phone Number: (020) 7831 3110
Website: www.ciwem.org.uk

Engineering Council EC(UK)
10 Maltravers Street
London WC2R 3ER
Phone Number: (020) 7240 7891
Website: www.engc.org.uk

Energy Institute
61 New Cavendish Street
London
W1G 7AR
Phone Number: (020) 7467 7100
Website: www.energyinst.org.uk

ETB (Engineering Technology
Board)
10 Maltravers Street,
London
WC2R 3ER.
Phone Number: (020) 7240 7333
Website: www.etechb.co.uk

Institute of Acoustics (IOA)
77A St Peters Street
St Albans
Herts AL1 3BN
Phone Number: 01727 848195
Website: www.ioa.org.uk

Institution of Agricultural
Engineers (IAgrE)
West End Road
Silsoe
Bedford MK45 4DU
Phone Number: 01525 861096
Website: www.iagre.org

Institution of Civil Engineers (ICE)
1–7 Great George St
London SW1P 3AA
Phone Number: (020) 7222 7722
Website: www.ice.org.uk

Institute of Cast Metals Engineers
(ICME)
ICME Metalforming Centre
47 Birmingham Road
West Bromwich
West Midlands B70 6PY
Phone Number: 0121 601 6979
Website: www.icme.org.uk

Institution of Chemical Engineers
(IChemE)
165–189 Railway Terrace
Rugby CV21 3HQ
Phone Number: 01788 578214
Website: www.icheme.org

Institution of Engineering
Designers (IED)
Courtleigh
Westbury Leigh
Westbury
Wilts BA13 3TA
Phone Number: 01373 822801
Website: www.ied.org.uk

Institution of Electrical Engineers
(IEE)
Savoy Place
London WC2R 0BL
Phone Number: (020) 7240 1871
Website: www.iee.org

Institution of Fire Engineers (IFE)
148 New Walk
Leicester LE1 7QB
Phone Number: 0116 255 3654
Website: www.ife.org.uk

Institution of Gas Engineers and Managers (IGEM)
Charnwood Wing
Ashby Road
Loughborough
Leicester LE11 3GH
Phone Number: 01509 282728

Institute of Healthcare Engineering & Estate Management (IHEEM)
2 Abingdon House
Cumberland Business Centre
Northumberland Road
Portsmouth PO5 1DS
Phone Number: (023) 9282 3186
Fax Number: (023) 9281 5927
Website: www.iheem.org.uk

Institute of Highway Incorporated Engineers (IHIE)
De Morgan House
58 Russell Square
London WC1B 4HS
Phone Number: (020) 7436 7487

Institution of Highways & Transportation (IHT)
6 Endsleigh Street
London WC1H 0DZ
Phone Number: (020) 7387 2525
Website: www.iht.org

Institution of Incorporated Engineers (IIE)
Savoy Hill House
Savoy Hill
London WC2R 0BS
Phone Number: (020) 7836 3357
Website: www.iie.org.uk

Institution of Lighting Engineers (ILE)
Lennox House
9 Lawford Road
Rugby CV21 2DZ
Phone Number: 01788 576492
Website: www.ile.co.uk

Institute of Materials, Minerals and Mining (IOM[3])
1 Carlton House Terrace
London SW1Y 5DB
Phone Number: (020) 7451 7300
Website: www.iom3.org

Institute of Marine Engineering, Science and Technology (IMarEST)
80 Coleman Street
London EC2R 5BJ
Phone Number: (020) 7382 2600
Website: www.imarest.org

Institute of Measurement and Control (InstMC)
87 Gower Street
London WC1E 6AA
Phone Number: (020) 7387 4949
Website: www.instmc.org.uk

Institution of Mechanical Engineers (IMechE)
1 Birdcage Walk
London SW1H 9JJ
Phone Number: (020) 7222 7899
Website: www.imeche.org.uk

Institution of Nuclear Engineers
1 Penerley Road
London SE6 2LQ
Phone Number: (020) 8698 1500
Website: www.inuce.org.uk

Institute of Physics (IOP)
76 Portland Place
London W1B 1NT
Phone Number: (020) 7470 4800
Website: www.iop.org

Institute of Physics &
Engineering in Medicine (IPEM)
Fairmount House
230 Tadcaster Road
York YO24 1ES
Phone Number: 01904 610821
Website: www.ipem.org.uk

Institute of Plumbing (IoP)
64 Station Lane
Hornchurch
Essex RM12 6NB
Phone Number: 01708 472791
Website: www.plumbers.org.uk

Institution of Railway Signal
Engineers (IRSE)
Savoy Hill House
Savoy Hill
London WC2R 0BS
Phone Number: (020) 7240 3290
Website: www.irse.org

Institution of Structural Engineers
(IStructE)
11 Upper Belgrave Street
London SW1X 8BH
Phone Number: (020) 7235 4535
Website: www.istructe.org.uk

Institution of Water Officers
(IWO)
4 Carlton Court
Team Valley
Gateshead
Tyne & Wear NE11 0AZ
Phone Number: 0191 422 0088
Website: www.iwo.org.uk

Royal Academy of Engineering
29 Great Peter Street
Westminster
London SW1P 3LW
Phone Number: (020) 7222 2688
Website: www.raeng.org.uk

Royal Aeronautical Society
(RAeS)
4 Hamilton Place
London W1V 0BQ
Phone Number: (020) 7499 3515
Website: www.raes.org.uk

Royal Institution of Naval
Architects (RINA)
10 Upper Belgrave Street
London SW1X 8BQ
Phone Number: (020) 7235 4622
Website: www.rina.org.uk

Society of Engineers
Guinea Wiggs, Nayland
Colchester
Essex CO6 4NF
Phone Number: 01206 263332
Website: www.society-of-engineers.
org.uk

Society of Environmental
Engineers (SEE)
The Manor House
High Street
Buntingford
Herts SG9 9PL
Phone Number: 01763 271209
Website: www.environmental.
org.uk

Society of Operations Engineers
(SOE)
22 Greencoat Place
London SW1P 1PR
Phone Number: (020) 7630 1111
Website: www.soe.org.uk

Welding Institute (TWI)
Granta Park
Great Abington

Cambridge CB1 6AL
Phone Number: 01223 891162
Website: www.twi.co.uk

► KEY EUROPEAN ENGINEERING SOCIETIES

Commission des Titres d'Ingenieur (CTI)
135, Avenue de Rangueil
31077 Toulouse Cedex 4
Phone Number: +33 5 61 55 95 11
Website: www.commission-cti.fr

Conseil National des Ingenieurs et Scientifiques de France (CNISF)
7 Rue Lamennais
F-75008
Paris
Phone Number: +33 1 44 13 66 88
Website: www.cnisf.org

European Committee of Civil Engineers (ECCE)
ECCE Secretariat
3 Springfields
Amersham
Bucks
United Kingdom HP6 5JU
Phone Number: +44 01494 723369
Website: www.eccenet.org

European Federation of Chemical Engineering (EFChE)
DECHEMA e.V.
Theodor-Heuss-Allee 25
D-60486 Frankfurt am Main
Phone Number:
+49–69–7564–143/209
Website: www.efce.info

EurETA (European Higher Engineering and Technical Professionals Association)
EurEta Secretary General
162 Sylvan Rd
London SE19 2SA
Phone Number: +44 (0)20 8652 1694
Website: www.eureta.org

EUREL (Convention of National Engineering Societies of Electrical Engineers in Europe)
EUREL General Secretariat
Avenue Roger Vandriessche
18 B-1150 Brussels
Phone Number: +32 (0) 2646.76.00
Website: www.eurel.org

FEANI (European Federation of National Engineering Associations)
Rue du Beau Site 21
B-1000 Bruxelles
Belgium
Phone Number: +32 2 6390390
Fax Number: +32 2 6390 299
Website: www.feani.com

*Koninklijk Instituut Van
Ingenieurs (KIVI)*
23 Prinsessegracht
P.O. Box 30424
2500 GK The Hague
The Netherlands
Phone Number: +31 70 391 99 00
Website: www.ingenieurs.net

*Nederlandse Ingenieursvereniging
(NIRIA)*
Van Stolkweg 6
P.O. Box 84220,
NL-2508 AE THE HAGUE

Phone Number: +31 70 3 522 141
Website: www.niria.nl

*Verein Deutscher Ingenieure
(VDI)* e.V.Graf-Recke-Str.
84 40239 Düsseldorf
Postfach 10 11 39 40002
Düsseldorf Germany
Phone Number: +49 (0) 211 62
14–0
Email Address: kundencenter
@vdi.de
Website: www.vdi.de

▶ MAIN US ENGINEERING SOCIETIES

*Accreditation Board for
Engineering and Technology
(ABET)*
111 Market Pl., Suite 1050
Baltimore, MD 21202
Phone Number: (410) 347 7700
Fax Number: (410) 625 2238
Website: www.abet.org

*American Academy of
Environmental Engineers
(AAEE)*
130 Holiday Court, Suite 100
Annapolis MD 21404
Phone Number: (410) 266 3311
Website: www.aaee.net

*American Association of
Engineering Societies
(AAES)*
1828 L Street, NW
Suite 906
Washington D.C 20036
Phone Number: (202) 296 2237
Fax Number: (202) 296 1151
Website: www.aaes.org

*American Congress on Surveying
and Mapping (ACSM)*
6 Montgomery Village Ave., Suite
403
Gaithersburg MD 20879
Phone Number: (240) 632 9716
Website: www.survmap.org

*American Institute of Aeronautics
and Astronautics (AIAA)*
1801 Alexander Bell Drive
Suite 500
Reston, VA 20191 4344
Phone Number: (703) 264 7500
Website: www.aiaa.org

*American Institute of Chemical
Engineers (AIChE)*
Three Park Avenue
New York NY 10016–5901
Phone Number: (212) 591 7338
Website: www.aiche.org

*American Industrial Hygiene
Association (AIHA)*
2700 Prosperity Avenue, Suite 250

Fairfax, VA 22031
Phone Number: (703) 849 8888
Website: www.aiha.org

American Inst. of Mining,
Metallurgical and Petroleum
Engineers (AIME)
Three Park Avenue
New York NY 10016–5998
Phone Number: (212) 705–7676
Website: www.aimeny.org

American Nuclear Society (ANS)
555 North Kensington Avenue
La Grange Park IL 60526
Phone Number: (708) 352 6611
Website: www.ans.org

American Society of Agricultural
Engineers (ASAE)
2950 Niles Road
St. Joseph MI 49085
Phone Number: (269) 429 0300
Website: asae.org

American Society of Civil
Engineers (ASCE)
1801 Alexander Bell Drive
Reston, VA 20191–4400
Phone Number: (800) 548–2723
Website: www.asce.org

American Society for Engineering
Education (ASEE)
1818 'N' St., NW
Suite 600Washington DC 20036
Phone Number: (202) 331–3500
Website: www.asee.org

American Society of Heating,
Refrigerating and Air-
Conditioning Engineers (ASHRAE)
1791 Tullie Circle, N.E.
Atlanta GA 30329
Phone Number: (404) 636–8400

Website: www.ashrae.org

American Society of Mechanical
Engineers (ASME)
Three Park Avenue
New York NY 10016–5990
Phone Number: (212) 591–7722
Website: www.asme.org

Institute of Electrical and
Electronics Engineers (IEEE)
Corporate Office
Three Park Avenue 17th Floor
New York NY 10016–5997
Phone Number: (212) 419–7900
Website: www.ieee.org

Institute of Industrial Engineers
(IIE)
3577 Parkway Lane Suite 200
Norcross, GA 30092
Phone Number: (770) 449–0460
Website: www.iienet.org

ISA – The International Society for
Measurement and Control
67 Alexander Drive P.O. Box
12277
Research Triangle Pk NC 27709
Phone Number: (919) 549–8411
Website: www.isa.org

National Academy of Engineering
(NAE)
National Academy of Engineering
500 Fifth Street, NW
Washington, DC 20001
Phone Number: (202)-334–1628
Website: www.nae.edu

National Council of Examiners for
Engineering and Surveying
(NCEES)
P.O. Box 1686
Clemson SC 29633–1686

Phone Number: (803) 654–6824
Website: www.ncees.org

National Society of Professional Engineers (NPE)
1420 King Street
Alexandria VA 22314
Phone Number: (703) 684–2800
Website: www.nspe.org

Society of Automotive Engineers (SAE)
400 Commonwealth Drive
Warrendale PA 15096
Phone Number: (724) 776–4841
Website: www.sae.org

Society of Manufacturing Engineers (SME)
One SME Drive
Dearborn MI 48121
Phone Number: (313) 271–1500
Website: www.sme.org

Society for Mining, Metallurgy and Exploration, Inc. (SME-AIME)
8307 Shaffer Parkway
Littleton CO 80127–4102
Phone Number: (303) 973–9550
Website: www.smenet.org

Society of Naval Architects and Marine Engineers (SNAME)
601 Pavonia Avenue
Jersey City NJ 07306
Phone Number: (201) 798–4800
Website: www.sname.org

Society of Petroleum Engineers (SPE)
P.O. Box 833836
Richardson TX 75083–3836
Phone Number: (972) 952–9393
Website: www.spe.org

The Minerals, Metals and Materials Society (TMS)
184 Thorn Hill Road
Warrendale, PA 15086
Phone Number: (724) 776–9000
Website: www.tms.org

United Engineering Foundation (UEF)
Three Park Avenue
New York
NY 10016–5902
Website: www.uefoundation.org

▶ REFERENCES

Cambridge Market Intelligence, 1997. *The engineering profession, CMI Ivanhoe Career Guide.* London: Cambridge Market Intelligence.

Carel, 2003. *Key organizations.* Carlisle: Carel Press.

CBD Research Ltd, 1995. *Directory of European professional and learned societies.* 5th ed, Beckenham: CBD Research Ltd.

CBD Research Ltd, 2002. *Directory of British associations and associations in Ireland.* 16th ed, Beckenham: CBD Research Ltd.

Engineering Council, 2003. *UK Standard for Professional Engineering Competence Chartered Engineer and Incorporated Engineer Standard.*

Engineering Council, 2003. *UK Standard for Professional Competence Engineering Technician Standard.*

Engineering Council, 2003. *A guide to the engineering profession.*

Engineering Council, 2002. *Facts about the engineering profession.* www.engc.org.uk/publications/facts.asp

Engineering Council, 2002. *Survey of Registrants.* London: Engineering Council.

ICE, IMechE, IMarEST, et al., 2002. *Engineering Opportunities for students and graduates 2003.* Bury St Edmunds: Professional Engineering Publishing.

Gale, 2003. *Encyclopedia of associations, international organisations. An associations unlimited reference.* 40th ed, Detroit: Gale.

Gale, 2003. *Encyclopedia of associations, national organizations of the United States.* Detroit: Gale.

Hagstrom, A., and Poyry, S., 1998. *FEANI Handbook 1999.* Brussels: FEANI.

Hamilton, J., 2000. *The engineering profession.* London: Engineering Council.

Hollis, 2002. *Ask Hollis the directory of UK associations 2003.* 2nd ed, Teddington: Hollis Publications.

IEE, 2001. *Requirements for electrical installations BS 7671.* Stevenage: Institution of Electrical Engineers.

IMechE, IEE, ACE, 2001. *Model form of general conditions of contract including forms of tender, agreement, sub-contract, performance bond and defects liability demand guarantee for use in connection with home or overseas contracts for the supply of electrical, electronic or mechanical plant- with erection (MF/1; rev 4).* London: Institution of Mechanical Engineers.

Pullin, J., 1997. *Progress through mechanical engineering. The first 150 years of the Institution of Mechanical Engineers.* London: Quiller Press.

Reynard, K. W., 2002. *Aslib directory of information sources in the United Kingdom.* 12th ed, London: Europa Publications.

Union of International Associations, 2003. *Yearbook of International organizations.* 40th ed., Munich: K. G. Saur Verlag.

14 Information Sources in Aerospace and Defence

John Harrington

▶ INTRODUCTION

Aerospace is a strategically important global business, not only because it makes a vital contribution to the preservation of national and international security, but it also enables the worldwide movement of people and goods. By continually pushing the boundaries of exploration and innovation, the industry is a fertile source of scientific progress and inspiration, and traditionally has occupied one of the leading roles in the global acquisition and dissemination of information and data.

Perhaps not surprisingly, therefore, aerospace engineers have been one of the most highly studied engineering communities in terms of their information needs and information seeking behaviour. This body of research has demonstrated the importance of information to an industry which is characterised by high investment, high risk, complexity, and a high incidence of technical and economic uncertainty. Numerous studies have shown that aerospace engineers and scientists spend a significant proportion of their work time discovering, using and communicating information (Pinelli, 1997; Hanley, 1998; Harrington, *et al.*, 2002).

The multidisciplinary nature of the aerospace business means that it has a very diverse range of information requirements, ranging from science and technology to business, marketing and psychology. Inevitably, therefore, this chapter is as much about 'information sources of interest to aerospace and defence engineers', as it is about aerospace and defence engineering information in the strictest sense. These studies have also shown that although access to information is affected by commercial and security restrictions there is still an enormous amount of relevant and useful information available in the public domain.

Indeed the amount of information available, its highly dispersed nature, and the importance of matching information needs to the most appropriate sources, all present barriers and challenges to the would-be aerospace information user. Searching behaviour and the selection of information sources is invariably influenced by 'least effort' perceptions and is constrained partly by access issues but perhaps most worryingly by low levels of awareness, both of the existence of resources and the benefits of using them. This chapter is partly an attempt to address this awareness problem.

▶ FUSING 'FORMAL' AND 'INFORMAL' INFORMATION SOURCES

The information needs of engineers are often driven by well-defined problem solving imperatives of one sort or another. Engineers generally therefore tend to favour 'information rich' sources that offer a synthesis of information, informed by knowledge and experience. Discussion of these problems with immediate work colleagues or others within the organisation is normally an engineer's first thought, rather than to go to a library, search a database or to read a book or journal. Ease of access is also a powerful determinant and indeed one recent study has shown that, amongst aerospace engineers in industry, the internet has become the 'formal' information resource of first choice (Harrington, et al., 2002).

A number of initiatives are trying to capitalise on the popularity of the Web in order to fuse together the best characteristics of so-called 'informal' and 'formal' information resources to provide a more interactive environment in which to communicate and discover information. Much of the drive to present access to information within the common framework of a web portal (of which more later) is certainly part of this process. Particularly good examples of initiatives that are trying to embody interactivity between the information provider and the user, and between the users themselves in an aerospace and defence context are as follows:

▶ INSTITUTION OF ELECTRICAL ENGINEERS PROFESSIONAL NETWORKS

The IEE has been developing a series of Professional Networks dedicated to bringing like-minded individuals together to discuss and debate the key issues. Each Network represents a world-wide group of people with common technical and professional interests, based on an industrial sector, an academic discipline or an underpinning activity such as management. They provide online access to up to date sector-specific news, a library of technical articles and the opportunity to get together with peer groups through dedicated discussion forums.

The Aerospace Professional Network (www.iee.org/OnComms/pn/aerospace/) has some 7,000 members engaged in electronics, electrical and systems engineering within the international aerospace community. The scope of the Aerospace PN encompasses a broad range of aerospace and defence related disciplines.

The Aerospace PN also provides access to an electronic library of documents drawn from a mixture of IEE publications and conferences, and other full text sources available through the internet. These papers can be browsed or searched. In addition a website directory of quality aerospace and defence websites is provided by Cranfield University's AERADE information portal (see below).

▶ SOCIETY OF BRITISH AEROSPACE COMPANIES (SBAC) INTELLIGENCE CENTRES

The concept of information sharing, including the ability to disseminate as well as to retrieve information, is being promoted by the UK aerospace trade association, the Society of British Aerospace Companies (SBAC), through the establishment of information and intelligence centres. The three already set up are the UK Aerospace Marketing Centre, (www.aerospacemarketingcentre.com), the Airports Intelligence Centre (www.airportsintelligence.co.uk) and the Best Practice Centre (www.bestpracticecentre.com). As part of the services offered, members gain free access to data provided by several key aerospace, air transport and defence information providers. The Marketing Centre also includes market forecasts, supply chain mappings for major aerospace programmes such as the Airbus A380, A400M and Joint Strike Fighter (JSF), daily press headlines and country data for priority markets produced exclusively for the centre.

Members of the Best Practice Centre can draw on its internet-based Best Practice Database to source research findings, case studies and publications from the SBAC's Best Practice Programme which focuses on a number of themes including supply chains, e-Business and people management. The BPC acts as an information portal for the UK Lean Aerospace Initiative (UK-LAI) a joint academic and industry group formed by the Universities of Warwick, Bath, Cranfield and Nottingham. The Centre also provides access to aerospace and defence databases, forthcoming events, privileged research reports from government, universities and trade association sources and links to partners engaged in Best Practice Campaigns. As part of an initiative between the DTI and SBAC, free membership of the BPC is currently available to any recognised organisation within the UK Aerospace industry.

▶ PRIMARY INFORMATION PROVIDERS

International organisations

The aerospace and defence industries are highly competitive. However, the design, manufacturing and operation of aircraft and spacecraft are fraught with technical complexity and high risk, and require considerable planning and investment. Consequently, organisations often choose to undertake these challenges by working in a variety of collaborations, consortiums and partnerships. At an international level, there are many organisations whose primary function is to encourage co-ordination of these activities.

The International Council of the Aeronautical Sciences (ICAS) and the International Society for Air Breathing Engines (ISOABE), for example, both sponsor major biennial congresses. The International Academy of Astronautics (IAA), International Astronautical Federation (IAF), Committee on Space Research (COSPAR) of the International Council of Scientific Unions (ICSU), are all similarly active in the fields of astronautics. The United Nations Office for Outer Space Affairs (UNOOSA) is the United Nations office responsible for promoting international co-operation in the peaceful uses of outer space. UNOOSA maintains the Register of Objects Launched into Outer Space and in 1968, 1982 and 1999 sponsored three United Nations Conferences on the Exploration and Peaceful Uses of Outer Space (UNISPACE). UNOOSA also prepares, and distributes reports, studies and publications on various fields of space science and technology applications and international space law. The website (www.unvienna.org) provides access to online indexes of these publications and where available links to the full text of specific documents.

Trade associations

Trade associations promote the interests of the aerospace and air transport industries. Their primary roles include enhancing competitive development, advocacy and representation, strategic planning, collaboration and co-ordination, marketing and promotion, and adherence to technical and quality standards.

The European Association of Aerospace Industries (AECMA) represents the aerospace industry in Europe in all matters of common interest on the level of aircraft/systems, engines, equipment and components. The AECMA website provides a useful list of aerospace trade associations in Europe (such as the SBAC in the UK, GIFAS in France, BDLI in Germany, AIAD in Italy and ATECMA in Spain) which contains web address and/or e-mail contact information (www.aecma.org/CompnInst.htm). In the US, the Aerospace Industries Association is the primary trade association representing manufacturers of commercial, military and business aircraft, helicopters, engines, missiles, spacecraft, materiels, and related components and equipment. In April 2004 the three major associations representing the aeronautic, space and defence industry in Europe announced their decision to merge. AECMA, EDIG (European Defence Industries Group) and EUROSPACE will form the Aerospace and Defence Industries Association of Europe (ASD). See www.asd-europe.org/main.html, for the latest news on this development.

Many air carriers in Europe are members of the Association of European Airlines (AEA), while the Air Transport Association (ATA) is the trade organisation that represents the principal US airlines. The ATA publishes a wide range of reference documents including specifications, manuals, and handbooks. These include the Airline Handbook, which provides an overview of the history, structure, economics and operations of the airline industry, as well as a glossary of commonly used airline terminology. It is available in print and is freely accessible online (www.airlines.org/public/publications/display1.asp?nid=961).

The International Air Transport Association (IATA) is the prime vehicle for inter-airline co-operation to promote safe, reliable, secure and economical services. IATA produces a wide range of published information aimed at the airlines, airports, cargo, and travel agent sectors of the air transport industry. IATA publications in electronic and print formats cover reference manuals (technical, planning, design, handling and financial), passenger and cargo data, and business information and intelligence including statistics, analysis, forecasting, benchmarking and market research. IATA also produces electronic databases such as the Airport and Obstacle Database (AODB) and World Air Transport Statistics (WATS). The WATS database provides detailed information on more than 200 IATA member airlines, including passenger and freight traffic and employee and fleet data.

The Airports Council International (ACI) is the international association of the world's airports. The ACI produces a range of handbooks, reference manuals, position statements and other guidance material as well as conference proceedings and statistics (www.airports.org/publications/pub_frame.htm).

Professional societies and associations

The professional interests of engineers and scientists involved in aerospace and related disciplines are represented by many individual member associations and societies.

Founded in 1866, The Royal Aeronautical Society (RAeS) claims to be the only professional body which caters for all spectrums of the aerospace community. The Society's library and archives have collections of remarkable historic and contemporary importance. Other professional societies with very strong links to the aerospace and defence community include the Institution of Mechanical Engineers (IMechE) and the Institution of Electrical Engineers (IEE).

In the US there is a number of associations with memberships that include many aerospace and defence engineers. Formed in 1963 through a merger of the American Rocket Society (ARS) and the Institute of Aerospace Sciences (IAS), the American Institute of Aeronautics and Astronautics (AIAA) claims to be the world's largest professional society devoted to the progress of engineering and science in aviation, space, and defence. Over the past sixty-five years, the AIAA and its predecessor organizations have published more than 350 books and 250,000 technical papers. The AIAA continues to produce a magazine, seven technical journals, more than 40 standards, and an increasing number of electronic products.

The American Society of Mechanical Engineers (ASME), the Society of Automotive Engineers (SAE International), AHS International (formerly the American Helicopter Society), the Institute of Electrical and Electronics Engineers (IEEE), SPIE-The International Society for Optical Engineering, International Society of Allied Weight Engineers (SAWE), the American Astronautical Society (AAS), and the American Society of Civil Engineers (ASCE) also organise professional activities and events and produce information for the aerospace and defence sectors. SAE has recently launched a new SAE Aerospace website (www.sae.org/technology/aerospace.htm).

Research organisations and access to technical reports

Historically, research driven organisations such as the National Advisory Committee for Aeronautics (NACA) in the US (the predecessor of NASA), and the UK's Aeronautical Research Council (ARC), favoured the technical report as a primary mechanism for disseminating research results. Comparatively cheap and quick to produce, and normally containing more detailed information than either journals or conference papers, technical reports in the past tended to be physically distributed between producers via exchange agreements.

Nowadays, where commercial and security considerations permit, technical report producers are more likely to utilise the Web as an even more convenient way of publishing this sort of material. This is especially true in the US where succeeding Federal Governments have encouraged agencies to make unlimited distribution material widely available. However, the resulting plethora of web publishing initiatives can be difficult for would-be users to track, especially now that some organisations have taken the decision to end hard copy distribution completely. For a wider discussion of the issues affecting access to technical reports, see Chapter 3.

▶ INTERNATIONAL SOURCES

NATO Research and Technology Organisation (RTO)

The RTO was formed in 1998 by the merger of two NATO bodies: AGARD (the Advisory Group for Aerospace Research and Development) and DRG (the Defence Research Group). Support for, and co-ordination, of RTO activities is provided by the Research and Technology Agency (RTA).

The RTA now publishes all RTO reports up to and including NATO Unclassified and NATO/PfP Unclassified in electronic format on the Web. The NATO Research and Technology Organization Full Text Publication Library provides access to a collection of full text documents produced by the RTO and its predecessor, the Advisory Group for Aerospace Research & Development (AGARD) (www.rta.nato.int/Abstracts.asp).

Von Karman Institute For Fluid Dynamics (VKI)

The Von Karman Institute is a non-profit international educational and scientific research organisation which provides post-graduate education and training in fluid dynamics. The Institute is supported by subsidies from NATO member countries and income derived from contract research.

The VKI produces a range of primary research material including technical notes, technical memoranda, theses and reprints. A selection of these can be accessed on the VKI website (www.vki.ac.be/research/publi/index.html).

In addition, the extensive notes produced as part of the VKI short courses for continuing education are published as proceedings in the renowned VKI Lecture Series Monographs (www.vki.ac.be/educat/lect-ser/monographs1.html).

▶ US SOURCES

NASA

NASA produces an enormous amount of aerospace scientific and technical information (STI) as a result of basic and applied scientific and technical research and mission-related activities. This includes research reports, journal articles, conference and meeting papers, technical videos, mission-related operational documents, preliminary data and technical photos. Primary responsibility for the acquisition and dissemination of this material resides with the NASA STI Program. This administers STI from the twelve NASA centres and through exchange from over fifty countries worldwide. While the NASA STI Program offers many products and services to the wider aerospace community, free registration to the Program is primarily limited to NASA and to US government agencies and contractors via the NASA Center for AeroSpace Information (CASI).

NASA Technical Reports and NASA Technical Report Server (NTRS)

There are currently six NASA STI Report Series as follows: Technical Publications (TP), Conference Publications (CP), Special Publications (SP), Technical Memoranda (TM), Contractor Reports (CR), and Technical Translations (TT). Since it first went online in June 1994, the NASA Technical Report Server (NTRS) has become a primary mechanism for facilitating access to this material via the Web (techreports.larc.nasa.gov/cgi-bin/NTRS).

The goal of the NTRS is in effect to provide a one-stop-shop for NASA technical reports. It provides links to, and in most cases cross searching of, technical report servers located at the NASA centres as well as several other full text and bibliographic databases. It is open to all members of the Internet/World Wide Web community (Nelson, *et al.*, 1996).

NACA Technical Reports and the NACA Technical Report Server (NACATRS)

The National Advisory Committee for Aeronautics was chartered in 1915 and was operational from 1917 until 1958. As NASA's predecessor organisation, NACA played an integral role in the development of the United States' fledgling aeronautics industry as the main research body for a collection of federal, commercial and university interests.

The main product of NACA's research was its multi-tiered report series. Although the exact number of NACA reports published is unknown, most estimates place this number between 20,000 and 30,000. This collection of work remains in high demand even today, especially for the basic fundamentals of flight.

NASA began the ongoing digital conversion of their NACA report collection in 1995. The result of this effort is the NACA Technical Report Server (naca.larc.nasa.gov) (Nelson, 1999). The NACA Technical Report Server provides search and browse access to the full text of over 7,000 reports. Access to the NACATRS from the UK and Europe has been recently enhanced with the establishment of a mirror service hosted at Cranfield University (naca.central.cranfield.ac.uk).

NASA Image eXchange (NIX)

Established in May 1997, NIX is a web-based database of photographic digital images and QuickTime animation and video (nix.nasa.gov). It currently links the internal image databases of seven NASA centres, and has an estimated 500,000 images. (Not all NASA images are available through NIX).

US Department of Defense (DoD) Defense Technical Information Center (DTIC)

The Defense Technical Information Center (DTIC) is the central facility for the collection and dissemination of scientific and technical information for the Department of Defense (DoD). Much of this information is made available by DTIC in the form of technical reports about completed research, and research summaries of ongoing research.

DTIC's flagship online research service for accessing technical report and other primary research documents is STINET. This is available in two formats, Public STINET and Secure STINET. Public STINET (stinet.dtic. mil) contains all unclassified, unlimited citations to documents added into DTIC from late December 1974 to present. There are also full-text versions of all unclassified, unlimited documents recently added into the DTIC technical reports collection from September 1998 to present. Public STINET is free of charge.

US Department of Transportation (DoT)

For commercial aeronautics (air transport, general aviation) in the United States the technical, economic, and safety regulatory framework is primarily the responsibility of the Department of Transportation (DoT). Operationally the DoT exercises its responsibilities through fourteen administrations, including the Federal Aviation Administration (FAA) and the Transportation Security Administration.

The DoT and its operating agencies provide many valuable sources of research and regulatory information (described in the regulatory section below).

The National Transportation Library (NTL) / Transportation Research Information Services (TRIS) – TRIS Online

The National Transportation Library (ntl.bts.gov) was established in 1998 as a mechanism for assisting US Federal, State, and local transportation information users. It provides search and browse access to a large collection of digital documents, as well as to the DoT's premier online bibliographic database, TRIS Online. Containing almost 450,000 records, TRIS Online is one the largest and most comprehensive sources of information on transportation research on the Web (199.79.179.82/sundev/search.cfm). It not only provides access to bibliographic records and abstracts but it also provides value-added links to the full text of public domain documents and document suppliers. Currently there are over 9,100 TRIS records with links to electronic copies of the full-text of the reports or papers.

Federal Aviation Administration (FAA)

A good many FAA technical reports and regulatory materials are now available in full text on the Web. However, because these are produced by a variety of FAA offices they tend to be rather scattered. A selection of some useful FAA sites includes the William J. Hughes Technical Center Library (actlibrary.tc.faa.gov), FAA Office of Aviation Research (AAR) (research.faa.gov/tech_reports.asp), FAA Office of Aerospace Medicine / Civil Aerospace Medical Institute (CAMI) (www.cami.jccbi.gov/AAM-400A/index.html), and the Office of the Associate Administrator for Commercial Space Transportation (AST) (ast.faa.gov).

Transportation Research Board (TRB)

The TRB is a unit of the National Research Council, a private, non-profit institution that is the principal operating agency of the National Academy of Sciences and the National Academy of Engineering.

The TRB addresses all modes and aspects of transportation through the work of its standing technical committees and task forces. These produce a number of report series including Conference Reports and Conference Proceedings, TRB Special Reports, Millennium Papers, and Transportation Research Records. Details of all TRB reports, studies and other documents can be found on the website (www4.trb.org/trb/onlinepubs.nsf).

National Technical Information Service (NTIS)

It should be noted that despite all of this direct publishing to the Web, NTIS (www.ntis.gov/index.asp) is still a major source for Federal scientific, technical, engineering, and business-related information. Annually, NTIS receives tens of thousands of new publications, technical reports, and other products, including around 2,500 in aeronautics and aerodynamics, 2,300 in space technology, and 1,700 in combustion, engines, and propellants.

▶ UK GOVERNMENT REPORTS

Compared to the US situation, public access to technical reports produced by UK Government and other sources is rather more problematic. Reports tend to be scattered across many libraries and there is no straightforward way of identifying holding locations, especially as the cataloguing of individual items is rather patchy.

Aeronautical Research Council (ARC) and Royal Aerospace Establishment (formerly Royal Aircraft Establishment)

The ARC, which for many years was the UK's chief advisory body for aeronautics, produced a key historic collection of technical reports. Originally established as the Advisory Committee for Aeronautics in April 1909, the ARC was reconstituted in March 1920 as the Aeronautical Research Committee. It was disbanded in December 1980.

ARC reports were produced in four series: Reports & Memoranda (R&M), Current Papers (CP), Typed Reports (T), and the unprefixed papers. Many libraries in the UK, the US and elsewhere have collections of ARC reports. Both the UK Public Records Office (catalogue.pro.gov.uk) and Cranfield University (unicorn.central.cranfield.ac.uk/uhtbin/webcat/) offer publicly accessible library catalogues which enable item level searching for individual ARC reports. Cranfield University has also digitised some 3000 ARC R&Ms and CPs as part of the Managing Access to Grey Literature Collections (MAGiC) project (Needham, 2002).

The Royal Aircraft Establishment (RAE) was the largest corporate producer of research reports for the ARC and many titles can be found in both ARC and RAE reports series. The RAE existed between 1918 and 1988, after which it became part of the Defence Research Agency (DRA later DERA, see below). RAE reports are to be found in collections scattered throughout the UK. A good starting point for understanding this source is the detailed account of the history of the reports series produced by the RAE and its predecessors (Thornton, 1979).

QinetiQ / Defence Science and Technology Laboratory (DSTL)

In July 2001 the UK Government's Defence Evaluation and Research Agency (DERA) was split into two organisations, Defence Science and Technology Laboratory (DSTL) and QinetiQ Group plc. DSTL remains part of the Ministry of Defence (MOD) and continues to handle the most sensitive areas of defence research. Under a Public-Private Partnership arrangement, QinetiQ has become a Government owned PLC and remains one of Europe's largest research organisations, with business interests in defence, transport, space, energy and health care technologies. QinetiQ produces its own technical reports, and these together with those produced by DERA and its predecessor organisations are held in store at an information warehouse at Boscombe Down.

DSTL also produces research reports, copies of which are held as part of the MOD scientific reports collection at Kentigern House in Glasgow. DSTL Knowledge Services (www.dstl.gov.uk/info_store/index.htm) administers the collection which contains over three-quarters of a million reports dating back to World War Two. The collection contains both unlimited distribution as well as protectively marked material.

▶ OTHER SOURCES OF RESEARCH REPORTS

- **Office National d'Études et de Recherches Aérospatiale (ONERA)** – The ONERA website provides search and browse access to publications produced by ONERA staff). A few of these are available in full text in the database (www.onera.fr/SEARCH/BASIS/public/web_en/document/sf).
- **Nationaal Lucht- en Ruimtevaartlaboratorium / National Aerospace Laboratory (NLR)** – NLR makes available technical publications and reports released since 1997 via a web database (www.nlr.nl/public/library/lib-search.cgi?).
- **FOI – Totalförsvarets forskningsinstitut / Swedish Defence Research Agency** – The results of FOI research are published in reports, of which there are 150 – 200 each year. The research reports are in most cases unclassified. These can be searched and browsed online (www.ffa.se/english/index.html). Individual documents are sorted under the producing department.
- **Defence Research and Development Canada (DRDC)** – The website contains a database of publicly accessible Defence Research Reports produced by the agency's five research centres. The Defence Research Reports web database (pubs.drdc-rddc.gc.ca/pubdocs/pcow1_e.html) includes details of unlimited distribution publications produced over the past fifty years, and there are currently well over 8,000 bibliographic records for documents which are authored or co-authored by DRDC or its previous incarnations. The database covers virtually all defence-relevant scientific and technical areas. It is a sub-set of the larger CANDID (CANadian Defence Information Database), which is

itself a component of the CANadian Defence Information System (CANDIS), a resource containing almost one million bibliographic records. Access to CANDIS, is however, restricted to Department of National Defence staff.

*   **Defence Science and Technology Organisation (DSTO)** – Part of Australia's Department of Defence, DSTO's Scientific and Technical Publications Database provides access to selected reports, journal articles, and conference papers (www.dsto.defence.gov.au/corporate/reports/).

▶ STANDARDS, RECOMMENDED PRACTICES AND PROCEDURES – THE REGULATION OF AEROSPACE AND DEFENCE

Like any industry in which safety and environmental impact are major (if not overriding) concerns, the aeronautics, air transport, and space sectors are all very highly regulated. Access to current rules, regulations, standards, and recommended practices and procedures is therefore a major information requirement.

It is a challenging and diverse industry. For example, in the UK the CAA is responsible for licensing, approving and monitoring: 200 aeroplane and helicopter operators and nearly 80 balloon operators, 145 aerodromes, 48,300 professional and private pilots, 11,400 maintenance engineers, 800 design and manufacturing organisations, 2,400 air traffic controllers, and 1,800 tour operators selling holidays to twenty-nine million people.

The complexity of the tasks involved and the importance of establishing consistency and harmonization inevitably means that there is often an international as well as a national dimension to much of this regulatory effort.

▶ INTERNATIONAL REGULATORS

International Civil Aviation Organization (ICAO)

The ICAO is the United Nations Specialized Agency responsible for establishing international standards, recommended practices and procedures covering the technical, economic and legal fields of international civil aviation operations.

The ICAO produces a wide range of documents including air navigation rules and regulations, air transport studies, reports and manuals, Annexes to the Convention on International Civil Aviation (SARPS), and Procedures /Air Navigation Services (PANS), including Aircraft Operations

(OPS) and Rules of the Air Traffic Services (RAC). It also produces a regular series of key statistical digests. The separate compilations are titled: *Airport and Route Facilities, Airport Traffic Civil Aircraft on Register, Civil Aviation Statistics of the World, Financial Data-Commercial Air Carriers, Fleet-Personnel-Commercial Air Carriers, On-flight Origin and Destination, Traffic by Flight Stage,* and *Traffic-Commercial Air Carriers.*
Availability (216.46.2.37/mainpage.ch2).

▶ AIR TRANSPORT AND AIR TRAFFIC MANAGEMENT IN EUROPE

Of all forms of transport, air travel has seen by far the most impressive growth in the European Union over the last twenty years. In terms of passenger-kilometres, traffic increased by an average of 7.4% a year between 1980 and 2001, while traffic at the airports of the fifteen Member States has increased five-fold since 1997. Key players in coordinating efforts to solve these challenges include the European Commission (EC), EURO-CONTROL, the European Civil Aviation Conference (ECAC), the Joint Aviation Authorities (JAA), and eventually the European Aviation Safety Agency (EASA).

The European Commission

The Air Transport website (europa.eu.int/comm/transport/air/index_en. htm) provides an overview and description of the key themes that shape the European Commission's policies for air transport. The description includes links to relevant EEC regulations, where these are referred to in the text. Key policy documents and regulations are collected together in the legislation section.

EUR-Lex (europa.eu.int/eur-lex/en/index.html) is the portal to European Union law, covering legislation in force and new legislation as it is enacted. Two sections from the EUR-Lex site are of particular relevance to the aerospace community:

- **The EUR-Lex Directory of Community Legislation in Force and Preparatory Acts** – Air Transport (europa.eu.int/ eur lex/en/lif/reg/en_register_0740.html) provides coverage of competition rules, market operation, market access, route distribution, prices and terms, air safety, structural harmonization, international relations, consultation procedures and conventions with non-member countries.

- **European Commission: Air Transport: Legislation**
  (europa.eu.int/comm/transport/air/legislation/index_en.htm)
  provides access to the text of Commission Decisions, Council
  Directives and Regulations, which are listed under the headings of
  internal market, state aid, competition rules, air traffic
  management, air safety, environment, protection of passengers,
  working conditions and other.

EUROCONTROL

EUROCONTROL, the European Organisation for the Safety of Air
Navigation, has been Europe's Air Traffic Management body for over forty
years. Research and Development (R&D) is a key activity for EURO-
CONTROL. The website provides search and browse access to a collection
of EEC technical reports and technical notes issued since 1994/95
(www.eurocontrol.fr).

European Civil Aviation Conference (ECAC)

ECAC is an intergovernmental organisation which aims to promote the
continued development of a safe, efficient and sustainable European air
transport system. The ECAC website (www.ecac-ceac.org) provides online
access to a number of ECAC reports and other documents, including reso-
lutions, symposium proceedings, studies and codes of conduct.

Joint Aviation Authorities (JAA)

The JAA is an associated body of the European Civil Aviation Conference
(ECAC) representing the civil aviation regulatory authorities of a number of
European states who have agreed to co-operate in developing and implementing common safety regulatory standards and procedures. Among the
JAA's many functions is the development and adoption of the Joint Aviation
Requirements (JARs) in the fields of aircraft design and manufacture, aircraft
operations and maintenance and the licensing of aviation personnel. The full
text of section 1 of the Joint Airworthiness Requirements (JARs) can be
viewed online (www.jaa.nlsection1/jarsec1.html), but note that none of the
guidance material is made available as this must be purchased separately.

European Aviation Safety Agency (EASA)

In June 2000 the Council of the EU Transport Ministers asked the
Commission to develop an EU Regulation for a European Aviation Safety
Agency (EASA) which will be responsible for rulemaking, certification

and standardisation for the application of rules by the national aviation authorities.

▶ NATIONAL REGULATORY AUTHORITIES

Civil Aviation Authority (CAA)

The CAA is the UK's independent aviation regulator, with all civil aviation regulatory functions (economic regulation, airspace policy, safety regulation and consumer protection) integrated within a single specialist body. The legal separation of National Air Traffic Services Limited (NATS) from the CAA on 31 March 2001 established clear division between the provision and the regulation of air traffic services in the UK.

The CAA produces regulatory/guidance documents as well as research reports and CAPs (Civil Aviation Papers). The CAA's publications site (www.caa.co.uk/publications/) offers print and browse access to the documents.

United Kingdom Department For Transport (DFT)

The DFT's Aviation website (www.aviation.dft.gov.uk) enables the Department to disseminate information relating to current and past consultations including the Future Development of Air Transport in the United Kingdom.

United Kingdom Air Accidents Investigation Branch (AAIB)

The AAIB is part of the Department for Transport and is responsible for the investigation of civil aircraft accidents and serious incidents within the UK. The AAIB produces a series of reports and bulletins some of which are reproduced in full text on the AAIB's website (www.aaib.dft.gov.uk).

Federal Aviation Administration (FAA)

In the US it is the FAA that oversees the safety of civil aviation. The FAA's function includes the issuance and enforcement of regulations and standards related to the manufacture, operation, certification and maintenance of aircraft. In addition to air transport the FAA regulates and encourages the US commercial space transportation industry, with responsibility for licensing commercial space launch facilities and private sector launches.

Selected key FAA and DoT regulatory information sources include:

- **The FAA Regulatory and Guidance Library (RGL)**
  (www.airweb.faa.gov/Regulatory_and_Guidance_Library/rgWebcom
  ponents.nsf/HomeFrame?OpenFrameSet) – provides access to a set
  of searchable databases which contain regulatory and aviation
  product information. These include Federal Aviation Regulations
  (FARs) and Special Federal Aviation Regulations (SFARs).
- **Regulation and Rulemaking** (www1.faa.gov/avr/arm/index.cfm).
- **Regulation and Certification Group (AVR)**
  (www.faa.gov/avr/index.cfm).
- **The DoT Docket Management System (DMS)**
  (dms.dot.gov). The DMS provides access to information about
  proposed and final regulations, copies of public comments on
  proposed rules, and related information.
- **Department of Transportation Library** (dotlibrary.dot.gov).
  The DoT library provides full text access to some very useful
  historical 'grey' literature resources. This includes the digitisation
  of a selection of historic aerospace technical and regulatory
  materials such as: Civil Aeronautical regulations (CARs), Civil
  Aeronautical Manuals (CAMs), Historical Aircraft Accident Reports
  (1934–1965), and Historical Federal Aviation Regulations (FARs).
  There are also online bibliographies covering various aspects of air
  safety and security (dotlibrary.dot.gov/bibliographies/intro.htm).

National Transportation Safety Board (NTSB)

The National Transportation Safety Board is an independent Federal agency
that investigates every civil aviation accident in the United States and significant accidents in other modes of transportation, conducts special
investigations and safety studies, and issues safety recommendations to
prevent future accidents.

The NTSB produces a range of information resources including databases and reports including: Aircraft Accident Reports, Aviation Studies
and Special Reports, Aviation Statistical Reports, Aviation Accident
Statistical Tables, and the Aviation Accident and Synopses Database. These
resources are accessible from the NTSB website (www.ntsb.gov/Publictn/
publictn.htm).

▶ OTHER REGULATORY SOURCES AVAILABLE ON THE INTERNET

Various other national civil aviation authorities and organisations have a
strong web presence. A selection of the best sources includes:

- **Bureau Enquetes Accidents (BEA)** (www.bea-fr.org/anglaise/index.htm). The BEA is the official French organisation responsible for technical investigations of civil aviation accidents and incidents. The site includes a searchable database of accident reports.
- **Service De L'Information Aeronautique (SIA)** – (www.sia.aviation-civile.gouv.fr/default_uk.htm). Within the French General Directorate of Civil Aviation (DGAC) and the Air Navigation Directorate (DNA), the SIA is responsible for providing Aeronautical information Services for national and international air navigation. The SIA publishes regulations related to air traffic operation (RCA), aircraft airworthiness and operations (RTA), commercial transport operations (OPS) and flight crew licences (FCL).
- **Civil Aviation Authority of New Zealand** (www.caa.govt.nz).
- **Civil Aviation Safety Authority Australia (CASA)** (www.casa.gov.au).
- **Department of Transport and Regional Services: Aviation and Airports Policy (Australia)** (www.dotrs.gov.au/avnapt/index.htm).
- **Transport Canada: Civil Aviation Program** (www.tc.gc.ca/CivilAviation/menu.htm).

▶ STANDARDS

The design, manufacture, testing and operation of aircraft and spacecraft are informed by a great many standards. There are numerous military, industry and professional agencies and organisations that play a key role in producing and maintaining standards aimed specifically at the aerospace and defence sector.

However, over the last ten years or more there has been something of a shift in policy on military standardardisation in many countries including the US, UK and other NATO member states. Defence procurement goals are now focussed on achieving equipment interoperability, compatibility, and integration. This has led to the increasing adoption of performance-based specifications and standards or nationally-recognised private sector standards, rather than the development or retention of separate specialist military standards. For example, where it is possible to do so, maximum use is being made of procuring Commercial-Off-The-Shelf (COTS) equipment for the armed services.

This places an increased emphasis on the use of civil standards for military materiel standardisation. Many of the national and international authorities that either produce, administer or co-ordinate standards programmes are generally very well known, such as the International Organization for Standardization (ISO), International Electrotechnical Commission (IEC), European Committee for Standardization (CEN), the UK's British Standards Institution (which has its own BSI aerospace series) and the US American National Standards Institute (ANSI).

A selection of the key specialist military standards series includes the following:

UK Defence Standardisation (DSTAN) – These are produced only where there is a clear advantage and when no suitable British or other type of standard is available which fulfils the need. Since March 2000 all extant Defence Standards which are unclassified are available in electronic format for downloading in full text via the DStan website (www.dstan.mod.uk). A comprehensive list of all extant UK Defence Standards is contained in Def Stan 00–00 (Part 3) Section 4, which is published annually.

US Military Specifications and Standards (Mil Specs & Mil Stds) – The US Department of Defense (DoD) standardisation policy is managed by the Defense Standardization Program (www.dsp.dla.mil). DoD policy is to state requirements in performance terms, and wherever practical to replace its detailed military specifications with performance specifications, interface standards, and commercial specifications and standards. Nevertheless the use of detailed military standards and specifications still continues where these appear to offer the most cost-effective solution.

Information about, and access to, US Defense specifications, standards and related documents is now readily available through a number of routes including several web database formats.

- **ASSIST (Acquisition Streamlining and Standardization Information System)** – ASSIST-Online (assist.daps.dla.mil/online/), provides direct access to over 104,000 digital document images. The major component of the database consists of documents listed in DODISS (Department of Defense Index of Specifications and Standards).
- **ASSIST Quick Search** (assist2.daps.dla.mil/quicksearch/) enables users to search the ASSIST database for unrestricted documents without having to register.
- **Defense Technical Information Center's Scientific and Technical Information Network (STINET)** – DODISS Search (stinet.dtic.mil/str/dodiss4_fields.html). This is an alternative to ASSIST in that it presents a different interface for searching for DODISS documents using some additional parameters.

NATO Standardisation Programme

Standardisation amongst NATO forces makes a vital contribution to the combined operational effectiveness of the military forces of the Alliance and enables opportunities to be exploited for making better use of economic resources. Operational, materiel and administrative standards are published in the form of NATO Standardization Agreements (STANAG) which define common procedures systems and equipment, and Allied Publications (AP). Many of these are now available via the NATO Online Library (www.nato.int/docu/standard.htm).

▶ TRADE ASSOCIATION / INDUSTRY STANDARDS

- **AECMA-STAN** – the recognised body in Europe for the preparation and promotion of European Standards (EN) for aerospace civil and military applications and an Associated Body (ASB) to CEN, the European Committee for Standardisation. The AECMA-STAN website (www.aecma-stan.org) provides access to the ESSAS online facility for searching and purchasing copies of standards and other documents.
- **AECMA-CERT** – qualifies standard aerospace products and approves the quality system of their manufacturers so as to establish conformity with applicable standards, particularly EN standards and ensures that the requirements underlying the qualification are observed.
- **European Organisation for Civil Aviation Equipment (EUROCAE)** – develops performance specifications for airborne electronic equipment. These documents are considered by Joint Aviation Authorities to be referenced by the JAA Joint Technical Standard Orders and other regulatory documents.
- **Aerospace Industries Association (AIA)** – National Aerospace Standards (NAS) – The NAS series of standards is best known for its high strength precision fasteners. In addition to all types of screws, nuts, and rivets, NAS define high pressure hoses, electrical connectors, splices and terminations, rod end bearings and many other types of hardware and components.
- **Air Transport Association (ATA) Specifications** – These specifications address a range of engineering, maintenance and material requirements.
- **Airlines Electronic Engineering Committee (AEEC) / ARINC Inc** – The AEEC establishes consensus-based, voluntary form, fit, function, and interface standards that are published by ARINC and are known as ARINC Standards. ARINC Standards specify the air transport avionics equipment and systems used by more than 10,000 commercial aircraft worldwide.

- • **Avionic Systems Standardisation Committee** – The role of the ASSC is to enable both customers and suppliers to derive the maximum commercial advantage from the standards applicable to UK military avionic systems.
- • **RTCA Inc** – Is a private, not-for-profit organisation that develops consensus-based recommendations regarding communications, navigation, surveillance, and air traffic management (CNS/ATM) system issues. Although its primary focus is US-based, many non-U.S. government and business organizations also belong to RTCA.

▶ STANDARDS PRODUCED BY ASSOCIATIONS, SOCIETIES AND OTHER PROFESSIONAL ORGANISATIONS

In the US, professional associations such as the AIAA, SAE, IEEE and SAWE all produce aerospace standards. Indeed, the SAE describes itself as the world's largest producer of non-government aerospace standards. The Society annually publishes many new, revised, and reaffirmed standards in two specifically aerospace related series: Aerospace Standards (AS) and Aerospace Material Specifications (AMS).

Consultative Committee for Space Data Systems

Since it was established in 1982, CCSDS has been actively developing recommendations for data- and information-systems standards. CCSDS documents are given colour coded covers (so-called white, red, green, blue, and yellow books) which visually indicate their status and maturity.

NASA Technical Standards Program

The NASA Technical Standards Program website (standards.nasa.gov) acts as a common access point for technical standards either developed by NASA, or adopted for use on NASA programmes.

European Co-operation for Space Standardization (ECSS)

This is an initiative established to develop a coherent, single set of user-friendly standards for use in all European space activities. ECSS standards are harmonised with international standards or working practices where these have been, or are in the course of being, generally adopted by the European space industry. ECSS drafts documents for project management, product assurance and safety for space programmes and engineering which are submitted to the European Committee for Standardization (CEN) for publication as European Standards. ECSS Standards include specifications, guidelines, manuals, handbooks and procedures. As with CCDS a colour coded system is applied to distinguish between these categories. Full text and download access to standards is provided by the ECSS website (www.ecss.nl).

▶ ELECTRONIC AND PRINTED AEROSPACE AND DEFENCE JOURNALS

Titles published in the aerospace and defence field range from the popular press catering for the enthusiast, modeller and historian, through trade journals, to the highly technical and specialised publications, produced by academic publishers and learned societies. The focus of the selection presented below is very much on the more academic end of the market, along with a selection of the key trade publications.

▶ IDENTIFYING KEY JOURNALS

The first selection of key aerospace and defence journals is presented in ranked order by ISI Impact Factor, as presented in the 2001 Science edition of the *ISI Journal Citation Report*. JCR is a unique tool for journal evaluation and comparison based on the collection and analysis of citation data.

ESA Bulletin (European Space Agency) – This is the Agency's quarterly 'house journal'. Each issue contains feature articles on ESA programmes and missions, as well as brief news items, programme status reports, and a list of recent ESA publications. *ESA Bulletin* is freely distributed by ESA Publications Division, European Space Research and Technology Centre (ESTEC), and is published electronically in full text (esapub.esrin.esa.it/bulletin/bullets.htm).

Progress in Aerospace Sciences: an international review journal – This journal is devoted primarily to the publication of specially commissioned review articles. It covers aero- and gas-dynamics, structures, flight mechanics, materials, vibrations, aeroelasticity, acoustics, propulsion, avionics and occasionally related areas such as hydrodynamics (www.elsevier.com/locate/paerosci).

IEEE Transactions on Aerospace and Electronic Systems – This is principally aimed at those individuals who are working or studying in the areas of aerospace electronic systems, including command, control, and communications systems, avionics, aircraft control, aircraft navigation, missile guidance, multisensor systems, electronic warfare systems, energy conversion systems, intelligent systems, radar systems, robotics systems, space systems and support systems (www.ieee.org/products/periodicals. html).

AIAA Journal – The AIAA's flagship journal covers all topics of broad interest to the membership as opposed to the more narrowly focused scope of the AIAA's other journals

Journal of Aircraft – This AIAA specialist journal focuses on significant advances in aircraft, the operation of aircraft, and applications of aircraft technology to other fields.

Journal of the American Helicopter Society – This is the peer reviewed quarterly journal of the AHS (www.vtol.org/journal/journal.html).

Advances in Space Research (including the Cospar Information Bulletin) – The journal presents information on fundamental research obtained by utilising aerospace vehicles and is primarily of interest to physicists, astronomers, and the general field of space science. It includes the proceedings of COSPAR organised symposia and other scientific meetings organized by the Committee (www.elsevier.com/locate/asr).

Journal of Guidance, Control, and Dynamics – This is another of the AIAA's specialist technical journals. The aim of the journal is to publish papers that contain and describe significant technical knowledge, exploratory developments, design criteria, and applications in aeronautics, astronautics, celestial mechanics, and related fields.

Journal of Propulsion and Power – This is the AIAA technical journal that covers combustion, power generation and use, and overall propulsion systems and components as they relate to the fields of aeronautics, astronautics, and space sciences.

Journal of Spacecraft and Rockets – Yet another of the AIAA's titles.

International Journal of Satellite Communications and Networking – The journal covers all aspects of the theory and practice of satellite systems and networks (www.interscience.wiley.com/jpages/1542–0973/).

Aerospace Science and Technology – The journal was created by a merger *of La Recherché Aérospatiale* and *ZFW* (*Zeitschrift für Flugwissenschaften und Weltraumforschung*), formerly both leading journals in France and Germany. This is a refereed journal which is now published in conjunction with Elsevier. It contains original papers and review articles and condensed versions of recently completed Ph.D. theses (www.elsevier.com/locate/issn/12709638).

Transactions of the Japan Society for Aeronautical and Space – This journal is published quarterly by the Japan Society for Aeronautical and Space Sciences (JSASS) in English.

Journal of Aerospace Engineering – Published by the American Society of Civil Engineers, this quarterly journal promotes the implementation and development of space and aerospace technologies, and their transfer to other civil engineering applications. It focuses on information related to the civil engineering aspects of aerospace engineering, primarily structural aspects of space engineering, applied mechanics, aeronautics, and astronautics (ojps.aip.org/aso/).

Aeronautical Journal – This is the long-established monthly technical journal of the Royal Aeronautical Society (RAeS). The coverage and content of the journal is guided by the Society's specialist committees.

IEEE Aerospace and Electronic Systems Magazine – Produced by the IEEE's Aerospace and Electronic Systems Society (AESS), the scope and content of the magazine therefore reflect the interests of AESS members. (www.ieee.org/products/periodicals.html).

Journal of Astronautical Sciences – Published quarterly by the American Astronautical Society (AAS), this is the Society's forum for more technical and research oriented articles concerned with the science and technology of astronautics (www.astronautical.org/pubs/thejournal.html).

Space Communications – This peer-reviewed quarterly journal covers all aspects of the satellite communication, satellite navigation, and satellite broadcast fields (www.iospress.nl/site/html/09248625.html).

Acta Astronautica: Journal of the International Academy of Astronautics – This journal features papers on space science technology related to peaceful scientific exploration of space and its exploitation for human welfare and progress, and the conception, design, development and operation of space-borne and Earth-based systems. It includes selected proceedings of the Annual International Astronautical Congress in a special volume. In addition to regular issues of contributed papers, the journal publishes the Transactions of the Academy and special issues on topics of current interest (www.elsevier.com/locate/issn/00945765).

International Journal of Turbo & Jet-Engines – (www.angelfire.com/il/freund/TurboASc.html).

Aerospace America – The AIAA's monthly trade magazine contains informative articles of interest to those within the field of aeronautics and space science rather than the more technical articles and papers presented in other AIAA publications. (www.aiaa.org/publications/index.hfm?pub=1).

Aerospace Engineering – The SAE's monthly news and trade journal is intended to provide technical assistance and state-of-the-art technology of interest to designers, manufacturers, and project managers of aerospace systems and components. (www.sae.org/aeromag/current.htm).

Journal of Aerospace Engineering, Proceedings of the Institution of Mechanical Engineers Part G – The journal contains papers on both theoretical and practical aspects of all types of civil and military aircraft and spacecraft and their support systems (www.pepublishing.com/frm_journal.asp).

Aviation Week and Space Technology (AWST) – First published in 1916, this is one of the most established and renowned aerospace and aviation trade magazines. Being a weekly publication the magazine aims to provide broad coverage of the aerospace industry with an emphasis on news, forecasts and analysis. McGraw-Hill, who publish AWST also produce the AviationNow website (www.aviationnow.com). This offers industry news and analysis organised around a number of news channels including airports, business and commercial aviation, homeland security and defence, and overhaul and maintenance.

Aircraft Engineering and Aerospace Technology – This provides a broad coverage of the materials and techniques employed in the aircraft and aerospace industry. The journal tends to focus on the UK and European aerospace industry (isacco.emerald-library.com/vl=921702/cl=106/nw=1/rpsv/aeat.htm).

Izvestiya Vysshikh Uchebnykh Zavedenii Aviatsionnaya Tekhnika – This is the sole scientific-technical journal in Russia which publishes articles on fundamental research, application, and development works in the field of aeronautical, space, and rocket science and engineering that are carried out in higher institutions, research institutes, design bureaus, and branch enterprises. The journal is translated cover-to-cover from Russian into English and published by Allerton Press, Inc., USA under the title 'Russian Aeronautics'.

▶ OTHER IMPORTANT RESEARCH TITLES

The ISI JCR aerospace journal rankings do not include a number of academic and research journals that cover many of the disciplines which underpin aerospace and defence engineering

- *Journal of Aerospace Computing, Information, and Communication* (AIAA, new in 2004)
- *Journal of Thermophysics and Heat Transfer* (AIAA)
- *Journal of Applied Mechanics* (ASME)
- *Journal of Fluids Engineering* (ASME)
- *Journal of Heat Transfer* (ASME)
- *Journal of Engineering for Gas Turbines and Power* (ASME)
- *Journal of Turbomachinery* (ASME)
- *Journal of Dynamics Systems, Measurement, and Control* (ASME)
- *Journal of Vibration and Acoustics* (ASME)
- *Journal of Engineering Materials & Technology* (ASME)
- *Journal of Microelectromechanical Systems* (IEEE / ASME)

► TRADE MAGAZINES AND NEWS SERVICES

Some of the more significant trade titles include the following:

Flight International – This is one of the world's leading aerospace trade magazines. Since it was first published in 1909, Flight has become noted for its features, occasional cut-away drawings as well as directories that provide overviews of industry sectors including maintenance facilities, simulators, engine manufacturers, and world airlines (www. flightinternational.com/fi_home.asp).

Airline Business – A monthly publication, *Airline Business* reports on the operations of individual companies, developments in specific countries or regions, and issues affecting the industry as a whole. There are annual special reports on the state of the world's top airlines and airports (www.airlinebusiness.com).

Air Transport Intelligence – *Flight International* and *Airline Business* are both searchable electronically as part of *Air Transport Intelligence* (ATI), Reed's subscription specialist online news and data service for the aerospace and air transport industries (www.rati.com). Aimed very much at the corporate market, ATI's core service provides access to real-time industry news, profiles of some 1,800 airlines using data provided by Airclaims (see www.airclaimsv1.com), airports, aircraft and fleet information, leading industry manufacturers, suppliers and maintenance organisations, and passenger and cargo schedules from OAG (Official Airline Guide (www.oag.com).

ATI also provides access to several additionally priced 'premium' data modules. The Online Airline Product Database (OAPD), produced by the International Air Transport Association (IATA), contains data on airline products and services on both long and short haul flights provided by major airlines (www.iata.org/air/productsandservices/oapd.htm). Market I, the result of collaboration between Reed and Airclaims, provides aircraft and engine trading information. Finally ATI is also a source of US DOT filing data and the Lexis Nexis global news service (www.lexisnexis.com).

Air Transport World (ATW) – This monthly trade magazine is aimed primarily at the airline and airport management market (www.atwonline.com).

Jane's Defence Weekly (JDW) – Published by Jane's Information Group, this weekly trade magazine is aimed at the international defence industry. It provides news of the latest developments in military technology and analysis of current geopolitical and industry issues (jdw.janes.com). In addition Jane's Information Group produce an extensive list of specialist defence and security analysis magazines and newsletters such as *Defence Industry, Navy International, International Defense Review*, and *Intelligence Review* (www.janes.com).

▶ OTHER TRADE TITLES

Popular commercial titles include *Interavia: Business and Technology* (Aerospace Media Publishing SA), *AIR International* (Key Publishing – www.airinternational.com), *Aviation News* (HPC Publishing – www. airpictorial.com/index.html), *Defence & Public Service Helicopter*, and *Unmanned Vehicles* (both Shephard Press – www.shephard.co.uk), and *Helicopter International* (Avia Press www.aviapress.freeserve.co.uk).

    Titles aimed specifically at the air transport industry include *Jane's Airport Review* (Jane's Information Group – jar.janes.com), and the series of Euromoney Aviation Group titles including *Air Finance* (www.airfinancejournal.com/contents/publications/afj/), *Aircraft* Economics (www.aircrafteconomics.com), and *Air Traffic Management* (www. airtrafficmanagement.net).

▶ MAGAZINES AND NEWSLETTERS FROM PROFESSIONAL SOCIETIES AND ASSOCIATIONS

Professional societies and other professional organisations are also major providers of news, magazines, newsletters, and news services. Good examples of these include:

- *ICAO Journal* – (www.icao.int/cgi/goto.pl?icao/en/jr/jr.cfm).
- *Aerospace International* – This is the flagship publication of the Royal Aeronautical Society.
- *Mechanical Engineering* – ASME's monthly printed news and trade magazine (www.memagazine.org).
- *Vertiflite* – The official journal of AHS International (American Helicopter Society (www.vtol.org/vertiflite/vertiflite.html).
- *Space Times* – This is the American Astronautical Society's (AAS) bi-monthly magazine (www.astronautical.org/pubs/spacetimes.html).

▶ CONFERENCE PROCEEDINGS AND PAPERS

Some conferences papers, such as those produced by the AIAA, can be searched and ordered online and/or are included on bibliographic databases. However with hundreds of events held each year, it is not surprising that bibliographic control of many of these can be uneven.

There is a number of companies that specialise in the organisation of events and the publication and supply of proceedings, which are specifically targeted at the aerospace, air transport and defence communities. Examples of these include:

- Jane's (www.janes.com/company/conference/)
- Shephard (www.shephard.co.uk/exhib/index.htm)
- Aviation Week (www.aviationweek.com/conferences/)
- Aviation Industry Conferences (www.aviation-industryconferences.com)
- Institute for Defense & Government Advancement (www.idga.org)
- Commercial Aviation Events (www.commercialaviation.net/)

▶ SOCIETY AND ASSOCIATION MEETING PAPERS

The organisation of events and the publication of meeting papers are also important functions of the professional societies and associations. Some examples include:

International Council of the Aeronautical Sciences (ICAS)

In addition to its own biennial conference, ICAS will also co-sponsor other congresses with organisations such as the AIAA, ISOABE and SAE. Details of past and forthcoming events are published on the ICAS website (www.icas.org).

International Society for Air Breathing Engines (ISOABE)

ISOABE organises an International Symposium on Air Breathing Engines (ISABE). Symposium papers typically cover a range of topics including advanced power plant concepts, engine and component design, engine/vehicle integration, design and off-design performance and characteristics, fuels, fuel control and combustion, fluid mechanics and gas dynamics, advanced materials, diagnostic measurement and health monitoring, operations, life cycle costs and economics, airworthiness, type certification, testing and evaluation, and manufacturing, maintenance and reliability.

Royal Aeronautical Society

The Royal Aeronautical Society holds approximately twenty conferences each year, many of which are backed by a full set of proceedings. The RAeS website provides details of forthcoming conferences and lectures (www.raes.org.uk/raes/First/conferences.asp?sessid=).

Details of forthcoming lectures and conferences at the Society's HQ at Hamilton Place and at the Branches and Divisions are also included the exclusive membership journal, *Aerospace Professional*, which is published monthly as a supplement to *Aerospace International*.

Institution of Mechanical Engineers

The IMechE website provides search and browse access to descriptive details all of the Institution's technical conferences, seminars and workshops (www.imeche.org.uk/conferencesandevents/). In addition to acting as a repository for the Institution's output of technical papers, the Information and Library Service has abstracted all proceedings, conferences and seminars published since 1984. These records, held on the Library Database, cover all events including those proceedings which were never 'officially' published. The abstracts are available for searching via the website (195.157.148.163/olibcgi/ntxcgi.exe).

American Institute of Aeronautics and Astronautics

The AIAA publishes approximately 3,500 papers each year from 20 to 30 technical conferences covering all aspects of aerospace. The website contains a calendar of events (www.aiaa.org/calendar/index.hfm?cal=1).

The site also contains a searchable database of meeting papers which is available free of charge (www.aiaa.org/Research/index.hfm?res=3).

Society of Automotive Engineers

The SAE sponsors and/or administers more than twenty-five international meetings and exhibitions each year that cover all aspects of technology related to design, manufacture, and total life cycle technology for the automotive, aerospace, and other related mobility industries. The SAE publishes about 2,000 papers each year. Finding SAE papers can sometimes be a problem, as although the best are included in the annual SAE transactions volumes, many of the others will appear in separately titled SAE proceedings (P) or special publications (SP) book series.

SAE Transactions, Section I – Journal of Aerospace

Published annually the SAE Transactions provide a compilation of the best of the Society's meeting papers. The papers are peer-reviewed and judged by a panel of qualified experts for inclusion. There are seven transactions volumes which together contain over 1000 papers. The Journal of Aerospace features the best papers.

Electronic access to SAE papers

Obtaining SAE papers and standards electronically is becoming more straightforward now that SAE technical papers published since February 1998, all aerospace material specifications (AMS), and most aerospace standards (AS) (and all current SAE Ground Vehicle Standards (J-Reports) can be individually ordered and downloaded online as PDF format files. Alternatively the SAE Digital Library (www.sae.org/products/digitallibrary. htm) offers a subscription-based internet or intranet subscription. This currently contains over 8,000 documents including SAE technical papers since 1998 as well as the AMS and AS series specifications and standards. Annual collections of SAE technical papers are also available on a series of CD ROM collections. These include papers contained in the SAE proceedings and special publications book series, as well as those selected for the SAE Transactions.

Additionally the SAE produces a variety of resources for identifying and locating meeting papers:

- **Website browsing and searching**
  Bibliographic information (title, paper number, author, meeting where presented, and associated book number) relating to SAE aerospace (and ground vehicle) papers published since February 1998 can be browsed or searched online free of charge. If a paper was published as part of the (P) or (SP) series, the order number of that book is listed as well.
- **Annual Index/Abstracts of SAE Technical Papers**
  This printed reference source contains bibliographic citations and abstracts of papers produced in any particular year.
- **Global Mobility Database**
  The Global Mobility Database covers all types of self-propelled vehicles on land, at sea, in the air and in space. It contains more than 125,000 citations with detailed abstracts of conference papers, journal and magazine articles, standards and specifications, technical books, and research reports not just from the SAE but also from leading technology sources around the world. SAE offers access to the database in a number of formats including web

subscription, CD ROM, dial-up online via STN International and as a tailored intranet solution.

- **SAE Publications and Standards Database**
  The Publications & Standards Database contains detailed summaries and bibliographic data for nearly 77,000 documents published by SAE, including technical papers since 1906, magazine articles, books, all ground vehicle and aerospace standards, specifications, and research reports. The Publications & Standards Database is available in two formats: via the World Wide Web (updated monthly) and on CD-ROM (updated annually). Webdex, a web-based index of current and past SAE publications, is marketed as an affordable variation that includes bibliographic citations, but lacks the abstracts.

American Society of Mechanical Engineers

The ASME website provides access to information relating to forthcoming ASME conferences (www.asme.org/events/) and to the published proceedings of past conferences (www.asme.org/pubs/press.html). The ASME Digital Store now offers online ordering of electronic editions of its conference proceedings. Details of conference titles and individual papers can be searched or browsed online (store.asme.org/search_cp.asp).

The International Gas Turbine Institute (IGTI), a technical institute of ASME, is dedicated to supporting the international exchange and development of information to improve the design, application, manufacture, operation and maintenance, and environmental impact of all types of gas turbines and related equipment. The IGTI organises the world's largest technical meetings and exhibitions exclusively for the exchange of gas turbine technology. The IGTI's flagship event, *ASME TURBO EXPO*, is held annually and attracts thousands of engineers, scientists, educators, military personnel, researchers, technical managers and gas turbine users from around the world.

The IGTI maintains an archive of ASME gas turbine related papers dating back to 1947. The archive of papers from 1990 can be searched and browsed online (www.asme.org/igti/services/pubs/paper_archive/index.html).

Institute of Electrical and Electronics Engineers

The IEEE sponsors more than 300 conferences each year, including technical conferences, workshops, professional/careers/technical/policy meetings, and standards working group meetings. These conferences are hosted by a range of IEEE groups, including Technical Societies, Sections and Chapters, Regions, the Standards Association, the Educational Activities Board, and IEEE-USA. In addition, the IEEE is involved in almost 200 'topical interest' meetings, either as consultants to the technical program or as other non-financial partners.

Information on IEEE conferences can be found using the IEEE Conference Database (www.ieee.org/conferencesearch/). It contains details of all meetings run by, or in association with, the IEEE.

AHS International – The Vertical Flight Society

The AHS International website (www.vtol.org) provides information about the society, provides a calendar of forthcoming events (including the Annual Forum), and an extensive programme of specialist technical, as well as local and international, chapter meetings. These all generate published proceedings of presented papers. The site also includes an AHS Online Documents Catalogue, a searchable database of articles and other documents (www.vtol.org/dbsearch/). This contains bibliographic details and abstracts of documents derived from the AHS Journal, Vertiflite, AHS Annual Forum Proceedings, specialist technical meetings and book and technical reports from the AHS library.

SPIE-The International Society for Optical Engineering

Part of SPIE's mission is to create global forums that facilitate the interaction of members of the optics and photonics communities with each other, with those in other technical disciplines, and with their suppliers and customers. To achieve this goal SPIE organises conferences and educational programs on emerging technologies. Details of forthcoming events are published on the SPIE website (spie.org/app/conferences/).

The SPIE Proceedings contains papers on new research and applications in optical, photonic, imaging, and optoelectronic technologies. The website (spie.org/app/Publications/index.cfm?fuseaction=proceedings) includes a database with links to citations from more than 3,400 proceedings and more than 100,000 abstracts. AeroSence (sensors), remote sensing, microelectronic and MEMS technology, non-destructive examination and smart structures, are among the titles and topics for which individual paper abstracts are available.

American Astronautical Society (AAS)

The AAS has long been recognised in the community for the excellence of its national meetings, symposia and publications as well as for the impact these have had on shaping the U.S. space programme. Papers prepared for AAS conferences and symposia are collected in individually titled books which are published in a number of series.

American Society of Civil Engineers (ASCE)

ASCE holds fifteen to twenty technical conferences annually, with an average total attendance of 10,000. The Civil Engineering Database (CEDB) provides access to over 100,000 bibliographic and abstracted records covering the period from 1970 to the present (www.pubs.asce.org/cedbsrch.html). The database provides citation and abstracts for a range of publication types including conference proceedings, journal articles, technical notes, books standards, manuals and reports.

▶ REFERENCE SOURCES AND DESIGN GUIDES

Testing proposed engineering solutions is invariably expensive and time consuming. Access to information that has already been validated, or is derived from an acknowledged, authoritative and reliable source can therefore be invaluable to the engineer and customer alike. In order to achieve that degree of recognition, providers of trusted design information are invariably long established such as the following examples:

ESDU International

ESDU provides subscription based validated and authoritative design data and methods for aerospace, chemical, mechanical, process and structural engineering. ESDU information is presented in a collection of data sheets, with supporting software. In total ESDU engineering design information is divided into twenty-two series with more than 270 volumes that contain over 1250 data item design guides, over 150 ESDUpac FORTRAN calculation codes, and over 100 VIEWpac executable codes.

There are ESDU series covering aerodynamics, aircraft noise, composites, dynamics, engineering structures, fatigue – endurance data, fatigue – fracture mechanics fluid mechanics, internal flow, fluid mechanics, internal flow (aerospace), heat transfer, mechanisms, performance, physical data – chemical engineering, physical data – mechanical engineering, process and environmental technology, sound propagation, stress and strength, structures, transonic aerodynamics, tribology, vibration and acoustic fatigue and wind engineering. ESDU also produces the *Metallic Materials Data*

Handbook, which contains data sheets covering a wide range of materials in common use in the aerospace industry.

The quality and relevance of ESDU data items are underpinned by voluntary technical committees of practicing subject experts, who monitor and steer the work of ESDU's own engineering team.

Now that its documents have been digitised, ESDU can offer integrated online access to all data items (www.esdu.com). A searchable database of ESDU data item abstracts is also available via the AERADE internet information portal (aerade.cranfield.ac.uk).

Jane's Information Group

Jane's Information Group Ltd is a leading commercial provider of specialist international defence, geopolitical, transport and law enforcement information and analysis. Its portfolio of information products includes its renowned yearbooks, magazines and newsletters, all of which are offered in a wide range of electronic and print formats. Jane's publications, conferences and other information services are fully described on the Jane's website (www.janes.com).

Jane's yearbooks / reference manuals typically provide a world wide listing of defence and transport related products, components and manufacturers and include development histories, descriptions, specifications, photographs and cut-away and sectional drawings. In addition to the long-established '*All the Worlds' Fighting Ships and Aircraft*, Jane's produce a much expanded range of titles including aero engines, air launched weapons, aircraft components, aircraft upgrades, air traffic control, avionics, airports, equipment and services, helicopter markets and systems, unmanned aerial vehicles and targets, and world airlines.

Jane's also publish the *International ABC Aerospace Directory*, which is one of the most comprehensive sources for product/service, supplier and contact information for the aerospace and defence sector.

► DATABASES AND DISCOVERY TOOLS

In order to search, identify and retrieve information about many of the primary sources described above, there is a wealth of 'discovery tools' available to aerospace STI users. Traditionally described as 'secondary' sources these tools include bibliographic databases, with and without value-added links to the full text, and internet portals or gateways (depending on functionality and/or definition).

A selection of some of the best databases for aerospace and defence engineering are as follows:

NASA STI database

The NASA STI database is one of the world's premier bibliographic databases for aerospace science, engineering, and related technologies. It contains over three million bibliographic citations and abstracts to worldwide aerospace related information on aeronautics, astronautics, chemistry and materials, engineering, geosciences, life sciences, mathematical and computer sciences, physics, social sciences, and space sciences, published from 1915 to the present.

In practice the database is available in a number of different formats and the level of access is determined by the affiliation of the would-be user.

NASA RECONplus is the dial-up online version that can be accessed by any terminal that can emulate a VT100 terminal. However RECONplus is password controlled and available only to NASA and US Federal Government employees and contractors who are registered at the NASA Center for AeroSpace Information.

NASA Database via GEM (European Information Network Services – EINS)

For many years an information exchange agreement between NASA and the European Space Agency (ESA), guaranteed aerospace STI users based in ESA member access to the NASA RECONplus database. The database was originally hosted by ESA-IRS, the Agency's own information retrieval service. Here it sat alongside the European Aerospace Database (EAD) developed by ESA-IRS. This covered mainly unpublished aerospace literature in Europe, i.e. technical reports and conference proceedings acquired by ESA in close cooperation with national aerospace organisations and industry in ESA Member States. In addition to unrestricted distribution documents EAD also included documents of controlled distribution like ESA Optional Programme Contractor Reports ESA-CR(X) and industrial technical reports.

After 1996 the closure of ESA-IRS led to the European version of the NASA database being transferred to the European Information Network Service (EINS), now being marketed as GEM (www2.eins.org).

However, the subsequent cancellation of the information exchange agreement with NASA has left something of a vacuum in terms of collaboration over the provision of aerospace STI with that, both the EAD and NASA databases have been left in limbo. The NASA database has been stripped of potentially useful records relating to documents supplied to NASA through third party agreements, and it has not been updated since April 1999.

Center for AeroSpace Information Technical Report Server (CASI TRS)

This web-based database is a subset (NASA RECONselect) of publicly available materials from the NASA STI (NASA RECON) Database. The CASI TRS database contains over 2.2 million records some of which describe documents dating back to 1915. It includes bibliographic citations for Scientific and Technical Aerospace Reports (STAR file series), journal articles, and conference proceedings (Open Literature file series), and citations from the NACA collection. Note in September 2003, NASA withdrew the CASITRS server. The contents and database are now accessed via the NASA Technical Reports Server (NTRS).

Aerospace & High Technology Database

The Aerospace Database provides bibliographic coverage of basic and applied research in aeronautics, astronautics, and space sciences dating back to 1962. The database also covers technology development and applications in complementary and supporting fields such as chemistry, geosciences, physics, communications, and electronics.

In addition to journals and conference literature, the database also includes coverage of technical reports issued by NASA, other U.S. government agencies, international institutions, universities, and private firms.

The database is essentially the work of the AIAA, but is now licensed by Cambridge Scientific Abstracts (CSA). It contains around 2.5 million records, with some 2,500 new items added each month. It now incorporates links to full text documents such as AIAA meeting papers.

International Aerospace Abstracts (IAA)

The AIAA also produces this monthly indexing and abstracting journal, the content of which is incorporated into the Aerospace & High Technology Database. IAA contains 3,000 or more citations per issue. In addition to complete coverage of AIAA conference papers, journals, and books, it includes international conference proceedings, particularly in the fields of microgravity, intelligent materials, fluid mechanics, aircraft design, space technology, and propulsion.

Transport database

Produced by SilverPlatter International, this is a bibliographic database of transportation research information, which includes air transport as well as other modes. It is produced by the 25-nation Organisation for Economic Co-operation and Development (OECD), headquartered in Paris, together with the United States' Transportation Research Board (TRB) and the European Conference of Ministers of Transport (ECMT). It encompasses three contributing databases: Transportation Research Information Services (TRIS), International Transport Research Documentation (ITRD), and TRANSDOC.

ITRD (formerly the International Road Research Documentation (IRRD) database), contains 200,000 abstracts on highway research provided by OECD member countries. TRANSDOC from ECMT contains 37,000 abstracts of transportation economics literature as well as bibliographic records provided by the International Union of Railways (UIC). These records are present in the database prior to 2000 only.

▶ OTHER BIBLIOGRAPHIC DATABASES

In addition to the above databases which are aimed specifically at aerospace and defence STI users, there are a number of others that offer significant coverage of aerospace and related technology areas as part of a broader science, technology, engineering and/or management remit. These include: Compendex, Mechanical and Transportation Engineering Abstracts, and Mechanical Engineering Abstracts, Inspec, Metadex and Engineered Materials Abstracts.

Science Citation Index references and cited references taken from titles published by the AIAA, IEEE, and the Institution of Civil Engineers.

▶ INTERNET RESOURCE DISCOVERY

The vast majority of the information sources described above, whether free or subscription-based, can be accessed via the Web. However, locating an appropriate source from amongst all of the sites, documents and other information resources now published on the web can be very time consuming and frustrating and/or fascinating depending on the viewpoint of the searcher.

Whilst generic search engines will continue to be hugely popular, they do not discriminate in terms of the quality and reliability of a resource, nor do they operate in a subject specific context. The development of subject-based web portals is very much a response to the challenge of enhancing the visibility and accessibility of appropriate resources.

A number of web portals aimed specifically at the aerospace and defence community are available. These include:

AERADE

Cranfield University's Aerospace and Defence portal (aerade.cranfield. ac.uk) provides links to over 3,000 quality assessed Internet resources, including websites and documents. AERADE offers cross-searching of a web resources database, a special collection of resources designed to meet the needs of the armed forces (DEVISE), and a database of abstracts and citations to data items provided by ESDU International. The AERADE service provides a link to Internet Aviator, an interactive tutorial which is designed to show users how to locate high quality aerospace and defence internet resources, (www.vts.rdn.ac.uk/tutorial/aviator/). AERADE also provides access to the latest news stories in the relevant fields, a listing of forthcoming conferences and events and links to over 1,700 technical reports that have been integrated into the service from the NASA Langley Technical Reports Server.

AERADE is also part of the EEVL, the Internet Guide to Engineering, Mathematics and Computing (www.eevl.ac.uk), which is itself a major subject component (or 'hub') of the UK JISC-funded Resource Discovery Network (www.rdn.ac.uk).

International Aerospace Information Network (IAIN)

Developed by an AGARD working group, IAIN (www.iainetwork.net) is premised on the need to identify major collections of data relevant to aerospace R&D; to provide mechanisms to access these data and information resources; and to create a vehicle to stimulate the integration and access of multidisciplinary data related to aerospace R&D. IAIN provides search and browse access to a large repository of links to aerospace and related sources of information.

Embry-Riddle Aeronautical University Virtual Libraries

Embry-Riddle Aeronautical University (ERAU) provides access to over 2,000 web resources divided between the Aerospace and the Aviation virtual libraries (www.erau.edu/libraries/virtual/). The focus of the Aerospace collection is on advanced R&D and contains link to NASA resources, and websites of university departments, manufacturers and businesses amongst others. The Aviation virtual library contains more resources and is wider in scope, covering individual aircraft, airline, pilot, and military websites.

▶ KEEPING UP TO DATE

A selection of specialist resources that either alert their users to new material and/or attempt to tailor information to meet the specific interests of their target audience is as follows:

STAR – Scientific and Technical Aerospace Reports

Scientific and Technical Aerospace Reports (STAR) is a free online information resource listing citations and abstracts of NASA and world wide aerospace-related STI (www.sti.nasa.gov/Pubs/star/Star.html). Updated biweekly, STAR highlights the most recent additions to the NASA STI Database. STAR includes citations to R&D results reported in NASA, NASA contractor, and NASA grantee reports, reports issued by other U.S. Government agencies, domestic and foreign institution, universities, and private companies, translations, NASA-owned patents and patent applications, other U.S. Government agency and foreign patents and patent applications, and domestic and foreign dissertations and theses.

SCAN (Selected Current Aerospace Notices)

Selected Current Aerospace Notices (SCAN) is a free electronic current awareness journal, which is electronically published twice monthly. SCAN announces new report literature, conference proceedings, and journal articles in 191 aerospace-related topics. The service covers the full spectrum of aeronautics and aerospace information, but segments it into subject groupings or topics, which are narrower in scope than those provided by Scientific and Technical Aerospace Reports (STAR). Each of the 191 SCAN topics is carefully tailored to fit the needs of a specialised research activity. New topics are added as the need arises, and others are retired or redefined as research demands dictate. SCAN can be searched and browsed at the NASA STI website free of charge (www.sti.nasa.gov/scan/scan.html).

RTO technical publications: a quarterly listing

This is a quarterly listing of unclassified NATO RTO technical publications. The bibliography can be viewed and or downloaded free of charge in PDF format (www.sti.nasa.gov/Pubs/Agard/Agard.html).

NASA patent abstracts bibliography

This bibliography is published semi-annually as a service to companies, firms, and individuals seeking new, licensable products for the commercial market. Included are citations and abstracts describing NASA-owned inventions covered by U.S. patents and patent applications. When available, a key technical illustration of the invention is included.

AIAA biblio alerts

The AIAA makes available some 2,000 prepared bibliographic reports covering a wide range of disciplines including aerospace, automotive and mechanical engineering, manufacturing, engineering management and computing and IT. Individual reports contain current information derived from journals, books, patents, and conference proceedings. Each report provides full bibliographic information and abstracts. Examples of the sort of very specific topics covered include *Intermetallics for Aerospace Applications*, *Fatigue of Aircraft and Their Components*, *Non-Destructive Testing for Aerospace Applications*, *Aircraft Gas Turbine Engines – Noise Reduction and Vibration Control*, and *Aircraft Systems – Computer Applications* (www.biblioalerts.com/biblio/default-aiaa.asp).

▶ MONOGRAPHS AND TEXTBOOKS

Aerodynamics

Anderson, J. D., 2001. *Fundamentals of aerodynamics.* 3rd ed.,Boston: McGraw-Hill.
Anderson, J. D., 2000. *Introduction to flight.* 4th ed, Boston: McGraw-Hill.
Barnard, R. H., and Philpott, D., 1995. *Aircraft flight: a description of the physical principles of aircraft flight.* 2nd ed, Harlow: Longman.
Bertin, J. J., 2002. *Aerodynamics for engineers.* 4th ed., Upper Saddle River, NJ: Prentice Hall.
Houghton, E. L., and Carpenter, P. C., 2003. *Aerodynamics for engineering students.* 5th ed, Oxford: Butterworth-Heinemann.
Kermode, A. C., 1996. *Mechanics of flight,* 10th rev. ed., Harlow: Longman
Kuethe, A. M., and Chow, Chuen-Yen, 1998. *Foundations of aerodynamics: bases of aerodynamic.* 5th ed., New York: John Wiley.
Seddon, J., and Newman, S., 2002. *Basic helicopter aerodynamics: an account of first principles in the fluid mechanics and flight dynamics of the single rotor helicopter,* Oxford: Blackwell Science.

Aeroelasticity, flight dynamics, performance, handling and stability

Anderson, J. D., 1999. *Aircraft performance and design.* Boston: WCB McGraw-Hill.

Abzug, M. J., and Larrabee, E.E., 2002. *Airplane stability and control: a history of the technologies that made aviation possible.* 2nd ed., Cambridge: Cambridge University Press.

Asselin, M., 1997. *An introduction to aircraft performance.* Reston, VA: American Institute of Aeronautics and Astronautics.

Boiffier, J-L., 1998. *Dynamics of flight: the equations.* Chichester: John Wiley.

Cook, M. V., 1997. *Flight dynamics principles.* London: Arnold.

Eshelby, M. E., 2000. *Aircraft performance: theory and practice.* London: Arnold.

Etkin, B. and Reid, L. D., 1999. *Dynamics of flight: stability and control, 3rd ed.,* New York: Wiley.

Hancock, G. J., 1995. *An introduction to the flight dynamics of rigid aeroplanes.* New York: Ellis Horwood.

Hodges, D. H., and Pierce, G. A., 2002. *Introduction to structural dynamics and aeroelasticity.* Cambridge: Cambridge University Press.

Smetana, F. O., 2001. *Flight vehicle performance and aerodynamic control.* Reston, VA: American Institute of Aeronautics and Astronautics.

Aircraft materials, structures and design

Ball, R. E., 2003. *The fundamentals of aircraft combat: survivability analysis and design.* 2nd ed., Reston, VA: American Institute of Aeronautics and Astronautics.

Fielding, J. P., 1999. *Introduction to aircraft design.* John P. Fielding, Cambridge, Cambridge University Press.

Howe, D., 2000. *Aircraft conceptual design synthesis.* London: Professional Engineering Publishing.

Megson, T. H. G., 1999. *Aircraft structures for engineering students.* 3rd ed., Oxford: Butterworth-Heinemann.

Nui, M. C-Y., 1999. *Airframe stress analysis and sizing.* 2nd ed., Hong Kong: Conmilit Press.

Niu, M. C-Y., 1999. *Airframe structural design: practical design information and data on aircraft structures.* Hong Kong: Conmilit Press.

Nui, M. C-Y., 1992. *Composite airframe structures: practical design information and data.* Hong Kong: Conmilit Press.

Raymer, D. P., 1999. *Aircraft design: a conceptual approach.* 3rd ed., Reston, VA: American Institute of Aeronautics and Astronautics.

Stinton, D., 2001. *The design of the aeroplane.* 2nd ed., Oxford: Blackwell Science.

Wilkinson, R., 2001. *Aircraft structures and systems.* 2nd ed., St Albans: Mechaero Publishing.

Aircraft systems and avionics

Collinson, R. P. G., 2003. *Introduction to avionics systems*. 2nd ed., Dordrecht, Kluwer
Moir, I. R. M., and Seabridge, A., 2003. *Civil avionics systems*. Bury St Edmunds:
    Professional Engineering Publishing: Reston, VA, American Institute of
    Aeronautics and Astronautics.
Siouris, G. M., 1993. *Aerospace avionics systems: a modern synthesis*. San Diego: Academic
    Press.

Spacecraft design

Brown, C. D., 2002. *Elements of spacecraft design*. Reston, VA: American Institute of
    Aeronautics and Astronautics.
Fortescue, P., Stark, J., and Swinerd, G., 2002. *Spacecraft systems engineering*. 3rd ed.,
    Chichester: John Wiley.
Werts, J. R., and Larson, W. J., eds, 1999. *Space mission analysis and design*. 3rd ed.,
    Torrance, CA: Microcosm Press Dordrecht: Kluwer Academic Publishers.
Wie, B., 1998. *Space vehicle dynamics and control*. Reston, VA: American Institute of
    Aeronautics and Astronautics.

Aerospace propulsion

Boyce, M. P., 2002. *Gas turbine engineering handbook*. 2nd ed., Boston: Gulf.
Cumpsty, N. A., 1997. *Jet propulsion: a simple guide to the aerodynamic and thermodynamic
    design and performance of jet engines*. Cambridge University Press.
Lefebvre, A. H., 1998. *Gas turbine combustion*. 2nd ed., London: Taylor and Francis.
Mattingly, J. D., Heiser, H., and Pratt, D.T., 2002. *Aircraft engine design*. 2nd ed., Reston,
    VA: American Institute of Aeronautics and Astronautics.
Oates, G. C., 1997. *Aerothermodynamics of gas turbine and rocket propulsion*. 3rd ed.,
    Reston, VA: American Institute of Aeronautics and Astronautics.
Walsh, P. P., and Fletcher, P., 1998. *Gas turbine performance*. Oxford: Blackwell
    Science.

Air transport engineering (excludes air transport management, economics and finance

Ashford, N., and Wright, P. H., 1992. *Airport engineering*. 3rd ed., New York: John
    Wiley.
Kazda, A., and Caves, R. E., 2000. *Airport design and operation*. Amsterdam:
    Pergamon.
Wells, A. T., 2000. *Airport planning and management*. 4th ed., New York:
    McGraw Hill.

Human factors engineering

Ernsting, J., Nicholson, A. N., and Rainford, D. J., eds, 1999. *Aviation medicine.* 3rd ed., Oxford: Butterworth-Heinemann.

Hawkins, F. H., 1993. *Human factors in flight.* 2nd ed., Aldershot: Avebury Technical.

Helmreigh, R. L., and Merritt, A. C., 1998. *Culture at work in aviation and medicine: national, organizational and professional influences.* Aldershot: Ashgate.

Orlady, H. W., and Orlady, L. M., 1999. *Human factors in multi-crew flight operations.* Aldershot: Ashgate.

Reinhart, R. O., 1999. *Fit for flight: flight physiology and human factors for aircrew.* 2nd ed., Ames, Iowa: Iowa State University Press.

▶ REFERENCES

Hanley, K. J., et al., 1998. *Aerospace information management (AIM-UK): final report.* Cranfield: Cranfield University Press.

Harrington, J., et al., 2002. *Aerospace Information Europe – (AIM-Eu) Final Report.* European Space Agency.

Needham, P., 2002. *Management of access to grey literature collections (MAGiC) Final Report (in MS Word).* (www.bl.uk/concord/docs/magic-final.doc).

Nelson, M. L., et al., 1996. *Optimizing the NASA Technical Report Server, Internet Research: Electronic Network Applications and Policy, vol. 6, no. 1, August 1996, pp. . 64–70.* (techreports.larc.nasa.gov/ltrs/papers/NASA-96-ir-p64).

Nelson, M. L., 1999. *A Digital Library for the National Advisory Committee for Aeronautics, NASA/TM-1999–209127.*

Pinelli, T. E., et al., 1997. *Knowledge diffusion in the U.S. aerospace industry: managing knowledge for competitive advantage.* Greenwich, CT: Ables Publishing Corporation.

Thornton, S. A., 1979. *Report, Technical Note and Technical Memoranda series issued by the RAE and its antecedents between 1912 and 1978.* Report RAE/Lib Bib-370.

15 Bioengineering/ Biomedical Engineering

Peter Richards

▶ INTRODUCTION

In introducing a chapter whose subject definition is unfamiliar to those who do not work in the field and controversial to those that do, it was thought best to display all its intended wares at the outset so that readers can assess quickly its suitability or otherwise for their needs.

- Bioengineering is normally equated with Biomedical Engineering and this is the application of engineering principles to the study, treatment and enhancement of human health and performance. This chapter is not concerned with Biotechnology, Genetic or Agricultural Engineering, all areas that might be argued as legitimate claimants for inclusion under the bioengineering banner.
- In preparing this chapter, it was considered that the main readership would be the engineer who is not currently working in the field, but who would want some understanding of its scope, and then an easy introduction to information on areas of interest.
- It was thought also that the selected readership might obtain benefit from a simple guide into the concepts and vocabulary of the unfamiliar partner disciplines of the Life Sciences.
- Words that define subject areas or that might prove useful to consider as keywords are emboldened and italicised.
- One of the major differences between this and the previous edition is the intervening development of the World Wide Web and the need to form strategies for web based information retrieval.
- References are grouped under headed subject areas with a content that includes simple/introductory books, more advanced monographs and websites. Journals and Conference proceedings

are not listed as it is considered that their existence can be accessed through those Library and Society websites given here and elsewhere in this volume.

For students making the transfer from the Physical Sciences to the Life Sciences, one major difference they notice is that whilst the former tend to be mathematical in their descriptions, the latter are 'full of words.' However, the conventions and words used in Anatomy have evolved over several hundred years, and their use can be as precise as any mathematical formulae.

It is a sad fact that those who named the subjects that unite engineering and the life sciences were not rigorous in their choice of language; this has led to confusion. The result of these past demeanours is that almost every worker has his or her own definition of the subject area of this chapter, and many of the societies, institutions and educational establishments involved in the field spend what seems to be an inordinate proportion of their various mission statements describing the limitations they would put on the their own definition of the subject. As will be seen later, this work is no exception in presenting its own definitions; it does not, however, claim their superiority, they are included to enable progress.

▶ DEFINITIONS

1. General

Biomedical Engineering is defined, as 'the application of engineering principles to the study treatment and enhancement of human health and performance'.

Even with such a simple and seemingly straightforward definition it can be seen that it is a huge field for information retrieval, spanning all of engineering, all of medicine, many of the major life sciences and areas of sports science, computing and even some social sciences.

Biomedical Engineering forms part of an umbrella discipline known as '*Bioengineering*' in which the same principles are applied to all life forms. In truth, the word bioengineering is so broad in its concept and meaning as to be of little use in telling us what it does. However, historically it has had a medical/health aspect and in many organisations and minds it is a case of 'for Bioengineering, read Biomedical Engineering!'

2. Biology and the life sciences

Biology is the word for the science for the study of living things. Although there have been people studying living things since antiquity, the word itself is relatively new; its derivation is from the Greek *bios* = life and *logos* = study. Without contradiction in any of the major religions, humans are living things, and from the above definition it could follow therefore that any study of ourselves must be a part of Biology!

On a broad scale we classify living things into three main '*kingdoms*', these are *plants, animals* and *micro organisms*. This leads to further great subdivisions of biology. These are:-

- *Botany* the study of plants
- *Zoology* the study of animals (Greek *zoon* = animal, *logos* = study)
- *Microbiology* which is the study of all organisms that we usually define as being unicellular. *Bacteriology* and *Virology* are subsections of microbiology.

Botany, Zoology and Microbiology deal with the broad aspects of study of 'Life'. The following 'ologies' relate to more specific areas of study of a single living creature or organism.

If the '*structure*' or '*morphology*' (from Greek *Morph* = form and *logos* = study) of an organism is examined and, rather than just look at the surface structure, the organism is cut into and dismantled, then although still a part of morphology, this study becomes what is called '*Anatomy*' (from Greek *ana* = up and *tome* = cutting). The anatomy of any organism from a rose to an elephant can be studied, so that what is referred to as plain 'Anatomy' should strictly always be qualified by the species being studied: our concern in medicine is strictly '*Human Anatomy*' but plain 'Anatomy' does!

If morphology is explored further by examining fine detail using a magnifying glass or microscope (i.e. *Microanatomy* is carried out), then it is found that in humans the organs displayed by the cutting up process of anatomy are composed of collections of similar '*cells*' and any **extracellur matrix** that these cells may manufacture. Such conglomerates are referred to as '*Tissues*'. The study of the structure of tissues is called '**Histology**' (from Greek *histos* = tissue and *logos* = study). Study at a greater magnification to show the structure of cells is called '**Cytology**' (from Greek *Kytos* = a hollow vessel and *logos* = study). If structure is investigated in greater detail and the stage is reached where the larger component molecules of the living organism are examined, the field of '*Molecular Biology*' has been reached. The study of the interaction of the smaller molecules is **Biochemistry**.

If interest is now transferred from structure to '*function*', then the investigation becomes known as **Physiology** (Greek *physis* = nature and *logos* = study).

If organisms are diseased, then the study of disease is called **Pathology** (from Greek *Pathos* = suffer + *logos*) and it follows that *patho* can be added into the system to produce further word permutations. For instance the study of structural changes in diseased tissue becomes **Histopathology**, study of functional changes becomes **Pathophysiology** and so on, almost without limit.

▶ THE SCOPE OF BIOMEDICAL ENGINEERING

The scope of biomedical engineering is huge. One way to illustrate this is to present it in terms of objects and processes. Thus biomedical engineering can be said to extend from walking sticks to artificial hearts, from designer molecules to wheelchairs, from hip implants to cardiac pacemakers, from heart lung machines to bandages, from mattresses to MRI scanners. Such a collection however does not yield easily to a classification by subject. That used here roughly follows that given on the website of the U.S. based Biomedical Engineering Society:-

Biomechanics is the oldest branch of biomedical engineering applying classical mechanics (statics, dynamics, fluids, solids and thermodynamics) to biological or medical problems.

Historically, biomechanical studies have centred on the musculoskeletal system and its action in the movements of walking (*Gait*). Galileo is thought to be the first 'modern' scientist to have worked in the field of biomechanics whilst the first book on the subject, 'De Motu Animalium', was written by Giovanni Alfonso Borelli and published the year after his death in 1679 (this was translated into English from Latin for the first time by Maquet in 1989). Borelli's work is of fascinating historical interest and he should be credited with extending the application of biomechanics beyond the skeleton and movement into other sectors of body function; however, it is of little current experimental or practical interest. Historical works still of current practical interest however are the late 19th century publications on Gait by Braune and Fischer (published in English translation, from the original German, in the late 1980s). The modern breadth of biomechanics now includes, as well as the study of motion, the deformation of materials, fluid flow within the body and transport of chemical constituents across biological membranes and between body compartments.

Research in biomechanics has led to the development of artificial joint replacements, as well as a better understanding of the function of bone, cartilage, intervertebral discs, ligaments and the tendons of the musculoskeletal systems and their interaction in movement. In the fluid systems, it has led to the development of the artificial heart and heart valves, and a better understanding of the heart, lungs, blood vessels and capillaries.

The application of mechanics to explain biological phenomena in the seventeenth and eighteenth centuries, led to the 'Mechanists versus Vitalists' debate. The former thought that living processes could be explained in terms of the laws of the physical sciences, whilst the Vitalists believed that there was something extra to the living process, a sort of vital fluid energy, that could not be explained by physical science. This debate has largely disappeared from scientific thinking with the Mechanists accepted as victors, but occasionally it reappears in arguments on the initiation of thought processes and the problem of the 'Soul' (see e.g. Changeaux, 1986).

Borelli's words 'When dead, that is when the soul stops working, the animal machine remains inert and immobile' still echoes today.

In this technological age, it is difficult to understand why the Vitalists held sway for so long, but it must be remembered that the physical sciences were not well developed in previous centuries. It is difficult to equate levers and forces and moments with the non locomotive living processes; the defeat of the Vitalists was mainly at the hands of Chemists (see Hunter, 2000).

Orthopaedic Bioengineering is a direct medical offspring of the application of statics and dynamics in biomechanics; it is described as the speciality where methods of engineering are applied to the understanding of the function of bones, joints and muscles, and to design artificial joint replacements. Its practitioners must analyse the friction, lubrication and wear characteristics of natural and artificial joints (*Tribology*); perform stress analysis of the musculoskeletal system and develop suitable bone replacement materials. Orthopaedic Bioengineers also perform gait and motion analyses for sports and to monitor patient recovery.

Biomaterials includes investigation of both living tissue and the artificial materials used to replace them in implantation surgery. Understanding the properties and behaviour of living material is vital in the design and selection of replacements. Replacement materials must be non-toxic, non-carcinogenic, chemically inert, stable, and mechanically strong enough to withstand repeated use over many years. The human body reacts, usually unfavourably, to any material that is not 'self'.

Biomaterial scientists are therefore interested in producing materials that in some way placate the body's defence (mainly Immune) system. *Biocompatibility, bioactivity* and *osseointegration* are somewhat loosely defined subjects that deal with the interactions between Biomaterials and Immunology. In this area, of particular importance are the cells and chemicals of the *non-specific* or *innate immune system* and the *acute inflammatory response*. Where biomaterials are associated with the cardiovascular system, the biomedical engineer must be aware of phenomena associated with *blood rheology* and the reactions of the systems that stop leakage and bring about repair of the blood vessels (*haemostasis*).

Bioinstrumentation is the application of electronics and measurement techniques to develop devices used in diagnosis and treatment of disease. Instrumentation in diagnosis contributes to *physiological measurement* which detects deviations in *homeostasis*, the maintenance of a constant internal environment, caused by disease or attempts at cure. In treatment, it can include the replacement of the input of damaged nerves to muscle as is found in *functional electrical stimulation (F.E.S.)*.

Medical Imaging combines knowledge of a unique physical phenomenon (sound, radiation, magnetism, etc.) with high speed electronic data processing, analysis and display to generate an image. Often, these images can be obtained with minimal or completely non-invasive procedures.

Medical Imaging might be considered part of Bioinstrumentation or equally of Medical Physics. It is doubtful if workers in both fields would accept such a marriage.

Cellular/Tissue Engineering uses advances in the long established technique (Harrison, 1907) of *cell* or *tissue culture*, particularly recent identification of various cell modifying *growth factors* combined with designed *biodegradable* biomaterial *scaffolds*, to enable tissue re-growth in the laboratory (in-vitro).

Its simplest concept takes cells from a patient and grows them in the laboratory on an artificial matrix which forms a synthetic equivalent of the *extracellular matrix* of the tissue it is intended to replace. After accelerated growth in the laboratory, the cells and artificial scaffold are implanted. Within the body, the artificial scaffold/matrix then gradually breaks down as it is replaced by natural extracellular matrix and a new tissue is formed. Not surprisingly there are many imponderables: – Can the patient's mature cells be modified to take on the role performed by *pluripotent stem cells* in the original embryonic tissue formation? Are stem cells needed and should these be from the patient or from another source? Are there problems of immune reactions?

Another strategy of tissue engineering implants the artificial scaffold/matrix direct into the body so that cell re-growth is in the body (in-vivo). Yet another tissue engineering approach incorporates **Nanotechnology,** envisaging miniature devices delivering compounds that can stimulate or inhibit cellular processes at precise target locations.

It is a fascinating field, full of noble intent but also of premature claims. The biological problems to be solved are fundamental to the whole understanding of how cells differentiate. It is likely that its clinical applications will not be as rapid as the media claim.

Clinical Engineering and **Rehabilitation Engineering** are not so much subjects as job or role concepts. The clinical engineer is a member of the hospital health care team along with physicians, and nurses. Clinical engineers are responsible for developing and maintaining computer databases of medical instrumentation and equipment records and for the team's purchase and use of sophisticated medical instruments. They may also work with physicians to adapt instrumentation to specific needs. Rehabilitation engineers on the other hand are tasked to enhance the capabilities and improve the quality of life for individuals with physical and cognitive impairments. They are often concerned with the biomechanics of posture support and the rehabilitation of amputees or those with spinal injuries. This can encompass both orthopaedic biomechanics (including gait analysis) and Bioinstrumentation.

 Systems Physiology is the term used to describe that aspect of biomedical engineering in which engineering strategies are used in the study of the integrative function of the physiological systems necessary for homeostasis. These are highly regulated feedback control systems and any intellectual contribution that can be used to formulate predictions and an understanding of the related effects of the interference in one system on the function of others could be an important factor in the future of drug administration – it might avoid unwelcome side effects!

► WEB SEARCH STRATEGIES

If the reader is based in a University or Government Department, he or she will have access to many of the specialised academic information retrieval systems covered elsewhere in this volume. The private individual or small company on the other hand will not have this backup. Until recently, such workers were greatly disadvantaged. This section is aimed at them in the belief that there is now little to prevent those working at home with a good Web connection from retrieving most of the information that for instance the authors of the previous edition of this chapter could only access in 1994/5 by using full university library backup facilities.

There are a number of sources likely to provide information for Biomedical Engineering websites, these include:-

- Societies
- Professional Bodies
- Government Establishments
- Educational Establishments
- Journals
- Companies
- Interested Individuals
- Newsgroups

Their reasons for doing this are varied and it does sometimes help to remember possible ulterior motives! A selection of these sites has been listed here. If specific information is required fairly quickly however, the most logical starting place is to select a good Search Engine and type in a few keywords. There are several of these search engines and although you may well end up with a favourite, it pays, at first, to try a number and to explore the 'Advanced' facilities on the engine before deciding. You can gain confidence with a particular engine by searching for something for which you already have more than average knowledge and seeing if it agrees with or can improve on this.

► SOCIETIES

Societies that have useful information on Biomedical Engineering, fall into two main types:

- General Scientific or Engineering Societies that either have sections for those interested with Biomedical Engineering applications, occasionally publish subject related papers in their Journals, or have Websites that may give useful links.
- Societies dedicated to the subject of Biomedical Engineering or Bioengineering

In the following list, the name, address, telephone, fax number and home web address are given and any selected useful links page. As well as the links page (which will give related international contacts) it is always worth investigating any Education, Resources, or Publications section on the site.

General scientific societies:

The Institution of Electrical Engineers (IEE)
Runs many meetings on medical applications of electronics
IEE
Savoy Place,
London WC2R 0BL,UK
Tel: +44 (0)20 7240 1871
Fax: +44 (0)20 7240 7735
www.iee.org

The Institute of Electrical and Electronics Engineers (IEEE)
IEEE EMBS (Engineering in Medicine and Biology Society)
EMBS Executive Office
IEEE
445 Hoes Lane
Piscataway, NJ 08855–1331
USA
www.eng.unsw.edu.au/embs/index.
html or www.ieee.org/

The Institute of Materials
1 Carlton House Terrace,
London SW1Y 5DB, UK
Tel: +44 (0)20 7451 7300
Fax: +44 (0)20 7839 1702
www.instmat.co.uk/iom

Institution of Mechanical Engineers
Particularly useful web links to Standards, also has links to other Engineering Societies/Institutions. Publications include *Journal of Engineering in Medicine.* Table of contents and abstracts available free online. The publisher, MEP, also publishes *Advances in Bioengineering*, annually, about a year in arrears.
Institution of Mechanical Engineers
1 Birdcage Walk, Westminster,
London SW1H 9JJ, UK
Tel: +44 (0)20 7222 7899
Fax: +44 (0)20 7222 4557
www.imeche.org.uk

The Institute of Physics
Has a Biosciences group. Publishes *Physics in Medicine and Biology* Table of contents and abstracts available free online.
Institute of Physics
76 Portland Place
London W1B 1NT, UK
Tel: +44 (0)20 7470 4800
Fax: +44 (0)20 7470 4848
www.iop.org

*The Royal Academy of
Engineering*
Has held several one day
conferences on Biomedical
Engineering Applications.
The Royal Academy of Engineering
29 Great Peter Street, Westminster,
London SW1P 3LW, UK
Tel: +44 (0)20 7222 2688
Fax: +44 (0)20 7233 0054
www.raeng.org.uk
www.raeng.org.uk/policy/ukfocus

The Royal College of Surgeons
Their library pages are useful in
indicating sources of medical
journals online
The Royal College of Surgeons of
England
35–43 Lincoln's Inn Fields,
London WC2A 3PE, UK.
Tel: +44 (0)20 7405 3474
www.rcseng.ac.uk
Royal College of Surgeons links,
see particularly under Education
Resources and Revision Aids
www.rcseng.ac.uk/links/index_html

The Royal Society of Medicine
1 Wimpole Street
London W1G 0AE, UK
Tel: +44 (0)20 7290 2900
www.rsm.ac.uk

The Royal Society
'Useful links' page is very helpful in
accessing information on structure
of science in UK.
The Royal Society,
6–9 Carlton House Terrace,
London SW1Y 5AG, UK
Tel: +44 (0)20 7839 5561
Fax: +44 (0)20 7930 2170
www.royalsoc.ac.uk

Specific societies:

*Institute of Physics and
Engineering in Medicine*
Fairmount House
230 Tadcaster Road
York YO24 1ES, UK
Tel: +44 (0)1904 610821
Fax: +44 (0)1904 612279
www.ipem.org.uk

*The Biomedical Engineering
Society*
This has a very useful website (you
do not have to be a member to
access quite a lot of infor-
mation). Its publications are:-
*Annals of Biomedical Engineering.
BMES Bulletin.*
BMES
8401 Corporate Drive, Suite 225,
Landover MD 20785, USA
Tel: +1 (301) 459 1999
Fax: +1 (301) 459 2444
www.bmes.org

Society For Biomaterials
13355 Tenth Avenue North,
Suite 108,
Minneapolis MN 55441–5510,
USA
Tel: +1 (763) 543 0908
Fax: +1 (763) 765 2329
www.biomaterials.org

Institute of Biological Engineering
This is a site for those who were
disappointed in the omission of
Biotechnology etc., from the main
thrust of this chapter.
Institute of Biological Engineering
13355 Tenth Avenue North,
Suite 108
Minneapolis, MN 55441
Tel: +1 (763) 765 2300
Fax: +1 (763) 765 2329
www.ibeweb.org/ibe.htm

▶ WEB LINKS

Some Search Engines:

Alta Vista, uk.altavista.com
Lycos, www.lycos.com
Google, www.google.com
Ask Jeeves, www.ask.co.uk
All the Web, www.alltheweb.com
Elsvier BioMedNet, www.bmn.com
TEOMA, www.teoma.com

A gentle warning about the new technology (December 2002) may be found at news.bbc.co.uk/1/hi/technology/2570731.stm

General biomedical engineering sites:

If allowed only two sites to list, they would be these:-
The *Biomedical Engineering network,* www.bmenet.org/BMEnet
Gives links to most of the specialised Biomedical Engineering Societies in the world.
Biomechanics World Wide, www.per.ualberta.ca/biomechanics
If you cannot find it on the Biomedical Engineering network, it will probably be found here.

Academic & government resources:

UK:
Academic internet resources link indexes for biology and medicine:
bubl.ac.uk (click on link 5:15)
bioresearch.ac.uk
omni.ac.uk
EEVL Engineering resources site, click on Bioengineering, www.eevl.
ac.uk
Site to access all the main UK Research Councils, www.rcuk.ac.uk
LTSN-01 Learning and Teaching Support Network subject centre for
Medicine, Dentistry and Veterinary Medicine, www.ltsn-01.ac.uk
British Library Telemedicine Information Service, www.teis.nhs.uk
Bandolier Evidence based Healthcare, www.jr2.ox.ac.uk/bandolier
eMedicine (formerly Clinical Knowledge Base online), www.emedicine.com
Department of Health, www.doh.gov.uk
General Practice Notebook, www.gpnotebook.co.uk

National Electronic Library for Health, www.nelh.nhs.uk
National Institute for Medical Research, www.nimr.mrc.ac.uk
NHS Direct (UK), www.nhsdirect.nhs.uk
Parliamentary Office of Science & Technology links, www.parliament.uk/post/
Surgical Tutor, www.surgical-tutor.org.uk

USA:
National Institute of Ageing, www.nia.nih.gov
United States National Library of Medicine, www.nlm.nih.gov
National Centre for Biotechnology information, www.ncbi.nih.gov
National Institute of Health, www.nih.gov
The National Institute for Biomedical Imaging and Bioengineering (NIBIB) is the newest of the research institutes at the National Institutes of Health (NIH), www.nibib.nih.gov

World:
World Health Organisation, www.who.int/en
Swiss Health on the Net Foundation, www.hon.ch

Publishers:

The following four publishers have probably commissioned the largest number of Biomedical Engineering related titles. Their catalogues are worth investigation as they, like that of Amazon, can be used almost like search engines in finding specialised books. The Advanced Book Exchange shows that someone, somewhere, has just about any book ever published for sale!

CRC Press, www.crcpress.com
Marcel Dekker, www.dekker.com
Elsevier, www.elsevier.com
Springer Verlag, www.springeronline.com
Amazon (the US site is much larger than the UK site), www.amazon.com
The Advanced Book Exchange, www.abebooks.com

Companies:

One or two companies are mentioned in the pages that follow, but the following site is probably the best one site for access to many companies.

Medical Devices Industry, www.devicelink.com

Educational establishments:

Many universities have very useful sites. Their form and usefulness however changes with whoever has the time to keep them up to date.

Biomedical Engineering Program Home Pages, (www.whitaker.org/academic/biomed-homes.html), coupled with a visit to the Institute of Physics and Engineering in Medicine website, should provide the names of most of the world's biomedical engineering graduate training establishments

Wayne State University Biomedical Engineering is a good website (particularly Dr Grimm's homepage lectures, ttb.eng.wayne.edu/~grimm/BME/index.html)

▶ LARGE REFERENCE VOLUMES

Bronzino, J. D., ed., 1999. *The biomedical engineering handbook.* 2nd ed. Boca Raton: CRC Press.

Coatrieux, M. N. and Bronzino, J. D., 2004. *The biomedical engineering dictionary.* London: Academic Press.

Duck, F. A., 1997. *Physical properties of tissues: a comprehensive reference book.* London: Academic Press.

Webster, J. G., 1988. *Encyclopaedia of medical devices and instrumentation.* 4 vols. Chichester: Wiley.

Williams, D. F., 1999. *The Williams dictionary of biomaterials.* Liverpool: Liverpool University Press.

▶ BIOLOGY – HISTORY & PHILOSOPHY

These are mainly texts concerned either with vocabulary or some of the philosophy of Biology and its relations with the Physical Sciences. If the need is to learn more introductory Biology, then the websites listed provide useful starting points.

Hunter, G. K., 2000. *Vital forces: the discovery of the molecular basis of life.* London: Academic Press.

Ho, M.-W., 1999. *The rainbow and the worm: the physics of organisms.* 2nd ed. London: World Scientific Pub Co.

Savory, T. H., 1971. *The principles of mechanistic biology.* Watford: Merrow.

Scmidt-Nielson, K., 1984. *Scaling: why is animal size so important.* Cambridge: Cambridge University Press.

Thompson, D'A. W., 1917. *On growth and form.* Cambridge: Cambridge University Press.

An Online Biology Book, www.emc.maricopa.edu/faculty/farabee/BIOBK/
   BioBookTOC.html
University of Arizona Biology Teaching Project, www.biology.arizona.edu
A Hotlist of Life Processes, www.angelfire.com/sc2/rvcscience/Lifeprocesses.html#cat4,
   is essentially for children, but a good introduction to the beginner, with plenty of
   animations/videos.

▶ ANATOMY & PHYSIOLOGY

The texts by Marieb, Saladin, and Tortora and Grabowski, each give a
good working background in these subjects for the Biomedical Engineer.
They do not, however, give references for further reading. For anatomy,
these can be found in the specialised text by the Aiellos and Dean. More
detailed anatomy of joint function is found in the texts by Kapandji. The
Anatomy Society and other websites can lead to more advanced or
specialised anatomical resources.

   The texts by Berne *et al.* and Vander *et al.* have extensive bibliogra-
phies for those requiring slightly more advanced Physiology. (See also the
Systemic Physiology section). The Pathophysiology text by McCance and
Huether has information for those wanting knowledge of disease states.
The titles of other texts in the list should be self explanatory.

Aiello, L., Dean, C. and Aiello, A., 1990. *An introduction to human evolutionary anatomy.*
   London: Academic Press.
Berne, R. M., *et al.*, eds., 2003. *Physiology.* 5th ed. St.Louis: Mosby.
Kapandji, I. A., 1982. *Physiology of the joints (upper limb).* Vol. 1. Edinburgh: Churchill
   Livingstone.
Kapandji, I. A., 1987. *Physiology of the joints (lower limb).* Vol. 2. Edinburgh: Churchill
   Livingstone.
Kapandji, I. A., 1974. *Physiology of the joints (the trunk and the vertebral column).* Vol. 3.
   Edinburgh: Churchill Livingstone.
Marieb, E. N., 2003. *Human anatomy and physiology.* 6th ed. California:
   Benjamin/Cummings.
McCance, K. L. and Huether, S. E., 2001. *Pathophysiology.* 4th ed. St Louis: Mosby.
Saladin, K. S., 2002. *Anatomy and physiology: the unity of form and function.* 3rd ed.
   Boston: McGraw-Hill.
Tortora, G. J. and Grabowski, S. R., 2002. *Principles of anatomy and physiology.* 10th ed.
   Chichester: Wiley.
Vander A., Sherman, J. and Luciano D., 2001. *Human physiology.* 8th ed. New York:
   McGraw-Hill.

The Anatomical Society of Great Britain, www.anatsoc.org.uk; under their
Education section, see, for example: website of Dr D. R. Johnson, www.
leeds.ac.uk/humbmods.html

American Medical Association Atlas of the Body, www.ama-assn.org/ama/pub/
category/7140.html
Human Anatomy online (elementary), www.innerbody.com
The e-Skeletons project on elementary comparative anatomy, www.eskeletons.org
The History of Anatomy is fascinating, linking with Renaissance Art and 19th century
literature – if you want more information try these websites:
www.channel4.co.uk/science/microsites/A/anatomists/findout1.html#1 and
www.english.upenn.edu/%7Ejlynch/Frank/Contexts/dissect.html
Anatomy and Art History, www.nlm.nih.gov/exhibition/dreamanatomy/da_gallery.html
Muscle Physiology from U. California, San Diego, muscle.ucsd.edu/musintro/jump.shtml

▶ BIOMECHANICS

This has been divided into general biomechanics, the biomechanics of movement and gait, orthopaedics, animal biomechanics and fluids.

Fung, Y. C., 1993. *Biomechanics: mechanical properties of living tissues.* 2nd ed. Heidelberg:
Springer Verlag.
Fung, Y. C., 1990. *Biomechanics: motion, flow, stress, and growth.* Heidelberg: Springer
Verlag.
Fung, Y. C., 1996. *Biomechanics.* Heidelberg: Springer Verlag
Fung, Y. C., 2001. *Introduction to bioengineering.* Singapore: World Scientific Pub. Co.

▶ GAIT & MOVEMENT

Braune, W. and Fischer, O., 1987. *The human gait.* Translators, Maquet, P.G.J. and
Furlong, R. Heidelberg: Springer Verlag.
Bronstein, B. Bronstein, A. M., and Wollacott, M. H., eds., (new edition due June 2004)
Clinical disorders of balance, posture and gait. London: Edward Arnold.
Craik, R. L. and Oatis C. A., 1995. *Gait analysis: theory and application.* St Louis: Mosby.
Gage, J. R., 1991. *Gait analysis in cerebral palsy.* Oxford: Blackwells.
Gowitzke, B. A. and Milner, M., 1988. *Scientific bases of human movement.* 3rd ed.
Baltimore: Williams & Wilkins.
Jones, K. and Barker, K., 1996. *Human movement explained.* Oxford: Butterworth
Heinemann.
Kreighbaum, E. and Bartiels, K. M., 1996. *Biomechanics – a qualitative approach for
studying human movement.* New York: Macmillan.
Low, J. and Reed, A., 1996. *Basic biomechanics explained.* Oxford: Butterworth
Heinemann.
Nordin, M. and Frankel, V. H., eds., 2001. *Basic biomechanics of the musculoskeletal
system.* 3rd ed. Philadelphia: Lippincott Williams & Wilkins.

Norkin, C. C. and White, D. J., 1995. *Measurement of joint motion: a guide to goniometry.* 2nd ed. Philadelphia: Davis.

Roberts, T. M., 1995. *Understanding balance: the mechanics of posture and locomotion.* London: Chapman & Hall.

Sutherland, D. H., 1984. *Gait disorders in childhood and adolescence.* Philadelphia: Lippincott, Williams & Wilkins.

Tozeren, A., 2000. *Human body dynamics: classical mechanics and human movement.* Heidelberg: Springer Verlag.

Whittle, M. W., 2001. *Gait analysis: an introduction.* 3rd ed. Oxford: Butterworth-Heinemann.

Winter, D. A., 1990. *Biomechanics and motor control of human movement.* 2nd ed. New York: Wiley.

Gait and Clinical Movement Analysis Society, www.gcmas.org

Clinical Gait Analysis, guardian.curtin.edu.au/cga

University of Michigan Kinesiology website, www.umich.edu/~divkines/kinweb/index.html

University of South Australia Biological Sciences, www.unisanet.unisa.edu.au/10906/biosc101.htm, has a degree programme on Human Movement, useful introduction to locomotion lectures.

► ORTHOPAEDICS

Carter, D. R. and Beaupré G. S., 2001. *Skeletal function and form: mechanobiology of skeletal development, aging and regeneration.* Cambridge: Cambridge University Press.

Dowson, D., ed., 1997. *Advances in medical tribology: orthopaedic implants and implant materials.* Bury St Edmunds: MEP.

Dowson, D. and Wright, V., 1981. *Introduction to the biomechanics of joints and joint replacement.* Bury St Edmunds: MEP.

International Society for Fracture Repair, www.fractures.com/isfr

Southern California Orthopaedic Institute, www.scoi.com

The Orthoteers Orthopaedic Education Resource, www.orthoteers.co.uk
    Very useful site for Orthopaedics.

Biomet, www.biometmerck.co.uk/home.htm

UK orthopaedic implant manufacturer.

► ANIMAL BIOMECHANICS

Most of what we know about nerve conduction, muscle contraction, genetics and metabolism has been found by studying animal material ('models').

Alexander, R. M., 2003. *Principles of animal locomotion.* New Jersey: Princeton University Press.

Borelli, G. A. 1989. *On the movement of animals.* Translated by Maquet, P. Heidelberg: Springer Verlag.

Hildebrand, M., 1994. *Analysis of vertebrate structure.* 4th ed. Chichester: Wiley.

A useful website on many aspects of Vertebrate locomotion may be found at: www.biology.leeds.ac.uk/staff/jmvr/BLGY3120/Loco/index.htm

University of California (Berkeley) site on animal locomotion and robotics at: polypedal.berkeley.edu/

▶ FLUIDS

Caro, C. G., et al., 1978. *The mechanics of the circulation.* Oxford: O.U.P.

Denny, M. W., 1993. *Air and water: the biology and physics of life's media.* New Jersey: Princeton University Press.

Leyton, L., 1975. *Fluid Behaviour in Biological Systems.* Oxford:O.U.P.

Strackee, J., Westerhof, N. and Westerhof, N., eds., 1993. *The physics of heart and circulation.* Bristol: Institute of Physics.

European Society of Cardiology, www.escardio.org/index.htm

British Heart Foundation, www.bhf.org.uk

▶ BIOMATERIALS

This has been divided into the properties of biological materials and a section on immunology and biocompatibility. Knowledge of the basics of immunology is vital in understanding what happens when the body is subjected to the presence of an unwanted foreign body – an implant.

Barbucci, R., ed., 2002. *Integrated biomaterials science.* New York: Plenum Pub Corp.

Vincent, J. F. V., 1993. *Structural biomaterials.* 2nd ed. London: MacMillan.

Vincent, J. F. V., 1996. *Biomechanics – materials: a practical approach.* Oxford: IRL Press.

Society for Biomaterials, www.biomaterials.org

Texas A&M University Biomaterials Links, biomed.tamu.edu/

Immunology and Biocompatibility

Black, J., 1999. *Biological performance of materials: fundamentals of biocompatibility.* 3rd ed. New York: Marcel Dekker.

Brunette, D. M., Tengvall, P. and Textor, M., 2001. *Titanium in medicine: material science, surface science, engineering, biological responses and medical applications.* Heidelberg: Springer Verlag.

Cameron, H. U., 1994. *Bone implant interface.* St Louis: Mosby.

Dee, K. C., Puleo, D. A. and Bizios, R., 2002. *An introduction to tissue-biomaterial interactions.* Chichester: Wiley.

Eales, L. J., 2003. *Immunology for life scientists.* 2nd ed. Chichester: Wiley.

Janeway, C. A., et al., 2001. *Immunobiology.* 5th ed. New York: Garland Pub.

Roitt, I., 2001. *Roitt's Essential Immunology.* 10th ed. Oxford: Blackwell.

Silver, F. H. and Christiansen, D. L., 1999. *Biomaterials science and biocompatibility.* Heidelberg: Springer Verlag.

Immune system site, www.albany.net/~tjc/immune-system.html

Virginia Medical School Site on Inflammation, bme.virginia.edu/ley/index.html

Birmingham Medical Site on Acute Inflammation, medweb.bham.ac.uk/http/mod/3/1/a/acute.html

▶ CELLULAR OR TISSUE ENGINEERING

Tissue Engineering references and those on introductory cell biology are intermingled. The works by Alberts *et al.* and Lodish *et al.* have become the 'bibles' of undergraduate biologists. However, they contain more than enough information to leave the beginner comatose. The works by Cooper, and Bolsover *et al.* are more beginner-friendly. The works on cell-culture by Davis, Freshney and Paul give the technical basics of the biology involved in tissue engineering.

Alberts, B., et al., 2002. *Molecular biology of the cell.* 4th ed. New York: Garland.

Bolsover, S. R., et al., 1997. *From genes to cells.* Chichester: Wiley-Liss.

Cooper, G. M., 2003. *The cell: a molecular approach.* 3rd ed. Washington: ASM Press.

Davis, J. M., 2002. *Basic cell culture: a practical approach.* 2nd ed. Oxford: IRL Press.

Freshney, R. I., 2000. *Culture of animal cells: a manual of basic technique.* 4th ed. Chichester: Wiley.

Harrison, R. G., 1907. Observations on the living developing nerve fibre. *Proceedings of the Society for Experimental Biology and Medicine,* 4, 140.

Huard, J. and Fu, F. H., eds., 2000. *Gene therapy and tissue engineering in orthopaedic and sports medicine.* Basel/Boston: Birkhauser.

Langer, R. and Vacanti, J. P., 1993. Tissue engineering. *Science* 260, 920–926.

Lanza, R. P., Langer, R. and Vacanti, J. P., eds., 2000. *Principles of tissue engineering.* 2nd ed. London: Academic Press.

Lewandrowski, K.-U., et al., eds., 2002. *Tissue engineering and biodegradable equivalents: scientific and clinical applications.* New York: Marcel Dekker.

Lodish, H., et al., 2003. *Molecular cell biology.* 5th ed. New York: Freeman.

Palsson, B. O. and Bhatia, S. N., 2003. *Tissue engineering.* New Jersey: Prentice Hall.

Sipe, J. D., Kelley, C. A. and McNicol L. A., eds., 2003. *Reparative medicine: growing tissues and organs.* New York: New York Academy of Sciences.

A Beginners Guide to Molecular Biology, www.rothamsted.bbsrc.ac.uk/notebook/courses/guide

Cells Alive, www.cellsalive.com
    A beginners site with lots of pictures

Cell Biology (teaching) site at University of Arkansas for Medical Sciences, www.cytochemistry.net

Smith & Nephew, www.smiths-medical.com

UK Company most involved in Tissue Engineering research

Tissue Engineering Society, www.ptei.org/tes

European Tissue Engineering Society, etes.tissue-engineering.net

Tissue Engineering pages, www.tissue-engineering.net

Tissue Engineering Society International www.tesinternational.org/index.html Associated with journal *Tissue Engineering*

▶ SYSTEMS PHYSIOLOGY

Almost any advanced physiology text will lead into the basics of Systems Physiology. Bernard and Cannon are the physiological parents of the subject. *Cybernetics* (see websites) is a close relative. Introductory texts on the Nervous System are included here, because of its central role in control mechanisms.

Aidley, D. J., 1990. *The physiology of excitable cells.* 3rd ed. Cambridge: Cambridge University Press.

Bernard, C., 1957. *An introduction to the study of experimental medicine.* Translated by Green, H. C. New York: Dover.

Boyd, C. A. R. and Noble, D., 1993. *The logic of life: the challenge of integrative physiology.* Oxford: Oxford University Press.

Cannon, W. B., 1939. *The wisdom of the body.* Rev. ed. Norton: New York.

Carpenter, R. H. S., 2002. *Neurophysiology.* 4th ed. Arnold: London.

Changeaux, J.-P., 1986. *Neuronal man.* Oxford: Oxford University Press.

Horrobin, D. F., 1970. *Principles of biological control.* Aylesbury: MTP

The Research Resource for Complex Physiologic Signals, www.physionet.org/resource.shtml

The Control Systems Group, www.ed.uiuc.edu/csg

Principia Cybernetica Webpage on Homeostasis, pespmc1.vub.ac.be/homeosta.html

Neuroscience for Kids, faculty.washington.edu/chudler/neurok.html
    A wonderful introductory site.

▶ BIOINSTRUMENTATION

Webster, J. G., 1997. *Medical instrumentation: application and design.* 3rd ed. Chichester: Wiley.

Webster, J. G., 2001. *Minimally invasive medical technology.* Bristol: Institute of Physics.

Gad, S. C., 2002. *Safety evaluation of medical devices.* 2nd ed. New York: Marcel Dekker.

▶ REHABILITATION ENGINEERING

Aspects of this may also be called *Assistive technology*.

Bader, D. L., ed., 1990. *Pressure sores, clinical practice and scientific approach.* Basingstoke: Macmillan.

Chamberlain, M. A., Tennant, A. and Neumann, V., eds., 1997. *Traumatic brain injury rehabilitation: services, treatments and outcomes.* London: Chapman & Hall.

Cooper, R. A., 1995. *Rehabilitation engineering applied to mobility and manipulation.* Bristol: Institute of Physics.

Graupe, D. and Kohn, K. H., 1994. *Functional electrical stimulation for ambulation by paraplegics: twelve years of clinical observations and system studies.* Florida: Krieger Publishing Company.

Greenwood, R., et al., eds., 2002. *Handbook of neurological rehabilitation.* 2nd ed. Edinburgh: Churchill Livingstone.

Kralj, A. and Bajd, T., 1989. *Functional electrical stimulation: standing and walking after spinal cord injury.* Boca Raton: CRC Press.

Letts, R. M., ed., 1991. *Principles of seating the disabled.* Boca Raton: CRC Press.

Loeb, G. E. and Gans, C., 1986. *Electromyography for experimentalists.* Chicago: University of Chicago Press.

Simonds, K. A., ed., 1996. *Non-invasive respiratory support.* London: Chapman & Hall.

Smith, R. V. and Leslie Jr., J. H., eds., 1990. *Rehabilitation engineering.* Boca Raton: CRC Press.

Webster, J. G., 1989. *Electronic devices for rehabilitation.* Chichester: Wiley.

Webster, J. G., 1991. *Prevention of pressure sores: engineering and clinical aspects.* Bristol: Adam Hilger.

16 Chemical Engineering

Martin Pitt

▶ INTRODUCTION

What we know as chemical engineering today arose about 100 years ago in the British chemical industry, and at the same time in the American petrochemical industry. The later development of the European chemical and pharmaceutical industries (particularly in Germany and Switzerland) was another major and separate influence. There are thus three major traditions in the literature, two English and one German language.

A short history of the subject in the UK is given in Freshwater, D., 1995, *People, Pipes and Processes*, IChemE, and more fully in Divall, C., and Johnston, S. F., 2001, *Scaling Up – The Institution of Chemical Engineers and the Rise of a New Profession*, Kluwer. The Chemical Heritage Foundation publishes a number of books on historical aspects, including Aftilion, A., 2001, *A History of the International Chemical Industry*, 2nd ed., and a quarterly journal, *Chemical Heritage*. A History of Chemical Engineering website is available at: www.pafko.com/history/.

Some books and journals are still published in German, though some major series have completely switched to English. English translations are normally specialist technical monographs and thus fairly expensive. English translations from Eastern Europe are starting to become more common.

It is a disadvantage for Europeans that many otherwise excellent American chemical engineering textbooks do not use the SI system of units, or give it only passing attention, though US scientific journals expect it as standard.

The special feature of chemical engineering is that its practitioners design processes rather than equipment, so the term *'process engineering'* is sometimes used. Likewise, chemical engineering skills are applied in many areas apart from chemicals, such as food, biotechnology, materials, or water treatment. These are the so-called *process industries*.

In general, a process involves the transfer and conversion of matter and energy. Chemical reactions are often not involved at all. Chemistry and thus the chemical literature therefore only play a minor part. The task of a chemical engineer is principally to analyse and optimize the mass and energy flows, then consider different portions, the so-called *'unit operations'* and specify (rather than design) the equipment required. Actual equipment may be bought off the shelf or designed by specialists.

The chemical engineer therefore draws upon fundamental science and engineering which is common to other disciplines. Unfortunately books on these topics specifically intended for chemical engineers are quite likely to end up elsewhere in bookshops and libraries. Thus information on heat transfer may be shelved by the library in the section for mechanical engineering, fluid flow texts may be split between civil and mechanical engineering, whereas thermodynamic data may be in chemistry or physics!

However, chemical engineers commonly have to deal with chemists and other engineers in order to get their processes built, so they may be expected to have some familiarity with the other disciplines, and at least know where to look things up.

In practice, much useful information relating to processes tends to be defined by the end use. So far as the chemical engineer is concerned, pumping chocolate or pumping concrete is much the same, but relevant data and know-how will be found in quite different sources. Similarly, a heat exchanger to boil custard and another to boil nitric acid may have similar throughputs and thermal duties, but will require information from separate sources about materials compatibility and practical details of operation before they can be specified.

The technology is progressing and it is important to keep up to date, so this chapter concentrates on recent publications, except where earlier items are still in print and have not been superseded. For a substantial list of earlier publications, consult Ray, M. S., 1991, *Chemical Process and Plant Design Bibliography (1959–1989)*, Noyes Data Corp [out of print since the publishers changed to William Andrew, but copies may be available from booksellers].

▶ INSTITUTIONS

There are two main institutions which have members worldwide and produce the majority of professional texts. They have a reciprocal agreement to supply each other's publications.

In the UK is the *Institution of Chemical Engineers* (known as the **IChemE**), 165–189 Railway Terrace, Rugby CV21 3HQ (tel 01788–578214, fax 01788–547262), (www.icheme.org). Its Education Subject Group has a website with an extensive list of links of interest to students and teachers of chemical engineering at: ed.icheme.org/edlinks.html. This includes some complete books online!

The IChemE publishes:

- *Symposium Series*: more than 130 collections of conference proceedings;
- *Guides*: short books on professional topics; many related to safety, but also practical operation of equipment, costing and management techniques;
- *Safety training modules*: multi-media packages for self or group instruction;
- and a small range of other publications such as monographs on technical topics.

In the USA is the *American Institute of Chemical Engineers* (known as the **AIChE**), 345 E 47th St, New York, NY 10017 (www.aiche.org), which publishes:

- *Symposium Series*: more than 100 collections of conference proceedings;
- *Guidelines*: substantial books mainly on safety topics;
- and a small range of other publications.

Other relevant institutional publishers are:

DECHEMA, a German society with extensive technical publications, some in English, and reciprocal arrangements with the above. DECHEMA e. V., Theodor-Heuss-Allee 25, D-60486 Frankfurt am Main, Germany, (www.dechema.de).

The Institute of Petroleum, 61 New Cavendish Street, London W1G 8AR (known as the **IP**), (www.petroleum.co.uk).

The *American Petroleum Institute*, 1271 Avenue of the Americas, NY 10020 (known as the **API**), (www.api.org).

The *Instrumentation, Systems and Automation Society* (formerly the *Instrument Society of America)*, 67 Alexander Drive, P.O. Box 12277, Research Triangle Park, NC 27709 (known as the **ISA**), (www.isa.org).

The IP, API and ISA produce extensive numbers of standards and codes of practice which are used in chemical engineering and not just in the petroleum industry.

▶ HANDBOOKS, DICTIONARIES AND ENCYCLOPAEDIAS

The best-known general book is *Perry's Chemical Engineers' Handbook*. 7th ed., 1998, by Perry, R. H., and Green, R. W., McGraw-Hill, which is a compendium of data and short descriptions of equipment and chemical engineering practice. For a small library wishing to have a single book on the topic, this is the obvious choice. Recently the same edition has appeared in various versions such as 'platinum' and 'student' with, and without, a CD-ROM.

While chemical engineering is not limited to the chemical process industries, it is of major importance within them. The two major source of data and process descriptions are the encyclopaedias known as 'McKetta' in the USA, and 'Kirk-Othmer' in Europe, namely the *Encyclopedia of Chemical Processing and Design*, (1976–2001) edited by J. McKetta and published by Dekker, which has 68 volumes and a supplement, and the *Kirk-Othmer Encyclopaedia of Chemical Technology*, 4th ed. [27 volumes + supplement and index], 1998, Wiley Europe. It is also available by subscription on-line (www.mrw.interscience.wiley.com/kirk/). A shorter version is available, namely *Kirk-Othmer Encyclopaedia of Chemical Technology, Concise*, 2001, Wiley Europe.

Another source is *Ullmann's Encyclopedia of Industrial Chemistry*, 6th ed., 2002, [40 volumes], a German production but available in English from Wiley-VCH (Cambridge). It is also available by subscription on-line (www.mrw.interscience.wiley.com/ueic/) and as CD-ROMs.

Books giving details of common industrial processes include:

Matar, S., and Hatch, L. F., 2000. *Chemistry of Petrochemical Processes*. 2nd ed., Gulf.

Meyers, R. A., 1996. *Handbook of Petroleum Refining Processes*. McGraw Hill.

Moulijn, J. A., Makkee, M., and van Diepen, A., 2001. *Chemical Process Technology*, Wiley.

Weissermul, K., 2002. *Industrial Organics Chemistry*. Wiley-VCH.

Wittcoff, H. A., and Reuben, B. G., 1996. *Industrial Organic Chemicals*. Wiley.

A useful book (in English or German) is Noether, D., and Noether, H., 1992. *Encyclopedic Dictionary of Chemical Technology*. Wiley-VCH.

Comyns, A. E., 1999. *The Encyclopedic Dictionary of Named Processes in Chemical Technology*, CRC, is precisely what it says.

► BASIC STUDENT TEXTBOOKS

In a typical degree course, students will study complementary subjects, usually chemistry and mathematics, possibly biology and physics. At the same time they will learn the principles of chemical engineering. They go on to take specialist courses, usually in fluid mechanics, heat transfer, mass transfer, unit operations, transport processes, chemical reactors, and process control. They may possibly study particle technology, biochemical engineering or biotechnology. In the higher levels there will be at least some study of management, economics, safety and environmental protection.

In the UK all students carry out a major design project and possibly a research project. Both of these will require a literature review with access to documents apart from undergraduate textbooks. While the Internet search engines have value, the literature search will normally be expected to include a more thoughtful inspection of the library journals, whether hardcopy or on electronic subscription. They may require access to patents and national standards.

US graduates take a Professional Engineering (PE) or License examination after some industrial experience. Some books for this purpose are:

Das, D. K., and Prabhudesia, R. K., 1996. *Chemical Engineering: License Problems and Solutions.* Engineering Press at OUP, and

Robinson, R. N., 1996. *Chemical Engineering Reference Manual for the PE Exam.* 5th ed., Crisp, which has a companion volume Robinson, R. N., 1996. *Solutions Manual for the Chemical Engineering Reference Manual,* 5th ed., Crisp.

The most widely used textbook set is: '*Coulson & Richardson's Chemical Engineering*' (Butterworth Heinemann / Elsevier). This is in 6 volumes, but note that the contents and authors have moved around between volumes with editions, which is the source of some confusion. From the third edition of volumes 1 and 2, and the second edition of volume 6, they have been fully SI. Earlier editions are called '*Chemical Engineering*' later ones '*Coulson & Richardson's Chemical Engineering*'. Volumes 1, 2, and 6 have been fairly consistent, and represent the core of years 1, 2 and 3 of a typical chemical engineering degree. Volume 6 is particularly helpful for the design project. Current individual volumes are:

Vol 1: Fluid flow, heat transfer and mass transfer. 6th ed., 1999, Richardson, J. F., Coulson, J. M., Backhurst, J. R., and Harker, J. H.

Vol 2: Particle Technology and Separation Processes. 5th ed., 2002, Richardson, J. F., Backhurst, J. R., and Harker, J. H.

Vol 3: Chemical and Biochemical Reactors and Process Control. 3rd ed., 1994, Peacock, D. G., and Richardson, J. F.

(Vol 4) Solutions to Problems in Volume 1. 2001, Backhurst, J. R., Harker, J. H, and Richardson, J. F.

(Vol 5) Solutions to Problems in Volumes 2 & 3. 2002, Backhurst, J. R., and Harker, J. H., and Richardson, J. F.

Vol 6 Chemical Engineering Design. 3rd ed., 1999, Sinnott, R. K.

As of 2002, the solutions manuals are no longer labelled volumes 4 and 5, though the content seems the same. In 2004 it is planned to produce volumes as follows:

Introduction, Bowen, H., and Rhodes, E.

Vol 3: Process Control and Instrumentation.

Vol 4: Chemical Reaction Engineering. Lee, J. C.

Vol 5: Biochemical Engineering. Jones, M., and Lovett, R.

Other first year texts are:

De Nevers, D., 2001. *Physical and Chemical Equilibria for Chemical Engineers.* Wiley.

Felder, R. M., and Rousseau, R. W., 1999. *Elementary Principles of Chemical Processes.* 3rd ed., Wiley.

Himmelblau, D. M., 1996. *Basic Principles and Calculations in Chemical Engineering.* 6th ed., Prentice Hall.

Thomson, W. J., 2000. *Introduction to Transport Phenomena.* Prentice Hall.

Some books that cover a wide part of the field for students or graduates are:

Baasal, W. D., 1990. *Preliminary Chemical Engineering Plant Design.* 2nd ed., Kluwer.

Bird, R. B., Stewart, W. E., and Lightfoot, E. N., 2001. *Transport Phenomena.* 2nd ed., Wiley.

Branan, C., 2002. *Rules of Thumb for Chemical Engineers.* 3rd ed., Gulf.

Cheremisinoff, N. P., 1999. *Chemical Engineer's Condensed Encyclopedia of Process Equipment.* Gulf.

Chopey, N. P., ed., 1993. *Handbook of Chemical Engineering Calculations,* 2nd ed., McGraw-Hill.

Cussler, E. L., 1997. *Diffusion: Mass Transfer in Fluid Systems.* Cambridge University Press.

Cussler, E. L., and Moggridge, G. D., 2001. *Chemical Product Design.* Cambridge University Press.

Cutlip, M. B., and Shacham, M., 1998. *Problem Solving in Chemical Engineering with Numerical Methods.* Prentice Hall.

Douglas, J. M., 1988. *Conceptual Design of Chemical Processes.* McGraw Hill.

Duncan, T. M., and Reimer, J., 1998. *Chemical Engineering Design and Analysis.* Cambridge University Press.

Erwin, D., and McCombs, K., eds., 2002. *Industrial / Chemical Process Design.* Higher Education US.

Foley, H. C., 2002. *An Introduction to Chemical Engineering Analysis Using Mathematica.* Academic.

Fryer, P. J., Fryer, P., and Pyle, D. L., 1996. *Chemical Engineering for the Food Industry.* Kluwer.

Furusaki, S., Garside, J., and Fan, L. S., eds., 2002. *The Expanding World of Chemical Engineering.* Taylor & Francis.

Griskey, R. G., 2000. *Chemical Engineer's Portable Handbook.* McGraw-Hill.

Jones, D. S. J., 1996. *Elements of Chemical Processing.* Wiley.

Ogden, J, 1999. *Handbook of Chemical Engineering.* Research & Education Association, USA.

Polyanin, A. D., Kutepov, A.M., Vyazmin, A. V., and Kazenin, D.A., 2001. *Hydrodynamics, Mass and Heat Transfer in Chemical Engineering.* Taylor & Francis.

Reynolds, J. P., Jeris, J. S., and Theodore, L., 2002. *Handbook of Chemical and Environmental Engineering Calculations.* Wiley.

Shaheen, E. I., 1983. *Basic Practice of Chemical Engineering.* 2nd ed., Intl. Inst. Tech.

Speight, J., 2001. *Chemical Process and Design Handbook.* McGraw-Hill.

Seider, W. D., Seader, J. D., & Lewin, D. R, 2000. *Process Design Principles: Synthesis, Analysis and Evaluation, Simulation of Process Flowsheets.* Wiley.

Turton, R., Bailie, R. C., Whiting, W. B., and Shaeiwitz, J. A., 2002. *Analysis, Synthesis and Design of Chemical Processes.* 2nd ed., Prentice Hall.

Varma, A., and Morbidelli, M., 1997. *Mathematical Methods in Chemical Engineering.* Oxford University Press.

▶ DATA COMPILATIONS

The most widely used sources of physical and chemical data must be *Perry's Handbook* referred to above, and the Chemical Rubber Co's *Handbook of Chemistry and Physics* (annual – 2003 was the 84th edition, edited by Lide, D. R.).

The largest single source [14 volumes, but a total of over 40 bound books] is the DECHEMA *Chemistry Data Series* (1978–2001), available from DECHEMA e.V., Frankfurt, or Scholium International, Port Washington, New York. It gives relevant properties of single substances and mixtures. The text is in English.

Physical properties of pure substances for chemical engineering use are given in 9 volumes (but 38 books) *Physical Data, Chemical Engineering* by ESDU International plc, London. They also have collections on fluid flow and heat transfer.

The most complete single volume is probably:

Yaws, C. L., 1998. *Chemical Properties Handbook: Physical, Thermodynamic, Transport and Safety Properties for Organic and Inorganic Compounds.* McGraw-Hill. (The safety data is based on US health standards.)

Note that it is common nowadays for data to be provided not in terms of look-up tables, but in the form of constants to be put into mathematical models which can then be manipulated by computer. Some compilations are:

Barin, I., and Platzki, G., 1997. *Thermochemical Data of Pure Substances.* 2nd ed., Wiley-VCH.

Binnewies, M., and Milke, E., 2002. *Thermochemical Data of Elements and Compounds.* 2nd ed., Wiley-VCH.

Daubert, T. E., and Danner, R. P., 1996. *Physical and Thermodynamic Properties of Pure Chemicals.* [5 vols], Taylor & Francis.

Lide, D. R., Kheiaian, H. V., and Birdi, K. S., 1994. *CRC Handbook of Thermophysical and Thermochemical Data.,* CRC.

Mezaki, R., Mochizuki, M., Ogawa, K., 1999. *Engineering Data on Mixing.* Elsevier.

Poling, B. E., Prausnitz, J. M., and O'Connell, J. P., 2000. *The Properties of Gases and Liquids.* 5th ed., McGraw-Hill.

Raal, J. D., and Muhlbauer, A., 1997. *Vapor-Liquid Equilibrium Measurements and Calculations.* Taylor & Francis.

Walas, S. M., 1985. *Phase Equilibria in Chemical Engineering.* Butterworth.

Specialist data for the oil and gas industries is given in:

API, 2000. *Technical Data Book – Petroleum Refining (Metric) API 822–99949.* API.

Yaws, C. L., 1995. *Handbook of Thermal Conductivity.* [3 vols], Gulf).

Yaws, C. L., 1997. *Handbook of Chemical Compound Data for Process Safety.* Gulf.

Yaws, C. L., 1997. *Handbook of Viscosity.* [4 vols], Gulf.

A journal specializing in data for single substances or well-defined mixtures is: *Journal of Chemical & Engineering Data*, ACS, 6/yr.

► STEAM TABLES

The energy involved in the vaporization and condensation of water at various temperatures and pressures is collected together in something popularly known as 'the Steam Tables', which are essential in chemical engineering. It is perhaps remarkable that the properties of water should be the subject of copyright and competition between publishers of very expensive books, but this is so.

For most student purposes any of the following inexpensive versions will do:

Grigull, U., 1969. *Properties of Water and Steam in SI units.* Springer.

Haywood, R. W., 1990. *Thermodynamic Tables in SI (Metric) Units.* Cambridge University Press.

Rogers, G. F. C., and Mayhew, Y. R., 1994. *Thermodynamic and Transport Properties of Fluids.* 5th ed., Blackwell.

In fact, the summary tables given in standard handbooks or as an appendix in standard first-year texts are often sufficient (e.g. Coulson & Richardson volume 1, Felder & Rousseau, Himmelblau).

It is probable that anyone needing more precise calculations today would pay for software rather than printed versions (see below) but the following are available. (Be careful to get the SI tables since non-SI versions are still on sale at high prices)

Haar, L., 1984. *NBS/NRC Steam Tables.* Taylor & Francis.

Keenan, J. H., Keyes, F. G., Hill, P. G., and Moore, J. G., 1992. *Steam Tables: Thermodynamic Properties of Water Including Vapor, Liquid, and Solid Phases (International System of Units – S. I.).* Krieger.

Parry, W. T., Gallagher, J. C., Bellows, J. S., and Harvey, A. H., 2000. *ASME International Steam Tables for Industrial Use.* ASME.

Wagner, W., and Kruse, A., 1998. *Properties of Water and Steam, IAPWS-IF97.* Springer-Verlag.

▶ COMPUTER DATABASES

It is increasingly common for chemical engineers to access data by computer. Physical property data is often provided as part of the package or as an add-on for design programs such as simulators which require it. Separate data compilations can be obtained from DECHEMA e.V. (www.dechema.de), the Design Institute for Physical Properties (www.aiche.org/dippr/), ESDU International (www.esdu.com), and the NEL Physical Property Data Service (www.ppds.co.uk). Free data sources online are given in the webpage: ed.icheme.org/chemengs.html.

The online database *Ei Compendex* provides access to some data compilations and can be used to search journals for data. Technical Indexes Ltd have an on-line database of manufacturers' information *e4data process* via: www.info4education.com. ACHEMA is the name of an annual congress and exhibition which publishes a CD-ROM called WOICE which is largely a catalogue of suppliers of chemical engineering equipment and services. It is available from DECHEMA. Literature databases are dealt with later.

▶ UNIT OPERATIONS AND GENERAL DESIGN

Chemical process plant is designed by reducing it to a set of sub-processes which can be individually dealt with. A *mass and energy balance* is carried out on each of these *unit operations* and is balanced for the process overall. An important group of unit operations involves material passing from one physical phase to another, which is known as *mass transfer*. Unit operations involving the transfer of energy and/or material are sometimes called *transport processes*.

Process analysis is concerned with understanding the overall requirements and the interactions of different parts. *Process synthesis* means putting portions together to make an effective overall design. The *chemical engineering design* of a unit operation will specify the physical conditions (temperature, pressure etc), the flows and general necessary dimensions, plus the number of stages or the amount of treatment (e.g. number of distillation stages, or length of catalyst bed) and materials requirement. It is then necessary to select standard items such as pumps or have a mechanical design procedure for equipment to be fabricated.

The following deal with these areas:

Bausbacher, E., and Hunt, R., 1993. *Process Plant Layout and Piping Design.* Prentice Hall.

Beigler, L.T., Grossman, I. E., and Westerberg, A. W., 1997. *Systematic Methods for Chemical Process Design.* Prentice Hall.

Bertucco, A., and Vetter, G., eds., 2001. *High Pressure Process Technology: Fundamentals and Applications.* Elsevier.

Bloch, H. P., and Soares, C., 1998. *Process Plant Machinery.* 2nd ed., Butterworth-Heinemann.

Branan, C., 1999. *Rules of Thumb for Chemical Engineers.* 2nd ed., Gulf.

Cheremisinoff, N. P., 1998. *Liquid Filtration.* Butterworth-Heinemann.

Cheremisinoff, N. P., 1999. *Chemical Engineer's Condensed Encyclopedia of Process Equipment.* Gulf.

Cheremisinoff, N. P., 2000. *Handbook of Chemical Processing Equipment.* Butterworth-Heinemann.

Cussler, E. L., 1997. *Diffusion: Mass Transfer in Fluid Systems.* Cambridge University Press.

Doherty, M. F., and Malone, M. F., 2001. *Conceptual Design of Distillation Systems.* McGraw-Hill.

Douglas, J. M., 1988. *Conceptual Design of Chemical Processes.* McGraw-Hill.

Edgar, T. F., and Himmelblau, D. M., 2001. *Optimization of Chemical Processes.* McGraw Hill.

Geankopolis, C. J., 1993. *Transport Processes and Unit Operations.* 3rd ed., Prentice Hall.

Giddings, J. C., 1991. *Unified Separation Science.* Wiley.

Hewitt, G. F., 1999. *Multiphase Science and Technology.* Taylor & Francis.

Humphrey, J. L., 1997. *Separation Process Technology.* McGraw Hill.

Jones, A. G., 2001. *Crystallization Process Systems.* Butterworth-Heinemann.

Kister, H. Z., 1989. *Distillation Operations.* McGraw Hill.

Kister, H. Z., 1992. *Distillation Design.* McGraw Hill.

Kohl, R., and Nielson, R. B., 1997. *Gas Purification.* 5th ed., Gulf.

Koolen, J. L. A., 2001. *Design of Simple and Robust Chemical Plants.* Taylor & Francis.

Leung, W. W-F., 1998. *Industrial Centrifugation Technology.* McGraw Hill.

Ludwig, E. E., 2001. *Applied Process Design for Chemical and Petrochemical Plants Volume 1.* 3rd ed., Gulf.

Ludwig, E. E., 1997. *Applied Process Design for Chemical and Petrochemical Plants Volume 2.* 3rd ed., Gulf.

Ludwig, E. E., 2000. *Applied Process Design for Chemical and Petrochemical Plants Volume 3.* 3rd ed., Gulf.

McCabe, W. L., Smith, J. C., and Harriott, P., 2001. *Unit Operations of Chemical Engineering.* 6th ed., McGraw-Hill.

Mersmann, A., 2001. *Crystallization Technology Handbook.* Dekker.

Mullin, J. W., 2001. *Crystallization.* 4th ed., Butterworth-Heinemann.

Myerson, A. S., 2002. *Handbook of Industrial Crystallization.* Butterworth-Heinemann.

Peters, M. S., Timmerhaus, K. D., and West, R., 2003. *Plant Design and Economics for Chemical Engineers.* 5th ed., McGraw-Hill.

Plawsky, J. L., 2001. *Transport Phenomena Fundamentals.* Dekker.

Polyanin, A. D., Kutepov, A. M., Vyazmin, A. V., and Kazenin, D. A., 2002. *Hydrodynamics, Mass and Heat Transfer in Chemical Engineering.* Taylor & Francis.

Prentice, G., 1991. *Electrochemical Engineering Principles*. Prentice Hall.

Rautenbach, and Albrecht, R., 1989. *Membrane Processes*. Wiley.

Rousseau, R. W., 1987. *Handbook of Separation Process Technology*. Wiley.

Rushton, A., 2000. *Solid-Liquid Separation Technology*. 2nd ed., Wiley-VCH.

Schweitzer, P. A., ed., 1997. *Handbook of Separation Techniques for Chemical Engineers*. 3rd ed., McGraw Hill.

Seader, J. D., and Henley, E. J., 1998. *Principles of Separation Operations*. Wiley.

Slattery, J., 1999. *Advanced Transport Phenomena*. Cambridge University Press.

Stichlmair, J., and Fair, J., 1998. *Distillation: Principles and Practice*. Wiley-VCH.

Svarovsky, L., 2000. *Solid-Liquid Separation*. 4th ed., Butterworth-Heinemann.

Treybal, R. E., 1981. *Mass Transfer Operations*. 3rd ed., McGraw-Hill.

Van Heuven, J. W., and Beek, W. J., 1999. *Transport Phenomena*. Wiley.

Walas, S. M., 1988. *Chemical Process Equipment: Selection and Design*. Butterworth-Heinemann.

Wesselingh, J. A., Krishna, R., 1990. *Mass Transfer*. Ellis Horwood.

Woods, D. R., 1995. *Process Design and Engineering Practice*. Prentice Hall.

Zlokarnik, M., 2002. *Scale-up in Chemical Engineering*. Wiley-VCH.

Zlokarnik, M., 2001. *Stirring in Theory and Practice*. Wiley-VCH.

▶ ENGINEERING DRAWING

Technical drawing books and courses for mechanical and civil engineers are generally not very useful for chemical engineers, who make more use of diagrams. The key drawing skill focuses on the flowsheet, a semi-symbolic representation of items and material flows in a process. It is usual to start with a block diagram, and from this develop a flowsheet, which may be further refined into an engineering line diagram (ELD) and/or a piping and instrumentation diagram (PID). Where mechanical details are shown, they are normally by simple section drawings, rather than orthographic projections. Graduates in industry may deal with piping isometrics.

Sufficient information for typical student use is given in Coulson & Richardson, volume 6 (by R. Sinnott). This includes extracts from the following British Standards. However, it is preferable to have the full standards available.

BS1553 Part 1: 1977. *Graphical symbols for general engineering – Part 1: Piping systems and plant*. BSI.

BS5070: Part 3: 1988. *Engineering diagram drawing practice. Part3. Recommendations for mechanical/fluid flow diagrams*. BSI.

Various computer packages now include some symbolic drawing facility. Drawing packages may have a chemical engineering library. Simulators commonly include a flowsheeting module.

► CHEMICAL REACTORS

The design of industrial equipment for carrying out chemical reactions involves many physical processes as well. The chemical engineer needs to balance chemical kinetics with diffusion, agitation, heat transfer and other factors not covered in purely chemical books. (Biochemical reactors are given later.)

Aris, R., 2000. *Elementary Chemical Reactor Analysis.* Dover.

Baldyga, J., and Bourne, J. R., 1999. *Turbulent Mixing and Chemical Reactions.* Wiley.

Coker, A. D., 2001. *Modeling of Chemical Kinetics and Reactor Design.* Gulf.

Davis, M. E., and Davis, R. J., 2002. *Fundamentals of Chemical Reaction Engineering.* McGraw Hill.

Deckwer, W. D., 1991. *Bubble Column Reactors.* Wiley.

Fogler, H. S., 1998. *Elements of Chemical Reaction Engineering.* 3rd ed., Prentice Hall.

Ford, M. E., 2000. *Catalysis of Organic Reactions (Chemical Industries).* Dekker.

Froment, G. F., and Bischoff, K., 1990. *Chemical Reactor Analysis and Design.* 2nd ed., Wiley.

Hayes, R. E., 2001. *Introduction to Chemical Reaction Analysis.* Harwood Academic.

Levenspiel, O., 1999. *Chemical Reaction Engineering.* 3rd ed., Wiley.

Metcalfe, I. S., 1997. *Chemical Reaction Engineering: A First Course.* Oxford Science.

Missen, R., Mims, C., and Saville, B., 1999. *Introduction to Chemical Reaction Engineering and Kinetics.* Wiley.

Mizrahi, J., 2002. *Developing an Industrial Chemical Process: an Integrated Approach.* CRC.

Morbidelli, M., Gavriilidis, A., and Varma, A., 2001. *Catalyst Design: Optimal Distribution of Catalyst in Pellets, Reactors, and Membrane.s* Cambridge University Press.

Nauman, B., 2001. *Handbook of Chemical Reactor Design, Optimization and Scale-up.* McGraw-Hill.

Rase, H. F., 2000. *Handbook of Commercial Catalysts.* CRC.

Sadeghbeigi, R., 2000. *Fluid Catalytic Cracking.* 2nd ed., Gulf.

Varma, A., Morbidelli, M., and Wu, H., 1999. *Parametric Sensitivity in Chemical Systems.* Cambridge University Press.

Walas, S. M., 1995. *Chemical Reaction Engineering Handbook of Solved Problems.* Taylor & Francis.

Westerterp, K. R., Van Swaaij, W. P. M., and Beenackers, A. A. C. M., 1987. *Chemical Reactor Design and Operation.* Wiley.

Wijngaarden, R. I., Westerterp, K. R., and Kronberg, A., 1998. *Industrial Catalysis.* Wiley-VCH.

Winterbottom, J. M., and King, M. B., 1999. *Reactor Design for Chemical Engineers.* Nelson Thornes.

▶ PHYSICAL CHEMISTRY

Many standard chemical textbooks, and texts on thermodynamics for mechanical and general engineering, may be used (see Chapter 23), but the following are especially relevant.

Come, G-M., 2001. *Gas-Phase Thermal Reactions: Chemical Engineering Kinetics*. Kluwer.
Houston, P. L., 2001. *Chemical Kinetics and Reaction Dynamics*. McGraw-Hill.
Kyle, B. G., 2000. *Chemical and Process Thermodynamics*. 3rd ed., Prentice Hall.
Prausnitz, J. M., Lichtenhaler, R. N., and de Azevedo, E. G., 1998. *Thermodynamics of Fluid-Phase Equilibria*. 3rd ed., Prentice Hall.
Sandler, S. I., 1998. *Chemical and Engineering Thermodynamics*. 3rd ed., Wiley.
Smith, J. M., 1981. *Chemical Engineering Kinetics*. 3rd ed., McGraw-Hill.
Smith, J. M., Van Ness, H. C., and Abbott, M. M., 2001. *Introduction to Chemical Engineering Thermodynamics*. 6th ed., McGraw-Hill.

▶ FLUID MECHANICS

The movement of fluids is fundamental to many processes. The basic theory is covered in books intended for general engineering. Some that are specially written for, or well suited to, chemical engineering, or cover special applications are as follows.

Student texts:

Darby, R., 2001. *Chemical Engineering Fluid Mechanics*. Dekker.
de Nevers, N., 1991. *Fluid Mechanics for Chemical Engineers*. 2nd ed., McGraw-Hill.
Denn, M. M., 1980. *Process Fluid Mechanics*. Prentice Hall.
Holland, F. A., and Bragg, R., 1995. *Fluid Flow for Chemical Engineers*. 2nd ed., Butterworth-Heinemann.
Schaschke, C., 1998. *Fluid Mechanics: Worked Examples for Engineers*. IChemE.
Wilkes, J. O., and Bike, S. G., 1998. *Fluid Mechanics for Chemical Engineers*. Prentice Hall.

Specialist texts:

Chhabra, R. P., and Richardson, J. F., 1999. *Non-Newtonian Flow: fundamentals and engineering applications*. Butterworth-Heinemann.
Crowe, C., Sommerfield, M., and Tsuji, Y., 1997. *Multiphase Flows with Droplets and Particles*. CRC Press.
DeKee, D., and Chhabra, R. P., 2002. *Transport Processes in Bubbles, Drops and Particles*. Taylor & Francis.

Jamal, S., 2002. *Fluid Flow Handbook*. McGraw-Hill.

Larson, R. G., 1999. *The Structure and Rheology of Complex Fluids*. Oxford University Press.

Loy Upp, E., and LaNasa, P. J., 2002. *Fluid Flow Measurement*. Butterworth-Heinemann.

Probstein, R. F., 1994. *Physicochemical Hydrodynamics: An Introduction*. 2nd ed., Wiley.

Sirignano, W. A., 1999. *Fluid Dynamics and Transport of Droplets and Sprays*. Cambridge University Press.

Stanek, V., and Sharp, D., 1994. *Fixed Bed Operations: Flow Distribution and Efficiency*. Ellis Horwood.

In addition, ESDU International plc (London) has a set of regularly updated data books (11 volumes, 16 books) *Fluid Mechanics, Internal Flow*, which is suitable for chemical engineering design usage.

► HEAT EXCHANGERS, HEAT PUMPS AND REFRIGERATION

Devices for heating and cooling are of major concern to chemical engineers. Many are used to conserve energy by transferring energy gained in one operation to material in the same or a different operation which requires heat input. These are called *heat exchangers*, but the same general term and technology is used for simple heaters, coolers, boilers and condensers.

The most complete combination of theory, practice and data (in 5 volumes with quarterly updates) is probably given by:

Hewitt, G., 1998. *Heat Exchanger Design Handbook*. 2nd ed., Begell House.

The special use of high temperature liquids is covered by:

Wagner, W., 1997. *Heat Transfer Practice with Organic Media*. Begell House.

Heat pumps are machines for redistributing energy. This generally means to produce a higher temperature than the energy source, although in fact refrigerators are actually heat pumps producing lower temperatures.

The basic physics of heat transfer and heat pumping is common to other fields, notably mechanical engineering, physics and fuel and energy studies (see Chapter 23). However, texts particularly relevant to chemical engineering are as follows.

Student texts

The theory is covered in Coulson & Richardson volume 1, and the design of heat exchangers in volume 6. The following are more complete and specialist course books.

Carey, V. P., 1992. *Liquid-Vapor Phase-Change Phenomena.* Taylor & Francis.

Hewitt, G. F., Shires, G. L., and Bott, T. R., 1994. *Process Heat Transfer.* Begell House.

Holman, J. P., 2001. *Heat Transfer.* 8th ed., McGraw-Hill.

Incropera, F. P., and Dewitt, D. P., 2001. *Fundamentals of Heat and Mass Transfer.* 5th ed., Wiley.

Incropera, F. P., and Dewitt, D. P., 2001. *Introduction to Heat Transfer.* 4th ed., Wiley.

Fraas, A. P., 1989. *Heat Exchanger Design.* 2nd ed., Wiley.

Kaviany, M., 2001. *Principles of Heat Transfer.* Wiley.

Kreith, F., and Bohn, M. S., 2001. *Principles of Heat Transfer.* Brooks Cole.

Levenspiel, O., 1998. *Engineering Flow and Heat Exchange.* Kluwer/ Plenum.

McKetta, J. J., 1991. *Heat Transfer Design Methods.* Dekker.

Middleman, S., 1997. *An Introduction to Mass and Heat Transfer.* Wiley.

Mills, A. F., 1998. *Basic Heat and Mass Transfer.* 2nd ed., Prentice Hall.

Moran, M. J., Shapiro, H. N., Munson, B. R., and DeWitt, D. P., 2002. *Introduction to Thermal Systems Engineering: Thermodynamics, Fluid Mechanics, and Heat Transfer.* Wiley.

Ozisik, M. N., 1985. *Heat Transfer: A Basic Approach.* McGraw-Hill.

Smith, E. M., 1997. *Thermal Design of Heat Exchangers: A Numerical Approach: Direct Sizing and Stepwise Rating.* Wiley.

Welty, J. R., Wicks, C. E., Wilson, R. E., and Rorrer, G. L., 2000. *Fundamentals of Momentum, Heat and Mass Transfer.* 4th ed., Wiley.

Industrial or graduate texts

Cheremisinoff, N. P., ed., 1986. *Handbook of Heat and Mass Transfer; Vol 1: Heat Transfer Operations.* Gulf Publishing.

Cheremisinoff, P. N., and Cheremisinoff, N. P., 1993. *Heat Transfer Equipment.* Prentice Hall.

Hesselgreaves, J. E., 2001. *Compact Heat Exchangers: Selection, Design and Operation.* Pergamon.

Kakac, S., ed., 1991. *Boilers, Evaporators and Condensers.* Wiley.

Kakac, S., and Hongtan, L., 2002. *Heat Exchangers: Selection, Rating and Thermal Design.* CRC Press.

Kays, W. M., and London, A. L., 1998. *Compact Heat Exchangers.* Krieger.

Kraus, A. D., Aziz, A., and Welty, J., 2001. *Extended Surface Heat Transfer.* Wiley.

Kuppan, T., 2000. *Heat Exchanger Design Handbook.* Dekker.

Ludwig, E. E., 2001. *Applied Process Design for Chemical and Petrochemical Plants, Volume 3.* 3rd ed., Gulf.

Rohsenow, W., Hartnett, J., and Cho, Y. I., 1998. *Handbook of Heat Transfer.* 3rd ed., McGraw-Hill.

Shenoy, U. V., 1995. *Heat Exchanger Network Synthesis.* Gulf.

Walker, G., 1990. *Industrial Heat Exchangers – A Basic Guide.* Taylor & Francis.

A set of data books (13 volumes) for heat transfer and design of heat exchangers is available from ESDU International plc, London. The AIChE produces a series of volumes of *Transport Properties and Related Thermo-dynamic Data of Binary Mixtures* from volume 1 (1994) to volume 5 (1998) covering to date more than 2000 mixtures.

Both the AIChE and IChemE have regular conferences on this topic, with published proceedings.

▶ PARTICLE TECHNOLOGY

There are comparatively few publications devoted to the handling of solid materials in a chemical engineering context. The main refereed journal is *Powder Technology*, Elsevier. The AIChE publishes conference proceedings on this topic. The most common undergraduate text is volume 2 of *Coulson and Richardson's Chemical Engineering* (latest edition by Richardson *et al.*). A general undergraduate textbook is:

Rhodes, M., 1998. *Introduction to Powder Technology*. Wiley.

The following books are substantially relevant:

Brown, C. J., 1998. *Silos – Fundamentals of Theory, Behaviour and Design*. Spon.
Fayed, M., and Otten, L., eds., 1997. *Handbook of Powder Science and Technology*. Kluwer.
Gupta, C. K., and Sathiyamoorthy, D., 1998. *Fluid Bed Technology in Materials Processing*. CRC Press.
Heiskanen, K., 1993. *Particle Classification*. Kluwer.
Hoyle, W., ed., 2001. *Powders and Solids: Developments in Handling and Processing Technologies*. Royal Society of Chemistry.
Institution of Mechanical Engineers, 2000. *From Powder to Bulk: International Conference on Powder and Bulk Solids Handling*. Professional Engineering.
Jackson, R., 2000. *The Dynamics of Fluidized Particles*. Cambridge University Press.
Kaye, B. H., 1997. *Powder Mixing*. Kluwer.
Klinzing, G. E., Marcus, R. D., Rizk, F., and Leung, L., 1997. *Pneumatic Conveying of Solids: A Theoretical and Practical Approach*. Kluwer.
Levy, A., and Kalman, H., 2001. *Handbook of Conveying and Handling of Particulate Solids*. Elsevier.
Mills, D., 1990. *Pneumatic Conveying Design Guide*. Butterworth-Heinemann.
Molerus, O., 1993. *Principles of Flow in Disperse Systems*. Kluwer.
Richardson, J. F., Backhurst, J. R., and Harker, J. H., 2002. *Chemical Engineering Vol 2: Particle Technology and Separation Processes*. 5th ed., Butterworth-Heinemann.
Weinekotter, R., and Gericke, H., 2000. *Mixing of Solids*. Kluwer.
Woodcock, C. R., and Mason, J. S., 1987. *Bulk Solids Handling*. Kluwer.
Yang, W., 1999. *Fluidization Solids Handling and Processing*. Noyes.

▶ BIOCHEMICAL ENGINEERING, BIOPROCESSING AND BIOTECHNOLOGY

Engineering involving living cells (or materials such as enzymes derived from them) has special requirements, both in the biochemical processes and in subsequent operations such as separation and purification. Developments in the field are sufficiently rapid that books over ten years old have limited value. Publications generally address one of (a) biological processes for synthesis of products (b) biological processes for waste treatment, including remediation of contaminated soil, or (c) broader environmental issues.

Papers may be published in the regular chemical engineering journals, or in:

Biotechnology & Bioengineering (28/yr, Wiley SCI),
Engineering in Life Sciences (12/yr, Wiley VCH)
Journal of Chemical Technology & Biotechnology (12/yr, Wiley).

A 12-volume, multi-author work entitled *Biotechnology* is published by Wiley-VCH (2nd edition complete in 1996 but with some supplementary volumes 11A, 11B, 11C and a new index in 2001). Volumes 3 and 11 seem especially relevant.

Rehm, H-J., Reed, G., Pûhler, A., Stadler, P., 1996. *Biotechnology, Volumes 1–12 + Index*. 2nd ed., Wiley-VCH.

DECHEMA has an annual conference with published proceedings on the topic of Biotechnology and related matters.

Biochemical reactors (and basic biology / biochemistry) are covered in *Coulson & Richardson's Chemical Engineering, volume 3* (Richardson & Peacock, 1994) and in Winterbottom, J. M., and King, M. B., 1999. *Reactor Design for Chemical Engineers*. Nelson Thornes. The following are more specialist texts:

Blanch, H. W., and Clark, D. S., 1996. *Biochemical Engineering*. Dekker.
Cabral, J. M. S., Mota, M., and Tramper, J., 2001. *Multiphase Bioreactor Design*. Taylor & Francis.
Demain, A. L., Davies, J. E., and Atlas, R. M., 1999. *Manual of Industrial Microbiology and Biotechnology*. American Society for Microbiology.
Hall, S. J., Stanbury, P. F., and Whitaker, A., 1999. *Principles of Fermentation Technology*. Butterworth-Heinemann.
Johnson, A. T., 1998. *Biological Process Engineering: An Analogical Approach to Fluid Flow, Heat Transfer, and Mass Transfer Applied to Biological Systems*. Wiley.
Ladisch, M. R., 2001. *Bioseparations Engineering: Principles, Practice and Economics*. Wiley.
Leeson, A., and Alleman, B. C., 1999. *Bioreactor and Ex-Situ Biological Treatment Technologies*. Battelle [latest in a series of symposium reports].

Lee, J. M., 2001. *Biochemical Engineering.* 2nd ed., (available for purchase only as an ebook from: www.geocities.com/eBioChE/)

Liese, A., Seelbach, K., and Wandrey, C., 2000. *Industrial Biotransformations.* Wiley-VCH.

Lyderson, B. K., Nelson, K. L., and D'Elia, N., 1994. *Bioprocess Engineering.* Wiley.

Nielsen, J. H., and Roy, R., 2002. *Bioreaction Engineering Principles.* Kluwer/Plenum.

Payne, G., Bringi, V., Prince, C., and Shuler, M., 1993. *Plant Cell and Tissue Culture in Liquid Systems.* Wiley.

Schügerl, K., 1987. *Bioreaction Engineering Volume 1.* Wiley.

Schügerl, K., 1991. *Bioreaction Engineering Volume 2.* Wiley.

Schügerl, K., 1997. *Bioreaction Engineering Volume 3.* Wiley.

Schügerl, K., and Bellgardt, K. H., 2000. *Bioreaction Engineering: Modeling and Control.* Springer.

Schuler, M. L., and Kargi, F., 2002. *Bioprocess Engineering.* 2nd ed., Prentice Hall.

Stanbury, P. F., Whitaker, A., and Hall, S., 1998. *Principles of Fermentation Technology.* 2nd ed., Butterworth-Heinemann.

Uhlig, H., ed., 1998. *Industrial Enzymes and their Applications.* Wiley.

Vogel, H. C., and Todaro, C. L., 1996. *Fermentation and Biochemical Engineering Handbook: Principles, Process Design, and Equipment.* Noyes.

Walsh, G., 1998. *Biopharmaceuticals: Biochemistry and Biotechnology.* Wiley.

▶ CONTROL

(See also Chapter 23)

Process control can mean different things in different disciplines. The Institute of Measurement and Control (London) publishes a few guides on process measurement as well as a yearbook. The Instrumentation Systems and Automation Society (ISA) in the USA publishes more than 170 books and many standards and guides, including Murrill, P. W., 2000. *Fundamentals of Process Control Theory*, 3rd ed., Corripio, A. B., 1998. *Design and Application of Process Control Systems*, Nisenfeld, A. E., and Leegwater, H., 1996. *Batch Control*, and McMillan, G. K., 1994. *pH Measurement and Control*.

The following from other publishers are relevant to chemical engineering.

Brosilow, C., and Joseph, B., 2002. *Techniques of Model Based Control.* Prentice Hall.

Center for Process Safety, 1992. *The Safe Automation of Chemical Processes.* AIChE.

Chau, P. C., 2002. *Process Control: A First Course with MATLAB.* Cambridge University Press.

Chopey, N. P., 1996. *Instrumentation and Process Control.* McGraw Hill.

Coughanowr, D. R., 1991. *Process Systems Analysis and Control.* 2nd ed., McGraw-Hill.

Erickson, K. T., and HEdrick, J. L., 1999. *Plantwide Process Control.* Wiley.

Felder, T. M., 2002. *Process Technology Systems.* Prentice Hall.

Fltzgerald, B., 1999. *Control Valves for the Chemical Process Industries.* McGraw Hill.

Ikonen, E., and Najim, K., 2001. *Advanced Process Identification and Control.* Dekker.

Johnson, C. D., 2000. *Process Control Instrumentation Technology.* 6th ed., Prentice Hall.

Kalani, G., 2002. *Industrial Control Systems: Advances and Applications.* Butterworth Heinemann.

Kane, L. A., ed., 1999. *Advanced Process Control and Information Systems for the Process Industries.* Gulf.

Luyben, W. L., 1996. *Essentials of Process Control.* McGraw-Hill.

Luyben, W. L., 2002. *Plantwide Dynamic Simulators in Chemical Processing and Control.* Dekker.

Luyben, W. L., Tyreus, B. D., and Luyben, M., 1998. *Plantwide Process Control.* McGraw Hill.

Marlin, T. E., 2000. *Process Control.* 2nd ed., McGraw-Hill.

McMillan, G. K., 1999. *Process/Industrial Instruments and Controls Handbook.* McGraw Hill.

Ogunnaike, B., and Ray, W. H., 1995. *Process Dynamics, Modeling and Control.* Oxford University Press.

Paraskevopoulos, P. N., 2001. *Modern Control Engineering: Modelling and Simulation of Organic Chemical Processes (Control Engineering).* Dekker.

Shinskey, F. G., 1996. *Process Control Systems: Application, Design and Tuning.* McGraw Hill.

Smith, C. A., and Corripio, A. B., 1997. *Principles and Practice of Automatic Process Control.* 3rd ed., Wiley.

Svrcek, W. Y., Mahoney, D. P., and Young, B., 2000. *A Real Time Approach to Process Control.* Wiley.

The IChemE has a regular conference on Process Control with published proceedings (6th in 2001).

▶ SAFETY

Safety is of course a prime requirement in chemical engineering, and there is an extensive literature ranging from abstruse mathematical modelling of complex technical processes to the practical management of human beings. As fires, explosions and chemical releases can be expensive as well as dangerous, the term '*loss prevention*' has been introduced to include action to prevent or reduce economic losses. In recent years, there has been increasing regulation, and handbooks tend to reflect the local legal approach, U.S. ones in particular. Helpful guides are produced by some government agencies such as the HSE in the UK. A website with extensive links is maintained by the Safety and Loss Prevention Subject Group of the IChemE at: slp.icheme.org/slplinks.html.

Safety techniques developed by chemical engineers (such as Hazop – hazard and operability studies) have been adopted elsewhere, and techniques from other disciplines are routinely used, so the literature is by no means clearly defined, (See Chapter 26). However, the following are particularly relevant.

The principal refereed journals are:

Journal of Hazardous Materials (16/yr, Elsevier).
Journal of Loss Prevention in the Process Industries (6/yr, Elsevier).
Process Safety Progress (4/yr, AIChE).
Process Safety and Environmental Protection (6/yr, IChemE),

A more practical publication is the *Loss Prevention Bulletin* (6/yr, IChemE) which includes advice, incident reports and information from the IChemE Accident Database. This latter is software available under license giving over 13,000 incidents and lessons learned.

The AIChE publishes proceedings of its annual Loss Prevention Symposium, and the IChemE of its series of Hazards Symposia, and Management of Safety Symposia.

The pre-eminent book on the subject is a two-volume compendium:

Lees, F., 1996. *Loss Prevention in the Process Industries.* 2nd ed., Butterworth Heinemann.

Trevor A. Kletz produces some particularly readable but scholarly books. His most famous is probably:

Kletz, T., 1993. *Lessons from Disaster: How Organizations have no Memory and Accidents Recur.* IChemE.

His autobiography is:

Kletz, T., 2001. *By Accident . . . a Life Preventing Them in Industry.* PFV.

Recent ones are:

Kletz, T., Chung, P., and Shen-orr, C., 1995. *Computer Control and Human Error.* IChemE.
Kletz, T. A., 1998. *Process Plants: a Handbook for Inherently Safer Design: A User-Friendly Approach.* Taylor and Francis.
Kletz, T., 1998. *What went Wrong? Case Histories of Process Plant Disasters.* Gulf.
Kletz, T., 2000. *Hazop and Hazan.* 2nd ed., IChemE.
Kletz, T., 2001. *An Engineer's View of Human Error.* Taylor & Francis.
Kletz, T., 2001. *Learning from Accidents.* 3rd ed., Butterworth-Heinemann.

In the USA, the Center for Chemical Process Safety produces many guides and reviews for practising engineers. These are published via the AIChE. Examples are:

(1993) *Guidelines for Engineering Design for Process Safety*
(1995) *Guidelines for Process Safety Fundamentals in General Plant Operations*
(1996) *Plant Safety*

(2000) *Guidelines for Chemical Process Quantitative Risk Analysis,* 2nd ed.
(2000) *Evaluating Process Safety in the Chemical Industry*
(2002) *Guidelines for Analyzing and Managing the Security Vulnerabilities of Fixed Chemical Sites.*

Other books by and/or for chemical engineers are:

Barton, J., 2001. *Dust explosion prevention and protection: a practical guide.* IChemE.
Barton, J., and Rogers, R., 1997. *Chemical Reaction Hazards: a guide to safety.* IChemE.
Burns, T., 2002. *Serious Incident Prevention: How to Sustain Accident-free Operations in your Plant Company.* Butterworth-Heinemann.
Cheremisinoff, N. P., 2000. *Practical Guide to Industrial Safety: Methods for Process Safety Professionals.* Dekker.
Crowl, D., and Louvar, J., 2001. *Chemical Process Safety: Fundamentals with Applications.* Prentice Hall.
European Process Safety Centre, 2000. *Hazop: Guide to Best Practice.* IChemE.
European Process Safety Centre, 1996. *Safety Performance Measurement.* IChemE.
Flynn, A. M., and Theodore, L., 2001. *Health, Safety and Accident Management in the Chemical Process Industries.* Dekker.
Fullwood, R., 1999. *Probabilistic Safety Assessment in the Chemical and Nuclear Industries.* Butterworth-Heinemann.
Gillett, J. E., 1997. *Hazard Study and Risk Assessment in the Pharmaceutical Industry.* Global Engineering Documentation.
Grewer, T., 1994. *Thermal Hazards of Chemical Reactions.* Elsevier.
Marshall, V., and Ruhemann, S., 2001. *Fundamentals of Process Safety.* IChemE.
Marshall, V., and Townsend, A., 1991. *Safety in Chemical Engineering Research and Development.* IChemE.
Pitblado, R., and Turney, R., 1996. *Risk Assessment in the Process Industries.* IChemE.
Sanders, R. E., 1999. *Chemical Process Safety: Learning from Case Histories.* 2nd ed., Butterworth-Heinemann.
Ramiro, J. M. S., Aisi, P. N. B., and Hutchinson, J., 1997. *Risk Analysis and Reduction in the Chemical Process Industry.* Kluwer.
Skelton, R., 1996. *Process Safety Analysis: an Introduction.* IChemE.
Steinbach, J., 1998. *Safety Assessment for Chemical Processes.* Wiley-VCH.
Urben, P., and Pitt, M. J., 1999. *Bretherick's Handbook of Reactive Chemical Hazards.* 6th ed., Butterworth-Heinemann.
Vinnem, J. E., 1999. *Offshore Risk Assessment: Principles, Modelling and Applications of QRA Studies.* Kluwer.
Wells, G., 1996. *Hazard Identification and Risk Assessment.* IChemE.

In addition, reference may be made to the following hazard databases available on CD-ROM:

Bretherick's Reactive Chemicals Database V. 3.0, 1999. Butterworth-Heinemann.
The Accident Database V. 4.0, 2000. IChemE.
Loss Prevention on CD-ROM. 2002. 2nd ed., AIChE.

► ENVIRONMENT

Chemical engineers have always been concerned with the environment, particularly by the efficient use of energy and the minimizing of the amount and effect of waste. In recent years they have been increasingly concerned with the concept of *sustainability*. The term *green chemistry* is used for chemical processes which minimize environmental impact by limiting waste and using sustainable resources. The American Chemical Society has an annual conference on Green Chemistry and Engineering. In addition, legislation such as the European *Seveso II Directive* has expanded risk assessment to require environmental impact as well as the danger to human life to be considered. Wastewater treatment and land disposal is normally categorized under civil engineering, though it could well be considered chemical engineering. There is a large area of literature devoted to energy production, and its byproducts such as CO_2. [See Chapter 20].

The principal refereed journals are:

Environmental Progress (quarterly) AIChE.
Process Safety and Environmental Protection (6/yr), IChemE.

The following is a selection of particularly relevant books.

Allen, D. T., and Rosselot, K. S., 1996. *Pollution Prevention for Chemical Processes*. Wiley.
Allen, D. T., and Shonnard, D. R., 2002. *Green Engineering: Environmentally Conscious Design of Chemical Processes*. Prentice Hall.
Anastas, P. T., and Warner, J. C., 1998. *Green Chemistry: Theory and Practice*. Oxford University Press.
Boyle, G., ed., 1996. *Renewable Energy: Power for a Sustainable Future*. Oxford University Press.
Calow, P., 1997. *Controlling Environmental Risks from Chemicals: Principles and Practice*. Wiley.
Calow, P. ed., 1997. *Handbook of Environmental Risk Assessment and Management*. Blackwell.
Christ, C., ed., 1999. *Production-Integrated Environmental Protection and Waste Management in the Chemical Industry*. Wiley-VCH.
El-Halwagi, M., 1997. *Pollution Prevention Through Process Integration*. Academic.
Hocking, M. B., 1998. *Handbook of Chemical Technology and Pollution Control*. Academic.
Institution of Chemical Engineers, 1997. *Controlling Industrial Emissions: Practical Experience*. IChemE, (conference proceedings).
Institution of Chemical Engineers, 2002. *Sustainability Metrics*. IChemE, (also available on-line at: www.icheme.org/sustainability/sustainabilitymetrics.pdf)
Kirchsteiger, C., Christou, M., and Papadakis, G., eds., 1998. *Risk Assessment and Management in the Context of the Seveso II Directive*. Elsevier.
Lancaster, M., 2002. *Green Chemistry: An Introductory Text*. Royal Society of Chemistry.
Lankey, R. L., and Anastas, P. T., 2002. *Advancing Sustainability Through Green Chemistry and Engineering*. Oxford University Press.

McMillan, G., 1999. *Industrial Water Reuse and Wastewater Minimization.* McGraw Hill.

Reynolds, J. P., Jeris, J. S., and Theodore, L., 2002. *Handbook of Chemical and Environmental Engineering Calculations.* Wiley.

Rossiter, A. P., Nalven, G., and Rossiter, A. P., 1997. *Environmental Management and Pollution Prevention.* AIChE.

Sharrat, P., and Spearshot, M., 1996. *Case Studies in Environmental Technology.* IChemE.

Shepherd, W, and Shepherd, D. W., 1998. *Energy Studies.* Imperial College Press.

▶ SOFTWARE

More than 2000 programs and data sets are available commercially. Most are listed and briefly described in an annual supplement to the journal *Chemical Engineering Progress*, (www.cepmagazine.org/features/software/). It is increasingly common for software versions of books to be produced, and certain books have computer disks with them.

▶ JOURNALS

Chemical engineers may publish in, and refer to, journals of mathematics, science and general engineering, and of course business publications related to the process industries. However, they have their own distinct set of literature. Despite the name, most chemical journals are rarely consulted. The following are publications with significant chemical engineering content.

UK: published by the Institution of Chemical Engineers (Rugby)

The Chemical Engineer: topical news and technical articles (fortnightly) (online at: www.tce.com)
Transactions: Learned Journal, refereed research papers
Part A: Chemical Engineering Research and Design (10/yr).
Part B: Process Safety and Environment Protection (6/yr).
Part C: Food and Bioproduct Processing (4/yr).
Loss Prevention Bulletin: accident reports and articles on safety (6/yr).

UK: for the Society of Chemical Industry (by Wiley)

Chemistry & Industry (fortnightly) news, reviews and short papers.
Journal of Chemical Technology & Biotechnology (12/yr) technical papers.

USA: published by the American Institute of Chemical Engineers

AIChE Journal (12/yr) technical papers.
Biotechnology Progress (4/yr) technical papers.
Chemical Engineering Progress (12/yr) news and general articles.
Environmental Progress (4/yr) technical papers.
Process Safety Progress (formerly Plant/Operations Progress) (4/yr)
   technical papers.

Other journals

Publications of research findings are given in:

Advances in Biochemical Engineering/Biotechnology (Springer 4/yr).
Applied Catalysis A: General (Elsevier 8/yr).
Biochemical Engineering Journal (Elsevier 8/yr).
Bioprocess and Biosystems Engineering (Springer 6/yr).
Canadian Journal of Chemical Engineering (Can Soc Chem Eng. 12/yr)
Catalysis Today (Elsevier 4/yr).
Chemical and Petroleum Engineering (Plenum translation of Russian
   journal)
Chemical & Engineering Technology (Wiley-VCH 12/yr).
Chemical Engineering and Processing (Elsevier 12/yr).
Chemical Engineering Journal (Elsevier 12/yr).
Chemical Engineering Science (Elsevier fortnightly).
Combustion and Flame (Elsevier 16/yr).
Computers and Chemical Engineering (Elsevier 12/yr).
Filtration and Separation (Elsevier 8/yr).
Fuel (Elsevier 15/yr).
Fuel Processing Technology (Elsevier 15/yr).
Green Chemistry (Royal Society of Chemistry 6/yr).
Heat and Mass Transfer (Springer 6/yr).
Industrial & Engineering Chemistry Research (ACS 26/yr).
International Journal of Heat and Mass Transfer (Pergamon 26/yr)
International Journal of Refrigeration (Elsevier 8/yr)
Journal of Catalysis (Elsevier 16/yr).
Journal of Chemical & Engineering Data (ACS 6/yr).
Journal of Chemical Engineering of Japan (Soc Chem Eng Jap 12/yr).
Journal of Environmental Engineering (ACS 12/yr).
Journal of Hazardous Materials (Elsevier 12/yr).
Journal of Process Control (Elsevier 8/yr).
Minerals Engineering (Elsevier 12/yr).
Powder Technology (Elsevier 15/yr).

Process Biochemistry (Elsevier 12/yr).
Separation and Purification Technology (Elsevier 13/year).
Theoretical Foundations of Chemical Engineering (Kluwer – translation of Russian journal).

News items and technical review articles are given in:
Chemical & Engineering News (ACS weekly).
Chemical Engineering (Chemical Week Publishing 12/yr).
Chemical Engineering Education (Am Soc for Engineering Education, 4/yr).
Chemical Engineering and Processing (Elsevier 9/yr).
Chemie-Ingenieur-Technik (Wiley-VCH Germany: German with English abstracts 12/yr).
Hydrocarbon Processing (Gulf 12/yr).
International Journal of Heat and Fluid Flow (Elsevier 6/yr).
Journal of Chemical Thermodynamics (Academic 12/yr).
Journal of Loss Prevention in the Process Industries (Elsevier 6/yr).
Oil & Gas Journal (Pennwell weekly).
Petroleum Review (Institute of Petroleum 12/yr).
Progress in Energy and Combustion Science (Elsevier 6/yr).
A serial publication by Academic Press is *Advances in Chemical Engineering*, of which Volume 28 (ed. Wei, J.) was published in 2001.

▶ LITERATURE ABSTRACTS AND DATABASES

Most academic chemical engineering publications are given in the *Science Citation Index* and the *Ei Compendex*. Reference is sometimes made to the *Chemical Abstracts Service* of the American Chemical Society (www. cas.org).

An important literature database is: *Chemical Engineering and Biotechnology Abstracts* CEABA. This is available online, and in printed form from DECHEMA in sections as follows:

Biotechnology Apparatus and Equipment
(formerly Biotechnologie-Verfahren, Anlagen, Apparate)

Current Biotechnology
(formerly Current Biotechnology Abstracts)

Process and Chemical Engineering
(formerly Chemical Engineering Abstracts)

Theoretical Chemical Engineering
(formerly Theoretical Chemical Engineering Abstracts)

In addition, the following abstracts are relevant:

Catalysts and Catalysed Reactions (Royal Society of Chemistry 12/yr or online).

Chemical Hazards in Industry (Royal Society of Chemistry 12/yr or online).

Fuel and Energy Abstracts (Elsevier 6/yr).

17 Civil Engineering

Mike Chrimes

▶ INTRODUCTION

Of all the engineering disciplines civil engineering is perhaps the most difficult to define. At its broadest, and in its original eighteenth century sense, it embraces all branches of engineering outside the military sphere. This is not particularly helpful as many aspects of the work of military engineers such as the provision of roads and bridges would generally be considered as civil engineering. In 1827, Thomas Tredgold attempted an all embracing definition for the Institution of Civil Engineers' first Royal Charter (1828). It began 'Civil engineering is the art of directing the great sources of power in nature for the use and convenience of man'. Today it is generally seen to embrace those branches of engineering that are particularly concerned with the planning, design and construction of the man-made environment which embraces civilisation as we know it today. Taking a more detailed view the following specialisms have been selected for discussion – geotechnical engineering, maritime engineering, structural engineering, transport engineering, and water engineering.

Inevitably in such a broad brush subject there is a varying overlap with other engineering disciplines, sciences and technologies, including what might be considered the social sciences. Although developments in management techniques might be more obviously identified with the work of mechanical engineers in the manufacturing industry, project management has always been an important if not key aspect of the work of the civil engineer, and there is now an abundance of information regarding this aspect of the profession. Closely allied with this are methods of procurement and construction law, which over the last twenty years have produced considerable literature. The impact of the Latham and Egan reports has been to encourage partnership rather than confrontation in construction contracts, whereas worldwide encouragement of private funding for public infrastructure projects has led to a reconsideration of traditional roles of client/consultant/

contractor. There has been a rash of new forms of contract from relevant professional bodies and trade associations to reflect these changes, and the ICE's *New Engineering Contract* (www.newengineeringcontract.com) has gained widespread acceptance as a result of these developments. Much construction is done under the auspices of the building contracts issued by the Joint Contracts Tribunal rather than ICE and its partners.

Materials play an important part in this work of the civil engineer, particularly concrete and steel, but also more traditional building materials such as timber and natural stone, and newer materials such as man-made polymers. Sustainability is an important topical issue, while the history of civil engineering is the key to the understanding of modern civilised life.

With these main themes identified, it is intended to inform the reader where and how to find out about civil engineering. What follows must inevitably be selective; space precludes any other approach. For example in the UK alone there are more than fifty organisations involved with cement and concrete. The sources listed here are those generally found to be most useful; they should be able to guide the enquirer to the appropriate sources of more detailed information.

Civil engineering is a world-wide industry, many important projects cross national boundaries, or are funded by international bodies, and executed by multi-national consortia, and for those reasons alone an international view has been taken of information sources. More importantly, some of the 'best' sources are non-UK. Indeed one could add that certain subjects are best served by acquiring a knowledge of German or Japanese! Generally, learned institutions produce the leading journals, with ASCE, ICE and JSCE being most prolific.

In the listings below contact details are restricted to websites, unless addresses are likely to be elusive, or a visit is expected, e.g. to a library, etc.

► PROFESSIONAL INSTITUTIONS, CIVIL ENGINEERING EDUCATION AND RESEARCH

Under the auspices of the Engineering Council/ (and Technology Board) (www.engc.org.uk, www.etechb.co.uk see Chapter 13) a number of UK professional bodies concern themselves with the education, training and promotion of civil engineering. Of these the oldest and most important in terms of its size and breadth of interests is the Institution of Civil Engineers. All combine an active interest in promoting engineering as a career and maintaining educational standards with learned society activities – publishing and organising meetings. Although most would field enquiries regarding their subject area, only the Institutions of Civil and Structural Engineers have a Library and Information Service of sufficient depth to be of detailed help.

Although it is possible to study certain aspects of civil engineering at the secondary level, civil engineering is largely taught at the tertiary level in the UK, to a number of standards, 'technician' and 'degree' level. Although some universities have specialist departments dealing with disciplines like transport engineering, most first degrees are more general and courses in geotechnical engineering are generally aimed at post-graduates. Information on appropriate and approved courses of study is available from the relevant professional institutions. While full (chartered) membership of a professional body is the sole indicator of professional status in the UK, the situation is different on Continental Europe where engineering courses are generally longer, and successful attendance at specialist schools such as the Ecole des Ponts et Chaussees in France may be the recognised route to practice. In the United States of America engineers have to register with each State to practice, while in Britain there is no legal control over the term 'civil engineer' at all. Thus routes to professional engineering status are varied and information must be sought from the relevant body in each country.

Although the contribution of universities to the professional status of civil engineers may vary from country to country, the important contribution of academic research to developments in civil engineering is recognised everywhere. Much is published in contributions to journals and conferences, but individual university websites describe ongoing research which may help identify expert sources of information in academia which may not be evident from other sources. Universities are, however, essentially concerned with their own academic community, and cannot always be regarded as a resource for the general public.

Most countries support research laboratories and institutes which concern themselves with civil engineering. In the UK these were traditionally directly government funded, but now, although much revenue comes from government contracts, most have been privatised, with a consequent restriction on their ability and willingness to provide free information.

Trade Associations, while obviously anxious to promote their members' activities, are also restricted in the information they can provide. Few have libraries, most can provide a restricted amount of free information, but access to latest research is frequently restricted to members, and free technical support rare.

Institutions

(see also specialist listings below; for comprehensive listings visit the links on the ICE website).

American Society of Civil Engineers (ASCE) (www.asce.org). 1801 Alexander Bell Drive, Reston, VA 20191 Tel: + 800 548 2723. Founded in 1852, ASCE is the world's largest civil engineering learned society, publishing a wide range of journals, conference papers, and increasingly, standards. Their Civil Engineering Database (CEDB) provides bibliographic access to all ASCE publications since 1975. Online versions of their journals are available on subscription/pay per view via the American Institute of Physics.

Association of Consulting Engineers (www.acenet.co.uk). The leading trade association in the UK for consulting engineers, producing standard forms and scales of fees for consulting engineer's services and, work with ICE and the contractors to develop conditions of contract.

Association for Planning Supervisors (www.aps.org.uk).

Association for Project Management (www.apmgroup.co.uk).

Canadian Society for Civil Engineering (CSCE) (www.csce.ca). The CSCE site includes a brief introduction on civil engineering history. Their learned journal *Canadian journal of civil engineering* is published by the National Research Council of Canada.

Chartered Institution of Wastes Management (CIWM) (www.ciwm.co.uk).

Civil Engineering Contractors Association (www.ceca.co.uk) was established in November 1996 to represent the interests of civil engineering contractors registered in the UK.

Construction Federation, formerly Building Employers Federation (www.thecc.org.uk).

Construction Industry Council (www.cic.org.uk). An industry-wide body, given great impetus by the recommendations of the Latham and Egan reports.

County Surveyors Society (www.cssnet.org.uk).

European Council of Civil Engineers (www.eccenet.org). A pan-European inter-institutional forum and pressure group on EC issues. ECCE Secretariat, 3 Springfields, Amersham, Bucks, HP6 5JU, U.K.

Institution of Civil Engineers (www.ice.org.uk). One Great George Street, Westminster, London SW1P 3AA. Tel: 020 7222 7722; Fax: 020 7222 7500. Founded in 1818, the world's first professional engineering institution and the model for similar bodies worldwide. With an international membership and structure, it organises events all over the world. Technical enquiries are answered by the Library, but other departments deal with education, training and professional qualifications, etc.

Institution of Engineers and Shipbuilders in Scotland (www.iesis.org). Clydeport, 16 Robertson Street, Glasgow G2 8DS. Tel: 0141 248 3721; Fax: 0141 221 2698. Organise meetings and publish annual Transactions.

Institution of Engineers, Australia (www.ieaust.org.au). Publish a weekly journal, civil engineering transactions, and a number of specialist conferences.

Institution of Engineers, Ireland (www.iei.ie). Publish a monthly journal, transactions and organise meetings.

Institution of Engineers, Malaysia (www.jaring.my/iem/). Publish a monthly journal, transactions and organise meetings.

Institution of Professional Engineers, New Zealand (www.ipenz.org. nz/ipenz/). Publish a monthly journal, transactions and organise meetings.

International Federation of Municipal Engineers (www.ifme-fiim.org). Organise international conferences between member societies.

Japan Society of Civil Engineers (www.jsce.or.jp/e/). The most important civil engineering society outside the English speaking world. Responsible for a large number of publications, increasingly in English, including important seismic codes.

National Joint Utilities Group (NJUG) (www.njug.org.uk). UK trade grouping for the Utilities in street works.

Society of Construction Law (www.scl.org.uk).

South African Institution of Civil Engineers (www.civils.org.za). Publish journals and organise meetings.

Verein Deutscher Ingenieure (Association of German Engineers) (www.vdi. de/vdi/ie4x.php). The VDI organise conferences and meetings.

Universities and research

The Internet provides the best route into university information; there are two well established directories.

Commonwealth universities yearbook. London: Association of Commonwealth Universities.

World of learning. London: Europa (i.e., Taylor & Francis). (www. worldoflearning.com).

Leading research bodies

Civieltechnisch Centrum Uitvoering Research en Regelgeving (CUR) (www. bouwweb.nl/CUR/home.html). Responsible for a number of design manuals, now available in English.

Civil Engineering Research Foundation (CERF) (www.cerf.org). CERF was established by the ASCE to foster civil engineering research.

Construction Industry Research and Information Association (CIRIA) (www.ciria.org.uk). 6 Storey's Gate, London SW1P 3AU. Tel: 020 7222 8891; Fax: 020 7222 1708. Despite its title, CIRIA is primarily a research organisation with a major publishing programme.

Ecole Nationale des Ponts et Chaussées (www.enpc.fr/eng/sommaire.html). 28 rue des Saint-Pères, 75007 Paris, France. Tel: +33 1 42 60 34 13 (see also Libraries below).

Laboratoire Centrale des Ponts et Chaussées (www.lcpc.inrets.fr).

SKAT – Swiss Centre for Development Co-operation in Technology and Management (www.skat.ch).

United States Corps of Engineers (www.usace.army.mil). The ASCE is publishing a growing number of the Corps' Engineering Manuals. Subsidiary sites include the Cold Regions Engineering Laboratory (www.crrel.usace.army.mil).

▶ MAJOR LIBRARY RESOURCES

Most civil engineers use information published within the previous 10–15 years, an increasing proportion of which is available electronically. Those with direct access to major university libraries are particularly able to benefit from this trend as they have been able to exploit consortium deals with major publishers. Excepting universities, national libraries are the most obvious repository for any country's published literature. However, much engineering literature is 'grey literature' which copyright libraries have never been particularly successful in acquiring. For that reason, and because leading engineers and researchers are able to exploit international contacts, the most important library collections are in fact specialist libraries, rarely comprehensive, overlapping and complementing each other. The great collections date back around 200 years and are major historical resources as well as continuing to serve practising engineers today. Most, but not all, are attached to an academic institution.

For professional librarians in the UK one can contact The Construction Industry Information Group (CIIG), 26 Store Street, London WC1E 7BT. Tel: 020 7637 1022; Fax: 020 7580 9641. Membership includes institution, academic, commercial and company libraries. It organises meetings and produces a newsletter.

Delft University of Technology, Delft (www.tudelft.nl/home.html). The Library building is itself a fascinating example of construction.

Ecole Nationale des Ponts et Chaussées. Founded in 1747, perhaps the most comprehensive library in the field. The Library is now in Cité Descartes: 6 et 8 avenue Blaise Pascal, Cité Descartes, Champs-sur-Marne, 77455 Marne-la-Vallée cedex 2 Tel: 33 (0)1 64 15 30 00 – 33 (0)1 64 15 30 00

Eidgenössischen Technischen Hochschule (ETH) Zürich. (www.ethbib. ethz.ch/index_e.html) Rämistrasse 101, CH-8092 Zurich, Switzerland. Tel: +411 632 21 35; Fax: +411 632 10 87. The ETH-Bibliothek is the largest library in Switzerland and the main library of the Swiss Federal Institute of Technology. Special emphasis is given to electronic resources accessible to the faculty, staff and students at ETH-Zurich.

La Escuela Técnica Superior de Ingenieros de Caminos, Canales y Puertos de Madrid. (www.upm.es/centros/etsiccp.html). Founded 1802 on the model of the Ecole des Ponts et Chaussees.

Imperial College of Science, Technology and Medicine, London (www.imperial.ac.uk/library/). Collections include the Science Museum Library, and the Department of Civil Engineering Library, with a number of special, historical collections attached.

St Petersburg State Transport Communications University (www.ofko.spb.ru/english/liizt_eng.htm). Formerly the Institute of Railway Engineers, St Petersburg, founded 1809. Houses probably the world's largest civil engineering collection.

Institution of Civil Engineers, London. library@ice.org.uk Library founded in 1819, c.100,000 titles. International in its coverage, with books dating back to the 15th century.

Kungl Tekniska Högskolan Stockholm (www.kth.se/eng/). One of the leading collections in Scandinavia.

Linda Hall Library (www.lhl.lib.mo.us). Provides library services for ASCE members whose collection it houses.

The Mitchell Library, Glasgow (www.glasgowlibraries.org). North Street, Glasgow G3 7DN. Arguably the best engineering collections of any public library in the UK.

Norwegian Geotechnical Institute, Oslo (www.ngi.no). Best known for housing the Terzaghi collection. This is probably the world's leading geotechnical library.

Technical University, Berlin (www.ub.tu-berlin.de). Founded 1799, the oldest academic collection in the field in Germany.

Technical University, Hannover (www.tib.uni-hannover.de./kooperationspartner/). Although there were a number of technical universities established in modern Germany in the nineteenth century, which all have important collections today, TIB is the central specialist library in Germany for Technology/Engineering and associated sciences.

University of Texas at Austin (www.lib.utexas.edu/engin/). Possibly the largest engineering Library in the USA; the Library is distinguished by the high quality of its user documentation.

▶ STANDARDS AND REGULATIONS

British Standards Institution (BSI) (www.bsi.org.uk/index.xalter). 389 Chiswick High Road, London W4 4AL. Tel: 020 8996 9000; Fax: 020 8996 7400. BSI, initially established by the ICE, was the first national standards body in the world, and ICE still are heavily involved.

Eurocodes (www.eurocodes.co.uk). The ICE have developed a website for all those interested in the development of Eurocodes, which was launched in March 2003.

Health and Safety Executive (www.hse.gov.uk). Broad Lane, Sheffield S3 7HQ. Tel: 0114 892 345; Fax: 0114 892 333.

International Conference of Building Officials (ICBO) (www.icbo.org). ICBO is best known for the *Uniform Building Code* whose seismic provisions are widely referenced. This is being replaced by the *International Building Code*.

▶ ABSTRACTING AND INDEXING SERVICES

(See Chapter 9 and specialisms below for details)

American Society of Civil Engineers (ASCE): *Civil Engineering Database* (CEBD) (www.pubs.asce.org/cedbsrch.html). Access to bibliographic and abstracted records published by the American Society of Civil Engineers from January 1973 to date.

Aqualine (Cambridge Scientific Abstracts).

Chemical Abstracts (www.info.cas.org/casdb.html). Although regarded as the prime information source for chemists, it provides perhaps the most comprehensive source of information on materials such as cements.

Civil Engineering Abstracts (Cambridge Scientific Abstracts). Selective indexing of over 3,000 journal titles, many largely irrelevant to practising civil engineers.

Cold Regions Bibliography (lcweb.loc.gov/rr/scitech/coldregions/welcome.html).

Ei Engineering Index (www.ei.org/eivillage/). Engineering index has its origins in the 1880s when it was largely confined to indexing US engineering literature. Although this bias remains it is the single most important source of bibliographic information in the world's engineering literature.

ICE Abstracts (of foreign engineering literature) 1875–1940 (last published as railway engineering abstracts in 1962).

ICONDA – International Construction Database (1974-) (Fraunhofer-Gesellschaft Informationzentrum Raum und Bau (IRB)). Excellent on European coverage but poor on British coverage since *c.*1990 due to lack of input. Available on CD-ROM from SilverPlatter.

International Civil Engineering Abstracts (Emerald) (www.leporello.emeraldinsight.com/vl=4613822/cl=36/nw=1/rpsv/abstracts/icea/about.htm). This international civil engineering database, formerly available on CD-ROM, currently indexes 150 leading civil engineering titles, covering articles from 1972 to the present in its printed form. The Internet version covers 1976–

Transport CD (www.oecd.org/pdf/M00000000/M00000678.pdf). Developed as part of the *International Road Research Database (IRRD)* under the auspices of OECD. Marketed by Silver platter.
Transportation Research Board (TRB). *TRIS Online* (www.ntl.bts.gov/tris).
WELDASEARCH (Cambridge Scientific Abstracts). Produced by TWI – The Welding Institute, an excellent specialist source.

▶ DICTIONARIES, HANDBOOKS AND DIRECTORIES

Handbooks and Directories

EMAP publishes a range of annual directories and yearbooks which cover most aspects of construction engineering. The following are a selection: *Concrete Yearbook, Ground Engineering Yearbook, NCE Road Construction & Traffic Directory, Steel Construction Yearbook, Underground Directory, Waste, Recycling and Environmental Directory, Water Directory.*

Berlow, L. H., 1998. *The reference guide to famous engineering landmarks of the world.* Chicago: Fitzroy Dearborn.

Blake, L. S., 1994. *Civil Engineers Reference Book,* 4th ed. London: Butterworth.

Chen, W. F., 1995. The Civil Engineering Handbook. Boca Raton: CRC.

Construction Statistics Annual. London: TSO.

Davis, J., and Lambert, R., 2002. *Engineering in Emergencies.* 2nd ed. London: ITDG.

Merritt, F. S., *et al.,* 1995 *Standard Handbook for Civil Engineers.* 4th ed. New York: McGraw-Hill.

Stephens, J. H., 1976. *Guinness book of structures.* Enfield: Guinness Superlatives.

Dictionaries

Bucksch, H., [various]. *Dictionary of Civil Engineering and Construction Machinery and Equipment.* Wiesbaden: Bauverlag, various editions, (German/English) and (French/English).

Forbes, J. B., 1988. *Dictionary of Architecture and Construction.* Paris: Lavoisier. (English/French).

Gutierrez, M. F., 1991. *Elsevier Dictionary of Civil Engineering.* Amsterdam: Elsevier. (English, German, Spanish, French). Digital format available.

Montague, D.,1996. *Dictionary of Building and Civil Engineering.* London: Spon. (English/French).

Routledge, 1986. *Arabic Dictionary of Civil Engineering.* London: Routledge.

Routledge, 1997. *German Dictionary of Construction.* London: Routledge, 1997. (English/German).

Scott, J. S., 1991. *Penguin Dictionary of Civil Engineering*. 4th ed. London: Penguin.

Webster, L. F., 1997. *The Wiley Dictionary of Civil Engineering and Construction: English-Spanish/Spanish-English*. New York: Wiley.

► MONOGRAPHS

In print catalogues are available from: TSO (The Stationery Office), British Standards Institution, Building Research Establishment, CIRIA, professional institutions (e.g., ICE/TTL, IStructE,), research institutes and trade associations (e.g., BCA, SCI, TRADA, BDA), Health and Safety Executive, commercial publishers (e.g., Blackwell, Butterworths, Longman, Spon, Wiley, etc.). Most are readily accessible on the Internet. The Government drive to make all publications available electronically is significant in this regard.

► OTHER RESOURCES

Civil Engineering-Virtual Library (www.ce.gatech.edu/WWW-CE/home. html). Based at Georgia Tech, acts as a portal to a range of sites and information.

Construction Best Practice Programme (www.cbpp.org.uk). The Construction Best Practice Programme provides support to individuals, companies, organisations and supply chains in the construction industry seeking to improve the way they do business.

The Disaster Research Center (DRC) (www.udel.edu/DRC/homepage.htm). This centre, at the University of Delaware, conducts research on preparations for, response to, and recovery from natural and technological disasters and other community-wide crises. The site includes a publications list.

Electronic journal in civil engineering (www.civag.unimelb.edu.au/ejse/).

Institution of Civil Engineers. Virtual Library, etc. (www.iceknowledge. com). Full text of ICE proceedings etc. 1836–date.

Munich Reinsurance Group (www.munichre.com). A mine of information about risk, insurance and disasters, with the full text of many downloadable publications

NBS (www.nbsservices.org.uk). The main purpose is to write, revise and publish the National Building Specification. The NBS was first launched in 1973. In 1988, the documents were completely revised to take account of the Common Arrangement of Work Sections, part of the CPI (Co-ordinated Project Information) initiative.

Rethinking construction (www.rethinkingconstruction.org/rc/). Contains the full text of the Egan report on rethinking construction.

Technical Indexes Limited (TI) mktg@techindex.co.uk. Willoughby Road, Bracknell, Berkshire RG12 8DW. Tel: 01344 426311; Fax: 01344 424971. Developing from a microfilm based library and product information service, TI is now arguably the most important UK provider of civil engineering documentation. Rapidoc is the document supply division. They act as authorised distributors for BSI, ITU, ETSU, TSO, EIA and many other publishers.

The RIBA.ti Construction Information Service is produced jointly with RIBA Enterprises Ltd. Its target audience includes civil and structural engineers. The service can be delivered online or on CD-ROM. Although TI is aimed at civil engineers, there are certain important categories of documentation which are not available, such as ICE publications. On the other hand, TI agreements with Network Rail and the Highways Agency mean a lot of key data is available from a single source. Network Rail Company Standards are a required source of information for any organisation carrying out work in the railway environment. They are available on CD-ROM, as hard copy, and at www.rgsonline.co.uk/main.html.

▶ CIVIL ENGINEERING MATERIALS

Civil engineers' use of materials is overwhelmingly concerned with the use of concrete and mild steel, with asphalt/bitumen thrown in for highway engineers. With the properties of these materials specified for civil engineering uses in standards, the need for civil engineers to concern themselves with materials science on a daily basis might be considered limited, but in fact higher performance materials are frequently sought for specialist applications, and to reduce the mass or cost of structures. Moreover, 'new' materials such as plastics have gained an increasingly important role in reinforced materials, ground strengthening through geotextiles, and membrane technology in waste containment and treatment. More traditional materials such as timber and glass have enjoyed something of a revival, with jointing and joining methods facilitating timber construction, while the adventurous use of glass by architects has been facilitated by a better understanding of the structural properties among engineers. Materials like cast iron are generally associated with older structures like mill buildings, but continue to have specialist uses, while a newer metal like aluminium which enjoyed a minor vogue in the 1950s continues to be important where lightness and strength are required.

Engineering structures have a long design life – decades if not centuries, and so the durability of materials, and their decay and corrosion mechanisms are ultimately as important as their strength.

While standards and specifications for most materials are produced by the leading national standard organisations, when new developments take place engineers have to turn to industry standards and manufacturers' specifications for guidance until the 'official' standards have caught up. The problem in seeking such information is that in many fields such specialist organisations proliferate – more than sixty are involved in concrete in the UK alone. The Internet and the concept of the 'one-stop-shop' can help, but what follows is intended to provide guidance on the most important such organisations and sources.

General sources

American Society for Testing and Materials (ASTM) (www.astm.org). Organised in 1898, ASTM is probably the most important body for materials standards aside from national standards bodies. It publishes standard test methods, specifications, and guides to terminology, as well as state of the art conferences and specialist journals.

Addleson, L., and Rice, C., 1991. *Performance of Materials in Buildings: A Study of the Principles and Agencies of Change.* Butterworth-Heinemann.
Doran, D. K., 1992. *Construction Materials Reference Book.* Butterworth-Heinemann.

Concrete

While concentrating on UK and other English Language sources, other countries, notably Germany and Japan, have a number of active societies in this area, and an extensive literature.

American Concrete Institute (ACI) (www.aci-int.org). The world's leading learned society for concrete construction, publishing in English and Spanish. The *ACI Manual of Concrete Practice* (MCP) includes all the ACI standards, specifications, recommendations, and guides used for concrete structures (available on CD-ROM).

British Cement Association (BCA) (www.bca.org.uk). Riverside House, 4 Meadows Business Park, Station Approach, Blackwater, Camberley GU17 9AB. Tel: 01276 607140; Fax: 01276 607141. The British Cement Association, formerly the Cement and Concrete Association, has published a large number and range of *Technical reports, Interim technical notes,* etc, and audio visual material. Their database *Concquest,* an online service for publications relating to concrete design and construction from the British Cement Association, is being redeveloped with BRE and the Concrete Society as Concrete Information Ltd (www.concreteinfo.org).

Concrete Society (www.concrete.org.uk). Riverside House, 4 Meadows Business Park, Station Approach, Blackwater, Camberley GU17 9AB.

Tel: 01276 607140; Fax: 01276 607141. Publishes many technical reports, guides and digests. Now taking the lead with BCA in developing Concrete information, a one-stop-shop for UK concrete information.

Fédération Internationale de Beton (FIB) (International Concrete Federation) (fib.epfl.ch). An international organisation formed by the merger of FIP and CEB for the development of structural concrete; it publishes via Thomas Telford the journal *Structural concrete*, many recommendations, and state-of-the-art reports, on both reinforced and prestressed concrete.

Beton kalender (annual) Berlin: Ernst. Provides useful summaries of german (DIN) standards. Available electronically.

Concrete year book (www.nceplus.co.uk/cyb/?ChannelID=38).

ICE Bibliography on Prestressed Concrete 1920–1957.

Neville, A. M., 1995. *Properties of Concrete*. 4th ed. London: Prentice Hall, 1995.

Reynolds, C. E., and Steedman, J. C., 1988. *Reinforced Concrete Designers Handbook*. 10th ed. London: Spon. Despite criticism of its age, this handbook is a useful compendium of information on subjects not readily found elsewhere, e.g. weights of various materials.

Steel

American Institute of Steel Construction (AISC) (www.aisc.org). Standards activities and publications include: *Manual of Steel Construction*, Specifications and Codes. They publish *Engineering Journal* and *Modern Steel Construction*.

American Iron and Steel Institute (AISI) (www.steel.org). Produce standards.

American Welding Society (AWS) (www.aws.org). The AWS site includes a buyer's guide and research supplements to the *Welding Journal*.

British Constructional Steelwork Association Ltd (BCSA), 4 Whitehall Court, London SW1A 2ES. Tel: 020 7839 8566; Fax: 020 7976 1634. Produces manuals and handles the sales of publications of other organisations such as: AISC, European Convention for Constructional Steelwork (ECCS).

Concrete Reinforcing Steel Institute (CRSI) (www.crsi.org). CRSI publish a *Design Handbook* and *Manual of Standard Practice* which relate to ACI Standards. Their site includes several full-text publications.

Corus (www.corusconstruction.com). The major British producer of structural steel; their website contains technical documents on piling, etc. Technical advice on 01724 405060

Steel Construction Institute (SCI) (www.steel-sci.org). Silwood Park, Ascot, Berkshire SL5 7QN. Tel: 01344 23345; Fax: 01344 22944. A membership based research institute which produces design guides, commentaries on codes of practice and manuals relating to the use of structural steel. The *Steel Designers Manual,* 6th ed. was published by Blackwell Scientific in 2003.

TWI (The Welding Institute) (www.twi.co.uk). Granta Park, Great Abington, Cambridge CB1 6AL. Tel: 01223 891162; Fax: 01223 892588.

Timber

In the UK, TRADA are the leading source although both the BRE and CIRIA also publish much useful information on timber. Many other countries have institutes equivalent to TRADA.

American Institute of Timber Construction (www.aitc-glulam.org). Produce a manual and other key publications on US practice.

Timber Research & Development Association (TRADA) (www.trada. co.uk). Stocking Lane, Hughenden Valley, High Wycombe, Buckinghamshire HP14 4ND. Tel: 01494 563091; Fax: 01494 565487.

Baird, J. A., and Ozelton, E. C., 2002. *Timber Designers Manual.* 3rd ed. Oxford: Blackwell.

Centrum Holst, 1995. *Timber Engineering: STEP 1* and *STEP 2.* B J Almere.

▶ OTHER MATERIALS

Adhesives and Sealants

British Adhesives and Sealants Association, 33 Fellowes Way, Stevenage, Hertfordshire SG2 8BW. Tel: 01438 358514; Fax: 01438 742565.

Institution of Structural Engineers, 1999. *Guide to the Structural Use of Adhesives.* London: IStructE.

Aluminium

Aluminum Association (AAI) (www.aluminum.org). The Aluminum Association is a US trade association. It publishes Aluminum Standards.

Aluminum Federation (www.alfed.org.uk). The UK equivalent.

Corrosion

Shreir, L. L., *et al.*, 1994. *Corrosion*. 3rd ed., 2 vols. Oxford: Butterworth.

Glass

Dutton, H., and Rice, P., 1995. *Structural Glass*. 2nd ed. London: Spon.
Amstock, J. S., 1997. *Handbook of Glass in Construction*. New York: McGraw-Hill.
Institution of Structural Engineers, 1999. *Structural Use of Glass in Buildings*. London: IStructE.
Schittich, C., 1999, *Glass Construction Manual*. Wiesbaden: Birkhauser.

Iron

British Cast Iron Research Association (BCIRA), Cast Metals Technology Centre, Alvechurch, Birmingham B48 7QB. Tel: 01527 66414; Fax: 01527 585070.

Angus, H.T., 1976. Cast iron: physical and engineering properties. 2nd ed. London: Butterworth.

Masonry

The term 'masonry' includes natural stone, and bricks; particularly in the US it is sometimes used to describe mass concrete (without reinforcement).

Brick Development Association (BDA) (www.brick.org.uk). Woodside House, Winkfield, Windsor, Berkshire SL4 2DX. Tel: 01344 885651; Fax: 01344 890129. The BDA publishes design guides, notes and technical information papers.

British Masonry Society, c/o CERAM Research (see below). This society publishes a journal and organises regular conferences.

CERAM Research (formerly British Ceramic Research Limited) (www.ceram.co.uk). Queens Road, Penkhull, Stoke-on-Trent ST4 7LQ. Tel: 01782 45431; Fax: 01782 412331. CERAM has published research papers and Special Publications, and specifications such as the *Model specification for clay and calcium silicate structural brickwork*.

Stone Federation of Great Britain (www.stone-federationgb.org.uk). 82 New Cavendish Street, London W1M 8AD. Tel: 020 7580 5588; Fax: 020 7631 3872.

Paint and coatings

British Coatings Federation Limited (www.coatings.org.uk). James House, Bridge Street, Leatherhead, Surrey KT22 7EP. Tel: 01372 360660; Fax: 01372 376069.

Paint Research Association (www.pra.org.uk). 8 Waldegrave Road, Teddington, Middlesex TW11 8LD. Tel: 020 8977 4427; Fax: 020 8943 4705.

Plastics

Snook, S., 1994. *Engineering Plastics and Elastomers: A Design Guide*. London: Institute of Materials.

ASCE, 1985. *Structural Plastics Selection Manual*. New York: ASCE.

ASCE, 1984. *Structural Plastics Design Manual*. New York: ASCE.

▶ ENVIRONMENTAL ENGINEERING

'The environment' has for so long now been the flavour of the month that the term has almost become devoid of meaning, as it has been adopted by successive governments and pressure groups. In the US, environmental engineering is generally seen as embracing all aspects of public health engineering, particularly sewage. Here the environment is treated in the broadest sense, embracing planning considerations and pollution control, but not sewerage systems which are dealt with under water engineering.

Beim, H. J., et al., 1998. *Rapid Guide to Hazardous Air Pollutants*. New York: Van Nostrand Reinhold. Based on the US Clean Air Act.

Cunningham, W. P., et al., 1998. *Environmental Encyclopedia*. Detroit: Gale. Covers subjects as varied as defoliation, dune erosion, ISO 14000, and the environmental effects of war.

Lewis, R. J., 1996. *Sax's Dangerous Properties of Industrial Materials*. New York: Van Nostrand Reinhold. Digital format available.

Tolley's (Garner's) environmental law. London: Butterworths. (available in loose leaf/hard copy and on CD-ROM).

Liu, D. H. F., and Liptak, B. G., 1997. *Environmental Engineers' Handbook*. Boca Raton, FL: Lewis.

Viguri, A., 1999. *Comparative Environmental Laws*. Southampton, MA: WIT Press, 1999. Compares European environmental protection laws with those in the United States and Latin America.

Bioengineering (see also Chapter 15)

Biotechnical techniques have been particularly successfully applied to slope stabilisation.

Benyus, J. M., 1997. *Biomimicry: Innovation Inspired by Nature.* New York: William Morrow & Co. Inc.

Hong Kong. Geotechnical Engineering Office, 2000. *Technical Guidelines on Landscape Treatment and Bioengineering for Man-made Slopes and Retaining Walls.* Kowloon: GEO Civil Engineering Department.

International Navigation Association (PIANC), 2002. *Recreational Navigation and Nature.* Brussels: PIANC.

Morgan, R. P. C., and Rickson, R. J., 1995. *Slope Stabilisation and Erosion Control: A Bioengineering Approach.* London: E & FN Spon.

Schiechtl, H. M., and Stern, R., 1996. *Ground Bioengineering Techniques for Slope Protection and Erosion Control.* Oxford: Blackwell Science.

Schiechtl, H. M., and Stern, R., 1997. *Water Bioengineering Techniques for Watercourse Bank and Shoreline Protection.* Oxford: Blackwell Science.

Environmental impact assessment

Bregman, J. I.,1999. *Environmental Impact Statements.* Boca Raton, FL: Lewis. Useful for understanding the development of environmental impact statements in the USA.

DETR, 2000. *Environmental Impact Assessment: A Guide to Procedures.* London: DETR.

Rogers, M., 2001. *Engineering Project Appraisal.* Oxford: Blackwell Scientific.

Sustainability

CIRIA, 2001. *Sustainable Construction: Company Indicators.* C563.

ICE, 1996. *Sustainability and Acceptability in Infrastructure Development.* London: Thomas Telford Limited.

Nienhuis, P. H., *et al.*, eds., 1998. *New Concepts for Sustainable Management of River Basins.* Leiden: Backhuys Publishers.

Ove Arup and Partners, 1996. *Green Construction Handbook.* Bristol: J T Design Build Limited.

▶ GEOTECHNICAL ENGINEERING

Geotechnical engineering is a relatively young branch of civil engineering, its development largely taking place since the Second World War, building on the work of Karl Terzaghi in particular. Concerned with the engineering behaviour of soils and rocks, it impacts on foundation design, slope stability, pavements and permanent way design. The behaviour of ground under earthquake loads has almost become an academic discipline in its own right. Many countries have developed national geotechnical research facilities; in the UK this was done at BRE. Academic departments in many universities have supplemented these.

Today many countries have their own geotechnical society; these publish their own journals and organise conferences, although the international and regional conferences of the International Society for Soil Mechanics and Geotechnical Engineering (ISSMGE), are the chief source for state-of-the-art developments. The most comprehensive index of the literature is *Geotechnical abstracts*, dating back to the 1960s and now available on CD-ROM – this is difficult to use and there is no facility for geographical searches. For that reason other sources such as Engineering Index or TRIS may be preferred despite their more limited coverage. The online catalogue of the Swedish Geotechnical Institute is easy to use and answers many queries.

Specialist literature is often only to be found where active research is carried out. In the UK the Civil Engineering Department at Imperial College is one, but by no means the only example.

Institutions

There are a number of major international societies in this field catering for specialist interests, most with national groups, such as the British Geotechnical Association at ICE. These International societies organise major international conferences as well as regional and specialist events. Their involvement is normally an indication of the status of the event.

Association of Engineering Geologists (AEG) (www.aeg.tamu.edu). The US society for engineering geologists, publishing a journal.
Association of Geotechnical and Geoenvironmental Specialists (www.ags.org.uk).
British Geological Survey (www.bgs.ac.uk). Keeps borehole records for the UK as well as producing geological maps and memoirs.
Deep Foundations Institute (Englewood Cliffs USA) (www.dfi.org). Organise regular conferences.
Federation of Piling Specialists (www.fps.org.uk).
Geological Society of London (www.geolsoc.org.uk). Home to an excellent library and hosts the UK Engineering Geology Group.
International Association for Engineering Geology and the Environment (IAEG) (www-cgi.ensmp.fr/iaeg/)
International Geosynthetics Society (www.igs.rmc.ca).

ISRM – International Society for Rock Mechanics (www-ext.lnec.pt/ISRM/).

International Society for Soil Mechanics and Geotechnical Engineering (ISSMGE) (www.issmge.org).

Seismological Society of America (SSA) (www.seismosoc.org). The SSA publishes the *Bulletin of the Seismological Society of America* (BSSA), *Seismological letters* etc. The website provides an index for BSSA.

Abstracts and bibliographies

Geotechnical Abstracts 1970–1993; CD ROM available 1989–2001 (Research Resources Inc) (www.geotechnical-abstracts.com).

ICE Bibliography on Soil Mechanics 1920–1959.

KWIK Index of Rock Mechanics Literature, 3 vols. Pergamon.

Schriftung uber Bodenmechanik, 3 vols (Forschungs-Arbeiten aus dem Strassenwesen).

Other sources

Bell, F. G., 1997. *Ground Engineers Reference Book*. London: Butterworth

Electronic journal in geotechnical engineering (www.geotech.civen.okstate.edu/ejge/index.htm).

Geotechnical Engineering – Virtual Library (www.ejge.com/GVL/).

Geotechnical engineering handbook. 3 vols. Berlin: Ernst, 2003.

Ground engineering year book (www.nceplus.co.uk/ground/?ChannelID=47) Hong Kong Geotechnical Central Office (www.ced.gov.hk/eng).

International Society for Soil Mechanics and Foundation Engineering, 1981. *Technical terms, symbols and definitions in English, French, German, Italian, Portuguese, Spanish and Swedish used in soil mechanics and foundation engineering*. Toronto: ISSMFE.

Van der Tuin, J. D., 1997. *Elsevier's Dictionary of Soil Mechanics and Geotechnical Engineering*. New York: Elsevier. (English, French, Spanish, Dutch, and German).

Contaminated land

The Environment Agency's website provides important guidance on contaminated and derelict land, with many CLR reports available to download (www.environment-agency.gov.uk/subjects/landquality/).

Cairney, T., 1995. *The Reuse of Contaminated Land*. Chichester: Wiley.

Contaminated Land (www.contaminatedland.co.uk). Excellent website.

Fleming, G., ed., 1995. *Recycling Contaminated Land*. London: TTL.

GLR, 1993. *Geotechnics of Land Remediation*. 2nd ed. Berlin: Ernst.

SDU, 1995. *Leidraad bodembescherming*, 2 vols. The Hague: SDU. Contains widely quoted standards.

Earthquakes and seismology

(see also Structures and Buildings below).

Abstract Journal in Earthquake Engineering 1971–1997.

National Information Services for Earthquake Engineering (NISEE) (www. nisee.ce.berkeley.edu). NISEE is located at the Pacific Earthquake Engineering Research (PEER) Center and provides access to the *Earthquake Engineering Abstracts* database. The site contains full-text papers.

Quakeline (www.mceer.buffalo.edu/utilities/quakeline.asp). Easy to use online database.

Soil Liquefaction Web Site (www.ce.washington.edu/~liquefaction/html/ main.html).

Surfing the Internet for Earthquake Data (www.geophys.washington.edu/ seismosurfing.html).

Virtual Earthquake (www.vcourseware2.calstatela.edu/VirtualEarthquake/ VQuakeIntro.html). An interactive computer program indicating how an earthquake epicentre is located and how the Richter magnitude of an earthquake is determined.

Earthworks

CIRIA, 2001. *Infrastructure Embankments – Condition, Appraisal and Remedial Treatment.* C550. London: CIRIA.

Nichols, H. L., and Day, D. A., 1996. *Moving the Earth.* 4th ed. New York: McGraw-Hill.

Puller, M., 1996. *Deep Excavations.* London: Thomas Telford Limited.

Trenter, N. A., 2001. *Earthworks: A Guide.* London: Thomas Telford Limited.

Engineering geology

Rose, E. B. F., and Nathaniel, C. P., 2002. *Geology and warfare.* London: Geological Society.

US Bureau of Reclamation, 1998. *Engineering Geology Field Manual.* 2 vols., Washington, DC: US Department of the Interior.

Foundations

Curtins, W. G., 1994. *Structural Foundations Designers' Manual.* Oxford: Blackwell Scientific.

Fleming, W. G. K., *et al.*, 1992. *Piling Engineering.* Glasgow: Blackie.

Freeman, T. J., *et al.*, 2002. *Has Your House Got Cracks?* 2nd ed. London: Thomas Telford Limited for ICE and BRE.

Tomlinson, M. J., 2001. *Foundation design and Construction.* 7th ed. Harlow: Prentice Hall.

Geosynthetics and geotextiles

International Geosynthetics Society (www.geosyntheticssociety.org). Produce a *Geosynthetics Bibliography* as well as conferences, etc.

Shukka, S. K., 2002. *Geosynthetics and their applications.* London: TTL.

Numerical modelling

NUMOG conferences. Contact *GNPande@swan.ac.uk*

Tunnels and tunnelling

British Tunnelling Society. Based at ICE.
The Institute of Materials, Minerals and Mining (IOM^3) (www. iom3.org). Created from the merger of The Institute of Materials (IOM) and The Institution of Mining and Metallurgy (IMM); the former IMM regularly organised international tunnelling conferences, and their publications and databases are of great relevance particularly to tunnelling in hard ground.
International Tunnelling Association (ITA) (www.ita-aites.org). Publish *Tribune*, and recommendations via the *International journal of tunnelling and underground space technology.*
United Kingdom Society for Trenchless Technology (www.ukstt. org.uk). Based at ICE.

Megaw, T. M., and Bartlett, J. B., 1981–1982. *Tunnels: planning, design and construction* Chichester: Ellis Horwood.
Muir-Wood, A. M., 2000. *Tunnelling: management by design.* London: E & F N Spon.
Stack, B., 1995. *Encyclopaedia of tunnelling, mining and drilling equipment.* 3 vols. Hobart, Australia: Muden Publishing.

▶ MARITIME ENGINEERING

The sea probably produces the greatest regular challenge for the civil engineer, requiring a knowledge of tides, waves and the wind. To protect shipping, breakwaters of various forms have been developed, and offshore structures have been designed for ever greater depths of water. Design guidance is often more problematic and engineering decisions more difficult than in other areas.

Institutions

The Institute of Marine Engineering, Science and Technology (IMarEST) (www.imarest.org). An international professional membership body and learned society for all marine professionals. Their database and library have excellent coverage of material relating to offshore structures.

International Navigation Association (PIANC) (www.pianc-aipcn.org). With its origins in the nineteenth century, PIANC hold major conferences and produce guidelines relating to both ocean and inland navigation, on topics such as locks, dredging etc. The UK committee are based at ICE. General Secretariat, PIANC, Graaf de Ferraris building – 11th floor, Blvd. du Roi Albert II, 20 – Box 3, B-1000 Brussels (Belgium) Tel: +32 2 553 71 60, Fax: +32 2 553 71 55.

International Society of Offshore and Polar Engineers (ISOPE) (www.isope.org). ISOPE organise conferences as well as publishing a journal. ISOPE, P.O. Box 189, Cupertino, California 95015-0189, USA Tel: + 1–408–980–1784; Fax: + 1–408–980–1787.

Offshore Engineering Society (OES) (www.oes.org.uk). Based at ICE.

Research organisations

British Maritime Technology (www.bmt.org). BMT comprise a number of divisions; the work of BMT Fluid Mechanics is most relevant to civil engineers.

Det Norske Veritas (www.dnv.com). DNV are involved in research into offshore structures as part of their regulatory and registering activities, and as producers of some of the most widely referenced standards for marine structures.

Proudman Oceanographic Laboratory (www.pol.ac.uk). UK centre for surveying and research in oceanography.

United Kingdom Hydrographic Office (www.ukho.gov.uk). Based in Taunton, the UKHO produce admiralty charts, pilots and tide tables.

United Nations Conference on Trade and Development (UNCTAD) (www.unctad.org). UNCTAD produce important guidelines for port management and development.

US Corps of Engineers Waterways Experiment Station (www.wes.army.mil). The Waterways Experiment Station (WES) is headquarters for the U.S. Army Engineer Research and Development Center (ERDC). A number of publications including the widely cited *Shore Protection Manual* can be downloaded from the site.

Bibliographies etc

BMT abstracts.
PIANC, *Rivers, Canals and Ports: bibliographic notes, 1885–1930*. 6 vols.

Other publications

BMT, 1986. *Global Wave Statistics*. Woking: Unwin, 1986.
PIANC, *Illustrated Technical Dictionary in Six Languages*. Brussels:
PIANC, various editions and parts
(French/German/English/Spanish/Italian/Dutch).
Offshore Research Focus. Latest information on UK offshore research.
Health and Safety Executive, 122A, Thorpe Road, Norwich, NR1
1RN. Fax: +44 (0)1603 828 055
International Conference on Coastal Engineering. Held every two years and
generally published by ASCE.

▶ DOCKS AND HARBOURS

Associations

International association of ports and harbors (www.iaphworldports.org).
Hold regular conferences and publish *Ports and Harbors*.
Port and Harbour Research Institute (Japan) (www.pari.go.jp/english/
30-kenky/english/html/etitle.htm). Publish technical reports and notes.

Publications

Abbott, M. B., and Price, W. A., 1994. *Coastal, Estuarial and Harbour Engineer's Reference
Book*. London: E & F N Spon.
Bruun, P., 1984–90. *Port Engineering*. 2 vols., 4th ed. Houston: Gulf Publishing.
Lloyd's List Ports of the World. London: Informa.

Dredging

Conferences are regularly organised by the World Organisation of Dredging
Associations, WODA (www.woda.org/congr.htm) and Central Dredging
Association (www.dredging.org). UK contact ICE.

Herbich, J.B., 2000. *Handbook of Dredging Engineering*. 2nd ed. New York: McGraw-Hill.

Lighthouses

IALA are the international body for navigation aids, with many of their publications downloadable (www.iala-aism.org/web/pages/presentation/cadrepresent.html).

Offshore structures

Offshore Mechanics and Arctic Engineering Conference (ASME) (www.ooae.org).
Offshore Technology Conference (OTC) (www.spe.org).
Gerwick, B. C., 2002. *Construction of Offshore Structures*. New York: Wiley.

► STRUCTURES AND BUILDINGS

Structural engineering is the discipline within civil engineering which seizes the imagination of the public and inspires youngsters to join the profession. It emerged as a discipline in the early twentieth century with the development of reinforced concrete and steel-framed structures, most spectacularly with the skyscrapers of Chicago and New York. While much of the work of the structural engineer is involved with more mundane questions relating to building regulations approval for domestic housing extensions, etc., it is the interface of structural engineers with modern architecture which understandably attracts media attention.

Since the nineteenth century, increasingly sophisticated methods of analysis have been developed to design structures, today dominated by computer programmes. Codes have changed to reflect these developments, and an increasing number of British structures are now based on Eurocodes.

The design of modern building structures is closely allied with the provision of building services, and the concept of 'intelligent buildings'.

Institutions

Association for Specialist Fire Protection (www.asfp.org.uk).
Chartered Institute of Building (CIOB) (www.ciob.org.uk). Englemere, Kings Ride, Ascot, Berkshire SL5 8BJ. Tel: 01344 23355; Fax: 01344 23467. Primarily aimed at construction managers, the Institute has an Information Centre, and publishes a journal and reports which cover technology, management and best practice in construction.
Construction Industry Computing Association (CICA) (www.cica.org.uk). Guildhall Place, Cambridge CB2 3QQ. Tel: 01223 311246;

Fax: 01223 62865. The CICA is a source of information and advice about the use of computers and software in construction.

Institution of Structural Engineers (IStructE) (www.istructe.org.uk). 11 Upper Belgrave Street, London SW1X 8BH. Tel: 020 7235 4535; Fax: 020 7235 4294. IStructE publishes *The Structural Engineer*, technical reports, symposia etc. The Library is an important specialist resource.

International Association for Bridge and Structural Engineering (IABSE), ETH-Hönggerberg, CH-8093, Zürich, Switzerland. Tel: +41 1 377 2647; Fax: +44 1 371 2131. IABSE organise conferences as well as publishing a journal and state-of-the-art reports.

International Council for Building Research Studies and Documentation (CIB), PO Box 1837, NL 3000 BV Rotterdam, Netherlands. Tel: +31 10 411 0240; Fax: +31 10 433 4372. A number of conferences and commercially published journals are produced under CIB auspices.

National House Building Council (NHBC) (www.nhbc.co.uk). Buildmark House, Chiltern Avenue, Amersham, Buckinghamshire HP6 5AP. Tel: 01494 434477; Fax: 01494 728521. Produce standards and codes of practice.

Réunion Internationale des Laboratoires d'Essais et de Recherches sur les Matériaux et Constructions (RILEM), Avillon du Crous, 61 Avenue de Président Wilson, F-94235, Cachan, CEDEX France. Tel: +33 1 47 40 08 59; Fax: +33 1 47 40 01 13. Publishes *Materials and Structures*, symposia, and other journals.

SCOSS – the Standing Committee on Structural Safety (www.scoss. org.uk/about/index.html). Established by ICE, IStructE and others in 1976 to maintain a continuing review on the safety of structures. The website contains full text of all their reports.

Research bodies etc

The Building Centre (www.buildingcentre.co.uk). 26 Store Street, London WC1E 7BT. Tel: 020 7637 1022; Fax: 020 7580 9641. Information on construction products and materials. The Building Bookshop is one of the few specialist shops of this type in the UK. There are regional Building Centres.

Building Research Establishment (BRE) (www.bre.co.uk). Bucknalls Lane, Garston, Watford, Hertfordshire WD2 7JR. Tel: 01923 894040; Fax: 01923 664010. Also at BRE Scotland, Kelvin Road, East Kilbride, Glasgow G75 0RZ. Tel: 01355 576200; Fax: 01355 576210; eastkilbride@bre.co.uk. Publishes a range of material including *BRE Digests*, *BRE Reports*, *Good Building Guides* etc. Although library services are now minimal, this is the national source for building and geotechnical information.

Building regulations

The UK building regulations are available from TSO, and on subscription via Knights/Tolley.

Knowles, C. C., and Pitt, P. H., 1972. *The History of Building Regulations in London 1189–1972*. London: Architectural Press.

Documentation databases

Barbour Index (www.barbour-index.co.uk/content/aboutservices/cfm.asp). Barbour Index has a range of information services for built environment professionals. It is more relevant for the building and architectural professions than TI (above) who provide more information of relevance to engineers. Barbour, like TI, have developed from a microfiche based product library. They produce a number of services etc: Building Product Compendium – a building product directory; Building Product Expert, a building product database containing detailed technical and product information from manufacturers of building products; Construction Expert, an integrated database of technical and product information for construction professionals; Specification Expert [Incorporating the National Engineering Specification], a specification writing tool for building services engineers.
Construction Information Service (Technical Indexes Ltd) described above.

Bibliographic sources

Building (construction) References 1946–1990 (MPBW/PSA).
BRE Bibliography of Structural Failures 1850–1970.
Building Science Abstracts 1926–1976.
Instruct (1923–). This covers a wide range of books, periodicals and related publications held in the library of the Institution of Structural Engineers. This includes all articles in *The Structural Engineer* from 1923–date.

Other electronic resources

Great buildings online (www.greatbuildings.com/search.html).
    Spreadsheets for structural engineering (www.structural-engineering.fsnet.co.uk).
CTBUH Review, the journal of the Council on Tall Buildings and Urban Habitat. (www.lehigh.edu/ctbuh/journal/).
    Structurae (www.structurae.de/en/).

Monographs

Adler, D., ed., 1999. *Metric Handbook*. Oxford: Architectural Press.

Chen, Wai-Fah, *Structural Engineering Handbook*. Boca Raton, FL: CRC, 1998. Digital format.

Gaylord, E. H., *et al.*, 1997. *Structural Engineering Handbook*. New York: McGraw-Hill.

Mainstone, R. 1998. *Developments in Structural Form*. 2nd ed. Oxford: Architectural Press.

Young, W. C., and Budynas, R. C., 2002. *Roark's Formulas for Stress and Strain,* 7th ed. New York: McGraw Hill.

United Nations (UNECE) *Annual Bulletin of Housing and Building Statistics for Europe and North America*.

Bridges, aqueducts and viaducts

Bridge site (www.bridgesite.com). Something for everybody.

Jakkula, A. A., 1941. *A History of Suspension Bridges in Bibliographic Form*. Texas A&M University.

Chen, Wai-Fah, and Lian Duan. 1999. *Bridge Engineering Handbook*. Boca Raton, FL: CRC.

Podolny, W., and Scalzi, J. B., 1986. *Construction and design of cable stayed bridges*, 2nd ed. New York: Wiley.

Ryall, M. J., *et al.*, 2000. *Manual of Bridge Engineering*. London: Thomas Telford Limited.

Tilly, G., 2002. *Conservation of Bridges*. London: Spon.

Cladding

Centre for Window and Cladding Technology (www.bath.ac.uk/cwct/). Is a leading information provider in the field of building envelopes and glazing.

Earthquake loads (see also geotechnical engineering).

Earthquake Engineering Research Institute (EERI) (www.eeri.org). Several information resources are available at this site.

International association for earthquake engineering (IAEE) (www. iaee.or.jp). An international society with national and regional activities, which organise major international conferences, supports a journal: *Earthquake Engineering & Structural Dynamics*, and produce the definitive: *Regulations for Seismic Design – A World List* 1996, with *Supplement-* 2000. The UK secretariat is at ICE.

National Information Services for Earthquake Engineering (NISEE) (nisee.ce.berkeley.edu).

Paz, M., 1994. *International Handbook of Earthquake Engineering*. New York: Chapman and Hall.

Impact and blast loads

Jones, N., 1989. *Structural Impact*. Cambridge: UP, 1989.

ASCE. 1999. *Structural Design for Physical Security*. ASCE.

Bangash, M. Y. H., 1993. *Impact and Explosion*. Oxford: Blackwell. (new edition, Springer, in press.)

Mays, G.C., and Smith, P.D., 1995. *Blast Effects on Buildings*. London: Thomas Telford Limited.

Shells and spatial structures

International Association for Shell and Spatial Structures (www.iass-structures.org). Publish a *Bulletin,* and organise conferences.

Tall buildings

Council on Tall Buildings and Urban Habitat (www.lehigh.edu/ctbah). Based at Lehigh University, they have organised many conferences and produced a significant body of research.

Zaknic, I., et al., 1998. *100 of the World's Tallest Buildings*. Corte Madera, CA: Gingko.

▶ TRANSPORTATION SYSTEMS

In the civil engineering context transport engineering is concerned with the planning and management of transportation systems, and the construction, maintenance and renewal of the infrastructure. While this includes knowledge of the moving loads operating in the system, vehicle design is the province of the mechanical engineer, while the electrical engineer interfaces with the civil engineer in the design of electrical power systems and traffic control/signalling.

Transport affects people in their daily lives and when transport systems fail to operate efficiently, as has been witnessed in Britain in recent years, the work of the civil engineer is taken into the world of politics.

Institutions

Institute of Logistics and Transport (www.iolt.org.uk). Incorporates the former Chartered Institute of Transport.

Transportation Research Board (TRB) (www.nas.edu/trb). The Transportation Research Board is part of the National Research Council. TRB publishes the TRIS database which is freely available. Descriptions of the Research in Progress projects are available (rip.trb.org).

Transport Research Laboratory (TRL)(www.trl.co.uk/1024/mainpage.asp). Old Wokingham Road, Crowthorne, Berkshire RG45 6AU. Tel: 01344 770007; Fax: 01344 770880; Edinburgh office email: scotland @trl.co.uk. Although largely concerned with highway/road related research, in its field it is the leading research body, a major publisher of research and with comprehensive library holdings.

US Department of Transportation (DOT). National Transportation Library (NTL) (www.ntl.bts.gov).

Directories, etc.

Road, rail & transport yearbook (www.nceplus.co.uk/road_rail/ ?ChannelID=53).

Nelson, P. M., (1997). *Transportation noise reference book*. London: Butterworths.
United Nations (UNECE) *Annual bulletin of transport statistics*.

Airport engineering

The expansion of air transport has been mirrored by a growth of literature on airport design, which had previously been largely confined to industry standards.

International Civil Engineering Organization (ICAO) (www.icao.int). Produce international standards and codes of practice for airport design.

United States Federal Aviation Administration (USFAA) (www1.faa.gov). Responsible for an enormous volume of research and documentation in the sector.

Railways

In Britain prior to rail privatisation information on modern railway research and practice was very much provided in-house for British Rail, centred on the Research and Development Division in Derby, with industry standards influenced also by international bodies like UIC and ORE. The development of high-speed rail since the 1960s has been largely external to the UK and as a consequence much of the research and literature is foreign, including important work published in Japanese in the 1960s.

Since privatisation the involvement of private consultants and contractors has meant industry standards have become more widely available. Despite the volume of railway publications, the chief sources for information on the historic infrastructure remain with Network Rail and the National Archives in Kew, Edinburgh and Aberystwyth.

Sources

American Railway Engineering and Maintenance of Way Association (AREMA) 8201 Corporate Drive, Suite 1125, Landover, Maryland 20785–2230. Tel + 301 459 3200. Their *Manual* is the America railway civil engineer's bible.

Channel tunnel rail link (www.ctrl.co.uk).

Network Rail (www.networkrail.co.uk). Network Rail have, in their regional plans offices, detailed drawings of the railway infrastructure, which they make available to their own staff and consultants. They are also responsible for drawing up a whole range of standards, distributed through TI.

Permanent Way Institution (www.permanentwayinstitution.org.uk). Publish a *Journal* and *British railway track*.

UIC (www.uic.asso.fr/s_apropos/apropos/presentation_en.html). The UIC was founded in 1922, in the wake of the intergovernmental conferences, with the aim of creating uniform conditions for the establishment and operation of railways. They produce international standards for railways, as well as publishing a journal, *Rail international*.

Directories etc.

Jane's Urban Transport Systems. Coulsdon: Jane's Information Systems.

Jane's World Railways. Coulsdon: Jane's Information Systems (both available digitally).

UIC. *Lexique general des termes ferrorviares*, 4th ed. Paris: UIC, 1988.

Road engineering

Investment in roads has characterised most Western economies since the 1930s, and there is an enormous literature on the subject which is generally readily accessible via the most successful cooperative database – IRRD, developed by OECD. Although the UK Department of Transport/Highways Agency through its various changes has produced standards and codes of practice for many years, ready access has only been made possible via the transfer of sales to TSO, and their publication on the Internet. It is an area where American practice has played a significant role, and despite the proliferation of Highways Agency documentation, a large number of other bodies produce important guidelines on best practice and specialist areas like heavy duty pavements.

Institutions

American Association of State Highway and Transportation Officials (AASHTO) (www.aashto.org). The leading provider of US standards for highway engineers; the materials standards overlap with those of the ASTM. Publications include *Standard Specifications for Transportation Materials and Methods of Sampling and Testing*, *Standard Specifications for Highway Bridges*, etc.

Institute of Transportation Engineers (ITE) (www.ite.org). The Institute is one of five organisations designated by the US Department of Transportation to develop standards.

The Institution of Highways and Transportation (www.iht.org). IHT have been endeavouring to broaden their brief and appeal outside the road engineering community who first established the Institution. They publish a journal, organise conferences and produce important guidelines. They do not have a Library service at present, although they are looking into such a service. 6 Endsleigh Street, London, WC1H 0DZ. Tel: +44 (0)20 7391 9977; Fax: +44 (0)20 7387 2808.

PIARC (www.piarc.lcpc.fr/siege-e.htm). The World Road Association (PIARC) has ninety-seven national or federal government members, 2,000 collective or individual members in 129 countries. In addition to organising conferences, PIARC via its technical committees produce guidance on subjects such as road tunnels. World Road Association, AIPCR / PIARC, La Grande Arche, Paroi nord, niveau 8, 92055 LA DEFENSE (France). Tel: +33 (1) 47 96 81 21Fax: +33 (1) 49 00 02 02.

Abstracts and indexing services

Road Abstracts 1934–1968 (continued in *Transport CD* (www.oecd.org/pdf/M00000000/M00000678.pdf) developed as part of the International Road Research Database (IRRD) under the auspices of OECD).

Other publications

Atkinson, K., 1997. *Highway Maintenance Handbook*, 2nd ed. London: TTL.

Brockenbrough, R. L., and Boedecke, K. J., 2002. *Highway Engineering Handbook: Building and Rehabilitating the Infrastructure*. 2nd ed, New York: McGraw-Hill.

Department for Transport (DfT). *Transport Statistics: Great Britain*. London: TSO.

Highways Agency. *Design Manual for roads and bridges*. (www.highways.gov.uk).

Lamm, R., *et al.*,1998. *Highway Design and Traffic Engineering Handbook*. New York: McGraw-Hill.

Motorway Archive Trust (2002–). *The Motorway Achievement*. 3 vols. London: TTL.

United Nations. *Annual Bulletin of Transport Statistics for Europe and North America* (UNECE).

US Department of Transportation (DOT). Federal Highway Administration (FHA). *Highway Statistics*. (www.bts.gov/ntda/fhwa/prod.html).

US Transportation Research Board. 1994. *Highway Capacity Manual*. Washington, DC: National Research Council. (*Special Report 209*).

Wignall, A., *et al.*, 1999. *Roadwork, Theory and Practice*. 4th ed. Oxford: Butterworth-Heinemann.

Pavements

Asphalt Institute (US) (www.asphaltinstitute.org). Produce a number of manuals aimed at the practitioner, together with useful FAQS on their website. They played a major role in the establishment of the International Society for Asphalt Pavements, 400 Selby Avenue, Suite 1, St. Paul, MN, USA 55102 -Tel: (651) 222–1128 – Fax: (651) 293–9193 who publish a major series of conferences. A parallel organisation, the International Society for Concrete Pavements (www.iscp.tamu.edu) organise meetings and activities on rigid/concrete pavements.

Croney, D., and Croney, P., 1997. *Design and Performance of Road Pavements*, 3rd ed. New York: McGraw-Hill.

Shell bitumen handbook. 2003. London: TTL.

▶ WATER TRANSPORT (SEE ALSO MARITIME ENGINEERING)

In the UK the use of inland waterways has been increasingly devoted to leisure. The network has enjoyed something of a renaissance partly due to the Heritage Lottery funding, and the enthusiasm of a young group of British Waterways engineers. On Continental Europe and countries such as the USA with major river systems water transport has an important role

in freight transport, and links are still being built between Eastern and
Western Europe.

ASCE. 1998. *Manual 94: Inland Navigation*. Reston: ASCE.
British Waterways. 1999. *Design Manual*, 3 vols. Watford: BW.
McKnight, H., 1978. *The Guinness Guide to Waterways of Western Europe*. Enfield:
    Guinness.
PIANC. 1986. *Final Report study of locks*. Brussels: PIANC (*supplementary bulletin no.55*).

▶ WATER ENGINEERING

Probably the most significant contribution to modern society by civil engineers is the provision of safe drinking water. Closely allied with this is the
treatment and disposal of wastewater – both from industry and in the form
of sewage and agricultural wastes. Water supply involves the design of
dams, reservoirs and water towers, as well as pipelines and aqueducts.
These involve a knowledge of hydraulics and fluid mechanics, as well as
geotechnical and structural engineering. Water purification requires a
knowledge of chemistry and biology, a clear overlap with science. The principal information source in the UK has been the Water Research Centre,
although other research institutes such as Hydraulics Research (now HR),
and the Institute of Hydrology (now CEH) are sources of specialist advice.

Water engineering can also be seen in other aspects of the control of
the natural environment – river engineering to control flooding and make
navigation possible. Artificial navigation is seen in the construction of
canals, and man-made channels are also required for irrigation schemes,
also the work of the civil engineer. These are closely allied with drainage
engineering.

Flood control is often associated with land reclamation and most
dramatically in coastal protection schemes. The cost of such works is
causing reconsideration of land engineering in the form of sea walls, and
an acceptance of some loss of land to flooding and the sea and an effort
to use natural processes to protect the coasts.

Institutions

American Water Resources Association (www.uwin.siu.edu/~awra/
    awrahome.html). Publish a journal and organise conferences.
American Water Works Association (AWWA) (www.awwa.org). The
    American Water Works Association (AWWA) produces standards
    and specifications, a journal, and conference proceedings, including
    an important series on water reuse.

CEH Wallingford (www.nwl.ac.uk/ih). Formerly the Institute of Hydrology, the Centre for Ecology & Hydrology carries out research into the effects of land use, climate, topography and geology on the volume and character of surface water resources. A new Joint Centre for Hydro-Meteorological Research has been established in partnership with The Met Office.

Chartered Institution of Water and Environmental Management (CIWEM) (www.ciwem.org.uk). Formed as the result of series of mergers of societies for engineers and scientists in the water and environmental field CIWEM produce two journals, organise conferences, and publish state of the art manuals. The multi-volume *Manual of British Water Engineering Practice*, although no longer up to date, remains the best general source of information on topics such as water supply and river engineering.

HR Wallingford (www.hrwallingford.co.uk). Provides research, and consultancy services on hydraulic engineering in its broadest sense.

International Water Association (www.iwap.co.uk). IWA sponsor a number of journals, and organise major conferences related to water supply and wastewater treatment.

OFWAT: Office of Water Services (www.ofwat.gov.uk). The regulator for the privatised water industry in the UK, producing reports, industry reviews and codes of practice, mostly available free, or downloadable from their website.

UNESCO (upo.unesco.org). UNESCO publish a number of series and reports relevant to water engineers including Studies in hydrology, and discharge records for selected (major) rivers.

Water UK (www.water.org.uk). Based at 1 Queen Anne's Gate, Westminster, membership comprises the water and wastewater suppliers of the UK. Funded by the members who all have representation on the council, they publish reports on the water industry, and statistics.

Water, Engineering and Development Centre, Loughborough University (www.lboro.ac.uk/departments/cv/wedc/). The UK's leading institute involved in infrastructure development for the third world.

Water Environment Federation (WEF) (www.wef.org). Based in Alexandria, Virginia WEF compliment AWWA in their activities.

World Health Organisation (WHO) (www.who.int/water_sanitation_health/). WHO producing drinking water guidelines and sponsor a number of initiatives linking water, sanitation and health.

WRc Group (www.wrcplc.co.uk). The former Water Research Centre, provide consultancy services related to water, wastewater, and the environment, and are prolific publishers of reports and standards/codes of practice for the UK water industry.

Abstracting and indexing services

Aqualine Comprehensive coverage, from the 1950s, concerning water supply and wastewater treatment, and environmental effects of water pollution. Articles are drawn from journals and conference proceedings, scientific reports, books and theses. Previously published by WRc in England, Aqualine is now produced in joint cooperation with WRc and Cambridge Scientific Abstracts. Email: sales@csa.com

National Ground Water Association (NGWA) (www.ngwa.org). NGWA provides subscriber access to the database *Ground Water On-Line*.

Water Pollution Research Abstracts 1927–1975 (continued in Aqualine).

Water Resources Abstracts (NISC) available on line and on CD ROM.

Other sources

The Water Librarians' Home Page (www.wco.com/~rteeter/waterlib.html).

Van der Tuin, J. D., 1997. *Elsevier's Dictionary of Water and Hydraulic Engineering*. New York: Elsevier, (available digitally).

Dams and reservoirs

International Commission on Large Dams (ICOLD) (www.genepi.louis-jean.com/cigb/index.html). ICOLD has membership in eighty-two countries, holds regular conferences and produces bulletins of good practice, and a world register of large dams. Their publications are indexed on their website. Many national societies, including the British Dam Society (based at ICE) have produced national directories and histories of dams. Most are held in the ICE Library. ICOLD Central Office , 151 Boulevard Haussmann, 75008 Paris. Tel. +33 1 40 42 68 24; Fax: +33 1 40 42 60 71.

ICOLD. *Technical Dictionary on Dams*. Paris: ICOLD, various editions, (French/English/German/Spanish/Italian/Portuguese).

Floods and floodworks

Environment agency (www.environment-agency.gov.uk/subjects/flood/).

Responsibility for dealing with flooding has traditionally been a divided responsibility in the UK. Around five million people, in two million properties, live in flood risk areas in England and Wales. The Environment Agency's website has a lot of helpful information:

Hydraulics and fluid mechanics

International Association for Hydraulic Research (www.iahr.nl). With member associations in most countries IAHR have an extensive meetings and publishing programme.

Hydrology and groundwater

American Institute of Hydrology (AIH) (www.aihydro.org).
International Association of Hydrological Sciences (www.cig.ensmp. fr/~iahs/index.html).
  The society publishes a journal, and produces two series of publications, a series of symposia, and specialist reports. The association has national associated societies. The British Hydrological Society is based at ICE, but the IAHS has a presence at CEH Wallingford, who distribute their publications.

Irrigation and drainage

Food and Agriculture Organization of the United Nations (www.fao.org).
  Responsible for several series of publications relevant to the work of civil engineers.
International Commission on Irrigation and Drainage (www.icid.org). The International Commission on Irrigation and Drainage (ICID) was established in 1950 as a Non-Governmental International Organization (NGO) with headquarters in New Delhi. Their *Irrigation and drainage in the world* provides nation by nation summaries of major schemes. The UK member society is based at ICE. ICID 48 Nyaya Marg, Chanakyapuri, New Delhi 110021, India. Tel: 91–11–26116837, Fax: 91–11–26115962.

ICID *Bibliography on Irrigation, Drainage and Flood Control* 1954–
ICID. *Multilingual Technical Dictionary on Irrigation and Drainage* (produced by ICID national committees) (English/French/Italian/Spanish/Turkish/Japanese/German).

▶ HISTORY OF CIVIL ENGINEERING AND CONSTRUCTION

The history of civil engineering can scarcely be regarded as an academic discipline; yet civil engineering is by definition as old as civilisation as we would now describe it, and construction with which it is intimately connected as old as early man making his first efforts to build shelters as protection from the elements, or positioning a log or stones to bridge a stream. Interest in the history of civil engineering has always been strong among certain members of the profession, yet while the history of science and the history of architecture are represented by academic departments all over the world, the history of technology has rarely attained this status. Although the history of civil engineering is offered as an option in some UK universities, its practical value as a teaching aid to engineers has yet to be widely accepted. Much that has been written therefore is that of the engineer turned amateur historian, or by historians with only a passing interest in the subject. One consequence is that much of the published material on the history of civil engineering has been overlooked by the traditional historical abstracting services as it is contained in professional engineering journals, whilst that written by historians rarely comes under the scrutiny of the engineer.

In broad terms those interested in the history of civil engineering since the second half of the eighteenth century, when the profession can be recognised in some form in most European countries, are relatively well served by secondary sources. For the period before then the situation is less simple. Whilst most accounts of Roman civilisation discuss the Roman roads and water supply, what happened in mediaeval times is far more elusive. Looking at the international picture certain countries such as Spain have made available considerable resources to enable their patrimony of bridges to be thoroughly explored; similar authoritative works exist or are being compiled in the Netherlands and Germany. In the USA for more than sixty years the Historical American Engineering Record has been recording the nations' engineering heritage. In some of these countries one can identify an academic community of engineering historians. Unfortunately, knowledge tends to be restricted to a specific country. One can read monographs on the construction of military roads in Scotland under Hanoverian monarchs in the eighteenth century, but the relationship, if any, to near contemporary efforts in Hanover to reshape the Electorate's road network are unclear.

Thus if one is seeking a broad review of the civil engineering associated with early civilisations, or the industrial world, secondary sources are available. For those seeking information on civil engineering c.400AD-1760AD, in Britain one will have to turn to the publications of local history societies, and archaeological groups, or research primary material in local or public records offices. Even for the period after 1760 much information remains unpublished in record offices while practising engineers seeking information on old structures regularly make use of contemporary accounts such as those contained in F.W. Simms' *Practical Tunnelling* (1844, etc.).

Finding aids

The Archon Directory (www.hmc.gov.uk/archon/).
A2A – Access to Archives (www.a2a.pro.gov.uk).
National Register of Archives (www.hmc.gov.uk/nra/search_nra.htm).
Repertorium der technischen literature, 1823–. Berlin, Leipzig
Royal Society. *Catalogue of scientific papers, 1800–1900*. London and Cambridge, 1867–1923.

Institutions and government agencies

Both ICE and IStructE have historical groups, and significant library resources.

The Association for Industrial Archaeology (www.industrial-archae-ology.org.uk). C/o School of Archaeological Studies, University of Leicester, Leicester LE1 7RH. Tel: 0116 252 5337; Fax: 0116 252 5005.

The Construction History Society (www.fp.rdg.ac.uk/wkcl/chs/). C/o The Chartered Institute of Building, Englemere, Kings Ride, Ascot, Berkshire SL5 8BJ. Tel: 01344 630734; Fax: 01344 630777.

Construction Industry Resource Centre Archive (CIRCA), Kimmins Hill, Meadow Lane, Dudbridge, Gloucestershire GL5 5JP. Tel: 0117 968 7850 (evening) 07966 227 575 (daytime); Fax: 0117 962 6614. Possibly worth contacting if more conventional, i.e., ICE/IStructE/RIBA sources fail.

English Heritage (www.english-heritage.org.uk). Have London offices in Savile Row, W1, and regional centres.

Historic Scotland (www.historic-scotland.gov.uk). Longmore House, Salisbury Place, Edinburgh EH9 1SH. Tel: 0131 668 8600; Fax: 0131 668 8669.

The National Archives of Scotland, Register House, 2 Princes Street, Edinburgh EH1 3YY. Tel: 0131 535 1334; Fax: 0131 535 1328; enquiries@nas.gov.uk

The Newcomen Society, The Science Museum, London SW7 2DD. Tel/Fax: 020 7371 4445; (www.newcomen.com). Their *Transactions* are the most important source in the field.

Royal Commission on the Ancient and Historical Monuments of Scotland (www.rcahms.gov.uk). John Sinclair House, 16 Bernard Terrace, Edinburgh EH8 9NX. Tel: 0131 662 1456; Fax: 0131 662 1499.

The US National Parks Service (www.cr.nps.gov/buildings.htm). 'Links to the Past'. Provides links to the Historic American Engineering Record site at (www.lcweb2.loc.gov/ammem/hhquery.html).

Background reading

Davey, N., 1961. *A History of Building Materials.* London: Phoenix House.

Pannell, J. P. M., 1964. *An Illustrated History of Civil Engineering.* London: Thames & Hudson.

Straub, H., 1952. *A History of Civil Engineering.* London: Leonard Hill. (a later German edition is available).

Structural appraisal

Sutherland, R. J. M., *et al.*, 2001. *Historic Concrete: Background to Appraisal.* London: Thomas Telford Limited.

SCI. 1997. *Appraisal of Existing Iron and Steel Structures.* SCI.

Institution of Structural Engineers. 1996. *Appraisal of Existing Structures.* 2nd ed. London: IStructE.

Biography

Day, L., and McNeil, I., 1998. *Biographical Dictionary of the History of Technology.* New York: Routledge.

Marshall, J., 2003. *Biographical Dictionary of Railway Engineers.* 2nd ed. Railway and Canal Historical Society.

Skempton, A. W., *et al.*, eds., 2002. *Biographical Dictionary of Civil Engineers. Vol. 1, 1500–1830.* London: Thomas Telford Limited.

18 Electrical, Electronic and Computer Engineering

Jonathan Dell

▶ INTRODUCTION

There has been an immense acceleration in the deployment of advanced electronics and computing systems, in the last few years, across almost every industrial enterprise. An ever-increasing body of professional information has kept pace with this acceleration and this chapter aims to provide a summary of the various sources available. A large proportion of current professional papers, conference proceedings and more general data is available on-line, and reference to these will be made where appropriate.

Modern electronics and computing stems from the invention of the transistor in 1947 by Bardeen, Brattain and Shockley which brought about a fundamental change in the technology utilised for the fabrication of electronic devices. Transistor devices depend on the semi-conducting properties exhibited by germanium and silicon, as well as some other compounds, when certain impurities are present in very small quantities. These impurities give rise to a surplus or deficiency of electrons. It was found that a three-terminal, current controlled device could be fabricated when these materials were formed into a minute three-layer structure. The basic operational characteristics of these transistors had many parallels with the earlier thermionic valves that they replaced. Valves utilised rather inconvenient and unreliable heated filaments and high voltage supplies. As a result, vastly superior system reliability was achieved as well an enormous reduction in physical size. The use of transistors became prevalent in the 1960s when almost all electronic applications such as radio receivers and Television sets made use of them.

It was soon discovered that several transistors, as well as other components including resistors and capacitors, could be fabricated on the same small slice of high purity silicon. This technique, which became known as the integrated circuit (IC), also improved reliability because fewer external connections were required and the circuit was able to operate at lower power levels, reducing thermal stresses still further. As progressive developments in IC technology became available during the 1970s and 1980s, the number of transistors that could be fabricated on the same 'chip' increased dramatically, and still continues today. This has lead to improvements in the functionality and ease of application of these components. Today many thousands of transistors are fabricated within a few square millimetres of silicon in the most advanced designs. Complexity has increased to such an extent that complete systems can now be fabricated on a single chip (SoC).

The wide availability of modern digital computers has been made possible by the development of integrated circuits to provide highly reliable logic, memory and arithmetic functions on which they rely. Each of these functions utilises many thousands of electronic logic gates and each gate is formed from a small group of transistors. Historically, as IC developments continued, a rapid increase in the level of integration that could be practically achieved became possible and the functionality of computing circuits grew, eventually enabling the development of the advanced microprocessors and powerful computing machines that are an established feature of every office today.

Communications and telecommunications was another branch of electronics to greatly benefit from the advanced components that became available with the advent of transistors. Most telecommunications channels now exploit integrated circuits and digital techniques to enable many 'conversations' to share the same physical circuits. This in turn helped to accommodate the explosion in demand for these services that has taken place. The introduction of the mobile telephone network was made possible by the availability of advanced integrated circuits to provide the system functions. Another development that has been of particular benefit to communications can be traced back to the realisation of a semi-conductor laser in 1961 using fabrication techniques similar to those employed for transistor and integrated circuit manufacture. The subsequent development of a low-loss optical fibre for guiding the laser beam achieved practical performance over several kilometres in the early 1970s, and enabled the implementation of communication systems which can operate at hundreds of million bits per second. These systems now form the main links between telephone exchanges throughout the UK and in other countries with a well-developed communications industry. Together with satellite communication channels high-speed data links are readily available in many parts of the world.

The consumer electronics industry has also seen rapid developments with the availability of advanced integrated circuit components, these enabled applications such as video recorders, the compact disk (CD), calculators, watches and electronic games in the early stages. The most recent developments which have taken place in consumer electronics, such as the introduction of digital Radio and Television services, have also relied heavily on the availability of advanced electronic components to provide the high speed digital circuits on which these systems are based.

Electronics has an impact on almost every individual in the developed world and constitutes a major world industry. In the UK alone the turnover of electronics companies runs into many millions of pounds. What follows is a short review of professional organisations as well as primary and secondary information sources that can be consulted to gain an insight into various aspects of the subject.

▶ ORGANISATIONAL SOURCES

In the field of electronics and computing, the professional organisations provide an extremely rich source of general information, standards and peer reviewed research publications which give an insight on the latest developments that are taking place. Contributors come from all branches of industry and academia where electronics research and development is being undertaken.

Learned societies

Learned societies, with their extensive histories, now occupy central positions in the structure of the electronics industry as well as its education, literature and standards. This chapter will review the three major institutions, the IEE, the IEEE and the ACM, as well as one of the smaller ones, the IIE.

IEE: The Institution of Electrical Engineers (www.iee.org)

The Institution of Electrical Engineers was founded in the UK in 1871, although its present title dates back to 1888. The IEE was awarded a Royal Charter in 1921 and now has more than 130,000 men and women members in 128 countries throughout the world.

The remit of the IEE is to promote electrical engineering and information technology by representing its members and communicating with industry, academia and government. To this end it publishes a wide range of books and periodicals in electrical and electronic engineering, physics, computing, control, software engineering and related subjects in information technology. It also provides the on-line Information Services for the Physics and Engineering Communities (INSPEC) (see below, under 'Abstracting and Indexing Services').

The IEE library in London, which incorporates the British Computer Society Library and that from the Institution of Manufacturing Engineers, offers an extensive collection of books, journals and conference proceedings from which photocopies can be obtained. Its Technical Information Unit specialists can answer enquiries on almost any aspect of the subject by making searches of literature, market data, supplier listings and the press. The unit has on-line access to over 1,000 databases from which customised searches can be made.

IEEE: The Institute of Electrical and Electronic Engineers (www.ieee.org/theinstitute)

The Institute of Electrical and Electronic Engineers, based in the USA, is the world's largest technical professional society. It was founded in 1884 and it is now comprised of over 320,000 members throughout the world. Its objectives mirror those of the IEE and focus on the advancement of both theory and practice in electronics and computing. To realise its objectives it sponsors technical conferences, symposia, workshops and local meetings throughout the world, publishing nearly 25% of the world's technical papers in electrical, electronic, computer engineering and closely related subjects. Most of these publications are also available on-line through IEEE Xplore (see later). It has thirty-six technical societies for different specialist subject areas and these publish more than seventy transactions as well.

IEEE Computer Society

With nearly 100,000 members, the IEEE Computer Society is the world's leading organisation of computer professionals. Founded in 1946, it is the largest of the thirty-six societies of the IEEE. It aims to be a leading provider of technical information and services to the world's computing professionals.

The Society is dedicated to advancing the theory, practice, and application of computer and information processing technology. Through its conferences, applications-related and research-oriented journals, local and student chapters, distance learning campus, technical committees, and standards working groups, the Society promotes an active exchange of information, ideas, and technological innovation among its members. In addition, the Society maintains close ties with the US Computing Sciences Accreditation Board and Accreditation Board for Engineering and Technology, monitoring and evaluating curriculum accreditation guidelines.

With over 40% of its members living and working outside the United States, the Computer Society fosters international communication, cooperation, and information exchange. To meet the needs of its members conveniently and efficiently, it maintains service centre offices in Brussels and Tokyo, in addition to a publications office in Los Alamitos, California, and its headquarters in Washington, DC.

ACM: The Association for Computing Machinery (www.acm.org)

The Association for Computing Machinery was formed in 1947 and is now a major force in advancing the skills of information technology professionals across the world. It has over 75,000 members and provides for its membership computing literature, authoritative publications and conferences. It has thirty-four Special Interest Groups, and these offer publications, conferences and resource archives to promote technical expertise and provide details of the latest developments and trends. The ACM provides an on-line Digital Library which gives access to published information and training course materials.

IIE: The Institution of Incorporated Engineers (www.iie.org.uk)

The Institution of Incorporated Engineers, based in the UK, is the largest institution for the multidisciplinary engineering community. It represents the interests of approximately 40,000 Incorporated Engineers (IEng) and Engineering Technicians (EngTech), providing professional recognition and career development support for the modern practical professional. It provides an on-line library through which members can access various technical articles. It has nine Special Interest Groups and each group delivers regularly updated news and detailed technical articles.

Trade associations

A number of trade associations represent the interests of the electronics equipment and component manufacturing industry and provide information on the electrical, electronic and computer engineering market. There are two trade associations based in the UK and two in America, although these have a world-wide presence.

Intellect (www.intellectuk.org)

Intellect is a recent amalgamation of FEI Federation of Electronic Industries and CSSA Communications Support Services Association now catering for all in the field of Information Technology and Electronics manufacturing. Intellect represents over 1,000 companies in the information technology, telecommunications and electronics industries based in the UK. Intellect is primarily concerned with improving the environment in which its members do business, promoting their interests and providing them with high value services. It provides on-line resources through which its members can view a selection of publications, business guidance documents, statistics, research, market intelligence and advice on issues particularly relevant to its membership.

afdec (www.afdec.org.uk)

The members of the Association of Franchised Distributors of Electronic Components represent over 80% of all electronic component distribution sales in the UK. It provides extensive monthly statistics and a very convenient on-line database that can be searched to determine the source of particular components or subsystem.

AeA (www.aeanet.org)

The American Electronics Association was originally formed in 1943 and is committed to the advancement of high technology business, it is the largest high-technology trade association in the USA. The AeA represents more than 3,000 companies with 1.8 million employees. These companies span the high-technology spectrum, from software, semiconductors, medical devices and computers to Internet technology, advanced electronics and telecommunications systems and services. The association has seventeen regional councils in the USA and has offices in Brussels and Beijing. Through these it offers a unique global policy making capability and a wide portfolio of valuable business services and products for the high-technology industries. It sponsors a series of conferences and publishes regular business summaries for the market sector.

EIA: Electronic Industries Alliance (www.eia.org)

The Electronic Industries Alliance is a partnership of high-tech associations and companies and comprises 2,500 member companies. These companies provide products and services ranging from the smallest electronic components to the most complex systems used by defence, space and industry, including the full range of consumer electronic products. Its mission is to promote market development and competitiveness of the U.S. high-tech industry through domestic and international policy making efforts. It does considerable work in the definition of standards and certification of components. Through its joint venture, the Internet Security Alliance, the EIA also seeks to highlight the security and survivability of the Internet.

Research centres

National research centres have a very wide brief but can provide technical support and consultancy services for the electrical, electronic and computer engineering industries. Their staff publish useful reports periodically on their latest work and new advances, but frequently contribute to the learned journals of the IEE and IEEE.

ERA (www.era.co.uk)

ERA Technology works at the leading edge of many advanced technologies and provides specialist, technology-based services including design and development, testing, assessment and expert advice. It also assists businesses that rely on substantial infrastructures, such as power generators, railways, telecoms, airports and oil refineries. ERA reports and conference proceedings provide their clients with the leading-edge information that they require to develop their businesses in an increasingly competitive commercial environment. For example, a report into microelectromechanical systems has recently been published.

SIRA (www.sira.co.uk)

The SIRA Group specialises in electronic imaging, measurement, measuring instruments and control systems that are an essential part of many diverse industries. As well as its consultancy services the institute publishes regular technical reviews, organises meetings and provides training courses for professional engineers. Recent initiatives include ROSE 'Remote Optical Sensing Evaluation' for open-path gas monitoring equipment and FARADAY organising partnerships for the introduction of high-technology into Small and Medium scale businesses.

Government organisations

The DTI (www.dti.gov.uk) Department of Trade and Industry sponsors various programmes in electronics and appoints various working parties with the particular objective of transferring the results of electronics research to industry, improving the competitive edge of UK industries in the process. The DTI also commissions reports on particularly important developments.

▶ PRIMARY SOURCES

The principal sources of information for electrical, electronic and computer engineers and researchers are the materials published in journals, conference proceedings, product data and standards. Many of these are now available on-line which greatly enhances search possibilities.

Journals

Journals can be conveniently divided into three main categories, these being journals from the learned societies IEE and IEEE, from commercial publishing houses and the major electronic industries.

Learned society journals

The IEE and IEEE dominate the publishing of learned journals in the field of electronics and computing, but the ACM also makes a significant contribution particularly in computing techniques.

IEE

The *IEE Proceedings* is historically the most important journal, its origins dating back to 1872, and is divided into twelve bi-monthly parts. All the contributed papers are peer reviewed to ensure that the highest standards are maintained. The most important journals for practising electronic or computing engineers are probably *Computers and Digital Techniques*, *Circuits, Devices and Systems*, *Communications*, *Optoelectronics*, *Software* and *Vision, Image and Signal Processing*. Special issues are published periodically to provide a collection of papers on a specific subject area of topical interest. A full list of the IEE Proceedings is given in the Table below.

IEE Proceedings	IEE Engineering Journals
Circuits, Devices and Systems	Computing and Control Engineering
Communications	Electronics and Communications Engineering
Computers and Digital Techniques	Engineering Management
Control Theory and Applications	Engineering Science and Education
Electric Power Applications	Manufacturing Engineer
Generation, Transmission and Distribution	Power Engineering
Microwave, Antennas and Propagation	
Optoelectronics	
Radar, Sonar and Navigation	
Science Measurement and Technology	
Software	
Vision, Image and Signal Processing	

The fortnightly IEE learned journal *Electronic Letters* provides rapid publication of short contributions describing research advances in electronic engineering, computing, telecommunications and optoelectronics, reflecting current and on-going research across the industry.

The IEE publishes a series of six Engineering Journals, bi-monthly, which provide an in-depth coverage of new work that will be both informative and accessible to a wide spectrum of engineers. The most important of these are *Electronics and Communication Engineering* and *Computing and Control Engineering*.

IEE On-line Publications provides unlimited access to all the Proceedings, Professional Magazines, Conference Proceedings and Electronic Letters when an appropriate subscription is in place.

IEEE

The IEEE publishes an extensive series of journals which includes the excellent, award winning, magazine *Spectrum* (monthly) where advances in technology and their significance in society are discussed from a professional viewpoint. The *IEEE Proceedings* (monthly) contains papers of broad significance to electronic engineers as well as papers describing original work, reviews and tutorials. Over seventy *Transactions* (usually monthly) are produced by the thirty-six IEEE specialised technical societies, these cover an extremely wide area of interest. A number of other specialist journals, usually bi-monthly, such as *IEEE Journal of Solid-State Circuits* and the *IEEE Micro*, dealing with 'chips, systems, software and applications', cater for more specific areas of interest.

IEEE Xplore

Provides on-line full-text access to IEEE transactions, journals, magazines and conference proceedings published since 1998 as well as all current standards. Anyone can browse and access tables of contents but a membership subscription is required to access the full-text documents within a particular group of publications.

IEEE Computer Society Digital Library

Several specialist societies have been established within the IEEE and the Computer Society is one of the largest. The society publishes a series of specialised magazines and journals itself and provides on-line access for its members through the Digital Library to twenty society magazines and transactions and over 1,000 selected conference proceedings.

ACM

The ACM publishes its *Communications of the ACM* journal monthly as well as maintaining an extensive portfolio of on-line training courses on all aspects of computing. Membership gives access to these courses and the journal articles through the ACM Digital Library. The library also provides an extensive collection of pioneering concepts and fundamental research since its inception and includes biographic information, abstracts, reviews and full texts. An optional subscription gives access to an on-line guide which includes 500,000 bibliographic citations extending far beyond the ACM literature itself.

Other learned journals

Several commercial publishing houses produce high quality learned journals containing peer reviewed articles on theoretical electronics and research topics. The monthly *International Journal of Electronics* (Taylor and Francis) and the monthly *Microprocessors and Microsystems* (Elsevier) are good examples.

Commercial journals

Commercial industry-oriented journals are produced by a number of publishers. In general these fall between peer reviewed learned journals proper and more popular journals aimed at hobbyists. They are often described as controlled-circulation journals.

For example the monthly journal *Electronic Design* (Penton Media Inc., www.penton.com), with over 50 years of publication, is one of the most widely known, and it includes technical articles and application ideas, news of the electronic industry and product reviews. The title *Components in Electronics* (SMG Magazines Ltd., www.smg.plc.uk.cie) provides a monthly update on component and industry news.

The weekly journals *Electronics Weekly* (www.electronicsweekly. com) Reed Electronics Group) and *EE Times* (www.eetuk.com) cover news of products, people, jobs and the industry.

Popular journals

There are many popular journals aimed at the home electronics enthusiast or hobbyist, these frequently contain construction projects and technical feature articles as well as more general review articles. The *Electronics World* (monthly, Highbury Business Communications) and *Elektor Electronics* (monthly, Elektor Electronics publishing) provide high quality articles and well planned construction projects. Other examples such as *Everyday Practical Electronics* (Wimbourne Publishing) have a wide circulation and usually contain a number of product reviews and simpler projects.

House journals

The vast majority of electronics companies, large and small alike, have websites which describe their products and their work, and some also publish house journals to bring their technical developments to a world-wide audience and promote internal communications. When companies have a significant research activity their staff will also contribute articles to the peer reviewed journals. Examples of these publications include the Lucent™ *Bell Labs Technical Journal* (Wiley InterScience), the *IBM Systems Journal* (quarterly, IBM (www.research.ibm.com/journal)) and the *BT Technology Journal* (quarterly, BTexact Technologies (www.btexact.bt.com/publications/bttj).

Conferences proceedings

The majority of conferences, symposia and workshops are organised by the major professional bodies who also publish their proceedings. A panel of professionals working in related subject areas review all the papers that are presented at such events. This ensures that the highest possible technical quality of the accepted contributions is achieved. In many cases conference proceedings are made available on-line by their organising body.

The IEE is again of central importance and typically organises about twenty major conferences each year, the present series started in 1961, as well as more than one hundred and fifty colloquia. Comprehensive conference proceedings are published, recent examples include the Third international conference on 3G mobile communication technologies (no. 489) and the First international conference on power electronics, machines and drives (no. 487).

The IEEE has an extensive programme of some three hundred conferences annually, many of these are held outside the USA, and comprehensive conference proceedings are published for each. Recent examples include the IEEE International Symposium on Circuits and Systems (ISCAS), 2002, the IEEE International Conference on Microelectronic Test Structures, (ICMTS 2003) and the IEEE Symposium on Radio Frequency Integrated Circuits (RFIC), 2001.

The ACM has an extensive programme of conferences which provides an objective arena for the discussion of cutting-edge and often competing ideas. Many ACM special interest group (SIG) conferences have become premier world events.

International conferences are frequently organised jointly by the IEE, IEEE and ACM as well as other bodies. The annual International Broadcasting Convention (IEE, IEEE, EBU) held in the UK is a good example.

Product data

Accurate and comprehensive product data is essential to any practising engineer, and manufacturers of components go to great lengths to provide adequate information to facilitate design with their products. The first step in the process of selecting a component or sub-system is to consult a suitable industry-wide directory. In the UK the primary publication of this nature is the *Electrical and Electronic Trades Directory Blue Book* (IEE, 1998), which provides an extensive classified listing of products, materials, services, manufacturers and their agents.

Directories of electronic products, components and sub-assemblies are also available for companies outside the UK. For European listings the *European electronics directory 1996* by C. G. Wedgwood (Elsevier) provides information on suppliers of components and sub-assemblies, manufacturers, their agents and applications. Information about manufacturers in the USA can be found in the *Electronic Manufacturers Directory 2003* (Frank Carlsen, Harris Infosource).

Component data

For the detailed information required in original design work it is best to refer to the component manufacturers themselves. Most component manufacturers now provide component data sheets on-line to reduce a vast duplication cost and facilitate component selection based on parameters that are of direct relevance to the application in question. Good examples of major manufacturers and their on-line services are Philips Semiconductors (www.semiconductors.philips.com) and Texas Instruments (www.ti.com). Electronic components are usually supplied through a network of distributors except when very large volumes are required. These distribution companies can provide on-line information regarding price and delivery as well as component data in some cases.

A large number of manufacturers are involved in the production of electronic components and semiconductors in particular, so cross-reference information can be very useful. Several companies provide such cross-reference information, listing equivalent types and a short summary of the main specification parameters, including connection details. The *I.C. Master* (www.icmaster.com) (Hearst Business Communications, New York) is the foremost provider in this field and provides a searchable on-line database split into nine major categories. These cover the main component classifications from manufacturers in all parts of the world and include discrete devices, integrated circuits and special application functions. The listings, which group components by generic family include both current and discontinued types, outline drawings and manufacturers' addresses. The database is updated regularly and the registered users can access some other useful facilities.

Materials data

Electronics systems would not have achieved their prominence today without a plentiful supply of raw materials having both appropriate and well-defined properties. The realisation of the transistor in 1948 was only possible as a result of nearly a decade of research and development centred on the materials needed for its construction. Most electronic materials can be classified under one of the following types: conductor; semiconductor; insulator; dielectric; magnetic. In many applications of dielectric or magnetic materials a synthetic material is favoured over a naturally occurring material on account of the superior properties which can be obtained. A good example is found in magnetic materials, naturally occurring iron has very poor properties and a complex alloy is needed even to form an effective permanent magnet. In very high storage density computer disks systems the digital read/write heads employ various synthetic ceramic materials to provide the required performance in the very small physical dimensions.

The electrical and magnetic properties of natural materials and the most common synthetic materials can be found in standard texts such as Kaye, G. W. C. and Laby, T. H., 1986, *Table of Physical and Chemical Constants,* 15th ed., Longmans. A detailed explanation of electronic materials, the physical theory and their applications is given in Schroder, D. K., 1998, *Semiconductor Material and Device Characterisation,* 2nd ed., Wiley Interscience. This includes a very useful collection of information on the properties of semiconductor materials as well as many references to other information sources.

For information on the highly developed magnetic materials that can be used in the construction of inductors and other electro-magnetic devices it is best to consult the data provided by one of the specialist manufacturers. A good example is Ferroxcube (www.ferroxcube.com); this company is a leading supplier of ferrite-ceramic technology offering a broad range of soft ferrite cores for application in a wide range of electronic systems.

Research into new electronic materials continues in many institutions and recent advances enabled the realisation of optical fibre communication systems, mentioned previously, and high-temperature superconductors. Current research papers can be found in the *Journal of Electronic Materials* published by the IEEE as well as subject related journals such as the *IEEE Transactions on Magnetics.*

Application data

Component manufacturers often produce useful application data and typical designs for their products, but for a more fundamental introduction it is frequently more convenient to consult a compendium of applications. Hughes, F. R., 1993, *Op-Amp Handbook,* 3rd ed., Prentice Hall, and Lancaster, D., 1997, *CMOS Cookbook,* 2nd ed., Newnes, are good examples. With the more advanced and highly integrated components applications information and suggested circuits are essential. For devices such as the Texas Instruments family of Digital Signal Processors extensive applications information is available on-line and covers the hardware, the software and the interface requirements.

Standards and specifications

Standards and specifications are extremely important in the electronics and computing industry, for example the European Directive (89/336/EEC) on Electro-Magnetic Compatibility (EMC) affects every manufacturer of electronic equipment even when their product is embedded within other products like a car or washing machine.

European standards are established by CENELEC (European Committee for Electrotechnical Standardization) (www.cenelec.org), which was founded in 1973 and it has been officially recognised as the European Standards Organisation in its field by the European Commission. In order to harmonise standards across Europe CENELEC produces a series of standards under the CECC (CENELEC Electronic Components Committee) which supersede national standards in the member countries. In developing standards it sponsors workshops to bring together experts in a particular field and some of its most recent work has been to establish the standards for the new Digital Television broadcast service. It currently has over 4,000 active standards.

The British Standards Institute (www.bsi.org.uk) is responsible for the implementation of European Standards in the UK and the ISO9000 Quality Management System is particularly relevant to the electronics and computing industry.

IEE and IEEE

The IEEE has an important role in establishing standards and has numerous technical committees working in this area. An example of this work is the series of standards established under the IEEE 802 committee, which cover local area computer network implementation technologies. The standards related to wireless computer networks have been a recent feature of its work. Another example is the IEEE 488 standard that applies to the interconnection of programmable measuring instruments. This ensures that an automated system can be built up with equipment from a diversity of manufacturers. The IEE has a similar role in developing standards and providing training for engineers, such as the recent series of courses on the European EMC Directive, its implications on equipment design and testing procedures. This course in particular is available as a series of Videos for distance learning.

▶ SECONDARY INFORMATION SOURCES

Abstracts and Indexes form the principle source of information in this category but reference works have also been included for completeness.

Abstracts and indexes

The IEE provides one of the world's major abstracting publications through its INSPEC database service, which was established in 1898 as Science Abstracts and currently contains records for more than seven million scientific and technical papers. The contents of over 4,000 journals and some 2,000 published conference proceedings as well as books and reports are regularly scanned and records are added at a rate of 350,000 per year. Although INSPEC provides a comprehensive index to the literature in physics, electrical/electronic engineering, computing, control engineering and information technology, it also has significant coverage in areas such as materials science, oceanography, nuclear engineering, geophysics, biomedical engineering and biophysics. The powerful classification system was devised by INSPEC (INSPEC Classification, 1992) and includes terms from the INSPEC Thesaurus 1993.

Electrical and Electronic Engineering abstracts can be accessed in several different ways. The Abstracts Journal is published in three volumes, *Physics* twenty-four issues per year, *Electrical and Electronic* twelve issues per year and *Computing and Control* twelve issues per year. A cumulative index is provided every six months and these are collected into a four-yearly index periodically, the last issue being 1989–92. The other forms of access involve the current awareness service where data is retrieved for particular subjects that have been carefully selected from dynamic areas of the database. INSPEC can provide the current awareness service as a weekly email alert to keep users abreast of globally published literature in engineering, physics, electrotechnology, computing and information technology. The service can take one of three forms:

INSPEC Alerts use standard search profiles, producing typically 5–50 records per week.

Subject Updates use more extensive search profiles that allow data to be grouped under different headings and producing typically 50–250 categorised records per week.

Custom Alerts use user-specified search profiles, producing up to 100 records per week.

The INSPEC database from 1989 onwards is also available on CD-ROM and can be searched using special software running on an IBM-PC compatible. The CD-ROM is updated quarterly and gives users the opportunity to run their own profiles of retrospective searches.

The Technical Information Unit of the IEE has access to over 1,000 on-line databases covering technical, business, marketing, company and news data as well as all the IEEE publications. It compiles its own database on sales and market forecasts in the electrical, electronic, computing and information technology sectors.

IEEE

Ask*IEEE is an automated document delivery service, powered by Infotrieve, which can obtain the papers and articles required from thousands of different publishers. Whether the request is for a journal paper, magazine article or conference paper, Ask*IEEE will assist in the location and purchase of the documents and can deliver them via fax, mail or electronically.

ACM

An optional element of the ACM Digital Library gives access to a bibliographic database that includes over half a million citations extending far beyond the ACM publications themselves.

Handbooks and reference books

Graf, R. F., and Sheets, W., 1998, *Encyclopaedia of Electronic Circuits,* Vol 7, McGraw-Hill/TAB Electronica, covers nearly 7,000 topics in a non-academic format and is thoroughly indexed and cross-referenced. Useful Handbooks are available from several publishers. Christiansen, D., ed., 1996, *The Electronic Engineers' Handbook,* 4th ed., McGraw Hill Professional, and Jones, G. R., *et al.,* 2002, *Electronic Engineer's Reference Book,* Butterworth-Heinemann, both cover the full spectrum of components, assemblies and systems used in linear and digital systems. Kaufman, M., and Siderman, A. H., eds., 1984, *The Handbook for Electronic Engineering Technicians,* 2nd ed., McGraw Hill, provides useful reference material on electronic laboratory measuring instruments and signal observation techniques.

Textbooks and monographs

The enormous breadth of electronics as a subject means that no single textbook can possibly provide an adequate overview of the field. Even when the subject of interest is identified precisely a choice between introductory and advanced texts will have to be made. Some illustrative examples are given below for the particular subject areas that are most frequently encountered. It should be noted that electronics textbooks do not reflect the current state of development for very long because rapid advances are taking place in nearly all aspects of the subject. However, some books are now established as standard texts and are widely recommended in academic circles.

Electronics textbooks are available from very many publishers, of particular note McGraw-Hill has published an extensive series on electronics and many new titles are added each year as the field advances. Other major publishers such as Prentice Hall, John Wiley, Addison-Wesley,

Chapman & Hall and Macmillan produce texts on both introductory and advanced topics that are widely recommended. The significant contribution of other publishers should not be overlooked.

The professional organisations, the IEE and the IEEE, are also involved in the publication of electronics textbooks. In general these are aimed at the more specialised areas of the subject that have a smaller readership. A significant number of new titles are commissioned each year as major developments and advances are made in particular fields of topical interest.

The foundation theories of electronics as well as the advanced techniques employed, particularly in communications, computer networks and image processing rely heavily on a good understanding of mathematical tools and techniques. A good reference which is widely used in academic courses is Stroud, K. A., 1995, *Engineering Mathematics*, 4th ed., Macmillan.

A general introduction to modern electronic components and their application in system design can be found in Horowitz, P., and Hill, W., 1989, *The Art of Electronics,* 2nd ed., Cambridge University Press, and Millman, J., and Grabel, A., 1987, *Microelectronics,* 2nd ed., McGraw Hill.

Most electronic engineers will have to become proficient at computer programming at some point in their careers but, although there are a profusion of textbooks, few of these approach the subject from an engineering perspective. However, Tyrrell, A. M., Smith, S. L., and Dell, J. A., 1998, *The Essence of C for Electronic Engineers*, Pearson Education, is a good example that does. Another very effective approach to the solution of a particular problem can be made through the use of standard numerical processing examples and a good source of these is Nakamura, S., 1993, *Applied Numerical Methods in C*, Prentice-Hall.

At a fundamental level electronics is divided between two distinct types of system and many textbooks follow this division. Analogue systems form one branch and at a simple level the op-amp is an almost universal building block. Digital systems form the other branch and make extensive use of the logic component families. A wide range of textbooks on these and more specialised subjects are available, some examples are given below. For digital systems Stoneman, T. J., 1996, *Digital Logic Techniques,* 3rd ed., Van Nostrand Reinhold, and Wakerly, J. F., 2000, *Digital Design Principles and Practices,* 3rd ed., Prentice-Hall International, are recommended. For analogue systems Franco, S., 2002, *Design with Operational Amplifiers and Analogue Integrated Circuits,* 3rd ed., McGraw Hill, and Dailey, J., 2001, *Electronic Devices and Circuits*, Prentice Hall, are recommended.

Some examples of textbooks that deal with more advanced concepts and specific subject areas such as analogue and digital systems, communications, computing, instrumentation, semiconductor devices and optoelectronics will now be given. Techniques for advanced analogue system design is presented in Gray, P. R., and Meyer, R. G., 1993, *Analysis and*

Design of Analogue ICs, Wiley. For an introduction to communications techniques O'Riley, J. J., 1989, *Telecommunication Principles,* 2nd ed., Van Nostrand Reinhold, is recommended and more advanced references are Glover, I. A., 1998, *Digital Communication Systems,* Prentice Hall, and Stallings, W., 1998, *High-Speed Networks,* Prentice Hall. For instrumentation systems Bentley, J. P., 1995, *Principles of Measurement Systems,* 3rd ed., Longman, is an excellent reference, and Wilmshurst, T. H., 1990, *Signal Recovery,* Adam Hilger, provides a description of useful techniques for practical measurement situations. In the field of semiconductor devices, works such as Streetman, B. G., 1995, *Solid State Electronic Devices,* 4th ed., Prentice Hall, and Chang, C. Y., and Sze, S. M., 1996, *VLSI Technology,* McGraw Hill, are good references. A reference for optoelectronics is Gower, J., 1993, *Optical Communication Systems,* 2nd ed., Prentice Hall, and a reference for computer system design is Hennessey, J. L., 2003, *Computer Architecture,* Morgan Kaufmann.

With the vast increase in the utilisation of digital electronic systems in all fields of the subject, a profusion of texts have been published. Many of these deal with the fundamentals of digital systems ignoring the broader considerations of large-scale system design and test. A good reference dealing with the principles of effective large-scale design and optimisation is Gajski, D. D., 1997, *Principles of Digital Design,* Prentice-Hall. Most large digital designs utilise a high-level hardware description language, such as VHDL, which is widely accepted in the industry. The more advanced works by Smith, M. J. S., 1997, *Application Specific Integrated Circuits,* Addison-Wesley, and Roth, C. H., 1997, *Digital System Design using VHDL,* PWS Publishing, introduce these concepts very effectively.

There are relatively few books covering the highly specialised application fields such as Avionics but an excellent reference in this particular area is Collinson, R. P. G., 1996, *Introduction to Avionics,* Chapman and Hall. Texts from the IEE and IEEE frequently provide the most up to date references in these areas of electronic application.

▶ CONCLUSION

This chapter has attempted to classify the principle sources of information in the field of electrical, electronic and computer engineering but it should be appreciated that this represents only a snapshot of the present situation. An attempt has been made to quote web addresses correctly and use the most recent book references, but details are always changing in this fast moving area.

19 Engineering Design

*Steve J. Culley and
Chris A. McMahon*

▶ INTRODUCTION

The engineering design process is the process by which a need for an artefact is translated into a description of the artefact for manufacture, and as
such is a vitally important activity. It is the means by which a company
turns what it has learned about its product domains and its markets into
products for sale. Holmes (1999) notes that the quality and performance
of these products is paramount in determining the success of the company,
and thus investment in the product design process can be among the most
cost-effective investments that any firm can make. Key to the performance
of the design process, and thus a central factor in this investment, is effective information provision to the process.

Design can be one of the most difficult collaborative activities undertaken by people. For complex products such as aircraft or automobiles, the
design process may involve thousands of participants in different companies
distributed over many geographic locations and working over many years.
The quality and performance of today's products comes in many cases
from the detailed effort that can be applied by distributing the work over a
large team. In such a process, the communication and sharing of knowledge
and information among the participants are very important issues.

Today, design teams work under increasing pressure to develop products of high performance and reliability at low cost and in shorter and
shorter time-scales. Increasingly, design responsibilities for complex assembles are devolved to the suppliers of the sub-assemblies and parts that make
up the assembly, and these suppliers may be located anywhere in the
world. Design is also increasingly interdisciplinary in nature. Electronic and
computing technologies are an integral part of products that were traditionally almost entirely mechanical, such as internal combustion engines,
and there has been a great growth in complex systems such as modern
buildings, ships or aircraft.

The issues that have been described above have led to a great interest in the nature of the design process, in the development of design techniques and in the development of computer-based aids for design. The role of information is often central in the design process and in the effective use of design techniques and, increasingly, computer aids are being used to assist designers in their information needs. In this chapter, we will first explore the nature of the design process before examining the supply and provision of engineering design information and the way in which information is presented to engineers.

▶ THE NATURE OF DESIGN

In this first section, we consider aspects of design and of the design process that influence the information needs of the designer.

Design process

Finger and Dixon, in their comprehensive review of engineering design research (1989a, 1989b), noted that there are both prescriptive and descriptive models or descriptions of the design process. Prescriptive models suggest how design should be carried out in order to achieve good results. Descriptive models describe how design is actually carried out in practice, based on observations of the process. There is considerable variation in the descriptions given in the design literature, both in terminology and in detail, but in general they agree that design progresses in a step-by-step manner from some statement of need through identification of the problem (the specification of requirements), a search for solutions and development of the chosen solution to manufacture, test and use.

A well-known prescriptive model of the design process, shown in Figure 1, is that proposed by Sharing Experience in Engineering Design (SEED) and used in the SEED Design Activity Model (Kimber *et al.*, 1985) and by Pugh (1991). In this model, the process is described as comprising six main phases, each of which presents different challenges in the provision of information, and which may be summarised as:

- The market phase, which is the initial phase in the total design activity and is the phase in which knowledge and understanding are acquired about the context for which the product is intended. It involves gathering and sifting information on such topics as customers needs, competitors' products, technological forecasts, relevant legislation, standards and patents, and so on (Pugh, 1991).
- The specification phase, which is closely linked to the market phase, and involves collecting information about the design

requirements and the constraints on the design, and describing these in a product design specification. Figure 19.1 also shows the elements that should be considered in such a specification.

- The concept design phase, which involves establishment of the functions to be included in the design, and identification and development of suitable solutions.
- The detail design phase, in which the dimensions, tolerances, materials and form of individual components of the design are specified in detail for subsequent manufacture.
- The manufacture phase, in which the production system and tooling are designed and acquired, and the product is then manufactured.
- The sales phase, in which the product is sold in the market.

Many variations on the models of the design process may be identified. Models used by specific companies or industries may be very much more detailed – in the aerospace industry, for example, as many as fourteen phases are identified in the 'Product Introduction Process', with specific conditions that have to be achieved before a project may pass through a 'gateway' from one phase to the next. In practice, the main phases of real processes are not always clearly defined, and there is invariably feedback to previous phases and often iteration between phases. Increasingly, also,

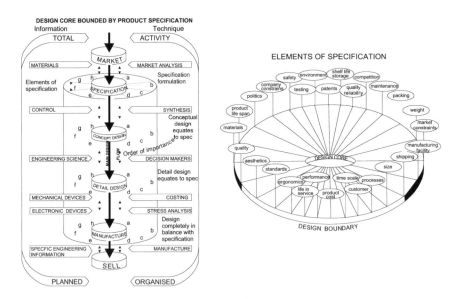

Fig. 19.1: The SEED Design Activity Model (Kimber et al., 1985)

the pressures on the design process to effect reductions in time to market have led to compression and parallelisation of the phases of the design process. This has occurred not just because of the requirement to reduce programme timescales, although this has been one of the major benefits, but because of the complexity and dynamism of today's product technologies, with the resulting imperative to share product and technical knowledge. This compression and parallelisation is known as 'concurrent engineering', which aims to improve on traditional sequential processes, by bringing together a design team with the appropriate combination of specialist expertise to consider, early in the design process, all elements of the product life cycle from conception through manufacture and use in service to maintenance and disposal (Prasad, 1996). This team can thus include not just specialists in manufacturing and design analysis, but also representatives of the customer and those responsible for maintenance and for the eventual disposal of the product.

The traditional approach to product development is often described as an 'over the wall' approach, because each department involved in the process tends to complete its work and then metaphorically throw it over the wall to the next department. These barriers in communication between phases of product development are broken down in concurrent engineering to enable faster and more responsive product development and a higher product quality. In Figure 19.2 (based on Prasad, 1995 and Solhenius, 1992), the sequential and concurrent approaches are compared.

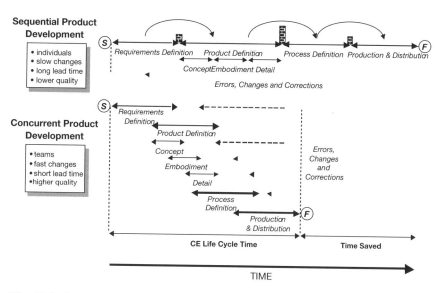

Fig. 19.2: Sequential vs. Concurrent Engineering (McMahon and Browne, 1998)

Design contexts

Many criteria have been used to try to classify design context. The obvious one perhaps is the professional discipline – software engineering, mechanical engineering, civil engineering, etc. Perhaps surprisingly, this is not always very helpful as an indicator of the required design approach. It may be more useful to consider firstly the place of the activity in the supply chain – from raw material supplier through component supplier to original equipment manufacturer – and secondly the volume of production ranging from mass production through batch production to made-to-order and then engineer-to-order. A further classification that is regularly applied is the degree of originality in the new design. Pugh (1991) considers a spectrum of designs from conceptually dynamic, in which a novel solution principle is chosen at the concept stage, to conceptually static, in which an existing solution principle is reused. Pahl and Beitz (1995) extend this classification into original, adaptive and variant design, where:

- **original** design involves developing a novel solution principle to solve a new or existing problem;
- **adaptive** design involves adapting a known system (often with original design of parts or assemblies), and –
- **variant** design involves varying the size/arrangement of aspects of a system, the function and solution principle remaining unchanged.

Table 1 shows examples from the different classes from a number of engineering disciplines.

Table I Design Classification by Degree of Originality

Original	Adaptive	Variant
First Sony Walkman	VHS video recorder	Headphones
ABS brakes	Diesel engine	Automobile clutch
Space shuttle	Airbus aircraft	Airliner seat
Object-oriented DBMS	Relational DBMS	Database schema
Syndey opera house	Channel tunnel	Motorway bridge
Stereolithography machine	CNC machine tool	Carbide tool insert
Maglev train	TGV train	Railway vehicle axle
Electrically assisted steering	Hydraulic power steering	Steering rack
Magnetostrictive actuator	Hydraulic actuator	Solenoid

Aspects of design

Within any design problem, the designed artefact has to be considered at a number of levels of granularity, and, for each level of granularity, a choice has to be made between selecting a standard design or design element, typically from the product range of a supplier company, and designing a design element especially for use in the new artefact. The levels of granularity and the division between design and selection approaches and design examples at each level include the following considerations:

Level 1: System level, such as the choice between a light rail system and a tracked bus system.

Level 2: Sub-system level, such as the choice between a diesel or a petrol engine, and approach to power transmission, and so on.

Level 3: Unit level, concerned with the main distinguishable sub-system elements used in a product. An example of unit **selection** is the selection of a clutch or a motor in a machine, a storage module in a computing device, a window unit is a building, and so on. Unit **design** involves the design (often from standard parts) of a bespoke sub-system, such as a cam mechanism or a control unit.

Level 4: Component level, concerned with the individual component parts used in a product. An example of component **selection** is the selection of a gear or a sprocket in a machine, a resistor in an electrical device, a gutter for a building, and so on. Component **design** involves the design of a bespoke component, such as a drive shaft or a circuit board.

Level 5: Production level, concerned with the design of detailed aspects of the product to reflect manufacturing considerations such as selection of surface condition, limits and fits, and so on.

It is perhaps pertinent to note that there is a close interaction between the level of the design activity and the degree of difficulty. System level design is often original, whereas unit and component design is often variant, but conversely for adaptive designs, original steps are often taken at sub-system level (consider, for example, the introduction of ABS in automotive braking systems).

Representing the product

During the design process, the design team produces representations of the product in order to allow the design intent to be communicated, and to allow the participants in the design process to cope with the complexity of their work. The representation of discrete manufactured parts has traditionally been by drawings that describe in the abstract the characteristics that the design is to have. The structure of systems of interconnected parts is shown in diagrams, for example for electrical or fluid power systems. For some forty years, engineers have also worked on computer-based representations of designs, including three-dimensional geometric models using a variety of representation schemes.

The important characteristics of the design comprise much more than just shape. During the design process, a whole range of properties of the new artefact have to be defined. These are the design parameters and are definitive or descriptive – they are the properties which affect the manufacture of the object, and include the form, dimension, surface condition, material properties and specific manufacturing instructions associated with a design (McMahon *et al.*, 1995), (Suh, 1990). They are the attributes recorded in engineering drawings and diagrams.

In addition to the design parameters, a number of further properties of the emerging design are identified during the design process. These are the performance parameters, which are judgements, performance-related assessments, or emergent properties – they do not need to be known to manufacture the object, but they emerge or can be derived from the design parameters, and are used to assess the suitability of the object (McMahon *et al.*, 1995), (Suh, 1990). Performance parameters might include the estimated performance, strength, wear resistance and durability of an emerging design. They are derived by considering the design, described by design parameters, subjected to a set of external influences on the artefact, such as the applied loads (these will often be maximum loads that the design has to support, or 'worst case' influences).

The design process is the process by which a statement of need or a requirements specification is transformed into a final design which enables an artefact to be manufactured. During this process, the design team will need to identify the functional requirements of the artefact, and the constraints within which they work such as manufacturing process or materials capabilities. During the conceptual design phase, design parameter models will be proposed for design solutions that may meet the functional requirements. The design process proceeds by developing the design parameter models via a sequence of activities that gradually develop and refine the models. Concurrently, the functional requirement model and constraint models may be refined as information is fed back from the design activity, from customers and from other external sources.

Also concurrent with the development of design parameter models is the elaboration of assessments and judgements about the implicit properties of the proposed designs, by the designer or by specialists who contribute to the design process. In some cases, these may be derived directly by examination or manipulation of the design parameter models (for example, a judgement on the aesthetic merit of an artefact may be made by examination of a model of the external form and colour), but in most cases the evaluation will require an additional **auxiliary** model, created for the purposes of making the appraisal. Examples of auxiliary models are mathematical models used in automatic control, or Finite or Boundary Element models for stress or vibration analysis. Auxiliary models may be transient – developed for the purposes of making an assessment, but no longer required except for the purposes of recording the design history once the assessment is made. They may also be more permanent, and developed and refined as the design progresses. For example, a finite element model may be refined or adapted in the light of changes in the emerging design.

In some cases, the performance parameters of a design will be complex functions of its other properties. For example, an evaluation of the durability of an automotive suspension system would be based on an evaluation of stress states in the component parts, in turn based on analysis of the loads arising from dynamic loading of the suspension system through the tyre and from cornering and braking loads. Performance parameters may thus be evaluated from other performance parameters, through series of auxiliary models constructed for different purposes. This implies a series of potentially complex interconnections and interactions between design parameter, performance parameter and auxiliary models, again carried on in parallel with the development of an understanding about the functional characteristics of the design, and of the design constraints.

▶ INFORMATION AND KNOWLEDGE

The focus of the subsequent sections is on information. However it is necessary to briefly understand the role and nature of knowledge in engineering design to set the role and nature of engineering information in context.

In his book, Ullman (1992) proposes three types of knowledge that engineering designers make use of and refer to during their work:

- *General knowledge,* gained through everyday experiences and general education. The information used in updating this knowledge is that which most people know and apply without regard to the specific domain that they are working in.
- *Domain-Specific Knowledge,* gained through study and experience within the specific domain that the designer works in. Information is on the form or function of individual items or groups of items.
- *Procedural Knowledge,* gained from experience of how to undertake one's tasks within the enterprise concerned. This form of knowledge is often based upon a combination of the previous two.

Vincenti (1993) argues, through his observations of the historical developments in aeronautical engineering, that engineering knowledge is developed and formalised to meet the needs of engineering designers in a particular domain and that some items of this knowledge are clearly distinguishable, whilst others are not.

Eder (1989) notes the distinction between *prescriptive* or *descriptive* design knowledge. The former is that commonly referred to as the 'know-how' of design and includes:

- Design knowledge related to the technical system to be designed (knowledge about natural phenomena, knowledge about how to apply that science, etc)
- Design knowledge related to the design process (knowledge about general strategic approach to designing, knowledge about tactics and methods for designing, etc)

and the latter as the 'know-that' of design and includes:-

- Design knowledge related to the technical system to be designed (knowledge about properties and constituents of socio-technical and technical systems, knowledge of theories of properties)
- Design knowledge related to the design process (knowledge about design processes, knowledge about using working means).

For the rest of this chapter, the focus will be on the particular characteristics of *engineering design information*. In particular, some basic definitions of 'Type' and 'Sources' of engineering information will be presented along with a discussion of supply and information flow issues. The final section will consider the factors associated with information delivery.

► ENGINEERING DESIGN INFORMATION

A preliminary list of factors relating to engineering design information can be readily generated from the often vast quantity of information found within an engineering enterprise, which comprises many different types, even in the smallest enterprise. This engineering design information is provided in many different formats, consists of many different types of information, and may be accessed from many different sources. In this regard, it is important to differentiate between an information type and an information source (Court *et al.*, 1993)

The types of engineering design information

The following definition of Information Type is proposed (Court, 1995).

> *TYPE* of information is *WHAT* information is required to undertake a particular task. Examples include material strength, production lead time, why a certain design was used in the past or how the design is to be installed in the working environment.

A hierarchical tree has been developed, using this definition as a basis and combining it with the elements of the PDS identified by Pugh (1991).

TYPES OF INFORMATION

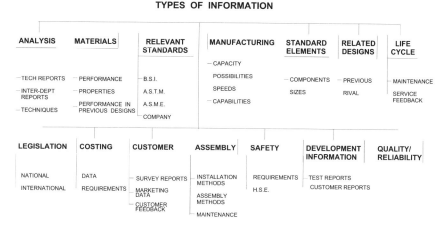

Fig. 19.3: Types of Design Information (Court *et al.*, 1993)

The resulting tree comprises thirteen core types of information and thirty-three sub-types (Figure 19.3). The tree does not provide an exhaustive set of information types, rather it consists of the essential elements proposed by Court and is intended to illustrate what is meant by the term 'type' of information.

The sources of engineering design information

The term *'information source'* has also been widely considered by design information researchers, and there is a general consensus of what the main sources of engineering design information should be. The term, 'source of information' is sometimes used synonymously with information type, but it is considered important to distinguish between the two. The following definition of *'information source'* is proposed (Court, 1995):

> **SOURCE** is defined as **WHERE** such information can be obtained – for example a textbook, a journal, a drawing, a colleague, etc.

In a similar manner to the treatment of type of information, it is useful to develop and present a hierarchical structure showing core sources of information (Figure 19.4). Once again, this structure does not aim to be all-encompassing, but rather to provide an example of what is meant by the term 'source of information'.

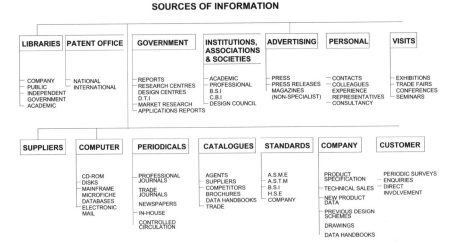

Fig. 19.4: Sources of Design Information (Court *et al.,* 1993)

Information delivery

Engineers access information from a variety of locations and systems, including personal collections, working group information stores and company systems. Some large companies will have company systems comprising collections of millions of computer-aided design files, analysis files and engineering documents, and may be continually reusing these over a period of many years (consider, for example, the design of a large passenger aircraft or of a generating station). They therefore need systems to index and manage these large quantities of information in a sort of electronic vault. Such systems are known as Product Data Management systems.

Product Data Management (PDM)

PDM systems have been available in various forms to assist engineers in their work. These systems act as an engineer's working environment, capturing new and changed data as it is generated, and thus providing a track of the development of a product (Hewlett-Packard (www.pdmic.com/undrstnd.html), Williams (www.pdmic.com/evoltech.html)). Storga *et al.* (2001) give the basic requirements of a PDM system:

- Secure storage of documents and product information
- Management of previews designs
- Management of alternative variants of design object

- Management of the inspection and approval procedures
- Management of the recursive division of design objects into smaller components
- Management of multiple structural views of a design object
- Software tool integration
- Component and supplier management.

The last bullet point highlights a topic of particular importance to the design engineer. Although some information is available via the PDM route, the designer also receives information about this topic from a variety of other sources. The four major mechanisms are:

- Distributed – paper or CD-ROM based information.
- Internet – Internet based information.
- Intranet – Intranet based information (stored on a local company network specifically for that company).
- Extranet – Extranet based information (stored by one company specifically for another company).

Paper based information from the supplier

Paper catalogues are still the most frequently used source of supplier information for the engineering designer (Boston *et al.*, 1998). This is mainly owing to historical reasons: the ease of publication on the part of the supplier, and the familiarity and ease (albeit time consuming) of component sourcing by the designer. However, arguably, there is also something comforting and familiar with the use of paper. This is to do with what Sellen and Harper (2001) refer to as *affordances* in their book, 'The Myth of the Paperless Office'. Until recently, information from suppliers was sourced solely from paper catalogues (e.g. Parker, 1997). This information is sent out to the customer by suppliers on request, as well as at regular intervals using mailing lists. As a consequence of this, areas in a design office need to be set aside for the storage of this information (Finger, 1998). Finger discusses the use of a reference librarian, who catalogues and then disseminates the incoming information, according to projects in progress. While this has large benefits, namely, that of an organised information storage area which is up to date and with someone who knows where the information is, it is typically reserved for larger organisations who can justify such expenses of staffing and room allocation. For the smaller design office, Finger mentions the 'expert consultant'. She comments that in case studies undertaken, these design consultants would oversee the creation of the designs, and assist in supplying information via their own developed indexing schemes. In a survey conducted by Boston *et al.* (1998), 84% of respondents stated that, within their organisations, a collection of standard supplier literature was stored in some form of global library. The report goes on to state that, in addition, 75% of the respondents had a personal collection of supplier literature. We can also observe that, when a design engineer wishes to source a third-party (Business-to-Customer) component, they will tend to utilise a favoured supplier or catalogue, due to familiarity and historical links with that supplier.

Electronic catalogues

Technologies have advanced at a substantial rate over the last decade, especially in the Internet and distributed media areas. As a consequence, there is a wealth of electronic tools for the identification of individual components. Initially, catalogues for the distribution and presentation of information published using computers – 'electronic catalogues' – were typically supplied on floppy disks, then on CD-ROM media (e.g. Lee Spring, 2001). Increasingly today, catalogues are provided by suppliers on Internet sites, although CD-ROMs continue to be used, although less widely than before.

Standards

At present, there are no standards that provide and give guidance for the publishing of electronic catalogues. In the field of engineering, however, there are various standards that are in use for data representation. The Initial Graphics Exchange Specification (IGES) is a US standard that allows for the transfer of basic geometric data between computer-aided design (CAD) systems. Further developments to this incorporated more complete product descriptions, such as the Product Data Exchange Standard (PDES), which allows for CAD to computer-aided manufacture (CAM) as well as CAD to CAD data exchange. Both of these have been superseded by the Standard for the Exchange of Product Model Data (STEP), a set of ISO standards which provide for the exchange of engineering product data (International Standards Organisation, 1994), owing to its broad coverage of modelling data (PDES Inc., 2000), although IGES is still widely used for CAD data exchange. STEP aims to standardise the way that engineering data is represented for a product throughout its life (Owen, 1997). However, much of its implementation to date relates to purely geometric information, mainly around CAD/CAM systems; it does not encompass the performance data necessary in order to represent information for search criteria, and has not at present digressed into the catalogue area. The PLib standard (ISO 13584) is an exchange format for digital libraries of technical components (Pierra *et al.*, 1998, Toshiba (www.toplib.com/en/Standardization.html)). It is closely linked with STEP, and utilises information models described using the same EXPRESS language. It is again a set of ISO standards which provide a computer-interpretable representation and which allow for exchange of parts specification data. At present, it is not widely used, although there has been research in its use in a number of industries (e.g. Concurrent Technologies Corporation describes its use in shipping (tdaextprod.ctcgsc.org/STEP/standard.html)).

Some catalogues have made use of the proprietary 'DXF' drawing format to allow output of engineering component drawing information from the catalogue. However, this file format relates to the structure of data that describes the geometry of engineering components – it does not provide for the interfacing and non user-initiated exchange of data between applications.

Types of CD-ROM Catalogue

As noted, one widely used mode of delivery of electronic catalogues uses CD-ROM media. It is possible to characterise these catalogues by the main role that they serve. The CD catalogues listed are available from the appropriate suppliers.

- *Distributed CD-ROM Catalogues*
  Examples include RS Components Ltd., FAG Ltd and HES
- *Sales Based CD-ROM Catalogues*
- *Design Based CD-ROM Catalogues*
  Examples: Gates Power Drives supply a CD-ROM catalogue containing installable software on the CD-ROM, including video clips that, for example, can give instruction on how best to fit a product (ACI Ltd.).
- *CAD Integrated CD-ROM Catalogues*
  Examples: Sun's hydraulic catalogue is similar to that of Vickers Ltd.,
- *Demonstration CD-ROM Catalogues*
  An example of this is the Interactive Product Guide CD-ROM from ACI Ltd., which shows applications of their products.

Internet based systems

With the increased use of the Internet, many companies are starting to expand their catalogues to utilise this medium. In addition to catalogue contents being incorporated on websites, email is used to notify engineers of the latest information. One example that shows a steady increase in use is the Engineeringtalk (www.engineeringtalk.com) email newsletter, which is published weekly, with a current circulation in excess of 40,000. Another example, indicating the use of the Internet by engineering designers, is the Design Research News email newsletter, which is published once a month and has a circulation in excess of 6,300.

Online Services

There are various online services available through the World Wide Web other than electronic catalogues that are potentially very useful to the engineering designer, such as EEVL: The Internet guide to Engineering, Mathematics and Computing (www.eevl.ac.uk). EEVL contains Engineering Design and Product Design sections, and presents a selection of websites hand-picked against various quality criteria to highlight the fact that these are quality sites on offer, not just a randomly selected list. This site is primarily for the higher education and research community, but can be used free of charge by anyone. Subscription-based online bibliographic databases have long provided quick and sophisticated access to a vast wealth of information. Databases such as Compendex, Inspec, ANTE, and Metadex are available from various hosts, and are covered more fully elsewhere in this book.

Industrial Technology Magazine (www.industrialtechnology.co.uk), as well as providing a good manufacturing and component magazine, provides a very informative website and weekly email newsletter, which contains vast amounts of information, including articles from previous magazines, and links to many other sites. (Other such magazines may be found [e.g. via EEVL]. Titles include *Machine Design, Cadence, Design Engineering, Eureka, co-design, Medical Equipment Designer*). The Institution of Mechanical Engineers (www.imeche.org) website is similar, with information for members, but also many useful links and information for companies. The Institution of Engineering Designers (www.ied.org.uk) website has an Internet database, which gives a substantial number of links to different products and suppliers. This site is aimed at ease of use, the main benefit being the categorisation of products, which aids the task of information retrieval, as well as not requiring users to wade through irrelevant data that may be picked up in an automated search engine. This is an area of information provision that is expanding at a considerable rate and the availability of 'portal' sites such as EEVL, and the University of Queensland's DesignSurfer '02 site (www.catalyst.uq.edu.au/designsurfer), is of considerable importance to enable engineers to monitor and keep up to date with current trends and current information sources.

Summary

Information for engineering comes from a wide variety of sources and through a variety of delivery media and systems. Information is used in different forms throughout the design process. In addition to the references given in this chapter, details of a number of the more useful general design engineering websites, together with a collection of recommended books, are given in the Bibliography at the end of this chapter.

▶ REFERENCES

Boston, O. P., Culley, S. J., and McMahon, C. A., 1998. *Suppliers in engineering design: a survey of information & integration issues.* Bath: University of Bath.

Court, A. W., Culley, S. J., and McMahon, C. A., 1993. *A survey of information access and storage amongst engineering designers.* Bath: The University of Bath.

Court, A. W., 1995. *Modelling and classification of information for engineering designers.* PhD Thesis. University of Bath, Department of Mechanical Engineering.

Design Research News, www.drs.org.uk. Digital newsletter of the Design Research Society.

Finger, S., and Dixon, J. R., 1989a. A review of research in mechanical engineering design. Part I: Descriptive, prescriptive, and computer-based models of design processes. *Research in Engineering Design,* 1(1), 51–68.

Finger, S., and Dixon, J. R., 1989b. A review of research in mechanical engineering design. Part II: Representations, analysis, and design for the life cycle. *Research in Engineering Design.* 1(2), 121–138.

Holmes, M., 1999. Keynote address. *In: Proc. 11th international design theory and methodology conference: ASME design engineering technical conferences, Las Vegas.* New York: ASME.

International Standards Organisation, ISO 10303-1: 1994 Industrial automation systems and integration – product data representation and exchange – Part 1: overview and fundamental principles.

Kimber, M. D., *et al.,* 1985. *Curriculum for design: engineering undergraduate courses,* Hatfield: SEED.

Lee Spring, 2001. Spring Catalogue.

McMahon, C. A., and Browne, J., 1998. *CADCAM: principles, practice and manufacturing management.* Harlow: Addison-Wesley Longman.

McMahon, C. A., Xianyi, M., Brown, K. N. and Sims Williams, J. H. 1995. A parallel multi-attribute transformation model of design. *In: Proc. 7th international design theory and methodology conference: ASME design engineering technical conferences, Boston, MA, 17–21 September.* Vol.2, 341–350. New York: ASME.

Owen, J., 1997. *STEP: an introduction.* Winchester: Information Geometers Ltd.

Pahl, G., and Beitz, W., 1995. *Engineering design: a systematic approach.* 2nd ed. Berlin: Springer Verlag.

Parker Motion & Control, 1997. *Parker product program hydraulic controls.* Parker Motion & Control.

PDES Inc., 2000. *Results of STEP testing worldwide,* pdesinc.scra.org/whatsnew/step_overview.html

Pierra, G., *et al.,* 1998. Exchange of component data: the PLib (ISO 13584) model, standard and tools. *In: Proceedings of the CALS Europe '98 conference, 16–18 September 1998, Paris, France,* 160–176.

Prasad, B., 1995. Sequential versus concurrent engineering – an analogy. *Concurrent Engineering: Research and Applications.* 3(4), 250–5.

Prasad, B., 1996. *Concurrent engineering,* Upper Saddle River, NJ: Prentice Hall.

Pugh, S., 1991. *Total design: integrated methods for successful product engineering.* Wokingham: Addison-Wesley.

Sellen, A. J., and Harper, R. H. R., 2001. *The myth of the paperless office.* Boston: MIT Press.

Solhenius, G., 1992. Concurrent engineering. *Annals of the CIRP,* 41(2), 645–55.

Storga, M., Pavlic, D., and Marjanovic, D., 2001. Reducing design development cycle by data management within the design office. *In: Design research – theories, methodologies, and product modelling: proc. international conference on engineering design, Glasgow, August 2001,* 429–436.

Suh, N. P., 1990. *The principles of design.* New York: Oxford University Press.

Ullman, D. G., 1992. *The mechanical design process.* Columbus, OH: McGraw-Hill.

Vincenti, W. G., 1993. *What engineers know and how they know it: analytical studies from aeronautical history.* Baltimore: The Johns Hopkins University Press.

▶ BIBLIOGRAPHY

General

Stanford Joint Program for Design. Books for designers, design.stanford.edu/PD/books.html

Carvill, J., 1994. *Mechanical engineer's data handbook.* Oxford: Butterworth-Heinemann

Beitz, W. and Kuettner, K. H., eds., 1994. *DUBBEL: handbook of mechanical engineering.* Berlin: Springer-Verlag.

British Standards Institution, BS 7000–1: 1999. *Design management systems: guide to managing innovation*

British Standards Institution, BS 7000–2: 1999. *Design management systems: guide to managing the design of manufactured products*

British Standards Institution, BS 7000–3: 1999. *Design management systems: guide to managing service design*

British Standards Institution, BS 7000–4: 1999. *Design management systems: guide to managing design in construction*

Approaches to product design

Ulrich, K. T., and Eppinger, S. D., 1999. *Product design and development.* 2nd ed. Columbus, OH: McGraw-Hill Education.

Ullman, D. G., 2002. *Mechanical design process.* Columbus, OH: McGraw-Hill Education

Pahl, G., and Beitz, W., 1996. *Engineering design: a systematic approach.* 2nd ed. Berlin: Springer-Verlag.

Hubka, V., and Eder, W. E., 1995. *Design science: introduction to needs, scope and organization of engineering design knowledge.* Berlin: Springer-Verlag.

Cross, N., 2000. *Engineering design methods: strategies for product design.* Chichester: John Wiley.

Smith, P. G., and Reinertsen, D. G., 1997, *Developing products in half the time: new rules, new tools*. Hoboken, NJ: John Wiley & Sons Inc.

Machine design

Shigley, J. E., 2001. *Mechanical engineering design*. Columbus, OH: McGraw-Hill Education

Shigley, J. E., and Mischke, C. R., 2002. *Mechanical engineering design*. Columbus, OH: McGraw-Hill College

Hurst, K., ed., 1994. *Rotary power transmission design*. Maidenhead: McGraw-Hill Education – Europe.

Materials

Ashby, M. F., 1999. *Materials selection in mechanical design*. Oxford: Butterworth Heinemann.

Ashby, M. F., and Johnson, K., 2002. *Materials and design: the art and science of material selection in product design*. Oxford: Butterworth-Heinemann.

Matweb. Material property data, www.matweb.com.

Wegst, C. W., ed., 2001. *Stahlschlussel (key to steel): a cross-reference book for steel standards and designation*. Marback am Weckar: Verlag Stahlschlussel Wegst.

Manufacturing processes

Swift, K. G., and Booker, J. D., 2003. *Process selection: from design to manufacture*. 2nd ed. Oxford: Butterworth-Heinemann.

Kalpakjian, S., and Schmid, S. R., 2001. *Manufacturing engineering and technology*. 4th ed. Upper Saddle River, NJ: Prentice Hall.

British Standards Institution, PD 6470:1981: 1981. *The management of design for economic production*. Standardization philosophy aimed at improving the performance of the electrical and mechanical manufacturing sectors

Boothroyd, G., Dewhurst, P., and Knight, W., 2001. *Product design for manufacture and assembly*. 2nd ed. New York: Marcel Dekker.

Bralla, J. G., 1998. *Design for manufacturability handbook*. Columbus, OH: McGraw-Hill Education.

Design data

Carvill, J., 1994. *Mechanical engineer's data handbook*. Oxford: Butterworth-Heinemann.

Beitz, W., and Kuettner, K. H., eds., 1994. *DUBBEL: handbook of mechanical engineering*. Berlin and Heidelberg: Springer-Verlag.

Amiss, J. M., et al., 2000. *Machinery's handbook guide*. 26th ed. New York: Industrial Press, Inc.

Pohanish, R., and McCauley, C. J., eds., 2000. *Machinery's handbook pocket companion*. New York: Industrial Press, Inc.

Avallone, E. A., and Baumeister, T., III., eds., 1996. *Marks' standard handbook for mechanical engineers*. Columbus, OH: McGraw-Hill Education.

Tapley, B. D., ed., 1990. *Eshbach's handbook of engineering fundamentals*. Hoboken, NJ: John Wiley & Sons Inc.

The Engineering Technology Site, www.engineers4engineers.co.uk. Technical information for the professional engineer.

EFUNDA, www.efunda.com. Information and calculation pages covering materials, standard formulae, hematics, process, units and standard parts.

Findlay Publications, www.findlay.co.uk. Site covering engineering information magazines, product and supplier databases and industry research data.

Ergonomics

Salvendy, G., ed., 1995. *Handbook of human factors and ergonomics*. Chichester: John Wiley & Sons.

British Standards Institution, BS EN ISO 7250: 1998. *Basic human body measurements for technological design*.

British Standards Institution, BS DD 202: 1991, ENV 26385: 1990, ISO 6385: 1981. *Ergonomic principles in the design of work systems*.

Noyes, J., 2001. *Designing for humans*. Hove: Psychology Press.

Safety and reliability

Smith, D. J., 2000. *Reliability, maintainability and risk*. 5th ed. Oxford: Butterworth-Heinemann.

Computer-aided design

McMahon, C. A., and Browne, J., 1998. *CADCAM:, princples, practice and manufacturing management*. Harlow: Addison Wesley Longman.

Zeid, I., 1991. *CAD/CAM theory and practice*. Columbus, OH: McGraw-Hill Education.

Quality

Revelle, J., et al., 1997. *The QFD handbook*. Hoboken, NJ: John Wiley & Sons Inc.

Terninko, J., 1997. *Step-by-step QFD: customer driven product design*. Boca Raton, FL: St Lucie Press.

Beauregard, D. M., 1996. *Basics of FMEA*. Quality Resources.

Creveling, C. M., 2002. *Design for six sigma in technology and product development.* Englewood Cliffs, NJ: Prentice Hall.

Fowlkes, W. Y., and Creveling, C. M., 1995. *Engineering methods for robust product design: using Tagichi methods in technology and product design.* Englewood Cliffs, NJ: Prentice Hall.

Cohen, L., 1995. *Quality function deployment: how to make it work.* Reading, MA: Addison Wesley.

Design analysis

Durka, F., *et al.*, 2002. *Structural mechanics: loads, analysis, design and materials.* Englewood Cliffs, NJ: Prentice Hall.

Adams, V., 1999. *Building better products with finite element analysis.* Ashville, NC: High Mountain Press.

Young, W. C., Budynas, R. D. and Ludewig, L., eds., 2001. *Roark's formulas for stress strain.* Columbus, OH: McGraw-Hill Education

General websites

Technical Indexes, www.ti.com. The website of Technical Indexes, a major supplier of technical information

The Institution of Engineering Designers, www.ied.co.uk. The site gives a categorised list of component suppliers

The Institution of Mechanical Engineers, www.imeche.org.uk. Gives access to consultant services, publications and educational services

ESDU, www.esdu.co.uk. A very valuable source of validated engineering data, methods and software for the engineer.

Darnell, M. J., *Bad human factors designs,* www.baddessigns.com. How not to do it!

How things work, www.howthingswork.com. A suprisingly valuable and informative site on complex mechanisms and systems.

EFUNDA, www.efunda.com. Source of a range on engineering information including engineering equations; simple ones available freely, others on a subscription service.

The Design Council, www.designcouncil.com. The website of the Design Council, with a lot of up to date information on product design and design services.

RAPRA Technology Ltd., www.rapra.net. The site of the former Rubber and Plastics Research Association, gives a range of information on polymers, with additional information on subscription.

Journals

Journal of Engineering Design, published by Taylor & Francis.

Research in Engineering Design, published by Springer Verlag.

Journal of Design Computing, web based journal,
     www.arch.usyd.edu.au/kcdc/journal/IJDC2.
AI-EDAM, published by Cambridge University Press.
Computer Aided Design, published by Elsevier.
Design Studies, published by Elsevier.
International Journal of Production Research, published by Taylor and Francis.
International Journal of Computer Integrated Manufacture, published by Taylor and Francis.
Concurrent Engineering: Research and Applications Journal (CERA-J), published by Sage
     Publishing.
Computers and Industrial Engineering, published by Elsevier.
Journal of MechanicaL Design, published by the American Society of Mechanical
     Engineers.
Advanced Engineering Informatics, published by Elsevier.
International Journal of Product Development, published by Inderscience [to be published in
     2004]

20 Environmental Engineering

Ruth Harrison

Environmental engineering, as this branch of civil engineering became known in the late 20th century, incorporates issues of central concern for human society. At its heart is water supply – capture, treatment and distribution – and this was recognised as such by the Roman, Greek and Egyptian societies many centuries ago; all developed some form of a water supply system. It was not until the 19th century, however, when industrialisation gathered in pace, that major advances were made.

When the pump was invented in the 19th century, engineers were able to increase the capacity of supply, and together with considerable social and economic developments, began to develop a more sophisticated system than had previously existed. In the UK, industrialisation led to a boom in urban living, accompanied with the less welcome spread of ill health and disease, such as cholera, through poor sanitary arrangements. The effects of this led to the creation of a sanitary reform movement successfully lobbying for legislation leading to the Public Health Acts, the first in 1848, followed by a more comprehensive act in 1875 (the first did not include London), and the River Pollution Act in 1876. There is now a wealth of legislation that environmental engineers need to be aware of, including UK Acts of Parliament, and standards as well as EU directives and US legislation.

However, at the earlier stage, government involvement was a new development, as prior to the changes influenced by sanitary reform, water supply had been overwhelmingly financed privately. Drainage had not been funded under similar arrangements, meaning that local and national government had had to take limited action. Continued public awareness of sanitary and health issues, and the impact of these upon engineering, provided the base for the establishment of a professional body in the UK: the Association of Municipal & Sanitary Engineers & Surveyors was formed in 1873. Since this time a number of merges and changes to various other bodies has resulted in the current institution: the Chartered Institution of Water and Environmental Management (CIWEM). Its American counterpart is the American Water Works Association (AWWA).

The changes that affected the development of the professional bodies reflected the changes that were taking place within sanitary and public health engineering throughout the 20th century. The issue of water supply is now only one of a myriad of areas in which environmental engineers study and work. Crucial developments in scientific research such as those in bacteriology, epidemiology and chemistry have all contributed to the growth of the subject, for example leading to better water purification and sewage treatment.

What has also seen a shift is the way in which professionals have described their job function, moving from 'sanitary engineer' when the emphasis was on water supply, drainage and sewerage, to the more recent 'environmental engineer'. The latter has been used to encompass a wider range of concerns with which engineers deal, such as the effect of pollution on the natural environment, in the air and sea, and on land. Again, as awareness has grown, government has become increasingly involved, meaning a rise in environmental protection and pollution prevention. Additionally, research departments and centres have proliferated, as have NGOs providing access to research and resources to less developed areas of the world.

All of these issues mean that an environmental engineer's role is not only one of mere engineering, but one that includes social and economic awareness of the environment they are working in, as well as a constant process of maintaining current practices, as new legislation and increased environmental protection is introduced. Environmental engineers are very much involved in ensuring that the basic tenet, water supply, is feasible, but to ensure this is an even more complex task than it ever has been; additionally they now work within a large variety of interests. Areas of key importance include: air quality control; water supply and distribution; wastewater collection, treatment and disposal; stormwater management; solid waste management; hazardous waste management; biology; chemistry; environmental science; environmental impact assessment; industrial hygiene; noise control; oceanography and radiography.

There is, therefore, a wide range of resources available for environmental engineering, and a key selection of these are described on the following pages. In addition to books, there are internationally published journals, as well as legislation, and report material, published electronically and on paper. This chapter will outline the resources available for the main areas of environmental engineering.

General information

A large number of handbooks have been written as introductions to different aspects of the subject; titles are given in the next section.

Handbooks would be recommended as one of the best places to begin, particularly for students and researchers, as well as professionals, who are new to a subject, or need background information.

Dictionaries, encyclopaedias and handbooks

Gilpin, A., 2000. *Dictionary of environmental law.* Cheltenham: Elgar.

Quentin Grafton, R., Pendleton, L. H., and Nelson, H. W., 2001. *A dictionary of environmental economics, science and policy.* Cheltenham: Elgar.

Porteous, A., 1996. *Dictionary of environmental science and technology.* 2nd ed. Chichester: Wiley.

Chereminisoff, P., ed., 1989– *Encyclopaedia of environmental control technology.* Houston: Gulf.

McGraw-Hill encyclopedia of science and technology. 2002. 9th ed. London: McGraw-Hill.

Corbitt, R. A., ed., 1998. *Standard handbook of environmental engineering.* 2nd ed. New York: McGraw-Hill.

Boulding, J. R., 1995., *Practical handbook of soil, vadose zone, and ground-water contamination: assessment, prevention and remediation.* Boca Raton: Lewis Publishers.

Frank, K., ed., 1994., *Handbook of solid waste management.* New York: McGraw-Hill.

Freeman, H. M., 1997., *Standard handbook of hazardous waste treatment and disposal.* 2nd ed. New York: McGraw-Hill.

HDR Engineering inc., 2001. *Handbook of public water systems.* 2nd ed. New York: Wiley.

Higgins, T. E., ed., 1995. *Pollution prevention handbook.* Boca Raton: Lewis Publishers.

Liu, D. H. F., and Liptak, B. G., 1997. *Environmental engineers' handbook.* 2nd ed. Boca Raton: Lewis Publishers.
Available online via CRC Press subscription services, (www.engnetbase.com).

Mays, L. W., ed., 1996. *Water resources handbook.* New York: McGraw-Hill.

Oh, C. H., 2001. *Hazardous and radioactive waste treatment technologies handbook.* Boca Raton: Lewis Publishers.
Available online via CRC Press subscription services, (www.engnetbase.com).

Petts, J., ed., 1999. *Handbook of environmental impact assessment.* 2 vols. Oxford: Blackwell Science.

Bitton, G., 1997. *Formula handbook for environmental engineers and scientists.* New York: Wiley.

Introductory and review series

Chartered Institute of Water and Environmental Management: Introductory books: series of eight introductions to wastes management; river management; water supply in the UK;

drinking water quality; water quality in rivers, coastal waters and estuaries; industrial wastewater treatment and disposal; wastewater treatment; and sustainable development.

Handbooks on UK wastewater practice: series of six books on preliminary processes; tertiary treatment; activated sludge; biological filtration and other fixed film processes; primary sedimentation; and a glossary.

Handbooks on sewage sludge: series of four books on treatment and management; utilisation and treatment; stabilisation and disinfection; and conditioning, dewatering, thermal drying and incineration.

Details of further series will be available at the CIWEM website: *see Selected organisations* section below.

Royal Society of Chemistry:
Issues in Science and Technology, 1994-
2 issues are published per year, edited by R.E. Hester and R.M. Harrison.

Two examples include:

Air quality management, 1997
Waste incineration and the environment, 1994

More information is available at the RSC website, (www.rsc.org).
A good introductory text book to environmental engineering is:

Kiely, G., 1996. *Environmental engineering.* New York: McGraw-Hill.

Current awareness

A number of institutions publish magazines providing information on current developments, and as environmental concerns continue to rise, it is important that practitioners are able to keep ahead on any possible changes to policy etc. The ICE publishes the *NCE* (New Civil Engineer) weekly, and CIWEM produces a monthly publication, *Water & Environment Manager*. In the US, the ASCE *Civil Engineering* (monthly) provides regular updates.

In addition, electronic publishing means there is a variety of information sources accessible online, of which one of the most notable is Edie (environmental data information exchange), (www.edie.net). Subscribers to the website can receive a weekly newsletter by email – this reports on UK, European and international news in the field – as well as access to other services including the Edie library, literature reviews, a job centre, discussion forums and so on. Providing a similar service, but focussed on Europe, is Environmental Data Services (ENDS), (www.ends.co.uk).

The World Resources Institute has developed EarthTrends, an environmental information portal, (earthtrends.wri.org), which presents a wealth of information on such areas as coastal and marine ecosystems, water resources and freshwater ecosystems, climate and atmosphere, population, health and human well-being, and so on. There is much statistical and background data at this website, for example, country profiles, which provide basic environmental information and sources for each topic covered by the portal.

Bibliographic databases

For literature searching in environmental engineering it would be advisable to consult one or more of the bibliographic databases that can be accessed online or on CD-ROM. These should be available in most academic libraries, as well as at the British Library, and all index a variety of journal articles, technical reports, and conference papers. Those to note include:

Ei Compendex: This is a vast general engineering database produced by an American company called Engineering Information Inc (Ei), and includes over six million records. Its size means it is highly comprehensive, and is likely to be of use to the environmental engineer despite its less specific nature compared to the other databases mentioned below. Source items include journals, conference papers, books, theses, reports and unpublished papers, and with over six million records is a recommended starting point for literature searches.

Science Citation Index: This is another very large bibliographic database that covers a range of multidisciplinary science and engineering subjects. However, coverage extends as far back as 1945, and over 5,700 journals from across the world are indexed, so there is very comprehensive access to published research. The database is produced by an international company called ISI (the Institute for Scientific Information) and can be accessed through a service called ISI Web of Science.

Aqualine: This database includes abstracts from over 300 journals, as well as conference proceedings, reports, books and theses on subjects such as water resources and supplies management, water legislation, water quality, potable water distribution, wastewater collection, water treatment technologies, wastewater and sewage treatment, and ecological and environmental effects of water pollution. It is produced jointly by the Water Resources Centre (WRc) in the UK, and Cambridge Scientific Abstracts (CSA).

Environmental Engineering Abstracts: This database is produced by Cambridge Scientific Abstracts, and covers such areas as air and water quality, environmental safety and energy production, and includes abstracts from over 700 journals, as well as books and theses. Again, there is an emphasis on international coverage.

Pollution Abstracts: This has been compiled to provide information on government policy and assistance on compliance, as well as abstracting scientific research on the most current concerns in pollution control. Journals, conference proceedings and less commercially available publications are indexed from 1981. Areas of coverage include air pollution, marine pollution, freshwater pollution, sewage and wastewater treatment, waste management, land pollution, toxicology and health, noise, radiation, and environmental action. As with the other Abstracts titles listed here, it is produced by and can be accessed at the Cambridge Scientific Abstracts service.

Water Resources Abstracts: Again, this database is available from Cambridge Scientific Abstracts and is compiled from international sources including journals, books, conference proceedings, reports, and government and legal publications. Subject coverage focuses mainly on water supply and treatment. It used to be published by the United States Geological Survey, and in 1994 was taken over by CSA; as such, the material has a strong US bias, but has been broadened to include publications outside the US in recent years.

The Abstracts titles mentioned here also make up the *Environmental Sciences & Pollution Management Database*, produced by Cambridge Scientific Abstracts. This has abstracts from publications covering a wide range of environmental engineering subjects; it is made up of twelve smaller abstract services all of which can be searched individually or as a whole.

There is also a number of other databases relating to research in biology and chemistry which may be of use such as Chemical Abstracts, published by the American Chemical Society and *Biological Sciences*, published by Cambridge Scientific Abstracts.

Report material

As with all disciplines, research organisations, government departments, NGOs and universities all produce their own published material, and this is a valuable area of information, as well as providing access to the most recent research. Organisations which publish report series, or other forms of publications, vary in the types of access they provide, but it is increasingly possible to find research summaries if not whole reports online; they can otherwise be obtained in paper format from the publishing body.

Foundation for Water Research, www.fwr.org
Water Research Centre, www.wrcplc.co.uk

Centre of Ecology and Hydrology, www.nwl.ac.uk/ih

Construction Industry Research and Information Association, www.ciria. org.uk

Department of the Environment, Food and Rural Affairs, www.defra. gov.uk

Department for International Development, www.dfid.gov.uk

Environment Agency, www.environment-agency.gov.uk

Environmental Protection Agency (US), www.epa.gov

Department of Energy (US), www.energy.gov

International Institute for Environment and Development, www.iied.org

Institute for European Environmental Policy, www.ieep.org.uk

Selected organisations

The following professional bodies will all be valuable sources of information, either in the form of their libraries, or that which can be found on their websites.

American Society of Civil Engineers, www.asce.org

American Water Works Association, www.awwa.org

Chartered Institute of Water and Environmental Management, www. ciwem.org.uk

Institute of Air Quality Management, www.iaqm.co.uk

Institute of Environmental Management and Assessment, www.iema.net

Institution of Civil Engineers, www.ice.org.uk

▶ WATER TREATMENT

This is an aspect of environmental engineering that generates much concern in both developed and developing countries. In the latter, a healthy supply of water is often lacking despite technological advances, and the support of aid agencies and voluntary organisations which provide assistance with water pumps, wells and distribution as well as treatment. The Water, Engineering and Development Centre (WEDC) based at Loughborough University, (www.lboro.ac.uk/departments/cv/wedc/index.htm) is committed to research, education and training, and promoting better infrastructures, such as the provision of clean water, in developing countries. Its website is well organised and provides access to a wealth of research and further information. Sustainable development, or sustainability, is another key area of improving focus throughout many disciplines, and is a major consideration in urban planning, of which water treatment is one part. Journals such as *Urban Water* have been established with this as one of their central remits.

A key text is Twort (2000), widely recommended, as well as the AWWA publication (1999), as listed below. Such texts are constantly being revised in line with the legislative and procedural changes that take place internationally.

American Water Works Association, 1999. *Water quality and treatment: a handbook of community water supplies.* 5th ed. New York: McGraw-Hill.

Binnie, C., Kimber, M., and Smethurst, G., 2002. *Basic water treatment.* 3rd ed. London: Thomas Telford.

Hammer, M. J., 2001. *Water and wastewater technology.* 4th ed. Upper Saddle River, NJ: Prentice Hall.

McGhee, T. J., 1991. *Water supply and sewerage.* 6th ed. New York: McGraw-Hill.

Masschelein, W. J., 1992. *Unit processes in drinking water treatment.* New York: Marcel Dekker.

Qasim, S. R., Motley, E. M., and ZHU, G., 2000. *Water works engineering: planning, design and operation.* Upper Saddle River, NJ: Prentice Hall.

Twort, A. C., Ratnayaka, D. D., and Brandt, M. J., 2000. *Water supply.* 5th ed. London, Arnold: IWA Publishing.

Anon. 1991. *Water treatment handbook.* 6th ed. Paris: Reuil-Malmaison, Degrémont.

Journals and magazines

Many journal titles will cover water and wastewater treatment, but the following are a key selection and will provide access to major research. There are also several industry based magazines enabling professionals and students to keep up-to-date with technical issues, including equipment news, and legislative matters.

American Water Works Association Journal
Environmental Science and Technology
Journal of Water Resources, Planning and Management (ASCE)
Urban Water
Water 21
Water and Environmental Management (CIWEM)
Water and Maritime Engineering (ICE)
Water and Waste Treatment
Water and Wastewater International
Water Engineering and Management
Water Science and Technology
Waterlines This title focuses on matters affecting developing countries
World Water and Environmental Engineering
Water Science and Technology is published as a journal, but it is worth noting that each issue is the proceedings of a conference, and it is common for researchers to find reference to the conference without

it being clear this is the case. The publisher's website, (www.iwapub-lishing.com), provides an index, and the British Library Public Catalogue records for the conferences usually note the appropriate journal reference to aid in tracking them down.

It will be necessary also to ensure that any guidelines in whichever country an engineer is working are consulted. The texts above will provide advice on these, although they focus on practices in the US and the UK.

▶ WASTEWATER TREATMENT

Wastewater treatment is of equal concern as water treatment, and again there are many books dealing with this, and increasing amounts of research. It will be necessary to consult a number of books when needing informa-tion about design problems, although Cheremisinoff (2002) has written a comprehensive introduction to this area. A number of other titles commonly used include Metcalf & Eddy (1991), Tebbutt (1992) and Hammer (2001). For undergraduate purposes, texts such as Butler (2000) and Williams (1998) should also be noted, but all the titles listed below should provide reliable advice on various aspects of wastewater treatment. It is likely that books written on water treatment will deal with issues in this area, and vice versa.

Butler, D., and Davies, J. W., 2000. *Urban drainage.* London: Spon.

Cheremisinoff, N. P., 2002. *Handbook of water and wastewater treatment technologies.* Boston: Butterworth-Heinemann.

Cooper, P. F., and Findlater, B. C., eds., 1990. *Constructed wetlands in water pollution control.* Oxford: Pergamon.

Hammer, M. J., 2001. *Water and wastewater technology.* 4th ed. Upper Saddle River, NJ: Prentice Hall.

Horan, N. J., 1990. *Biological wastewater treatment systems.* Chichester: Wiley.

Metcalf and Eddy inc., 1991. *Wastewater engineering: treatment, disposal, and reuse.* 3rd ed. New York: McGraw-Hill.

Read, G. F., and Vickrage, I., eds., 1996. *Rehabilitation and new construction. Vol. 1: repair and renovation.* London: Butterworth-Heinemann.

Tebbutt, T. H. Y., 1992. *Principles of water quality control.* 4th ed. Oxford: Pergamon.

Vesilind, P. A., 1979. *Treatment and disposal of wastewater sludges.* Rev. ed. Ann Arbor: Ann Arbor Science Publishers.

Water Environment Federation, 1998. *Design of municipal wastewater treatment plants.* 4th ed. Alexandria: Water Environment Federation.

Water Research Centre, 2001. *Sewerage rehabilitation manual.* 2 vols. 4th ed. Swindon: Water Research Centre.

Williams, P. T., 1998. *Waste treatment and disposal.* Chichester: Wiley.

Developing countries

Cairncross, S., and Feachem, R. G., 1993. *Environmental health engineering in the tropics: an introductory text*. 2nd ed. Chichester: Wiley.

Feachem, R. G., et al., 1983. *Sanitation and disease: health aspects of excreta and wastewater management*. Chichester: Wiley.

Mara, D. D., 1976. *Sewage treatment in hot climates*. London; Wiley.

Journals and magazines

Again, there are many journals which will cover wastewater treatment in their research papers, and these are a key selection. The majority are highly respected research titles from the major research and professional bodies.

Environmental Science and Technology
International Journal of Water
Journal of Environmental Engineering (ASCE)
Process Biochemistry
Waste Management and Research
Water 21
Water and Environmental Management (CIWEM)
Water and Waste Treatment
Water and Wastewater International
Water Research
Water Science and Technology. See note in previous section on Water Treatment
Waterlines This title focuses on matters affecting developing countries
World Water and Environmental Engineer

▶ WATER POLLUTION

Hand in hand with water treatment and supply is the ability to deal with and remove water pollutants, another essential in ensuring good health and decreasing the spread of disease. Viessmann (1998) and Trudgill (1999) are well recommended along with the ASCE design guide (1998). Water quality modelling, examining and producing mathematical models for water flow and so on, has become another focal research topic: Chapra (1997) and James (1992) can be consulted for further information.

Abel, P. D., 1996. *Water pollution biology*. 2nd ed. London: Taylor & Francis.

ASCE/AWWA, 1998. *Water treatment plant design*. 3rd ed. London: McGraw-Hill.

Chapra, S. C., 1997. *Surface water-quality modelling*. New York: McGraw-Hill.

Eckenfelder, W. W., 1989. *Industrial water pollution control.* 2nd ed. New York: McGraw-Hill.

Harrison, R. M., ed., 2001. *Pollution: causes, effects and control.* 4th ed. Cambridge: Royal Society of Chemistry.

Institute of Water Pollution Control, 1972–1987. *Manuals of British practice in water pollution control.* Maidstone: Institute of Water Pollution Control.

See also the CIWEM series as mentioned in the introductory section of this chapter.

James, A., ed., 1992. *An introduction to water quality modelling.* 2nd ed. Chichester: Wiley.

Mason, C. F., 1996. *Biology of freshwater pollution.* 3rd ed. Harlow: Longman.

Moss, B., 1998. *Ecology of fresh waters: man and medium, past to future.* 3rd ed. Oxford: Blackwell.

Trudgill, S. T., Walling, D. E., and Webb, B. W., eds., 1999. *Water quality: processes and policy.* Chichester: Wiley.

Viessman, W., and Hammer, M. J., 1998. *Water supply and pollution control.* 6th ed. Menlo Park, CA: Addison Wesley.

Journals and magazines

This aspect of pollution is a central area of research, and many journals publish much of this. Below is a selection of the key titles.

Environmental Pollution
Environmental Science and Technology
European Environmental Law Review
Ground Water
International Journal of Environment and Pollution
International Journal of Environment and Sustainable Development
International Journal of Water
Journal of Environmental Engineering (ASCE)
Journal of Environmental Management
Marine Pollution Bulletin
Urban Water
Water 21
Water and Environmental Management (CIWEM)
Water Environment Research
Water Research
Water Science and Technology. See note in previous section on Water Treatment

▶ SOLID AND HAZARDOUS WASTES

As with other potential pollutants, solid and hazardous wastes have received more and more attention in the past few decades because of their environmental impact. The treatment of such wastes is therefore crucial, and it is essential that engineers have access to environmental control guidance as well as the latest research on disposal techniques. The ASCE journal, *Practice Periodical of Hazardous, Toxic and Radioactive Waste Management*, will give access to such research, and may be a good starting point for current literature.

ASTM., [s.d.], *Annual book of standards, vol. 11.04. Environmental assessment, hazardous substances and oil spill responses.* West Conshohocken, PA: ASTM.

Cheremisinoff, N. P., 2003. *Handbook of solid waste management and waste minimisation technologies.* Amsterdam: Butterworth Heinemann.

Department of The Environment, 1976–1991. *Waste management papers, nos. 1–28.* London: HMSO.

> Publications under this series title continued to be produced into the 1990s, with revised and new editions being added.

Pescod, M. B., ed., 1991. *Urban solid waste management.* Firenze: IRIS for World Health Organisation.

Henstock, M. E., ed., 1983. *Disposal and recovery of municipal solid waste: a review of realistic options facing the public authorities and industry.* London: Butterworths.

Holmes, J. R., ed., 1984. *Managing solid wastes in developing countries.* Chichester: Wiley.

Porteous, A., ed., 1985. *Hazardous waste management handbook.* London: Butterworths.

Nemerow, N. L., and Dasgupta, A., 1991. *Industrial and hazardous waste treatment.* New York: Van Nostrand Reinhold.

Wentz, C. A., 1995. *Hazardous waste management.* 2nd ed. New York: McGraw-Hill.

A highly respected conference series is that which was held annually at Purdue University, between 1944 and 1997, called the Purdue Industrial Waste Conference. These conferences are an important reference tool, and were highly regarded internationally amongst waste management professionals for the quality of research papers given each year.

Waste disposal of this kind is closely related to the issues of soil pollution and contaminated land, an example of how environmental engineering can cross over to other scientific concerns. Much research has been conducted in recent years about how landfill affects the environment, and the part played by waste disposal, and, as such, there are a number of titles that can be consulted.

Cairney, T., and Hobson, D. M., eds., 1998. *Contaminated land: problems and solutions.* London: Spon.

Hester, R. E., and Harrison, R. M., eds., 2001. *Assessment and reclamation of contaminated land.* Cambridge: Royal Society of Cambridge.

Petts, J., Cairney, T., and Smith, M., 1997. *Risk-based contaminated land investigation and assessment.* Chichester: Wiley.

Sarsby, R., 2000. *Environmental geotechnics.* London: Thomas Telford.

> This book contains useful chapters on waste disposal and contaminated land, although the overall emphasis is on geotechnical engineering, as the title suggests.

Journals

There are not many titles dealing specifically with solid and hazardous wastes, but material will be found in those journals listed in other sections as well as those listed below.

Environmental Engineering Science
International Journal of Environment and Pollution
Journal of Environmental Health and Science. Part A: Toxic Hazardous Substances and Environmental Engineering
Journal of Hazardous Materials
Practice Periodical of Hazardous, Toxic and Radioactive Waste Management (ASCE)
Waste Management
Waste Management and Research

Various newsletters are published concerning hazardous waste policy, management, guidance, and case law, the majority of these in the US; examples include:

Hazardous Materials Control: industrial effluent and sewage treatment, published in the UK
SANDEC News is published by Swiss Federal Institute for Environmental Science and Technology and includes information on research activities concerning waste management in developing countries
The Hazardous Waste Regulatory Update Service
Waste News

▶ AIR POLLUTION

Air pollution is hardly a problem common to the 20th and 21st centuries, given the effects of industrialisation has affected skies since the 19th century. However, the rate at which pollution has spread and endangered not only the earth's atmosphere, but public health, water supplies, and soil, is verging on catastrophic, certainly for very near generations. Governments are leading efforts to clean up globally, but environmentalists have been arguing their case vociferously for years. Environmental engineers have to be aware of the effects that society has had and will continue to have on its surrounding environment, and clean air is crucial to this.

The books below are a selection of what is available on air pollution; government policies and legal controls are, as with all areas of engineering, particularly important, and it is advisable to check that standards are as up-to-date as are available.

Buonicore, A. J., and Davis, W. T., eds., 1992. *Air pollution engineering manual*. New York: Van Nostrand Reinhold.

Chereminisoff, P. N., ed., 1993. *Air pollution control and design for industry*. New York: Marcel Dekker.

Colls, J., 2002. *Air pollution*. 2nd ed. London: Spon.

Department of The Environment, 1997. *The United Kingdom National Air Quality Strategy*. London: Stationery Office.

Department of The Environment, Transport and The Regions, 1999. *Report on the review of the National Air Quality Strategy: proposals to amend the strategy*. London: DETR.

De Nevers, N., 1995. *Air pollution control engineering*. New York: McGraw-Hill.

Elsom, D., 1992. *Atmospheric pollution: a global problem*. 2nd ed. Oxford: Blackwell.

European Commission, 1996. Council directive on 96/62/EC of 27 September 1996 on ambient air quality assessment and management. *Official Journal* L 296, 21/11/1996, 0055–0063.
  Otherwise known as the *EU Air Quality Framework Directive*.

Expert Panel on Air Quality Standards, 1994–1998. *Reports on air pollutants*. London: HMSO/Stationery Office.

Harrison, R. M., ed., 2001. *Pollution: causes, effects and control*. 4th ed. Cambridge: Royal Society of Chemistry.

Heinsohn, R. J., and Kabel, R. L., 1999. *Sources and control of air pollution*. Upper Saddle River, NJ: Prentice-Hall.

Licht, W., 1988. *Air pollution control engineering: basic calculations for particulate collection*. 2nd ed. New York: Marcel Dekker.

Theodore, L., and Buonicore, A. J., 1988. *Air pollution control equipment*. 2 vols. Boca Raton: CRC Press.

Wellburn, A., 1994. *Acid rain and climate change: the biological impact*. 2nd ed. Harlow: Longman Scientific.

Journals

Many titles which publish research on pollution will contain valuable material on air quality. The journals below focus specifically on air pollution.

Air and Waste: Journal of the Air and Waste Management Association
Air Quality Management (newsletter)
Atmospheric Environment Part A and Part B
Journal of Atmospheric and Terrestrial Physics
Water, Air and Soil Pollution

▶ NOISE

Noise can be an environmental hazard, and one that needs to be controlled both in a work and social environment. Again, legislative controls should be adhered to, and guides to these are listed below. There is a vast range of noise control standards produced by the British Standards Institution, depending on the type of machinery being used, the environment being worked in, the type of industry producing noise, and so on, and these may also have to be consulted.

Technically, acoustics is the study of noise, and there are a number of texts written on this aspect: a small variety is listed below.

Adams, M. S., and McManus, F., 1994. *Noise and noise law.* London: Wiley.

Sharland, I., 1990. *Woods practical guide to noise control.* 6th ed. Colchester: Woods Acoustics.

Bies, D. A., and Hansen, C. H., 1996. *Engineering noise control: theory and practice.* 2nd ed. London: Spon.

HEalth and SAfety Executive, 1998. *Reducing noise at work: guidance on the noise at work regulations 1989.* Sudbury: HSE Books.

Anderson, J. S., and Bratos-Anderson, M., 1993. *Noise: its measurement, analysis, rating and control.* Aldershot: Avebury Technical.

Sound Research Laboratories, 1991. *Noise control in industry.* 3rd ed. London: Chapman & Hall.

Roberts, J., and Fairhall, D., eds., 1989. *Noise control in the built environment.* Aldershot: Gower.

McMullan, R., 1991. *Noise control in buildings.* London: BSP.

Barber, A., 1993. *Handbook of noise and vibration control.* 6th ed. Oxford: Elsevier.

Smith, B. J., Peters, R. J., and Owen, S., 1996. *Acoustics and noise control.* 2nd ed. Harlow: Longman.

Hansen, C. H., and Snyder, S. D., 1997. *Active control of noise and vibration.* London: Spon.

Journals

The journals listed below will guide engineers to the technical aspects of noise control, and, as such, should enable professionals to keep up-to-date with the latest developments. They represent a small number compared to other areas of environmental engineering, but should be useful nevertheless.

Journal of Sound and Vibration
Journal of Vibration and Acoustics
Noise and Vibration Worldwide

► ODOUR

Odour is an area of concern especially when handling and treating wastes, and material on odour will be found within that on air pollution, so refer also to that section of this chapter. However, texts focusing specifically on this subject can be found; journals and conference proceedings are likely to include papers on this subject, so check bibliographic databases for recent research. Journals such as those listed below should be good starting points.

Cheremisinoff, P. N., 1992. *Industrial odour control.* Oxford: Butterworth-Heinemann.

Connor, E. S., and Bruce, A. M., eds., 1984. *Stabilisation, disinfection and odour control in sewage sludge treatment: an annotated bibliography covering the period 1950–1983.* Chichester: Ellis Horwood.

Valentin, F. H. H., and North, A. A., eds., 1980. *Odour control: a concise guide.* Stevenage: Warren Spring Laboratory.

Stuetz, R., and Frechen, F.-B., eds., 2001. *Odours in wastewater treatment: measurement, modelling and control.* London: IWA.

Vincent, A., and Hobson, J., 2001. *Odour control.* London: Terence Dalton.

Woodfield, M., and Hall, D., eds., 1994. *Odour measurement and control: an update.* Abingdon: AEA Technology.

The International Water Association (IWA) began holding an annual conference in 2001 entitled, *Odour and VOCs [volatile organic compounds]: measurement, regulation and control techniques*, which should introduce researchers to, and expand their knowledge of, current research in odour control. The IWA is one of the leading professional bodies for environmental engineers. There have, of course, been other conferences held, and these can be located as suggested above.

Journals

As indicated above, much research material will be presented at conferences, but some journals will publish related papers. Bibliographic databases would be best at locating such material, but the following titles will be of use.

Water Science and Technology. See note in previous section on Water Treatment

Journal of Air and Waste Management Association

► ENVIRONMENTAL IMPACT ASSESSMENT (EIA)

EIA has recently become a much larger focal issue than it was only a decade or so ago; the US led the way in introducing EIA procedures twenty years ago, and other countries have in the past few years begun to take it more seriously. This has led to a proliferation of material on practice and policy, some of which is outlined below. Attention is on the impact that public and private projects will have socially, environmentally and economically, in compliance with EC Directive 97/11/EC (see below), and engineers need to ensure that they have taken all guidance on such assessment before starting work.

For the UK, the *Town and Country Planning (Environmental Impact Assessment) (England and Wales) Regulations 1999 (SI No 293)* implements the Directive. Access to this document is freely available online at the HMSO website, (www.hmso.gov.uk).

Council Directive 97/11/EC of 3 March 1997 amending Directive 85/337/EEC on the assessment of the effects of certain public and private projects on the environment. *Official Journal* L 073, 14/03/1997, 0005 – 0015, (europa.eu.int/eur-lex/en/index.html).

Strategic environmental assessment (SEA) is the latest development, examining the environmental impacts of policies, plans and programmes. EC Directive 2001/42 has been issued to implement this process and member states have to implement this into their own legislation by 2004. The EIA Centre based at the University of Manchester is a good source of information, (www.art.man.ac.uk/EIA/eiac.htm).

Wood, C., 2003. *Environmental impact assessment: a comparative review*. 2nd ed. Harlow: Prentice Hall.
This has a comprehensive and wide international scope.
Canter, L. W., 1996. *Environmental impact assessment*. 2nd ed. New York: McGraw-Hill.
Petts, J., and Eduljee, G., 1994. *Environmental impact assessment for waste treatment and disposal facilities*. Chichester: Wiley.
This is written from both the UK and EU perspectives, and, although slightly dated now, there are useful chapters on assessment on types of pollutant.
Biswas, A. K., and Agarwala, S. B. C., 1992. *Environmental impact assessment for developing countries*. Oxford: Butterworth-Heinemann.
Lee, N., and George, C., eds., 2000. *Environmental assessment in developing and transitional countries: principles, methods and practice*. Chichester: Wiley.
Gilpin, A., 1995. *Environmental impact assessment (EIA): cutting edge for the twenty-first century*. Cambridge: Cambridge University Press.
Turnbull, R. G. H., ed., 1992. *Environmental and health impact assessment of development projects: a handbook for practitioners*. London: Elsevier.
Glasson, J., Therivel, R., and Chadwick, A., 1999. *Introduction to environmental impact assessment: principles and procedures, process, practice and prospects*. 2nd ed. London: UCL Press.
Morris, P., and Therivel, R., eds., 2001. *Methods of environmental impact assessment*. 2nd ed. London: Spon.
Department of The Environment, Transport and The Regions, 2000. *Environmental impact assessment: a guide to procedures*. Tonbridge: Thomas Telford.

Smith, D. A., 1993. *Being an effective expert witness*. London: Thames.
  Helpful advice given for novices in legal situations, although with regards to the date of publishing, any reference to legislation should be checked.
Donnelly, A., Hughes, R., and Dalal-Clayton, B., compilers, 1998. *A directory of impact assessment guidelines*. London: International Institute for Environment and Development.
Bell, S., and McGillivray, D., 1999. *Ball and Bell on environmental law: the law and policy relating to the protection of the environment*. 5th ed. London: Blackstone Press.
  EC and UK law coverage
Gillies, D., 1999. *A guide to EC environmental law*. London: Earthscan.
Sunkin, M., Ong, D. M., and Wight, R., eds., 1998. *Sourcebook on environmental law*. London: Cavendish.
Therivel, R., and Rosario Partidario, M., 1996. *The practice of strategic environmental assessment*. London: Earthscan.
Rosario Partidario, M., and Clark, R., eds., 2000. *Perspectives on strategic environmental assessment*. Boca Raton: Lewis Publishers.

Journals

There is a small number of research journals, but it is highly likely that this number will increase over the next few years.

Environmental Monitoring and Assessment
Environmental Law and Management
European Environmental Law Review
International Journal of Environment and Sustainable Development
Journal of Environmental Assessment Policy and Management
Sustainable Development

▶ RELATED AREAS

In addition to the main subjects as listed above, environmental engineers will find that aspects of other engineering fields will be applicable to their work, such as hydrology, groundwater engineering, chemistry and biology. While it would not be possible to provide references for all these areas, it is likely that information source guidance will be available in similar reference tools. Organisations such as CIWEM publish useful introductions as well, as outlined in the opening paragraphs of this chapter. The handbooks and other introductory texts listed should also be consulted for further references to any related sub-areas.

The following titles would be recommended as starting points:

Lester, R. N., and Birkett, J. W., 1999. *Microbiology and chemistry for environmental scientists and engineers*. 2nd ed. London: Spon.

Domenico, P. A., and Schwartz, F. W., 1998. *Physical and chemical hydrogeology*. 2nd ed. New York: Wiley.

Chow, V. T., Maidment, D. L., and Mays, L. M., 1988. *Applied hydrology*. New York: McGraw-Hill.

Reed, D., and Faulkner, D., *et al.*, eds., 1999. *Flood estimation handbook*. 5 vols. Wallingford: Institute of Hydrology.

Previously known as the *Flood studies report*; this is a detailed analysis of flood data collated by the Institute of Hydrology for the UK.

Hillel, D., 1998. *Environmental soil physics*. San Diego, CA: Academic Press.

Douglas, J. F., Gasoriek, J. M., and Swaffield, J. A., 2001. *Fluid mechanics*. 4th ed. Harlow: Prentice Hall.

Burroughs, W. J., 2001. *Climate change: a multidisciplinary approach*. Cambridge: Cambridge University Press.

▶ BIBLIOGRAPHY

British Medical Association, 1998. *Health and environmental impact assessment*. London: Earthscan.

Corbitt, R. A., ed., 1998. *Standard handbook of environmental engineering*. 2nd ed. New York: McGraw-Hill.

Department of The Environment, Transport and The Regions, 2000. *Environmental impact assessment: a guide to procedures*. Tonbridge: Thomas Telford.

Glasson, J., Therivel, R., and Chadwick, A., 1999. *Introduction to environmental impact assessment: principles and procedures, process, practice and prospects*. 2nd ed. London: UCL Press.

Kiely, G., 1996. *Environmental engineering*. New York: McGraw-Hill.

Smith, D., ed., 1999. *Water-supply and public health engineering*. Aldershot: Ashgate Publishing Limited.

21 | Manufacturing Engineering

Jim Corlett and Peter Rayson

▶ INTRODUCTION

The aims of this chapter are two-fold: firstly, to provide a vision of the development of the manufacturing enterprise and the ways in which issues of information and knowledge will be addressed; and secondly, to see how those 'traditional' manufacturing information sources dealt with by previous editions of this work are developing within this context.

▶ THE INTELLIGENT MANUFACTURING ENTERPRISE

As we stand at the dawn of the 21st century, the ability of an enterprise, manufacturing or otherwise, to persist, grow and survive will be predicated on its ability to adapt to new conditions, manage the change and become a de-facto element of a revenue food-chain. From an economic standpoint, adaptability is a function of being able to generate and affect new responses quickly. Currently, the state of our toolset to deal with enterprise design is analogous to the level of engineering design tools available to the early aviation pioneers. This has implications for both industry and academia.

Whilst many of our technical capabilities (CRM, SRM, CNC, CAE, CAD, MRP, PDM, UML and IP Networks) developed in the 20th century are presented as standard methods, particularly in manufacturing organisations, their application has always been somewhat experiential, piecemeal and dependent upon the maturity of the concepts and technology. In hindsight, the consensus view of most business leaders today is that technology has failed to deliver on the business value that had been anticipated.

Technology companies are finding it very difficult to market messages of increased efficiency and performance on the basis of acquiring pieces of technology alone. It is now patently obvious that processes, organisation and culture really do have to be effectively addressed if investments are to produce the desired business performance results. This failure to take on board the organisational and cultural dimensions has in a large part contributed to the recent collapse of this sector.

This should not have been a great surprise. The external market conditions of enterprises have been and remain highly volatile. This has a direct impact on the goals and strategies that enterprises pursue. The business team is always challenged with constructing and implementing organisational, technological and human capital responses, i.e. value processes. To be successful, these processes must align with the enterprise strategies and need to be enhanced by effective use of knowledge, information, data and technology tools.

Intelligent enterprise

According to Jonathan Spira, CEO & Chief Analyst, Basex, (www.basex. com/web/tbghome.nsf/pages/home), a US-based collaborative business knowledge company, by the year 2006, more than 40% of all knowledge workers will work remotely. Business organisations and their constituencies will rely upon, and thrive on, advanced iterations of the knowledge exchange and collaboration solutions available today. In his view, for any enterprise, the power to compete effectively will depend on the ability to plan for, deploy, and support this new environment.

To do so, he suggests users must develop a firm understanding of imminent changes to IT and business landscape that will support the transformation. Today, he sees the broad range of collaborative, knowledge and content sharing solutions as confusing and complex. Nevertheless, the ability to make the right choices now, within the context of a sound strategy, is critical. While the required investments and risks are profound, the rewards will be unprecedented, so the mantra goes. Therein lies the rub: how are these unprecedented rewards to be achieved?

Systems thinking

As most engineers know, if you want a system to perform, then you have to design the system such that it can reliably achieve its given performance criteria or goal, which also has to be declared, otherwise you will not know when you have succeeded. Natural and artificial systems, such as aircraft, automobiles and manufacturing enterprises, comprise hierarchies of subsystems interconnected in such a manner to allow the system to perform to specification.

Our experience to date with Product Design has taught us that good designs are those where we understand the functional requirements, and what design parameters are available to achieve them, which then allow the identification of the process variables required to realise the design. Professor Nam Pyo Suh (2001) has declared what he describes as 'axioms of design' and has provided a theoretical framework called Axiomatic Design.

He argues that Design is ubiquitous across human activity; whilst each field of endeavour may use different databases and practices, what is common is that the designers must all do the following:

1.   *Know* or understand their *customers needs*
2.   *Define the problem* they must solve to satisfy the needs
3.   *Conceptualise the solution through synthesis*
4.   Perform *analysis* to optimise the proposed solution
5.   *Check the resulting design solution* to see if it meets the original customer needs.

There are some serious implications arising from this view, rooted in the rate at which new designs are created and deployed in a competitive free market economy. The plethora of new products, technology standards, methods and formats provide us with a vast array of design parameters that we can choose from to satisfy our system functional requirements. Examples are: collaborative technologies from organisations such as IBM, Microsoft, Oracle, SAP, PTC and Groove, where the virtual teaming spaces are predicated upon relatively new approaches like peer to peer using technology manifestations such as Portals, XML and Web Services.

The challenge for manufacturing businesses is that this manufacturing enterprise system design need is usually not their core competence. Invariably, the competence lies in the nature of the product the enterprise produces. The 'time-to-cash' need of the business requires that enterprise systems must be assembled quickly and efficiently in cost effective support of the business goal. It is this business goal which provides the context for determining the functional requirements of the system.

Changing business models

Many traditional businesses today started life as product companies, but the world moves on and their once innovative commercial product is now a commodity and their business model is no longer product-centric but service-centric. The speed with which this occurs is accelerating due to the inherent difficulty in generating truly differentiated products, as opposed to innovating existing developments. The business model becomes one of service level agreements and back-to-back contracts with value predicated on performance metrics.

In England, ignorance of law is no defence; there is a similar observation for manufacturing systems when it comes to being aware of the design parameters available that can be used to fulfil functional requirements. Navigating through the technology options space of commercial versus open source software, mobile versus fixed platforms, network topologies, bandwidth, in-house ICT versus outsourced, is fraught with danger. Poorly designed systems projects can consume large amounts of a company's resources – people, cash and time – and can become a distraction from the key business goal. It has, however, until recently been a lucrative market for System Integrators.

With the persistent and continued relaxation of national trade barriers, all enterprises – private or public – exist and interact within the global market environment. The basis of their business model is invariably a product or service that the market consumers want; the margin that can be commanded is determined by supply and demand. Variations in the market demand are complex and driven by many factors such as world events, new fashions or changes in cultural behaviour and changed expectations. The rate and scale and awareness of change we face as a global society is intense, ranging across GM foods, global warming, nanotechnology, mobile technology, transport and health services, all constrained by finite energy reserves.

Adapt and survive

For manufacturing companies, the competitive landscape is global in nature and the responses they make to the marketplace will determine their ability to survive and thrive. By analogy with biological organisms, (e.g. a virus), human organisations will have to be adaptive to be able to persist and survive. This has a direct impact on the design of organisation, its people and their information systems. Since the 1960s, information systems have been largely developed as personal productivity tools. The 90s' move to groupware tools by companies such as Lotus was enabled by the proliferation of IP networks providing connectivity and availability via high performance personal computers. The killer applications were email, spreadsheets, relational databases, word processing, browsers, http, URLs. These tools generated data, provided unstructured data, managed structured data and gave us connectivity and communication within our organisations.

Manufacturing was at the heart of the growth of MRP, through MRPII to today's ERP systems which effectively aggregate the common business applications required to operate a business from payroll to dynamic scheduling of a manufacturing plant. Engineering Design followed suit by aggregating the various applications for product definition, analysis, simulation, verification and product data management.

These two technology developments crashed into each other when engineering design parts lists met manufacturing bills of material, two hierarchical structures generated for different purposes but with essentially the same content. These structures are invariably configured, changed and modified by customers, engineering, manufacturing and service support. This change in turn impacts the part numbering and component identification which proliferates across all data items related to the component such as jigs and fixture, repair manuals, suppliers and, of course, customers.

Change is always expensive; as Henry Ford is said to have remarked, ' . . . you can have any colour you like as long as it is black'. Unfortunately, the 21st century world we live in is one of ever increasing and accelerating change. We do not have the luxury of creating organisational systems that are monolithic and brittle; they must be designed to be adaptive. This means that technology companies' market responses have to be tools that can be configured on demand for a designed process and defined human roles.

Information technology tools are in effect becoming utilities much like gas, electricity and water in support of business processes that have to produce value. The real value of processes is in the data, customer/supplier information content and knowledge that can be brought to bear in support of the business goals. The role that information technology plays is its ability to provide connection, facilitate communication and co-operation between value processes. However, it must be easily deployable, reconfigurable and humans must be able to rapidly and intuitively relate to the environment allowing them to achieve their role-based goals.

Value chains and responding

Enterprises, organisations are made up of hierarchies of interconnected value processes. Invariably, as you move away from the shop floor, these processes are not designed but described loosely by mission statements, people trees and procedures. The argument usually runs along the lines of design being an intellectual activity, not dealing with physical materials i.e. fuzzy, too difficult to quantify. The reality is that virtual product definition is every much as real as physical product realisation.

Whilst the objects are not *atom*-based but are *bit*-based, it is becoming an imperative for these virtual definitions to be validated and verified prior to physical realisation. Due to the globally federated nature of enterprise, brought about by the need to share risk and profits across an extended value chain, the use of collaborative, analytical and transactional patterns of business involving digital objects is now inescapable. The technology/SI company terminology currently in vogue to describe this scenario is loosely called Product Lifecycle Management (PLM).

However, this serial type of PLM view rather misses the point, as what we are dealing with is the need for 'design of enterprise'; the enterprise is a 'System' responding to marketplace patterns and signals. The response the enterprise makes determines its quality of life and continued survival. The types of response an enterprise may make can be categorised:

1.	Conditioned Responding System	(S-R)
2.	Discriminative Learning System	(S-O-R)
3.	Generative Processing System	(S-P-R)
4.	Organisational Processing System	(S-OP-R)
5.	Market Processing System	(S-PP-R)

This argument applies to the design and realisation of the organisation, people and processes which in turn are the framework for realising physical product and services designs. Today, we have to be consciously designing adaptive capability into our enterprise designs. This is not just a technology issue but involves people capabilities and cultural behaviours. This is why the term Intelligent Enterprise (IE) is preferred rather than PLM, which still tends towards technology solutions.

What are we selling?

The real economic products going forward will be service products that in many cases will have a physical product or digital definition or intellectual property as their economic platform. Early examples can be observed in the mobile market where the device is a platform to consume services. Similarly, Amazon and eBay represent services built on digital data and augmented by customer feedback and content. These services in effect will emanate from value zones within the enterprise and they will be consumed externally by customers to generate revenue or internally between value zones to reduce costs.

However, they will all have to be designed and the key interdependent design architectures of service product definition, processes, performance, organisation and technology will have to be configured. Today's extended enterprise designs are driven by marketplace changes, time-to-market, time-compression, cost reduction and risk sharing. The current inherent lack of design will be a significant contributor to their failure to prosecute opportunities and generate value for stakeholders, but it does not have to be this way.

Defining an extended enterprise is just as much a 'Design' exercise as the product design of a new or modified Jet Engine; the problem is that 'Enterprise Design' does not have the maturity and rigour associated with 'Product Design'. With this in mind, there is now a need to launch a generative international centre, an Intelligent Enterprise Foundation (IEF), having at its core the mission of Enterprise Design,

The Foundation would draw together competencies in the studies of social networks, human behaviour, cultural modes, entertainment technology, organisational process structures, programme management, knowledge-based technologies, complex adaptive systems, ICT, pattern recognition and axiomatic design. The purpose of the Foundation would be to develop 'Design Capability for Enterprise' that can be used to quantitatively provide robust business solutions in the same manner as is routinely expected from electro-mechanical product design activity.

Enterprise by design

The Foundation is required to explore and understand how Enterprises can respond to conditions of change, which are just like waves on the ocean; these waves of change build up, crest and diminish. In terms of the global marketplace, they may begin as sources of differentiated advantage, crest as the source of advantage, and then attenuate as new conditions build force. It was not so long ago that we witnessed one particular historical 'trough': the receding of the mechanical revolution, while, simultaneously, the so-called ICT revolution was gaining strength.

The marketplace can be considered to have waves or phases that can be labeled as Generative, Innovative, Commercial, Commodity and Attenuated. For many businesses, these phases are accelerating, as they are themselves impacted by the conditions of change. The advent of the Internet technologies in particular has generated a wave of change that has propagated across society, enterprises and business processes, creating significant ripples of change in its wake.

This phenomenon has its roots in the new ICT product industries of software, computers and telecommunications networks. Much of this capability, emerging during the cold war period, was put into service to facilitate time-to-market compression and reduced costs for traditional mechanical and pharmaceutical product businesses. The core tenet was to digitise the data, visual or audio, and move it quickly to the points of decision within the organisation.

As traditionally closed markets became open to global competition, the pressure to reduce costs became a key driver. This led the drive to reduce unnecessary headcount and significant downsizing of both blue and white collar direct labour force as well as the associated supply chain community. In response, modern organisations have, over the last 20 years, moved steadily away from the hierarchical control structures, inherited from the military, to flatter, networked, matrix-type organisations which are federated, being driven and coordinated by specific project goals and objectives.

This move toward collaborative environments is gaining momentum. The dynamics of doing business are changing rapidly. In many companies, virtual teams comprising workers around the globe are crucial to major projects. Nevertheless, the benefits of Intelligent Enterprise can only be realised by integrating core business processes and communications with knowledge management techniques and technologies. This requires major shifts in corporate culture, including the way people think about doing work. Moreover, corporate managers will be forced to understand, assess and implement a host of solutions which may well seem foreign today.

This shift to the new workplace requires significant analysis, planning, policy-making, and technology assessments, as well as large investments to support the transition. As a result, the new workplace, its stages of deployment and underlying elements, and the affected business operations, are all at risk.

Entering the age of unreason

Charles Handy (1995) brought to our attention the idea that individuals will have a portfolio of work, based on the view that rapid change causes unpredictable economic outcomes. Projects today typically generate work packages for individuals that are instantiated for a fixed period; the project leader assembles the mosaic of human capital required for the execution of the programme.

One metric of an Enterprise's business fitness is the speed and agility with which it can adapt to new opportunities or threats. Many analysts and observers point to the impact of what they call cultural inertia, when organisations fail to respond or execute the prosecution of a new business model. What they are really identifying is the lack of human capital development investment. The perceived enterprise responses and behaviour in the marketplace are emergent behaviours founded on the internal organisational culture, human capabilities and conditioned responses.

This organisational latency or extended learning curve stems from a lack of attention to a number of dimensions that impact human growth and development. These observations have very significant issues for educational institutions and those technology companies currently creating collaborative solutions for pan-enterprise virtual teams. The issues of knowledge, interaction, trust and value are of huge importance for successful projects.

21st Century performers

The changes in organisational control conditions led to a move away from conditioned performers who were fully dependent, as exemplified by the Taylor model of production systems. People were required to become involved in understanding the process preceding action. The organisational authorities still explored the data and they also retained control of understanding the strategic goals. However, they did delegate the tactical goals.

This resulted in performers participating in decision making and problem solving activities. They became involved in designing systems to achieve the goals, taking responsibility for the implementation of the systems. To do this, they needed to expand their repertoire of responses to manage their new responsibilities. In today's world, this translates into a concept described as *On Demand Workplace*, where the role-based process is configured online and surfed up using portal technology to the user on demand. The marketplace pressure and need to shorten the 'time-to-cash' cycle for projects means that traditional approaches to manufacturing systems design are inadequate.

We have seen a transition from the Industrial Age performer valued for dependency, to the Data Age performer valued for independent contribution. These independent performers were differentiated by their accumulated repertoires of response. They related laterally as well as vertically in participative settings to share known responses, e.g. quality circles, team building and consensus building. These performers are characterised by corporate identification, as opposed to corporate obedience; their welfare and that of the corporation are linked. The critical change is that they shared in the understanding of the goals before acting on the programmes.

The advent of this participative learning organisation served to increase the response repertoire and enabled performers to work smarter. Unfortunately, the problem that we now face is that the task requirements are changing so rapidly that we quickly exhaust known responses. Prior to the Internet, working smarter simply meant that the performer collected and selected from the available best practices for productive task performance. Today, performers are required to operate best knowledge processes for creating new and better responses.

The driver for this is the customer, who wants more personal service, more customisation, more value – on demand. The service-centric nature of the engagement with their customers means companies must establish an enterprise system that is interconnected from end-to-end with all aspects of their business processes both internally and externally – in real time. In this way, every relevant resource is leveraged in every interaction with the customer. Without this level of integration, the energy of a company – human interaction, customer data, pricing information, supply management – cannot be focused into value service flows through the business to the customer.

Only when people inside and outside the organisation and all business applications are interconnected can businesses adapt immediately to meet unpredictable market conditions and demands, i.e. innovative response or commodity response.

Cultural change realities

The most distinguishing characteristic of the Industrial Age was that people were asked to act – not to think. They were prepared by being conditioned or reinforced to make the appropriate conditioned response. In the paradigm of human processing, someone higher in the hierarchy explored the data, understood the goals, then allocated the action tasks to totally dependant performers.

While conditioned responding may be appropriate under specified and unchanging conditions, it becomes increasingly inappropriate with changing conditions. Spiralling changes in conditions condemn conditioned response training efforts to failure, the responses becoming functionally autonomous or autistic.

People change their attitudes and response only if they see the point of the change and agree with it at least enough to give it a go. Psychologists talk of cognitive dissonance, a mental state arising when people find their beliefs are inconsistent with their actions. The implication for organisations is that if people believe in its overall purpose, they will be happy to change their behaviour. To do this requires a meaningful and understandable story that can be related to all the people involved in making change happen.

Motivating people by conditioning and positive reinforcement such as reporting structures, measurement procedures, setting targets means that they all have to be consistent with the behaviour that people are asked to adopt. To adopt change means equipping people with skills they need to adopt. Alvin Toffler (1970) defined 'future shock' as 'a feeling of unease and apprehension, associated with the loss of a sense of permanence and caused by rapid and unrelenting change'. Not only are the infrastructures of modern enterprises changing, but the social fabrics that kept them together are also changing. There is no longer any single dominant common value system overshadowing all others.

It is a paradox that, whilst people are bombarded with universal images and icons, they are becoming more differentiated and tribal in their self-identification. Racial and ethnic divisions, age and gender gaps, and a proliferation of social and political agendas are taking away the comfortable sense of certainty and simple answers. The key observation is that people with a high psychological need for structure and order (e.g. as often found in engineering and manufacturing enterprises) will face increasing stress as the rules and answers become increasingly less clear. Conversely, the skill that psychologists call 'tolerance ambiguity' will become increasingly important for a person who wants to thrive, succeed and lead others in this new age of Intelligent Enterprise, which builds upon the Information Age.

Enterprise performance

In today's enterprise, the need is for continuous generation of new and more productive responses. The spiraling changes create the conditions for generative thinking. The difference between participative learning and generative thinking is that between best practices and best processes for creating new and better responses, i.e. thinking better. The capability required is that the performer can generate new and more productive ways of doing things under all circumstances, particularly, for instance, at a distance as part of an extended virtual team.

As authorities or bosses are overwhelmed by information overload from the information super highway and the web technologies, in particular, e-mail and voice mail, they must share the responsibility for total processing. This is particularly noticeable in Manufacturing – as the time to respond is ever reduced, the window for profit more fleeting, the need for collaborative knowledge-based extended enterprise value chains becomes more pronounced.

The head of the food chain has to delegate the entire database for processing, (e.g. engine design and manufacture), ceding responsibility for exploring experiences, understanding the goals and acting upon the programmes. To do so, the performers have to learn a whole new set of processing skills to deal with the information available and to be able to process it interdependently. A key skill is the ability to filter and evaluate the quality of what you see, hear and read. In support of 21st century manufactures, it will be critical to identify sources of high quality information, with content that is trustworthy. Even more important will be being part of/gaining access to expert networks and communities of practice

To put this in perspective, by 2004 the US will have 18,000 magazine titles, 200 television channels, 2,400 Internet radio stations and 20 million Internet sites. In five years, the amount of knowledge that now exists will double, and will continue to double every five years. Basically, we are unable to take it all in, much less remember it. Even if we store it electronically, we probably won't remember we have it or why we needed it. As soon as almost any information reaches us, it is already obsolete or on the way to obsolescence. This scenario requires that manufactures have organisational and cultural strategies to manage and direct the business towards relevant, pragmatic data, information and methods via know ledge hubs, expert networks, avatar technology and knowledge transfer specialists, etc.

This is so important because, within any manufacturing organisation, the people population will be a mosaic of capability; the earlier cultural waves of conditioning that performers were subject to will mean that there will most likely still be a significant population of dependent performers, but with an increasing population of independent performers. The big challenge is to grow people as interdependent performers with a tolerance for ambiguity.

Going global

For global enterprises, the challenge is magnified as people are sourced from a variety of national and social backgrounds. This move to independent and subsequently interdependent performers can also be detected as they proactively take personal responsibility for their own development. Convergent with this are virtual collaborative spaces which bridge time and distance, allowing companies to work 24/7 on what is called 21st Century time. Unfortunately, this virtual environment brings with it a new set of problems, as knowledge workers form virtual teams but never meet face to face, telecommuters face isolation, and the relationships formed around the coffee vending machine are never formed.

In modern society and enterprises, this scenario translates into the need for provision of a knowledge ecosystem, coaching portals that nurture self-help with appropriate validation of content and interdependent mentoring. It is an unfortunate fact that western society is moving from an oral and written tradition to a pictorial tradition. The popular media, whence most people derive their 'knowledge' of the contemporary world, are securely in the hands of commercial enterprise, whose route to value creation is via entertainment, not knowledge and intellect.

However, it is clear that, as spiralling change increases the complexity of the global working environment, interdependent manufactures will require a breadth of knowledge. People who can reach beyond the current topic of pre-occupation to find inspiration, meaning, context, examples, analogies, metaphors, lessons and primal themes have the edge when it comes to figuring out what comes next. Unfortunately, the pool of available knowledge is growing exponentially, but can be filtered by establishing an organisational leadership competency map in conjunction with sets of sources of high quality information and ideas that can be trusted. This need is driving the evolution of knowledge hubs and educational programmes where simple content aggregation and learning scheduling now has to be augmented by *filtering, categorising and configuring information* from knowledge sources to support the diverse needs of the interdependent performer.

▶ MANUFACTURING INFORMATION SERVICES

Before moving to consider the implications and future direction of the intelligent enterprise and the integration of services involved therein, we need to look at what many would describe as 'traditional' manufacturing information sources, where they are now in relation to enterprise developments, and how they may be integrated into knowledge hubs, both for the intelligent enterprise and the area which will do much to feed it, i.e. academia. This area is only a part – but an important part – of the scenario envisaged above. There are signs that moves are afoot to make many of the sources at least potentially applicable. This overview differs substantially from that given in the previous edition of this work largely in the *mode of delivery* and the way *bundles of products* are being put together, rather than in the products themselves.

The current scene still has a very intermediate feel about it. Some interesting products are beginning to emerge to take advantage of the Web and the medium of electronic delivery. Highlights include:

- aggregated, cross-searchable collections of full-text manufacturing books and journals
- the first examples of truly multimedia manufacturing e-books
- significant individual publisher full-text electronic collections
- freely-available full-text patent information and freely searchable standards databases

as well as the more traditional electronic information sources, such as bibliographic databases and on-line book and video catalogues. (See Chapters 2 and 8 for fuller details on electronic sources in general)

Electronic delivery of easily retrievable full-text documents is what the customer demands, as a key component of a knowledge hub. This is being addressed to a certain extent at the moment

- by aggregators gathering together products from different publishers and allow both searching and browsing of the complete collection
- by single publishers offering the same facilities, but for their own collections only

Both offerings allow the user to search by (combinations of) keywords, and retrieve the information from wherever it may be, as well as going to specific (favourite?) individual journal or book titles. *Most offer free searching, but access to full-text is only by subscription or payment per article.*

This development is more widely available in the journal publishing world, although certain areas of book publishing are making some headway. Many key titles will, as mentioned, be familiar from the previous edition, but in a different guise. The lists below are intended to provide examples of the sort of titles now available electronically, to illustrate developments occurring.

Books

An interesting and powerful tool in the context of **e-reference books** (handbooks/data books, etc) is provided by Knovel, (www.knovel.com). Knovel aims to provide a reference service, and, to this end, collects handbooks and data books from different publishers. Both the text and the data from these books are searchable, with a limited amount of interaction with the data. Examples of current titles which may be of interest to manufacturing engineers include:

- *The handbook of adhesives and sealants*
- *Paint and surface coatings – theory and practice*
- *Ceramic cutting tools*
- *Advanced ceramic processing and technology*
- *Handbook of composites*
- *Handbook of materials for product design*
- *Manufacturing engineers' reference book*
- *Engineering documentation control handbook*
- *Juran's quality handbook*
- *Dimensioning and tolerancing handbook*
- *Machinery's handbook*
- *Metal machining – theory and practice*
- *Roark's formulas for stress and strain*
- *Welding materials handbook*
- *Handbook of mould, tool and die repair welding*
- *Handbook of plastics joining*
- *Injection moulding handbook*
- *Materials selection deskbook*

New works are added to the collection regularly.

Another valuable collection of specifically **manufacturing reference works** is hosted by Ebrary, (www.ebrary.com/libraries/dbcollections.jsp). This is SME Source, consisting of some 4,000 books, journals and technical papers in manufacturing engineering published by the Society of Manufacturing Engineers, including the nine-volume Tool and Manufacturing Engineers Handbook series, and current and back volumes of *Journal of Manufacturing Systems* and *Journal of Manufacturing Processes.*

An example of a **single-publisher source** of online books is ENGnetBASE, (www.engnetbase.com), a collection of handbooks from CRC Press. Items with a manufacturing flavour include:

- *Composites manufacturing: materials, product, and process engineering*
- *Computational intelligence in manufacturing handbook*
- *Computer-aided design, engineering, & manufacturing: systems techniques and applications. 7 vols*
- *Run-to-run control in semiconductor manufacturing*

However, few publishers are taking full advantage of the technological possibilities in terms of e-publications. Professor Paul Ranky, of NJIT and CIMware, (www.cimwareukandusa.com), is one of the few to truly address this area. His case-based/problem-based teaching/learning approach provides 3D e-Book case studies involving leading experts and processes and takes full advantage of 3D web-browser readable multimedia technology with text and images, interactive 2D and 3D videos, 3D objects and panoramas, and active code, such as requirements analysis, risk analysis, statistical quality control, design of experiments, computer assisted assessment tools, and others, for faculty and students to calculate with their own data. Current 3D e-Book cases include:

- *Introduction to computer networking and the internet with engineering examples*
- *Case-based introduction to IMI Norgren's reengineering project*
- *Case-based introduction to component oriented disassembly (process) failure risk analysis [6 vols.]*
- *Case-based introduction to component oriented disassembly and user interface requirements analysis [vol.1 of 8 published]*
- *Case-based introduction to advanced CAM (computer aided manufacturing)*
- *Rapid prototyping solutions*
- *Introduction to the US national electronics manufacturing initiative's (NEMI) plug and play factory project*
- *Digital factory and digital, telematic car modelling*
- *IBM's solution to digital telematic cars*
- *Introduction to total quality management and the international quality standards*
- *Key R&D and e-Transition trends in US and international collaborative design and manufacturing enterprises*

Details of forthcoming case studies may be found on the website.

Other libraries of e-books are starting to appear, such as netLibrary and eBooks.com, and there are other sites with links to relevant books (such as: www.hopcottebooks.com/ebooks/manufacturing.html), although the number of manufacturing e-books currently available still seems low.

Some authors use the Web to provide **e-supplements** to the information in their hard-copy books. This trend may increase. One example is at: www.ulrich-eppinger.net for the book by Ulrich and Eppinger on Product Design and Development. One way to find free full-text material is via sites like EEVL (www.eevl.ac.uk/engineering/catalogue.htm), which offer searching by resource type (including *full-text e-books*) and subjects (including *Manufacturing Engineering*).

To find the latest **non-e-books** on manufacturing, it is worth looking at mainstream publishers sites. For example, the Industrial Engineering section, which includes manufacturing, at Wiley (www.wiley.com/WileyCDA/Section/id-2745.html) and at Elsevier (www.elsevier.com/inca/tree/?mode=advanced&key=A440&sarea=saf), Prentice-Hall's Mech/Manufacturing/Industrial Tech section at: vig.prenhall.com/catalog/academic/discipline/0,4094,3784,00.html or Kluwer (including Chapman & Hall)'s Manufacturing Technology at: www.wkap.nl/home/topics/1/A/ with further sections on factory automation and flexible manufacturing systems, all provide the requisite details. A useful, if dated, list of publishers in the Manufacturing area may be found on the World Wide Web Virtual

Library site at: www.uwstout.edu/mevl/mevl5.html. For those looking for guides towards achieving world-class manufacturing, Productivity Press (www.productivityinc.com/press/index.html) produces books, videos and training materials on process/productivity improvements (techniques such as lean manufacturing, six sigma, SMED, JIT, TPM, the Baldrige Award criteria, benchmarking, etc)

Of **professional societies**, the SME – www.sme.org/cgi-bin/books-vids. pl?15&&SME&BK& – has books listed under the following topics:

- Assembly
- Composites manufacturing
- Electronics manufacturing
- Finishing and coating
- Forming and fabricating
- Lean manufacturing
- Machining and material removal processes
- Manufacturing engineering and management
- Manufacturing systems, automation and IT
- Materials
- Measurement, inspection & testing
- Plastics moulding & manufacturing
- Product design management
- Quality
- Rapid technologies and additive manufacturing (RTAM)
- Research and development/new technologies
- Robotics and machine vision
- Welding

Videos, under most of the same headings, may be found at: www.sme.org/cgi-bin/books-vids.pl?15&&SME&VT&

Other societies such as

- ASME (members.asme.org/catalog/index.cfm?ProductType=A)
- IMechE (www.pepublishing.com/frm_bookshop.htm)
- ASM (www.asmInternational.org/Template. cfm?Section=BrowsebyTopic&template=Ecommerce/ Topic.cfm&TopicID=19)

also publish relevant books (and sometimes videos).

Journals

Some may be surprised at the inclusion of Business Source Premier as an example of an **aggregator** here. Despite its name, it includes a collection of full-text journals and directories/yearbooks within the manufacturing area:

- *American machinist*
- *Automotive design and production*
- *Automotive engineer*
- *CAD/CAM update*
- *Engineering management journal*
- *Fabricated metal products industry yearbook*
- *General industrial machinery yearbook*
- *Industrial management*
- *Industrial management and data systems*
- *International journal of computer integrated manufacturing*
- *International journal of operations and production management*
- *International journal of production research*
- *International journal of reliability, quality and safety engineering*
- *International journal of robotics research*
- *Journal of management in engineering*
- *Leadership and management in engineering*
- *Machine design*
- *Maintenance management*
- *Manufacturing and service operations management*
- *Manufacturing systems*
- *Material handling management*
- *Materials and manufacturing processes*
- *Metalworking digest*
- *Metalworking machinery industry yearbook*
- *Metalworking production*
- *Modern machine shop*
- *Modern materials handling*
- *Plastic materials industry yearbook*
- *Proceedings of the IMechE B [Engineering manufacture]*
- *Proceedings of the IMechE D [Automobile engineering]*
- *Proceedings of the IMechE G [Aerospace engineering]*
- *Proceedings of the IMechE L [Materials, design and applications]*
- *Production planning and control*
- *Products finishing*
- *Quality assurance*
- *Quality engineering*
- *Warehousing management*
- *Welding design and fabrication*
- *Works management*

Some of the more academically-oriented journals above have embargos on their latest issues, and there are further journals relevant to manufacturing which may be searched, but contain only abstracts rather than full-text of articles.

Another aggregator with substantial holdings in the manufacturing field is ingenta. Journals available include:

- *Assembly automation*
- *Industrial robot*
- *Integrated manufacturing systems*
- *International journal of computer integrated manufacturing*
- *International journal of flexible manufacturing systems*
- *International journal of operations & production management*
- *International journal of production research*
- *International journal of quality & reliability management*
- *International journal of quality science*
- *Journal of intelligent manufacturing*
- *Journal of materials processing and manufacturing science*
- *Proceedings of the IMechE Part B: journal of engineering manufacture*
- *Production planning and control*
- *Supply chain practice*

Similarly, EBSCOhost offers

- *Artificial intelligence for engineering design analysis & manufacturing*
- *Composites Part A: applied science and manufacturing*
- *Computer-aided design*
- *Computer integrated manufacturing systems*
- *Human factors and ergonomics in manufacturing*
- *IEEE transactions on components, hybrids and manufacturing technology*
- *IEEE transactions on components, packaging, and manufacturing technology, Parts A, B, C*
- *IEEE transactions on electronics packaging manufacturing*
- *IEEE transactions on semiconductor manufacturing*
- *Integrated manufacturing systems*
- *International journal of advanced manufacturing technology*
- *International journal of computer integrated manufacturing*
- *International journal of environmentally conscious design & manufacturing*
- *International journal of flexible manufacturing systems*
- *International journal of machine tools and manufacture*
- *Journal of advanced manufacturing systems*
- *Journal of computer-aided materials design*
- *Journal of electronics manufacturing*
- *Journal of engineering design*
- *Journal of intelligent manufacturing*
- *Journal of manufacturing science and engineering*
- *Journal of materials processing & manufacturing science*
- *Journal of mechanical design*
- *Journal of sustainable product design*
- *Manufacturing & service operations management*

- *Materials and manufacturing processes*
- *Robotics and computer-integrated manufacturing*

For those seeking **trade articles** and up-to-date **news** of the industry, Tradepub.com, (www.tradepub.com) offers the opportunity to subscribe to a number of leading industry publications. It has an Industry and Manufacturing section. These publications are free to those who qualify. In addition, websites such as e4engineering.com, manufacturing.net, NDX.com, or themanufacturer.com, offer the content of a range of such magazines from their publishers. Manufacturing and Technology News may be searched freely, but articles are viewable on a pay-per-view or subscription basis only. Using EEVL (www.eevl.ac.uk/engineering/catalogue.htm), resource type (*full-text e-journals*) and subject (*Manufacturing Engineering*), and inputting '*manufacturing*' as a search term, is an easy way to find individual magazines' websites, such as Advanced Manufacturing, Manufacturing Computer Solutions, Assembly Magazine, Tooling and Production, Machine Design, etc.

Finally, but not least, **professional societies** again provide a rich source of journal literature:

- The SME has on its website both free and subscription-based journals, including the magazines, *Manufacturing Engineering and Forming & Fabricating*, and scholarly journals, *Journal of Manufacturing Systems* and *Journal of Manufacturing Processes*.

Other sites are accessible on a subscription-only basis, including

- IEEE Xplore (includes all IEEE and IEE journals, and also IEEE/IEE manufacturing conferences)
- IEE Manufacturing Division (includes the *Manufacturing Engineer* magazine)
- ASME (contains, inter alia, the *Journal of Manufacturing Science and Engineering*)
- IMechE (offers the Proceedings of the Institution of Mechanical Engineers: *Journal of Engineering Manufacture (Part B)*; *Journal of Automobile Engineering (part D)*, and *Journal of Aerospace Engineering (part G)*.

Individual publishers also have sites which offer full-text searching and retrieval of source documents to subscribers (or individual papers on a pay-per-view basis). Examples include Elsevier ScienceDirect:

- *Composites Part A: applied science and manufacturing*
- *Computer-aided design*
- *Computer integrated manufacturing systems*
- *Computers & industrial engineering*
- *Computers in industry*
- *International journal of industrial ergonomics*

- *International journal of machine tools and manufacture*
- *International journal of production economics*
- *Journal of materials processing technology*
- *Journal of operations management*
- *Robotics*
- *Robotics and autonomous systems*
- *Robotics and computer-integrated manufacturing*

Inderscience Publishers:

- *International journal of automotive technology and management*
- *International journal of computer applications in technology*
- *International journal of integrated supply management*
- *International journal of manufacturing technology and management*
- *International journal of materials and product technology*
- *International journal of nanotechnology*
- *International journal of product development*
- *International journal of product lifecycle management*
- *International journal of six sigma and competitive advantage*
- *International journal of vehicle design*
- *International journal of vehicle safety*
- *International journal of vehicle noise and vibration*

Emerald (MCB Press journals) :

- *Assembly automation*
- *Industrial lubrication and tribology*
- *Industrial robot*
- *Integrated manufacturing systems*
- *International journal of operations & production management*
- *International journal of quality & reliability management*
- *Rapid prototyping journal*
- *Sensor review*
- *Soldering & surface mount technology*
- *Supply chain management*
- *TQM magazine*

There are some important resources, published on a regular basis, still **paper-based** only, such as *CIRP Annals* and *CIRP Journal of Manufacturing Systems*. (CIRP is the International Institute for Production Engineering Research).

Electronic subject gateways

The disadvantages of global search engines like Google is that they are both unfocused and unselective. **Subject gateways** try to rectify this by being focused (on particular subject areas) and selective (in [hand-]picking resources against particular quality criteria). They also generally supply a fuller description of the sites than do the global engines. Their weakness, of course, is the relatively small number of resources compiled.

Within manufacturing, the already-mentioned EEVL (www.eevl. ac.uk) contains a substantial Manufacturing section within its Engineering coverage. EEVL is an award-winning free service, created and run by a team of information specialists from various UK universities and institutions, and is part of the Resource Discovery Network (RDN), funded by the Joint Information Systems Committee (JISC). Three sections cover

- manufacturing engineering (general);
- manufacturing operations and systems (manufacturing operations and systems (general), automated manufacturing systems, machinery and machine tools, manufacturing processes, materials handling and packaging, and robotics); and
- product design and development (product design and development (general), CAD/CAM/CAPP issues, materials and energy recycling and reuse, mechatronics, and rapid prototyping (and any other prototype development)).

There are multi-subject gateways, some of which include reasonable collections of Web-related information. For instance, Academic Info has a list of manufacturing sites (www.academicinfo.net/engringman.html), as do the dmoz site (dmoz.org/Science/Technology/Manufacturing), the Scout Report archives (scout.wisc.edu/archives), and the World Wide Web Virtual Library (WWWVL) (www.uwstout.edu/mevl).

Bibliographic databases

There is one free bibliographic database which concentrates on manufacturing: Recent Advances in Manufacturing (RAM) (www.eevl.ac.uk/ram), which brings together both engineering and management aspects of the topic. It currently contains some 40,000 items.

There are other freely available specialist services such as

- GrayLIT, (www.osti.gov/graylit/) – includes free full-text papers on manufacturing from DTIC, DOE, and NASA [although manufacturing is not the prime topic of the database]
- NTIS, (www.ntis.gov/search/index.asp?loc=3–0-0) – covers US Government-sponsored research, with topic headings including Manufacturing Technology, which offers access to abstracts only
- SAE Technical Papers, (www.sae.org/servlets/techtrack?PROD_TYP=PAPER) – lists, among other subjects, manufacturing and product development papers in the automotive industry, again offering free searching

Otherwise, manufacturing topics may be retrieved from well-established **subscription-based services,** such as Inspec and Compendex [available from various hosts, but cross-searchable via the Ei Village2 system]. (See Chapter 9)

Other such databases include:

- ANTE: Abstracts in New Technologies and Engineering,
- Engineered Materials Abstracts (polymers, composites and ceramics),
- Mechanical Engineering Abstracts,
- Metadex, and
- Polymer Library (formerly Rapra Abstracts).

These are all available from CSA (sun5.csa1.co.uk/csa/ids/databases-collections.shtml) and are cross-searchable. Another database always worth a visit (because of its sheer size and cross-disciplinary nature) is Zetoc (zetoc.mimas.ac.uk).

Conferences

There are many conferences in the manufacturing area; here is a selection of some held regularly:

Annual Design for Manufacturing Conference [ASME]
Annual North American Manufacturing Research Conference
Annual International Conference of the Association for Manufacturing
    Excellence [SME]
Annual International Lean Manufacturing Conference
International Conference on Composite Materials [SME]
International Conference on Flexible Automation and Intelligent
    Manufacturing
International Conference on Integrated Design and Manufacturing in
    Mechanical Engineering
International Conference on Metal Forming
International Scientific Conference on Production Engineering
International Conference on Manufacturing Research (incorporating the
    National Conference on Manufacturing Research)
National Conference on Rapid Prototyping, Tooling and Manufacturing
Rapid Prototyping and Manufacturing Conference [SME]

Papers from those already published should be picked up via the bibliographic databases, while their announcements may be found on sites such as: www.manufacturingsystems.com/events/,www.e4engineering.com/events.asp, the events section of www.engineering.com, or on the various institutions' websites. Details of individual conferences may most easily be found using search engines such as Google (www.google.com).

Patents and standards

Chapter 5 deals specifically with patents and standards in an engineering context. Suffice it to note that, with regard to standards in terms of manufacturing specifically, bodies such as the SAE (www.sae.org/servlets/techtrack?PROD_TYP=STD), ASTM (www.astm.org), or ASME (www.asme.org/codes) offer free searching and information, with the opportunity to order hard copy or, on some, pay-per-view online.

Directories

Engineer-it, (www.info4engineering.com), a subscription-based service from Technical Indexes, is an online collection of up-to-date product catalogues for designers, specifiers and purchasers. The complete database includes over 85,000 full-text catalogues, data sheets, handbooks, reference manuals, selector guides and brochures from more than 15,000 UK sources.

www.electronics.org.uk/index.htm – the Applegate Directory for industry and technology in the UK and Ireland. The Applegate Directory has information on more than 46,000 companies cross-referred to 18,000 products

dir.yahoo.com/Business_and_Economy/Business_to_Business/Manufacturing/Directories – includes:

- ThomasRegister.com, (www.thomasregister.com) – North American, free information upon free registration; currently 8,000 online supplier catalogues and Web links available
- TREM – Thomas Register of European Manufacturers, (tremnet.tipcoeurope.com) – includes searchable listings for suppliers of industrial products across a variety of European countries
- Asian Manufacturers Journal, (www.asianmfrs.com) – directory of manufacturers and trade events
- Australian Manufacturers' Guide, (www.ausmanufacturers.com.au) – definitive guide/search engine to the Australian manufacturing industry
- Irish Manufacturing Directory, (www.irishmanufacturing.com) – dedicated to promoting Irish manufacturers worldwide
- Taiwan Products Online, (www.taiwansource.com)

Representative organisations

The following list provides the names and addresses of selected bodies which represent manufacturing in various areas and/or countries (mainly UK or USA).

- The DTI Manufacturing Advisory Service (MAS), (www.dti.gov.uk/manufacturing/mas) – an integrated service providing free information and advice for all UK manufacturers. The service is delivered through Regional Centres for Manufacturing Excellence (RCMEs), Centres of Expertise in Manufacturing (CEMs), and the MAS Website.
- CIRP (International Institute for Production Engineering Research), (www.cirp.net)
- International Institute of Welding, (www.iiw-iis.org)
- Advanced Manufacturing Technology Research Institute (AMTRI) , (www.amtri.co.uk)
- Manufacturing Technologies Association [MTA – previously, MTTA], (www.mta.org.uk)
- Institute of Measurement and Control, (www.instmc.org.uk)
- British Quality Foundation, (www.quality-foundation.co.uk)
- American Society of Quality, (www.asq.org)
- EFQM, (www.efqm.org) (European Foundation for Quality Management)
- SME, (www.sme.org) (Society of Manufacturing Engineers)
- IEE Manufacturing Division, (www.iee.org/oncomms/sector/manufacturing)
- IMechE Manufacturing Industries Division, (www.imeche.org.uk/manufacturing)
- ASME Manufacturing Engineering Division, (www.asme.org/divisions/med)
- ASM International, (www.asm-intl.org) (the Materials Information Society)

Useful lists of US associations and societies may be found at sites such as: www.tmanet.com/industry/all.asp#associations, while EEVL (www.eevl.ac. uk/engineering/catalogue.htm) again offers searching by resource type (this time, *society/institution*) and subjects (*Manufacturing Engineering*).

► SERVICES INTEGRATION

However, manufacturing is not just about technology, either machinery, systems or information. It is also about processes and cultural change. Ignoring these aspects constitutes a recipe for failure. To succeed, managers must develop – and sell – a viable pragmatic vision. This requires innovation leadership teams, comprised of key decision-makers and users whose goal is to develop and sell the intelligent enterprise vision internally. The selling 'campaign' must be framed around business issues and metrics. The investment justification and ROI analysis must be clearly and satisfactorily presented. In most cases, there should be a phased transition to a new environment, allowing for feedback and improvement. Begin with a manageable constituency. Empower users and determine ownership of designed business processes.

Where do we go from here?

We can see in the manufacturing extended enterprise the emergence of an 'n-tier architecture' for knowledge provision that can enable a learning organisation, providing personal role-based content and experience to the different categories of performer, who span the range of dependent, independent and interdependent. There is a need for *enterprise knowledge ecosystems* or portals of this nature to provide an environment for human capital development within modern manufacturing organisations, which directly impacts the organisation's ability to perform and achieve its business objectives.

Intelligent Enterprise strategies and business applications are driven by technological developments that better serve business needs. A beneficial side effect of such knowledge support systems may well be that they act as a pre-emptive stabilising context for people joining the organisation, who experience future shock from within the cultures and societies from which they are drawn.

The ICT industry serving Manufacturing is being driven by new economics. These include leased functionality, on-demand and utility computing, outsourcing (offshore or otherwise), leveraged partnerships, Open Source, and xSPs. For example, many core applications, services, and other IT capabilities are offered over the Internet through annuity-based pricing schemes. For some enterprises, offshore application development and other services are saving enterprises more than 50% of their costs. Within the scope of possibilities, a new ecology of interrelationships between technology, infrastructure, people, and business models is critical. Each aspect must support and enhance the others' viability.

The challenge for Manufacturing is to leverage the opportunities, while controlling risk. First, the perception of how to manage business must change. We must move faster: be more flexible, heighten our responsiveness, and our competitiveness. We want to take advantage of the opportunities. We want our IT investments to support these goals, not get in the way. The new set of IT economics will produce systems that can stretch and shrink to fit changing needs, deploy and grow new capabilities more rapidly, and reach out to connect us to partners, suppliers, and customers.

At this point I would like to share here the views of *Line56* editor James A. Alexander from his article 3rd of June, 2003, (www.line56.com/articles/default.asp?ArticleID=4692&KeyWords=alexander) in the context of moving towards Intelligent Enterprise:

'Smart executives in product companies have known for a long time the revenue and profit contribution of a solid services organisation. Not only do strong services complement and add value to the product, they contribute directly to growth and margin targets.

A global research project that I completed for AFSM International confirms this reality. Executives and managers from 370 companies in 29 countries show that, today, services have average gross margins that are more than 50 percent higher than products, and the current annual growth rate of services is more than double that of products, with a significant acceleration planned within two years. In consideration of continuing pressures on product profit margins, the future for services looks very bright indeed.

However, a select group of organisations has broken the code when it comes to yielding the power of services to drive exceptional performance. This same study revealed that top performing 's-businesses' (organisations that push services to pull products) are averaging 61 percent average gross margins and 30 percent annual growth rate for their services offerings. These elite services-focused, services-measured, and indeed, services-driven organisations are dramatically delivering new streams of revenue and increased profitability by creating and selling what customers are demanding – more and better services. I would challenge all readers to compare the performance metrics of their organisation against these benchmarks – maybe a new business approach is in order.

A core differentiator between top-performing s-businesses and the rest of the pack is their attitude toward services at the strategic level. In fact, the aforementioned research project found that there were six best practices separating these two groups. Think about whether your organisation implements each practice as you read through the listing.

S-Business Strategy: Six Best Practices
1. The overall strategy is based on 'pushing services' and 'pulling products.' With rare exceptions, customers see no difference between the product offerings of the top suppliers in any market space. What they value most are the services that maintain product uptime, enhance an application, or (better yet) drive business performance. The smart companies sell the value of these services and then drag the product along with the services sale.
2. The top management team includes individuals with services management experience. Product folks think (and act) differently from services people – different ways of viewing the business,

different ways to measure success, different ways of marketing, selling, etc. If you are going to be services-driven, there needs to be services horsepower on the bridge to help chart a new business heading.

3. A strategic services plan is in place. The operative word here is 'strategic.' Services must be an integral part of the overall business plan and not just a few paragraphs in the operations section.

4. The services organisation(s) sets its own financial targets. To truly unleash its potential, services must be set up as distinct profit centres responsible (and accountable) for setting and meeting financial objectives.

5. Services are *not* organised by geography. In reality, services organisations that organise geographically are implementing a 'worst practice.' Top performing services businesses organise by industry, or even better, they organise by account.

6. Services are integrated. Again, the key here is taking the customer's perspective. They prefer one-stop shopping, or at least dealing with organisations that focus on selling and delivering in a hassle-free way. To do this means aligning and packaging different services offerings and sometimes services businesses. For those organisations attempting to offer 'total solutions,' this means that the professional services group, product-support services team, and the product function must all work together to promote, sell, and deliver one complete package to the customer.'

I believe that James A. Alexander has highlighted here the most fundamental point for developing Intelligent Enterprise Manufacturing Systems, as they are all part of service process chains that provide service streams to you and I, the customer.

► READING LIST (1): THE INTELLIGENT MANUFACTURING ENTERPRISE

Carkhuff, R. R., and Berenson, B. G., 2000. *The possibilities organization.* Possibilities Publishing.

Handy, C., 1995. *The age of unreason.* Arrow Business Books.

Holland, J. H., 1992. *Adaption in natural and artificial systems.* MIT Press.

Ohno, T., 1988. *Toyota Production System: beyond large-scale production.* Productivity Press.

Papows, J., 1999. *Enterprise.com.* Nicholas Brealy Publishing.

Robertson, B., and Sribar. V., 2002. *The adaptive enterprise.* Addison-Wesley.

Schonberger, R. J., 1996. *World class manufacturing*. The Free Press.

Senge, P. M., 1990. *The fifth discipline: the art and practice of the learning organization.* Doubleday.

Simon, H. A., 1982. *The science of the artificial*, MIT Press.

Skyttner, L., 2001. *General systems theory: ideas and applications*. World Scientific.

Slywotzky, A. J., and Morrison, D. J., 1998. *The profit zone*. New York: Wiley.

Suh, N. P., 2001. *Axiomatic design: advances and applications*. Oxford: Oxford University Press.

Toffler, A., 1970. *Future shock*. Oxford: Bodley Head.

▶ READING LIST (2): MANUFACTURING BOOKS POST–1996

Anon, 2001. *Machining data handbook*. 2 vols. 3rd ed. Cincinnati: Institute of Advanced Manufacturing Sciences.

Askin, R. G., 2001. *Design and analysis of lean production systems*. New York: Wiley.

Banerjee, P., and Zetu, D., 2001. *Virtual manufacturing*. New York: Wiley.

Benhabib, B., 2003. *Manufacturing: design, production, automation and integration*. New York: Dekker.

Boothroyd, G., and Knight, W., 2001. *Product design for manufacture and assembly*. Rev. ed. New York: Dekker.

Bruce, R., Neely, G., *et al.*, 2003. *Modern materials and manufacturing processes*. 3rd ed. Upper Saddle River, NJ: Prentice Hall.

Chakravarty, A. K., 2000. *Market driven enterprise: product development, supply chains and manufacturing*. New York: Wiley.

Chua, C. K., Leong, K. F., and Lim, C. S., 2003. *Rapid prototyping: principles and applications*. 2nd ed. Singapore: World Scientific.

Cooper, K. G., 2001. *Rapid prototyping technology*. New York: Dekker.

Creese, R. C., 1999. *Introduction to manufacturing processes and materials*. New York: Dekker.

De Lit, P., 2003. *Integrated design of product family and its assembly system*. Boston: Kluwer.

Degarmo, E. P., 2002. *Materials and processes in manufacturing*. 9th ed. New York: Wiley.

Delchambre, A., 1997. *CAD method for industrial assembly: concurrent design of products, equipment and control systems*. New York: Wiley.

Dudzinski, D., 2002. *Metal cutting and high speed machining*. New York: Kluwer.

Erdel, B. P., 2003. *High speed machining: machining, material removal, metal cutting, tooling, tools*. Dearborn: Society of Manufacturing Engineers.

Feld, W. M., 2001. *Lean manufacturing: tools, techniques and how to use them*. Boca Raton: St. Lucie Press.

Fitzpatrick, M., 2004. *Machining and CNC technology*. McGraw-Hill.

Frontini, G., and Kennedy, S., 2003. *Manufacturing in real-time*. Oxford: Butterworth-Heinemann.

Garside, J., 1999. *Make it! The engineering manufacturing solution*. Oxford: Butterworth-Heinemann.

Gershwin, S. B., Papadopoulos, and C. R., Dallery, Y., 2002. *Analysis and modelling of manufacturing systems*. New York: Kluwer.

Groover, M. P., 2000. *Automation, production systems and computer-integrated manufacturing*. 2nd ed. Upper Saddle River, NJ: Prentice Hall.

Groover, M. P., 2003. *Fundamentals of modern manufacturing: materials, processes and systems*. 2nd ed. New York: Wiley.

Gunasekaran, A., ed., 2001. *Agile manufacturing: the 21st century competitive strategy*. New York: Elsevier.

Hilton, P. D., 2000. *Rapid tooling: technologies and industrial applications*. New York: Dekker.

Ihinaera, W. T., and Campbell, R. G., 2002. *Integrated product design and manufacturing using geometric dimensioning and tolerancing*. New York: Dekker.

IRani, S. A., ed., 1999. *Handbook of cellular manufacturing*. New York: Wiley.

Hyer, N., and Wemmerlöv, U., 2002. *Reorganizing the factory: competing through cellular manufacturing*. New York: Productivity Press.

Jameson, E. C., 2001. *Electrical discharge machining*. Dearborn: Society of Manufacturing Engineers.

Kalpakjian, S., and Schmid, S., 2000. *Manufacturing engineering and technology*. 4th ed. Reading, MA: Addison Wesley.

Kalpakjian, S., 2002. *Manufacturing processes for engineering materials*. 4th ed. Upper Saddle River, NJ: Prentice Hall.

Krar, S., Gill, A., and Smid, P., 2001. *CNC simplified*. NewYork: Industrial Press.

Kusiak, A., 2000. *Computational intelligence in design and manufacturing*. New York: Wiley.

McDonald, J. A., Ryall, C. J., and Wimpenny, D. I., 2001. *Rapid prototyping casebook*. London: Professional Engineering Publishing.

Marinescu, I. D., Bobac, D., and Ispas, C., 2002. *Handbook of machine tool analysis*. New York: Dekker.

Mather, H., 1999. *Competitive manufacturing*. Oxford: Butterworth-Heinemann.

Mayers, A. R. and Slattery, T. J., eds., 2001. *Basic machining reference handbook*. New York: Industrial Press.

Montgomery, D. C., 2000. *Introduction to statistical quality control*. 4th ed. New York: Wiley.

Nelson, D. H. and Schneider, G., 2000. *Applied manufacturing process planning: with emphasis on metal forming*. Upper Saddle River, NJ: Pearson.

Nof, S. Y., ed., 1999. *Handbook of industrial robotics*. 2nd ed. New York: Wiley.

Poli, C., 2001. *Design for manufacturing*. Oxford: Butterworth-Heinemann.

Priest, J. W., and Sanchez, J. M., 2001. *Product development and design for manufacturing*. New York: Dekker.

Quirk, M., 1998. *Manufacturing, teams and improvement: the human art of manufacturing*. Upper Saddle River, NJ: Pearson.

Rehg, J. A., and Kraebber, H. W., 2000. *Computer-integrated manufacturing*. 2nd ed. Upper Saddle River, NJ: Prentice Hall.

Rehg, J. A., 2002. *Introduction to robotics in CIM*. 5th ed. Upper Saddle River, NJ: Prentice Hall.

Rennie, A. E. W., Jacobson, D. M., and Bocking, C. E., 2002. *Rapid prototyping, tooling and manufacturing*. London: Professional Engineering Publishing.

Ribbens, J., 2000. *Simultaneous engineering for new product development: manufacturing applications*. New York: Wiley.

Scallan, P., 2003. *Process planning: the design/manufacturing interface*. Oxford: Butterworth-Heinemann.

Schey, J., 1999. *Introduction to manufacturing processes*. 3rd ed. Boston: McGraw-Hill.

Shaw, M. J., 2001. *Information-based manufacturing*. New York: Kluwer.

Sommer, C., 2000. *Non-traditional machining handbook*. Houston: Advanced Publishing.

Stein, R.E., 2003. *Re-engineering the manufacturing system: applying the theory of constraints*. 2nd ed. New York: Dekker.

Swamidass, P. M., ed., 2000. *Encyclopedia of production and manufacturing management*. New York: Kluwer.

Swamidass, P. M., 2002. *Innovations in competitive manufacturing*. New York: Amacom.

Theis, H. E, 1999. *Handbook of metalforming processes*. New York: Dekker.

Usher, J. M., Roy, U., and Parsaei, H., eds., 1998. *Integrated product and process development*. New York: Wiley.

Vardeman, S. B., and Jobe, J. M., 1998. *Statistical quality assurance methods for engineers*. New York: Wiley.

Worthington, S. L. S., and Boyes, W., 2001. *E-business in manufacturing: putting the Internet to work in the industrial enterprise*. Pittsburgh: ISA.

Wright, P., 2000. *21st century manufacturing*. Upper Saddle River, NJ: Pearson.

Wright, P. K., and Trent, E., 2000. *Metal cutting*. 4th ed. Oxford: Butterworth-Heinemann.

22 Materials Engineering

David Cebon
and Michael F. Ashby

▶ INTRODUCTION

When selecting a material for a developing design, the engineer needs data for its properties. Engineers are often conservative in their choice, and reluctant to consider materials with which they are unfamiliar. One reason is that data for the old, well-tried materials are reliable, familiar, easily-found; data for newer, better performing materials may not exist or, if they do, may not inspire confidence. Another is that material property data is complex, of varying types and qualities – and can be difficult to obtain, analyse and navigate. Yet innovation is often made possible by new materials. So it is important to know where to find material data and to what extent it can be trusted. As a design progresses from concept to detail, the data needs evolve in two ways. At the start, the need is for low-precision data for all materials and processes, structured to facilitate 'screening' (eliminating unsuitable materials). Near the end, the need is for accurate data for one or a few materials, but with the richness of detail needed for precise design calculations and to assist with some difficult aspects of the selection: corrosion, wear, cost estimation and the like. The data sources that help with the first are not necessarily useful for the second.

This chapter surveys data sources from the perspective of the designer seeking information at each stage of the design process. Long-established materials are well documented; less-common materials may be less so, posing problems of checking and, sometimes, of property estimation. The chapter ends with a discussion of how this can be done.

References are listed in the section on Further Reading. The Appendix is a catalogue of data sources, with brief commentary. It is intended for reference. When you *really* need data, this is the section you want.

▶ MATERIAL DATA NEEDS FOR DESIGN

Types of Data

Material properties are not all described in the same way. Table 1 sets out some of the data types that are typically required to handle information about materials and processes.

Some properties, like the atomic number, or a minimum 'allowable' design value, can be described by a *point* value ('the atomic number of copper = 29'); others, like the typical modulus or the thermal conductivity can be characterised by a *range* ('Young's modulus for low density poly-ethylene = 0.1 – 0.25 GPa', for instance). In some cases, the point or range is a *function* of one or more independent variables: (e.g., the strength of a material can be a function of temperature, and exposure time.)

Corrosion resistance is a property that is too complicated to charac-terise by a single number. For screening purposes, it can be ranked on a simple *discrete* scale: for example, A (very good) to E (very poor), but with further information stored as text files or graphs. Forming character-istics, similarly, can be described by a *list* ('mild steel can be rolled, forged, or machined'; 'Zirconia can be formed by powder methods') with case-studies, guidelines and warnings to illustrate how it should be done. Such a list is often implemented through a set of *Boolean* attributes, which can take values of yes/no or true/false: Can the material be Cast? (yes/no); Can it be Forged? (yes/no) . . . . The best way to store information about microstructures, or the applications of a material, or the functioning of a process, may be as an *image*. Finally, references to external documents can be stored as *hyperlinks*, enabling them to be followed-up quickly via a web browser.

From testing machine to selection data

Material property data is generated by a process which starts with indi-vidual test records, measured on a testing machine. Such tests are often repeated many times for different batches of material, and the results are processed statistically to generate 'allowable' values: minimum values of strength, modulus, etc, which can be reliably used for design purposes. Measured property values for various temperatures, strain rates, etc. may then be collected-together to provide 'functional' data: e.g. strength vs temperature (see Table 1). This process, illustrated in Figure 1, is very time consuming and very expensive, since many hundreds or even thousands of individual tests may be required to characterise a single material. These days, it is essential to use automated systems – normally based on a data-base – to process the huge quantity of information involved.

Table I Material Data Types

Data type	Example	Data value
Numeric point	Atomic number of magnesium:	12
Numeric range	Thermal conductivity of polyethylene:	0.28 – 0.31 W/mK
Boolean	304 stainless steel can be welded:	Yes
Discrete	Resistance to tap water (scale A to E):	A
Text	Supplier for aluminium alloys:	Alcan, Canada . . . .
Date	Record last updated:	April 21, 2003
Hyperlink	URL for material supplier:	**www.alcan.com**
Functional data	Strength vs temperature	

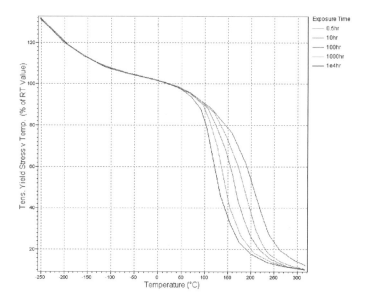

Image　　　　**Micrograph**

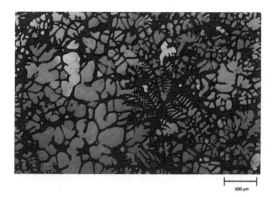

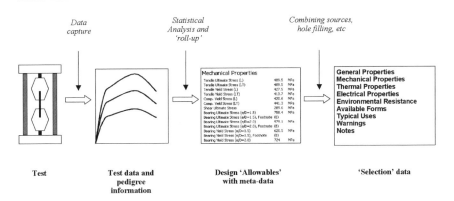

Fig. 22.1: The process of converting raw laboratory test data into design and selection data.

Three main types of data are involved in this process. First, the raw test data, and all associated information about its pedigree (e.g. information about the material batch, the testing procedure, etc) needs to be saved for data auditing purposes. Second, the 'design' data ('allowables') is needed for use in detailed design calculations. Note that it is important to be able to trace the source of the design data. It is therefore highly desirable for each record in the design data to be accompanied by considerable 'meta data' (information about the testing conditions and statistical analyses that were performed to generate the data). It is also desirable that the data is linked to the raw data that was used to generate it. Such design data may come from in-house sources in large corporations, but otherwise, is usually provided by standards organisations, specialist data providers, or sometimes material suppliers' data sheets.

There is one further level of abstraction required if materials information is to be used for purposes of *optimal selection*. *Selection* databases (right side of Figure 22.1) must satisfy a number of special requirements. If they don't, selection software that use them will not yield optimal results. This means that there may be a better material for the application from within the allowable list of candidates (e.g. a company's preferred list of materials). These special requirements are detailed in the next section.

It is necessary to process and collate the design data in a variety of ways to generate selection data. The resulting database often contains 'typical' values rather than 'allowable' values, as a consequence of the wide variety of sources that are normally used to create it. It is desirable to link each record in the *selection* data to all records in the *design* data that were used to make it.

Table 2 summarises some of the key features of the three types of material data tables: test, design and selection data.

Table 2 Features of the three main types of materials data tables

	Selection Data	Design Data	Test Data
Scope	Comprehensive: All relevant classes	Specific material classes	Individual test records
Record types	Generic material grades	Specific material grades	Partial records – individual tests
Attribute types	Universal attributes	Class-specific attributes	Test data
Holes	Complete (estimates)	Holes	Holes
Sources	Variety of sources	Pedigree sources (single)	Testing machine
Data class	Typical values	Design allowables	Extracted parameters
Typical data types	Ranges	Point values	Point values, raw test data
Common use models	Optimal Selection, Data Analysis/mining	Design calculations, search, export to FE	Archive, QA, re-analysis

Figure 22.2 compares two records for Ti-13V-11Cr-3Al: a *design* data record from MIL-HDBK-5 (United States Department of Defense, 1998), and a *selection* data record from the CES4 MATERIALUNIVERSE database, (Granta Design, 2003). Note that the *design* data record (Fig. 22.2a) contains point values (design allowables), whereas the *selection* data record (Fig 22.2b) contains ranges of typical values.

General		
Common Name	Ti-13V-11Cr-3Al	
Material Designation/Specification	MIL-T-9046, Comp. B-1	
UNS	R58010	
Finish Heat Treatment/Conditioning	Solution treated and aged	
Form	Sheet	
Characteristic dimensions	Thickness: <=4.000 in	
Statistical Basis	S Basis	
Source table number	5.5.1.0(b)	

Physical Properties
| Density | 4.816 | Mg/m^3 |

Mechanical Properties at Room Temperature
Tensile Ultimate Stress (L)	1172	MPa
Tensile Ultimate Stress (LT)	1172	MPa
Tensile Ultimate Stress (ST)	1172	MPa
Tensile Yield Stress (L)	1103	MPa
Tensile Yield Stress (LT)	1103	MPa
Tensile Yield Stress (ST)	1103	MPa
Comp. Yield Stress (L)	1117	MPa
Comp. Yield Stress (LT)	1117	MPa
Comp. Yield Stress (ST)	1117	MPa
Shear Ultimate Stress	724	MPa
Bearing Ultimate Stress (e/D=1.5)	1710	MPa
Bearing Ultimate Stress (e/D=2.0)	2158	MPa
Bearing Yield Stress (e/D=1.5)	1496	MPa
Bearing Yield Stress (e/D=2.0)	1703	MPa
Elongation (L)	4e4	µstrain
Elongation (ST)	4e4	µstrain
Modulus of Elasticity (L)	106.9	GPa

Available Forms
| Sheet | ✓ |

(a)

General			
Tradenames			
VCA ALLOY, Manufacturer unknown ();			
Designation			
Ti-alloy: Ti-13V-11Cr-3Al, STA			
Density	4.792 - 4.84	Mg/m^3	
Energy Content	750 - 1250	MJ/kg	
Price	* 25 - 35	GBP/kg	
Recycle Fraction	* 0.55 - 0.65		

Composition
Composition (Summary)			
Ti/13V/11Cr/3Al			
Base	Ti		
Al (Aluminium)	3	%	
Cr (Chromium)	11	%	
Ti (Titanium)	73	%	
V (Vanadium)	13	%	

Mechanical
Bulk Modulus	93.7 - 99	GPa	
Compressive Strength	889 - 1117	MPa	
Compression Strength with Temperature	713.5 - 896.5	MPa	ℹ 📈
Elongation	2 - 6	%	
Elastic Limit	1103 - 1219	MPa	
Elastic Limit with Temperature	879.7 - 972.3	MPa	ℹ 📈
Endurance Limit	420 - 460	MPa	
Fatigue Strength Model	* 392.2 - 490	MPa	ℹ 📈
Fracture Toughness	75 - 80	MPa.m^1/2	
Hardness - Vickers	450 - 460	HV	
Loss Coefficient	* 1e-3 - 2e-3		

(b)

Fig. 22.2: Partial database records for Ti-13V-11Cr-3Al from the CES4 (Granta Design, 2003) (a) Design data from Mil-HDBK 5H-CN1 (US Department of Defense, 1998) (b) Selection data from the CES MATERIALUNIVERSE database (Granta Design, 2003)

▶ SCREENING AND RANKING: DATA STRUCTURE AND SOURCES

Data Structure for Screening and Ranking

To 'select' means: 'to choose'. But from what? Behind the concept of selection lies that of a *universe of entities* from which the choice is to be made. The universe of materials means: all metals, all polymers, all ceramics and glasses, all composites, as in Figure 22.3. If it is *materials* we want to select, then the universe is all of these; leave out part, and the selection is no longer one of all materials but of some subset of them. If the choice is limited to polymers from the start, then the universe becomes a single family of materials, that of polymers.

There is a second implication to the concept of selection; it is that all members of the universe must be regarded as candidates – they are, after all, *viable choices* – until, by a series of selection stages, they are shown to be otherwise. From this arises several key requirements of a data structure for the Selection database (represented by circles in Fig 22.4). The selection table must be *comprehensive* (includes all members of the universe). It should be *structured* – like the information shown in Figure 22.2b, – it must contain attributes that are *universal* (apply to all members of the universe) and the attributes should be *discriminating* (have recognisably different values for different members of the universe). Similar considerations apply to any selection exercise (Cebon and Ashby, 2000).

In the universe of materials, many attributes are universal and discriminating: density, bulk modulus and thermal conductivity are examples.

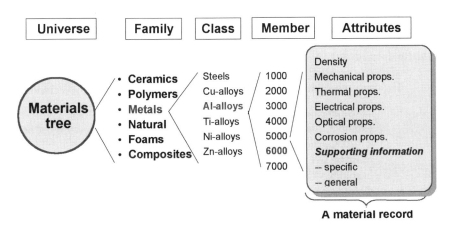

A material record

Fig. 22.3: Taxonomy of the Material 'Universe' (NB the 'Member' branch can be broken down into several further levels of classifcation.)

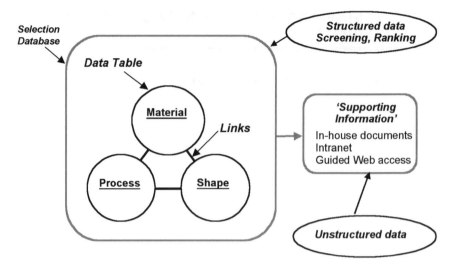

Fig. 22.4: Structure of a materials information system. The *structured* database on the left contains several tables, linked together in a relational structure. The *unstructured* data on the right contains information in a wide range of formats.

Universal attributes can be used for *screening and ranking*, the initial stage of any selection exercise (Selection Database in Figure 22.4).

If the values of one or more screening attributes are grossly inaccurate or missing, that material will be eliminated by default. It is important, therefore, that the database be *complete* (have no holes or gaps in the records which would make a material fail a selection by default due to absence of data) and be of high *quality*, meaning that the data in it can be trusted. This creates the need for data checking and estimation, which are tackled by methods described later.

The screening and ranking process is normally quantitative, and is ideally carried out by linking the technical and economic requirements of the design to the attribute profiles stored in the database.

The two types of selection criteria are 'constraints' and 'objectives.'

- *Constraints* are design requirements that must be satisfied: for example, the minimum working temperature of a material must be $\leq -20°C$; the strength must be ≥ 400 MPa; the fracture toughness must be ≥ 15 MPam$^{0.5}$, and so on. Constraints *screen* out unsuitable choices.
- *Objectives* are design criteria that must be maximised or minimised to *optimise* the performance of a component.
  Their function is to *rank* the materials and facilitate selection of the best candidates. In the case of materials selection, the objectives can be used to generate 'material performance indices,'

which are combinations of material properties that characterise performance in a given application. Typical examples are the specific stiffness of a material E/ρ , and the specific strength σ_f / ρ (E is the Young's modulus, σ_f is the failure strength and ρ is the density). These particular indices can be used to select the optimum material for a *light, stiff* tie rod, or a *light, strong* tie rod respectively. Many material performance indices have been derived and tabulated for standard design cases in mechanical, structural, thermo-mechanical, and electro-mechanical engineering (Ashby, 1999).

Data sources for screening and ranking (See also Appendix)

Level 1 – Conceptual Design

Data needs evolve as a design develops. In the *conceptual* stage (Level 1 in Figure 22.5), the designer requires approximate data for the widest possible range of materials. At this stage, all options are open: a polymer could be the best choice for one concept, a metal for another, even though the function is the same. Breadth is important; precision is less so. Data for this first-level screening is found in wide-spectrum compilations like the material property charts developed by Ashby (1999), and general handbooks such as ASM International's *Guide to Engineered Materials* (Anon, 2001) and the Chapman and Hall *Materials Selector* (Waterman and Ashby, 1996). It is the *selection* data in Figure 22.1. These are the primary sources, but they are clumsy to use because their data structure is not well-suited to screening. Comparison of materials of different classes is possible but difficult because data are seldom reported in comparable formats: there is too much unstructured information, requiring the user to filter out what he needs; and the data tables are almost always full of holes.

Electronic sources for generic screening can overcome these problems. If properly structured, they allow direct comparison across classes and selection by multiple criteria, and it is possible (using the methods described in Ways of Checking and Estimating Data) to arrange that they have no holes. A good example is the *MaterialUniverse* database from Granta Design Ltd, (Granta Design, 2003).

Level 2 – Embodiment Design

The calculations involved in deciding on the scale and layout of the design (the *embodiment* stage in Figure 22.5) require more complete information than before, but for fewer candidates. Data enabling this second-level screening are found in the specialised compilations that include handbooks and computer databases. For examples, see *Smithells Metals Reference Book* (Brandes and Brook, 1992) and ASM International's *Alloy Center*, (ASM International, 2003). Similar data is also available in data books published by associations or federations of material producers. These publications list, plot and compare properties of closely-related materials, and provide data at a level of precision not usually available in the broad, level 1, compilations. And, if they are doing their job properly, they provide further information about processability and possible manufacturing routes. Because they contain much more detail, their breadth (the range of materials and processes they cover) is restricted, and access is more cumbersome.

Level 3 – Detailed Design

The final, detailed design stage (Level 3 in Figure 22.5) requires data at a still higher level of precision and with as much depth as possible, but for only one or a few materials. They can be found in standards (e.g. the *US MIL-HDBK-5*, (United States Department of Defense, 1998), which

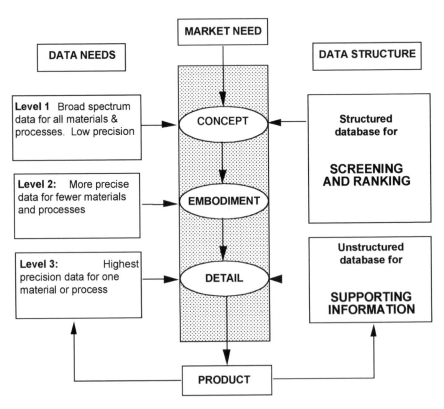

Fig. 22.5: Data needs and data structure for screening/ranking and for the supporting information step.

contains 'design allowables' for aerospace alloys), and the data-sheets issued by the producers themselves.

A given material (low-density polyethylene, for instance) has a range of properties that derive from differences in the way different producers make it. At the detailed-design stage, a supplier should be identified, and the properties of his product used in the design calculation. But sometimes even this is not good enough. If the component is a critical one, (meaning that its failure could be disastrous), then it is prudent to conduct in-house tests, measuring critical properties on samples of the material that will be used to make the component itself. Parts of power-generating equipment (the turbine disk for instance), or aircraft (the wing spar, the landing-gear) and nuclear reactors (the pressure vessel) are like this; for these, every new batch of material is tested, and the batch is accepted or rejected on the basis of the tests.

As we have seen, screening and ranking identifies a set of viable candidates. We now need their family history. That is the purpose of the 'supporting information' step (Figures 22.4 and 22.5).

▶ SUPPORTING INFORMATION: DATA STRUCTURE AND SOURCES

Data Structure for Supporting Information

The data requirements in the Supporting Information step differ greatly from those for Screening and Ranking (Figure 22.4, right half). Here, we seek additional details about the few candidates that have already been identified by the screening and ranking step. Typically, this is information about availability and pricing; exact values for key properties of the particular version of the material made by one manufacturer; case studies and examples of uses, with cautions about unexpected difficulties (e.g. 'liable to pitting corrosion in dilute acetic acid' or 'material Y is preferred to material X for operation in industrial environments'). It is on this basis that the initial short list of candidates can be narrowed down to one or a few prime choices.

Sources of supporting information typically contain specialist knowledge of a relatively narrow range of materials or processes. The information may be in the form of text, tables, graphs, photographs, computer programs, even video clips. The data can be large in quantity, detailed and precise in nature, but it there is no requirement that it be comprehensive or that the attributes it contains be universal. The most common media are handbooks, trade association publications and manufacturers' leaflets and catalogues. Increasingly, such information is becoming available in electronic form, particularly on the Internet. Because the data is in 'free' format, the search strategies differ completely from the numerical optimisation procedures used for the screening/ranking step. The simplest approach is to use an index (as in a printed book), or a keyword list, or a computerised full text search, as implemented in many multi-media systems.

Data sources for supporting information (see also Appendix)

By 'supporting information', we mean data sources which, potentially, can contain everything that is known about a material or a process, with some sort of search procedure enabling users to find and extract the particular details that they seek. The handbooks and software that are the best sources for screening also contain supporting information, but because they are edited only infrequently, they are seldom up to date. One key encyclopaedic reference for metals is the ASM International's *Handbooks Online*, (ASM International, 2002). Trade organisations, listed in the Appendix, do better, providing their members with frequent updates and reports (e.g., Anon, 1999). The larger materials suppliers (Dow Chemical, Ciba-Geigy, Inco, Corning Glass, etc) publish design guides and compilations of case studies. All suppliers have data-sheets describing their products.

There is an immense resource here. The problem is that of access to a range of diverse data sources in an efficient and integrated way. One approach is to search a wide body of electronic reference sources on topic strings such as 'aluminium bronze *and* corrosion *and* sea water'. The Internet provides an ideal venue for this.

Data sources on the Internet

The Internet contains a rapidly expanding spectrum of information sources. Some, particularly those on the *World-Wide Web*, contain information for materials, placed there by standards organisations, trade associations, material suppliers, learned societies, universities, and individuals – some rational, some eccentric – who have something to say. There is no control over the contents of Web pages, so the nature of the information ranges from useful to baffling, and the quality from good to appalling. The Appendix includes websites which contain materials information, but the rate-of-change here is so rapid that it cannot be seen as comprehensive.

The *Material Data Network*, (matdat.net) enables full-text searching of numerous high-quality resources. These include *ASM Handbooks Online* (features the complete content of twenty one encyclopaedic ASM Handbook volumes); *ASM Alloy Center Online* (contains all ASM's property data, performance charts, and processing guidelines for specific metals and alloys); *NPL 'MIDAS'* (from the National Physical Laboratory in the

UK: specialises in material property measurement technology and standards); *UKSteel 'SteelSpec'* (contains summaries of British, European and some International steel standards, together with selected proprietary steel grades); *TWI 'JoinIT'* (from TWI, UK contains comprehensive information about welding and joining processes); *MIL-HDBK-5* (data contains information from Granta Design's MIL-Handbook-5 database incorporating data from MIL-HDBK-5H CN1); *IDES ResinSource* (contains summary data sheets for more than 40,000 plastics from 390 global suppliers); and *MatWeb* (a database of manufacturer's data sheets for more than 31,000 metals, plastics, ceramics, and composites). The *Material Data Network* is evidence of the beginnings of a useful 'supporting information' tool.

Expert systems

The main drawback of the simple, common-or-garden, database is the lack of qualification. Some data are valid under all conditions, others can properly be used only under certain circumstances. The qualification can be as important as the data itself. Sometimes the question asked of the database is imprecise. The question: 'What is the strength of a steel?' could be asking for yield strength or tensile strength or fatigue strength, or perhaps the least of all three. If the question were put to a materials expert as part of a larger consultation, he would know from the context that was wanted, would have a shrewd idea of the precision and range of validity of the value, and would warn of its limitations. An ordinary database can do none of this. Expert Systems can.

Expert Systems have the potential to solve problems which require reasoning, provided they are based on rules that can be clearly defined: using a set of geometries to select the best welding technique, for instance; or using information about environmental conditions to choose the most corrosion resistant alloy. It might be argued that a simple check-list or a table in a supplier's data sheet could do most of these things, but an Expert System combines qualitative and quantitative information using its rules (the 'expertise'), in a way which only someone with experience can. It does more than merely look up data; it qualifies it as well, allowing context-dependent selection of material or process. In the ponderous words of the British Computer Society, 'Expert systems offer intelligent advice or take intelligent decisions by embodying in a computer the knowledge-based component of an expert's skill. They must, on demand, justify their line of reasoning in a manner intelligible to the user.'

This context-dependent scheme for retrieving data sounds just what we want, but things are not so simple. An expert system is much more complex than a simple database: it is a major task to elicit the 'knowledge' from the expert; it can require massive programming effort and computer power; and it is difficult to update. A full expert system for materials selection is decades away. Success has been achieved in specialised, highly focused applications: guidance in selecting adhesives from a limited set, in choosing a welding technique, or in designing against certain sorts of corrosion. It is only a question of time before more fully developed systems become available. They are something about which to keep informed.

► WAYS OF CHECKING AND ESTIMATING DATA

The value of a database of material properties depends on its precision and its completeness – in short, on its quality. One way of maintaining or enhancing quality is to subject data to validating procedures. The property ranges and dimensionless correlations, described below, provide powerful tools for doing this. The same procedures fill a second function: that of providing estimates for missing data. This is essential for material screening when no direct measurements are available.

Property ranges

Each property of a given class of materials has a characteristic *range*. A convenient way of presenting the information is as a table in which a low (L) and a high (H) value are stored, identified by the material class. An example listing Young's Modulus, E, for the generic material classes is shown in Table 3, in which E_L is the lower limit and E_H the upper one.

Table 3 Ranges of Young's Modulus E for Broad Material Classes

Material Class	E_L (GPa)	E_H (GPa)
All Solids	0.00001	1000
Classes of Solid		
Metals: ferrous	70	220
Metals: non-ferrous	4.6	570
Fine Ceramics*	91	1000
Glasses	47	83
Polymers: thermoplastic	0.1	4.1
Polymers: thermosets	2.5	10
Polymers: elastomers	0.0005	0.1
Polymeric foams	0.00001	2
Composites: metal-matrix	81	180
Composites: polymer-matrix	2.5	240
Woods: parallel tograin	1.8	34
Woods: perpendicular to grain	0.1	18

* Fine ceramics are dense, monolithic ceramics such as SiC, Al_2O_3, ZrO_2 etc.

All properties have characteristic ranges like these. The range becomes narrower if the classes are made more restrictive. For purposes of checking and estimation, (see also below), it is helpful to break down the 'family' of *metals* into the 'classes': cast irons, steels, aluminium alloys, magnesium alloys, titanium alloys, copper alloys and so on (e.g. see Figure 22.3). Similar subdivisions for polymers (thermoplastics, thermosets, elastomers) and for ceramics and glasses (engineering ceramics, whiteware, silicate glasses, minerals) increase resolution here also.

Correlations between material properties

Materials that are stiff have high melting points. Solids with low densities have high specific heat capacities. Metals with high thermal conductivities have high electrical conductivities. These rules-of-thumb describe correlations between two or more material properties which can be expressed more quantitatively as limits for the values of *dimensionless property groups.* They take the form

$$C_L < P_1 \, P_2{}^n < C_H \qquad (22.1)$$

or $$C_L < P_1 \, P_2{}^n \, P_3{}^m < C_H \qquad (22.2)$$

(or larger groupings) where P_1, P_2, P_3 are material properties, n and m are simple powers (often -1, -1/2, 1/2 or 1), and C_L and C_H are dimensionless constants – the lower and upper limits between which the values of the property-group lies. The correlations exert tight constraints on the data, giving the 'patterns' of property envelopes which appear on material property charts (Ashby, 1999). An example is the relationship between expansion coefficient, α (units: K^{-1}), and the melting point, T_m (units: K)

$$C_L \leq \alpha \, T_m \leq C_H \qquad (22.3a)$$

or, for amorphous materials, between α and the glass temperature T_g:

$$C_L \leq \alpha \, T_g \leq C_H \qquad (22.3b)$$

Equation (3) is a correlation with the form of equation (1). Values for the dimensionless limits C_L and C_H for this group are listed in Table 4 for a number of material classes. The values span a factor to 2 to 10 rather than the factor 10 to 100 of the property ranges. There are many such correlations (see Ashby, 1998). They form the basis of a hierarchical data-checking and estimating scheme, described next.

Table 4 Limits for the Group αT_m and αT_g for Broad Material Classes*

Correlation* $C_L < \alpha T_m < C_H$	$C_L \ (\times 10^{-3})$	$C_H \ (\times 10^{-3})$
All Solids	0.1	56
Classes of Solid		
Metals: ferrous	13	27
Metals: non-ferrous	2	21
Fine Ceramics*	6	24
Glasses	0.3	3
Polymers: thermoplastic	18	35
Polymers: thermosets	11	41
Polymers: elastomers	35	56
Polymeric foams	16	37
Composites: metal-matrix	10	20
Composites: polymer-matrix	0.1	10
Woods: parallel to grain	2	4
Woods: perpendicular to grain	6	17

*For amorphous solids the melting point T_m is replaced by the glass temperature T_g.

Data checking

The checking method is shown in Figure 22.6. Each datum is associated with a material class, or, at a higher level of checking, with a sub-class. It is first compared with the range-limits L and H for that class and property. If it lies within the range-limits, it is accepted; if it does not, it is flagged for checking.

Why bother with such low-level stuff? Because in compilations of material or process properties, the most common error is that a property value which is expressed in the wrong units, has been converted wrongly,

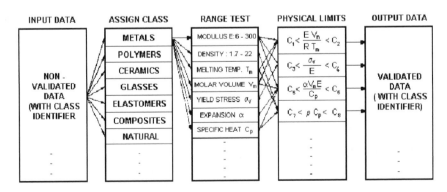

Fig. 22.6: A scheme for checking material properties

or is, for less obvious reasons, in error by one or more orders of magnitude (slipped decimal point, for instance). Range checks catch errors of this sort. If a demonstration of this is needed, it can be found by applying them to the contents of almost any standard reference data-book; none among those we have tried has passed without errors.

In the second stage, each of the dimensionless groups of properties like that of Table 4 is formed in turn, and compared with the range bracketed by the limits C_L and C_H. If the value lies within its correlation limits, it is accepted; if not, it is flagged for manual checking. Correlation checks are much more discriminating than range checks – particularly when properties are involved in several different correlations. They catch subtler errors, enabling the quality of data to be enhanced further.

Data estimation

The relationships have another, equally useful, function. There remain gaps in our knowledge of material properties. The fracture toughness of many materials has never been measured, nor has the electric breakdown potential; even moduli are not always known. The absence of a datum for a material would falsely eliminate it from a selection which used that property, even though the material might be a viable candidate. This difficulty is avoided by using the correlation and range limits described above to estimate a value for the missing datum, adding a flag to alert the user that they are estimates (Bassetti, Brechet, and Ashby, 1998).

In estimating property values, the procedure used for checking is reversed: the dimensionless groups are used first because they are the more accurate. They can be surprisingly good. As an example, consider estimating the expansion coefficient, α, of polycarbonate from its glass temperature T_g. Inverting equation (22.3) gives the estimation rule:

$$\frac{C_L}{T_g} \leq \alpha \leq \frac{C_H}{T_g} \qquad (22.4)$$

Inserting values of C_L and C_H from Table 3, and the value $T_g = 420$ K for a particular sample of polycarbonate gives the mean estimate

$$\bar{\alpha} = 63 \times 10^{-3} \text{ K}^{-1} \qquad (22.5)$$

The reported value for polycarbonate is

$$\alpha = 54 - 62 \times 10^{-3} \text{ K}^{-1}$$

The estimate is within 9% of the mean of the measured values, adequate for screening purposes. That it is an estimate must not be forgotten, however: if thermal expansion is crucial to the design, better data or direct measurements are essential.

Only when the potential of the correlations is exhausted are the property ranges invoked for estimating purposes. They provide a crude first-estimate of the range of values of the missing property, far less accurate than that of the correlations, but still useful in providing guide-values for screening.

▶ CONCLUSIONS

The systematic way to select materials or processes (or anything else, for that matter) is this:

(i)   Identify the taxonomy of the *universe* from which the selection is to be made; its *classes, subclasses* and *members.*

(ii) Identify the *attributes* of the members, remembering that they should be *universal* and *discriminating* within this universe.

(iii) Assess the *quality* and *completeness* of the data sources for the attributes; both can be increased by techniques of checking and estimation described here.

(iv) Reduce the large population of the universe to a short-list of potential candidates by *screening* and *ranking* the candidates on the basis of their attributes.

(v)   Identify sources of *supporting information* for the candidates: texts, design guides, case studies, suppliers' data sheets or (better) searchable electronic versions of these, including the Internet.

(vi) Compare full character-profiles of the candidates with requirements of the design, taking into account local constraints (preferences, experience, compatibility with other activities, etc.).

To do all this, you need to know where to find data, and you need it at three levels of breadth and precision. Conceptual design requires a broad survey at the low accuracy. Embodiment design needs more detail and precision, of the kind found in the handbooks and computer databases listed in the Appendix. The final, detailed phase of design relies on the yet more precise (and traceable) information contained in standards and material suppliers' data sheets.

The falling cost and rising speed of computing makes databases increasingly attractive. They enable fast retrieval of data for a material or a process, and the selection of the subset of entities that have attributes within a specified range. Commercially available databases already help enormously in selection, and are growing every year. Some of those currently available are reviewed in the Appendix.

▶ FURTHER READING

ASM International, 2002. *Handbooks online*, www.asminternational.org/hbk/index.jsp

ASM International, 2003. *Alloy center*, www.asminternational.org/alloycenter/index.jsp

Anon, 2001. *Guide to engineered materials (GEM)*, Advanced Materials and Processes, 159(12), Materials Park: ASM International.

Anon, 1999. *Megabytes on coppers II*, CD-ROM. New York: Copper Development Association.

Ashby, M. F., 1998. Checks and estimates for material properties. *Proceedings of The Royal Society*, A454, pp. 1301–1321.

Ashby, M. F., 1999. *Materials selection in mechanical design*. 2nd ed. Oxford: Butterworth-Heinemann.

Bessetti, D., Brechet, Y., and Ashby, M. F., 1998. Estimates for material properties: the method of multiple correlations. *Proceedings of The Royal Society*, A454, pp. 1323–1336.

Cebon, D. and Ashby, M. F., 2000. Information systems for materials and processes. *Advanced Materials and Processes*, 157(6), pp. 44–48.

Granta Design, 2003. *Cambridge Engineering Selector, CES4.*, Cambridge: Granta Design Limited, www.grantadesign.com.

Brandes, E. and Brook, G. E., eds., 1992. *Smithells metals reference book*. 7th ed. Oxford: Butterworth-Heinemann.

United States. Department of Defense, 1998. *Metallic materials and elements for aerospace vehicle structures (MIL-HDBK-5H-CN1)*. Columbus: Battelle Memorial Institute.

[*Replaced by* Rice, R. C., Jackson, J. L., et al., 2003. *Metallic materials properties development and standardization (MMPDS)*. Springfield, VA: National Technical Information Service.]

Waterman, N. A. and Ashby, M. F., 1996. *Materials selector*. London: Chapman and Hall.

▶ APPENDIX: DATA SOURCES FOR MATERIALS AND PROCESSES

Introduction

This Appendix suggests places to look for material property data. The sources, broadly speaking, are of three sorts: hard-copy, software and the Internet. The hard-copy documents can be found in most engineering libraries. The computer databases are harder to find: the supplier is listed, with contact information, as well as the hardware required to run the database, and an indication of the price, where it is known. Internet sites are easy to find but can be frustrating to use.

The number of Internet sites carrying information about materials increases daily. There is almost no control of website contents, which can vary enormously in nature and quality. The best are genuinely useful, establishing the Web as a potent 'supporting information' source. The sites listed here are a selection of ones that we have found to be useful.

The first section of the Appendix lists sources of information about database structure and functionality. The next twelve sections catalogue hardcopy and internet data sources for various classes of material, with a brief commentary where appropriate. Selection of material is often linked to that of processing; the following section provides a starting point for reading on processes. The next gives information about the rapidly-growing portfolio of software and dedicated websites for materials and process data and information. The final sections list various websites on which materials information can be found. These include supplier registers, government organisations, standards organisations and professional societies.

General references on materials databases

Waterman, N. A., Waterman, M. and Poole, M. E., 1992. Computer based materials selection systems. *Metals and Materials*, 8, pp. 19–24.

Sargent, P. M., 1991. *Materials information for CAD/CAM*. Oxford: Butterworth-Heinemann.
    A survey of the way in which materials databases work. No data.

Demerc, M. Y, 1990. *Expert system applications in materials processing and manufacture*. Warrendale: TMS Publications.

Data sources for all materials

Hard copy sources

Few hardcopy data-sources span the full spectrum of materials and properties. Several that attempt to do so in different ways are listed below.

Anon, 1997. Materials selector. *Materials Engineering*, Special Issue.
    Tabular data for a broad range of metals, ceramics, polymers and composites, updated annually. Basic reference work.

Waterman, N. A. and Ashby, M. F., 1996. *Materials selector*. London: Chapman and Hall.
    A 3-volume compilation of data for all materials, with selection and design guide. Basic reference work.

Bauccio, M. L., ed., 1994. *ASM engineered materials reference book*. 2nd ed. Materials Park: ASM International.
    Compact compilation of numeric data for metals, polymers, ceramics and composites.

Anon, 1974. Materials selector and design guide. *Design Engineering*.
    Resembles the ASM *Guide to Engineered Materials*, but less detailed and now rather dated.

Anon, 1992. *Handbook of industrial materials*. 2nd ed. Oxford: Elsevier.
> A compilation of data remarkable for its breadth: metals, ceramics, polymers, composites, fibres, sandwich structures, leather.

Brady, G. S. and Clauser, H. R., eds., 1986. *Materials handbook*. 12th ed. New York: McGraw Hill.
> A broad survey, covering metals, ceramics, polymers, composites, fibres, sandwich structures and more.

Goldsmith, A., Waterman, T. E., and Hirschhorn, J. J., 1961. *Handbook of thermophysical properties of solid materials*. New York: MacMillan.
> Thermophysical and thermochemical data for elements and compounds.

Bittence, J. C., ed., 1994. *Guide to engineering materials producers*. Materials Park: ASM International.
> A comprehensive catalogue of addresses for material suppliers.

Internet Sources of information on all classes of materials

ASM Materials Information, www.asminternational.org/matinfo/index.jsp

AZOM.com, www.azom.com

Design InSite, www.designinsite.dk

Goodfellow, www.goodfellow.com

K&K Associate's thermal connection, www.tak2000.com

Corrosion source (databases), corrosionsource.com/links.htm

Material data network, www.matdata.net

Materials (Research): Alfa Aesar, www.alfa.com

MatWeb, www.matweb.com

MSC datamart, www.mscsoftware.com

Space Environments and Technology Archive System (SETAS),
> setas-www.larc.nasa.gov/index.html

NPL MIDAS, midas.npl.co.uk/midas/index.jsp

All metals

Hard copy sources

Metals and alloys conform to national and (sometimes) international standards. One consequence is the high quality of data. Hardcopy sources for metals data are generally comprehensive, well-structured and easy to use.

Anon, eds., 1986, 1990– . *ASM metals handbook*. 10th ed. 21 vols. Materials Park: ASM International.
> Basic reference work, continuously upgraded and expanded.

Bauccio, M. L., ed., 1993. *ASM metals reference book*. 3rd ed., Materials Park: ASM International.
> Consolidates data for metals from a number of ASM publications. Basic reference work.

Brandes, E. and Brook, G. E., eds., 1992. *Smithells metals reference book*. 7th ed. Oxford: Butterworth-Heinemann.
A comprehensive compilation of data for metals and alloys. Basic reference work.

Robb, C., 1990. *Metals databook*. London: The Institute of Metals.
A concise collection of data on metallic materials covered by the U.K. specifications only.

Anon, 1986. *Guide to materials engineering data and information*. Materials Park: ASM International.
A directory of suppliers, trade organisations and publications on metals.

Bringas, J. E., ed., 1992. *The metals black book. Vol. 1. Steels.*, Edmonton: Casti Publishing Inc.
A compact book of data for steels.

Bringas, J. E., ed., 1993. *The metals red book., Vol.2. Nonferrous metals*. Edmonton: Casti Publishing Inc.

Anon, 2002. *MIL-HDBK-5H-CN1*, [now also known as *Metallic Materials Properties Development and Standardization (MMPDS)*], Columbus: Battelle Memorial Institute.
MIL-HDBK characterizes material properties for aircraft design. Also available in database format from Granta Design Ltd.

Brown, W. F. Jr, ed., 1999. *37th Aerospace structural metals handbook (ASMH)*. West Lafayette: Purdue University Institute for Interdisciplinary Studies.
A broad survey of metals used in aerospace and their properties. Contains data covering 205 alloys, fully analysed exclusively for this publication. Available as five print volumes (over 4,100 pages) or as PDF files on a single CD-ROM.

Holt, J. M., ed.,1996. *Structural alloys handbook*. West Lafayette: Purdue University Institute for Interdisciplinary Studies.
Includes representative and detailed characterization data for the more common metals and alloys important to construction, machine tool, heavy equipment, automotive, and general manufacturing industries. SAH covers wrought steel, cast iron, wrought stainless steel, cast steel, cast stainless steel, structural steels, wrought and cast aluminum, copper, brass, bronze, magnesium, and titanium. Three volumes, over 2,500 pages.

Internet sources for two or more metals classes

ASM International Handbooks, www.asminternational.org/hbk/index.jsp
ASM International, Alloy Center, www.asminternational.org/alloycenter/index.jsp
Carpenter Technology Home Page, www.cartech.com
CASTI Publishing Site Catalog, www.casti-publishing.com/intsite.htm
CMW Inc. Home Page, www.cmwinc.com
Engelhard Corporation-Electro Metallics Department, www.engelhard.com
Eurometaux, www.eurometaux.org
Materials (high performance): MatTech, www.mat-tech.com
Metsteel.com, www.metsteel.com

Rare earths: Pacific Industrial Development Corp., pidc.com
Rare Metals: Stanford Materials Inc. www.stanfordmaterials.com
Refractory Metals: Teledyne Wah Chang, www.twca.com

Pure metals

Hardcopy sources

Most of the sources listed in the previous section contain some information on pure metals. However, the publications listed below are particularly useful in this respect.

Emsley, J., 1998. *The elements*. 3rd ed. Oxford: Oxford University Press.
> A book aimed more at chemists and physicists than engineers, with good coverage of chemical, thermal and electrical properties but not mechanical properties.

Brandes, E. and Brook, G. E., eds., 1992. *Smithells metals reference book*. 7th ed. Oxford: Butterworth-Heinemann.
> Data for the mechanical, thermal and electrical properties of pure metals.

Goodfellow Cambridge Ltd., 1995–6. *Catalogue*. Cambridge: Goodfellow Cambridge Ltd.
> Useful though patchy data for mechanical, thermal and electrical properties of pure metals in a tabular format. Free.

ALFA AESAR, 1995–6. *Catalog*. Ward Hill, MA: Johnson Matthey Catalog Co. Inc.
> Coverage similar to that of the Goodfellow Catalogue. Free.

Samsonov, G.V., ed., 1968. *Handbook of the physiochemical properties of the elements*. Oldbourne: London.
> An extensive compilation of data from Western and Eastern sources. Contains a number of inaccuracies, but also contains a large quantity of data on the rarer elements, hard to find elsewhere.

Gschneidner, K. A., 1964. Physical properties and interrelationships of metallic and semimetallic elements. *Solid State Physics*, 16, pp. 275–426.
> Probably the best source of its time, this reference work is very well referenced, and full explanations are given of estimated or approximate data.

Internet sources

Winter, M, *WebElements*. Sheffield: University of Sheffield, www.webelements.com
> A comprehensive source of information on all the elements in the Periodic Table. If it has a weakness, it is in the definitions and values of some mechanical properties.

Martindale's: the virtual physics web pages, www.martindalecenter.com/GradPhysics.html

Non-ferrous metals

Aluminium alloys

Hardcopy Sources

Anon, 1990. *Aluminium standards and data*. Washington, DC: The Aluminium Association Inc.

Anon, 1981. *The properties of aluminium and its alloys*. Birmingham: The Aluminium Federation.

Anon, 1993. *Technical data sheets*. Kingston: ALCAN International Ltd, *and* Banbury: Banbury Laboratory.

Anon, 1993. *Technical data sheets*. Pittsburgh: ALCOA.

Anon, 1994. *Technical data sheets*. Paris: Aluminium Pechiney.

Internet Sources

Aluminium Federation, www.alfed.org.uk

Aluminium World, www.sovereign-publications.com/index.htm

International Aluminium Institute, www.world-aluminium.org

Babbitt Metal

The term 'Babbitt Metal' denotes a series of lead-tin-antimony bearing alloys, the first of which was patented in the USA by Isaac Babbitt in 1839. Subsequent alloys are all variations on his original composition.

ASTM Standard, B23–00. *White metal bearing alloys (known commercially as Babbitt Metal)*. (ASTM Annual Book of Standards. Vol. 02.04)

Beryllium

Anon, 1996. *Designing with Beryllium*. Cleveland: Brush Wellman Inc.

Anon, 1996. *Beryllium Optical Materials*. Cleveland: Brush Wellman Inc.

Brush Wellman, www.brushwellman.com

Cadmium

Anon, 1991. *Cadmium production, properties and uses*. London: International Cadmium Association.

Chromium

ASTM Standard A560–89, *Castings, Chromium-Nickel Alloy*. (ASTM Annual Book of Standards. Vol. 01.02).

Cobalt aloys

Betteridge, W., 1982. *Cobalt and its alloys*. Chichester: Ellis Horwood. A good general
introduction to the subject.

Columbium alloys: see Niobium alloys

Copper alloys

Hardcopy Sources

Anon, eds., 1990. *ASM metals handbook*. 10th ed. Materials Park: ASM International.,
West, E. G., 1979. *The selection and use of copper-based alloys*. Oxford: Oxford
University Press.
Anon. *Data sheets*, 26 (1988), 27 (1981), 31 (1982), 40 (1979), and *Publication* 82
(1982)., St Albans: Copper Development Association Inc.
Anon. *Megabytes on Coppers II*. CD-ROM. St Albans: Copper Development
Association.
Brandes, E. and Brook, G. E., eds., 1992. *Smithells metals reference book*. 7th ed. Oxford:
Butterworth-Heinemann.

Internet Sources

Copper Development Association, www.cda.org.uk
Copper page, www.copper.org

Dental Alloys

O'Brien, W. J. *Biomaterial properties database*,
www.lib.umich.edu/libhome/Dentistry.lib/Dental_tables.
An extensive source of information, both for natural biological materials and for
metals used in dental treatments.
Jeneric Pentron inc. *Casting alloys*, www.jeneric.com/casting
An informative commercial site.
ISO Standard, 1562: 1993. *Dental casting gold alloys*. Geneva: ISO.
ISO Standard, 8891: 1993. *Dental casting alloys with Noble metal content of 25% up to but
not including 75%*. Geneva: ISO.

Gold

Rand Refinery Limited, www.bullion.org.za/associates/rr.htm
South Africa Chamber of Mines website, contains useful information on how gold is
processed to varying degrees of purity.
See also the section on Dental Alloys.

Indium

The Indium Info Center, www.indium.com/metalcenter.html

Lead

Hardcopy Sources

ASTM Standard, B29–79. *Pig lead*. (ASTM Annual Book of Standards. Vol. 02.04).

ASTM Standard, B102–76. *Lead- and tin-alloy die castings*. (ASTM Annual Book of Standards. Vol. 02.04).

ASTM Standard, B749–85. *Lead and lead alloy strip, sheet, and plate products*. (ASTM Annual Book of Standards. Vol. 02.04).

Lead Industries Association, 1983. *Lead for corrosion resistant applications*. New York: LIA Inc.

Anon, eds., 1986. *ASM metals handbook*. 9th ed. Vol. 2, pp. 500–510.

See also Babbitt Metal *(above)*

Internet Sources

Lead Development Association International, www.ldaint.org/default.htm

India Lead Zinc Development Association, www.ilzda.com

Magnesium alloys

Anon, 1994. *Technical data sheets*. Swinton: Magnesium Elektron Ltd.

Anon, 1994. *Technical literature*. Salt Lake City: Magnesium Corp. of America.

Molybdenum

ASTM Standard, B386–85. *Molybdenum and molybdenum alloy plate, sheet, strip and foil*. (ASTM Annual Book of Standards. Vol. 02.04).

ASTM Standard, B387–85. *Molybdenum and molybdenum alloy bar, rod and wire*. (ASTM Annual Book of Standards. Vol. 02.04).

Nickel

A major data sources for Nickel and its alloys is the **Nickel Development Institute (NiDI)**, a global organisation with offices in every continent except Africa. NiDI freely gives away large quantities of technical reports and data compilations, not only for nickel and high-nickel alloys, but also for other nickel-bearing alloys, e.g. stainless steel.

Hardcopy Sources

ASTM Standard, A297–84. *Steel castings, iron-chromium and iron-chromium-nickel, heat resistant, for general application*. (ASTM Annual Book of Standards. Vol. 01.02).

ASTM Standard, A344–83. *Drawn or rolled nickel-chromium and nickel-chromium-iron alloys for electrical heating elements.* (ASTM Annual Book of Standards. Vol. 02.04).

ASTM Standard, A494–90. *Castings, nickel and nickel alloy.* (ASTM Annual Book of Standards. Vol. 02.04).

ASTM Standard, A753–85. *Nickel-iron soft magnetic alloys.* (ASTM Annual Book of Standards. Vol. 03.04).

Betteridge, W., 1984. *Nickel and its alloys.* Chichester: Ellis Horwood.
A good introduction to the subject.

INCO Inc., 1995. *High-temperature, high-strength nickel base alloys.* Birmingham: Nickel Development Institute.
Tabular data for over 80 alloys.

Elliott, P., 1990. *Practical guide to high-temperature alloys.* Birmingham: Nickel Development Institute.
Tabular data for over 80 alloys.

INCO Inc., 1978. *Heat and corrosion resistant castings.* Birmingham: Nickel Development Institute.

INCO Inc., 1969. *Engineering properties of some nickel copper casting alloys.* Birmingham: Nickel Development Institute.

INCO Inc., 1968. *Engineering properties of IN-100 alloy.* Birmingham: Nickel Development Institute.

INCO Inc., 1969. *Engineering properties of nickel-chromium alloy 610 and related casting alloys.* Birmingham: Nickel Development Institute.

INCO Inc., 1968. *Alloy 713C: technical data.* Birmingham: Nickel Development Institute.

INCO Inc., 1981. *Alloy IN-738: technical data.* Birmingham: Nickel Development Institute.

INCO Inc., 1976. *36% nickel-iron alloy for low temperature service.* Birmingham: Nickel Development Institute.

ASTM Standard, A658 (discontinued 1989). *Pressure vessel plates, alloy steel, 36 percent nickel.*

Anon, eds., 1986. *ASM metals handbook.* 9th ed. Vol. 3, pp. 125–178.

Internet Sources

Nickel Development Institute, www.nidi.org

INCO website, www.incoltd.com

Special Metals Corp., www.specialmetals.com

Steel & nickel based alloys, www.superalloys.co.uk/start.html

Niobium (Columbium) alloys

ASTM Standard, B391–89. *Niobium and niobium alloy ingots.* (ASTM Annual Book of Standards. Vol. 02.04).

ASTM Standard, B392–89. *Niobium and niobium alloy bar, rod and wire.* (ASTM Annual Book of Standards. Vol. 02.04).

ASTM Standard, B393–89. *Niobium and niobium alloy strip, sheet and plate.* (ASTM Annual Book of Standards. Vol. 02.04).

ASTM Standard, B652–85. *Niobium-hafnium alloy ingots.* (ASTM Annual Book of Standards. Vol. 02.04).

ASTM Standard, B654–79. *Niobium-hafnium alloy foil, sheet, strip and plate.* (ASTM Annual Book of Standards. Vol. 02.04).

ASTM Standard, B655–85. *Niobium-hafnium alloy bar, rod and wire.* (ASTM Annual Book of Standards. Vol. 02.04).

Palladium

ASTM Standard, B540–86. *Palladium electrical contact alloy.* (ASTM Annual Book of Standards. Vol. 03.04).

ASTM Standard, B563–89. *Palladium-silver-copper electrical contact alloy.* (ASTM Annual Book of Standards. Vol. 03.04).

ASTM Standard, B589–82. *Refined palladium.* (ASTM Annual Book of Standards. Vol. 02.04).

ASTM Standard, B683–90. *Pure palladium electrical contact material.* (ASTM Annual Book of Standards. Vol. 03.04).

ASTM Standard, B685–90. *Palladium-copper electrical contact material.* (ASTM Annual Book of Standards. Vol. 03.04).

ASTM Standard, B731–84. *60% palladium-40% silver electrical contact material.* (ASTM Annual Book of Standards. Vol. 03.04).

Platinum alloys

ASTM Standard, B684–81. *Platinum-iridium electrical contact material.* (ASTM Annual Book of Standards. Vol. 03.04).

Anon. *Elkonium Series 400 data sheets.* Indianapolis: CMW Inc.

Anon, eds. 1986. *ASM metals handbook.* 9th ed. Vol. 2, pp. 688–698.

Silver alloys

Hardcopy Sources

ASTM Standard, B413–89. *Refined silver.* (ASTM Annual Book of Standards. Vol. 02.04).

ASTM Standard, B 617–83. *Coin silver electrical contact alloy.* (ASTM Annual Book of Standards. Vol. 03.04).

ASTM Standard, B 628–83. *Silver-copper eutectic electrical contact alloy.* (ASTM Annual Book of Standards. Vol. 03.04).

ASTM Standard, B 693–87. *Silver-nickel electrical contact materials.* (ASTM Annual Book of Standards. Vol. 03.04).

ASTM Standard, B742–90. *Fine silver electrical contact fabricated materials.*, (ASTM Annual Book of Standards. Vol. 03.04).

ASTM Standard, B 780–87. *75% silver, 24.5% copper, 0.5% nickel electrical contact alloy.* (ASTM Annual Book of Standards. Vol. 03.04).

Anon, 1996. *Elkonium Series 300 data sheets.* Indianapolis: CMW Inc.

Anon, 1996. *Elkonium Series 400 data sheets.* Indianapolis: CMW Inc.

Internet Sources

Jeneric Pentron Inc. *Casting alloys*, www.jeneric.com.
An informative commercial site, limited to dental alloys.
Silver Institute, www.silverinstitute.org

Tantalum alloys

ASTM Standard, B365–86. *Tantalum and tantalum alloy rod and wire*. (ASTM Annual Book of Standards. Vol. 02.04).

ASTM Standard, B521–86. *Tantalum and tantalum alloy seamless and welded tube*. (ASTM Annual Book of Standards. Vol. 02.04).

ASTM Standard, B560–86. *Unalloyed tantalum for surgical implant applications*. (ASTM Annual Book of Standards. Vol. 21.01).

ASTM Standard, B708–86. *Tantalum and tantalum alloy plate, sheet and strip*. (ASTM Annual Book of Standards. Vol. 02.04).

Rembar Company inc, 1996. *Tantalum data sheet.*, Dobbs Ferry, NY: The Rembar Company.

Anon, eds., 1986. *ASM handbook*. 9th ed. Vol.3, pp. 323–325, 343–347.

Tin alloys

ASTM Standard, B32–89. *Solder metal*. (ASTM Annual Book of Standards. Vol. 02.04).

ASTM Standard, B339–90. *Pig tin*. (ASTM Annual Book of Standards. Vol. 02.04).

ASTM Standard, B560–79. *Modern pewter alloys*. (ASTM Annual Book of Standards. Vol. 02.04).

Barry, B.T.K. and Thwaites, C.J., 1983. *Tin and its alloys and compounds*. Chichester: Ellis Horwood.

Anon, eds., 1986. *ASM metals handbook*. 9th ed. Vol. 2, pp. 613–625.

See also Babbitt Metal (above)

Tin Research Association, www.tintechnology.com

Titanium alloys

Hardcopy Sources

Titanium Development Association, 1993. *Technical data sheets*. Boulder: Titanium Development Association.

Titanium Information Group, 1993. *Technical data sheets*. Melbourne, UK: The Titanium Information Group, c/o Inco Engineered Products.)

IMI Titanium Ltd, 1995. *Technical data sheets*. Birmingham: IMI Titanium Ltd.

Internet Sources

International Titanium Association, www.titanium.org
Titanium Information Group, www.titaniuminfogroup.co.uk

Tungsten alloys

ASTM Standard, B777–87. *Tungsten base, high-density metal.* (ASTM Annual Book of Standards. Vol. 02.04).

Yih, S. W. H. and Wang, C. T., 1979. *Tungsten.* New York: Plenum Press.

Anon, eds., 1986. *ASM metals handbook.* 9th ed. Vol. 7, p. 476.

Rembar Company inc, 1996. *Tungsten data sheet.* Dobbs Ferry, NY: The Rembar Company Inc.

British Aerospace Defence Ltd, 1996. *Royal Ordnance speciality metals data sheet.* Woverhampton: British Aerospace Defence Ltd.

Anon, 1996. *Data sheets.* Indianapolis: CMW Inc.

Tungsten: North American Tungsten, www.northamericantungsten.com

Uranium

Uranium Information Centre, Australia, www.uic.com.au

Ux Jan 96 Uranium Indicator Update, www.uxc.com/review/uxc_g_ind-u.html

Vanadium

Teledyne Wah Chang, 1996. *Vanadium brochure.* Albany, OR: TWC.

Zinc

Hardcopy Sources

ASTM Standard, B6–87. *Zinc.* (ASTM Annual Book of Standards. Vol. 02.04).

ASTM Standard, B69–87. *Rolled zinc.* (ASTM Annual Book of Standards. Vol. 02.04).

ASTM Standard, B86–88. *Zinc-alloy die castings.* (ASTM Annual Book of Standards. Vol. 02.02).

ASTM Standard, B418–88. *Cast and wrought galvanic zinc anodes.* (ASTM Annual Book of Standards. Vol. 02.04).

ASTM Standard, B791–88. *Zinc-aluminium alloy foundry and die castings.* (ASTM Annual Book of Standards. Vol. 02.04).

ASTM Standard, B792–88. *Zinc alloys in ingot form for slush casting.* (ASTM Annual Book of Standards. Vol. 02.04).

ASTM Standard, B793–88. *Zinc casting alloy ingot for sheet metal forming dies.* (ASTM Annual Book of Standards. Vol. 02.04).

Goodwin, F. E. and Ponikvar, A. L., eds., 1989. *Engineering properties of zinc alloys.* 3rd ed. Research Triangle Park, NC: International Lead Zinc Research Organization.

An excellent compilation of data, covering all industrially important zinc alloys.

Chivers, A. R. L., 1981. *Zinc diecasting.* (Engineering Design Guide no. 41). Oxford: OUP.

A good introduction to the subject.

Anon, eds., 1986. *ASM metal handbook.* 9th ed. Vol.2, pp. 638–645.

Internet Sources

International Zinc Association, www.iza.com

Zinc Industrias Nacionales S.A.- Peru, www.zinsa.com/espanol.htm

Eastern Alloys, www.eazall.com

India Lead Zinc Development Association, www.ilzda.com

Zirconium

ASTM Standard, B350–80. *Zirconium and zirconium alloy ingots for nuclear application.* (ASTM Annual Book of Standards. Vol. 02.04).

ASTM Standard, B352–85, B551–83, B752–85. *Zirconium and zirconium alloys.* (ASTM Annual Book of Standards. Vol. 02.04).

Teledyne Wah Chang, 1996. *Zircadyne: properties and applications.* Albany, OR: TWC.

Anon, eds., *ASM metals handbook.* 9th ed. Vol. 2, pp. 826–831.

Ferrous metals

Ferrous metals are probably the most thoroughly researched and documented class of materials. Nearly every developed country has its own system of standards for irons and steels. Recently, continental and worldwide standards have been developed, which have achieved varying levels of acceptance. There is a large and sometimes confusing literature on the subject. This section is intended to provide the user with a guide to some of the better information sources.

General Data Sources

Bringas, J. E., ed., 1995. *The metals black book – ferrous metals.* 2nd ed. Edmonton: CASTI Publishing.

An excellent short reference work.

Anon, eds., 1990. *ASM metals handbook.* Vol. 1.10th ed. *Materials* Park: ASM International.

Authoritative reference work for North American irons and steels.

Anon, eds., 1998. *ASM metals handbook desk ed.* 2nd ed. Materials Park: ASM International. A summary of the multi-volume ASM Metals Handbook.

Wegst, C. W. *Stahlschlüssel (Key to Steel).* Marbach: Verlag Stahlschlüssel Wegst GmbH. Published every 3 years, in German, French and English. Excellent coverage of European products and manufacturers.

Woolman, J. and Mottram, R. A., 1996. *The mechanical and physical properties of the British standard EN steels.* Oxford: Pergamon Press.

Still highly regarded, but is based around a British Standard classification system that has been officially abandoned.

Brandes, E. and Brook, G. E., eds., 1992. *Smithells metals reference book.* 7th ed. Oxford: Butterworth-Heinemann.

An authoritative reference work, covering all metals.

Waterman, N. A. and Ashby, M. F., eds., 1996. *Materials selector*. London: Chapman and Hall.
  Covers all materials – irons and steels are in Vol. 2.
Sharpe, C., ed., *Kempe's engineering yearbook*. Tonbridge: Benn.
  Updated each year – has good sections on irons and steels.

Iron and Steels Standards

Increasingly, national and international standards organisations are providing a complete catalogue of their publications on the World Wide Web. Two of the most comprehensive printed sources are listed below:

British Iron and Steel Producers Association, 1998. *Iron and steel specifications*. 9th ed. London: BISPA [now UKSteel]. Comprehensive tabulations of data from British Standards on irons and steels, as well as some information on European and North American standards. The same information is available on searchable CD.
ASTM annual book of standards. Vols. 01.01 to 01.07. The most complete set of American iron and steel standards. Summaries of the standards can be found at *www.astm.org*

Cross-Referencing of Similar International Standard Grades
It is difficult to match, even approximately, equivalent grades of iron and steel between countries. No coverage of this subject can ever be complete, but the references listed below are helpful:

Gensure, J. G. and Potts, D. L., 1998. *International metallic materials cross reference*. 3rd ed. New York: Genium Publishing.
  Comprehensive worldwide coverage of the subject, well indexed.
Bringas, J. E., ed., 1995. *The metals black book – ferrous metals*. 2nd ed. Edmonton: CASTI Publishing.
  Easy-to-use tables for international cross-referencing. (*See* General section for more information).
Anon., 1977. *Unified numbering system for metals and alloys*. 2nd ed. Washington, DC: Society of Automotive Engineers.
  An authoritative reference work, providing a unifying structure for all standards published by US organisations. No coverage of the rest of the world.
Anon, 1989. *Iron and steel specifications*. 7th ed. London: British Steel.
  Lists 'Related Specifications' for France, Germany, Japan, Sweden, UK and USA.

Cast Irons

Scholes, J. P., 1979. *The selection and use of cast irons*. Oxford: OUP.
Angus, H. T., 1976. *Cast iron: physical and engineering properties*. London: Butterworths.

Gilbert, G. N. J., 1977. *Engineering data on grey cast irons*. Birmingham: British Cast Iron Research Association.

Gilbert, G. N. J., 1986. *Engineering data on nodular cast irons*. Birmingham: British Cast Iron Research Association.

Gilbert, G. N. J., 1983. *Engineering data on malleable cast irons*. Birmingham: British Cast Iron Research Association.

Smith, L. W. L., Palmer, K. B., and Gilbert, G. N. J., 1986. *Properties of modern malleable irons*. Birmingham: British Cast Iron Research Association.

Palmer, K. B., 1988. *Mechanical and physical properties of cast irons at sub-zero temperatures*. Birmingham: British Cast Iron Research Association.

Palmer, K. B., 1986. *Mechanical and physical properties of cast irons up to 500 C.* Birmingham: British Cast Iron Research Association.

Cast Irons, American Standards

These can all be found in the *Annual Book of ASTM Standards*. Vol. 01.02:

ASTM Standard. A220M-88. *Pearlitic malleable iron.*
ASTM Standard. A436–84. *Austenitic gray iron castings.*
ASTM Standard. A532. *Abrasion-resistant cast irons.*
ASTM Standard. A602–70. *Automotive malleable iron castings.*

Cast Irons, International Standards

These are available from ISO Central Secretariat, 1, rue de Varembe, Case postale 56, CH-1211 Geneve 20, Switzerland:

ISO 185: 1988. *Grey cast iron – classification.*
ISO 2892: 1973. *Austenitic cast iron.*
ISO 5922: 1981. *Malleable cast iron.*

Cast Irons, British Standards

Compared with steels, there are relatively few standards on cast iron, which makes it feasible to list them all. The standards are available from BSI Customer Services, 389 Chiswick High Road, London, W4 4AL, UK.

British Standards Institution, BS 1452: 1990. *Flake graphite cast iron.*
British Standards Institution, BS 1591: 1975. *Specification for corrosion resisting high silicon castings.*
British Standards Institution, BS 2789: 1985. *Iron castings with spheroidal or nodular graphite.*
British Standards Institution, BS 3468: 1986. *Austenitic cast iron.*
British Standards Institution, BS 4844: 1986. *Abrasion resisting white cast iron.*
British Standards Institution, BS 6681: 1986. *Specification for malleable cast iron.*

Carbon & Low Alloy Steels

Anon, 1990. *ASM metals handbook*. 10th ed. Vol. 1. Materials Park: ASM International. Authoritative reference work for North American irons and steels.

Fox, J. H. E., [s.d.] *An introduction to steel selection. Part 1. Carbon and low-alloy steels.* (Engineering Design Guide, no. 34). Oxford: Oxford University Press.

Stainless Steels

Anon, eds., 1990. *ASM metals handbook*. 10th ed. Vol. 1. Materials Park: ASM International. Authoritative reference work for North American irons a nd steels.

Elliott, D. and Tupholme, S. M, 1981. *An introduction to steel selection. Part 2. Stainless steels.* (Engineering Design Guide, no. 43). Oxford: Oxford University Press.

Peckner, D. and Bernstein, I. M., 1977. *Handbook of stainless steels*. New York: McGraw-Hill.

Nickel Development Institute, 1991. *Design Guidelines for the Selection and Use of Stainless Steel.* (Designers' Handbook Series, no. 9014). Toronto: Nickel Development Institute.

(The Nickel Development Institute (NiDI) is a worldwide organisation that gives away a large variety of free literature about nickel-based alloys, including stainless steels. NiDI European Technical Information Centre, The Holloway, Alvechurch, Birmingham, B48 7QB, UK.)

General Internet Sites for Ferrous Metals

British Constructional Steel Work Association, www.steelconstruction.org
International Iron & Steel Institute, www.worldsteel.org
Iron & Steel Trades Confederation, www.istc-tu.org
National Assoc. of Steel Stock Holders, www.nass.org.uk
Steel Manufacturers Association, www.steelnet.org
Bethlehem Steel's website, www.bethsteel.com/index2.shtml
Corus home page, www.corusgroup.com/home/index.cfm
Automotive Steel Library, www.autosteel.org
Steels Construction Institute, www.steel.org.uk
SteelSpec, www.steelspec.org.uk/index.htm
Steelynx, www.steelynx.net
UK Steel, www.uksteel.org.uk
Wire & Wire Rope Employers Association, www.uksteel.org.uk/wwrea.htm
British Stainless Steel Association, www.bssa.org.uk/index.htm
Arcus Stainless Steel, www.arcus.nl
Great Plains Stainless, www.gpss.com

Polymers and elastomers

Polymers are not subject to the same strict specification as metals. Data tend to be producer-specific. Sources, consequently, are scattered, incomplete and poorly presented. Saechtling is the best; although no single hardcopy source is completely adequate, all those listed here are worth consulting. See also Databases and Software: some (Plascams, CES/OPS from Granta Design) are good on polymers.

Hardcopy Sources

Saechtling, H. J., ed., 1983. *Saechtling: international plastics handbook*. London: MacMillan Publishing Co.

The most comprehensive of the hard-copy data-sources for polymers.

Seymour, R. B., 1987. *Polymers for engineering applications*. Materials Park: ASM International.

Property data for common polymers. A starting point, but insufficient detail for accurate design or process selection.

Murphy, J., ed., [s.d.]. *New horizons in plastics, a handbook for design engineers*. London: WEKA Publishing.

Anon, 1989. *ASM engineered materials handbook. Vol 2. Engineering plastics*. Materials Park: ASM International.

Harper, C. A., ed., 1975. *Handbook of plastics and elastomers*. New York: McGraw-Hill.

Anon, 1987. *International plastics selector, plastics*. 9th ed. San Diego: Int. Plastics Selector.

Dominighaus, H., ed., 1992. *Die Kunststoffe and Ihre Eigenschaften.*, Dusseldorf: VDI Verlag.

Van Krevelen, D. W., 1990. *Properties of polymers*. 3rd ed. Amsterdam: Elsevier.

Correlation of properties with structure; estimation from molecular architecture.

Bhowmick, A. K. and Stephens, H. L., 1988. *Handbook of elastomers*. New York: Marcel Dekker.

Anon, 1981. *ICI technical service notes*. Welwyn Garden City: ICI Plastics Division, Engineering Plastics Group.

Anon, 1995. *Technical data sheets*. Brickendonbury, Herts: Malaysian Rubber Producers Research Association, Tun Abdul Razak Laboratory.

Data sheets for numerous blends of natural rubber.

Internet Sources

CAMPUS Plastics database, www.campusplastics.com

GE Plastics, www.ge.com/en/company/businesses/ge_plastics.htm

Harboro Rubber Co. Ltd., www.harboro.co.uk

IDES Resin Source, ides.com

MERL, www.merl-ltd.co.uk

Plastics.com, www.plastics.com

Ceramics and glasses

Sources of data for ceramics and glasses, other than the suppliers' data-sheets, are limited. Texts and handbooks such as the ASM's (1991) *Engineered Materials Handbook*, Vol. 4, Morell's (1985) compilations, Neville's (1996) book on concrete, Boyd and Thompson's (1980) *Handbook on Glass* and Sorace's (1996) treatise on stone are useful starting points. The *CES Ceramics Database* (Granta Design) contains recent data for ceramics and glasses. But, in the end, it is the manufacturer to whom one has to turn: the data sheets for their products are the most reliable source of information.

Ceramics and Ceramic-matrix Composites

Anon, 1991. *ASM engineered materials handbook. Vol 4. Ceramics and Glasses*. Materials Park: ASM International.

Waterman, N. A. and Ashby, M. F., 1996. *Materials selector*. London: Chapman and Hall.

Brook, R. J., ed., 1991. *Concise encyclopedia of advanced ceramic materials*. Oxford: Pergamon Press.

Creyke, W. E. C., Sainsbury, I. E. J., and Morrell, R., 1982. *Design with non ductile materials*. London: Applied Science.

Cheremisinoff, N. P., ed., 1990. *Handbook of ceramics and composites*. 3 vols. New York: Marcel Dekker Inc.

Clark, S. P, ed., 1966. *Handbook of physical constants, memoir 97*. Boulder: Geological Society of America.

Schwartz, M. M., ed., 1992. *Handbook of structural ceramics*. New York: McGraw-Hill. Lots of data, information on processing and applications.

Kaye, G. W. C.and Laby, T. H., 1986. *Tables of physical and chemical constants*. 15th ed. New York: Longman.

Kingery, W. D., Bowen, H. K., and Uhlmann, D. R., 1976. *Introduction to ceramics*. 2nd ed. New York: Wiley.

Anon, 2001. 'Guide to engineered materials (GEM)'. *Advanced Materials and Processes*, 159(12).

Morrell, R., 1995. *Handbook of properties of technical and engineering ceramics. Parts I and II*. Teddington: National Physical Laboratory.

Musikant, S., 1991. *What every engineer should know about ceramics*. New York: Marcel Dekker, Inc. Good on data.

Richerson, D. W., 1992. *Modern ceramic engineering*. 2nd ed. New York: Marcel Dekker.

The American Ceramics Society, www.acers.org

Glasses

Anon., 1991. *ASM engineered materials handbook. Vol 4. Ceramics and glasses*. Materials Park: ASM International.

Boyd, D. C., Thompson, D. A., 1980. *Glass*. [Reprinted from *Kirk-Othmer encyclopedia of chemical techology*. Vol. 11. 3rd ed. pp. 807–880]. New York: Wiley.

Oliver, D. S, 1975. *The use of glass in engineering*. (Engineering Design Guide 05). Oxford: Oxford University Press.

Bansal, N. P. and Doremus, R. H., 1966. *Handbook of glass properties*. New York: Academic Press.

Cement and Concrete

Cowan, H. J. and Smith, P. R., 1988. *The science and technology of building materials*. New York: Van Nostrand-Reinhold.

Illston, J. M., Dinwoodie, J. M., and Smith, A. A., 1979. *Concrete, timber and metals*. New York: Van Nostrand-Reinhold.

Neville, A. M., 1996. *Properties of concrete*. 4th ed. London: Longman Scientific and Technical.
  An excellent introduction to the subject.

Composites: PMCs, MMCs and CMCs

The fabrication of composites allows so many variants that no hard-copy data source can capture them all; instead, they list properties of matrix and reinforcement, and of certain generic lay-ups or types. The '*Engineers Guide*' and the '*Composite Materials Handbook*', listed first, are particularly recommended.

Composite, General

Weeton, J. W., Peters, D. M., and Thomas, K. L., eds., 1987. *Engineers guide to composite materials*. Materials Park: ASM International.
  The best starting point: data for all classes of composites.

Schwartz, M. M., ed., 1992. *Composite materials handbook*. 2nd ed. New York: McGraw-Hill.
  Lots of data on PMCs, less on MMCs and CMCs, processing, fabrication, applications and design information.

Anon, 1987. *ASM engineered materials handbook. Vol. 21., Composites*. Materials Park: ASM International.

Seymour, R. B., 1991. *Reinforced plastics: properties and applications*. Materials Park: ASM International.

Cheremisinoff, N. P., ed., 1990. *Handbook of ceramics and composites*. 3 Vols. New York: Marcel Dekker Inc.

Kelly, A., ed., 1989. *Concise encyclopedia of composite materials*. Oxford: Pergamon Press.

Middleton, D. H., 1990. *Composite materials in aircraft structures*. New York: Longman Scientific and Technical Publications.

Smith, C. S., 1990. *Design of marine structures in composite materials*. London: Elsevier Applied Science.

Metal Matrix Composites

See, first, the sources listed under 'All Composite Types', then, for more detail, go to:

Anon, 1995. *Technical data sheets.* San Diego: Duralcan USA.
Anon, 1995. *Technical data sheets.* St Paul, MN: 3M Company.

Foams and Cellular Solids

Many of the references given above for polymers and elastomers mention foam. The references given here contains much graphical data and simple formulae which allow properties of foams to be estimated from its density and the properties of the solid of which it is made, but in the end it is necessary to contact suppliers. See also Databases and Expert Systems as Software (below); some (Plascams, CES) are good on foams. For Woods and Wood-based Composites, see Section below.

Cellular Polymers. [journal, 1981–1996. Shawbury: RAPRA Technology].
Anon, 1980. *Encyclopedia of chemical technology.* Vol 2. 3rd ed. pp. 82–126. New York: Wiley.
Anon, 1985. *Encyclopedia of polymer science and engineering.* Vol 3. 2nd ed., Section C. New York: Wiley.
Gibson, L. J. and Ashby, M. F., 1997. *Cellular solids.* Cambridge: Cambridge University Press.
    Basic text on foamed polymers, metals, ceramics and glasses, and natural cellular solids.
Anon, 1992. *Handbook of industrial materials.* 2nd ed,. pp. 537–556. Oxford: Elsevier.
Hilyard, N. C. and Cunningham, A., eds., 1994. *Low density cellular plastics – physical basis of behaviour.* London: Chapman and Hall.
    Specialised articles on aspects of polymer-foam production, properties and uses.
PLASCAMS: Plastics Computer-Aided Materials Selector, 1995. Version 6. Shawbury: RAPRA Technology Limited.
Saechtling, H. J., ed., 1983. *Saechtling: international plastics handbook.* London: MacMillan Publishing Co.
Seymour, R. P., 1987. *Polymers for engineering applications.* Materials Park: ASM International.

Stone, Rocks and Minerals

There is an enormous literature on rocks and minerals. Start with the Handbooks listed below; then ask a geologist for guidance.

Atkinson, B. K., 1987. *The fracture mechanics of rock.* London: Academic Press.
Clark, S. P., Jr., ed., 1966. *Handbook of physical constants.* Memoir 97. New York: The Geological Society of America.

Old but trusted compilation of property data for rocks and minerals.

Lama, R. E. and Vutukuri, V. S., eds., 1978. *Handbook on mechanical properties of rocks.* 4 Vols. Clausthal: Trans Tech Publications.,

Griggs, D. and Handin, J., eds., 1960. *Rock deformation.* Memoir 79. New York: The Geological Society of America.

Sorace, S., 1966. Long-term tensile and bending strength of natural building stones. *Materials and Structures,* 29(Aug/Sept), pp. 426–435.

Woods and wood-based composites

Woods, like composites, are anisotropic; useful sources list properties along and perpendicular to the grain. The US Forest Products Laboratory '*Wood Handbook*' and Kollmann and Cotés' '*Principles of Wood Science, and Technology*' are particularly recommended.

General Information

Bodig, J. and Jayne, B. A., 1982. *Mechanics of wood and wood composites.* New York: Van Nostrand Reinholt Company.

Dinwoodie, J. M., 1989. *Wood, nature's cellular polymeric fibre composite.* London: The Institute of Metals.

Dinwoodie, J. M., 1981. *Timber, its nature and behaviour.* Wokingham: Van Nostrand-Reinhold.

Basic text on wood structure and properties. Not much data.

Gibson, L. J. and Ashby, M. F., 1997. *Cellular solids.* 2nd ed. Cambridge: Cambridge University Press.

Jane, F. W., *The structure of wood.* 2nd ed. London: A. and C. Black.

Kollmann, F. F. P. and Côté, W. A., Jr., 1968. *Principles of wood science and technology. Vol. 1. Solid wood.* Berlin: Springer-Verlag.

The 'bible'.

Kollmann, F., Kuenzi, E. and Stamm, A., 1968. *Principles of wood science and technology. Vol. 2. Wood based materials.* Berlin: Springer-Verlag.

Schniewind, A. P., ed., 1989. *Concise encyclopedia of wood and wood-based materials.* Oxford: Pergamon Press.

Woods, Data Compilations

Anon, 1996. *BRE information papers.* Watford: Building Research Establishment.

United States. Department of Agriculture. Forest Service. Forest Products Laboratory, 1989. *Handbook of wood and wood-based materials.* New York: Hemisphere Publishing Corporation.

A massive compliation of data for NorthAmerican woods.

Informationsdienst Holz, 1996. *Merkblattreihe holzarten.* Hamburg: Verein Deutscher Holzeinfuhrhäuser e.V.

Anon, 1978–9. *Timbers of the world.* 9 Vols. High Wycombe: Timber Research and Development Association.

Anon, 1991. *Information sheets.* High Wycombe: Timber Research and Development Association.

Wood and Wood-Composite Standards

Great Britain

British Standards Institution (BSI), 389 Chiswick High Road, GB-London W4 4AL, UK (Tel: +44 181 996 9000; Fax: +44 181 996 7400; e-mail: info@bsi.org.uk)

Germany

Deutsches Institut für Normung (DIN), Burggrafenstrasse 6, D-10772, Berlin, Germany (Tel +49 30 26 01–0; Fax: +49 30 26 01 12 31; e-mail: postmaster@din.de)

USA

American Society for Testing and Materials (ASTM), 1916 Race Street, Philadelphia, Pennsylvania 19103–1187 (Tel +00 1215 299 5400; Fax: +00 1215 977 9679).

ASTM European Office, 27 – 29 Knowl Piece, Wilbury Way, Hitchin, Herts SG4 0SX, UK (Tel: +44 1462 437933; Fax: +44 1462 433678).

Software and Internet Data Sources

CES Woods Database, www.grantadesign.com
> A database of the engineering properties of softwoods, hardwoods and wood-based composites. PC format, Windows environment.

Prospect. (Version 1.1), 1995. Oxford: Oxford Forestry Institute, Department of Plant Sciences, Oxford University.
> A database of the properties of tropical woods of interest to a wood user; includes information about uses, workability, treatments, origins. PC format, DOS environment.

Woods of The World, 1994. Burlington, VT: Tree Talk, Inc.
> A CD-ROM of woods, with illustrations of structure, information about uses, origins, habitat etc. PC format, requiring CD drive; Windows environment.

WoodWeb, www.woodweb.com

Natural fibres and other materials

Houwink, R., 1958. *Elasticity plasticity and structure of matter.* New York: Dover Publications.

Anon, *Handbook of industrial materials*. 2nd ed. Oxford: Elsevier.
   A compilation of data remarkable for its breadth: metals, ceramics, polymers,
   composites, fibres, sandwich structures, leather . . .
Brady, G. S. and Clauser, H. R., eds., 1986. *Materials handbook*. 12th ed. New York:
   McGraw Hill. A broad survey, covering metals, ceramics, polymers, composites,
   fibres, sandwich structures, and more.

Environmental and medical

Biomaterials Properties TOC, www.lib.umich.edu/dentlib/Dental_tables/toc.html
Pentron, www.pentron.com
British Metals Recycling Association, www.britmetrec.org.uk
Green Design Initiative, www.ce.cmu.edu/GreenDesign
IDEMAT, Environmental Materials Database,
      www.io.tudelft.nl/research/dfs/idemat/index.htm

Data for manufacturing processes

Hardcopy Sources

Alexander, J. M., Brewer, R. C., and Rowe, G. W., 1987. *Manufacturing technology. Vol. 2.
   Engineering processes*. Chichester: Ellis Norwood Ltd.
Bralla, J. G., 1986. *Handbook of product design for manufacturing*. New York: McGraw-
   Hill.
Waterman, N. A. and Ashby, M. F., 1996. *Materials selector*. London: Chapman
   and Hall.
CES: Cambridge Engineering Selector ProcessUniverse, www.grantadesign.com
   Software and data for process selection.
Dieter, G. E., *Engineering design,: a materials and processing approach. Ch. 7*. New York:
   McGraw-Hill.
Kalpakjian, S., 1984. *Manufacturing processes for engineering materials*. London: Addison
   Wesley.
Lascoe, O. D., 1989. *Handbook of fabrication processes*. Materials Park: ASM International
Schey, J. A., 1977. *Introduction to manufacturing processes*. New York: McGraw-Hill.
Suh, N. P., 1990. *The principles of design*. Oxford: Oxford University Press.

Internet Sources

Cast Metals Federation, www.castmetalsfederation.com
Castings Technologies International, www.castingstechnology.com
Confederation of British Metalforming, www.britishmetalforming.com
National Center for Excellence in Metalworking Technology, www.ncemt.ctc.com
PERA, www.pera.com
The British Metallurgical Plant Constructors' Association, www.bmpca.org.uk
TWI (The Welding Institute), www.twi.co.uk

Databases and expert systems in software

The number and quality of computer-based materials information systems is growing rapidly. A selection of these, with comment and source, is given here. There has been consumer resistance to on-line systems; almost all recent developments are in PC-format. The prices vary widely. Five price groups are given: free, cheap (less than $200 or £125), modest (between $200 or £125 and $2,000 or £1250), expensive (between $2,000 or £1,250 and $10,000 or £6,000) and very expensive (more than £10,000 or £6,000). The databases are listed in alphabetical order.

ACTIVE LIBRARY ON CORROSION. Materials Park: ASM International.
  PC format requiring CD ROM drive. Graphical, numerical and textual
  information on corrosion of metals. Price modest.
ASM HANDBOOKS ONLINE: Materials Park: ASM International,
  www.asminternational.org/hbk/index.jsp
  Annual license fee.
ALLOYCENTER: Materials Park: ASM International,
  www.asminternational.org/alloycenter/index.jsp
  Annual license fee.
ALUSELECT P1.0: Engineering Property Data for Wrought Aluminium Alloys, 1992. Dusseldorf:
  European Aluminium Association.
  PC format, DOS environment. Mechanical, thermal, electrical and environmental
  properties of wrought aluminium alloys. Price cheap.
CAMPUS: Computer Aided Material Preselection by Uniform Standards, 1995,
  www.campusplastics.com
  Polymer data from approx 30 suppliers, measured to set standards.
CETIM-EQUIST II: Centre Technique des Industires Mécaniques, 1997. Senlis: CETIM.
  PC format, DOS environment. Compositions and designations of steels.
CETIM-Matériaux: Centre Technique des Industires Mécaniques, 1997. Senlis: CETIM.
  On-line system. Compositions and mechanical properties of materials.
CETIM-SICLOP: Centre Technique des Industires Mécaniques, 1997. Senlis: CETIM.
  On-line system. Mechanical properties of steels
CES: Cambridge Engineering Selector, 1999–2004, www.grantadesign.com
  Comprehensive selection system for all classes of materials and manufacturing
  processes. Variety of optional reference data sources, connects directly to
  matdata.net. Windows and web format. Modest price.
CUTDATA: Machining Data System. Cincinnati: Metcut Research Associates Inc,
  Manufacturing Technology Division.
  A PC-based system which guides the choice of machining conditions: tool
  materials, geometries, feed rates, cutting speeds, and so forth. Modest price.
EASel: Engineering Adhesives Selector Program, 1986. London: The Design Centre.
  PC and Mac formats. A knowledge-based program to select industrial adhesives
  for joining surfaces. Modest price.
SF-CD: (replacing ELBASE): Metal Finishing/Surface Treatment Technology, 1992. Stevenage:
  Metal Finishing Information Services Ltd.

PC format. Comprehensive information on published data related to surface treatment technology. Regularly updated. Modest price.

MATDATA.NET: matdata.net

The Material Data Network provides integrated access to a variety of quality information sources, from ASM International, Granta Design, TWI, NPL, UKSteel, Matweb, IDES, etc.

M-VISION: 1990: www.mscsoftware.com

Materials selection and querying, report generation and development of customizable, electronic links to analysis programs. Workstation and web versions. Substantial database of reference materials. Very expensive.

MEGABYTES ON COPPERS II: Information on Copper and Copper Alloys, www.cda.org.uk

A CD-ROM with Windows search engine, containing all the current publications as well as interactive programs published by CDA on topics of electrical energy efficiency, cost effectiveness and corrosion resistance. Cheap.

PAL II: Permabond Adhesives Locator, 1996. Eastleigh: Permabond.

A knowledge-based, PC-system (DOS environment) for adhesive selection among Permabond adhesives. An impressive example of an expert system that works. Modest price.

PLASCAMS: Plastics Computer-Aided Materials Selector, 1995. Version 6. Shawbury: RAPRA Technology Limited.

PC format, Windows environment. Polymers only. Mechanical and processing properties of polymers, thermoplastics and thermosets. Easy to use for data retrieval, with much useful information. Selection procedure cumbersome and not design-related. Modest initial price plus annual maintenance fee. Updated regularly.

POLYMERGE, 1997: Frankfurt am Main: Modern Plastics International.

Allows CAMPUS disks to be merged, enabling comparison.

PROSPECT: Version 1.1, 1995. Oxford: Oxford Forestry Institute, Department of Plant Sciences, Oxford University.

A database of the properties of tropical woods of interest to a wood user; includes information about uses, workability, treatments, origins. PC format, DOS environment.

OPS: (Optimal Polymer Selector), www.grantadesign.com

Integrates Granta Design's generic '*PolymerUniverse*' database, with Chemical resistance data from RAPRA and grade-specific data for approx 6000 ISO polymers from CAMPUS and 35,000 ASJM polymer grades from IDES, to produce the only comprehensive polymer selection system available.

SteCal: Steel Heat-Treatment Calculations. Materials Park: ASM International.

PC format, DOS environment. Computes the properties resulting from defined heat-treatments of low-alloy steels, using the composition as input. Modest price.

Wegst, C. W., 1997. *Stahlschlüssel (Key to Steel).* 17th ed. Marbach: Verlag Stahlschlüssel Wegst GmbH.

CD ROM, PC format. Excellent coverage of European products and manufacturers.

SOFINE PLASTICS, 1997. Villeurbanne Cedex: Société CERAP.

Database of polymer properties. Environment and price unknown.

STRAIN: *Plastic Properties of Materials.* Livermore: Lawrence Livermore Laboratory, Materials Laboratory.
> PC format, DOS environment. Very simple but useful compilation of room-temperature mechanical properties of ductile materials. Free.

TAPP 2.0: *Thermochemical and Physical Properties,* 1994. Hamilton, OH: ES Microware.
> PC format, CD ROM, Windows environment. A database of thermochemical and physical properties of solids, liquids and gasses, including phase diagrams neatly packaged with good user manual. Modest price.

THERM: *Thermal Properties of Materials.* Livermore: Lawrence Livermore Laboratory, Materials Laboratory.
> PC format, DOS environment. Very simple but useful compilation of thermal data for materials: specific heat, thermal conductivity, density and melting point. Free.

UNSearch: *Unified Metals and Alloys Composition Search.* Materials Park: ASTM.
> PC format, DOS environment. A datbase of information about composition, US designation and specification of common metals and alloys. Modest price.

Woods of The World:1994. Burlington, VT: Tree Talk, Inc.
> A CD-ROM of woods, with illustrations of structure, information about uses, origins, habitat etc. PC format, requiring CD drive; Windows environment.

Metals prices and economic reports

American Metal Market On-line, www.amm.com
Business Communications Company, www.buscom.com
Daily Economic Indicators, www.bullion.org.za/Level2/Econ&stats.htm
Iron & Steel Statistics Bureau, www.issb.co.uk
Kitco Inc Gold & Precious Metal Prices, www.kitco.com/gold.live.html
London Metal Exchange, www.lme.co.uk
Metal Bulletin, www.metalbulletin.plc.uk
Metal Powder Report, www.metal-powder.net
Metallurgia, www.metallurgiaonline.com
Mineral-Resource, minerals.usgs.gov/minerals/
Roskill Reports www.roskill.com
The Precious Metal and Gem Connection, www.thebulliondesk.com/default.asp

Supplier Registers, Government Organisations, Standards and Professional Societies

Supplier Registers

AMM.com: Major Industry and Trade Associations,
> www.amm.com/index2.htm?/ref/trade.htm

IndustryLink Homepage, www.industrylink.com
Kellysearch, www.kellysearch.com
Metals Industry Competitive Enterprise, www.metalsindustry.co.uk
Thomas Register, www.thomasregister.com
Top 50 US/Canadian Metal Cos, www.amm.com/ref/top50.HTM

Government Organisations

Commonwealth Scientific and Industrial Research Org (Australia), www.csiro.au
National Academies Press, USA, www.nap.edu
National Institute for Standards and Technology (USA), www.nist.gov
The Fraunhofer Institute, www.fhg.de/english.html

Professional Societies and Trade Associations

Aluminium Federation, www.alfed.org.uk
ASM International, www.asminternational.org
ASME International, www.asme.org
British Constructional Steel Work Association, www.steelconstruction.org
Cast Metals Federation, www.castmetalsfederation.com
Confederation of British Metalforming, www.britishmetalforming.com
Copper Development Association, www.cda.org.uk
Institute of Cast Metal Engineers, www.ibf.org.uk
Institute of Spring Technology Ltd, www.ist.org.uk
International Aluminium Institute, www.world-aluminium.org
International Council on Mining and Metals, www.icme.com
International Iron & Steel Institute, www.worldsteel.org
International Titanium Association, www.titanium.org
International Zinc Association, www.iza.com
Iron & Steel Trades Confederation, www.istc-tu.org
Lead Development Association International, www.ldaint.org/default.htm
Materials Information Service, www.iom3.org/mis/index.htm
National Association of Steel Stock Holders, www.nass.org.uk
Nickel Development Institute, www.nidi.org
Pentron, www.pentron.com
Society of Automotive Engineers (SAE), www.sae.org
Steel Manufacturers Association, www.steelnet.org
Steels Construction Institute, www.steel.org.uk
The American Ceramics Society, www.acers.org
The British Metallurgical Plant Constructors' Association, www.bmpca.org.uk
The Institute of Materials, Minerals and Mining, www.instmat.co.uk
The Minerals, Metals & Materials Society, www.tms.org/TMSHome.html
Tin Research Association, www.tintechnology.com
UK Steel, www.uksteel.org.uk
Wire & Wire Rope Employers Association, www.uksteel.org.uk/wwrea.htm

Standards Organisations

ASTM, www.astm.org
BSI, www.bsi.org.uk
DIN Deutsches Institut für Normung e.V, www2.din.de/index.php?lang=en
International Standards Organisation, www.iso.org
National Standards Authority of Ireland, www.nsai.ie

Miscellaneous

Common unit of measure conversion, www.conweb.com/tblefile/conver.shtml
Information for Physical Chemists, www.liv.ac.uk/Chemistry/Links/links.html
K&K associate's thermal connection, www.tak2000.com
Thermal data, www.csn.net/~takinfo/prop-top.html

23 Mechanical Engineering

Michael Richards

The purpose of offering information sources is twofold: to provide students, practitioners, librarians and information scientists with the necessary contacts to obtain the information they require; and to equip them with enough details to establish a physical working library of any size or depth. While this is an enormous task with even small subject areas, mechanical engineering offers its own particular set of questions and ambiguities – mainly in the area of definitions.

Mechanical engineering, succinctly defined by James (1998), is the 'process, skills and technology used to achieve optimised >metamorphosis= of materials into components, machines and structures'. Thus, in engineering terms, anything – and everything – manmade, whatever its degree of sophistication, can healthily be argued to come under the heading of mechanical engineering. Even if the notion of machinery, defined by *The Oxford Shorter Dictionary* as 'an apparatus for applying mechanical power, consisting of a number of parts, each having a definite function', is introduced to reduce this universal manufactory warehouse, none of its components is actually obsoleted. Gloriously, the history of mechanical engineering traces the history and evolution of the human race.

Clearly, for our present purpose, such a broad perspective will not do, even before considering concepts such as fuel, energy, control, power and heat, so definitions provided by EEVL; the Internet guide to engineering, mathematics and computing (www.eevl.ac.uk/engineering/engsubjectguide.htm) are largely followed.

- **Mechanical engineering:** mechanics, design, drives and transmission, lubricants and lubrication, measuring instruments.
- **Automotive engineering:** automotive engines, buses, tractors, trucks.
- **Control engineering:** automatic control principles, applications, devices.

- **Fluid flow, hydraulics and pneumatics:** fluid flow, hydraulics, pneumatics, vacuum technology.
- **Fuel and energy technology:** fuel combustion, flame research, liquid and solid fuels, energy management.
- **Heat and thermodynamics:** heat and mass transfer, thermodynamics, industrial, furnaces and process heating, space heating and air conditioning, refrigeration and cryogenics.
- **Naval and marine engineering:** naval architecture, naval vessels, shipbuilding and shipyards, small craft and other marine craft, marine engineering.
- **Nuclear engineering:** nuclear reactors, radioactive materials, nuclear power plants.
- **Plant and power engineering:** hydro and tidal power plants, internal combustion engines, steam power plants, thermoelectric magnetohydrodynamic and other power generators, heat exchangers, turbines and steam engines, compressors and pumps, pipes, tanks and accessories.
- **Railway engineering:** railway plant and structures, railway rolling stock.
- **Selected websites.**

The contents of each section are divided into these categories with some variously omitted or adapted according to expediency.

- **Introduction.** Differences, exceptions and omissions from the definitions given above are noted. They occur mostly for reasons of space.
- **Texts.** Generally, texts are listed if believed to be available in the UK at the time of writing. Some text categories are offered, although it should be noted that classifications are acknowledged to be debatable or blurred.
- **Periodicals.** Periodicals are listed without sources.
- **Handbooks.** In most cases, a publication whose title contains 'handbook' is a handbook; what constitutes a practical hands-on guide differs from industry to industry and user to user. Some publications are clearly handbooks even if not entitled as such. For other comments, see 'Texts'.
- **Reference works.** These are dictionaries, directories, encyclopaediae and the like. For other comments, see 'Texts'.
- **Abstracts.** Few are listed but they are authoritative. All but one (see 'Nuclear Engineering') are available at the time of writing.
- **Standards.** Major or pervasive standards bodies are detailed in the first section, 'Mechanical Engineering'. It should be noted that major manufacturers often create and quote their own standards

on specifications which often creep into the public domain, even if not publicly available. Also, standards tend not to observe national borders and can be very expensive.

- **Legislation and government.** The global presence of corporations and their products ensures that research into legislative and gubernatorial requirements should be carefully handled. The existence of a national legislation on which the production of a product has been based does not guarantee applicability elsewhere.

- **Research.** As most universities holding courses carry out either notional, course-based or highly defined research activities, they are excluded from this list. Commercial companies undertaking research are also excluded as details are either necessarily unavailable or, by their very nature, fragmented. Only a few non-profit-making, non-university based research institutions are therefore listed.

- **Professional organisations.** Most of the professional organisations have libraries with access to papers and loans systems. Very often, they have supporting publishing houses with publications for sale. Umbrella or pervasive organisations are given in the first section, 'Mechanical Engineering', without repeating them later even if they have specified local application. Trades unions and employee representative organisations are omitted.

- **Commercial organisations.** If only because of the wealth of material available, this is a problematic area. By and large, inclusions are based on membership of professional associations and discoverable, working websites. But selections do not comment on the financial, ethical or engineering validity or value of the companies or their products; omission equally implies nothing.

- **Pressure and single issue groups.** Pressure and single issue groups are included if they have identifiable interests in the topic in question. The usual caveats attached to voices, opinions and information may well not apply here, as at least pressure groups' motives and agendas are self-proclaimed and blatant.

- **Collections.** UK museums and exhibitions with websites are listed in 'Automotive Engineering', 'Naval and Marine Engineering' and 'Railway Engineering'. UK nuclear reactors are listed in 'Nuclear Engineering'.

- **Websites.** A few virtual resources are offered. The websites quoted throughout this chapter were visited periodically to ensure working effectiveness. Most offer links whose usefulness are defined solely by the needs of the user.

► **MECHANICAL ENGINEERING**

This section offers sources for mechanical engineering. To prevent repetition, it includes the more general or global sources relating to disciplines in the rest of this chapter, particularly under 'Abstracts', 'Standards', 'Legislation and Government', 'Professional Organisations', 'Websites'.

Texts

Texts: mechanical engineering, mechanics, mechanical design

Bird, J. and Ross, C., 2002. *Mechanical engineering principles*. London: Butterworth-Heinemann.

Hannah, J. and Hillier, M. J., 1999. *Mechanical engineering science*. London: Prentice Hall.

Cowan, B. P., 1984. *Classical mechanics*. London: Kluwer Academic Publishers.

Gere, J. M., 2000. *Mechanics of materials*. Pacific Grove: Brooks/Cole Publishing.

Hannah, J. and Hillier, M. J., 1999. *Applied mechanics*. London: Longman.

Harrison, H. R. and Nettleton, T., 1994. *Principles of engineering mechanics*. London: Butterworth-Heinemann.

Hughes, J. H. and Martin, K. F., 1977. *Basic engineering mechanics*. London: Palgrave Macmillan.

Meriam, J. L., 2002. *Engineering mechanics: dynamics*. London: John Wiley & Sons.

Ryder, G. H. and Bennett, M. D., 1991. *Mechanics of machines*. New York: Industrial Press Inc.

Smith, P. and Smith, R. C., 1990. *Mechanics*. London: John Wiley & Sons.

Burr, A. H. and Cheatham, J. B., 1995. *Mechanical analysis and design*. London: Prentice Hall.

Phelan, R. M., 1970. *Fundamentals of mechanical design*. London: McGraw-Hill Education.

Shigley, J. E., 2001. *Mechanical engineering design*. London: McGraw-Hill Education.

Texts: lubricants and lubrication

Bannister, K. E., 1996. *Lubrication for industry*. New York: Industrial Press Inc.

Bloch, H. P., 2000. *Practical lubrication for industrial facilities*. New York: Marcel Dekker.

Denis, J. and Briant, J., 2000. *Lubricant properties: analysis and testing*. Paris: Editions Technip.

Mang, T. and Dressel, W., eds., 2001. *Lubricants and lubrication*. Weinheim. Wiley-VCH.

Mortier, R. M. and Orszulik, S., eds., 1996. *Chemistry and technology of lubricants*, London: Kluwer Academic Publishers.

Pirro, D. M. and Wessol, A. A., 2000. *Lubrication fundamentals*. New York: Marcel Dekker.

Texts: measuring instruments

Anderson, N. A., 1998. *Instrumentation for process measurement and control.* London: CRC Press.

Beckwith, T. G. *et al.*, 1993. *Mechanical measurements.* Boston: Addison Wesley.

Busch, T., 1989. *Fundamentals of dimensional metrology.* Albany: Delmar.

Dyer, S. A., 2001. *Wiley survey of instrumentation and measurement.* London: John Wiley & Sons.

Figliola, R. and Beasley, D., 2000. *Theory and design for mechanical measurements.* London: John Wiley & Sons.

Harlow Jr, R. H. and Thompson, R., 2002. *Fundamentals of dimensional metrology.* Albany: Delmar.

Hughes, T. A., 2002. *Measurement and control basics.* Pittsburgh: Instrument Society of America.

Nicholas, J. V. and White, D., 2001. *Traceable temperatures: an introduction to temperature measurement and calibration.* London: John Wiley & Sons.

Padmanabhan, T. R., 1999. *Industrial instrumentation: principles and design.* London: Springer-Verlag.

Webster, J. G., ed., 1999. *Mechanical variables measurement – solid, fluid and thermal.* London: CRC Press.

Periodicals

Archive of Applied Mechanics
Computational Mechanics
Computer Methods in Applied Mechanics & Engineering
Engineer
Engineering
European Journal of Mechanics
Experimental Mechanics
International Journal of Mechanical Engineering Education
International Journal of Mechanical Sciences
Journal of Engineering Tribology
Journal of Applied Mechanics
Journal of Engineering Design
Journal of Engineering Mechanics
Journal of Mechanical Design
Journal of Mechanical Engineering Science
Journal of Multi-Body Dynamics
Journal of Process Mechanical Engineering
Journal of Rheology
Journal of Tribology
Lubrication Engineering
Mechanical Engineering
Mechanical Systems and Signal Processing
Professional Engineering

Handbooks

Handbooks: mechanical engineering, mechanics, mechanical design

Amiss, J. M. et al., 2000. *Guide to the use of tables and formulas in Machinery's Handbook.* New York: Industrial Press Inc.

Avallone, E. A. and Baumeister III, T., 1996. *Marks' standard handbook for mechanical engineers.* London: McGraw-Hill Education.

Carvill, J., 1994. *Mechanical engineer's data handbook.* London: Butterworth-Heinemann.

Hicks, T. G., 1997. *Handbook of mechanical engineering calculations.* London: McGraw-Hill Education.

Kreith, F., ed., 1997. *CRC handbook of mechanical engineering.* London: CRC Press.

Oberg, F. D. J. E., 2000. *Machinery's handbook.* New York: Industrial Press.

Pohanish, R., ed., 2000. *Machinery's handbook pocket companion: a reference book for the mechanical engineer, designer, manufacturing engineer, draftsman, toolmaker, and machinist.* New York: Industrial Press Inc.

Pope, E. J., 1996. *Rules of thumb for mechanical engineers.* Houston: Gulf Publishing.

Shigley, J. E. and Mischke, C. R., 1996. *Standard handbook of machine design.* London: McGraw-Hill Education.

Timings, R., 1997. *Mechanical engineer's pocket book.* London: Newnes.

Young, W. C. and Budynas, R. G., 2001. *Roark's formulas for stress and strain.* London: McGraw-Hill Education.

Nwokah, O. D. et al., eds., 2001. *Mechanical systems design handbook: modeling, measurement, and control.* London: CRC Press.

Rothbart, H., 1996. *Mechanical design handbook.* London: McGraw-Hill Education.

Handbooks: lubricants and lubrication

Ash, M. and Ash, I., 2001. *Handbook of lubricants.* New York: Synapse Information Resources Inc.

Booser, E. R., 1994. *CRC Handbook of lubrication: theory and practice of tribology: monitoring, materials, synthetic lubricants, and applications.* London: CRC Press.

Caines, A. and Haycock, R., 1996. *Automotive lubricants reference book.* London: Mechanical Engineering Publications.

Neale, M. J., 1995. *Tribology handbook.* London: Butterworth-Heinemann.

Neale, M. J., 2000. *Lubrication and reliability handbook.* London: Butterworth-Heinemann.

Handbooks: measuring instruments

Battikha, N. E., 1997. *Condensed handbook of measurement and control.* Pittsburgh: Instrument Society of America.

Farago, F. T. and Curtis, M. A., 1994. *Handbook of dimensional measurement.* New York: Industrial Press Inc.

Liptak, B., ed., 1995. *Instrument engineers' handbook: process control*. London: Butterworth-Heinemann.

Liptak, B., ed., 1995. *Instrument engineers' handbook: process measurement and analysis*. London: Butterworth-Heinemann.

Liptak, B., ed., 2002. *Instrument engineers' handbook: process software and digital networks*. London: CRC Press.

Reference works

Chopra, S. B., 1994. *Dictionary of mechanical engineering*. New Delhi: Anmol Publications.

Engineering industry buyers' guide. London: CMP Information.

Kempe's engineers yearbook. London: Morgan-Grampian.

Nayler, G., 1996. *Dictionary of mechanical engineering*. London: Butterworth-Heinemann.

Schwartz, V. V., 1984. *Illustrated dictionary of mechanical engineering*. London: Kluwer Academic Publishers.

Sclater, N. and Chironis, N. P., 2001. *Mechanisms and mechanical devices sourcebook*. London: McGraw-Hill Education.

Smith, E. H., 1994. *Mechanical engineer's reference book*. Warrendale: Society of Automotive Engineers.

Abstracts

Applied Mechanics Reviews. New York: American Society of Mechanical Engineers.

Key Abstracts. London: Institution of Electrical Engineers.

Mechanical Engineering Abstracts. Cambridge Scientific Abstracts.

Standards

American Gear Manufacturers' Association, www.agma.org

American Institute of Chemical Engineers, www.aiche.org

American National Standards Institute, www.ansi.org

American Society for Testing and Materials, www.astm.org

American Society of Mechanical Engineers, www.asme.org

Association Francaise de Normalisation, www.afnor.fr

British Standards Institution, www.bsi-global.com and bsonline.techindex.co.uk

Canadian Standards Association, www.csa.ca

Deutsches Institut für Normung, www2.din.de

Institute of Electrical and Electronics Engineers, www.ieee.org

Instrument Society of America, www.isa.org

International Organisation for Standardisation, www.iso.ch

Japanese Standards Association, www.jsa.or.jp

National Standards Authority of Ireland, www.nsai.ie

National Institute of Standards and Technology, www.nist.gov

Legislation and government

European Union: europa.eu.int/eur-lex. UK outlets: Stationery Office Ltd,
    www.tso.co.uk; Context Electronic Publishers Ltd, www.justis.com
Health & Safety Executive, www.hse.gov.uk
Her Majesty's Stationery Office, www.hmso.gov.uk
National Measurement System Directorate, www.dti.gov.uk/nmd
UK Patent Office, www.patent.gov.uk
US Patent & Trademark Office, www.uspto.gov

Research

Engineering and Physical Sciences Research Council, www.epsrc.ac.uk/website

Professional organisations

American Association of Engineering Societies, www.aaes.org
American Gear Manufacturers' Association, www.agma.org
American Society of Civil Engineers, www.asce.org
American Society of Mechanical Engineers, www.asme.org
British Mechanical Power Transmission Association (aka British Gear Association),
    www.bga.org.uk
British Society of Rheology, www.ncl.ac.uk/rheology/bsr
Engineering Employers' Federation, www.eef.org.uk
European Mechanics Society, www.euromech.cz
Institute of Electrical and Electronics Engineers, www.ieee.org
Institution of Civil Engineers, www.ice.org.uk
Institution of Electrical Engineers, www.iee.org
Institution of Incorporated Engineers, www.iie.org.uk
Institution of Mechanical Engineers, www.imeche.org.uk
International Union of Theoretical and Applied Mechanics, www.iutam.net
Production Engineering Research Association, www.pera.com
Society for Experimental Mechanics, www.sem.org
Society of Tribologists and Lubrication Engineers, www.stle.org

Websites

www.engineeringvillage2.org gives entry by subscription to abstracts, US Patent &
    Trademark Office, technical standards, Compendex, INSPEC and similar
    bibliographic databases.
www.industrysearch.com only US-based, provides engineering buyers and suppliers
    comprehensive search and information facilities.

www.manufacturing.net is a free US-biased e-village for manufacturing buyers and
    suppliers.
www.official-documents.co.uk offers UK government documents and papers.

▶ AUTOMOTIVE ENGINEERING

This section covers four-wheel road vehicles propelled by the internal
combustion engine, and some electric vehicles and other alternative fuel-
driven systems. Texts about the theory of the internal combustion engine
can be found under Plant and Power Engineering. Global manufacturers
are listed if they have a UK base. A collection is listed only if a dedicated
website could be found. The reader is referred to the final part in this section
for information of collections not publicised by individual websites.
Minimal coverage of agricultural engineering is possible, but the final
website listed at the end of this section should provide the interested
specialist with satisfactory information resources. Space prevents coverage
of two-wheel, military, off-road construction, motorsport or the forty or
so UK automotive manufacturers, each producing annually no more than
double-figure quantities of handmade or kit vehicles.

Texts

Texts: fundamentals

Garrett, T. K., ed., 2000. *Motor vehicle.* London: Butterworth-Heinemann.
Heisler, H., 1998. *Vehicle and engine technology.* London: Butterworth-Heinemann.
Hillier, V. A. W., 1993. *Fundamentals of motor vehicle technology.* London: Nelson
    Thornes.

Texts: chassis, body

Barnard, R. H., 2001. *Road vehicle aerodynamic design.* St Albans: MechAero
    Publishing.
Daniels, J., 1996. *Anatomy of the car.* London: Simon & Schuster.
Gillespie, T.D., 1992. *Fundamentals of vehicle dynamics.* Warrendale: Society of
    Automotive Engineers.
Heisler, H., 2002. *Advanced vehicle technology.* London: Butterworth-Heinemann.
Hucho, W.-H., 1998. *Aerodynamics of road vehicles, from fluid mechanics to vehicle
    engineering.* Warrendale: Society of Automotive Engineers.
Milliken, W. F. and Milliken, D. L., 2002. *Chassis design, principles and analysis.* London:
    Professional Engineering Publishing.

Texts: engines

Blair, G. P. et al., 1990. *Basic design of two stroke engines.* Warrendale: Society of Automotive Engineers.

Blair, G. P., et al., 1996. *Design and simulation of two-stroke engines.* Warrendale: Society of Automotive Engineers.

Fenton, J., 1987. *Gasoline engine analysis for computer aided design.* London: Mechanical Engineering Publications.

Heisler, H., 1995. *Advanced engine technology.* London: Butterworth-Heinemann.

Hillier, V. A. W., 1996. *Fundamentals of automotive electronics.* London: Nelson Thornes.

Kienecke, U. and Nielsen, L., 2000. *Automotive control systems.* Warrendale: Society of Automotive Engineers.

Plint, M. and Martyr, A., 1998. *Engine testing, theory and practice.* London: Butterworth-Heinemann.

Poulton, M. L., 1994. *Alternative engines for road vehicles.* Southampton: WIT Press.

Poulton, M. L., 1994. *Alternative fuels for road vehicles.* Southampton: WIT Press.

Texts: heavy duty, agricultural machinery

Brady, R. N., 1997. *Heavy duty trucks: powertrains, systems and service.* New York: US Imports & PHIPEs.

Winkler, C. B., 2000. *Rollover of heavy commercial vehicles,* Warrendale: Society of Automotive Engineers.

Periodicals

Auto Asia
Autocar
Automobile Management International
Automobiltechnische Zeitschrift
Automotive Components Analyst
Automotive Design and Production
Automotive Emerging Markets
Automotive Engineer
Automotive Engineering
Automotive Environment Analyst
Automotive Industries
Automotive Manufacturing Analyst
Automotive News Europe
Automotive Powertrain Analyst
Automotive Quarterly
Automotive Sourcing
Car
Engine Technology International
European Automotive Design

Evo
Hybrid & Electric Vehicle Progress
International Journal of Automotive Technology and Management
International Journal of Crashworthiness
International Journal of Engine Research
International Journal of Heavy Vehicle Systems
International Journal of Vehicle Autonomous Systems
International Journal of Vehicle Design
International Journal of Vehicle Noise and Vibration
Journal of Automobile Engineering
LPG Car
Motortechnische Zeitschrift
Parker's Car Price Guide
Powertrain International
Testing Technology International
Top Gear
Traffic Injury Prevention
Vehicle News International
Ward's Auto World
World Automotive Manufacturing

Handbooks

Bosch, 1998. *Automotive electrics and electronics handbook.* Warrendale: Society of
    Automotive Engineers.
Bosch, 1999. *Gasoline engine management.* Warrendale: Society of Automotive
    Engineers.
Bosch, 2000. *Automotive handbook.* Warrendale: Society of Automotive Engineers
Fenton, J., 1996. *Handbook of vehicle design analysis.* London: Mechanical Engineering
    Publications.
Fenton, J., 1998 *Handbook of automotive power train and chassis design.* London:
    Mechanical Engineering Publications.
Owen, K. and Coley, T., 1995. *Automotive fuels reference book.* Warrendale: Society of
    Automotive Engineers.

Reference works

Directory of Automotive Electric/Electronics Suppliers. London: ims Publishing.
Directory of Automotive Interiors Suppliers. London: ims Publishing.
Directory of Automotive Materials Suppliers. London: ims Publishing.
Directory of Automotive Powertrain Suppliers. London: ims Publishing.
Directory of Automotive Safety. London: ims Publishing.
Directory of European Automotive Suppliers. London: ims Publishing.

Directory of European Vehicle Manufacturers. London: ims Publishing.

Directory of the Motor Industry. London: Society of Motor Manufacturers & Traders.

Directory of UK Automotive Suppliers. London: ims Publishing.

Georgano, N., ed., 2000. *Beaulieu encyclopaedia of the automobile.* London: Stationery Office.

Goodsell, D. L., 1995. *Dictionary of automotive engineering.* London: Butterworth-Heinemann.

McGeoch, J. J. and Randall, M., 1998. *Haynes automotive technical data book 1989–1998.* London: Haynes Publishing.

Schellings, A., 1996. *Elsevier's dictionary of automotive engineering.* London: Elsevier.

Storey, J., 2000. *World truck manufacturers.* London: Automotive World Publications.

Storey, J., 2002. *World 's car manufacturers: a financial and operating review.* London: Automotive World Publications.

Storey, J., 2002. *World 's truck manufacturers: a financial and operating review.* London: Automotive World Publications.

Ward's automotive yearbook. Southfield: Ward's Communications.

Yearbook of the world's motor industry. Paris: Organisation Internationale des Constructeurs d'Automobiles.

Abstracts

Automobile Abstracts, MIRA.
Automobile Business News, MIRA.
PowerGram, J.D. Power.
SAE Mobility CD-ROM, Society of Automotive Engineers.
SMMT Briefing, Society of Motor Manufacturers & Traders.
SMMT Bulletin, Society of Motor Manufacturers & Traders.

Standards

British Technical Council of the Motor and Petroleum Industries, www.btcmpi.org.uk
Society of Automotive Engineers, www.sae.org [UK contact: American Technical Publishers, www.ameritech.co.uk]

Legislation and government

Department of Transport, www.dft.gov.uk
US Department of Transportation, National Highway Traffic Safety Administration, www.nhtsa.dot.gov
Vehicle Certification Agency, www.vca.gov.uk
Vehicle Inspectorate, www.via.gov.uk

Research

Automotive Industry Action Group, www.aiag.org
Automotive Research Center, University of Michigan, arc.engin.umich.edu
Centre for Automotive Industry Research, www.cf.ac.uk/carbs/research/cair
European Automotive Initiative Group, www.autotrain.org
International Motor Vehicle Program, web.mit.edu/org/c/ctpid/www/imvp
United States Council for Automotive Research, www.uscar.org
Vehicle Safety Research Centre, www.lboro.ac.uk/research/esri/vsrc

Professional organisations

Association des Constructeurs Europeens d'Automobiles, www.acea.be
Association of Agricultural Engineers, www.aea.uk.com
Automobile Association, www.theaa.com
European Natural Gas Vehicle Association, www.engva.org
Institution of Agricultural Engineers, www.iagre.org
Motorsport Industry Association, www.the-mia.co.uk
Motorsport Manufacturing Group, Institute for Manufacturing,
        www.ifm.eng.cam.ac.uk/ig/motorsportmanufacturing.htm
RAC plc, www.racplc.co.uk
Society of Automotive Engineers, www.sae.org [UK contact: SAE-UK, PO Box 4966,
        Birmingham B29 S7Y]
Society of Motor Manufacturers & Traders, www.smmt.co.uk

Commercial companies

Commercial companies: passenger cars

Alfa Romeo (GB) Ltd, www.alfaromeo.co.uk
Aston Martin Lagonda Ltd, www.astonmartin.com
Audi UK, www.audi.co.uk
Bentley Motors Ltd, www.rolls-roycemotorsandbentley.co.uk
BMW (GB) Ltd, www.bmw.co.uk
Caterham Cars Ltd, www.caterham.co.uk
Citroen UK Ltd, www.citroen.co.uk
DaimlerChrysler UK Ltd, www.chryslerjeep.co.uk
Fiat Auto (UK) Ltd, www.fiat.co.uk
GM Daewoo UK Ltd, www.daewoo-cars.co.uk
Honda, www.honda.co.uk, www.hondaintheuk.co.uk
Hyundai Car (UK) Ltd, www.hyundai-car.co.uk
Isuzu (UK) Ltd, www.isuzu.co.uk
Jaguar Cars, www.jaguar.com/uk

Kia Motors, www.kia.co.uk
Lada UK Ltd, www.lada.co.uk
Lamborghini London, www.lamborghini.co.uk
Lexus (GB) Ltd, www.lexus.co.uk
Lotus Cars, www.lotuscars.co.uk
Mazda Motors Ltd, www.mazda.co.uk
McLaren Cars Ltd, www.mclarencars.co.uk
Mercedes-Benz (UK) Ltd, www.mercedes-benz.co.uk
MG Rover Group Ltd, www.mg-rover.com
Mitsubishi Motors, www.mitsubishi-cars.co.uk
Morgan Motor Co, www.morgan-Motor.co.uk
Nissan Motor (GB) Ltd, www.nissan.co.uk
Peugeot Talbot Motor Co Ltd, www.peugeot.co.uk
Porsche Cars GB Ltd, www.porsche.co.uk
Proton Cars (UK) Ltd, www.proton.co.uk
Renault UK Ltd, www.renault.co.uk
Rolls-Royce Cars, Goodwood, Chichester, West Sussex.
SEAT UK, www.seat.co.uk
Skoda, www.skoda.co.uk
Subaru (UK) Ltd, www.subaru.co.uk
Suzuki (GB) Cars Ltd, www.suzuki.co.uk
Toyota (GB) Ltd, www.toyota.co.uk
TVR Engineering Ltd, www.tvr.co.uk
Vauxhall, www.gmc.com
Volkswagen UK, www.volkswagen.co.uk
Volvo Car Corporation, www.volvocars.co.uk

Commercial companies: commercial vehicles

Dennis Eagle Ltd, www.dennis-eagle.co.uk
ERF, www.erf.com
Foden Trucks, www.foden.com
Isuzu Truck (UK) Ltd, www.isuzutruck.co.uk
Iveco (UK) Ltd, www.iveco.com
LDV Ltd, www.ldv.co.uk
London Taxis International, www.london-taxis.co.uk
MAN Truck & Bus UK, www.man.co.uk
Scania (Great Britain) Ltd, www.scania.co.uk
Volvo Truck and Bus Ltd, www1.volvo.com

Commercial companies: passenger cars, commercial vehicles

Ford Motor Co Ltd, www.ford.co.uk
General Motor Corp, www.gmc.com
Saab Great Britain Ltd, www.saab.com

Commercial companies: consultancies

AVL United Kingdom Ltd, www.avl.com
Cosworth Technology, www.cosworth-technology.co.uk
Hawtal Whiting Ltd, www.hawtalwhiting.com
Integral Powertrain, www.integralp.com
Millbrook Proving Ground Ltd, www.millbrook.co.uk
MIRA, www.mira.co.uk
Prodrive Ltd, www.prodrive.com
Ricardo Consulting Engineers, www.ricardo.com
Roush Technologies, www.roush.co.uk

Pressure and single issue groups

Clear Zones, www.clearzones.org.uk
Environmental Transport Association, www.eta.co.uk
In Town Without My Car!, www.local-transport.dft.gov.uk/eurocar

Collections

Dover Transport Museum, www.dovertransportmuseum.co.uk
Glasgow Museum of Transport, clyde-valley.com/glasgow/transmus.htm
Ipswich Transport Museum, www.ipswichtransportmuseum.co.uk
Kew Transport Museum, www.ktm.itgo.com
Museum of British Road Transport, www.mbrt.co.uk
Museum of Transport, www.gmts.co.uk
St Helens Transport Museum, www.sthtm.freeserve.co.uk

Collections: automotive

Atwell-Wilson Motor Museum, www.atwell-wilson.org
Automobilia, www.3mc.co.uk/automobilia
Bentley Wildfowl & Motor Museum, www.bentley.org.uk
Filching Manor Motor Museum, www.filchingmanor.co.uk.
Glenluce Motor Museum, www.dumfriesmuseum.demon.co.uk/glenmotor.html
Haynes Motor Museum, www.haynesmotormuseum.co.uk
Heritage Motor Centre, www.heritage.org.uk
Jaguar Daimler Heritage Trust, www.jdht.com
Lakeland Motor Museum, www.visitcumbria.com/sl/holkmus.htm
Manx Transportation Museum, www.iomguide.com/manxtransportationmuseum.php
Moray Motor Museum, www.moray.gov.uk/museums/facilities/moraymotor.html
National Motor Museum, www.beaulieu.co.uk

Collections: commercial vehicles

Birmingham & Midland Museum of Transport, www.bammot.org.uk
Cobham Bus Museum, www.geocities.com/kevin291/lbpt/lbpt.html
East Anglian Transport Museum, www.eatm.org.uk
Glasgow Bus Museum, www.glasgowbusmuseum.co.uk
Keighley Bus Museum, www.kbmt.org.uk
London Bus Preservation Trust, www.kevinmcgowan.org
London Transport Museum, www.ltmuseum.co.uk
Manchester Museum of Road Transport, www.gmts.co.uk
Oxford Bus Museum, www.geocities.com/MotorCity/Lane/5050/obm
Scottish Vintage Bus Museum, www.busweb.co.uk/svbm
Sheffield Bus Museum, freespace.virgin.net/neil.worthington/sheff/page1~1.htm
Trolley Bus Museum, www.sandtoft.org.uk

Collections: historic

Brooklands Museum Trust Ltd, www.brooklandsmuseum.com.
Historic Motor Centre, www.heritage.org.uk.
Lincolnshire Road Transport Museum, www.lvvs.freeserve.co.uk.
Llangollen Motor Museum, www.llangollenmotormuseum.co.uk.
Motoring Heritage Centre, www.motoringheritage.co.uk.
Myreton Motor Museum, www.netherabbey.co.uk/myreton.html.
Whitewebbs Museum, www.enfield-online.co.uk/edvvs.

Websites

secure.autoxperience.co.uk offers comprehensive coverage of the UK automotive
industry.
www.autoindex.org is an invaluable source for information about companies, products
and relationships.
www.autoline.org offers automotive industry information.
www.classicmotor.co.uk/museums/museums.htm claims to give a full list of UK motor
museums.
www.just-auto.com offers daily automotive news services.
www.motoring.gov.uk is a UK-government-sponsored website for motoring issues.
www.wardsauto.com is authoritative and widely respected, giving news and
assessments of road transport; heavy subscription fees, though.
www.ytmag.com/today is as full a resource for UK agricultural machinery as the
information scientist is likely to need.

▶ CONTROL ENGINEERING

Control Engineering falls into three sub-disciplines: control, mechatronics and artificial intelligence. While the texts and handbooks lists are shorter than might be expected, the periodicals are clearly the most useful source of information. Legislation and Government sources are adequately covered in the Mechanical Engineering section. A selection of commercial companies gives a flavour of who and what is available; even the most simplified internet wordsearch will yield thousands more components and systems manufacturers and consultancies.

Texts

Alciatore, D. G. and Histand, M. B., 1998. *Mechatronics.* London: McGraw-Education.

Bradley, D. *et al.*, 2000. *Mechatronics and the design of intelligent machines and systems.* Cheltenham: Nelson Thornes.

Considine, D. M., 1999. *Instrumentation and computer control in applied automation.* London: Kluwer Academic Publishers.

Hardy, J. E. *et al.*, 1999. *Flow measurement methods and applications.* London: John Wiley & Sons.

Lyvshevski, S. E., 2001. *Control systems theory with engineering applications.* Basel: Birkhauser Verlag AG.

Mareels, I. and Polderman, J. W., 1996. *Adaptive systems: an introduction.* Basel: Birkhauser Verlag AG.

Martin, A. J. and Banyard, C. J., 1998. *Library of system control strategies.* London: BSRIA Ltd.

Morris, N. M., 1991. *Control engineering.* London: McGraw-Hill Education.

Nilsson, N. J., 1982. *Principles of artificial intelligence.* London: Springer-Verlag.

Nilsson, N., 1998. *Artificial intelligence: a new synthesis.* London: Morgan Kaufmann.

Norton, J. P., 1986. *Introduction to identification.* London: Academic Press.

Ogata, K., 1995. *Discrete-time control systems.* London: Prentice Hall.

Ogata, K., 1998. *System dynamics.* New York: US Imports & PHIPEs.

Ogata, K., 2001. *Modern control engineering.* London: Prentice Hall.

Patel, R. V. and Munro, N., 1981. *Multivariable system theory and design.* Oxford: Pergamon.

Warwick, K., 1988. *Industrial digital control systems.* London: Peter Peregrinus.

Warwick, K., 1996. *Introduction to control systems.* London: World Scientific Publishing.

Wellstead, P. E. and Zarrop, P., 1991. *Self-tuning systems: control and signal processing.* London: John Wiley & Sons Ltd.

Winston, P. H., 1977. *Artificial intelligence.* Boston: Addison Wesley.

Periodicals

Adaptive Behavior
AI Magazine
Applied Artificial Intelligence
Artificial Intelligence
Artificial Intelligence in Engineering
Artificial Intelligence Review
Automatic Control and Computer sciences
Automatica
Automation and Remote Control
Autonomous Robots
Computation Intelligence
Computer and Control Engineering Journal
Control
Control and Instrumentation
Control Engineering
Control Engineering Practice
Control Platforms
Control Solutions
Control Systems
Decision Support Systems
Drives and Controls
Engineering Applications of Artificial Intelligence
Fuzzy Optimisation and Decision Making
Fuzzy Sets and System
IEEE Control Systems
IEEE Transactions on Automatic Control
IEEE Transactions on Neural Networks
IEEE Transactions on Robotics and Automation
International Journal of Adaptive Control and Signal Processing
International Journal of Applied Expert Systems
International Journal of Control
International Journal of General Systems
International Journal of Human-computer Studies
International Journal of Knowledge-Based Intelligent Engineering Systems
International Journal of Neural Systems
International Journal of Pattern Recognition and Artificial Intelligence
International Journal of Robotics Research
International Journal of Systems & Cybernetics
International Journal of Systems Science
International Journal of Uncertainty, Fuzziness and Knowledge-based Systems
Journal of Automated Reasoning
Journal of Computation Electronics
Journal of Dynamic Systems, Measurement and Control

Journal of Dynamical and Control Systems
Journal of Experimental and Theoretical Artificial Intelligence
Journal of Intelligent and Robotic Systems
Journal of Intelligent Systems
Journal of Robotic Systems
Journal of Systems and Control Engineering
Knowledge Engineering Review
Machine Learning
Measurement + Control
Mechatronics
Multibody System Dynamics
Neural Processing Letters
Optimal Control Applications and Methods
Pattern Recognition
Process Engineering
Transactions on Mechatronics

Handbooks

Considine, D. M., 1994. *Process industry instrumentation and control handbook*. London: McGraw-Hill Education.
Levine, W. S., 1995. *Control handbook. London*: CRC Press.
Parr, E. A., 1998. *Industrial control handbook*. London: Butterworth-Heinemann.
Salvendy, G., ed., 2001. *Handbook of industrial engineering*. London: John Wiley & Sons.

Reference works

Automation, systems, and instrumentation dictionary 2002. Pittsburgh: Instrument Society of America.
Borne, P. and Quayle, N., 1998. *Systems and control dictionary*. Paris: Editions Technip.
Considine, D., 1981. *Encyclopedia of instrumentation and control*. Melbourne FL: Krieger Publishing Company.
Instrument engineers' yearbook. London: Institute of Measurement and Control.
Noltingk, B. E., ed., 1995. *Instrumentation reference book*. London: Butterworth-Heinemann.
Singh, M. G., ed., 1987. *Systems and control encyclopaedia: theory, technology, applications. 8 vols,* Oxford: Pergamon.

Abstracts

Computer & Control Abstracts, Institution of Electrical Engineers.
Current Papers in Computing and Control, Institution of Electrical Engineers.

Standards

European Committee for Electrotechnical Standardization, www.cenelec.org
International Electrotechnical Commission, www.iec.ch

Professional organisations

American Association for Artificial Intelligence, www.aaai.org
American Society for Cybernetics, www.asc-cybernetics.org
Cybernetics Society, www.cybsoc.org
European Society for the Study of Cognitive Systems, www.esscs.org
GAMBICA Association Ltd, www.gambica.org.uk
Institute of Measurement and Control, www.instmc.org.uk
International Federation for Automatic Control, www.ifac-control.org
International Society for Measurement and Controls, www.isa.org
International Society for the Systems Sciences, www.isss.org
Robotic Industries Association, www.robotics.org
Society for the Study of Artificial Intelligence and Simulation of Behaviour,
     www.aisb.org.uk
United Kingdom Automatic Control Council, www.shef.ac.uk/acse/ukacc
World Organization of Systems and Cybernetics, www.cybsoc.org/wosc

Commercial companies

ABB Ltd, www.abb.com
Blackburn Starling & Co Ltd, www.blackburn-starling.co.uk
Cytek Projects Ltd, www.cytek.co.uk
Data Systems & Solutions Ltd, www.ds-s.com
Emerson Process Automation, www.emersonprocess.com
Expo-Telektron Safety Systems Ltd, www.expotelektron.com
Foxboro Great Britain Ltd, www.foxboro.com
Honeywell Control Systems Ltd, www.honeywell.com
IMI Watson Smith Ltd, www.watsonsmith.com
Measurement Technology Ltd, www.mtl-inst.com
Pepperl & Fuchs GB Ltd, www.pepperl-fuchs.com
Rockwell Automation Ltd, www.automation.rockwell.com
Siemens Process Automation, www.sea.siemens.com
Solartron Mobrey Ltd, www.solartronmobrey.com
VT Controls Ltd, www.vtplc.com

Websites

nusapcg.hypermart.net/directory is a small resource centre but effective for controls
     engineering.

▶ FLUID FLOW, HYDRAULICS AND PNEUMATICS

The recommended texts are divided into three categories: fluids, hydraulics and pneumatics, vacuum. Meaningful non-commercial websites are difficult to find; information found on professional organisations' websites is sparse when compared to similar knowledge centres in other branches of mechanical engineering.

Texts

Texts: fluids

Anderson, J. D., 1995. *Computational fluid dynamics*. London: McGraw-Hill Education.

Aris, R., 1990. *Vectors, tensors and the basic equations of fluid mechanics*. New York: Dover Publications.

Blazek, J., 2001. *Computational fluid dynamics*. London: Elsevier.

Chung, T. J., 2002. *Computational fluid dynamics*. Cambridge: Cambridge University Press.

Esposito, A., 2000. *Fluid power with applications*. New York: US Imports & PHIPEs.

Fay, J. A., 1994. *Introduction to fluid mechanics*. Cambridge, MA: MIT Press.

Ferziger, J. H. and Peric, M., 2001. *Computational methods for fluid dynamics*. London: Springer-Verlag.

Gallavotti, G., 2001. *Foundations of fluid dynamics*. London: Springer-Verlag.

Hodges, P., 1996. *Hydraulic fluids*. London: Butterworth-Heinemann.

Horsley, M. and Sherwin, K., 1996. *Thermofluids*. London: Nelson Thornes.

King, R. P., 2002. *Introduction to practical fluid flow*. London: Butterworth-Heinemann.

Kokernak, R. P., 1998. *Fluid power technology*. New York: US Imports & PHIPEs.

Lesieur, M., 1997. *Turbulence in fluids*. London: Kluwer Academic Publishers.

Massey, B. S. and Ward-Smith, J. 1998. *Mechanics of fluids*. London: Nelson Thornes.

Mitchell, R. J. and Pippenger, J. J., 1997. *Fluid power maintenance basics and troubleshooting*. New York: Marcel Dekker.

Munson, B. R., 2002. *Fundamentals of fluid mechanics*. London: John Wiley & Sons.

Nevers, N. de, 1991. *Fluid mechanics for chemical engineers*. London: McGraw-Hill Education.

Oosthuizen, P. and Carscallen, W., 1997. *Compressible fluid flow*. London: McGraw-Hill Education.

Pozrikidis, C., 1997. *Introduction to theoretical and computational fluid dynamics*. Oxford: Oxford University Press Inc.

Pozrikidis, C. 2001. *Fluid dynamics: theory, computation, and numerical simulation*. London: Kluwer Academic Publishers.

Smits, A. J., 2000. *Physical introduction to fluid mechanics*. London: John Wiley & Sons.

Stern, H., 2001. *Fluid power*. London: CRC Press.

Street, R. L., 1995. *Elementary fluid mechanics*. London: John Wiley & Sons.

Streeter, V. *et al.*, 1998. *Fluid mechanics*. London: McGraw-Hill Education.

Versteerg, H. K. and Malalasekera, W., 1995. *Introduction to computational fluid dynamics: the finite volume method*. London: Prentice Hall.

Wesseling, P., 2001. *Principles of computational fluid dynamics*. London: Springer-Verlag.

Texts: hydraulics, pneumatics

Andersen, B. W., 2001. *Analysis and design of pneumatic systems*. Melbourne FL: Krieger Publishing Company.

Callear, B. and Pinches, M. J., 1996. *Power pneumatics*. London: Prentice Hall.

Hamill, L., 2001. *Understanding hydraulics*. Basingstoke: Palgrave Macmillan.

Hwang, N. H. C. and Houghtalen, R. J., 1995. *Fundamentals of hydraulic engineering systems*. London: Prentice Hall.

Johnson, J. E., 1996. *Hydraulics for engineering technology*. London: Prentice Hall.

Kay, M., 1998. *Practical hydraulics*. London: Spon Press.

Lambeck, R. P., 1983. *Hydraulic pumps and motors: selection and application for hydraulic power control systems*. New York: Marcel Dekker.

Lobanoff, V. S. and Ross, R. R., 1992. *Centrifugal pumps: a practical reference stressing hydraulic design, performance prediction, analysis and evaluation*. Houston: Gulf Publishing.

Majumdar, S.R., 2002. *Oil hydraulic systems: principles and maintenance*. London: McGraw-Hill Education.

Mei, Z-Y., 1991. *Mechanical design and manufacture of hydraulic machinery*. Aldershot: Ashgate Publishing.

Muller, R., 1998. *Pneumatics: theory and application*. Warrendale: Society of Automotive Engineers.

Nelik, L., 1999. *Centrifugal and rotary pumps: fundamentals with applications*. London: CRC Press.

Parr, A., 1998. *Hydraulics and pneumatic.*, London: Butterworth-Heinemann.

Pippenger, J., 1984. *Hydraulic valves and controls: selection and application*. New York: Marcel Dekker.

Pippenger, J. J., 1980. *Industrial hydraulics*. London: McGraw-Hill Education.

Pippenger, J. J., 1993. *Zero downtime hydraulics*. Decatur: Amalgam Publishing.

Pippenger, J. J., 1994. *Basics for the fluid power mechanic*. Decatur: Amalgam Publishing.

Rohner, P., 1996. *Industrial hydraulic control*. London: John Wiley & Sons.

Simon, A. L. and Korom, S. F., 2002. *Hydraulics*. La Vergne, TN: Simon Publications.

Stacey, C., 1997. *Practical pneumatics*, London: Butterworth-Heinemann.

Stewart, H. L., 1977. *Hydraulic and pneumatic power for production*. New York: Industrial Press Inc.

Turner, I. C., 1995. *Engineering applications of pneumatics and hydraulics*. London: Butterworth-Heinemann.

Turner, I. C., 1998. *Practical pneumatics and engineering applications of pneumatics and hydraulics set*. London: Butterworth-Heinemann.

Turton, R. K., 1994. *Rotodynamic pump design*. Cambridge: Cambridge University Press.

Vockroth, R. W., 1994. *Industrial hydraulics*. Albany: Delmar.

Walters, R. B., 2001. *Hydraulic and electric-hydraulic control systems*. London: Kluwer Academic Publishers.

Texts: vacuum

Chambers, A. *et al.*, 1989. *Basic vacuum technology*. London: Institute of Physics.

Hablanian, M. H., 1997. *High-vacuum technology: a practical guide*. New York: Marcel Dekker.

Lafferty, J. M., 1998. *Foundations of vacuum science and technology*. London: John Wiley & Sons.

O'Hanlon, J. F., 1998. *User's guide to vacuum technology*. London: John Wiley & Sons.

Rosebury, F., 1993. *Handbook of electron tube and vacuum techniques*. London: Springer-Verlag.

Rozanov, R. L. and Hablanian, M., 2002. *Vacuum technique*. London: Taylor & Francis.

Zhu, W., 2001. *Fundamentals of vacuum microelectronics*. London: John Wiley & Sons.

Periodicals

Annual Review on Fluid Mechanics
Computers & Fluids
European Journal of Mechanics B/Fluids
Experimental Thermal and Fluid Science
Experiments in Fluids
Fluid Dynamics Research
Fluid Power
International Journal for Numerical Methods in Fluids
International Journal of Computational Fluid Dynamics
International Journal of Fluid Power
Journal of Fluid Mechanics
Journal of Fluids and Structures
Journal of Fluids Engineering
Journal of Mathematical Fluid Mechanics
Journal of Non-Newtonian Fluid Mechanics
Journal of Vacuum Science and Technology
Numerical Methods in Fluids
Physics of Fluids
Theoretical and Computational Fluid Dynamics
Vacuum
Vacuum Technology & Coating

Handbooks

Brater, E., 1996. *Handbook of hydraulics*. London: McGraw-Hill Education.

Fuhs, A. and Schetz, J., 1996. *Handbook of fluid dynamics and fluid machinery*. 3 vols. London: John Wiley & Sons.

Garay, P. N., 1996. *Pump application desk book*. London: Prentice Hall.

Hauser, B. A., 1996. *Practical hydraulics handbook.* London: CRC Press.

Hoffmann, D. M. *et al.*, 1997. *Handbook of vacuum technology* London: Academic Press.

Hunt, T. and Vaughan, N., 1996. *Hydraulic handbook.* London: Elsevier.

Jamal, S., 2002. *Fluid flow handbook.* London: McGraw-Hill Education.

Johnson, R. W., 1998. *Handbook of fluid dynamics* London: CRC Press.

Mobley, K., 1999. *Fluid power manual.* London: Butterworth-Heinemann.

Peyret, R., 1999. *Handbook of computational fluid mechanisms.* London: Academic Press.

Totten, G. E., 1999. *Handbook of hydraulic fluid technology.* New York: Marcel Dekker.

United States Army Material Command, 2000. *Engineering design handbook: hydraulic fluids.* Honolulu: University of Hawaii Press.

Weisand, J. G., 1998. *Handbook of cryogenic engineering.* London: Taylor & Francis.

Yeaple, F., 1995. *Fluid power design handbook.* New York: Marcel Dekker.

Zipparro, V. J. and Hasen, H., 1992. *Davis' handbook of applied hydraulics.* London: McGraw-Hill Education.

Reference works

2000/2001 Fluid power handbook and directory. Isleworth: Penton Media Inc.

Fluid power equipment in the UK and directory of members 2002–2003. Chipping Norton: British Fluid Power Association.

Glossary of terms used in vacuum technology, 1958. Oxford: Pergamon Press.

Hurrle, K., ed., 1973. *Technical dictionary of vacuum physics and vacuum technology.* Oxford: Pergamon Press.

Neubert, G., 1973. *Technical dictionary of hydraulics and pneumatics.* Oxford: Pergamon Press.

Weber, F. W., 1968. *Dictionary of high vacuum science and technology.* London: Elsevier Science.

Abstracts

Fluidex. New York: Elsevier Science.

Standards

National Fluid Power Association, www.nfpa.com

Legislation and government

British Vacuum Council, www.astec.ac.uk/vacsci/British-Vacuum-Council

Research

Fluid Power Net International, www.fluid.power.net

Professional organisations

American Vacuum Society, www.avs.org
Association of Vacuum Equipment Manufacturers International, www.avem.org
British Fluid Power Association, www.bfpa.co.uk
British Fluid Power Distributors Association, www.bfpa.co.uk
Fluid Power Society, www.ifps.org
Hydraulic Institute, www.pumps.org
International Union for Vacuum Science, Technique, and Applications, www.iuvsta.org
National Fluid Power Association, www.nfpa.com

Websites

www.dse.nl/~an2an/wwv.html deals with aspects of high and ultra high vacuum.

▶ FUEL AND ENERGY TECHNOLOGY

For this section, *fuel* is defined as an additive fed into an engine to assist its operation (oil, gas, petroleum, coal) and *energy* as its consequent reaction. Therefore, alternative elemental or meteorological sources of energy (air, water, sun) or their physical manifestations receive minor attention. Commercial companies are listed if they have UK bases.

Texts

Texts: combustion, flame technology

Borghi, R. and Destriau, M., 1998. *Combustion and flames*. Paris: Editions Technip.
Drysdale, D., 1998. *Introduction to fire dynamics*. London: John Wiley & Sons.
Eugene, L., 1993. *Applied combustion*. New York: Marcel Dekker.
Fristrom, R. M., 1995. *Flame structure and processes*. Oxford: Oxford University Press.
Griffiths, J. F. and Barnard, J. A., 1995. *Flame and combustion*. London: Nelson Thornes.
Sarkar, S., 1990. *Fuels and combustion*. Pune: Sangam Books.

Texts: liquid fuels

Archer, J., 1986. *Petroleum engineering: principles and practice*. London: Kluwer Academic Publishing.
Berger, B. D. and Anderson, K., 1981. *Modern petroleum – a basic primer of the industry*. Tulsa: Pennwell Books.

Leigh-Jones, C., 1998. *Practical guide to marine fuel oil handling.* London: Institute of
  Marine Engineers.
McCain Jr, W. D., 1990. *Properties of petroleum fluids.* Tulsa: Pennwell Books.
Mian, M. A., 1991–2. *Petroleum engineering handbook for the practicing engineer.* 2 vols.
  Tulsa: Pennwell Books.
Modern petroleum technology, 2000. Institute of Petroleum. London: John Wiley & Sons.
Williams, A., 1990. *Combustion of sprays of liquid fuels.* London: Butterworth-Heinemann.

Texts: solid fuels

Berkowitz, N., 1994. *Introduction to coal technology.* London: Academic Press.
Loison, R. *et al.,* 1989. *Coke: analysis and production.* London: Butterworth-Heinemann.
Pitt, G. J. and Millward, G. R., eds., 1979. *Coal and modern coal processing: an introduction.*
  London: Academic Press.
Singhal, S. C. and Kendall, K., 2001. *High-temperature solid oxide fuel cells: fundamentals,*
  design and applications. London: Elsevier Science.
Speight, J. G., 1994. *Chemistry and technology of coal.* New York: Marcel Dekker.
Tillmann, D. A., 1991. *Combustion of solid fuels and waste.* London: Academic Press.
Tomeczek, J., 1994. *Coal combustion.* New York: Krieger Publishing Co.

Texts: energy management

Beggs, C., 2002. Energy management and conservation. London: Butterworth-
  Heinemann.
Brown, H. *et al.,* 1997. *Energy analysis of 108 industrial processes.* London: Prentice Hall.
Gottschalk, C., 1996. *Industrial energy conservation.* London: John Wiley & Sons.
Panke, R. A., 2001. *Energy management systems and direct digital control.* London: Prentice
  Hall.
Petrecca, G., 1993. *Industrial energy management: principles and applications.* London:
  Kluwer Academic Publishing.

Periodicals

Coal Age
Coal International
Coal Leader
Coal Preparation
Combustion and Flame
Energy Engineering
Fire Technology
Fuel
Hydrogen & Fuel Cell Newsletter
International Journal of Coal Geology
International Journal of Energy Technology and Policy
Journal of Canadian Petroleum Technology

Journal of Energy Engineering
Journal of Energy Resources Technology
Journal of Essential Oil Research
Journal of Petroleum Technology
Journal of the Japanese Association for Petroleum Technology
Oil & Gas Journal
Oil Information Technology Journal
OPEC Bulletin
Petroleum Intelligence Weekly
Petroleum Review

Handbooks

Bechtold, R. L., 2002. *Alternative fuels: transportation fuels for today and tomorrow.* Warrendale: Society of Automotive Engineers.

Hollingdale, A. C. *et al.*, 1992. *Charcoal production: a handbook.* Bath: eco-logic books.

Lyons, W. C., 2001. *Standard handbook of petroleum and natural gas engineering.* London: Butterworth-Heinemann.

Peyton, K. B., 2001. *Nalco fuel field manual.* London: McGraw-Hill Education.

Piper, J. E., 1999. *Operations and maintenance manual for energy management.* New York: M. E. Sharpe.

Schmidt, P. F., 1985. *Fuel oil manual.* New York: Industrial Press Inc.

Shell Group of Companies, 1983. *The Petroleum handbook.* London: Elsevier.

Tarek, A., 2002. *Reservoir engineering handbook.* London: Butterworth-Heinemann.

Turner, W. C., 2001. *Energy management handbook.* London: Prentice Hall.

Reference works

Gilpin, A., 1969. *Dictionary of fuel technology.* London: Newnes-Butterworth.

Hyne, N., 1991. *Dictionary of petroleum: exploration, drilling and production.* Tulsa: Pennwell Books.

Langenkamp, R. D., 1994. *Handbook of oil industry terms and phrases.* Tulsa: Pennwell Books.

Moureau, M. and Brace, G., 1993. *Comprehensive dictionary of petroleum science and technology.* Paris: Editions Technip.

Plunkett's energy industry almanac. Houston: Plunkett Research Ltd.

Rosenberg, P., 2001. *Illustrated energy dictionary.* London: Prentice Hall.

Slesser, M., 1988. *Macmillan dictionary of energy.* Basingstoke: Palgrave.

Stevens, P., 1988. *Dictionary of oil and gas: an encyclopaedic dictionary of economic and financial concepts and terms.* London: Macmillan Reference.

Tippee, B., 2001. *International petroleum encyclopedia.* Tulsa: Pennwell Publishing.

USA oil industry directory. Tulsa: Pennwell Books.

Williams, H. *et al.*, 1999. *Manual of oil and gas terms.* London: LexisNexis Matthew Bender.

Abstracts

Fuel and Energy Abstracts. London: Institute of Energy/Elsevier.

Standards

American Petroleum Institute, api-ec.api.org

Legislation and government

Coal Authority, www.coal.gov.uk
Office of Gas and Electricity Markets, www.ofgem.gov.uk
UK Department of Trade and Industry Oil and Gas Directorate, www.og.dti.gov.uk
UK Department of Trade and Industry Energy Group, www.dti.gov.uk/energy
US Department of Energy, www.energy.gov

Research

Combustion Institute, www.combustioninstitute.org
Global Petroleum Research Institute, pumpjack.tamu.edu/gpri
IEA Coal Research – The Clean Coal Centre, www.iea-coal.org.uk

Professional organisations

American Coalition for Ethanol, www.ethanol.org
American Gas Association, www.aga.com
American Institute of Mining, Metallurgical and Petroleum Engineers, www.aimehq.org
American Petroleum Institute, api-ec.api.org
American Solar Energy Society, www.ases.org
American Wind Energy Association, www.awea.org
Australian Institute of Petroleum, www.aip.com.au
Canadian Institute of Mining Metallurgy & Petroleum, www.petsoc.org
Canadian Petroleum Institute, www.cipid.com
Institute of Petroleum, www.petroleum.co.uk
International Energy Agency, www.iea.org
Japanese Association for Petroleum Technology, www.japt.org/html/english
National Hydrogen Association, www.hydrogenus.com
Organisation of Petroleum Exporting Countries, www.opec.org
Petroleum Equipment Institute, www.pei.org
Petroleum Exploration Society of Great Britain, www.pesgb.org.uk
Petroleum Transfer Technology Council, www.pttc.org

Society of Petroleum Engineers, www.spe.org
Solar Energy Industries Association, www.seia.org
Solid Fuel Association, www.solidfuel.co.uk
United Kingdom Offshore Operators Association, www.ukooa.co.uk

Commercial companies

Commercial companies: oil, petroleum

Agip (U.K.) Ltd, www.eni.it/english/home.html
Amerada Hess Ltd, www.hess.com
BG Group, www.bgplc.com
BHP Billiton Ltd, www.bhp.com
BP plc, www.bp.com
Burlington Resources UK Ltd, www.br-inc.com
ChevronTexaco, www.chevrontexaco.com
ConocoPhillips (UK) Ltd, www.conoco.com
ExxonMobil International Ltd, www.exxonmobil.com
John Swire & Sons Ltd, www.swire.com/activities/hk/marine.htm
Marathon Oil UK Ltd, www.marathon.com
Petro-Canada, www.petro-canada.com
Premier Oil plc, www.premier-oil.com
Shell UK Exploration and Production, www.shell.co.uk
Statoil (UK) Ltd, www.statoil.co.uk
TotalFinaElf Exploration UK PLC, www.totalfinaelf.com
Tullow Oil UK Ltd, www.tullowoil.com
Venture Production plc, www.vpc.co.uk

Commercial companies: solid fuel

Celtic Energy Ltd, www.coal.com
Coalite Smokeless Fuels, www.coalite.co.uk
E.H. Bennett & Co Ltd, www.ehbennett.co.uk
Maxibrite Ltd, www.maxibrite.co.uk
UK Coal plc, www.ukcoal.com

Pressure and single issue groups

Friends of the Earth, www.foe.co.uk

Websites

www.energyprojects.co.uk outlines renewable energy projects underway in the UK.

www.h2fuelcells.org leads to the Hydrogen Fuel Cell Institute whose website appears
    not to give a landmail address.
www.oilsite.com is a news and information internet source for the oil and gas
    industries.

▶ HEAT AND THERMODYNAMICS

Commercial companies are not detailed in this section covering the theory
and practice of heat. Legislation and Government sources are adequately
covered in the Mechanical Engineering section.

Texts

Texts: fundamentals

Barron, T. H. K., 1999. *Heat capacity and thermal expansion at low temperatures.* London:
    Kluwer Academic/Plenum Publishers.
Kakac, S., 1991. *Boilers, evaporators and condensers: design fundamentals.* London: John
    Wiley & Sons.
Maxwell, J. C., 2001. *Theory of heat.* New York: Dover Publications.
Moran, M. J. et al., 2002. *Introduction to thermal systems engineering: thermodynamics, fluid
    mechanics, and heat transfer.* London: John Wiley & Sons.
Rogers, G. F. C. and Mayhew, Y. R., 1992. *Engineering thermodynamics: work and heat
    transfer.* London: Longman.
Sears, F. W. and Lee, J. E., 1975. *Introduction to thermodynamics, the kinetic theory of
    gases, and statistical mechanics.* Boston: Addison Wesley.
Stoecker, W. F., 1989. *Design of thermal systems.* London: McGraw-Hill Education.
Yoshida, A., ed., 2001. *Smart control of turbulent combustion.* London: Springer-Verlag.

Texts: heat transfer

Incropera, F. P. and Dewitt, D., 2001. *Fundamentals of heat and mass transfer.* London:
    John Wiley & Sons.
Isachenko, V. P. et al., 2000. *Heat transfer.* University Press of the Pacific.
Kaviany, M., 2001. *Principles of heat transfer.* London: John Wiley & Sons.
Kays, W. M. and Crawford, M., 1993. *Convective heat and mass transfer.* London:
    McGraw-Hill Education.
Middleman, S., 1997. *Introduction to heat and mass transfer: principles of analysis and
    design.* London: John Wiley & Sons.
Modest, M. M., 1993. *Radiative heat transfer.* London: McGraw-Hill Education.
Siegel, R. and Howell, J. R., 1992. *Thermal radiation heat transfer.* London: Taylor &
    Francis.

Tannehill, J. C., 1997. *Computational fluid mechanics and heat transfer.* London: Taylor & Francis.

Welty, J. *et al.,* 2001. *Fundamentals of momentum, heat and mass transfer.* London: John Wiley & Sons.

Texts: refrigeration, cooling

Dossat, R. J. and Horan, T. J., 2001. *Principles of refrigeration.* London: Prentice Hall.

Howell, R. *et al.,* 2001. *Principles of heating, ventilating and air-conditioning.* Atlanta: American Society of Heating, Refrigerating and Air Conditioning Engineers.

Texts: temperature measurement

Childs, P. R. N., 2001. *Practical temperature measurement.* London: Butterworth-Heinemann.

McGee, T. D., 1998. *Principles and methods of temperature measurement.* Maidenhead: John Wiley & Sons.

Texts: thermodynamics

Adkins, C. J., 1983. *Equilibrium thermodynamics.* Cambridge: Cambridge University Press.

Annamalai, K. and Puri, I. K., 2001. *Advanced thermodynamics engineering.* London: CRC Press.

Cengel, Y. and Boles, M., 1997. *Thermodynamics: an engineering approach.* London: McGraw-Hill Education.

Eastop, T. D. and McConkey, A., 1993. *Applied thermodynamics: for engineering technologists.* London: Longman.

Fermi, E., 1937. *Thermodynamics.* New York: Dover Publications.

Gaskell, D. R., 1995. *Introduction to the thermodynamics of materials.* London: Taylor & Francis.

Goodger, E. M., 1984. *Principles of engineering thermodynamics.* London: Macmillan Education.

Graetzel, M. *et al.,* 2000. *Bases of chemical thermodynamics.* Florida: Universal Publishers.

Granet, I. and Bluestein, M., 1999. *Thermodynamics and heat power.* New York: US Imports and PHIPEs.

Honig, J. M., 1999. *Thermodynamics: principles characterizing physical and chemical processes.* London: Academic Press.

Mayhew, Y. R. and Rogers, G. F. C., 1994. *Thermodynamic and transport properties of fluids.* Oxford: Blackwell Publishers.

McGovern, J. A., 1996. *Essence of engineering thermodynamics.* Maidenhead: Prentice Hall.

Moran, M. J. and Shapiro, H. N., 1998. *Fundamentals of engineering thermodynamics.* London: John Wiley & Sons.

Rayner, J., 1996. *Basic engineering thermodynamics.* London: Prentice Hall.

Smith, J. M., 2001. *Introduction to chemical engineering thermodynamics.* London: McGraw-Hill Education.

Sonntag, R., 2002. *Fundamentals of thermodynamics*. London: John Wiley & Sons.
Van Ness, T. C., 1983, *Understanding thermodynamics*. New York: Dover Publications.
Wark Jr, K. J., and Richards, D. E., 1999. *Thermodynamics*. London: McGraw-Hill Education.
Wong, K-F. V., 2000. *Thermodynamics for engineers*. London: CRC Press.

Periodicals

Applied Thermal Engineering
Calorimetry and Thermal and Analysis
Continuum Mechanics and Thermodynamics
Experimental Heat Transfer
Experimental Thermal and Fluid Science
Heat and Mass Transfer
Heat Transfer – Asian Research
Heat Transfer Engineering
Heat Transfer Research
International Communications in Heat and Mass Transfer
International Journal of Applied Thermodynamics
International Journal of Enhanced Heat Transfer
International Journal of Heat & Technology
International Journal of Heat and Fluid Flow
International Journal of Heat and Mass Transfer
International Journal of Numerical Methods for Heat & Fluid Flow
International Journal of Refrigeration
Journal of Chemical Thermodynamics
Journal of Enhanced Heat Transfer
Journal of Heat Transfer
Journal of Thermal Analysis and Calorimetry
Journal of Thermophysics and Heat Transfer
Numerical Heat Transfer: Applications
Numerical Heat Transfer: Fundamentals

Handbooks

ASHRAE fundamentals handbook. Atlanta, American Society of Heating, Refrigerating and Air Conditioning Engineers.
ASHRAE refrigeration handbook. Atlanta, American Society of Heating, Refrigerating and Air Conditioning Engineers.
Bruno, T. J., 1995. *CRC Handbook for the analysis and identification of alternative refrigerants*. London: CRC Press.
Gallagher, P.K., ed., 1998. *Handbook of thermal analysis and calorimetry: principles and practice*. London: Elsevier.

Gilmore, D. G., 2002. *Spacecraft thermal control handbook: fundamental technologies.* Reston: American Institute of Aeronautics and Astronautics.

Guyer, E. C., and Brownell, D. L., 1989. *Handbook of applied thermal design.* London: McGraw-Hill.

Haines, R. W., and Wilson, C. L., 1998. *HVAC systems design handbook.* London: McGraw-Hill.

Heating, ventilation, air-conditioning applications handbook. 1999. Atlanta: American Society of Heating, Refrigerating and Air Conditioning Engineers.

Heating, ventilation, air-conditioning systems & equipment handbook. Atlanta: American Society of Heating, Refrigerating and Air Conditioning Engineers.

Hewitt, G. F., *et al.*, eds., 1998. *Heat exchanger design handbook.* New York: Begell House Inc.

Keenan, J. H., *et al.*, 1969. *Steam tables: thermodynamic properties of water including vapor, liquid, and solid phases.* London: John Wiley & Sons.

Krieth, F. K., 1999. *CRC handbook of thermal engineering.* London: CRC Press.

Liscic, B., *et al.*, 1992. *Theory and technology of quenching: a handbook.* London: Springer-Verlag.

Palmer, D. A., 1987. *Handbook of applied thermodynamics.* London: CRC Press.

Perry, R. H., and Green, D. W., 1998. *Perry's chemical engineers' handbook.* London: McGraw-Hill Education.

Rohsenow, W. M., *et al.*, 1998. *Handbook of heat transfer.* London: McGraw-Education.

Rudnev, V., *et al.*, 2002. *Handbook of induction heating.* New York: Marcel Dekker.

Sergent, J. E., and Krum, A., 1998. *Thermal management handbook: for electronic assemblies,* London: McGraw-Hill Education.

Shah, R. K., and Sekulic, D. P., 2003. Fundamentals of heat exchanger design. Hoboken: Wiley.

Vargaftik, N. B., *et al.*, 1993. *Handbook of thermal conductivity of liquids and gases.* London: CRC Press.

Wong, H.Y., 1977. *Handbook of essential formulae and data on heat transfer for engineers.* London: Longman.

Reference works

Hewitt, G. F., *et al.*, eds., 1997. *International encyclopedia of heat & mass transfer.* London: CRC Press.

James, A. M., 1976. *Dictionary of thermodynamics.* Macmillan.

Perrot, P., 1998. *Dictionary of Thermodynamics.* Oxford University Press.

Abstracts

Previews of Heat and Mass Transfer. Chicago, IL: Rumford Publishing Co Inc.

Standards

Air Conditioning & Refrigeration Institute, www.ari.org
American Society of Heating, Refrigerating and Air Conditioning Engineers,
www.ashrae.org

Research

International Centre for Applied Thermodynamics, www.icatweb.org
International Centre for Heat and Mass Transfer, www.ichmt.org

Professional organisations

Air Conditioning & Refrigeration Institute, www.ari.org
American Boiler Manufacturers Association, www.abma.com
American Society of Heating, Refrigerating and Air Conditioning Engineers,
www.ashrae.org
British Industrial Furnace Constructors Association, www.bifca.org
British Refrigeration Association, www.feta.co.uk/bra
Combined Heat and Power Association, www.chpa.co.uk
European Committee for the Advancement of Thermal Sciences and Heat Transfer,
termserv.casaccia.enea.it/eurotherm
Federation of Environmental Trade Associations, www.feta.co.uk
Heat Pump Association, www.feta.co.uk/hpa
Heat Transfer Society of Japan, www.htsj.or.jp
Heating, Ventilating & Air Conditioning Manufacturers Association,
www.feta.co.uk/hevac
Industrial Heating Equipment Association, www.ihea.org
International Ground Source Heat Pump Association, www.igshpa.okstate.edu
Japan Society for Calorimetry and Thermal Analysis,
wwwsoc.nii.ac.jp/jscta/e/society_1.html
Swiss Society for Thermal Analysis and Calorimetry, www.stk-online.ch

Websites

thermodex.lib.utexas.edu is a resource and formula-driven site for thermodynamists
run by the University of Texas at Austin.

▶ NAVAL AND MARINE ENGINEERING

Like other transportation engineering, naval and marine engineering is defined by the surface travelling engine-driven vessels move on or through – in this case, salt water. Consequently, the following are not covered: inland water craft engines, or leisure/sports, wind-powered or fishing craft. Some attention is paid to crime prevention and military applications. Commercial companies are listed if they have a UK presence. Passing acknowledgement is paid to off-shore engineering.

Texts

Barltrop, N. D. P., 1998. *Floating structures: a guide for design and analysis.* London: Centre for Marine and Petroleum Technology (CMPT).

Barnaby, K., 1992. *Basic naval architecture.* Southampton: Warsash Publishing.

Biran, A., 2003. *Ship hydrostatics and stability.* London: Butterworth-Heinemann.

Blank, D. A., and Bock, A. E., 1985. *Introduction to naval engineering.* Annapolis: Naval Institute Press.

Breslin, J. P., and Andersen, P., 1996. *Hydrodynamics of ship propellers.* Cambridge University Press.

Burcher, R., and Rydill, L. J., 1995. *Concepts in submarine design.* Cambridge University Press.

Bureau of Naval Personnel, 2001. *Principles of naval engineering.* University Press of the Pacific.

Design of ships structures. 1993. London: Stationery Office.

Erichsen, S., 1989, *Management of marine design.* London: Butterworth-Heinemann.

Eyres, D. J., 2001. *Ship construction.* London: Butterworth-Heinemann.

Faltinsen, O., 1993. *Sea loads on ships and offshore structures.* Cambridge University Press.

Frankel, E. G., 1987. *Port planning and development.* London: John Wiley & Sons.

Gillmer, T. C., and Johnson, B., 1985. *Introduction to naval architecture.* Annapolis, Naval Institute Press.

Griffiths, D., 1999. *Marine medium speed diesel engines.* London: Institute of Marine Engineering, Science and Technology.

Gritzen, E. F., 1986, *Introduction to naval engineering.* London: Kluwer Academic Publishers.

Hamlin, C., 1989. *Preliminary design of boats and ships.* Maryland: Cornell Maritime Press.

Henshall, S. H., 1997. *Medium and high speed diesel engines for marine use.* London: Institute of Marine Engineering, Science and Technology.

Kim, J. C., and Muehldorf, E. I., 1994. *Naval shipboard communication systems.* New Jersey: Prentice-Hall.

Knak, C., 1990. *Diesel motor ships' engines and machinery.* London: Institute of Marine Engineering, Science and Technology.

Laws, W., 1998. *Electricity applied to marine engineering.* London: Institute of Marine Engineering, Science and Technology.

Munro-Smith, R., 1997. *Ships and naval architecture.* London: Institute of Marine Engineering, Science and Technology.

Newman, J. N., 1977. *Marine hydrodynamics.* Massachusetts: MIT Press.

Nowacki, H., et al., eds., 1995. *Computational geometry for ships.* London: World Scientific Publishing.

Ochi, M. K., 1998. *Ocean waves: the stochastic approach.* Cambridge University Press.

Schneekluth, H., and Bertram, V., 1998. *Ship design for efficiency and economy.* London: Butterworth-Heinemann.

Stokoe, E. A., 1991. *Naval architecture.* Boston: Thomas Reed Publications Inc.

Swindells, N. S., ed., 1997. *Glossary of maritime technology.* London: Institute of Marine Engineering, Science and Technology.

Taylor, D., 1998. *Merchant ship construction.* London: Institute of Marine Engineering, Science and Technology.

Tupper, E. C., and Rawson, K. J., 2001. *Basic ship theory* (2 vols). London: Butterworth-Heinemann.

Tupper, E., 1996. *Muckle's introduction to naval architecture.* London: Butterworth-Heinemann.

Watson, D. G. M., 1998. *Practical ship design.* London: Elsevier Science.

Zubaly, R. B., 1996. *Applied naval architecture.* Maryland: Cornell Maritime Press.

Periodicals

Coastal Engineering Journal
IMarEST News
Journal of Engineering for the Maritime Environment
Journal of Offshore Technology
Journal of Water and Maritime Engineering
Marine Engineers Review
Marine Geophysical Researches
Maritime IT & Electronics
Naval Architect
Naval Engineers Journal
Parliamentary Maritime Review
Proceedings (of the US Naval Institute)
Safety at Sea International
Sea Technology
Seaways
Ship & Boat International
Ship Repair & Conversion Technology

Handbooks

Reed's Nautical Companion. Boston: Thomas Reed Publications Inc.

Reference works

Jones, S., *Lloyd's List marine equipment buyer's guide*. London: Informa Maritime and
    Transport.
Paasch, H., 1997. *Paasch's illustrated marine dictionary*. Connecticut: The Lyons Press.
Reed's nautical almanac. Boston: Thomas Reed Publications Inc.
Sullivan, E., 1999. *Marine encyclopaedic dictionary*. London: LLP Publishing.

Abstracts

Bryon, R. V., and Bryon, T. M., eds., 1993. *Maritime information: a guide to libraries and
    sources of information in the United Kingdom*. London: Maritime Information
    Association.
Marine Technology Abstracts. Institute of Marine Engineering, Science and
    Technology.

Standards

Lloyd's Register of Shipping, www.lr.org

Legislation and government

American Bureau of Shipping, www.eagle.org
ICC Commercial Crime Services, www.iccwbo.org
IMB Piracy Reporting Centre, www.iccwbo.org/ccs/menu_imb_piracy.asp
International Maritime Organisation, www.imo.org
Marine Accident Investigation Branch, www.maib.dft.gov.uk
Marine Consents and Environment Unit, www.mceu.gov.uk
Maritime and Coastguard Agency, www.mcga.gov.uk

Research

Centre for Marine and Petroleum Technology, www.cmpt.co.uk
Marr Vessel Management Ltd, www.j-marr.co.uk
Office for Naval Research, www.onrifo.navy.mil

Professional organisations

American Society of Naval Engineers, www.navalengineers.org
Association Technique Maritime et Aeronautique, www.ensta.fr

Bristol Steamship Owners' Association, 2 Downleaze, Avonmouth, Portishead, Bristol BS20 8BJ.
British Association of Ship Suppliers, Peartree Cottage, Nordham, North Cave, North Humberside HU15 2LT.
British Marine Equipment Association, 4th Floor, 30 Great Guilford Street, London SE1 0HS.
British Marine Federation, Marine House, Thorpe Lea Road, Egham TW20 8BF.
British Naval Equipment Association, 4th Floor, 30 Great Guildford Street, London SE1 0HS.
Cardiff and Bristol Channel Incorporated Shipowners' Association, c/o Welsh Industrial & Maritime Museum, Bute Street, Cardiff CF1 6AN.
Chamber of Shipping, www.british-shipping.org
Engineering and Marine Training Authority, www.emta.org.uk
European Marine Equipment Council, www.emec.net
Institute of Chartered Shipbrokers, www.ics.org.uk
Institute of Marine Engineering, Science and Technology, www.imare.org.uk
International Marine Contractors Association, www.imca-int.com
International Marine Purchasing Association, www.impa-assoc.org
International Ship Suppliers Association, www.shipsupply.org
Liverpool Ship Owners' and Port Users' Association, Number One Old Hall Street, Liverpool L3 9HG.
London Shipowners' and River Users' Society, Carthusian Court, 12 Carthusian Street, London EC1M 6EZ.
Marine Technology Society, www.mtsociety.org
Nautical Institute, www.nautinst.org
Royal Institution of Naval Architects, www.rina.org.uk
Society of Maritime Industries, www.maritimeindustries.org
Society of Naval Architects and Marine Engineers, www.sname.org
Standby Ship Operators Association Ltd, Chappetts Farm House, West Meon, Petersfield GU32 1NB.
US Naval Institute, www.usni.org
West European Confederation of Marine Technology Societies, www.wemt.nl

Commercial companies

Andrew Weir Shipping Ltd, www.aws.co.uk
Appledore Shipbuilders Ltd, www.appledore-shipbuilders.co.uk
BAE Systems Export Shipbuilding Ltd, www.baesystems.com
BAE Systems plc, www.baesystems.com
Bibby Line Group Ltd, www.bibbylinegroup.co.uk
BP Shipping Ltd, www.bpacomo.com
British Maritime Technology, www.bmt.org
BUE Marine Ltd, www.oamedia.co.uk/bue
Costain Ltd, www.costain.com

CP Ships Ltd, www.cpships.com
Cunard Seabourn Ltd, www.cunardline.com
David Brown Engineering Ltd, www.textronpt.com
Eidesvik Shipping Ltd, www.eidesvik.no
F.T. Everard & Sons Ltd, Candlewick House, 120 Cannon Street, London EC4N 6AS.
Farstad Shipping Ltd, www.farstad.no
First Marine International, www.firstmarine.co.uk
Fred Olsen Cruise Lines Ltd, www.fredolsen.co.uk
Halcrow Maritime, www.halcrow.com
Hart Fenton & Co Ltd, www.hart-fenton.demon.co.uk
James Fisher & Son plc, www.james-fisher.co.uk
Maersk Co Ltd, One Canada Square, www.maersk.co.uk
OT Africa Line Ltd, www.otal.com
P&O European Ferries (Irish Sea) Ltd, www.poirishsea.com
P&O Ferries Ltd, Channel House, Channel View Road, Dover CT17 9TJ.
P&O Nedlloyd Ltd, www.ponl.com
P&O Princess Cruises Ltd, www.poprincesscruises.com
P&O Stena Line Ship Management Ltd, www.posl.com
P&O Swire Containers Ltd, www.posl.com
Rolls-Royce plc – Commercial Marine, www.rolls-royce.com
Rolls-Royce plc – Naval Marine, www.rolls-royce.com
Royal Fleet Auxiliary, www.rfa.mod.uk
Royal National Lifeboat Institution, www.rnli.org.uk
Royal Navy, www.royal-navy.mod.uk, www.mod.uk
Sea Containers Ferries and Ports Ltd, www.seacontainers.com
Shell International Trading & Shipping Co Ltd, www.shell.co.uk
Southampton, Isle of Weight & South of England Steam Packet Co Ltd (Red Funnel),
        www.redfunnel.co.uk
Stena Line Ltd, Charter House, www.stenaline.com
Three Quays Marine Services Ltd, www.3quays.com
VT Shipbuilding Ltd, Victoria Road, Woolston, Southampton SO19 9RR,
        www.vtplc.com
Western Ferries (Clyde) Ltd, www.westernferriesclyde.com
Wightlink Ltd, www.wightlink.co.uk

Collections

Chatham Historic Dockyard, www.worldnavalbase.org.uk
Fleet Air Arm Museum, www.faam.org.uk
National Maritime Museum, www.nmm.ac.uk
National Waterways Museum, www.nwm.org.uk
Portsmouth Historic Dockyard, www.flagship.org.uk
Royal Naval Museum, www.royalnavalmuseum.org
Royal Navy Submarine Museum, www.rnsubmus.co.uk

Websites

www.lloydslist.com probably justly claims to be the world's leading source of maritime business news and information.

► NUCLEAR ENGINEERING

The focus is on nuclear power, not weapon or military applications. Statuses of UK nuclear reactors as of January 2003 are given; government, pressure group or other websites may post more current decisions as they occur.

Texts

Almenas, K., and Lee, R., 1992. *Nuclear engineering: an introduction.* London: Springer-Verlag.

Bell, G. I., 1979. *Nuclear reactor theory.* Melbourne FL: Krieger Publishing Company.

Benedict, M., 1981. *Nuclear chemical engineering.* London: McGraw-Hill.

Bennet, D. J., and Thomson, J. R., 1989. *Elements of nuclear power.* London: Longman.

Bodansky, D., 1996. *Nuclear Energy.* London: Springer-Verlag.

Cochran, R. G., and Tsoulfanides, N., 1999. *Nuclear fuel cycle: analysis and management.* American Nuclear Society.

Foster, A. R., 1983. *Basic nuclear engineering.* Boston: Allyn and Bacon.

Glasstone, S., and Sesonske, A., 1994. *Nuclear reactor engineering: reactor systems engineering.* London: Kluwer Academic Publishers.

Harms, A. A., 1987. *Principles of nuclear science and engineering.* London: John Wiley & Sons.

Knief, R. A., 1992. *Nuclear engineering: theory and technology of commercial nuclear power,* London: Taylor & Francis.

Lamarsh, J. R., and Baratta, A. J., 2001. *Introduction to nuclear engineering.* London: Addison Wesley.

Ligou, J. P., 1986. *Elements of nuclear engineering.* Amsterdam: Harwood Academic Publishers.

Marshall, W., 1984. *Nuclear power technology: volume 1, Reactor technology; volume 2, Fuel cycle; volume 3, Nuclear radiation.* Oxford University Press.

Mayo, R. M., 1998. *Introduction to nuclear concepts for engineers.* American Nuclear Society.

Murray, R., 2001. *Nuclear energy: an introduction to the concepts, systems and applications of nuclear processes.* London: Butterworth-Heinemann.

Nuclear communications: a handbook for guiding good communications practices at nuclear fuel cycle facilities. 1995. International Atomic Energy Agency.

Rahn, F., 1992. *Guide to nuclear power technology: a resource for decision-making.* Melbourne FL: Krieger Publishing.

Rozon, D., and Rouben, B., 1998. *Introduction to nuclear reactor kinetics.* Canada: Polytechnic International Press.

Saling, J. H., and Tang, Y. S., 2001. *Radioactive waste management.* London: Taylor & Francis.

Shultis, J. K., and Faw, R. E., 2002. *Fundamentals of nuclear science and engineering.* New York: Marcel Dekker.

Stacey, W. M., 2001. *Nuclear reactor physics.* London: John Wiley & Sons.

Todreas, N. E., and Kazimi, M. S., 1990. *Nuclear systems: volume 1, Thermal hydraulic fundamentals; volume 2, Elements of thermal design.* London: Taylor & Francis.

Wilpert, B., and Itoigawa, N., eds., 2001. *Safety culture in the nuclear industry.* London: Taylor & Francis.

Winterbottom, J. M., and King, M. B., 1999. *Reactor design for chemical engineers.* Cheltenham: Nelson Thornes.

Wolfson, R., 1994. *Nuclear choices: a citizen's guide to nuclear technology.* Massachusetts: MIT Press.

Periodicals

Atomic Energy
High Temperature
IAEA Bulletin
International Journal of Nuclear Energy Science and Technology
International Journal of Radioactive Materials Transport
Journal of Fusion Energy
Journal of Nuclear Materials
Journal of the ICRU
NEA News
Nuclear Energy
Nuclear Energy International
Nuclear Engineer
Nuclear Fusion
Nuclear Law Bulletin
Nuclear News
Nuclear Safety Newsletter
Nuclear Science and Engineering
Radiation Protection Dosimetry

Handbooks

Chao, A. W., and Tigner, M., eds, 1999. *Handbook of accelerator physics and engineering.* London: World Scientific Publishing.

Ronen, Y., 1987, *Handbook of nuclear reactors calculations.* London: CRC Press.

Reference works

Directory of nuclear research reactors. International Atomic Energy Agency.
Fossil fuel and nuclear power generation in the UK. 2002. London: Euromonitor
      International plc.
Glossary of terms in nuclear science and technology. 1986. American Nuclear Society.
Lau, F-S., 1987. *Dictionary of nuclear power and waste management: with abbreviations and
      acronyms*. London: John Wiley & Sons.
Nuclear research reactors in the world. International Atomic Energy Agency.
Safety review. International Atomic Energy Agency.
Sarbacher, R. I., 1959. *Encyclopaedic dictionary of electronics and nuclear engineering*,
      London: Pitman.

Abstracts

Radiation Protection Abstracts. Ceased publication December 2002. www.ntp.org.uk

Standards

American Nuclear Society, www.ans.org

Legislation and government

International Atomic Energy Agency, www.iaea.org
National Radiological Protection Board, www.nrpb.org
Nuclear Installations Inspectorate, www.hse.gov.uk/nsd/index.htm
Nuclear Safety Directorate, www.hse.gov.uk/nsd
OECD Nuclear Energy Agency, www.nea.fr
Radioactive Waste Management Advisory Committee, www.defra.gov.uk/rwmac

Research

Jet Joint Undertaking, www.ukaea.org.uk/culham/jet
Council for the Central Laboratory of the Research Councils: Chilbolton Facility,
      www.rcru.rl.ac.uk
Council for the Central Laboratory of the Research Councils: Daresbury Laboratory,
      www.dl.ac.uk
Council for the Central Laboratory of the Research Councils: Rutherford Appleton
      Laboratory, www.rl.ac.uk
United Kingdom Atomic Energy Authority Research Establishment,
      www.ukaea.org.uk/culham, www.fusion.org.uk

United Kingdom Atomic Energy Authority Research Establishment, Dounreay,
    www.ukaea.org.uk/dounreay
United Kingdom Atomic Energy Authority Research Establishment, Harwell,
    www.ukaea.org.uk/harwell
United Kingdom Atomic Energy Authority Research Establishment, Risley,
    www.ukaea.org.uk/risley
United Kingdom Atomic Energy Authority Research Establishment, Windscale,
    www.ukaea.org.uk/windscale
United Kingdom Atomic Energy Authority Research Establishment, Winfrith,
    www.ukaea.org.uk/winfrith

Professional organisations

American Nuclear Society, www.ans.org
British Nuclear Energy Society, www.bnes.com
British Nuclear Industry Forum, www.bnif.co.uk
European Nuclear Society, www.euronuclear.org
Institute of Physics and Power Engineering, www.rssi.ru
Institution of Nuclear Engineers, www.inuce.org.uk
Japan Atomic Industrial Forum, www.jaif.or.jp/english
Nuclear Energy Institute, www.nei.org
OECD Nuclear Energy Agency, www.nea.fr
Safegrounds, www.safegrounds.com
World Nuclear Association, www.world-nuclear.org
World Nuclear Transport Institute, www.wnti.co.uk

Commercial companies

AEA Technology plc, www.aeat.com
British Nuclear Fuels plc, www.bnfl.com
National Nuclear Corporation Ltd, www.nnc.co.uk
Nirex Ltd, www.nirex.co.uk
Nuclear Electric plc, www.nuclear-electric.co.uk
Nuclear Technologies plc, www.nuclear.co.uk
Scottish Nuclear Ltd, Redwood Crescent, Peel Park, East Kilbride, Glasgow G74 5PR,
    www.snl.co.uk

Pressure and single issue groups

N-Base, www.n-base.org.uk
Nuclear Information and Resource Service, www.nirs.com
World Information Service on Energy, www.antenna.nl/wise

UK nuclear reactors

Berkeley, Gloucester GL 13 9PA. Magnox reactor; undergoing decommissioning, July 2002.

Bradwell-on-Sea, Southminster, Essex CMO 7HP. Magnox reactor.

Calder Hall, Sellafield, Seascale CA20 IPG. Magnox reactor.

Chapelcross, Annan, Dumfriesshire DG12 6RF. Magnox reactor.

Dounreay, Thurso, Caithness KW14 7TZ. Prototype fast reactor; undergoing decommissioning, July 2002.

Dungeness A, Romney Marsh TN29 9PL. Magnox reactor.

Dungeness B, Romney Marsh TN 29 9PX. Advanced gas cooled reactor.

Hartlepool, Tees Road, Hartlepool TS25 2B2. Advanced gas cooled reactor.

Heysham, PO Box 4, Heysham, Morecambe LA3 2XN. Advanced gas cooled reactor.

Hinkley Point A, Bridgwater TA5 IUD. Magnox reactor; decommissioned

Hinkley Point B, Bridgwater TA5 IUD. Advanced gas cooled reactor.

Hunterston A, West Kilbride. Magnox reactor; undergoing decommissioning, July 2002.

Hunterston B, West Kilbride. Advanced gas cooled reactor.

Oldbury on Severn, Oldbury Naite, Thornburg BS IRQ. Magnox reactor.

Sizewell A, nr Leiston IP16 4UR. Magnox reactor.

Sizewell B, nr Leiston IP16 4UR. Pressurised water reactor.

Torness, Dunbar, East Lothian. Advanced gas cooled reactor.

Trawsfyndd, Blaenau Ffestiniog LL41 4D7. Magnox reactor; undergoing decommissioning, July 2002.

Windscale, Seascale CA20 IPF. Advanced gas cooled reactor; decommissioned

Winfrith, Dorchester DT2 8DH. Steam generating heavy water reactor; decommissioned

Wylfa, Anglesey LL67 0DH. Magnox reactor.

Websites

www.nucleartourist.com deals with all aspects of nuclear energy; as an example of an amateur specialist internet-based information, this regularly updated website is as good as it gets.

www.care2.com/channels/ecoinfo/nuclear energy lists some websites concerned with the use of, and protest against, nuclear energy.

► PLANT AND POWER ENGINEERING

Trying to capture the different types of engineered plant power is difficult. Texts and handbooks segregate into the various methodologies, along with details of facilities and maintenance. Details of internal combustion engines texts could just as well be placed in other sections. Legislation and

Government sources are adequately covered in the Mechanical Engineering section. Commercial companies are not covered.

Texts

Texts: fundamentals

Bloch, H. P., 1995. *Practical guide to compressor technology.* London: McGraw-Hill Education.

Drbal, L. F., *et al.*, 1995. *Power plant engineering.* London: Kluwer Academic Publishing.

Fehr, R. E., 2002. *Industrial power distribution.* London: Prentice Hall.

Frediani Jr, H. A., and Evans, K. M., 1996. *Power plant permitting.* Tulsa: Pennwell Books.

Glover, J. D., and Sarma, M. S., 2002. *Power system analysis and design.* Pacific Grove: Brooks/Cole Publishing.

Graham, F. D., and Buffington, C., 1984, *Power plant engineers guide.* London: Prentice Hall & IBD.

Khalil, E. E., 1989. *Power plant design.* London: Gordon & Breach.

Lindsley, D., 1999. *Power plant control and instrumentation: the control of boilers and heat-recovery steam generator systems.* London: Institution of Electrical Engineers.

Peters, M. S., and Timmerhaus, K. D., 1990. *Plant design and economics for chemical Engineers.* London: McGraw-Hill Education.

Potter, P. J., 1988. *Power plant theory and design.* New York: Krieger Publishing Company.

Robertson, J. L., and Nalven, G. F., 1996. *Plant operation and optimization.* American Institute of Chemical Engineers.

Ruan, D.,and Fantoni, P. F., 2002. *Power plant surveillance and diagnostics: applied research with artificial intelligence.* London: Springer-Verlag.

Thumann, A., 1999. *Plant engineers and managers guide to energy conservation.* London: Prentice Hall.

Tidal Power. 1988. Thomas Telford Ltd.

Weismann, J., 1985. *Modern power plant engineering.* London: Prentice Hall.

Wentz, C. A., and Kavianian, H. R., 1995. *Industrial process and plant design.* London: McGraw-Hill Education.

Texts: electric, gas, steam and diesel plant technology

Ganapathy, V., 1986. *Basic programs for steam plant engineers: boilers, combustion, fluid flow and heat transfer.* New York: Marcel Dekker.

Han, J. C., and Dutta, S. R. S., 2001. *Gas turbine heat transfer and cooling technology.* London: Taylor & Francis.

Kehlhofer, R. H., *et al.,* 1999. *Combined-cycle gas & steam turbine power plants.* Tulsa: Pennwell Books.

Maffezzoni, C., ed., 1984. *Modelling and control of electric power plants: workshop proceedings.* London: Pergamon Press.

Nolas, G. S., et al., 2001. *Thermoelectrics: basic principles and new materials developments.* London: Springer Verlag.

Russell, J., 2000. *Steam & diesel power plant operators examinations.* Las Vegas: James Russell Publishing.

Saravanamuttoo, H. I. H., et al., 2001. *Gas turbine theory.* London: Prentice Hall.

Technology of turbine plant operating with wet steam. 1989. London: Thomas Telford Ltd.

Woodruff, E. B., et al., 1998. *Steam plant operation.* London: McGraw-Hill Education.

Texts: facilities and maintenance

Dhillon, B. S., 2002. *Engineering maintenance: a modern approach.* London: Technomic Publishing Co.

Grossel, S. S., et al., 1996. *Plant safety.* American Institute of Chemical Engineers.

Mobley, K., 1999. *Maintenance fundamentals.* London: Butterworth-Heinemann.

Texts: heat exchanger, pipe technology

Allinson, G., 1999. *Heat exchanger design.* London: Taylor & Francis.

Faghri, A., 1995. *Heat pipe science and technology.* London: Taylor & Francis.

Fraas, A. P., 1989. *Heat exchanger design.* London: John Wiley & Sons.

Larock, B. E., et al., 1999. *Hydraulics of pipeline systems.* London: CRC Press.

Texts: internal combustion engines

Ferguson, C., and Kirkpatrick, A., 2000. *Internal combustion engines.* London: John Wiley & Sons.

Heywood, J. B., 1988. *Internal combustion engine fundamentals.* London: McGraw-Hill Education.

Pulkrabek, W. W., 1997. *Engineering fundamentals of the internal combustion engine.* New York: US Imports and PHIPEs.

Taylor, C. F., 1985. *Internal combustion engine in theory and practice, Volume 1, Thermodynamics, fluid flow, performance, Volume 2, Combustion, fuels, materials, design.* Massachusetts: MIT Press.

Periodicals

Asian Energy Infrastructure
Compressor Technology
Energy Sources
International Journal of Heat Exchangers
International Journal of Sustainable Energy
International Journal of Environment and Sustainable Development
International Journal of Global Energy Issues

International Journal on Hydropower & Dams
Journal of Engineering for Gas Turbines and Power
Journal of Hydraulic Research
Journal of Hydroinformatics
Journal of Power and Energy
Journal of Solar Energy Engineering
Plant Engineering
Power
Power Engineer
Power Engineering
Power Engineering International

Handbooks

Handbooks: fundamentals

Agrawal, K. C., 2001. *Industrial power engineering and applications handbook.* London: Butterworth-Heinemann.

Barber, A., 1996. *Pneumatic handbook.* London: Elsevier.

Elliott, T. C., *et al.*, eds., 1998. *Standard handbook of powerplant engineering.* London: McGraw-Hill.

Hanlon, P., 2001. *Compressor handbook.* London: McGraw-Hill Education.

Hehn, A., 1993. *Plant engineering's fluid flow handbook: system applications and components.* Houston: Gulf Publishing.

Hehn, A., 1993. *Plant engineering's fluid flow handbook: system design, maintenance and troubleshooting.* Houston, Gulf Publishing.

Heitmann, H-G., 1993. *Handbook of power plant chemistry.* London: CRC Press.

Kohan, A. L., 1995. *Plant operations and services handbook.* London: McGraw-Hill Education.

Lamping, D. A., 1999. *Electrical power system reliability handbook: for industrial and commercial facilities.* London: McGraw-Hill Education.

Mobley, K., 2001. *Plant engineer's handbook.* London: McGraw-Hill Education.

Moffat, D. W., 1991. *Plant engineer's handbook of formulas, charts, and tables.* London: Prentice Hall.

Nayyar, M. L., and Ludewig, L., 1999. *Piping handbook.* London: McGraw-Hill Education.

Rosaler, R., 2001. *Standard handbook of plant engineering.* London: McGraw-Hill Education.

Rowe, D. M., ed., 1995. *Handbook of thermoelectrics.* London: CRC Press.

Snow, D. A., 1991. *Plant engineer's reference book.* London: Butterworth-Heinemann.

Thake, J., 2001. *Micro-hydro Pelton Turbine manual: design, manufacture and installation for small-scale hydro-power.* Colchester: ITDG Publishing.

Wallingford, H. R., and Barr, D. I. H., *Tables for the hydraulic design of pipes, sewers and channels.* London: Thomas Telford Ltd.

Handbooks: diesel technology

Baranescu, R. and Challen, B. J., 1999. *Diesel engine reference book.* Warrendale: Society of Automotive Engineers.
Bosch, 1999. *Diesel engine management.* Warrendale: Society of Automotive Engineers.
Lilly, L. R. C., ed., 1984. *Diesel engine reference book.* London: Butterworth.

Handbooks: facilities, maintenance

Gustin, J. F., 2001. *Facility manager's handbook.* New York: Marcel Dekker.
Higgins, L. R., and Mobley, K., 2001. *Maintenance engineering handbook.* London: McGraw-Hill Education.
Levitt, J., 1997. *Handbook of maintenance management.* New York: Industrial Press Inc.
Lewis, B. T., 1999. *Facility manager's operation and maintenance handbook.* London: McGraw-Hill Education.
Liska, R. W., 1992. *Handbook of building and plant maintenance forms and checklists.* London: Prentice Hall.

Handbooks: gas technology

Boyce, M. P., 2001. *Gas turbine engineering handbook.* London: Butterworth-Heinemann.
Segeler, C. G., 1965. *Gas engineer's handbook.* New York: Industrial Press Inc.
Soares, C., 2002. *Handbook of gas turbine: design, applications and operations.* London: McGraw-Hill Education.

Handbooks: heat exchanger

Hewitt, G. F., 1989. *Hemisphere handbook of heat exchanger design.* London: Taylor & Francis.
Kuppan, T., 2000. *Heat exchanger design handbook.* New York: Marcel Dekker.

Reference works

Chambers, A., and Kerr, S. D., 1996. *Power industry dictionary.* Tulsa: Pennwell Books.
Diesel and gas turbine worldwide catalog. New York: Diesel and Gas Turbine Publications.
Laplante, P., *CRC comprehensive dictionary of electrical engineering.* London: CRC Press.
Plant engineering directory and specification catalog. Massachusetts: Cahners Pub Co.
Webster, J. G., 1999. *Encyclopedia of electrical and electronics engineering.* 24 volumes, London: John Wiley & Sons.

Abstracts

Power Engineering Society abstracts
Ray, M. S., 1991. *Chemical process and plant design bibliography (1959–1989).* New York: William Andrew Inc.

Standards

National Electrical Manufacturers Association, www.nema.org.

Research

Electric Power Research Institute, www.epri.com

Professional organisations

Association for Facilities Engineering, www.afe.org
Association Française des Ingénieurs et Responsables de Maintenance, www.afim.asso.fr
Association of Energy Engineers, www.aeecenter.org
British Hydropower Association, www.brit-hydro.cwc.net
Electricity Association, www.electricity.org.uk
Institute of Power Engineers, www.nipe.ca
Institution of Chemical Engineers, www.icheme.org.uk
Institution of Plant Engineers, www.iplante.org.uk
International Association for Hydraulic Engineering and Research, www.iahr.org
International Hydropower Association, www.hydropower.org
Power Engineering Society, www.ieee.org/organizations/society/power
World Energy Council, www.worldenergy.org

Websites

www.gridwatch.com is a very useful, although US-biased, internet resource. It lists links to fuel, power and plant engineering associations, companies and other power engineering concerns.

▶ RAILWAY ENGINEERING

Where a railway engine is locomotive power directed by a pre-constructed track system, its literature necessarily includes consideration of ulterior engineering questions. Trolleys, trams and steam railways are covered in passing; model railway activities are not. Standards are covered adequately in the Mechanical Engineering section and Her Majesty's Railway Inspectorate operated by the Health & Safety Executive listed below. Identities of railway collections are listed if dedicated websites have been discovered; the Heritage Rail Association's website details all UK collections.

Texts

Bhattacharjee, P. K., and Basu, A. K., 1979. *Textbook of railway engineering.* Pune, Sangam Books.

Bonnett, C. F., 1996. *Practical railway engineering.* London: Imperial College Press.

Brebbia, C. A., 1999. *Structural integrity and passenger safety.* London: WIT Press.

Edwards, J. T., 1990, *Civil engineering for underground rail transport.* London: Butterworth-Heinemann.

Faith, N., 2000. *Derail: why trains crash.* Edinburgh: Boxtree.

Kylov, V., 2001. *Noise and vibrations from high speed trains.* London: Thomas Telford Ltd.

Leach, M., ed., 1991. *Railway control systems.* London: A & C Black.

Manual for railway engineering. 1992. Washington, DC: American Railway Engineering Association.

Murthy, T. K. S., et al., eds., 1987. *Computations in railway installations, track and signalling.* Southampton, WIT Press.

Popp, K., and Schiehlen, W., eds., 2002. *System dynamics and long-term behaviour of railway vehicles, track and subgrade.* London: Springer-Verlag.

Profillidis, V. A., 2000. *Railway engineering.* Aldershot: Ashgate Publishing Ltd.

Railway infrastructure – Railway Technology Conference. 2001. London: Professional Engineering Publications.

Railway rolling stock – Railway Technology Conference. 2001. London: Professional Engineering Publications.

Ross, J., ed., 2000. *Railway Stations: planning, design and management.* London: Architectural Press.

Track Technology. 1985. London: Thomas Telford Ltd.

Whitaker, J. C., 1999. *Signal measurement, analysis, and testing,* London: CRC Press.

Periodicals

American Railway Engineering Association Manual For Railway Engineering
Asia Pacific Rail
Cityrail International
European Railway Review
International Railway Journal
IRSE News
ITF News
ITF Railway
Japanese Railway Engineering
Japanese Railway Technology Today
Journal of Rail and Rapid Transit
Journal of Transport Geography
Modern Railways
Passenger Rail Management
Rail Bulletin
Rail Engineering International

Railway Age
Railway Gazette International
Railway Technology International
Tramways & Urban Transit
World Railway Equipment and Technology

Reference works

Allan, J., *et al.*, eds., 2002. *Computers in railways VIII*. Southampton: WIT Press.
Bushell, C., *Railway directory*. London: Reed Information Services.
Jackson, A. A., 1996. *Railway dictionary: an A-Z of railway terminology*. Stroud: Sutton Publishing.
Jane's world railways. Annual series, London: Jane's Information Services.
Lewis, R. G., 1984. *Railway Age's comprehensive railroad dictionary*. Omaha: Simmons Boardman Publishing Co.
Pinkney, M., 1999. *Spon's railway construction price book*. London: Spon Press.
UK marketing presentations – Rail & light rail investment profiles. 2000. London: MSI Marketing Research for Industry.
UK reports – Rail & light rail: UK. 2000. London: MSI Marketing Research for Industry.

Legislation and government

British Railways Board, www.brb.gov.uk
Her Majesty's Railway Inspectorate, www.hse.gov.uk/railway/rihome.htm
Office of Passenger Rail Franchising, www.opraf.cgov.uk
Office of the International Rail Regulator, www.rail-reg.gov.uk/oirrhome.htm
Office of the Rail Regulator, www.rail-reg.gov.uk/oirrhome.htm
Railway Heritage Committee, www.rhc.gov.uk
Railway Passengers Council, www.rail-reg.gov.uk/rucc
Railway Safety, www.railwaysafety.org.uk
Strategic Railway Authority, www.sra.gov.uk

Research

Advanced Railway Research Centre, www.shef.ac.uk/uni/academic/A-C/arrc
Institute of Railway Studies & Transport History, www2.york.ac.uk/inst/irs/
Railway Technical Research Institute, www.rtri.or.jp
Railway Technology Strategy Centre, www.rtsc.org.uk

Professional organisations

Association of Train Operating Companies, www.atoc.org
Confederation of Passenger Transport, www.cpt-uk.org

UK Heritage Railway Association, ukhrail.uel.ac.uk

Institution of Railway Signal Engineers, www.irse.org

International Union of Railways, www.uic.asso.fr

Light Rail Transit Association, www.irta.org

Locomotive and Carriage Institution, www.lococarriage.org.uk

Rail Freight Group, www.rfg.org.uk

Rail Industry Training Council (RITC) Ltd, www.ritc.org.uk

Railway Forum, www.railwayforum.com

Railway Heritage Trust, PO Box 686, Melton House, 65/67 Clarendon Road, Watford
     WD17 1XZ.

Railway Industry Association, www.riagb.org.uk

Union of European Railway Industries, www.unife.org

Wagon Building & Repair Association, 48 Clifford Road, Poynton SK12 1HY.

Commercial companies

Commercial companies: UK operators

Anglia Railways, www.angliarailways.co.uk

C2C Rail Ltd (National Express Group London Lines), www.c2c-online.co.uk

Central Trains Ltd, www.centraltrains.co.uk

Chiltern Railway Co Ltd, www.chilternrailways.co.uk

Docklands Light Railway Ltd, www.tfl.gov.uk/dlr

Eurotunnel, www.eurotunnel.com

First Great Eastern (Great Eastern Railway Ltd), www.ger.co.uk

First Great Western (Great Western Trains Company Ltd), www.gwt.co.uk

First North Western (North Western Trains Company Ltd),
     www.firstnorthwestern.co.uk

Gatwick Express Ltd, www.gatwickexpress.co.uk

Great North Eastern Railway Ltd, www.gner.co.uk

Heathrow Express, www.heathrowexpress.co.uk

Hull Trains Ltd, www.hulltrains.co.uk

London Underground Ltd, www.thetube.com

Midland Main Line Ltd, www.midlandmainline.com

Network Rail, www.networkrail.com

Railtrack, www.railtrack.co.uk

ScotRail Railways Ltd, www.scotrail.co.uk

Silverlink Train Services Ltd (National Express Group London Lines), www.silverlink-
     trains.com

Virgin Trains, www.virgintrains.co.uk

Wales & Borders Trains Ltd, www.walesandborderstrains.co.uk

Wessex Trains Ltd, www.wessextrains.co.uk

West Anglia Great Northern Railway Ltd (National Express Group London Lines),
     www.wagn.co.uk

Commercial companies: UK infrastructure

Adtranz, DaimlerChrysler Rail System (UK) Ltd www.adtranz.com
AEA Technology Rail, www.aeat.com/rail
Alstom Railcare Ltd, www.transport.alstom.com
Balfour Beatty Railtrack Systems Ltd, www.bbrail.com
Bombardier Transportation UK Ltd, www.transport.bombardier.com
Carillion Rail, www.carillionplc.com
Corus Rail Consultancy, www.corusrailconsultancy.com
First Engineering Ltd, www.firstengineering.co.uk
GB Railways Group plc, www.gbrailways.com
Interfleet Technology Ltd, www.interfleet-technology.com
Invensys Rail Systems, www.invensysrail.com
Jarvis Rail, www.jarvisplc.com
Marconi Transportation, www.marconi.com/html/products/transportation.htm
National Railway Supplies Ltd, www.natrail.com

Pressure and single issue groups

Association for Commuter Transport, www.act-uk.com
Central Rail Users' Consultative Committee, First Floor, Golden Cross House,
    Duncannon Street, London WC2N 4JF.

Collections

Bowes Railway, www.bowesrailway.co.uk
Darlington Railway Centre and Museum, www.drcm.org.uk
Didcot Railway Centre, www.didcotrailwaycentre.org.uk
Mangapps Railway Museum, www.mangapps.org.uk
Museum of Rail Travel, www.vintagecarriagetrust.org
National Gauge Railway Museum, www.talyllyn.co.uk/ngrm
National Railway Museum, www.nrm.org.uk
National Tramway Museum, www.tramway.co.uk
Steam, Museum of the Great Western Railway, www.steam-museum.org.uk
Timothy Hackworth Victorian & Railway Museum, www.hackworthmuseum.co.uk
Vintage Trains, Vintage Trains Society, www.vintagetrains.co.uk

Websites

www.icivilengineer.com/Transportation_Engineering/Railway_Engineering gives a global
    view of the rail transport industry.
www.railwaydirectory.net provides information on the railway industry.
www.railway-technology.com claims to be a comprehensive resource to the rail
    industry.

► SELECTED WEBSITES

dart.stanford.edu/vlme sponsored by Stanford University, may not be as comprehensive as other lists but provides descriptions of aggregate websites referred to.

library.louisville.edu/library/kersey/org/mechanical.html gives the engineering resource library of University of Louisville, Kentucky.

www.analytics.co.uk/other_st.htm, organised by Austin Analytics, offers a full resource for those interested in public transport.

www.brainstorm.co.uk/TANC/Directory/ claims to be the web's most comprehensive directory of UK trade associations.

www.feani.org/UnitedKingdom.html is the website of the European Federation of National Engineering Associations and consequently gives a national overview of other useful websites and contacts.

www.nahste.ac.uk/corp/a/ sponsored by the University of Edinburgh, contains navigational aids for the history of science, technology and the environment.

www.parker.com/inphorminfo/Links/Societies.htm is Parker Hannifin Corporation's very useful resource mine.

► REFERENCES

James, M. N., 1998. Engineering materialism and structural integrity. *Journal of Engineering Design* 9(4), pp. 329–342.

24 Mining and Mineral Process Engineering

Tim Shaw

▶ INTRODUCTION

Mining is here defined as the recovery of minerals and hydrocarbons from the earth's crust for the benefit of mankind. As such it can claim to be probably the oldest profession, certainly the oldest engineering profession. It predates farming (as opposed to hunting and gathering) by millennia and it is arguable that one of the distinguishing features of the human species is the use of mining to recover the materials required to ensure humanity's comfort and survival. Mining then goes back to prehistory, to the start of human activity. Following this, the development of mankind has been chronicled by the attainment of skills to fashion tools first from flint, then from an alloy of copper and tin and subsequently from iron. The various ages of human history have thus been named after the dominant mined materials used, the stone age, the copper age, the bronze age, the Iron age, etc. Initially very few materials were mined, but over time the number has increased until now uses have been found for virtually all the elements in the periodic table and they are nearly all (other than the gases) recovered from mines. In addition, there is a large number of construction materials, industrial minerals, gemstones and fuels which are mined for themselves rather than for their contained elements. It can truly be said that there is currently nothing used by mankind which is not itself the product of a mine or did not require the products of mines for its production, transport and distribution. Mining is therefore an extremely broad discipline and covers a wide area of engineering. This chapter will, however, only deal with the mining of metals and industrial minerals.

Mining engineering as a discipline originally included mineral processing as a part of its body of knowledge. Ancient civilisations plus the Egyptians, Greeks and Romans accumulated substantial elementary knowledge of mineral resources and the mining and processing of ores in order to obtain base and precious metals, ceramics, glass, coloured pigments and gem stones. Several metals, for example gold, silver, tin, lead, copper and iron were extracted by direct smelting of ores but concentrates were also produced by manual sorting and selection of the minerals and by processes using water to separate minerals, methods which would be recognized today as gravity concentration. One of the earliest printed books *De re metallica* was written by Georgius Agricola (English translation; Hoover and Hoover, 1950) in 1556 who recorded and illustrated the practices of mining and mineral processing at that time in the Harz Mountains of Germany.

It is doubtful whether the knowledge base at that time could be considered truly a science, and both mining and mineral processing have been described much more recently as 'arts'. With such a long history mineral processing has obtained several synonyms including; mineral technology (recently), mineral dressing, ore dressing, beneficiation, mineral concentration and milling. The frequent use of water in mineral processing has led to the use of the term 'washing', still prevalent in the coal mining industry to describe coal preparation. In North America and elsewhere the mineral processing engineer may be known as a 'metallurgist' with reference to the part that mineral processing plays in the extraction of metals (Gilchrist, 1989) rather than the technology of forming, working and using metals.

The technology of both mining and mineral processing developed rapidly during the Industrial Revolution, particularly with mechanisation of the pumping of water from mines (Newcomen's first steam based engine was used to pump water from a mine), and mechanized mineral preparation replacing hand-sorting at coal mines which were called upon to provide fuel for the steam engines, coke for iron making, tar and domestic coal. During the first few decades of the twentieth century, significant advances in processing took place including the development of new separation processes such as froth flotation for the recovery of many base metals from their ores and cyanidation leaching of ores of gold and silver. Several legendary textbooks were printed during this period including Peele (1941), Richards and Locke (1940), Truscott (1923), Taggart (1927) and Gaudin (1939). Much of their content remains relevant and is certainly of interest but, clearly, a great many advances have taken place in the understanding and practice of mining and mineral processing since that time that were not included. Unfortunately, with the exception of Pryor (1965), it is only relatively recently that comprehensive textbooks have been printed to replace them.

Mineral process engineering is the recovery of product from mined materials, and is a multi-disciplinary subject requiring knowledge of geology, mineralogy, the properties of natural materials and material science, chemistry, process engineering and extractive metallurgy. The realisation of a mining project, including the mineral processing plant or mill, also requires that the engineer is familiar with the practices of mechanical, civil and electrical engineering. Thus, as perhaps with no other branch of engineering, it is likely that useful sources of information will often include textbooks and journals directed towards other engineering disciplines, especially chemical engineering.

Since the mineral industry is a large, basic wealth-creating activity which contributes significantly to the economies of most nations and dominates the economies of others, it is also necessary for the engineers within the industry to be closely concerned with finance, economics and business management.

Mining and mineral industry

Although several multinational mining companies exist with a wide range of mineral interests, clear divisions can be recognised within the mineral industry. The major divisions are between: (a) the production of metals, (b) the production of coal, (c) the production of construction aggregates and non-metalliferous industrial minerals, and (d) the production of gemstones. Interest in metals can be sub-divided into *(i)* iron ore and steel alloy metals, *(ii)* base metals, copper, lead. zinc, etc. *(iii)* precious metals, gold, and silver, *(iv)* aluminium, *(v)* nickel, and platinum group metals. This situation has promoted the publication of textbooks and journals catering for specific interests.

Organizational sources

There is a vast number of mining operations worldwide and the majority of them are privately owned. Even where there has been state ownership there is a move towards privatisation in most countries. However, mining tends to be dominated by a number of very large multinational organizations which own operations in a large number of countries. The mining companies can be researched in a number of publications particularly in the yearbooks which list all the most important mining organizations. The *Financial Times Business Global Mining Directory 2002* (ISBN: 1 904005 01 2) is an excellent source of information.

However, in these days of the internet the main resource of this nature is a number of sources on the web, and most of those listed here have links to the websites of the companies included in their directories. A good starting point when looking for a particular mining company is the Goldsheet Mining Directory at: www.goldsheetlinks.com. The Chamber of Mines of South Africa has another Mining Directory claiming to be 'the world's largest repository of mining and minerals related information on the internet' at: www.bullion.org.za/Level2/MinDirectory.htm. Then the US Department of Labour runs a web page titled A Directory for the Mining Industry at: www.msha.gov/MINELINK/MINELINK.HTM. All of these are valuable additions to the printed directories and will probably replace them.

In general there is remarkably free exchange of technical information within the mineral industry. The paucity of modern textbooks is compensated for by verbal exchange of information, meetings of institutions and societies and symposia and conferences. The journals, in particular, assume great importance as sources of information upon current practice and new developments. However, the aluminium, nickel, platinum and gemstone, especially diamond, industries tend to be vertically integrated from mining through processing to marketing of the finished product, and technical information is often confidential and difficult to obtain.

There are, therefore, also specialist directories for many sectors of the mining industry. Notable among these are *The Industrial Minerals Directory 2000* (Metal Bulletin Books) which covers all industrial minerals, and other more local publications such as *Spon's Quarry Guide*, 1990 (ISBN 0419167102), which lists all the quarries in the UK. There is also a wide range of publications dealing with coal but they are not covered in this chapter as they have already been dealt with elsewhere.

In the USA the major mining companies joined together to form a lobbying organisation based in Washington, the National Mining Association. The National Mining Association was formed as the result of the 1995 merger of the National Coal Association (NCA) and the American Mining Congress (AMC). While NMA is a relatively new organization in its current configuration, its predecessor organizations have a long history and tradition of representing the various segments of the mining industry. NCA was founded in 1917 and AMC in 1897. This organisation holds regular meetings, publishes a number of booklets which demonstrate the importance of mining and minerals to the USA and now publishes a weekly e.journal, *Mining Week*, at: www.nma.org/newsroom/miningweek/miningweek.asp

The governmental organisation associated with mining was the United States Bureau of Mines (USBM). However, this has now been disbanded and the United States Geological Survey is now responsible for much of the publication work that was done by the USBM. The USBM had been responsible for a vast amount of mining related research and published three regular series of research monographs. There is the Bureau of Mines Information Circular series of which there have been close to 10,000 produced. Secondly, there is the Bureau of Mines Report on Investigations of which again some 10,000 have been issued. The USBM now the USGS produces a regular *United States Department of the Interior; United States Geological Survey; minerals yearbook* (annual). This is now available on the web at: minerals.usgs.gov/minerals/pubs/myb.html. This deals with the production and statistics of the various mineral commodities, commodity by commodity. They also issue for each commodity a regular Mineral Commodity Profile which deals with the sources, producers, uses and statistics of the commodity concerned.

In the UK the mining companies have formed a number of industrial organizations, the ABMEC the Association of British Mining Equipment Companies at: www.abmec.org.uk and the Quarry Products Association at: www.qpa.org/home.htm. On the research side there is the Mining Industry Research Organization at: www.miro.co.uk. None of these organizations issues regular journals or publications in the public domain. In South Africa, the majority of the mining companies are members of the Chamber of Mines of South Africa at: www.bullion.org.za/welkome.htm. The Chamber of Mines reports regularly on the industry and publishes a *Chamber of Mines Newsletter* (bi-monthly). This organization also runs a research operation for mining and publishes research reports and a regular *COMRO Bulletin* giving news of research results. It also produces an annual report which contains a detailed statistical summary of the operations of the major gold, coal and uranium mines in South Africa. The Chamber of Mines also deals with safety matters and until 1992 published a monthly safety magazine, *The Reef.*

Professional societies

Mining is served by a large variety of professional societies. In the UK there were three which dealt directly with the mining industry. Two of these have now merged with the Institute of Materials into one large institution, the Institute of Materials, Minerals and Mining (IOM³), 1 Carlton House Terrace, London, SW1Y 5DB, UK at: www.iom3.org/index.htm. There is also an institute solely for the quarry industry, Institute of Quarrying (IQ) based in Nottingham. The IOM³ has a royal charter and is recognised by the Engineering Council as an institute able to grant chartered engineering status to its members. The Institute of Quarrying has not yet achieved that status. Each of these institutes publishes journals of one kind or another. The IOM³ publishes its *Transactions of the Institution of Mining and Metallurgy* (1892–) in three sections, *Section A – Mining Technology, Section B – Applied Earth Science* and *Section C – Mineral Processing and Extractive Metallurgy,* each of which is published three times each year. In addition it publishes a regular bi-monthly journal which contains news of the Institute activities and short technical contributions titled *Materials World.* The *Transactions* are fully refereed journals. Finally, the IOM³ runs an abstracting service which it markets both as a computer-based service called IMMAGE, currently available on CDROM and directly by modem connection, available at: www.imm.org.uk/esales/iindex.htm. This is probably the best computer abstracting service available to the industry as the vast majority of the abstracted material is also available in hard-copy from the IOM³. The IOM³ also runs a continuing series of conferences and publishes the proceedings of those conferences. Finally the IOM³ commissions books on various mining engineering topics and publishes these. The

Institute of Quarrying (IQ) (www.quarrying.org/iq/index.htm) publishes its activities in *Quarry Management* (QMJ Publishing Ltd.) (www.qmj.co.uk/qm/) monthly and also stocks a number of important quarrying texts. The organisation also runs regular conferences, but the proceedings are not always published.

There are equivalent institutions in all of the other countries of the English-speaking world. The Australasian Institute of Mining and Metallurgy (AusIMM) (www.ausimm.com.au), the Canadian Institute of Mining, Metallurgy and Petroleum (CIM) (www.cim.org/index2.html) and the South African Institute of Mining and Metallurgy (SAIMM) (www. saimm.co.za/index.html), are all similar in style to the IOM[3] and all publish transactions. The Australasian Institute publishes both *AusIMM Bulletin* (1983–) 6 per annum, and until recently *The AusIMM Proceedings* (1983–2003) biannually. However the *Proceedings* has just merged with the *Transactions of the Institution of Mining and Metallurgy* of the IOM[3]. The Canadian Institute publishes the *CIM Bulletin* monthly, and the South African Institute *The Journal of the SAIMM* (1984-) monthly. In South Africa there is also the Association of Mine Managers of South Africa. This organization prints the papers delivered at its meetings on a regular basis as *AMM Circulars*. On a biannual basis these papers are published in book form as the *Association of Mine Managers of South Africa – Papers and Discussions*. Normally each volume covers the previous two years papers and discussions.

In the USA there is the Society for Mining, Metallurgy and Exploration Inc. (SME) (www.smenet.org) which is an independent institution but is associated with and a part of the American Institute of Mining, Metallurgical and Petroleum Engineers (AIME) (www.aimehq.org). The SME publishes its proceedings in a monthly journal called *Mining Engineering* (1949-). This journal is a mix between a professional journal and a monthly magazine, but does publish refereed papers. The SME also commissions and publishes an extensive list of books with the result that many of the standard texts in mining are the publications of the SME. The book list of the SME, as for the IMM, also includes a large number of conference proceedings.

In the European Union there is Euromines, the European Association of Mining industries (www.euromines.org). There is also the Society of Mining Professors/Societät der Bergbaukunde (www.mineprofs.org/mineprofstart.htm), currently with its secretarial office in London at the Royal School of Mines, which has a largely European membership at present and deals mainly with the European Mining industry. The Society is associated with the journal *Mineral Resources Engineering* which has gone out of publication in 2003, but which is due to restart publication in 2004.

There are also specialized, usually international. institutions and societies dealing with various aspects of mining. The International Society for Rock Mechanics (www-ext.lnec.pt/ISRM/) which is associated with the

International Journal of Rock Mechanics and Mining Sciences (www.elsevier.nl/inca/publications/store/2/5/6/) and the International Society of Ventilation Engineers are probably two of the most important such associations.

Research centres

A number of research centres exist that are funded by national, federal or local government (to conduct research and development in the fields of mining and mineral processing in order to support an important wealth creating or export industry). These include:

Commonwealth Scientific and Industrial Research Organisation (CSIRO), Division of
   Mineral Process Engineering, Australia (www.csiro.au).
Council for Mineral Technology (MINTEK) Johannesburg, South Africa
   (www.mintek.ac.za).
Canadian Centre for Minerals and Energy Technology (CANMET), Ontario Research
   Foundation, Canada (www.nrcan.gc.ca/mms/hm_e.htm).
Bureau de Recherche, Geololiques et Minieres (BRGM), France (www.brgm.fr).
Institute of Geology and Mineral Exploration (IOME), Greece.
   (www.igme.gr/enmain.htm).
Mineral Research and Exploration General Directorate, (Maden Tetkik ve Arama Genel
   Müdürlügü), Turkey (www.mta.gov.tr).
Centro de Investigacion Minera y Metalurgica, (CIMM), Chile (http://www.cimm.cl).

Much of the work of such organizations is published in journals and proceedings of conferences.

Commercial research laboratories

There are many commercial research laboratories, some of which have been or continue to be partly funded by government including, for example, AEA Technology (formerly WSL) (www.aeat.com). A well known research centre is attached to a university: the Julius Kritschnitt Mineral Research Centre (JKMRC), (www.jkmrc.uq.edu.au) University of Queensland, Australia.

A large number of fully commercial laboratories are located near the major mining fields in USA, Canada, Australia and South Africa, for example Lakefield Research, Ontario; Kilborn Engineering, Toronto and Mountain State, Colorado. Several major mining companies have established research laboratories which may also undertake external research, for example RTZ, Anglo-American, De Beers, Noranda and BHP-Billiton. However, the results of their research are not generally available.

Research organisations

Two organisations which exist to identify the research needs of the mineral industry and manage collaborative research projects between industrial partners and both commercial and university research laboratories are:

Mineral Industry Research Organisation (MIRO), UK (www.miro.co.uk).
Australian Mineral Industries Research Association (AMIRA) (www.amira.com.au).

Universities

While the universities containing departments of, say, Civil or Chemical Engineering, are too numerous to mention, relatively few contain departments teaching degrees in mining, minerals engineering or mineral processing. There are only some 250 such universities world wide and a list of them with their web addresses can be found on the website of the Society of Mining Professors at: www.mineprofs.org.

Documentary sources

Journals

There is a large number of periodicals and serials which deal with various aspects of mining. Many of these are commercial publications and these are supplemented by the publications of the wide variety of institutions and societies, a lot of which have been mentioned above.

In the UK there is the weekly publication *The Mining Journal* (1835–), Mining Journal Ltd, (www.mining-journal.com/index1.htm). This is a newspaper-style journal which reports on developments within the industry. This is probably the leading weekly mining newspaper in the world and is extensively read worldwide. A sister publication of *The Mining Journal* is the *Mining Magazine* (1909–), Mining Journal plc, monthly. This has articles in depth on various mining operations around the world as well as reporting on technological developments in the industry. In addition to the above, in the UK there are *World Mining Equipment* (1976–), (www.wme.com), and *Industrial Minerals* (1967–), Metal Bulletin, (www.mineralnet.co.uk/index.html) monthly. *Mine, Quarry & Recycling* (1924–), IML Group, monthly, is the official journal of the UK Minerals Engineering Society (www.mineralsengineering.org).

Mining is relatively poorly served for independent refereed journals. The main such journals are the transactions of the various institutions mentioned above. There are, however, good ones in the area of rock mechanics, notably *The International Journal of Rock Mechanics and Mining Sciences* (1964–). Pergamon, 7 per annum, and *Rock Mechanics and Rock Engineering* (1929–), Springer Verlag, quarterly, but otherwise there are few to serve the rest of the discipline. *Mineral Resources Engineering,* which is currently suspended but publication of which should restart in 2004, will partially fill the gap. There are also the publications of the smaller societies such as the *MVS Journal*, being the journal of the South African Mine Ventilation Society (1948–), (www.mvssa.co.za) which publishes mine environmental material.

In the USA, other than the journals previously mentioned published by the professional and industrial associations, the leading mining journal is *E&MJ (Engineering and Mining Journal,* (1866–), Primedia, (www. e-mj.com) monthly.

From other countries there are *Australia's Mining Monthly* (1980–), (www.miningmonthly.com) monthly, the *Canadian Mining Journal* (1879–), Southam Mining Group, (www.canadianminingjournal.com), bi-monthly, and *The Northern Miner* (1918–), Southam Mining Group, Canada's weekly mining newspaper with a daily on line service (www.northernminer.com). From South America, for example, there are the Chilean published magazines *Mineria Chilena, Latinomineria* and *Ingeniero Andina*, all published by Editec Ltda of Chile, (www.editec.cl), and from South Africa comes *African Mining* (1995–), Brook Pattrick Publications, (www.mining.co.za), bi-monthly.

Statistical sources

There is a large variety of statistical sources of information on the mining industry available. Both the *Engineering and Mining Journal (E&MJ)* and the *Mining Magazine* produce annual review issues which cover the developments in the mining industry during the preceding year and give statistics on the production of the various mineral commodities. In addition to these, there is a variety of mining yearbooks and annual reviews produced. Probably the most comprehensive, although it normally appears about two to three years after the period it is covering, is the *United States Department of the Interior; United States Geological Survey; Minerals Yearbook* (USGPO). These are usually in three volumes and cover the mining and minerals industry of the world, commodity by commodity. They give greatest prominence to the US industry but do cover it all. They are now available on line at: minerals.usgs.gov/minerals/pubs/myb.html. The *Mining Annual Review* (Mining Journal) is another good review of the world's mining industry. There is also the *World Mineral Statistics* (British Geological Survey) some two years in arrears available at: www.bgs.ac.uk/mineralsuk/statistics/world/home.html. Most countries and particularly countries with a significant mining industry produce annual statistics of their mineral production. Thus there are the *United Kingdom minerals yearbook* (British Geological Survey, www.statistics.gov.uk/statbase/

Product.asp?vlnk=1142&More=N), *Canadian minerals yearbook* (Minerals and Metals Sector (MMS) of Natural Resources Canada, (www.nrcan.gc.ca/mms/cmy/pref_e.htm) and *Minerals South Africa; Statistical Tables* (South African Department of Minerals and Energy).

Conferences

The mining industry is very well served for conferences. The most important body of the mining literature is probably the volumes of the proceedings of the various conferences held. Certainly, there is more new material published at conferences than anywhere else. There are two major international general mining conferences. The World Mining Congress is held every two years and involves mining engineers from the entire world. The proceedings are published by the organising country. The other is the Council of Mining and Metallurgical Institutions conferences. These are held once every four years in countries which are, or were, members of the British Commonwealth and are major mining countries. The proceedings of these conferences are published by the host organization and include papers on most mining engineering topics.

Then there are specific conferences for various aspects of the mining discipline. For example, there are the APCOMs (The Application of Computers and Operations Research in the Minerals Industry). These are held about every eighteen months and alternately in the USA/Canada and in a country outside the North American continent. Again, the proceedings which are state of the art in the use of computing in mining, are published by the organisation hosting the particular conference,

As stated, the proceedings of these and other conferences form a very important part of the body of the literature in the field of mining engineering.

Conferences covering other areas of mining such as:

Mine Ventilation Conferences, e.g. *Proceedings of the 6th International Mine Ventilation Congress, R. V. Ramani (ed.), SME, Littleton, Colorado, 1997*; Proceedings of the 7th International Ventilation Congress. *S. Wasilewski (ed.). Electrical & Engineering and Automation in Mining (EMAG), June 17–22, 2001, Cracow, Poland; Proc. of the North American/ Ninth U.S. Mine Ventilation Symposium (Kingston, Canada), E. De Souza (Editor), Ashgate Pub Co, 2002*

Surface Mining Conferences, e.g. *Continuous Surface Mining, Proceedings of the 6th. International Symposium Continuous Surface Mining, Bergakademie Freiberg, 2001*

Rock Mechanics conferences, e.g. *9th International congress on rock mechanics – Proceedings; Vouille, G. / Berest, P. (eds / Comptes-rendus), Berichte, Paris, France, 1999*, and many more proceedings can be found at the website of the International Society for Rock Mechanics at: balkema.ima.nl/Scripts/cgiBalkema.exe/society?SctNo=8.

Abstracting and indexing services

As indicated in a previous section, the most important abstracting service in the field of mining and mineral process engineering is that run by the IOM[3], which offers a regular bi-monthly volume of abstracts and also offers the abstracts on the IMMAGE database for computers. This can be accessed online at: www.eins.org or can be purchased on CDROMs. IMMAGE (Information on Mining, Metallurgy and Geological Exploration) covers economic geology, mining and extraction technology and developments in the non-ferrous metals and industrial mineral fields. Also included are mineral economics and management, health and safety, environmental aspects, tunneling and underground excavation, including rock mechanics, instrumentation and automation. The geographic scope is worldwide. IMMAGE corresponds to the printed publication *IMM Abstracts*. Sources include journal articles, books and conference proceedings, collected from around the world, often by special arrangement with the publisher or originating authority.

The *Mining Journal* also runs a computer-based information service.

The Web

There is of course a number of resources on the web. First stop should always be one of the search engines such as Google or Lycos.

However, there are numerous specialist sites which contain information on mining and mineral process engineering. During the discussions of the journals and magazines mentioned above, the websites associated with them have been given, and all do of course have some information available on the web. But there are also web-only information sources for mining. Probably the most important one of these is InfoMine at: www.infomine.com which has a wide range of information raging from information on companies to a number of web-based, remote learning courses. Another is Mining Life at: www.mininglife.com. Both of these cover all aspects of mining and mineral processing. For an Australian oriented site there is MineBox at: www.minebox.com.au which though Australia-oriented does have a lot of general information on mining engineering as well. MineBox also provides a daily e-mail news service for those who want it.

Reference books, monographs and reports

Mining engineering is such a broad field that a large number of books exists in the general area. That said, there are areas of mining engineering which do not have a widely accepted text. The two best introductory texts in mining engineering are *Introductory Mining Engineering*, (Hartman and Mutmansky, 2002), and *An Introduction to Mining*, (Thomas, 1978).

The SME is the generally accepted source for the main general texts such as Cope and Rice (1992), Crickmer and Zegeer (1981), Hartman (1992), Hustrulid (1982), Kennedy (1990) and Stefanko (1983). For rock drilling there is a number of texts, many of them produced by the equipment manufacturers such as Atlas Copco (1982), Gardner-Denver (1976), Sandvik Coromant and Atlas Copco (1977a and 1977b), and Tamrock (annual). Other texts in this area include the works by the Australian Mineral Foundation listed under 'Blasting' below, and McGregor (1967).

Mining has a wide range of machinery specially designed for the purpose of mining. This machinery and equipment, especially that designed for use underground, is different from that used in any other discipline. There is no really modem text which covers the field of mining machinery but there have been conferences in this area. Probably the best modern source is Almgren *et al.* (1993) and there is also the *International Conference on Mining Machinery* (1979). Other sources of information in this area are Buchanan (1966), Bartholomae *et al.* (1983), which deals with machinery noise, Steele (1969), Manin (1982) and Stack (1982). As always there are also the materials supplied by the equipment manufacturers to consult as well.

In the area of blasting, the texts tend to be produced by the explosives manufacturers Atlas Powder Company (1987), Du Pont de Nemours & Co. (1977) and Nobel's Explosives Co. Ltd. (1972), although much good work has been done in Australia as well in this area by the Australian Mineral Foundation (1977 and 1983). Other important aspects of blasting are covered in Bollinger (1980), Dowding (1985), Gustafsson (1973), Health and Safety Commission (1988), Hemphill (1981), Konya and Walter (1990) and Langefois and Kihlstrom (1978).

Mining does affect the environment and there is a number of texts on the effects of mining on the environment such as Down and Stocks (1977). There is even more available on the clearing up of the environment after mining as Anon (1987), Department of the Environment (1986, 1988 and various dates), Littler (1990a and 1990b) and RMC Group (1987). Mining does have its management, and this is covered in Sloan (1983) and National Coal Board (1979). There are the usual economic concerns and thus there is a branch of studies called Mineral Economics. Gentry and O'Neil (1984), Gocehr *et al.* (1989) and Storrar (1981) deal with various aspects of this topic.

Specialized topics

The following specialized topics have been chosen to show the wide range of subject areas covered by the mining engineering discipline.

Surface mining

The vast bulk of the mineral recovered by mining is recovered from surface mines, some seventy percent or more of all material mined. This includes the mining of metals, fuels such as coal and the industrial minerals and structural materials required by civil engineering and other sectors. Surface mining of coal has been covered elsewhere in this series.

For metal mining, the surface mining techniques are somewhat different and are described well in Hustrulid and Kuchta (1995), Kennedy (1990) and Gertsch and Bullock *et al.* (1998). Surface mining equipment is specialized equipment and can be researched in Rozgonyi and Golosinski (1988) and by using the material supplied by the various manufacturers such as Caterpillar Inc. (1999). Most of these mines use large off-highway haulage systems and these have been covered in the proceedings of a conference on off-highway haulage (Golosinski and Srajer, 1989).

Many surface mines recover material that is already loose, such as river gravels or beach sands. When this is done to recover a valuable metal such as tin or gold, it is called placer mining. These methods of mining are covered by Cope and Rice (1992) and Basque (1999). However, similar deposits are worked for the sand and gravel themselves to provide building materials, and the methods used are treated in Department of the Environment (1988), Littler (1990a and 1990b) and Barksdale (1993).

Underground mining

Underground mining methods are very different from those used on the surface and form a study in themselves. The first major difference is of course access, which has to be through tunnels or shafts, and will be through shafts for all the deeper operations. The sinking of shafts is a study in itself and the various aspects of shaft sinking and operations can be referenced firstly through the Institution of Mining and Metallurgy (1989), Lutgendorf (1986), Bennen *et al.* (1985) and Health and Safely Executive (1985).

Mining engineers distinguish between rock which can be cut by heavy duty cutting machinery which is called 'soft rock', a typical example of which is coal, and rock which needs to be drilled and blasted, or 'hard rock', which is the type of rock usually mined in the recovery of metals. The mining methods for the two types of rock differ mostly in the kinds of equipment which can be used, which has an effect on the layout of the mines. For the machinery used in underground mines the material produced by the equipment manufacturers is again a good source, most of this is now best found on the web, such as Atlas Copco (www.atlascopco.com) and Tamrock (www.smc.sandvik.com).

For the mining methods used in hard rock mining there are a few good references such as Hustrulid (1982, 2001), Sturgul (2000) and Stewart (1981). Soft rock mining is mainly for coal, although other materials such as potash and salt are mined by these methods. This type of mining has been covered to an extent in another book under solid fuels, but in the context of these mining methods, texts worth consulting are Crickmer and Zeeger (1981) and Stefanko (1983).

Rock mechanics

The engineering material with which mining engineers work and in which they design their structures is rock. Rock is a non-homogeneous material, and in addition the engineer is constrained to work with the rock as it is found and is not able to design the material to its purpose. It is therefore important for the mining engineer to have a fundamental understanding of the behaviour of the material with which he will work, and this is rock mechanics. Over the last four decades a great deal has been learned in this area and some understanding of rock behaviour under varying stress conditions is now available. However, this remains one of the main areas of further research in the mining discipline. A good introductory text is Goodman (1988). For more advanced studies in rock mechanics consult Brady and Brown (1993), Franklin and Dusseault (1989), Hoek and Brown (1980), Hoek *et al.* (2000), Hudson (1989, 1992), Hudson and Harrison (2000) and Whitaker and Frith (1987).

The stability of the slopes in open pit mining is a critical factor in the design of these mines. It is critical both for the safety of the operation and for the optimization of the extraction of the ore through the minimization of the waste mined with it. Good texts for this area of rock mechanics are Hoek and Bray (1981) and Hustrulid *et al.* (2001).

The interaction of the openings with the rock and with the pre-existing stress field within which the opening has been cut is a very complex interaction. A variety of mathematical models has been, and is being, developed to help in the analysis of these interactions. Finite element, boundary elements and other mathematical and numerical techniques are used in the development of these models. The use of these methods in rock mechanics is covered by Panik *et al.* (1990).

Other texts of interest to the study of rock mechanics deal with some of the techniques used. See Price and Cosgrove (1990) and Priest (1985). As mentioned, there is a number of conferences held in this area and the proceedings of these conferences form a major portion of the literature. The subject of support systems for underground openings is covered in the general texts mentioned above, but the latest developments can also be gleaned from Kaiser and McCreath (1992) and Hoek *et al.* (2000).

Ventilation

The maintenance of an environment which is suitable for the workforce in an underground mine is of critical importance. This has been traditionally called ventilation but with the steady increase of concern, not just for the air within the mine, but also for the other working conditions such as light, sound, etc., the discipline has extended to become more broad and is called Mine Environmental Engineering. There is a number of texts which deal with all aspects of airflow in mines and the control of contaminants in that airflow. These topics are covered in Bossard (1983), Hall (1981), Hartman *et al.* (1997), Mine Ventilation Society of South Africa (1982), Misra (1989), National Coal Board (1978), Panigrahi (2001) and Sengupta (1987).

In addition to these more general texts there are numerous specific aspects of the ventilation of mines which tend to have their own texts. Thus, the drainage of methane in coal mining operations is comprehensively dealt with in Diamond (1994). The movement of the air in mines is controlled by the installation of fans and this information on fans is very important. A good text in this area is Fan Manufacturers' Association (1981). Owen and Pankhurst (1977) deals with the techniques and equipment for the measurement of airflow in mines in detail. Radchenko (1976) on the other hand covers the problem of dust, and the use of ventilation to assist in the elimination of dust in underground mines. Saxton (1986–1987) is an historical text which covers the history of ventilation in coal mines over the last 400 years or so.

Also in the area of ventilation due to many of the hazards associated with mining, and particularly with coal mining, as a result of the pick-up of gas by the mine air, it is now required that there be constant monitoring of gas levels in mines. This problem leads on to the general area of safety in mines and the need to plan for rescue should an accident happen. These aspects of mining are dealt with in Karmis (2001).

As mentioned previously there is a number of international and national Mine Ventilation Congresses held regularly. The proceedings of these are the best source of the most up-to-date thinking in the area of mine ventilation. However, in addition to these general conferences there are other congresses which cover specific topics in the area such the *First International Conference on Radiation Hazards in Mining*, edited by Gomez (1981).

Mineral Process Engineering

In essence, mineral process engineering encompasses *(i)* the mineralogical appraisal of an ore; *(ii)* the design of a process flowsheet to separate the valuable mineral by appropriate combination of unit processes; *(iii)* selection and specification of equipment within the flow-sheet; and *(iv)* commissioning, operation and control of the process plant. However, it may also extend to the supervision of construction and the transport and marketing of mineral concentrates or metals. Regrettably, few complete accounts or case histories have been published and none recently, but see Abu Rashid and Smith (1982), and Lewis and Martin (1983).

By its very nature, the mineral industry is often associated with large areas of land use and the general public will be concerned that the impact upon the environment is reduced to a minimum. Therefore it is most probable that mineral processing engineers will need to consider the environmental aspects of any process at the design stage and be familiar with technologies such as water treatment, gas cleaning and dust collection/suppression.

A notable feature of the mineral industry is the generation of waste mineral, gangue or tailings, which usually greatly exceeds the quantity of concentrate produced. The selection and design of an appropriate, safe and environmentally acceptable method of disposal in tips or tailings dams is an exercise in civil engineering for which the mineral processing engineer must accept some responsibility.

Finally, it is not uncommon for the plant manager to be responsible for the restoration and revegetation of abandoned mine workings and waste tips, a requirement of law in many countries. Some knowledge of techniques employed in agriculture and forestry is, therefore, useful.

The principal list processes and subjects of relevance to mineral process engineering are: Mineralogy; Comminution; Sizing; Mineral separation; Process modeling, simulation and control; Solid-liquid separation; and Bulk materials handling.

Therefore, it can be appreciated that information sources will include publications intended for chemical engineers, and mechanical engineers, in particular Backhurst *et al.* (Coulson and Richardson) (2001).

Mineralogy

Gribble (1988) and Dana (1949) provide introductory information on the identification, composition, occurrence and properties of minerals. A more comprehensive text is also available: Klein and Hurlbut (1993). However, the web is now the best source and an excellent and comprehensive mineralogical website is at: www.webmineral.com.

Comminution

The theoretical and practical aspects of the design of process plant for crushing and grinding of mineral ores are discussed in JKMRC (2000), and Kawatra (1997). More specific information is provided by McQuiston and Shoemaker (1975) and Austin, *et al.* (1984). The design of crushing plant to produce aggregates is the subject of Mellor (1990). Additional information can be found in the relevant chapters of texts upon chemical engineering, for example Backhurst *et al.* (2001).

Sizing

An introduction to the concepts and measurement of particle size is given by Allen (1990). The selection and application of vibrating screens is the subject of a chapter in Mular *et al.* (2002). The hydrocyclone classifier is in widespread use in the mineral industry as a sizing device and is discussed by Svarovsky and Thew (1992).

Mineral Separation

Mineral separation processes can be categorized as physical or chemical processing. One very important process, however, does not fit easily into either category and that is froth flotation. Mular *et al.* (2002) discuss the design of the mineral separation section of the plant.

Physical Separation Processes

The process exploits differences of physical properties, e.g. density, magnetism and electrical conductivity to separate the minerals. Separation on the basis of density includes processes known as dense-medium separation and gravity concentration. Gravity concentration processes, plant design and flowsheets are described in Burt and Mills (1984) and Honaker *et al.* (2003). Svoboda (1987) discusses magnetic methods of mineral separation and electrical separation is discussed by Inculet (1985).

Chemical Separation Processes

Also referred to as hydrometallurgy, these processes include leaching; solution purification by precipitation, solvent extraction or ion exchange; carbon adsorption for gold recovery, electro-winning and electro-refining. The most important applications are the production of alumina (aluminium), the recovery of gold by cyanidation and the leaching of copper and uranium from their ores.

The basic chemistry is discussed in Burkin (1966) and in American Cyanamid (1958). No single textbook has been devoted to the subject of hydrometallurgy, not even to the cyanidation of ores of gold and silver. However, much useful information can be obtained from collections of papers upon specific aspects of leaching practice. Examples are McQuiston and Shoemaker (1975) and Jergensen (1999).

Froth Flotation

There is probably more written upon froth flotation than any other aspect of mineral processing but, in part, this reflects the importance of the separation process to the modern industry. Most base metals, with the exception of tin and tungsten, and a significant proportion of precious metals are concentrated by froth flotation. In addition, it is applied to iron ores, coal and a wide variety of industrial minerals.

Although there has been substantial development, particularly of flotation reagents, and the size of flotation machines has increased dramatically in attempts to obtain economies of scale and energy consumption, the basic principles are unchanged. Therefore, many of the early texts remain useful and include Gaudin (1957), Sutherland and Wack (1955), and Glembotski *et al.* (1963). One of the most comprehensive reviews of the theory and application of flotation, undertaken to mark fifty years of industrial application of flotation, was edited by Fuerstenau (1962) and published by the SME. The conference held as a memorial to Professor Gaudin produced another important reference, Fuerstenau (1976). The most recent textbook with the title *Flotation* has been written by Crozier (1992) and the most recent important addition to the genre is Parekh and Miller (1999). An understanding of the surface chemistry of minerals and the function of flotation agents to alter the nature of this surface is fundamental to flotation. The science is discussed by Leja (1982). Discussion of flotation reagents constitutes a major part of Jones and Oblatt (1984) and Somasundaran and Moudgil (1987). Manser (1975) specifically reviewed the use of reagents for the flotation of silicate minerals.

Other than the introduction of specific reagents the most significant, recent development has been that of column flotation which is the subject of the textbook by Rubenstein (1995).

Solid-Liquid Separation

A comprehensive review has been given by Svarovsky (1992). Greater detail of the design procedures has been provided by Klimpel (1998). The subject is also dealt with in textbooks of chemical engineering by Backhurst *et al.* (Coulson and Richardson) (2001), and Perry and Green (1999).

Handbooks, data sources and directories

The most comprehensive, readily available data is Weiss (1985), and much useful data are also contained in Mular *et al.* (2002). On the web, Metso Minerals (www.metsominerals.com) a producer of much processing equipment can be assessed for information on the crushing, grinding, screening and handling equipment manufactured by that company. Pegson Ltd (www.bl-pegson.com) has a similar website where producers of crushed rock, sand and gravel can find assistance.

Manufacturers of flotation reagents, flocculants and other mining chemicals provide extensive technical literature of which American Cyanamid (1958) and Dow Chemical Co (1976) are well known and much used examples. Several compendia of mineral processing ftowsheets and accounts of operating experience provide useful comparative information for design purposes including Pickett (1978) and Woodcock (1980).

▶ REFERENCES

Abu Rashid, A. R., and Smith, M. R., 1982. *Development of a selective flocculation-froth flotation process to beneficiate a non-magnetic iron ore in Saudi Arabia. Proceedings of 14th International Mineral Processing Congress.* Toronto: CIM.

Agricola, G., 1556. *de re Metallica.* (Trans Hoover, H. C, and Hoover, L. H., 1912, 1989 ed. New York: Dover Publications).

Allen, T., 1990. *Particle size measurement.* 4th ed. London: Chapman and Hall.

Almgren, G. et al., eds., 1993. *Mine Mechanisation and Automation, Proceedings of the 2nd International Symposium on Mine Mechanisation and Automation.* Lulea, Sweden. 7–10 June 1993. Rotterdam; Balkema.

American Cyanamid Co., 1958. *Chemistry of cyanidation.* New York: American Cyanamid.

Ammen, C. W., 1997. *Recovery and Refining of Precious Metals.* 2nd ed. Kluwer Academic Publishers.

Anon, 1987. *A practical guide to restoration.* Egham: RMC Group.

Atlas Copco, 1982. *Atlas Copco manual.* 4th ed. Stockholm: Atlas Copco.

Atlas Powder Company, 1987. *Explosives and rock blasting.* Baltimore, MD: Atlas Power Co.

Austin, L. G., et al., 1984. *Process engineering and size reduction: ball milling.* Littleton, CO: SME/AIME.

Australian Mineral Foundation, 1977. *Drilling and blasting.* 2 vols, Sydney: AMF.

Australian Mineral Foundation, 1983. *Drilling arid blasting in open pits and quarries. Soft materials.* 2 vols. Sydney: AMF.

Backhurst, J. R., et al., 2001. *Coulson & Richardson's Chemical Engineering: Solutions to the Problems in Chemical Engineering (Coulson and Richardsons Chemical Engineering).* 3rd ed. New York: Butterworth-Heinemann.

Bandopadhyay, S., ed., 2002. *Application of Computers and Operations Research in the Mineral Industry: Proceedings of the 30th International Symposium.* Littleton, CO: SME/AIME.

Barksdale, R. D., ed., 1993. CD-ROM edition, *Aggregate Handbook.* National Stone Assn.

Bartholomae, R, C. et al., 1983. *Mining machinery noise control guidelines.* Washington, DC: USBM.

Basque, G., 1999. *Methods of Placer Mining.* Heritage House Pub Co Ltd.

Bennen, R. D., et al., 1985. *State-of-the-art construction technology for deep tunnels and shafts in rocks.* Technical Report WES/MP/ GL-BS-I. Vicksburg: US Amy Engineer Waterways Experimental Station.

Bise, C. J., 2003. *Mining Engineering Analysis.* 2nd ed. Littleton, CO: SME/AIME

Bollinger, G. A., 1980. *Blast vibration analysis.* Carbondale: Southern Illinois University Press.

Bossard, F., 1983. *Manual of mine ventilation design practices.* 2nd ed. Butte, MO: Floyd Bossard and Associates.

Brady, B. H. G., and Brown, E. T., 1993. *Rock Mechanics for Underground Mining.* 2nd ed. Chapman and Hall.

Buchanan, W., 1966. *Hydraulics applied to underground mining machinery.* London: Pitman.

Burkin, A. R., 1966. *The chemistry of hydrometallurgical processes.* London: Spon.

Burt, R. O., and Mills, C., 1984. *Gravity Concentration Technology (Developments in Mineral Processing, Vol. 5).* Netherlands: Elsevier Science.

Caterpillar Inc., 1999. *Caterpillar Performance Handbook.* 29th ed. Peoria, Illinois: Caterpillar Inc.

Cavender, B., 1999. *Mineral Production Costs: Analysis and Management.* Littleton, CO: SME/AIME.

Conveyor Equipment Manufacturers, ed., 1997. *Belt Conveyors for Bulk Materials.* 5th ed. Conveyor Equipment.

Cope, L. W, and Rice, L. R., eds., 1992. *Practical Placer Mining.* Littleton, CO: SME/AIME.

Crickmer, D. F., and Zegeer, D. A., eds., 1981. *Elements of practical Coal Mining.* Littleton, CO: SME/AIME.

Crozier, R. D., 1992. *Flotation.* Oxford: Pergamon.

Dana, E. S., 1949. *Minerals and how to study them.* 3rd ed. New York: Wiley.

Department of The Environment, 1986. *Landfilling wastes, Waste Management Paper No, 26.* London: HMSO.

Department of The Environment, 1988. *Marine dredging for sand and gravel.* London: HMSO.

Department of The Environment, 1991. *The control of landfill gas* rev. ed. Waste Management Paper No, 27, London: HMSO.

Department of The Environment, (various dates). *Minerals planning guidance.* London: HMSO.

De Souza, E., ed., 2002. *Mine Ventilation: Proceedings of the North American/Ninth US Mine Ventilation Symposium, Kingston, Canada, 8–12 June 2002.* Netherlands: A.A. Balkema.

Diamond, W. P., 1994. *Methane Control for Underground Coal Mines (Information Circular).* Pittsburgh, PA: U.S. Bureau of Mines.

Dow Chemical Co., 1976. *Flotation fundamentals and mining chemicals.* Midland, Dow Chemical Co.

Dowding, C. H., 1985. *Blast vibration monitoring and control.* New York: Prentice Hall.

Down, C. G., and Stocks, J., 1977. *Environmental impact of mining.* London: Applied Science.

Dravo Corporation, 1974. *Analysis of large-scale non-coal underground mining methods.* Springfield, VA: National Technical Information Service, sponsored by the US Bureau of Mines

Du Pont de Nemours & Co., 1977. *Blasters handbook.* 16th ed. Wilmington, DE: Du Pont de Nemours & Co.

Erlich, E. I., and Hausel, W. D., 2002. *Diamond Deposits: Origin, Exploration, and History of Discovery.* Littleton, CO: SME/AIME.

Fan Manufacturer's Association, 1981. *Fan application guide.* 2nd ed. Middlesex: Hevac Association Ltd.

Franklin, J. A., and Dusseault, M. B., 1989. *Rock engineering.* New York: McGraw Hill.

Fuerstenau, D. W., ed., 1962. *Froth flotation 50th anniversary volume.* Rocky Mountain Fund Series Littleton, CO: SME/AIME.

Fuerstenau, M. C., ed., 1976. *Flotation: A.M. Gaudin memorial volume.* 2 vols. Littleton, CO: SME/AIME.

Gardner-Denver, 1976. *Rock drilling data.* Sheffield: Gardner-Denver.

Gaudin, A. M., 1939. *Principles of mineral dressing.* New York: McGraw Hill.

Gaudin, A. M., 1957. *Flotation.* 2nd ed. New York: McGraw-Hill.

Gentry, D. W., and O'Neil, T. J., 1984. *Mine Investment Analysis.* Littleton,CO: SME/AIME.

Gertsch, R. E., and Bullock, R., eds., 1998. *Techniques in Underground Mining.* Littleton, CO: SME/AIME.

Gilchrist, J., 1989. *Extraction metallurgy.* 3rd ed. Oxford: Pergamon.

Glembotski, V. A., *et al.*, 1963. *Flotation* (Translated from Russian). New York: Primary Sources.

Goehr, W. R., *et al.,* 1989. *International mineral economics.* Berlin:Springer-Verlag.

Golosinski, T. S., and BOEHM, F.G., eds., 1987. *Continuous Surface Mining.* Clausthall-Zellerfeld: Trans Tech Publications.

Golosinski, T. S., and SRAJER, V., eds., 1989. *Off-Highway Haulage in Surface Mines.* Rotterdam/Brookfield: A.A. Balkema.

Golosinski, T. S., ed., 1995. *Proceedings, The AusIMM Underground Operators Conference.* Melbourne: The Australasian Institute of Mining and Metallurgy.

Golosinski, T. S., ed., 2000. *Mining in the New Millennium: Challenges and Opportunities,* Rotterdam/Brookfield: A.A. Balkema.

Gomez, M., ed., 1981. *First International Conference on Radiation Hazards in Mining: Control, Measurement and Medical Aspects.* New York: Society of Mining Engineers of AIME:

Goodman, R. E., 1988. *Introduction to rock mechanics.* 2nd ed. New York: Wiley.

Guo Yuguang and Golosinski, T. S., eds., 1996. *Mining Science and Technology '96.* Rotterdam/Brookfield: A A Balkema.

Gribble, C. D., 1988. *Rutley's elements of mineralogy.* 27th ed. London: Unwin Hyman.

Gustafsson, R., 1973. *Swedish blasting technique.* Gothenburg: SfJ.

Hall, C. J., 1981. *Mine ventilation engineering.* Littleton, CO: SME/AIME.

Han, K. N., 2002. *Fundamentals of Aqueous Metallurgy.* Littleton, CO: SME/AIME.

Hartman, H., and Mutmansky, J. M., 1998. *Introductory Mining Engineering.* 2nd ed. John Wiley & Sons.

Hartman, H., ed., 1992. *SME Mining Engineering Handbook.* 2nd ed. Littleton, CO: SME/AIME.

Hartman, H.L., *et al.*, 1997. *Mine Ventilation and Air Conditioning.* John Wiley & Sons.

Health and Safety Commission, 1988. *Explosives at quarries.* London: HMSO,

Health and Safety Executive, 1985. *Safe manriding in mines: supplement and corrigenda to the first and second reports of the National Commission for Safety of Manriding in Shafts and unwalkable Outlets.* London: HMSO.

Hemphill, G. B., 1981. *Blasting operations.* New York: McGraw.Hill.

Heping Xie and Golosinski, T. S., eds., 1999. *Mining Science and Technology ' 99.* Rotterdam/Brookfield: A.A. Balkema.

Hoek, E., 1980. *Underground excavations in rock.* London: Chapman and Hall.

Hoek, E., and Brown, E. T., 1980. *Underground excavations in rock.* London: IMM.

Hoek, E., and BRAY, J. W., 1981. *Rock slope engineering*. 3rd ed. London: E. & F. N. Spon.

Hoek, E., *et al.*, 2000. *Support of Underground Excavations in Hard Rock*. Rotterdam/Brookfield: A.A. Balkema.

Honaker, R.Q., *et al.*, eds., 2003. *Advances in Gravity Concentration*. Littleton, CO: SME/AIME.

Hoover, H. C., and Hoover, L. H., Trans., 1912, Agricola, G., 1556. *de re Metallica*. 1989 ed. New York: Dover Publications.

Hudson, J. A., 1989. *Rock mechanics principles in engineering practice*. London: Butterworths.

Hudson, J. A., 1992. *Rock engineering systems: theory & practice*. Chichester: Ellis Horwood.

Hudson, J. A., and Harrison, J. P., 2000. *Engineering Rock Mechanics*. Oxford: Pergamon Press.

Hudson, J. A., *et al.* eds., 1993.*Comprehensive rock engineering: principles, practice and projects*. Oxford: Pergamon.

Hudson, T. L., 1998. *Environmental Research Needs of Metal Mining*. Littleton, CO: SME/AIME.

Hustrulid, W. A., ed., 1982. *Underground Mining Methods Handbook*. Littleton, CO: SME/AIME.

Hustrulid, W. A., and Kuchta, M., 1995. *Open Pit Mine Planning and Design*. Rotterdam/Brookfield: A.A. Balkema.

Hustrulid, W. A., 1999. *Blasting Principles for Open Pit Mining*. Rotterdam/Brookfield: A.A. Balkema.

Hustrulid, W. A., *et al.*, eds., 2001. *Slope Stability in Surface Mining*. Littleton, CO: SME/AIME.

Hustrulid, W. A., and Bullock, R. L., eds., 2001. *Underground Mining Methods: Engineering Fundamentals and International Case Studies*. Littleton, CO: SME/AIME.

Inculet, I. I., 1985. *Electrostatic Mineral Separation (Electronic and Electrical Engineering Research Studies. Applications series, 5)*. Chichester: John Wiley & Sons.

Institution of Mining and Metallurgy, 1989. *Shaft engineering*. London: IMM.

Jergensen, II G. V., ed., 1999. *Copper Leaching, Solvent Extraction, and Electrowinning*. Littleton, CO: SME/AIME.

JKMRC, 2000. *Mineral Comminution Circuits, Their Operation and Optimisation*. Brisbane: Julius Kruttschnitt Mineral Research Centre.

Jones, M. J., and Oblatt, R., eds., 1984. *Reagents in the mineral industry*. London: IMM.

Kaiser, P. K., and McCreath, D., eds., 1992. *Rock Support in Mining and Underground Construction. International Symposium on Rock Support Proceedings*. Sudbury, Canada, 16–19 June, Rotterdam/Brookfield: Balkema.

Karmis, M., ed., 2001. *Mine Health and Safety Management*. Littleton, CO: SME/AIME.

Kawamoto, T., *et al.*, eds., 1993. *Assessment and Prevention of Failure Phenomena in Rock Engineering: Proceedings of the International Symposium on Assessment and Prevention of Failure Phenomena in Rock Engineering*. Rotterdam/Brookfield: Balkema.

Kawatra, S. K., ed., 1997. *Comminution Practices*. Littleton, CO: SME/AIME.

Kawatra, S. K., and Natarajan, K. A., eds., 2001. *Mineral Biotechnology: Microbial Aspects of Mineral Beneficiation, Metal Extraction, and Environmental Control.* Littleton, CO: SME/AIME.

Kennedy, B., ed., 1990. *Surface Mining.* 2nd ed. Littleton, CO: SME/AIME.

Klein, C., and Hurlbut, C., 1993. *Manual of mineralogy (after J. D. Dana).* 21st ed. New York: Wiley.

Kliche, C. A., ed., 1999. *Rock Slope Stability.* Littleton Co: SME/AIME.

Klimpel, R. R., 1998. *Introduction to Solid-Liquid Separation of fine particles.* Florida: NSF Engineering Research Center for Particle Science & Technology.

Klimpel, R. R., 1998. *Introduction to Solid-Solid Separation of Fine Particles by Physical Means.* Florida: NSF Engineering Research Center for Particle Science & Technology.

Klimpel, R. R., 1998. *Introduction to Solid-Solid Separation of Fine Particles by Froth Flotation.* Florida: NSF Engineering Research Center for Particle Science & Technology.

Kolsky, H., 1963. *Stress waves in solids.* New York: Dover.

Konya, C. J., and Walter, E. J., 1990. *Surface blast design.* Englewood Cliffs, NJ: Prentice Hall.

Langefois, U., and Kihlstrom, B., 1978. *Modern technique of rock blasting.* 3rd ed. New York: Wiley.

Leeser, R. C., 1996. *Engineer's Procurement Manual for Major Plant Equipment.* Upper Saddle River, NJ: Pearson Education.

Leja, J., 1982. *Surface chemistry of froth flotation.* New York: Plenum.

Lewis, P. J., and Martin, G. J., 1983. Mahd Al Dhabah gold silver deposit. Saudi Arabia: mineralogical, studies associated with metallurgical process evaluation. *Transactions. Institution of Mining and Metallurgy,* 92, 63–72.

Littler, A., 1990a. *Sand and gravel production.* Nottingham: Institute of Quarrying.

Littler, A., 1990b. *Sand and gravel planning and restoration.* Nottingham: Institute of Quarrying.

Lowrie, R. L., ed., 2002. *SME Mining Reference Handbook.* Littleton,CO: SME/AIME.

Lutgendorf, H. 0., 1986. 30 years of sliding shaft lining; a retrospect. *Gluckauf* 122, 310–316.

Manning, D. A. C., 1995. *Introduction to Industrial Minerals.* New York: Chapman and Hall.

McCarter, M. K., et al., eds., 2000. *Slope Stability in Surface Mining.* Littleton, CO: SME/AIME.

McGregor, K., 1967. *Drilling of rock.* London: C. R. Books.

McQuiston, F. W., and Shoemaker, R. S., 1975. *Gold and silver cyanidation plant practice.* Littleton, CO: SME/AIME.

McQuiston, F. W., and Shoemaker, R. S., 1978. *Primary crushing plant design.* Littleton, CO: SME/AIME.

Manser, R. M., 1975. *Handbook of silicate flotation.* Stevenage: Warren Spring Laboratory

Martin, J. W., 1982. *Surface mining equipment.* Golden, CO: Martin Consultants.

Mellor, S. H., 1990. *An introduction to crushing and screening.* Nottingham: Institute of Quarrying.

Mine Ventilation Society of South Africa, 1982. *Environmental engineering in South African mines.* Marshallown: Mine Ventilation Society of South Africa.

Misra, B., 1989. *Mine Environment and Ventilation,* India: OUP.

Mular, A. L., and Jergensen, G. V., 1982. *Design and installation of comminution circuits.* Littleton, CO: SME/AIME.

Mular, A. L., and Anderson, M. A., 1986. *Design and installation of concentration and dewatering circuits.* Littleton, CO: SME/AIME.

Mular, A. L., et al., 2002. *Mineral Processing Plant Design, Practice, and Control.* Littleton, CO: SME/AIME.

Myasnikov, A. A., and Patrushev, M. A., eds., 1983. *Principles of Coal Mine Ventilation Planning.* New Delhi: Amerind Publishing Co.

National Coal Board, 1978. *Ventilation in coal mines.* London: NCB, Mining Dept.

National Coal Board, 1979. *Work study in mines.* London: NCB, Mining Dept.

Nobel's Explosives Co., 1972., *Blasting practice.* 4th ed. Stevenson, Ayrshire: Nobel's Explosives Co.

Owen, E., and Pankhurst, R. C., 1977. *Measurement of air flow.* 5th ed. Oxford: Pergamon.

Panik, G. N., et al., 1990. *Numerical methods in rock mechanics.* Chichester: Wiley.

Panigrahi, D. C., ed., 2001. *Mine Environment and Ventilation.* Rotterdam/Brookfield: A.A. Balkema.

Parekh, B. K., and Miller, J. D., eds., 1999. *Advances in Flotation Technology.* Littleton, CO: SME/AIME.

Peele, R., 1941. *Mining Engineers' Handbook.* 3rd ed. New York: Wiley.

Perry, R., and Green, D. W., 1999. *Perry's Chemical Engineering Handbook.* New York: McGraw-Hill Osborne Media.

Petruk, W., ed., 1998. *Waste Characterization and Treatment.* Littleton, CO: SME/AIME.

Pickett, D. E., ed., 1978. *Milling practice in Canada.* Montreal: CIM.

Price, N. J., and Cosgrove, J. W., 1990. *Analysis at geological structures.* Cambridge: Cambridge University Press.

Priest, S. D., 1985. *Hemispherical projection methods in rock mechanics.* London: Allen & Unwin.

Primel, L., and Tourenq, C., eds., 2000. *Aggregates: Geology, Prospection, Environment, Testing Extraction, Specifications, Processing Plants Equipment, Quality.* Rotterdam/Brookfield: A.A. Balkema.

Pryor, E. J., 1965. *Mineral processing.* 3rd ed. Amsterdam: Elsevier.

Radchenko, G. A., 1976. *Ventilation for dust elimination in underground mines.* New Delhi: Amerind Publishing Co.

Ramani, R. V., ed., 1996. *Proceedings of the 26th International APCOM Symposium.* Littleton, CO: SME/AIME.

Ramani, R. V., ed., 1997. *Proceedings of the 6th International Mine Ventilation Symposium.* Littleton, CO: SME/AIME.

Richards, R. H., and Locke, C. E., 1940. *Textbook of ore dressing.* 3rd ed. New York: McGraw Hill.

RMC Group, 1987. *A practical guide to restoration.* Egham: RMC Group.

Rozgonyi, T. G., and Golosinski, T. S., eds., 1988. *Continuous Surface Mining: Equipment, operation and design.* Rotterdam/Brookfield: A.A. Balkema.

Rubinstein, J. B., 1995. *Column Flotation: Processes, Designs and Practices (Process Engineering for the Chemical, Metals and Minerals Industries, Vol 2).* London: Taylor & Francis.

Runge, I. C., 1998. *Mining Economics and Strategy.* Littleton, CO: SME/AIME.

Rustan, A., ed., 1998. *Rock Blasting Terms and Symbols.* Rotterdam/Brookfield: A.A. Balkema.

Sandvik Coromant and Atlas Copco, 1977a. *Rock drilling manual.* Sweden: Sandvik.

Sandvik Coromant and Atlas Copco, 1977b. *Rock drilling manual: Theory and technique.* Sweden: Sandvik.

Saxton, I., 1986–1987. *Coal mine ventilation from Agricola to the 1980s.* Published in serial form in *Mining Engineer.*

Sengupta, M., 1987. *Mine environmental engineering.* 2 vols. Boca Raton, FL.: CRC Press.

Sheorey, R., 1997. *Empirical Rock Failure Criteria.* Rotterdam/Brookfield: A.A. Balkema.

Shoemaker, R. S., 2002. *The Circulating Load: Practical Mineral Processing Plant Design by an Old-Time Ore Dresser.* Littleton, CO: SME/AIME.

Sloan, D. A., 1983. *Mine Management.* London: Chapman and Hall.

Somasundaran, P., and Moudgil, B. M., eds., 1987. *Reagents in Mineral Technology.* New York: Marcel Dekker.

Stack, B., 1982. *Handbook of mining and tunneling machinery.* Chichester: Wiley.

Steele, D. J., 1969. *Modern developments in mining machinery.* London: Virtue & Co.

Stefanko, R., ed., 1983. *Coal mining technology – theory and practice.* Littleton, CO: SME/AIME.

Stewart, D. R., ed., 1981. *Design and operation of caving and sublevel stoping mines.* Littleton, CO: SME/AIME.

Stocks, J. et al., 1979. *Mining and mineral processing.* Milton Keynes: Open University Press.

Stone, D., ed., 2001. *Minefill 2001: Proceedings of the 7th International Symposium on Mining with Backfill.* Littleton, CO: SME/AIME.

Storrar, C. D., ed., 1981. *South Africa mine valuation.* revised ed., Johannesburg: Chamber of Mines of South Africa.

Strang, L., and Mackenzie-Wood, P., 1987. *Manual of mines rescue, safety and gas detection.* 2nd ed., Golden, CO: Colorado School of Mines Press.

Sturgul, J. R., 2000. *Mine Design: Examples Using Simulation.* Littleton, CO: SME/AIME.

Sutherland, K. L., and Wack, L. W., 1955. *Principles of flotation.* Melbourne: AusIMM.

Svarovsky, L., and Thew, M. T., eds., 1992. *Hydrocyclones: Analysis and Applications (Fluid Mechanics and Its Applications, Vol 12).* New York: Kluwer Academic Publishers.

Svoboda, J., 1987. *Magnetic Methods for the Treatment of Minerals (Developments in Mineral Processing, No 8).* Netherlands: Elsevier Science Ltd.

Taggart, A. F., 1927. *Handbook of ore dressing.* New York: Wiley.

Tamrock, Annual. *Tamrock handbook of underground drilling.* Tampere: Tamrock.

Tamrock, Annual. *Tamrock handbook on surface drilling and blasting.* Tampere: Tamrock.

Thomas, L. J., 1978. *An Introduction to Mining.* Revised ed., Sydney: Methuen.

Tien, J. C., ed., 1999. *Proceedings of the 8th US Mine Ventilation Symposium.* Littleton, CO: SME/AIME.

Truscott, S. J., 1923. *Textbook of ore dressing.* London: Macmillan.

Van Zyl, *et al.*, eds., 1988. *Introduction to Evaluation, Design and Operation of Precious Metal Heap Leaching Projects.* Littleton, CO: SME/AIME.

Vogely, W. A., 1985. *Economics of the Mineral Industries.* Littleton, CO: SME/AIME.

Wala, A. M., ed., 1995. *Proceedings of the 7th US Mine Ventilation Symposium.* Littleton, CO: SME/AIME.

Walker, S. C., 1988. *Mine winding and transport.* Amsterdam: Elsevier.

Weiss, N. L., ed., 1985. *SME Mineral Processing Handbook.* Littleton, CO: SME/AIME.

Whittaker, B. N., and Frith, R. C., 1987. *Tunnelling: design, stability and construction.* IMM.

Woodcock, J. T., ed., 1980, Mining *and metallurgical practices in Australasia Monograph Series Volume 10.* Parkville: AusIMM.

Young, C., ed., 2000. *Minor Elements 2000: Processing and Environmental.* Littleton, CO: SME/AIME.

25 Nanotechnology

Andy Garland and Ottilia Saxl

▶ **INTRODUCTION**

Nanotechnology is rapidly moving to the forefront of the public consciousness – press coverage is on the increase, campaigners are calling for moratoriums and politicians are coming out in its defence. When many people think of nanotechnology, they think of exotic kinds of devices: nanomachines or medical applications in which tiny machines circulate in the bloodstream cleaning out fat deposits from our arteries. However, far from being a future technology, nanotechnology is already with us, and is not necessarily about manufacturing small things, but rather, making big things work better, with less waste. Novel textiles, sports equipment and cosmetics are already on the market based on advances in nanotechnology, as are CDs, air bag pressure sensors and inkjet printers.

Nanotechnology can perhaps be best defined as the ability to engineer new attributes through controlling features at a very small scale – at or around the scale of a nanometre. One nanometre is a *billionth* of a metre; or about 1/80,000 the width of a human hair. The use of materials at the 'nano' scale predates even the applications that are hitting the market now. Nanoparticles were used by the Romans to make glasses, and during the Renaissance period to make ceramic. However, although some elements were used in the past, it is the understanding of nanotechnology and how it can be used which is new. The nanoscale has become accessible both by application of new physical instruments and procedures and by further diminution of present microsystems.

Working at the nanometre level offers many opportunities for creating novel products; and any product, which possesses a characteristic, or attribute that involves some manipulation or measurement at or below 100 nanometres (or 0.1 of a micrometre), falls under the umbrella of nanotechnology. These include paints (with nanoparticles), medicines (coated drugs for targeted drug delivery), foodstuffs ('taste-burst' foods), clothing (stay-clean textiles with nano fibres), packaging (specially adapted polymers that prevent contamination and sense decay) and new materials for aerospace, automotive and construction applications (lightweight but tough, heat-resistant nanocomposites).

Nanotechnology unites the findings and processes from the living (biotechnology and genetic engineering) and 'non-living' worlds (chemistry, electronics, materials processing) with the unlimited potential to manufacture cost-effective, innovative products. It is likely that almost any product you care to think of within the next decade (or less!) will have some nanometre feature, and to quote one US source, in ten to fifteen years, $1trillion in products worldwide will be affected by nanotechnology.

► RESOURCES IN NANOTECHNOLOGY

New and potentially disruptive technologies always generate a huge amount of debate and hype, and it is often difficult to separate the fact from the fiction. This is a particular problem with nanotechnology as, especially in the press, the real science often gets entangled with fears about grey goo and rampaging nanobots. It is therefore necessary to separate the wheat from the chaff, as many of the concerns have little or nothing to do with nanotechnology. Only knowledge and research will help to allay these fears. According to one report, articles mentioning the word 'nanotechnology' have increased from 500 in 1999 to almost 6,000 in 2002. There is indeed a lot of information available, although, by its very nature, the amount may not compare with the more traditional engineering areas, which in some cases have been researched for many decades. The following are resources which have been found to be useful, informative and occasionally indispensable.

► GOVERNMENT RESOURCES

Governments worldwide are now spending close to £2.5billion on nanotechnology R&D, and this figure will continue to rise. The United States is leading the way, and full information is provided on their National Nanotechnology Initiative (www.nano.gov). This website is run by the National Science Foundation (NSF), and, as befits an initiative that will spend over US$847 million on nanotechnology in 2004, is the most comprehensive governmental website on nanotechnology, full of reports, facts and figures. The agencies involved with the initiative also have their individual websites on nanotechnology, including the Department of Defense (www.nanosra.nrl.navy.mil), NASA (www.ipt.arc.nasa.gov/gallery.html) and the Department of Energy (www.er.doe.gov/bes/NNI.htm).

A number of individual states also have their own nanotechnology initiatives, including Texas (www.texasnano.org), Virginia (www.inanova. org) and California (www.norcalnano.org). The National Nanofabrication Users Network (NNUN) provides users with access to nanofabrication technologies, with facilities open to all users from academia, government, and industry (www.nnun.org).

Japan is next in terms of spending, devoting over £500million in 2002, followed by South Korea. Nanotechnology is a key priority under Japan's Science & Technology S&T second basic plan, with the bulk of funding being provided by the Ministry for Education, Science & Technology (www.mext.go.jp/english) and the Ministry of Economy, Trade and Industry (www.meti.go.jp/english). Details on the initiatives in South Korea can be accessed at the Korea Institute of Science and Technology Information site (www.kisti.re.kr/kisti/english/index_english.jsp), where there are plans for an English website on nanotechnology.

Whilst individual governments in Europe have poorly publicised their efforts in nanotechnology, the European Union has been no slouch. Funds from the EU's Fifth Framework Programme were allocated to the creation of new pan-Europe nanotechnology 'network of networks' under the aegis of the 'Growth Programme,' called Nanoforum (www.nanoforum.org), lead by the Institute of Nanotechnology.

This brings together key players in nanotechnology across Europe, including VDI (www.vdi.de) and CEA/LETI (www-leti.cea.fr). Another valuable resource is the Cordis database (www.cordis.lu), which has an extensive search tool. Cordis is the European Commission's information service on European Research and Innovation activities. Germany has details on its nanotechnology programme (www.nanonet.de), but most countries' programmes and strategies receive insufficient publicity, though this is slowly changing. Exceptions include The Irish Nanotechnology Association (www.nanotechireland.com), but the best way to get information on government funding and policy in nanotechnology is by contacting the relevant government bodies direct, which are usually the Science Councils.

Other government resources of interest include Australia's strategic plan for nanotechnology (www.arc.gov.au/strat_plan/ARC_StratPlan.pdf) and the National Research Council Canada's Nanotechnology Initiative (www.nrc-cnrc.gc.ca/nanotech/nin_e.html).

▶ COMPANY RESOURCES

There are over 700 companies worldwide now involved in nanotechnology, ranging from university spin-outs to multinationals such as Degussa, Henkel, Intel and Johnson Matthey. The United States leads the way, followed by Japan, Germany and the UK. Most of the companies exploiting nanotechnology are start-ups and their websites are a rich resource, information ranging from technology outlines to animations. Sites worth visiting include Nano-Tex (www.nano-tex.com), Nanogate (www.nanogate.de), Allegro Technologies (www.allegro-technologies.com), Quantum Dot (www.qdots.com), QinetiQ Nanomaterials (www.nano.qinetiq.com), Oxonica (www.oxonica.com) and Angstrom Medica (www.angstromedica.com). These websites help to convey some of the technological possibilities of the nanoscale. For micro and nanotechnology companies seeking guidance and networking opportunities, the Institute of Nanotechnology recently launched the NanoMicroClub (www.nanomicroclub.com).

Most large companies are tentatively involved in nanotechnology at present, but there are a number taking advantage of the enhanced properties and functionalities at the nanoscale to gain a 'product advantage.' These include General Motors (www.gm.com/automotive/innovations/rnd/news/news_082801.html), who have incorporated nanocomposites into step assists for people carriers and BASF (www.basf.de/en/corporate/innovationen/praesentiert/0210/?id=V00—W2m863*.bsf500). Smith and Nephew has on the market a barrier dressing containing Nanocrystals (www.smith-nephew.com/businesses/W_Acticoat.html) and Kodak is producing OLEDs (organic light emitting diodes) made of nanostructured polymer film for use in car stereos and cell phones, cameras, PDAs, laptops and televisions (www.kodak.com/US/plugins/acrobat/en/corp/display/SID2000.pdf).

IBM has a nanotechnology image gallery (www.research.ibm.com/nanoscience).

► UNIVERSITY RESOURCES

Most universities are now conducting research in nanotechnology and are by and large driving the science. Governments are building on the research capability in universities through new facilities, new networks and increased funding for existing infrastructure. In the United States, a number of centres of excellence have been established by the NSF, including the Institute for Soldier Nanotechnologies (web.mit.edu/isn) at MIT and the Center for Biological and Environmental Nanotechnology (www.ruf.rice.edu/~cben) at Rice University. In the UK, there is the Nano-electronics centre at Glasgow (www.elec.gla.ac.uk/groups/nano) and the London Centre for Nanotechnology (www.london-nano.ucl.ac.uk/lcn/index2.htm). Information on two Interdisciplinary Research Collaborations in Nanotechnology can be found via the Oxford (www.lsi.ox.ac.uk/frames?page=/research/Bionanotechnology) and Cambridge (www.nanoscience.cam.ac.uk) websites.

There are several nanotechnology masters courses available in the UK at present, at Imperial College London (www.ch.ic.ac.uk/computational/mres/index.html), University of Cranfield (www.cranfield.ac.uk/sims/materials/education/msncourses), Leeds and Sheffield (www.ee.leeds.ac.uk/nanomsc) and Newcastle (www.ncl.ac.uk/postgraduate/taught/subjects/taught-bbsmd/courses/236).

For undergraduates there is the University of Sussex (www.nano.sussex.ac.uk) or St Andrews and Dundee (chemistry.st-and.ac.uk/materials), though most university taught scientific and engineering disciplines now have a strong nanoscale component.

▶ GENERAL INFORMATION

For the latest news and views in nanotechnology, it is hard to look past the IoN's own website (www.nano.org.uk). There is also a number of other worthy information sources, including Nanoworld (www.nanoworld.jp), which mainly focuses on events in Asia, and Small Times (www.smalltimes.com). However, there is still a dearth of good impartial information out there, with many websites favouring the 'any news on nanotechnology is good news' approach.

Most of the major Science magazines now have sections on their websites devoted to nanotechnology, including *Scientific American* (www.sciam.com) and *Science* magazine (www.sciencemag.org), with whom the Institute of Nanotechnology will be producing a special publication on nanotechnolgy in 2004.

▶ WHAT RESOURCES ARE REQUIRED TO WORK IN NANOTECHNOLOGY?

If you are an innovator, in terms of the basic technologies, some fairly sophisticated and expensive equipment is needed to produce and characterise your invention. But you may use nanotechnology by incorporating someone else's nanoproduct to improve your own. For example, the quantum dot 'barcodes' described above are being used by whisky companies to prevent counterfeiting; special sensors incorporated into the packaging of fresh food products will indicate tampering, or that the product has 'gone off'; and specially coated nanoparticles in cosmetics will act as a sunscreen while adding alluring light reflecting properties to the skin and impart a silkiness to the touch.

▶ WHAT SKILLS/TRAINING ARE REQUIRED?

For the user of the technology, a broad awareness of what is in the market-place, and what it can do is necessary. This can be achieved through attending events on new technologies, particularly those on topics slightly outside what would be considered immediately relevant, talking to technologists from a variety of disciplines, surfing the internet for new information, or joining a special interest group.

For the researcher or innovator, 'scientific depth first, breadth second' is the order of the day. It is generally agreed that a really good understanding of basic science or engineering (physics, chemistry, electronics or mechanical engineering, maths, biology, biochemistry) followed by a later exposure to other disciplines is a good route to being a nanotechnologist. Once the theory has been mastered, of course, this is only the first step along the road to success; and whether the next step is in industry or academia, the challenge is to identify a nanotechnology that solves an old problem in a new way.

Increasingly, UK Universities are offering post graduate courses that build on focused first degrees which provide a 'biased' insight into nanotechnology and are specially aimed at industrial applications – such as the food industry, fine chemical production, etc. These include Leeds, Imperial College (ICSTM) and Newcastle, and more are in the pipeline.

▶ WHAT SHOULD ENGINEERS DO ABOUT IT?

Above all – be aware! Nanotechnology is already here – it is only a matter of time before it could have a direct effect on the way we all work. For engineers, nanotechnology is affecting the design of basic construction materials, enabling the production of lightweight high strength 'concrete'; it is leading to long life coatings and paints that will prevent corrosion; the production of 'wonder' new adhesives for specialist applications; new embedded sensors that will detect and initiate the repair of weakening structures; ultra 'smart' controls for all domestic requirements including biometrically controlled domestic security; new materials such as self-cleaning glass; and wall-size lightweight displays – to name but a few.

▶ FURTHER READING

British Council Briefing Sheet on Nanotechnology, (www.britishcouncil.org/science/science/pubs/briefsht/BS13NanotechnologyJan2002.pdf)

Nanotechnology- Size Matters. Building a successful nanotechnology company, (www.nano.org.uk/NanoPaper.pdf)

New Dimensions for Manufacturing. A UK Strategy for Nanotechnology, (www.nano.org.uk/nanotechnologyreport.pdf)

Opportunities for Industry, (www.nano.org.uk/applications.pdf)

▶ FURTHER READING: JOURNALS

IEEE Transactions on Nanotechnology (Piscataway, NJ: IEEE)

International Journal of Nanotechnology (Olney: Inderscience Publishers)

Journal of Nanoscience and Nanotechnology (Stevenson Ranch, CA: American Scientific Publishers)

Nano Letters (Washington, DC: American Chemical Society)

Nanotechnology (London: Institute of Physics)

▶ FURTHER READING: BOOKS

Freitas, R. A., 1999. *Nanomedicine. Vol 1, Basic capabilities.* Lewisville, TX: J. A. Majors.

Hu, M. Z., and De Guire, M., eds. 2003 *Ceramic nanomaterials and nanotechnology.* Westerville, OH: American Ceramic Society.

Krummenacker, M., and Lewis, J., 1995. *Prospects in nanotechnology: toward molecular manufacturing.* New York: Wiley.

Lakhtakia, A., 2004. *The handbook of nanotechnology: nanometer structure theory, modelling, and simulation.* Bellingham, WA: SPIE.

Nalwa, H. S., 2003. *Encyclopedia of nanoscience and nanotechnology.* Stevenson Ranch, CA: American Scientific Publishers.

Nalwa, H. S., 1999. *Handbook of nanostructured materials and nanotechnology.* 5 vols. London: Academic Press.

Nance, J., ed., 2002. *Progress in nanotechnology.* Westerville, OH: American Ceramic Society

Nicolau, D. V., 2002. *Biomedical nanotechnology: architectures and applications.* Bellingham, WA: SPIE.

Poole, C. P., 2003. *Introduction to nanotechnology.* New York: Wiley.

Scientific American, 2003. *Understanding nanotechnology.* New York: Little, Brown & Company.

Taniguchi, N., 1996. *Nanotechnology:integrating processing systems for ultra-precision and ultra-fine products.* Oxford: Oxford University Press.

Varadan, V. K., 2002. *Smart electronics, MEMS, and nanotechnology.* Bellingham, WA: SPIE.

Whitehouse, D. J., 2003 *Handbook of surface and nanometrology.* Institute of Physics.

► NOTES

The Institute of Nanotechnology was established in 1997. It works throughout Europe, providing information on nanotechnology for industry, government and the public, running international events on new developments and supplying intelligence to business. The Institute leads one of the most important European nanonetworks, Nanoforum; which acts as a conduit for the European Commission to the nanocommunity and vice-versa.

Contact: Andy Garland, Head of Information (andy@nano.org.uk) Tel: +44 (0) 1786 447520

26 Occupational Safety and Health

Christine Middleton

This chapter aims to highlight and evaluate sources of information of use to researchers and practitioners working in the area of occupational safety and health. It does not intend to cover the theory of the topic in depth but rather to provide pointers to sources of further information for those already familiar with the subject.

▶ OVERVIEW

The International Labour Organization Convention on Occupational Health Services (1985), (www.ilo.org/public/english/protection/safework/cis/oshworld/ilostd/c161.htm), provides a useful definition to introduce this chapter. It advises that occupational health services should aim to prevent the occurrence of work-related ill health and should provide guidance related to:

1   'the requirements for establishing and maintaining a safe and healthy working environment which will facilitate optimal physical and mental health in relation to work.
2   the adaptation of work to the capabilities of the workers in the light of their state of physical and mental health'

The Health and Safety Executive have also produced two useful publications which offer advice in these areas:

* *Successful health and safety management. HSG 65.* 2nd ed. 2000. Sudbury: HSE.
* *Reducing error and influencing behaviour. HSG 48.* 2nd ed. 2000. Sudbury: HSE.

The approach recommended in HSG 65 is covered in the British Standard BS 8800:1996, *Guide to occupational health and safety management systems.* This standard extends the definition to cover all aspects of health and safety relevant to an organization. It 'seeks to improve the occupational health and safety performance of organizations by providing guidance on how the management of OH&S may be integrated with the management of other aspects of business performance, in order to:

- minimize risk to employees and others;
- improve business performance; and
- assist organizations to establish a responsible image within the marketplace.'

HSG 48 (page 11) highlights three key elements within the working environment and gives examples of problem areas which should be addressed in order to minimise the incidence of ill health. These are reproduced below:

- Job factors
  illogical design of equipment and instruments
  constant disturbances and interruptions
  missing or unclear instructions
  poorly maintained equipment
  high workload
  noisy and unpleasant working conditions
- Individual factors
  low skill and competence levels
  tired staff
  bored or disheartened staff
  individual medical problems
- Organisation and management factors
  poor work planning, leading to high work pressure
  lack of safety systems and barriers
  inadequate responses to previous incidents
  management based on one-way communications
  deficient co-ordination and responsibilities
  poor management of health and safety
  poor health and safety culture

Health and Safety Executive statistics based on self-reported work-related ill health, (www.hse.gov.uk/statistics/overall/hssh0102.pdf), indicate that whilst musculoskeletal disorders remain the most common problem, the prevalence of this is lower than a decade ago. However, stress related conditions are now the second most common complaint and the prevalence rate is around double the rate recorded in 1990. Stress related conditions also appear to contribute largely to the increase in working days lost from 18 million days in 1995 to 32.9 million days in 2001/2002. Other common occupationally related illnesses include respiratory problems, noise induced hearing loss, and headaches or eye strain.

The effect of some examples of work related ill health may only be seen many years later. Typical examples are the onset of deafness with age and also the cases of asbestosis arising from the common use of asbestos in the 1960s/70s. Due to the latency of such diseases, the full implications are not seen until several decades have passed (www.hse.gov.uk/campaigns/asbestos/index.htm). In response to these issues, legislation and codes of practice have been developed to protect workers against health hazards arising from their working conditions.

The Treaty of Rome (which first established the European Economic Community in 1957, and which the UK signed in 1972) did not initially include extensive provision for the safety and social aspects of work. However, a five-year plan was proposed in 1978 which led to the establishment of an ongoing series of EC Directives. These concentrated at first on protection against the risks of exposure to chemical, physical and biological agents at work, (www.europarl.eu.int/factsheets/4_8_1_en.htm). Safety at work was not fully addressed until the Treaty of Rome was modified by the Single European Act in 1986 and Article 138 (118a) was introduced to create standards to govern the working environment of employees (www.europarl.eu.int/factsheets/4_8_5_en.htm). Prior to this, health and safety had been subject to independently developed national requirements which resulted in varied approaches and standards across the European Union.

The directives developed under Article 138 specify minimum requirements concerning health and safety at work and the aim is to ensure that employees can expect the same minimum standards to apply throughout the European Community.

In addition to the EC Directives, a set of six regulations were introduced into UK legislation in January 1993:

- the Management of Health and Safety at Work Regulations 1992 (replaced by the Management of Health and Safety at Work Regulations 1999 (SI 1999 No. 3242))
- the Provision and Use of Work Equipment Regulations 1992 (PUWER) (replaced by the Provision and Use of Work Equipment Regulations 1998 (SI 1998 No. 2306))
- the Workplace (Health, Safety and Welfare) Regulations 1992 (SI 1992 No. 3004)
- the Personal Protective equipment at Work Regulations 1992 (SI 1992 No. 2966)
- the Manual Handling Operations Regulations 1992 (SI 1992 No. 2793)
- the Health and Safety (Display Screen Equipment) Regulations 1992 (SI 1992 No. 2792)

The Management of Health and Safety at Work Regulations introduced risk management into the legislation, and although it is not possible to eliminate all elements of risk from a workplace environment, it is essential to attempt to identify potential hazards and to minimise their effect.

The EC also continues to introduce additional measures. The European Agency for Health and Safety at work was established in 1994, and from 1996 – 2000 the Commission adopted a Community Programme on Health and Safety at Work in order to improve the implementation of health and safety guidelines.

► LEGISLATION

In the UK, adherence to health and safety regulations is enforced by the Health and Safety Executive (HSE). The HSE acts on the recommendations of the Health and Safety Commission (HSC) who are the official body responsible for the regulations relating to health and safety arising from work activities. Much of the legislation is enabled by the Health and Safety at Work Act 1974, by the directives of the European Union and by other initiatives already outlined.

Further information on the relevant legislation is available from the following sources.

UK legislation

HMSO (Her Majesty's Stationery Office), www.legislation.hmso.gov.uk
This website includes the full text of all legislation enacted by the UK Parliament covering Statutory Instruments (SI) from 1987, Public Acts from 1988 and Local Acts from 1991. These can be browsed by year which is the easiest way to navigate to a known act. Alternatively the site can be searched by keyword.

Regular use of the site will aid with current awareness, for example a search for health and safety, shows the Health and Safety (Miscellaneous Amendments) Regulations 2002 which came into force on 17th September 2002 and which details changes to the following:

- Amendment of the Health and Safety (First-Aid) Regulations 1981
- Amendment of the Health and Safety (Display Screen Equipment) Regulations 1992
- Amendment of the Manual Handling Operations Regulations 1992
- Amendment of the Workplace (Health, Safety and Welfare) Regulations 1992
- Amendment of the Provision and Use of Work Equipment Regulations 1998

Relevant acts which can be seen in full text include:

- The Working Time (Amendment) Regulations 2002 (SI 2002 No. 3128)
- The Control of Substances Hazardous to Health Regulations 2002 (SI 2002 No. 2677)
- The Management of Health and Safety at Work Regulations 1999 (SI 1999 No. 3242)
- The Disability Discrimination Act 1995
- The Health and Safety (Display Screen Equipment) Regulations 1992 (SI 1992 No. 2792)

Print and Braille copies of these and older acts (such as the Health and Safety (First Aid) Regulations 1981, the Health and Safety at Work Act 1974, and the Factories Act 1961) are available from The Stationery Office Ltd. Order online via the TSO Online Bookshop, by e-mail: customer. services@tso.co.uk, or by post to: TSO, PO Box 29, Norwich, NR3 1GN, tel. order line 0870 600 5522 or fax order line 0870 600 5533.

The Health and Safety at Work Act 1974 is reproduced online at: www.healthandsafety.co.uk/haswa.htm by Professional Health and Safety Consultants Ltd.

The First Aid Regulations are summarised at: www.hse.gov.uk/firstaid/legislation.htm

Prior to passing legislation, the Health and Safety Commission submits drafts for public consultation. These are referred to as HSC Consultative Documents and can be seen at: www.hse.gov.uk/consult

European legislation

The portal to European Union Law, EUR-Lex can be viewed online at: europa.eu.int/eur-lex/en. The site can be searched or alternatively browsed by an alphabetical index or by the analytical structure. The section giving EC Directives on Safety at Work is seen at: europa.eu.int/eur-lex/en/lif/reg/en_register_05202010.html

USA legislation

Information on USA laws and regulations is available from the US Department of Labor Occupational Safety and Health Administration (www.osha.gov). The relevant act is the Occupational Safety and Health Act of 1970 (Amended 1998) which is available in full text from this site.

Books on legislation

Barrett, B., and Howells, R., 2000. *Occupational health and safety law: text and materials.* 2nd ed. London: Cavendish.

Barrett, B., and Howells, R., 1997. *Occupational health and safety law*. 3rd ed. London: M & E Pitman.

Bradley, K., 2001. *The Health and Safety at Work Act 1974 explained*. London: Stationery Office.

Croner's A-Z essentials: health and safety, 2001. Kingston-upon-Thames: Croner Publications.

Croner's health and safety at work, 2002. Kingston-upon-Thames: Croner Publications.

Chandler, P., 1999. *An A-Z of health and safety law: a complete reference source for managers*. 3rd ed. London: Kogan Page.

Day, R., and Rowland, E., 2003. *Health, safety and environment legislation: a pocket guide*. Cambridge: Royal Society of Chemistry.

Duncan, M., and Cahill, F., 2003. *Health & safety at work essentials*. 2nd ed. London: Law Pack.

Kloss, D. M., 1998. *Occupational health law*. 3rd ed. Oxford: Blackwell Science. [4th ed. expected 2005]

Management of Health and Safety at Work regulations 1999 Approved Code of Practice and guidance. 2000. 2nd ed. London: HSE.

Ridley, J., and Channing, J., eds., 1999. *Safety at work*. 5th ed. Oxford: Butterworth-Heinemann. [Some chapters on legal aspects]

Stranks, J. W., 2001. *Health and safety law*. 4th ed. Harlow: Pearson Professional Education.

Tolley's health and safety at work handbook 2003. Croydon: Tolley.

In addition, the following online resource provides a useful summary:

MacGregor, P., *A general introduction to health and safety legislation* [online]. Produced by the Ranworth Association on behalf of the Institute for Independent Business (www.iib.org.uk/hands.htm). [Publication date not available].

For USA law see:

Byrum, L. L., 2001. *Occupational safety and health law handbook*. Rockville: Government Institutes.

▶ **ORGANISATIONS**

European Agency for Safety and Health at Work, europe.osha.eu.int
The European Agency for Safety and Health at Work was established to co-ordinate OSH related issues across Europe. This comprehensive site provides access to legislation, examples of good practice, research, statistics, publications, discussion fora and much more.

Health and Safety Executive, www.hse.gov.uk
The HSE website includes links to research, statistics and full-text publications in the field of occupational health. Lists of HSE publications are available at: www.hsebooks.co.uk.

International Labour Organisation, www.ilo.org/public/english
The International Labour Organization is a United Nations agency founded in 1919 to protect human rights. It produces standards covering the entire spectrum of work related issues and also provides technical advice on training and rehabilitation. It also produces the journal *World of Work*.

National Examination Board in Occupational Safety and Health (NEBOSH), www.nebosh.org.uk
NEBOSH is the QCA (Qualifications and Curriculum Authority) approved body offering a General Certificate in health and safety at work. Courses are offered throughout the UK and overseas.
Supporting texts are:

Hughes, P., 2003. *Introduction to health and safety at work: the handbook for the NEBOSH national general certificate.* Oxford: Butterworth-Heinemann.
Ridley, J., 2001. *Health and safety – in brief.* 2nd ed. Oxford: Butterworth-Heinemann.

National Institute for Occupational Safety and Health (NIOSH), www.cdc.gov/niosh/homepage.html
NIOSH is the American federal agency responsible for conducting research and making recommendations for the prevention of work-related disease and injury. The website includes details of the activities of the Institute and a searchable catalogue of their current publications. Topic sub-headings include: Chemical safety, Respirators, Traumatic injuries, Musculoskeletal disorders, Health care workers, Agriculture, Construction, Mining safety and health research, All occupational safety and health topics.

National Radiological Protection Board, www.nrpb.org
The NRPB is a source of information and advice on radiation matters. This covers ionising and non-ionising radiation and includes radioactive sources, lasers, electrical and magnetic fields, ultra-violet radiation (including exposure to UV in sunshine and protective clothing), microwaves etc.

Others . . .
A very large number of national and international organisations are listed within the Health and Safety section of the Steelynx web pages at: www.steelynx.net

▶ PROFESSIONAL SOCIETIES

UK

These can be found by doing a general web search or by using publications such as:

> *Directory of British associations & associations in Ireland.* 2002. Beckenham: CBD Research.

The information provided about each society summarises some of the activities undertaken and is not necessarily comprehensive. Further information can be found by visiting the relevant website.

Association of Occupational Health Nurse Practitioners, www.aohnp.co.uk
This UK professional organisation was founded to support the interests of occupational health nurse practitioners. It operates on a voluntary basis and is managed by an elected Board, supported by Regional directors and working parties. The Regional directors aim to support the occupational health needs of members operating within their region.

The Ergonomics Society, www.ergonomics.org.uk
The Ergonomics Society is a UK based professional society for all those specialising in ergonomics. It offers a range of membership grades, and its activities include running an annual conference.

The Faculty of Occupational Medicine of the Royal College of Physicians, www.facoccmed.ac.uk
Faculty members are qualified professionals operating in the field of occupational medicine. Full members (MFOM) will be registered medical practitioners specialising in occupational medicine. Those who have made outstanding contributions to the field may be considered for Fellowship. An Associate grade of membership also exists at the entry level. In addition to managing and promoting professional qualifications, the Faculty is also able to advise on policy issues and codes of practice relevant to all aspects of occupational medicine.

Institution of Occupational Safety and Health (IOSH), www.iosh.co.uk
IOSH is the professional body for safety and health practitioners in the UK. Corporate membership indicates a level of competence and experience in the field. IOSH members assist the government in producing draft legislation, codes of practice and guidance notes and sit on national and international committees. The Institution publishes the biannual journal *Policy and practice in health and safety,* and also the magazine *Safety and health practitioner* which is distributed free to members.

Society of Occupational Health Nursing, www.rcn.org.uk
The Society of Occupational Health Nursing is a special interest group of the Royal College of Nursing and the website is accessible to members from the RCN site. It provides a discussion forum for matters of mutual interest and also arranges an annual conference.

Society of Occupational Medicine, www.som.org.uk
The Society of Occupational Medicine provides a forum for discussion on topics of interest within occupational medicine such as the health of people at work and the prevention of work related injuries and disease. It provides newsletters and information on recent legislation, and offers opinion on consultative documents to government departments and to other professional societies.

USA

American Association of Occupational Health Nurses (AAOHN), www.aaohn.org
AAOHN is the American association for occupational and environmental health professionals and provides professional services for those concerned with health and safety in the workplace. It established an accreditation body, the American Board for Occupational Health Nurses, to provide a system of professional qualification.

American Board for Occupational Health Nurses, Inc. (ABOHN), www.abohn.org
The ABOHN is an independent certification board which implements and conducts a certification program for qualified occupational health nurses in the USA. It uses the standards of practice established by the AAOHN to set the criteria and standards for certification.

American Society of Safety Engineers, www.asse.org
ASSE is America's professional safety organisation. It provides training and professional services to its members, assists with the preparation of national and international standards, and arranges annual professional development conferences such as 'Safety 2003: Advancing the EH&S Profession' (June 22–25 in Denver, Colorado).

▶ RESEARCH INSTITUTES

Some of the following research institutes were located using the following:

Edwards, C. M., 2000. *Centres, bureaux and research institutes the directory of UK concentrations of effort, information and expertise.* Beckenham: CBD.

Links to many more institutes and to information on current research programmes and funding are available from the European Agency for Safety and Health at Work, at: europe.osha.eu.int/research

British Occupational Health Research Foundation (BOHRF), www.bohrf.org.uk
BOHRF provides funding for occupational health research. The website provides details of existing projects and guidelines for applying for funding.

Centre for Occupational and Environmental Health (COEH), www.coeh.man.ac.uk
This centre is a well established academic teaching and research unit based at the University of Manchester. It offers postgraduate training leading to professional qualifications, and has particular strengths in the incidence of diseases related to work or the environment.

Ergonomics and Safety Research Institute, www.lboro.ac.uk/research/esri
The Ergonomics and Safety Research Institute (ESRI) at Loughborough has been formed from the Research Institute for Consumer Ergonomics (RICE) and the Human Sciences Advanced Technology Research Institute (HUSAT). It is part of the Research School in Ergonomics and Human Factors at Loughborough University and comprises three research centres: Human Focused Design Centre; Transport Technology Ergonomics Centre; and Vehicle Safety Research Centre.

European Law Research Centre, www.research.salford.ac.uk/elrc
Based at the University of Salford, the European Occupational Health and Safety Law Research Centre is one of the leading European research centres concentrating on occupational health and safety law. It is involved with research programmes with the International Labour Organisation, the European Commission, the European Environment Agency, the Department of the Environment, Food and Rural Affairs and the Health and Safety Executive.

Health and Safety Ergonomics Unit, www.lboro.ac.uk/departments/hu/groups/hseu
The Health and Safety Ergonomics Unit based at Loughborough University undertakes research into the human factors aspects of health and safety. Areas of interest include tool design, job evaluation, risk assessment, the avoidance of accidents and strategies for health and safety management. It is one of a number of research groups within the Department of Human Sciences. This department also has links with the Ergonomics and Safety Research Institute mentioned previously. Further details can be seen at: www.lboro.ac.uk/departments/hu/groups/groups.html

Health and Safety Laboratory, www.hsl.gov.uk
The HSL is an Agency of the Health and Safety Executive providing research and investigative support to the HSE and to other Government Departments. The HSL also undertakes research for private organisations from two sites: one at Sheffield and the other at Buxton, Derbyshire. The Sheffield site has laboratories for biomedical, occupational hygiene and environmental measurements, and also undertakes engineering, risk assessment, ergonomics and behavioural studies. The site at Buxton concentrates on fire and explosion safety.

Institute for Occupational Ergonomics, www.virart.nottingham.ac.uk/ioe
The Institute for Occupational Ergonomics is a research and consultancy group based at the University of Nottingham. It specialises in a range of fields related to the ergonomic aspects of work, including engineering, health sciences and psychology. The IOE collaborates closely with two other research groups at the University of Nottingham: the Product Safety and Testing Group (PSTG) and the Virtual Reality Applications Research Team (VIRART). There is special interest in the human factors associated with rail transport and with seating research.

Institute of Occupational and Environmental Medicine, www.pcpoh-bham.ac.uk/ioem
This academic institute based at the University of Birmingham is engaged in research in the areas of occupational medicine, epidemiology, toxicology, industrial hygiene and other topics related to the control of health hazards in the workplace. It also offers consultancy and training facilities and has international influence through its activities with the World Health Organisation. The website provides access to *UK and Worldwide Occupational Health and Safety News* which is particularly useful for maintaining an awareness of recent developments in the field.

Institute of Occupational Medicine, www.iom-world.org
This is a major independent UK research centre based in Edinburgh and offering training and consultancy in occupational and environmental health, hygiene and safety.

Institute of Work, Health and Organisations (I-WHO), www.nottingham.ac.uk/iwho
I-WHO is a postgraduate research centre within the Faculty of Law and Social Science at the University of Nottingham. It specialises in the organisational psychology associated with occupational, environmental and public health. The Institute incorporates the Centre for Organizational Health and Development, which is a World Health Organization Collaborating Centre in Occupational Health. The Institute is also a Topic Centre for Stress at Work for the European Agency of Safety and Health at Work.

Robens Centre for Occupational Health Safety and Hygiene, www.eihms. surrey.ac.uk/rohshome.htm

The Robens Centre for Occupational Health and Safety offers training, research and consultancy services within the European Institute of Health and Medical Sciences (EIHMS) at the University of Surrey. It provides courses in health and safety training, and also training programmes for occupational health professionals. The Robens Centre for Health Ergonomics, (www.eihms.surrey.ac.uk/robens/erg/tcmsd.htm), is also involved in research into work related upper limb disorders and is a European Union Topic Centre for Musculoskeletal Disorders.

▶ REPORTS

Environment Health and Safety Reports, oshweb.me.tut.fi

Environment Health and Safety Reports produced by a large number of national and international commercial companies can be seen in full text via the EHS Reports link on the OSHWEB site. However, a number of the links appeared to be unreliable.

Health and Safety Executive reports, www.hse.gov.uk/research/publish.htm

HSE reports are freely available over the Internet. These are detailed on the website as follows:

- *Mainstream Research News* – quarterly newsletter for HSE's mainstream research programme
- *Offshore Research Focus* – quarterly newsletter for offshore research topics
- *Health Research Abstracts* – describes projects in HSE's occupational health research programme
- *Research Reports* (RR) – HSE's new single series for research reports, encompassing reports which would previously have been published as Contract Research Reports, Offshore Safety Reports or HSL Reports.
- *Contract Research Reports* (CRR) – reports produced as Contract Research Reports prior to the introduction of the Research Report Series
- *Health and Safety Laboratory Reports* (HSL) – HSL reports preceding the Research Report Series
- *Offshore Safety Reports* – reports preceding the Research Report Series
- *Strategic Research Projects Handbook* – provides summary details on the R&D projects currently underway or recently completed.

The link to Press releases from the main HSE website, (www.hse.gov.uk) is particularly useful for keeping up-to-date with events and for reports on recent prosecutions.

Useful publications include:

Commission of The European Communities, 1995. *Health and safety at work Community programme 1996–2000 European Commission.* Luxembourg: OOPEC.

Commission of The European Communities, 1999. *Health and safety at work in Europe: where next?* Luxembourg: OOPEC.

Committee of The Regions, 2002. *Opinion of the Committee of the Regions of 3 July 2002 on the communication from the Commission 'Adapting to change in work and society— a new Community strategy on health and safety at work 2002–2006' (COM(2002) 118 final and the proposal for a Council recommendation concerning the application of legislation governing health and safety at work to self-employed workers COM(2002) 166 final – 2002/0079 (CNS)).* Luxembourg: OOPEC.

European Agency for Safety and Health at Work, 2000. *Future occupational safety and health research needs and priorities in the member states of the European Union European Agency for Safety and Health at Work.* Luxembourg: OOPEC.

European Agency for Safety and Health at Work, 2001. *The state of occupational safety and health (OSH) in the EFTA countries European Agency for Safety and Health at Work.* Luxembourg: OOPEC.

▶ CONFERENCES

A good place to look for forthcoming conferences is the 'What's new' section of the hsedirect site at: baldwin.butterworths.co.uk/search/content/whatsnew_index.htm or on the Institute of Occupational and Environmental Medicine site at: www.pcpoh.bham.ac.uk/ioem. In addition, many of the organisations and professional societies mentioned previously will advertise conferences on their pages, see for example the events calendar at IOSH, (www.iosh.co.uk).

The following conferences are amongst those held on an annual basis:

- American Occupational Health Conference, www.aaohn.org
- Ergonomics Society Annual Conference, www.ergonomics.org.uk/events.htm
- Human Factors and Ergonomics Society Annual Meetings, hfes.org
- IOSH Annual Conference and Exhibition, www.iosh.co.uk
- RCN Society of Occupational Health Nursing Annual Conference, www.rcn.org.uk/events
- Safety and Health at Work Congress, www.safety-health-expo.co.uk

▶ JOURNALS

Although now a little out of date, the following publication produced by the Occupational Safety and Health Information Group (disbanded in 1999) is a useful source of reference for identifying relevant journal titles. The holdings information provided should be checked from more recent sources.

Occupational Safety and Health Information Group, 1993. *Health and safety journals: what's where.* Cambridge: Occupational Safety and Health Information Group.

Titles worth highlighting include:

AAOHN journal: official journal of the American Association of Occupational Health Nurses. Atlanta, GA: Published by SLACK Inc. for the AAOHN.
Accident analysis and prevention. Oxford, New York: Pergamon Press.
Applied ergonomics. Guildford: IPC Science and Technology Press.
Publications of the *European Agency for Safety and Health at Work.* Luxembourg: Office for Official Publications of the European Communities.
  Forum
  Magazine
  News
Health and safety bulletin. London: Industrial Relations Services, Eclipse Group.
Health & safety at work. Croydon: Maclaren Publishers, Ltd.
The Journal of the Society of Occupational Medicine. Edinburgh: E. & S. Livingstone.
Journal of occupational and organizational psychology. London: British Psychological Society.
Occupational ergonomics. Netherlands: IOS Press.
Occupational hazards. Cleveland: Penton Publishing.
Occupational health. London: Reed Business Information Ltd.
Occupational health & safety. Edmonton: Occupational Health & Safety Division.
Occupational health review. UK: IRS
Occupational medicine. Oxford: Oxford University Press.
OSH World: an electronic journal published by Sheila Pantry Associates Ltd, which continues Health and Safety World, (www.oshworld.com).
Process safety progress: a publication of the American Institute of Chemical Engineers. New York: American Institute of Chemical Engineers
Safety and health practitioner. Wigston: IOSH. (Published by IOSH and free to members.)
Safety science. New York: Elsevier.

▶ DATA

Researchers will need data to inform design decisions and to show trends in incidences of work related injuries and diseases. There are many authoritative sources providing this. There is anthropometric data available to advise ergonomic design, and additionally there is scientific data available to advise on the chemical properties of materials which may be hazardous to health. The following sections list sources providing good examples from these categories.

For those not familiar with statistics and data analysis, the following is a useful introductory text which uses examples relevant to occupational safety and health:

Janicak, C. A., 2000. *Applied statistics in occupational safety and health*. Rockville: Government Institutes.

UK statistics

UK Government statistics covering all aspects of life are available from: www.statistics.gov.uk. It is possible to do a keyword search or to browse by themes. Data relating to health and safety at work is within the Health section of Health and Care. Another relevant topic, Employment and Work, is contained within Labour Market.

HSE statistics, (www.hse.gov.uk/statistics)
The Health and Safety Executive provide authoritative data and statistics relating to workplace illnesses and injuries in the UK. Some data is available as an Excel spreadsheet. Other data is available within a pdf file or is presented in the form of a report.

Data covered includes:

- Overall summary
- Fatal injuries
- Kinds of accident/injury
- Statistics by industry
- Statistics by country/region
- By age, gender, etc.
- Working days lost
- Enforcement tables
- Gas safety
- Dangerous occurences.

European statistics

European Health and Safety Database (HASTE), www.occuphealth.fi/
e/eu/haste
This site, which is hosted by the Finnish Institute of Occupational Health,
does not provide access to actual data but refers to many European organisations which are collating data. The names and addresses of the
organisations are given, together with details of the statistical publications
available and a summary of the type of data that is collected. Organisations
are listed from Austria, Belgium, Czech Republic, Denmark, Finland,
France, Germany, Greece, Ireland, Italy, Luxembourg, Netherlands,
Norway, Portugal, Spain, Sweden and the UK.

Publications include:

European Commission, 2002. *European statistics on accidents at work (ESAW)
    methodology.* Luxembourg: OOPEC.
Nossent, S., De Groot, B., and Verboon, F., 1996. *European working environment in
    figures: availability and quality of occupational health and safety data in sixteen
    European countries.* Luxembourg: OOPEC.

USA statistics

Data on safety and health conditions in America is collected by the
Bureau of Labor Statistics (BLS). Detailed statistics are available from: stats.
bls.gov/data/home.htm. Details can be obtained of the most frequently
requested data or customised reports can be generated. Sub-headings
include:

- Employment and unemployment
- Prices and living conditions
- Compensation and working conditions (the most relevant section
  for this topic)
- Productivity and technology (this section contains a link to foreign
  labour statistics and includes some data relating to labour statistics
  from Australia, Canada, Japan, Korea, Switzerland and Taiwan in
  addition to the European countries already mentioned)
- Regional resources

Anthropometric data

Data from recent studies carried out by the Institute for Occupational
Ergonomics at the University of Nottingham are published in the following
texts:

Norris, B. J., and Wilson, J., 1995. *Childata: the handbook of child measurements and capabilities: data for design safety.* London: Consumer Safety Unit, Dept. of Trade and Industry.

Peebles, L., and Norris, B. J., 1998. *Adultdata: the handbook of adult anthropometric and strength measurements: data for design safety.* London: Dept. of Trade and Industry.

Peebles, L., and Norris, B. J., 2000. *Strength data for design safety – Phase 1.* URN 00/1070. London: Dept. of Trade and Industry.

Peebles, L., Reid, A., and Norris, B. J., 2000. *Strength data for design safety – Phase 2.* URN 01/1433. London: Dept. of Trade and Industry.

Smith, S., Norris, B. J., and Peebles, L., 2000. *Older adultdata: the handbook of measurements and capabilities of the older adult: data for design and safety.* London: Dept. of Trade and Industry.

A web search will result in a number of sites offering anthropometric data for adults, but the Anthrokids website at: ovrt.nist.gov/projects/anthrokids claims to be the only public domain online database of child anthropometric data. It is presenting data collected in 1975 and 1977 by the Consumer Product Safety Commission, (www.cpsc.gov), and is the result of a joint project between the CPSC and the National Institute of Standards and Technology, (www.nist.gov).

A major resource is the PeopleSize computer package produced by Open Ergonomics Ltd. (www.openerg.com/psz.htm) which 'gives data on human sizes through a visual interface'. It is possible to select nationality, age group and percentile value and then to click on patterns to ascertain physical dimensions. The basic package is currently priced at £149 + VAT.

Data on hazards

International Chemical Safety Cards (ICSCs), www.ilo.org/public/english/protection/safework/cis/products/icsc/index.htm
Data for over 1,300 chemicals can be searched by name, ISCS number or CAS number. The data given includes physical properties, molecular formulae and details of the hazards associated with the chemical including risk prevention and first aid and rescue procedures.

International hazard datasheets on occupations, www.ilo.org/public/english/protection/safework/cis/products/hdo/htmold/idhindex.htm
This site provides lists in English, Russian and Spanish of the types of hazards to which workers in a number of occupations may be exposed during their normal work.

The Physical and Theoretical Chemistry Laboratory at Oxford University, ptcl.chem.ox.ac.uk/MSDS
Under the heading 'Chemical and Other Safety Information', this site provides links to information on a whole range of chemicals which may be encountered in the home or in industry. There is also a link to material safety data sheets providing safety data for many thousands of substances.

Where to find Material Safety Data Sheets on the Internet, www.ilpi.com/msds
This site provides links to many freely available MSDS resources on the Internet. It also provides access to many other useful pages including a Frequently Asked Questions page, links to OSHA regulations, a glossary of related terms, software, and a forum for discussion.

▶ STANDARDS

To see the full text of official standards it will usually be necessary to purchase them from the publishing body. Catalogues are available in many public libraries.

A catalogue of British Standards can be searched at: bsonline. techindex.co.uk. Subscribers to the service are able to have unlimited online access to the full text of British Standards. However, it is possible search the bibliographic information freely and also to register for free access to summaries with the option to purchase printed copies of any documents of interest. A relevant example is the previously mentioned BS 8800:1996, Guide to occupational health and safety management systems.

Note that if the BSI has adopted a standard produced by another body or if there is a direct equivalence between the standards, then this will be indicated in the search results. From this site there is also a links page which offers access to other standards bodies including ISO, the International Organisation for Standards. The ISO catalogue may be searched at: www.iso.ch/iso/en/CatalogueListPage.CatalogueList.

Subscribers to the Occupational Health and Safety Information Service (OHSIS) (www.tionestop.com/tionestop/where/ohsis.htm) have full text access to a subset of the British Standards relating to health and safety. In addition the service provides access to key health and safety legislation and guidance material from the HSE and ROSPA, (www.rospa.com/CMS).

International Labour Standards including ILO Conventions and Recommendations can be searched through the ILOLEX service at: www.ilo.org/ilolex/english/index.htm

▶ CASE STUDIES

Case studies are useful for educational purposes, to achieve the benefit of hindsight and they provide interesting background reading. As an example, to discover the connection between swimming pools and processing salad vegetables, look at the relevant case study within the Work Environment section of the HSL case studies listed below.

Health and Safety Laboratory Case Studies, www.hsl.gov.uk/case-studies/index.htm
An interesting collection of case studies grouped under the headings:

- Fire, Explosion and Process Safety
- Engineering Control
- Work Environment
- Occupational and Environmental Health
- Behavioural and Social Science
- Risk Assessment

ErgoWeb, www.ergoweb.com/resources/casestudies
Examples of problems experienced and the solutions adopted are listed from a diverse range of manufacturing situations.

There is also a number of publications available which provide guidance and examples of good practice:

Akass, R., 1994. *Essential health and safety for managers: a guide to good practice in the European Union.* Aldershot: Gower.
European Agency for Safety and Health at Work, 2001. *Occupational safety and health and employability: programmes, practices and experiences.* Luxembourg: OOPEC.
Health and Safety Executive, 2001. *A pain in your workplace? Ergonomic problems and solutions.* Sudbury: HSE Books.

▶ ABSTRACTS AND INDEXES

As the previous paragraphs will have indicated, there is a wealth of freely accessible, good quality information on occupational safety and health available over the Internet. However, for a comprehensive search of the literature, it is necessary to use abstracting and indexing services to search for articles published within learned journals. Unfortunately, many of the following services are only available by subscription, although some libraries may hold printed copies which can be viewed by visitors. Note also that PubMed is freely available.

AMED (Allied and Complementary Medicine)

Subscription required. Further details can be found via: www.ovid.com. AMED indexes approximately 500 journals including those in the areas of occupational therapy and rehabilitation.

CINAHL (Cumulative Index to Nursing and Allied Health Literature), www.cinahl.com

Subscription required.

This service indexes over 500 journals and also books, nursing dissertations, conference proceedings and standards of professional practice. Relevant topics covered include occupational therapy and health education.

Ergonomics Abstracts, www.tandf.co.uk/ergo-abs

Subscription required but the publishers offer 24-hour free trials of Ergonomics Abstracts Online. The abstracts cover all aspects of ergonomics and human factors from 1969 to present.

Medline

Available online from a range of database providers. (See also PubMed)

Medline is compiled by the National Library of Medicine in America and is one of the most important medical databases. It provides access to approximately 3,700 medical journals, as well as some books and conference proceedings.

OSH-ROM, www.healthandsafety-centre.net/minisites/silverplatter.html

Subscription required.

This service allows the cross-searching of six bibliographic databases containing international occupational health and safety information with over 1.5 million citations from over 5,000 journals and 100,000 monographs and technical reports.

PubMed, www.pubmed.gov

PubMed is the publicly available version of Medline provided by the National Library of Medicine. It is possible to search by author, journal title, MeSH heading or to use the single citation matcher to retrieve a specific paper.

► ENCYCLOPAEDIAS, REFERENCE BOOKS AND OTHER KEY TEXTS

(Note that further texts are listed in the subject specific paragraphs within the section on Subject specific resources)

Encyclopaedias

Karwowski, W., ed., 2001. *International encyclopedia of ergonomics and human factors.* London: Taylor and Francis.

This encyclopaedia is published in three volumes with entries arranged alphabetically. Subjects covered include: general ergonomics; human characteristics; performance related factors; information presentation and communication; display and control design; workplace and equipment design; environment, system characteristics; work design and organisation; health and safety; social and economic impact of the system, and methods and techniques.

The following three volumes update the Occupational Ergonomics Handbook produced by CRC Press in 1998.

Karwowski, W., and Marras, W. S., 2003. *Occupational ergonomics engineering and administrative controls.* Boca Raton, FL: CRC Press.

Karwowski, W., and Marras, W. S., 2003. *Occupational ergonomics principles of work design.* Boca Raton, FL: CRC Press.

Karwowski, W., and Marras, W. S., 2003. *Occupational ergonomics design and management of work systems.* Boca Raton, FL: CRC Press.

Stellman, J. M., ed.,1998. *Encyclopaedia of occupational health and safety.* 4th ed., Geneva: International Labour Office.

The above encyclopaedia is extremely comprehensive and has been authored and edited by a panel of international experts. It is available either in print or as a CD. The print version is published in four volumes:

- Volume I covers health issues including health education, ethical issues, and occupational health and safety studies.
- Volume 2 concentrates on hazards such as air quality, noise, radiation and biological hazards. It also covers psychosocial factors such as stress and interpersonal issues.
- Volume 3 covers aspects specific to particular industries such as chemicals, agriculture, mining, metal production, textiles, transport, construction, and the power industries.
- Volume 4 comprises industry guides and chemical data.

Key texts

Bhattacharya, A., and McGlothlin, J. D., 1996. *Occupational ergonomics theory and applications.* New York: Marcel Dekker.

Friend, M. A., and Kohn, J. P., 2003. *Fundamentals of occupational safety and health.* 3rd ed. Rockville: Government Institutes. [aimed at American readers]

Health and Safety Executive, 1994. *Essentials of health and safety at work.* Sudbury: HSE Books.

Pantry, S., 1995. *Occupational health*. London: Chapman and Hall.

Ridley, J., and Channing, J., eds., 1999. *Safety at work*. Oxford: Butterworth-Heinemann.

Selwyn, N., 2001. *Guide to health and safety at work*. Kingston-upon-Thames: Croner Publications.

Stranks, J. W., 2001. *A manager's guide to health & safety at work*. London: Kogan Page.

Stranks, J. W., 2000. *One stop health and safety*. London: ICSA.

Glossaries and dictionaries

International Occupational Safety and Health Information Centre and International Labour Office, 1993. *Occupational safety and health glossary words and expressions used in safety and health at work: English, Francais, Deutsch, Espanol, Russkiei International Occupational Safety and Health Information Centre, International Labour Office*. Geneva: International Labour Office.

Koren, H., 1996. *Illustrated dictionary of environmental health and occupational safety*. Boca Raton: Lewis Publishers.

Stranks, J. W., 2002. *Health and safety at work key terms*. Oxford: Butterworth-Heinemann.

Bibliographies and further sources of information

Commission of The European Communities, 1999. *Health and safety at work reference texts*. Luxembourg: OOPEC. [lists relevant EC directives]

Pantry, S., 1997. *Health and safety: a guide to sources of information*. Birmingham: Royal Society for the Prevention of Accidents.

► ONLINE FULL-TEXT RESOURCES

Barbour Index, www.barbour-index.co.uk
The Barbour Index includes health and safety information services covering the areas of occupational health and safety, environmental health, food safety, trading standards and environmental protection. This is a commercial service and there are charges associated with it.

Croner, www.croner.co.uk
The Croner website includes a health and safety channel and a free news service. Croner customers can view subscriptions online from a range of information zones:

- Fire Safety
- Hazards and Work Activities
- Law and Official Guidance

- Manufacturing
- Risk Assessment
- Substances and Dangerous Goods
- Training

Croner also handles subscriptions to OSH Plus, a database containing the full text of many HSE and HSC documents.

Department of Health Publications and Statistics, www.dh.gov.uk/
PublicationsAndStatistics
This site gives full text access to Department of Health papers wherever possible.

HMSO, www.legislation.hmso.gov.uk
Full text of UK legislation is freely available
(See under Legislation, above)

HSC Consultative Documents, www.hse.gov.uk/consult
This site provides access to the full text of consultative documents and in some cases also offers the opportunity to take part in public consultations online.

Health, Environment and Work: Educational resources, www.agius.com/
hew/resource/index.htm
These full text resources have been made freely available by Prof. Raymond Agius, Professor of Occupational and Environmental Medicine and Director of the Centre for Occupational and Environmental Health at the University of Manchester Medical School. Other pages on the website are also worth a visit.

Health and Safety homepages, www.healthandsafety.co.uk
These pages are provided by Professional Health and Safety Consultants Ltd. and offer links to their consultancy services, but in addition there is access through the Information Library to many useful full text guidance leaflets.

OSHA Technical Manual, www.osha-slc.gov/dts/osta/otm/otm_toc.html
The Technical Manual of the American Occupational Health and Safety Administration is freely available.

Occupational Health and Safety Information Service (OHSIS), www.tion-estop.com/tionestop/where/ohsis.htm
A subscription is required for full text access but the index is freely searchable. The service provides a full-text collection of key health and safety, fire safety, and environmental health guidance material. It also includes UK legislation, standards and guidelines.

▶ WEB GATEWAYS

This chapter has already highlighted the wealth of information that is freely available on the Internet. However locating that information can be a very time consuming exercise. Doing a general search on one of the web search engines such as Google (www.google.co.uk) will result in a large number of hits which then need careful evaluation in order to assess their validity and the quality of information they contain. The following web gateways provide access to sites which have been categorised by subject for easier and more relevant searching. In addition, many of them have been vetted by subject specialists before being added to the gateways, thus giving them some authenticity. The RDN Virtual Training Suite packages detailed towards the end of the list are online tutorials designed to guide researchers through the variety of online resources available.

BIOME, biome.ac.uk
BIOME forms part of the Resource Discovery Network (RDN) which has been created through the collaboration of a number of UK educational and research organisations. It provides a searchable catalogue of quality Internet sites and resources in the areas of health and life sciences.

CCOHS: Canadian Centre for Occupational Health and Safety, www.ccohs.ca/resources
The Resources section of the CCOHS website provides access to a directory of Internet sites on health and safety, links to discussion groups, and also an alerting service relating to Canadian policy.

EEVL: the internet guide to engineering, mathematics and computing, www.eevl.ac.uk
Like BIOME, EEVL is a hub within the RDN. It is the primary gateway to quality assured engineering sites, and will therefore be mentioned elsewhere in this book. However, it is worth highlighting in this chapter that, in addition to the searching capability, there is also the option to browse for sites relevant to Occupational Safety and Health. From the home page, select the Engineering subject area followed by Occupational Safety and Health. You can then browse over 220 sites which have been selected for inclusion by subject experts.

Ergoworld, www.interface-analysis.com/ergoworld
This site produced by a Californian consultancy company, provides information on ergonomics (office ergonomics, industrial ergonomics, injury prevention/treatment) and human factors (HCI/usability, air & ground HF, product design). It also includes information on products, jobs, consultants/organisations, university programmes and industry events, but these are largely USA based.

Google Occupational Health and Safety, directory.google.com/Top/Health/
Occupational_Health_and_Safety
This is the Occupational Health and Safety section of the Google directory.
These sites have not all been quality checked.

Occupational and Environmental Health website, www.agius.com/hew
links
This is another reference to the pages provided by Prof. Raymond Agius,
Professor of Occupational and Environmental Medicine and Director of the
Centre for Occupational and Environmental Health at the University of
Manchester Medical School. These pages offer a directory of sites in occu-
pational and environmental health.

OHNet, www.occupational-health.net
To make best use of this site it is necessary to register. There are news
alerts, guidance on regulations, and information about forthcoming courses
and seminars.

Osh.Net: Gateway for Safety and Health Information Resources,
www.osh.net
Osh.Net is managed by a team of licensed occupational health and safety
experts and provides links to organisations, information resources and the
latest information on standards and regulations. There is also a bulletin
board providing a forum for discussion.

OSHWEB, oshweb.me.tut.fi
OSHWEB is an index of occupational safety and health resources on the
Internet developed by the Institute of Occupational Safety Engineering at
Tampere University of Technology, Finland. The resources are sorted in
subject hierarchies.

Our Healthier Nation, www.ohn.gov.uk
Our Healthier Nation is the government-wide health strategy for England
which was published in July 1999. The OHN Website provides links to
public health information, to NHS sites, and to health related work across
government sites. It aims to help professionals who are working to improve
health and reduce health inequalities.

RDN Virtual Training Suite, www.vts.rdn.ac.uk
This page contains links to a number of online tutorials prepared within
the Resource Discovery Network (also see BIOME and EEVL). The tutorials offer advice in techniques for searching for quality information on the
internet and highlight some of the key sites in each subject area. Within
the Internet for Further Education listing, there is a Health and Safety at
Work tutorial aimed at students within further education. There is also a

tutorial aimed at higher education called Internet for Health and Safety. This is listed within the EEVL titles (see earlier for more information about EEVL.)

WWWVL: Public health: Occupational Health and Safety, www.ldb.org/vl/top/top-ohs.htm
The WWW Virtual Library provides a subject hierarchy of Internet sites. This address points to the Occupational Health and Safety section within Public Health.

Yahoo! Public Health and Safety, dir.yahoo.com/Health/Public_Health_and_Safety
Yahoo is a directory which orders websites by subject category. This is the Public Health and Safety section of the directory.

▶ MAILING LISTS AND NEWSGROUPS

Mailing lists provide a means of generating email discussions between people interested in similar topics. Emails are sent to everyone on the list and it is possible to reply to the whole list or to specific individuals. In the UK, the JISCmail service maintains many publicly available lists. More information about the lists is available from: www.jiscmail.ac.uk. Relevant examples include:

- ECOHSE@jiscmail.ac.uk (European Centre for Occupational Health, Safety and the Environment)
- ergonomics@jiscmail.ac.uk
- occ-health@jiscmail.ac.uk
- occenvmed@jiscmail.ac.uk

With newsgroups, messages are posted to a bulletin board which has to be checked rather than arriving in personal email boxes. A useful list of newsgroups is available from the Google Groups website (groups.google.co.uk). The most relevant group is sci.med.occupational.
   Relevant discussion lists offered by other organisations include:

- Osh.Net Bulletin Board linked from: www.osh.net
- Vermont SIRI Archives of the Major Occupational Safety and Health Mailgroups, www.hazard.com/mail

Related sites include those where it is possible to post a question to an expert. Examples include:

- AllExperts.com: the Occupational (OHSA) and Environmental Hazard section, www.allexperts.com/getExpert.asp?Category=1417
- OSH Answers, www.ccohs.ca/oshanswers

▶ SUBJECT SPECIFIC RESOURCES

The resources discussed so far in this chapter have been general resources in the areas of occupational safety and health. However there are many additional resources which are appropriate for particular aspects within these areas. Some worthy of mention are listed in the following sections.

Safety and risk management

Adams, J., 1995. *Risk*. London: UCL Press.
Andrews, J. D., and Moss, T. R., 2002. *Reliability and risk assessment*. London: Professional Engineering Publishing.
Bateman, M., 2002. *Tolley's practical risk assessment handbook*. 3rd ed. London: Butterworths Tolley.
Dhillon, B. S., 2003. *Engineering safety: fundamentals, techniques and applications*. New York: Marcel Dekker. [American text].
Engineers and risk issues: code of professional practice. 1993. London: Engineering Council.
Gertman, D. I., and Blackman, H. S., 1993. *Human reliability and safety analysis data handbook*. Chichester: Wiley.
Harms-Ringdahl, L., 2001. *Safety analysis: principles and practice in occupational safety*. London: Taylor and Francis.
Kletz, T. A., 2000. *An engineer's view of human error*. 3rd ed. Rugby: Institution of Chemical Engineers.
Kletz, T. A., 2000. *Learning from accidents*. 3rd ed. Oxford: Gulf Professional.
Reeve, P., 2001. *Practical risk assessment*. London: Engineering Employers' Federation.
Sadhra, S. S., 1999. *Occupational health: risk assessment and management*. Oxford: Blackwell Science.
Wong, W., 2002. *How did that happen? Engineering safety and reliability*. London: Professional Engineering Publishing.

Journals

This is a selection of the titles available:
Accident analysis and prevention. Oxford, New York: Pergamon Press.
International journal of reliability and safety. Olney: Inderscience. [First issue due 2004]
International journal of risk assessment and management. Olney: Inderscience.
Journal of occupational accidents. Amsterdam: Elsevier.
Journal of hazardous materials. Amsterdam: Elsevier.
Journal of safety research. Amsterdam: Elsevier.
Policy and practice in health and safety. Wigston: IOSH. [continuation of IOSH Journal]
Safety science. Amsterdam: Elsevier.
Safety management. Waterford. Aspen Publishers.

Website

British Safety Council, ww2.britishsafetycouncil.org
The British Safety Council's mission is 'to promote health, safety and environmental
   best practice for the benefit of society and the increase of productivity'. The
   website includes details of a wide range of sources of health and safety
   information and also to training courses.

Human factors

Ergonomics

Alexander, D., and Rabourn, R., eds., 2001. *Applied ergonomics*. London: Taylor and
   Francis.
Bhattacharya, A., and McGlothlin, J. D., eds., 1996. *Occupational ergonomics theory and
   applications*. New York: Marcel Dekker.
Bridger, R. S., 2003. *Introduction to ergonomics*. 2nd ed. London: Taylor and
   Francis.
Corlett, E. N., and Clark, T. S., 1995, *The ergonomics of workspaces and machines:
   a design manual*. 2nd ed. London: Taylor and Francis.
Dul, J., and Weerdmeester, B. A., 2001. *Ergonomics for beginners: a quick reference guide*.
   2nd ed. London: Taylor and Francis.
Ergonomics Society, 2002. *Contemporary ergonomics*. London: Taylor and Francis.
   [a series of annual congresses].
Fraser, T. M., 1996. *Introduction to industrial ergonomics a textbook for students and
   managers*. Toronto: Wall and Emerson.
Hancock, P. A., ed., 1999. *Human performance and ergonomics*. San Diego, CA: Academic
   Press.
Harris, D., ed., 2001. *Engineering psychology and cognitive ergonomics*. Aldershot: Ashgate.
Helander, M., 1995. *A guide to the ergonomics of manufacturing*. London: Taylor and
   Francis.
Karwowski, W., ed. 2001. *International encyclopedia of ergonomics and human factors*.
   London: Taylor and Francis.
Kirwan, B., 1994. *A guide to practical human reliability assessment*. London: Taylor and
   Francis.
Kragt, H., ed., 1995. *Enhancing industrial performance experiences of integrating the human
   factor*. London: Taylor and Francis.
Kroemer, K. H. E., and Grandjean, E., 1997. *Fitting the task to the human: a textbook of
   occupational ergonomics*. 5th ed. London: Taylor and Francis.
Kroemer, K. H. E., and Kroemer, A. D., 2001. *Office ergonomics*. London: Taylor and
   Francis.
Meister, D., and Enderwick, T. P., 2002. *Human factors in system design, development, and
   testing*. Mahwah, NJ: L. Erlbaum.
Norman, D. A., 2000. *The design of everyday things*. London: MIT Press.

Norris, B. J., and Wilson, J. R., 1997. *Designing safety into products: making ergonomics evaluation a part of the design process.* Nottingham: University of Nottingham, Institute for Occupational Ergonomics.

Noyes, J. M., 2001. *Designing for humans.* Hove: Psychology Press.

Oborne, D. J., 1995. *Ergonomics at work human factors in design and development.* Chichester: Wiley.

Pheasant, S., 1996. *Bodyspace: anthropometry, ergonomics and the design of work.* 2nd ed. London: Taylor and Francis.

Phillips, C. A., 2000. *Human factors engineering.* New York: Wiley.

Salvendy, G., ed., 1997. *Handbook of human factors and ergonomics.* New York: Wiley.

Stanton, N., et al., eds., 2003. *Handbook of human factors and ergonomics methods.* London: Taylor and Francis.

Stanton, N., and Young, M. S., 1999. *A guide to methodology in ergonomics desiging for human use.* New York: Taylor and Francis.

Tayyari, F., and Smith, J. L., 1997. *Occupational ergonomics principles and applications.* London: Chapman and Hall.

Violante, F., Kilbom, A., and Armstrong, T., eds., 2000. *Occupational ergonomics: work related musculoskeletal disorders of the upper limb and back.* London: Taylor and Francis.

Wickens, C. D., Gordon, S. E., and Liu, Y., 1998. *An introduction to human factors engineering.* New York: Longman.

Wilson, J. R., and Corlett, N., eds., 1995. *Evaluation of human work: a practical ergonomics methodology.* 2nd ed. London: Taylor and Francis.

Environment

Boyce, P. R., 2003. *Human factors in lighting.* 2nd ed. London: Taylor and Francis.

Collins, L., and Schneid, T. D., 2001. *Physical hazards of the workplace.* London: Lewis Publishers.

Fahy, F. J., and Walker, J. G., 1998. *Fundamentals of noise and vibration.* London: Spon.

Health and Safety Executive ,1997. *Lighting at work.* 2nd ed. Sudbury: HSE Books.

Legislation for noise and vibration, 2000. Bury St. Edmonds: Professional Engineering Publishing.

Mansfield, N., 2003. *Human response to vibration.* London: Taylor and Francis.

National Aeronautics and Space Administration, 2001. *Handbook for industrial noise control.* Toronto: Books for Business.

Parsons, K. C., 2002. *Human thermal environments: the effect of hot, moderate and cold environments on human health, comfort and performance.* 2nd ed. London: Taylor and Francis.

Tregenza, P., and LOE, D., 1998. *The design of lighting.* London: E & F Spon.

Vicente, K. J., 1999. *Cognitive work analysis toward safe, productive, and healthy computer-based work.* Mahwah, NJ: Lawrence Erlbaum Associates.

Wreford, B. M., 1991. *Environmental assessment of the workplace.* Harrow: Scutari Projects for the Royal College of Nursing.

Stress

Cox, T., Griffiths, A., and Rial-Gonzalez, E., 2000. *Research on work-related stress.* Luxembourg: OOPEC.

Cox, T., 2000. *Organisational interventions for work stress a risk management approach.* Sudbury: HSE Books. [Prepared by: Institute of Work, Health and Organisations, University of Nottingham Business School for the Health and Safety Executive].

Crandall, R., and Perrewe, P. L., eds., 2003. *Occupational stress: a handbook.* 2nd ed. London: Taylor and Francis.

European Agency for Safety and Health at Work, 2002. *How to tackle psychosocial issues and reduce work-related stress.* Luxembourg: OOPEC.

European Agency for Safety and Health at Work, 2002. *Practical advice for workers on tackling work-related stress and its causes.* Luxembourg: OOPEC.

European Agency for Safety and Health at Work, 2002. *Work-related stress.* Luxembourg: OOPEC.

Health and Safety Executive, 1995. *Stress at work a guide for employers.* Sudbury: HSE Books.

Smith, A., et al., 2000. *The scale of occupational stress: the Bristol Stress and Health at Work Study.* Sudbury: HSE.

Journals

Ergonomics: the official journal of the Ergonomics Society and the International Ergonomics Association. London: Taylor and Francis.

International journal of industrial ergonomics. Amsterdam: Elsevier

Journal of occupational and organizational psychology. Leicester: British Psychological Society.

Journal of occupational psychology. Leicester: British Psychological Society.

Occupational ergonomics. Amsterdam: IOS Press.

Occupational hazards. Cleveland, OH: Penton Publishing.

Work and stress. London: Taylor and Francis.

Fire

Building regulations and fire safety: procedural guidance. 2001. London: Stationery Office.

The Building Regulations 2000, approved document B: fire safety. Amendments 2002 to approved document B., 2002. London: Stationery Office.

Burchett, R., 2001. *An introduction to fire safety for managers.* Leeds: H. and H. Scientific Consultants Ltd.

Dailey, W., 2000. *A guide to fire safety management.* Leicester: Perpetuity Press.

Fire safety: an employer's guide. 1999. London: Stationery Office.

Knight's guide to fire safety regulations. Issue 39, 2003. London: Butterworth Tolley.

McMahon, M., 2001. *Fire safety.* London: Sweet and Maxwell.

Miller, R., and Coules, K., 2003. *Tolley's fire safety management handbook.* 2nd ed. London: Tolley.

Thomson, N., 2001. *Fire hazards in industry.* Oxford: Butterworth-Heinemann.

Journals

Fire and materials. Chichester: Wiley.
Fire Safety Engineering. London: CMP Europe.
Fire Safety Journal. Amsterdam: Elsevier.
Fire Technology. London: Kluwer.

Websites

Fire Net, www.fire.org.uk
> A website for working fire fighters. Included information for the public and fire safety advice.

Fire Research, www.fire.nist.gov
> The website of the Building and Fire Research Laboratory at NIST (National Institute of Standards and Technology). Provides links to software, data and publications.

Fire Safety Engineering Group at the University of Greenwich, fseg.gre.ac.uk
> Details the research work of the group with links to publications.

National Fire Protection Association (USA), www.nfpa.org
> Links to an online catalogue of publications, news alerts, reports and opportunities for professional development.

Chemicals

Chemical hazards can be evaluated with the assistance of datasheets. Further guidance is available online through COSHH Essentials, (www.coshh-essentials.org.uk) which helps companies to assess the risks from chemicals and to apply appropriate controls. The Control of Substances Hazardous to Health Regulations 2002 (SI 2002 No. 2677) sets out characteristic properties of substances harmful to health:

- Very toxic: involves extremely serious acute or chronic health risk or death
- Toxic: involves serious acute or chronic health risk or death
- Harmful: involved limited health risks
- Corrosive: destroys living tissue on contact
- Irritant: Non-corrosive, but with immediate prolonged or repeated contact with tissues can cause inflammation
- Carcinogenic: may induce cancer or increase its incidence
- Teratogenic: may involve a risk of non-hereditable birth defects in offspring
- Mutagenic: may involve risk of hereditable genetic defects

Information on the toxicity of chemicals can be derived from a variety of sources:

- Labels on containers
- Manufacturers' or suppliers' data sheets as required by Section 6 of the HASAW Act 1974
- Trade journals
- Technical literature as follows

Alaimo, R. J., 2001. *Handbook of chemical health and safety*. Washington: American Chemical Society.

Barton, J., and Rogers, R., 1997. *Chemical reaction hazards: a guide to safety*. 2nd ed. Rugby: Institution of Chemical Engineers.

Carson, P., and Mumford, C., 2002. *Hazardous chemicals handbook*. 2nd ed. Oxford: Butterworth-Heinemann.

Coleman, R. J., 2000. *Hazardous materials dictionary*. 2nd ed. Lancaster, PA: Technomic Publishing Co.

Croner's dangerous substances [computer file], 2001. Kingston-upon-Thames: Croner Publications.

Eisler, R., 2000. *Handbook of chemical risk assessment: health hazards to humans, plants, and animals*. London: Lewis. [3 vol reference work concerning the effects of chemicals entering the environment].

Government Institutes Research Group, 2001. *Book of lists of regulated hazardous substances*. 10th ed. Rockville: Government Institutes. [refers to American legislation].

Greene, S. A., 2003. *International resources guide to hazardous chemicals: manufacturers, agencies, organizations, and useful sources of information*. Hitchin: Noyes Publications.

Health and safety: the control of major accident hazards regulations 1999. (SI 1999: 743). London: Stationery Office.

Health and Safety Executive, 2002. *Control of substances hazardous to health: the control of substances hazardous to health regulations 2002*. 4th ed. Caerphilly: HSE Books.

Kletz, T. A., 1998. *Process plants: a handbook for inherently safer design*. Philadelphia PA: Taylor and Francis.

Kletz, T. A., 1998. *What went wrong? Case histories of process plant disasters*. 4th ed. Houston, TX.: Gulf Publishing Co.

Kletz, T. A., 1999. *Hazop and hazan: identifying and assessing process industry hazards*. 4th ed. Rugby: Institution of Chemical Engineers.

Lewis, R. J., 2000. *Rapid guide to hazardous chemicals in the workplace*. 4th ed. Chichester: Wiley.

Lewis, R. J. Sr., 2000. *Sax's dangerous properties of industrial materials*. 10th ed. Chichester: Wiley.

Lewis, R. J. Sr., 2002. *Hazardous chemicals desk reference*. 5th ed. New York: Wiley-Interscience.

Meyer, E., 1998. *Chemistry of hazardous materials*. 3rd ed. Harlow: Pearson Professional Education.

Pybus, R., 2000. *Croner's guide to COSHH*. Kingston-upon-Thames: Croner.

Urben, P. G., and Pitt, M. J., 1999. *Bretherick's handbook of reactive chemical hazards*. 6th ed. Oxford: Butterworth-Heinemann.

Journals

Chemical hazards in industry. Royal Society of Chemistry. [the subscription includes
access to a corresponding online web database]
Journal of loss prevention in the process industries. Amsterdam: Elsevier.
Loss prevention bulletin. Rugby: Institution of Chemical Engineers.
Process safety progress. New York: American Institute of Chemical Engineers.

Website

European Process Safety Centre, www.epsc.org
The EPSC undertakes research in process safety and their web pages link to
their reports and other sources of information.

Construction industry

Barnard, M. J., 1999. *Tolley's construction health and safety*. London: Tolley Publishing Co.
Bielby, S. C., and Read, J. A., 2001. *Site safety handbook*. 3rd ed. London: Construction
Industry Research and Information Association.
Coble, R. J., Haupt, T. C., and Hinze, J., eds., 2000. *The management of construction safety
and health*. Rotterdam: Balkema.
Coble, R. J., 2001. *Construction safety and health management*. Welwyn Garden City:
Pearson Higher Education.
Davies, V. J., and Tomasin, K., 1996. *Construction safety handbook*. 2nd ed. London:
Thomas Telford.
European Agency for Safety and Health at Work, 2003. *Accident prevention in the
construction sector*. Luxembourg: OOPEC.
Goetsch, D. L., 2002. *Construction safety and health*. Upper Saddle River, NJ: Prentice
Hall.
Griffith, A., and Howarth, T., 2001. *Construction health and safety management*. Harlow:
Longman.
Health and Safety Executive, 2001. *Absolutely essential health and safety toolkit for the
smaller construction contractor*. INDG 344. Sudbury: HSE Books.
Health and Safety Executive, 1994. *Designing for health and safety in construction: a guide
for designers on the Construction (Design and Management) Regulations 1994*.
Sudbury: HSE Books.
Health and Safety Executive, 2001. *Health and Safety in Construction*. HSG 150. 2nd ed.
Sudbury: HSE Books.
Health and Safety Executive, 2001. *Managing health and safety in construction –
Construction (Design and Management) Regulations 1994 – Approved Code of Practice
and Guidance*. HSG 224. Sudbury: HSE Books.
Heberle, D., 1998. *Construction safety manual*. Maidenhead: McGraw-Hill.
Holt, A. St.-J., 2001. *Principles of construction safety*. Oxford: Blackwell Science.

Keller's official OSHA construction safety handbook. 2003. 4th ed. Ninan, WI: J.J. Keller and Associates. [relates to USA safety regulations].

Peyton, R. X., and Rubio, T. C., 1991. *Construction safety practices and principles.* Florence, KY: Van Nostrand Reinhold.

Websites

Construction confederation, www.thecc.org.uk
Selecting 'About us' from the home page of this website explains the benefits of being a member of the organisation. Benefits include the availability of help and advice on health and safety issues. Additionally, non-members can browse some interesting case studies and can access the 'Links' page which provides access to a range of construction related organisations and publications.

European Construction Institute, www.eci-online.org
This site has a Member's area and a Visitor's area. The Visitor's area contains information about their latest initiatives, and a Knowledge Bank with details of ECI publications. The Member's area includes details of the work of the Institute and task force reports.

Working well together, wwt.uk.com
'Working well together' is a health and safety campaign for the construction industry which has been developed by the Health and Safety Commission's Construction Industry Advisory Committee, (www.hse.gov. uk/aboutus/hsc/iacs/coniac). Registration is required to access many areas of the site including access to advice and guidance, examples of good practice, and health and safety statistics.

ukconstruction.com, www.ukconstruction.com
This site includes a health and safety channel.

Electrical industry

British Standards Institution, 1998. BS IEC 61508–3:1998. *Functional safety of electrical equipment.* London: British Standards Institution.

British Standards Institution, 2001, BS 7671:2001. *IEE wiring regulations.* 16th ed. London: IEE.

Cadick, J., 1999. *Electrical safety handbook.* 2nd ed. Maidenhead: McGraw-Hill.

Clapp, A. L., 2001. *National electrical safety code handbook.* 5th ed. Piscataway NJ: IEEE Standards Press. [relates to USA standards].

Grohmann, S., 2000. *Checking electrical safety measures.* New Delhi: Narosa Publishing House.

Health and Safety Executive, 2002. *Your guide to the essentials of electrical safety.* [compact disc audio]. Sudbury: HSE.

Kovacic, T. M., 2002. *An illustrated guide to electrical safety.* 5th ed. Chicago: American Society of Safety Engineers.

Marks, T. E., 2002. *Handbook on BS 7671: the IEE wiring regulations.* 6th rev. ed. Nottingham: Radikal Phase.

Marne, D. J., 2002. *McGraw-Hill's National Electrical Safety Code (NESC) Handbook.* Maidenhead: McGraw-Hill. [relates to USA regulations].

Scaddan, B., 2001. *IEE wiring regulations: explained and illustrated.* 6th ed. Oxford: Newnes.

Smith, K. O., and Madden, J. M., 2002. *Electrical safety and the law: a guide to compliance.* 4th ed. Oxford: Blackwell Science.

Wiggins, J. H., 2001. *Managing electrical safety.* Rockville: ABS Consulting.

Occupational health and medicine

Agius, R. M., and Seaton, A., 2002. *Practical occupational medicine.* 2nd ed. London: Arnold.

Bamford, M., ed., 2003. *Work and health: an introduction to occupational health care.* London: Chapman and Hall.

Baxter, P. J., et al., 2000. *Hunter's diseases of occupations.* 9th ed. London: Arnold.

Gee, D., et al., 1997. *Workplace health.* London: Health Education Authority.

Harrington, J. M., et al., 1998. *Occupational health.* 4th ed. Oxford: Blackwell Science.

Harris, J. S., 1999. *Quick reference to the occupational medicine practice guidelines: evaluation and management of common health problems and functional recovery in workers.* Beverly Farms, MA: OEM Press.

Hawkins, L., 2002. *Tolley's guide to managing employee health.* London: Tolley.

Koh, D., and Seng, C. K., eds., 2001. *Textbook of occupational medicine practice.* 2nd ed. Singapore: World Scientific Publishing.

Lee, Y-W., 2002. *Recording and notification of occupational accidents and diseases and ILO list of occupational diseases.* Geneva: ILO.

Levy, B. S., 2000. *Occupational health.* 4th ed. Philadelphia: Lippincott, Williams and Wilkins.

McCunney, R. J., 2002. *A practical approach to occupational and environmental medicine.* 3rd ed. Philadelphia: Lippincott, Williams and Wilkins.

Seaton, A., et al., 1994. *Practical occupational medicine.* London: Arnold.

SnashalL, D., and Patel, D., 2003. *ABC of work related disorders.* 2nd ed. London: BMJ.

Stansfeld, S. A., and Head, J., 2000. *Work-related factors and ill health: the Whitehall II study.* Sudbury: HSE Books.

Wald, P. H., 2002. *Physical and biological hazards of the workplace.* 2nd ed. Chichester: Wiley.

Wilkinson, C., 1997. *Managing health at work: a guide for managers and workplace health specialists.* London: Spon.

Journals

(in addition to those previously listed)

Journal of occupational and environmental medicine. Philadelphia: Lippincott, Williams and Wilkins.
Journal of occupational rehabilitation. London: Kluwer.
Occupational and environmental medicine. London: BMJ.

27 Petroleum and Offshore Engineering

Arnold Myers

The importance of the oil industry in providing fuel and raw materials for many synthetics hardly needs to be stated. Virtually every person on the planet uses petroleum products in one way or another. Most oil is buried underground and oil producers have to drill through the rock to reach it. The first rigs (drilling apparatus) were on land but ships and platforms can now be used to get oil from under the lakes and seabed. The ocean basins are too deep for oil drilling, so exploration and production takes place on the continental shelf. Oil is trapped in layers of rocks, and likely rock formations are detected by seismic surveying: using sound waves to build up a picture of the rock layers. These formations then have to be tested by exploratory drilling. Only then can the decision be made to invest in production drilling.

▶ THE INDUSTRY

Petroleum Engineering has developed an ethos and coherence of its own, fully expressed in its literature and information retrieval tools, although it could be regarded as a mere branch of some more general field of engineering. Its practitioners have been drawn from a variety of disciplines from geology through to process engineering: petroleum engineering itself is normally studied at postgraduate level following a grounding in one of the branches of engineering taught at first degree level, or in the geosciences.

Offshore Engineering as a concept has arisen from the challenge of exploiting hydrocarbon resources under the seabed: in its advanced forms a response to the economic and political situation in the 1960s and 1970s, and most notably exemplified by the development of North Sea oil and gas. Offshore Engineering is a 'bolt-on' to petroleum engineering. The concerns of petroleum engineering (such as seismic surveying, drilling, reservoir engineering) are present equally on land and offshore, but the engineering required to provide (literally and metaphorically) a platform for this in the marine environment is an expensive extra with its own information sources. The main areas of research in petroleum engineering are related to exploration techniques, drilling further (both vertically downwards and horizontally), and methods of extracting a higher proportion of the oil from the rock (reservoir and production engineering).

The oil industry is truly international, though in many aspects dominated by the United States of America. It meets a large and continuous demand for energy in the form of fuel, yet it is prone to boom and bust cycles (which can be monitored by plotting the price of oil). It has the wealth and drive to innovate on a grand scale, but it is in many ways conservative with an often old-fashioned outlook. This is reflected in its information generation and transmission.

Information flow

The petroleum industry handles the publication of information in ways which probably differ from other subject areas in this book. The proportion of industry-originated to university-originated publication in the petroleum industry is very much weighted to material coming from industry practitioners. Much of this could be characterised as industry experience rather than academic research. Nevertheless, this body of publication provides important data, information and opinion which independent and academic researchers as well as oil company engineers have to use. Developments are reported more promptly and in more detail at conferences than through other publishing media, and a petroleum library can be judged on the completeness of its holdings of conference papers.

The petroleum industry would appear to be well placed to exploit to the full the advantages of World-Wide Web publishing: its operations are truly world-wide, extending from the tropics to the arctic, the use of a single language (English) predominates, and developments in technical, commercial and political matters are rapid. However, the industry seems in many instances to prefer old-fashioned products, which are reliable and familiar. Although the first international Internet information system for the industry, *Sci.Geo.Petroleum*, was set up in 1994, large areas of its information provision are largely left to free enterprise, which continues to find print media profitable. The coverage of the petroleum industry in electronic journals is still meagre – examples such as *Proceedings – Institution of Civil Engineers: Water Maritime and Energy* include only a small fraction of the relevant literature. The situation may well improve, and it is always worth checking the current position in the Engineering E-journal Search Engine for full-text electronic journals, (www.eevl.ac.uk/eese).

EEVL, the Internet Guide to Engineering, Mathematics and Computing, includes in its catalogue of refereed high quality networked engineering resources over 100 petroleum-related sites, many of these concerned with the offshore industry. Since the EEVL service is free, well indexed and maintained, a long list of links is not necessary here. It can be searched from: www.eevl.ac.uk/engineering

▶ THE PATTERN OF PUBLISHING

Internal information dissemination

Information in petroleum and offshore engineering is a high-value commodity. Much of the most valuable information within companies is far removed from the public domain. Commercially sensitive information such as data from seismic exploration, drilling logs, etc., is naturally highly protected intelligence. Licensing authorities such as the UK and Norwegian governments may require companies who win exploration licences to deposit their exploration data in the public domain after a certain number of years. Although information about exploration activity in general is reported in the accessible literature, information about specific petroleum reserves, drilling activity and development plans is either out of the public domain or only available at a high price from consultancy firms.

Information sharing in the industry

The most substantial sector of petroleum industry publishing is that shared within the industry. The publications of bodies with company membership such as the American Petroleum Institute (API) (www.api.org), and especially the publications of professional societies, are all directly or indirectly subsidised by the industry.

Of the professional bodies, the most important and most active is the Society of Petroleum Engineers (SPE) (www.spe.org), based in the United States, but with world-wide membership. The SPE organises numerous professional conferences in the Americas, Europe and Asia, and organises the publication of the associated papers systematically. All meetings have their own published papers (generally on CD), and many are revised and reprinted in the Society's journals. The SPE e-Library is an online database of bibliographic details and full texts of more than 30,000 Society of Petroleum Engineers Technical Papers published since 1951 (www.spe.org).

The SPE e-Library website allows free of charge searching by author, title, year, publication, or paper number of the 30,000 references. Papers from 1997 are indexed in full text; for earlier papers only the abstract is searched. The electronic text (scanned or full text) of papers is offered through a shopping cart system to subscribers or by individual purchase.

The American Petroleum Institute (API) is the *de facto* international standards body for the industry, and its publications are indispensable in any petroleum-related work. API standards are available for sale in paper or download formats from Global Engineering Documents (www.global.ihs.com).

The Energy Institute (EI) (www.energyinst.org.uk), based in London, is both a personal membership and a company membership organisation. Many of its reports and standards are published by the Portland Press, Colchester. The EI website is one of the best-maintained and most user-friendly in the industry, and includes news, publications details, forthcoming meetings, etc. The Energy Institute was created in 2003 by the merger of the Institute of Petroleum and the Institute of Energy. The Norsk Petroleumsforening (Norwegian Petroleum Society) (www.npf.no) publishes mainly the proceedings of its conferences. Some of these are solely in the Norwegian language, but others are in English. The publishing arm of the Institut Française du Pétrole (French Petroleum Institute) (www.ifp.fr) is the publisher Technip, whose list includes not only French texts on oil and gas but also English translations and original works in English.

The American Association of Petroleum Geologists (AAPG) (www.aapg.org) is an international organisation of more than 31,000 members in 115 countries. The AAPG website contains articles from recent bulletins as PDF files, viewable using Adobe Acrobat reader software. The website also contains abstracts from past and future conferences and a large publications list. A related professional area is catered for by the Society of Exploration Geophysicists (www.seg.org), based in Tulsa, with extensive series of conference publications and a *Geophysics Reprints* series. In the UK, the Geological Society (www.geolsoc.org.uk) issues a series of *Special Publications* of major importance for oil exploration.

The International Association of Drilling Contractors (IADC) (www.iadc.org) is a company membership organisation in the area of oil and gas exploration and production, well servicing, and oil field manufacturing. IADC organises important technical meetings and publishes the resulting papers. The IADC website contains the text of the newsletter *Drill Bits Online*, accident statistics, a regular count of drilling rigs and news. The IADC document service offers a list of publications of interest to the drilling community. The site has full text PDF documents.

The United Kingdom Offshore Operators Association (www.ukooa.co.uk) is the representative organisation for the British offshore oil and gas industry. Its members are the companies licensed by the UK Government to explore for and produce oil and gas in UK waters. This site offers information about the organisation and its publications, and includes a glossary, a history of North Sea oil, information about safety policy and organisation, statistics, and press releases from the organisation. There is a large amount of background information, case studies, and briefings about the industry.

Some of the more important industry and professional journals are:

- *AAPG Bulletin* (American Association of Petroleum Geologists)
- *Journal of Canadian Petroleum Technology* (Canadian Institute of Mining and Metallurgy)
- *Journal of Offshore Engineering* (The Institute of Marine Engineering, Science and Technology)
- *Journal of Petroleum Technology* (Society of Petroleum Engineers)
- *Petroleum Review* (The Energy Institute)
- *Proceedings – Institution of Civil Engineers: Water Maritime and Energy*
- *SPE Drilling Engineering* (Society of Petroleum Engineers)
- *SPE Formation Evaluation* (Society of Petroleum Engineers)
- *SPE Production Engineering* (Society of Petroleum Engineers)
- *SPE Reservoir Engineering* (Society of Petroleum Engineers)
- *Underwater Technology* (Society for Underwater Technology)

The public domain

The prime information source here is the body of legislation. UK acts of Parliament and statutory instruments are now freely available through the Web. Information provision in the public domain includes some pure academic research (such as that funded by the Health and Safety Executive), and some government sponsored research. Of the latter, the work of the British Geological Survey (published in a series of *United Kingdom Offshore Regional Reports*) is particularly important.

In the UK, licensing and the promotion of the industry come under the Department of Trade and Industry who maintain an oil portal (www.og.dti.gov.uk/portal.htm). A report for the past year and historical account was formerly published annually by the DTI through the Stationery Office under various official titles, but always known in the industry as 'The Brown Book'. Since 2001 this official report on the UK oil industry has been published only on the Web (www.og.dti.gov.uk/information).

In the UK, much of the regulation of the industry comes under the Health and Safety Executive. HSE publishes and extensive series of 'Offshore Technology Reports' (Series OTO, OTH and OTI) and 'Research Reports' (Series RR). These reports include important sources of data not available elsewhere such as offshore accident statistics and other data which have by law to be notified by operating companies to government. Forthcoming and new reports are announced in the quarterly *Offshore Research Focus*. This periodical is only available online (www.orf.co.uk).

The Norwegian Petroleum Directorate (www.npd.no) server fulfils a comparable role in Norway, and issues an annual report on Norwegian Sector offshore developments under the title *Facts . . . the Norwegian petroleum sector*. The Norwegian Petroleum Directorate Web server, with pages in English and Norwegian, gives information on production, safety legislation applicable to the petroleum industry and details of research projects. Norwegian legislation is available free of charge through the Web. One of the most substantial free databases, *OIL*, contains all of the references in Oljeindeks (Oil Index) from 1974 to date, approximately 50,000 references, and covers both English-language and Norwegian language material of nordic origin.

Commercial publishing

Commercial publishing often has the appearance of gathering information from the industry and selling it back at inflated prices. Nevertheless, commercial publications form an important part of the overall picture. Some of the publishers with heavy investments in data gathering and a specialised clientele produce reports whose prices put them beyond the reach of many users and libraries where they would have potential use as background material for research. These include Wood Mackenzie, Edinburgh, with a track record of detailed publishing of North Sea fields, and Smith Rea Energy Analysts, Canterbury, with world-wide forecasts and offshore business reports, and Infield Systems Ltd, London, which maintains a comprehensive database of offshore developments and prospects (www.infield.com). Douglas-Westwood Ltd, also of Canterbury, publishes market forecasts for the industry. Some of the reports produced at this end of the market can hardly be regarded as conventional publications at all, they are rather multi-client studies.

For many years IBC Global Conferences Ltd and IBC UK Conferences Ltd have organised a large number of commercial conferences with industry presentations considerably out-numbering academic contributions. The published conference papers are often available only for a short period after the conference has been held, and in some cases amount to no more than speakers' presentation slides. The reporting of industry experience does, however, lead to information being included that is not available elsewhere. Other conference organisers about whose publications similar remarks could be made include International Quality & Productivity Centre Ltd (IQPC) and SMi Ltd.

Oilfield Publications Limited (OPL) is a prolific publisher of reference maps, books and registers of vessels and equipment for the international offshore oil and gas industry. OPL publications, most of which are regularly updated and re-published, include *Oil and Gas Activity and Concession Maps* and *Oil and Gas Field Development Guides* for major offshore regions worldwide, registers of mobile drilling units and other specialised vessels, and handbooks. These contain much factual information about specific oil fields and how they are being developed. Some of the vessel registers are available in online versions as well as on paper. The OPL maps, guides and registers have proved stable and reliable over many years and occupy a clearly-defined niche. Financial Times Business Ltd publish regular directories of oil and gas companies, and the detailed 'Guide to North Sea operators: a company-by-company review'.

One of the most active publishers in this field is PennWell, based in Tulsa, U.S.A. PennWell has an extensive list of journal titles, directories and textbooks, and is also active as an organiser of conferences. Hart Publications is another major publisher in the field particularly of news, with an informative website (www.eandpnet.com) and Gulf Publishing of Houston, Texas, has a strong list of petroleum publications. The so-called 'International Petroleum Encyclopedia' produced by PennWell is not an encyclopedia in the traditional sense, but a compilation of statistical series and reports of petroleum activity and prospects world-wide, some of the information culled from the same publisher's weekly *Oil and Gas Journal*. Some publishers are able to provide free products which are nevertheless useful, funded by advertising. An example is the substantial freely available industry trade directory, the *Pegasus Oil & Gas Directory* which is searchable by company name, location and keyword (www.pegasusoil-gasdirectory.co.uk).

The *Geotechnical & Geo-environmental Software Directory* (www.ggsd.com) catalogues some 1,500 programs in the fields of Geotechnical Engineering, Soil Mechanics, Rock Mechanics, Engineering Geology, Foundation Engineering, Hydrogeology, Geo-environmental Engineering, Data Analysis and Data Visualisation.

The major publishers of scholarly books such as Elsevier, Kluwer, Springer, Wiley, and Oxford University Press all have substantial lists in the area of petroleum and offshore engineering. Rather than list book publications here, readers are directed to the bibliography of the Offshore Engineering Information Service (www.eevl.ac.uk/offshore).

There are several useful news services on the Web, such as that provided by Financial Times Energy Publishing. The site contains about twenty full-text stories from current newsletters as well as information about the extensive range of energy publications from FT Energy Publishing. Although the full text of all publications is not available free of charge, sample issues of newsletters and executive summaries of many management reports can be downloaded. FT Energy – publications catalogue and free daily news service (www.ftenergy.com). Other news sites are

Oilsite with news and directory for the oil and gas industry (www.oilsite.com).

International Energy Annual (www.eia.doe.gov/emeu/iea/contents.html).

Petroleum Economist – regular energy news updates (www.petroleum-economist.com).

Meetings calendars

Most professional society websites include a calendar of meetings, some of which are not limited to meetings run by their own organisation. Several independent calendars having wider coverage and more comprehensive than these are maintained at websites such as:

- *Alexander's Gas & Oil Connections* (www.gasandoil.com/goc)
- *Offshore Engineering Information Service* (OEIS) (www.eevl.ac.uk/offshore). This is unique in having a back file.

Some of the more important commercially-produced academic journals are:

- *Geo-Marine Letters* (Springer)
- *Journal of Petroleum Science and Engineering* (Elsevier)
- *Marine and Petroleum Geology* (Elsevier)
- *Marine Geophysical Researches* (Kluwer)
- *Oil and Energy Trends* (Blackwell)

Some of the more important commercially produced trade journals are:

- *Asian Oil and Gas Monthly*
- *Drilling Contractor*
- *Hart's E & P*
- *Offshore (incorporating The Oilman)*
- *Offshore Engineer*
- *Oil and Gas Journal*
- *Petroleum Economist*
- *Petroleum Engineer International*
- *Pipeline and Gas Journal*
- *Pipeline Industry*
- *Pipeline World*
- *Quest Subsea Prospective Quarterly*
- *World Oil*

► STORAGE AND RETRIEVAL

Libraries

In the United Kingdom, libraries with good holdings include the Energy Institute and the Institute of Marine Engineering, Science and Technology in London, Heriot-Watt University in Edinburgh, and Aberdeen Public Library. The oil companies most active in the North Sea all used to maintain libraries, but many are now outsourced or run down. In Norway, the Norwegian Petroleum Directorate in Stavanger operates the leading technical library. The Norsk Oljemuseum (Norwegian Oil Museum) in Stavanger has a historical library.

Following the North Sea oil boom in the 1970s, many information professionals entered the area, and gave each other support in groups such as the Informal Group North Sea in Scotland and the Forum for Petroleum Information (FoP) in Norway. Professional matters have been discussed in the biennial series of UK-Norwegian *Offshore Information Conferences*, 1978–1996, the proceedings of which up to 1990 were published by the Institute of Offshore Engineering, Heriot-Watt University. The Energy Institute hosts and supports the London-based Information for Energy Group (IFEG) which continues to provide the UK professional forum in this area.

Bibliographies and databases

The Offshore Engineering Information Service maintained by the present author includes a regularly updated bibliographic database of petroleum engineering and marine technology.

Offshore Engineering Information Service (www.eevl.ac.uk/offshore) is a free service listing monographs and reports: as a consequence this chapter needs to cite few individual publications. This service supersedes the bibliography in:

Myers, A., Whittick, J., Edmonds, D., and Richardson, H.A., 1993. *Petroleum and Marine Technology Information Guide.* London: E. & F. N. Spon.

This in turn supersedes earlier offshore bibliographies published by ASR Marketing going back to 1981.

The Library of the Energy Institute has a freely available on-line catalogue which is itself a valuable bibliographic tool.

The material of most interest to academic engineers is, as in other fields, published in conference papers and journals. As noted above, substantial accounts of industry experience tend to be presented at conferences rather than written up for refereed journals, and the resulting publications are not always picked up by indexing and abstracting services. Academic contributions appear in both the conference and the journal literature.

Petroleum Abstracts, published by the University of Tulsa, is one of the most thorough and up-to-date abstracting services published on any topic. Over 25,000 abstracts are published annually. The abstracts are published in weekly Bulletins (printed copies up to and including 2000, electronic only subsequently). There are bound annual printed indexes up to and including 1993. A ten-year tranche of the abstracts and index is available on CD-ROM from the Dialog *OnDisc* service. The complete database, *TULSA*, is available to subscribers online. The coverage is international and includes reports and patents as well as the periodical and conference literature. The subject areas covered are: geology; geochemistry; geophysics; drilling; well logging; well completion and servicing; production of oil and gas; reservoir engineering and recovery methods; pipelining, shipping and storage; ecology and pollution; alternate fuels and energy sources; supplemental technology; and a few mineral commodities. Thus the scope 'petroleum exploration and production' is interpreted broadly and includes offshore technology and related technology.

Cambridge Scientific Abstracts (CSA) is an online information service which provides access to several databases. The databases available include *Aquatic Sciences and Fisheries Abstracts* (ASFA), which covers over 5,000 serial publications, books, reports, conference proceedings, translations and limited distribution literature. Coverage is from 1978 to the present. The database is updated monthly, with approximately 3,700 records added for each update. Major subject areas include aquatic pollution, environmental quality, oceanography; policy and legislation; and offshore technology. *Water Resources Abstracts*, which provides summaries of world technical and scientific literature on water-related topics covering the characteristics, conservation, control, pollution, treatment, use and management of water resources. Abstracts are drawn from journals, books, conference proceedings, and technical reports in the physical and life sciences, as well as from engineering, legal and government publications. This database complements the ASFA database, where there is greater coverage of the marine environment and biological material. Coverage is from 1967 to the present. Updates occur monthly, with approximately 1,300 records added per update. The major subject area is the water supply industry, but marine technology is also covered. *Oceanic Abstracts*, which covers world-wide technical literature pertaining to the marine environment, focussing on marine biology and physical oceanography, fisheries, non-living resources, meteorology and geology, plus environmental, technological, and legislative topics. Coverage is from 1981 to the present. Updates occur monthly, with approximately 1,210 records added per update. Major subject areas include: biological oceanography, ecology, physical and chemical oceanography, marine geology, geophysics, geochemistry, marine pollution, nonliving marine resources, navigation and communications, maritime law, ships, shipping, and marine biology.

MARNA (MARitiem NAutisch) (www.library.tudelft.nl/BTUD/eng/mic-e.htm) is an online database containing references to maritime publications. It is provided by the Technical University of Delft and is available through the web.

Elsevier's *Fluid Abstracts: Civil Engineering* commenced in 1991, superseding *Offshore Engineering Abstracts* which ceased in 1990 but can still be consulted for earlier material. The corresponding online database is *Fluidex*.

The Energy Institute maintains *International Petroleum Abstracts* (IPA) which is available at: www.energyinst.org.uk. Prior to 1996 this was a printed abstracts journal, which absorbed *Offshore Abstracts* in 1990.

Oil Index (www.npd.no/oil) is a reference database made available at no charge by the Norwegian Petroleum Directorate. Its coverage includes Scandinavian material not indexed elsewhere, much of which is relevant to the whole North Sea industry. Some of the material indexed is in the Norwegian language, much of it however is in English.

There are several online databases providing coverage of the geological literature relevant to petroleum engineering. these include *GEOBASE* with citations of world-wide literature on the earth sciences, *GEOLINE* with citations of the geoscience literature including, mineralogy, paleontology, sedimentology, environmental, marine, and petroleum geology, *GeoRef* (Geological Reference File) with citations of the literature of geology and geophysics, *GEOARCHIVE* with citations of the world-wide geoscience literature, geophysics, geochemistry, geology, paleontology, energy, exploration, mineral deposits, oceanography, petrology and water, and *GEOS* which covers aquatic and earth sciences.

Some services have operated by repackaging selected publications with an emphasis on legislation, regulations and standards, in an accessible and indexed form. These have included *OILRIG* and Barbour Index *Health and Safety Professional*.

Thesauri and classification

The *E&P Thesaurus*, developed by the University of Tulsa for indexing *Petroleum Abstracts*, is a well-organised and very thorough hierarchical thesaurus covering as does *Petroleum Abstracts*, exploration and production. New editions are published at intervals of a few years, and subscribers to *Petroleum Abstracts* can receive regular updates by e-mail on request. Terms for company names and for chemicals are published every six months. Complementing this, the University of Tulsa publishes a *Geographic Thesaurus* containing a listing of sedimentary basins, geographic features, and geographic area terms.

An alternative to this is the *Geoscience, Minerals and Petroleum Thesaurus* (GeMPeT), formerly the *Australian Geoscience, Minerals and Petroleum Thesaurus*. The 2003 printed edition was compiled and published by Jane Edinger and Tracy Barker, operating through Charted Information Services (www.chartedinfo.com.au/thesaurus.html).

In the 1980s the UK Department of Energy co-operated with the Norwegian Petroleum Directorate in an information handling system,

INFOIL. As part of this, a Norwegian language thesaurus covering offshore technology was translated into English and edited to be consistent with the *E&P Thesaurus.* This remains the only thesaurus devoted to offshore engineering.

Myers, A., ed., 1988. *INFOIL 2 thesaurus: terminology for the offshore industry.* London: H.M.S.O. for the Department of Energy (Offshore Technology Information OTI 88 505). ISBN 0 11 412912 6.

The only classification which has been widely used by petroleum libraries was developed fifty years ago and has not been updated:

Uren, L. C., 1953. *Decimal system for classifying data pertaining to the petroleum industry.* Berkeley and Los Angeles: University of California Press.

Current awareness publications

The most important current awareness tool is the weekly *Petroleum Abstracts* bulletin. This provides an excellent alerting service for recent reports, articles, conference papers, patents and other publications in the whole area of upstream petroleum, including offshore engineering. This weekly service is supplied by e-mail to subscribers on Fridays for fifty weeks of each year in either PDF or HTML format. A further useful service provided to subscribers by the University of Tulsa, the publishers of *Petroleum Abstracts,* is the 'Proceedings in Progress' e-mail alerting service available on request to subscribers. This gives details of published conference papers received by the University of Tulsa in advance of the publication of the abstracts.

The *Petroleum and Offshore Engineering Bulletin* available on subscription from the Offshore Engineering Information Service includes lists of recent publications and forthcoming meetings likely to give rise to published papers. This is available on paper or by e-mail in HTML format. More details are available at: www.eevl.ac.uk/offshore/homt.htm

Index

K·G·Saur Verlag

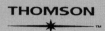

Guides to
Information Sources

Information Sources in **Art, Art History and Design**

Edited by Simon Ford
2001. XX, 220 pages Hardbound € 98.00. ISBN 3-598-24438-X

Like all sectors of the information profession, art librarianship is undergoing a period of major change. Recognition of the economic importance of the creative industries and the expansion of the further and continuing education sector, has meant an increasing number of people are seeking information on art, art history and design. The pressure to connect these people with multiplying fields of knowledge, accessible through an ever increasing variety of formats, has led to innovative new forms of service delivery.

Information Sources in Art, Art History and Design reviews current practice from a variety of perspectives, drawing on the subject knowledge of specialists based in the UK, USA and the Netherlands. Each chapter provides a guide to the best sources of information on a range of subjects, including "General reference sources", "The art book", "Auction catalogues" and "Multicultural art and design".

Information Sources in Art, Art History and Design is a welcome addition to the Guide to Information Sources series. It is edited by Simon Ford, Special Collections Bibliographer at the National Art Library, Victoria and Albert Museum, and written by experts who evaluate the best sources in their field.

Information Sources in **Music**

Edited by Lewis Foreman
2003. xix, 445 pages. Hardbound. € 110.00. ISBN 3-598-24441-X

From medieval chorales, to light operetta, to electronically generated 'musique concrete', this title offers meticulous coverage of musical composition and criticism, past and present. Information Sources in Music is an easy-to-use, evaluative guide to the wide range of published sources of information available.

Arranged by subject, each entry includes a brief description of the source, frequency of publication, and price and serial information where appropriate. As a time-saving resource this title will enable researchers to go straight to the information they need, indicating the range of sources available and offering a means of assessing which are the most useful.

www.saur.de

K·G·Saur Verlag
A Part of The Thomson Corporation

Postfach 70 16 20 · 81316 München · Germany
Tel. +49 (0)89 7 69 02-300 · Fax +49 (0)89 7 69 02-150/ 250
e-mail: saur.info@thomson.com   http://www.saur.de